OXFORD READINGS IN *OVID*

OXFORD READINGS IN CLASSICAL STUDIES

All available in paperback

Oxford Readings in *Ovid*

Edited by

PETER E. KNOX

OXFORD
UNIVERSITY PRESS

OXFORD

UNIVERSITY PRESS

Great Clarendon Street, Oxford ox2 6DP

Oxford University Press is a department of the University of Oxford.
It furthers the University's objective of excellence in research, scholarship,
and education by publishing worldwide in

Oxford New York

Auckland Cape Town Dar es Salaam Hong Kong Karachi
Kuala Lumpur Madrid Melbourne Mexico City Nairobi
New Delhi Shanghai Taipei Toronto

With offices in

Argentina Austria Brazil Chile Czech Republic France Greece
Guatemala Hungary Italy Japan Poland Portugal Singapore
South Korea Switzerland Thailand Turkey Ukraine Vietnam

Oxford is a registered trade mark of Oxford University Press
in the UK and in certain other countries

Published in the United States
by Oxford University Press Inc., New York

© Oxford University Press 2006

British Library Cataloguing in Publication Data

Data available

Library of Congress Cataloging in Publication Data

Data available

Typeset by SPI Publisher Services, Pondicherry, India
Printed in Great Britain
on acid-free paper by
Biddles Ltd., King's Lynn, Norfolk

ISBN 0–19–928115–7   978–0–19–928115–2
ISBN 0–19–928116–5 (Pbk.)   978–0–19–928116–9 (Pbk.)

1 3 5 7 9 10 8 6 4 2

Preface

The task of assembling a selection of papers on Ovid produced over the past several decades, as I quickly discovered when I undertook this project, is far from uncomplicated. The bibliography has swollen to Virgilian proportions, and the list of worthy titles that could not be included here is distressingly long. Much of the most important work of this period has emanated from critics working in Britain and the United States, and this volume inevitably tilts toward the anglophone. But Ovidian scholarship has also flourished in other venues, and while some of the papers reproduced here reflect the influential contributions of German and Italian scholars, inevitably their representation seems hardly adequate. In the meantime the appearance of the Cambridge and Brill Companions to Ovid in 2002 has made the study of our poet more accessible to students and scholars in related disciplines. In many respects this collection of papers is intended to complement those volumes by assembling some of the seminal works on which contemporary Ovidian studies have been based.

In preparing this book for publication I was aided by two able assistants, Courtney Roby and Michelle Soufl, whose technical expertise and keener eyes proved invaluable in translating the original publications into a new format. At an early stage Barbara Boyd, Stephen Hinds, and Carole Newlands responded generously to pleas for counsel; the anonymous readers for the Press also provided many helpful suggestions. I am grateful to the contributors to this book for checking and revising the digitized versions of their papers.

The final stages of assembling this volume were completed while I was a Visiting Fellow at that *locus amoenus* for classicists, Corpus Christi College in Oxford, with the support of a fellowship from the Loeb Classical Library Foundation. I cannot adequately express my gratitude to these benefactors, as well as to my home institution, the University of Colorado, for their tangible support, let alone that most crucial intangible, time.

Peter E. Knox

Contents

List of Illustrations

Introduction: Horizons in Ovidian Scholarship

Peter E. Knox

Sixty years ago it was possible for a scholar to write that 'about the merits and failing of the Roman poet Ovid there is, and has been for some considerable time, a remarkable unanimity among scholars . . . In Ovid's case, the reputation of the poet has been under a cloud for more than a hundred years' (Fränkel 1945: 10). Was there anyone who could then have believed that the road from that place led here (*ecquis ad haec illinc crederet esse uiam, Fast.* 2.8)? Ovid was never entirely neglected by scholars, to be sure, as is evidenced by von Albrecht and Zinn's collection of important essays (1968) produced over the first several decades of the past century or the fresh studies assembled by J. W. Binns (1973). And of course Ovid was continuously read and recontextualized by readers, translators, and artists (Martindale 1988; Anderson 1995; Ziolkowski 2005), even during periods when mainstream classical scholarship seemed to focus on a different subset of the canon of classical Latin authors. But it would be fair to say that the last three decades have witnessed a great increase both in the intensity of the critical engagement of professional classicists with Ovid's works and in the diversity of approaches employed. These trends are amply documented in recent bibliographical surveys (Myers 1999; Schmitzer 2002), which review the steadily increasing number of books, articles, and reviews dealing with every aspect of Ovid's output. The most recent manifestation of the surge of interest in Ovid is the nearly simultaneous publication of two companions for new readers (Boyd 2002; Hardie 2002*b*), produced by international teams of scholars and critics representing a broad spectrum of approaches. The horizon is, of course, an imaginary line, always receding as one approaches, also always simultaneously fading from view behind. The papers collected here illustrate several stages in the development of contemporary criticism of Ovid over the last thirty years and reflect the multiplicity of approaches that have informed scholarship during that time, including the dramatic impact of theoretical approaches. As the current generation of readers reviews the critical horizon whence we set out, some outlines may also begin to emerge of the horizon that we are approaching.

In the study of Latin poetry during the last decades of the twentieth century and continuing into the twenty-first, the dominant strain in criticism has been a deepening of our sense of the Roman poets' relationship to their literary forebears, their contemporaries, and the cultural imperatives of their times. The publication in 1986 of an English translation of two influential studies by G. B. Conte (1974; 1984) served as an important stimulus to further studies along these lines in the English-speaking world, leading to extensive critical engagement with notions of intertextuality in Roman poetry and the publication of new syntheses on the phenomenon (Hinds 1998; Edmunds 2001). Ovid's centrality in this discussion was secured from the first by Conte's frequently cited use of particular examples of intertextuality in the *Fasti* to inform his investigation of Virgil. Conte returned to a passage (*Fast.* 3.469–75) first discussed by Moriz Haupt (1876: 71–2) and again by Wilhelm Kroll (1924: 176–7), where Ovid retells the story of Ariadne in terms that clearly recollect Catullus' celebrated treatment in Poem 64. But in the middle years of the century, during much of which Latin literary studies were in the thrall of the New Criticism, the study of allusion in Latin poetry was largely in abeyance. It is no coincidence that this phase in the criticism of Roman poetry also coincides with the period when Ovid was most neglected by mainstream classicists. With the revived focus on intertextuality signalled by Conte's work, critics rediscovered in Ovid a rich field to till, for even in his earliest collections this poet is intensively engaged with his literary heritage. In Conte's analysis literary allusion is viewed as a kind of rhetorical figure, a sophisticated tool for deliberately importing into the text a discourse with earlier traditions. The same traits that an earlier generation of critics was inclined to dismiss as merely derivative might now be assessed on a higher critical plane as enriching the texture of the poetry.

The first group of papers assembled here illustrates many aspects of this concentrated focus on intertextuality in Ovid, which went hand in hand with a revised view of his relationship to the major cultural and political issues of his times. Again, just as Ovid was earlier viewed as a rather frivolous manipulator of inherited literary conventions (the standard descriptor, at once complimentary and dismissive, was 'clever'), so too his responses to the changing political and cultural environment of Augustan Rome tended to be viewed as superficial and mechanical. Stephen Hinds's important paper, which opens this collection, recontextualizes Ovid's works within the broader context of contemporary trends in Latin literary criticism, against inherited preconceptions on both these counts. Old truisms about Ovidian parody, the shallowness of his amatory verse, and the excessively literary orientation of the narrative poems are marshalled and refuted in this influential paper that has become a touchstone in new assessments of the poet and his work. In a related vein Niklas Holzberg demonstrates how, in the first-person voice found in most of his works, Ovid inscribes himself within the literary context as a self-constructed figure. This paper foreshadows the more fully developed argument of Holzberg's highly successful book on Ovid (1997), which brought Ovid to the notice of a wider reading public. What emerges from these studies is an approach to Ovid that probes beneath the glittering surface of verbal artifice, now generally characterized more respectfully as 'wit' rather than 'cleverness', and explores the complex associations of the poetry, beginning at the level of the individual word.

Other papers in the group on 'Contexts and Intertexts' exemplify the ways in which critics have turned the methodologies associated with intertextuality to good use in rehabilitating our readings of individual works. The *Heroides*, Ovid's fictional epistles composed in the voices of heroines from myth and literature, were for long dismissed as pale versifications of rhetorical school exercises until Duncan Kennedy taught us how to read these poems as sophisticated interpretations of earlier texts. On Kennedy's reading, the first poem in the collection is not simply a retelling of the story of the *Odyssey* from Penelope's point of view, but a close engagement with Homer's text and as such a critical treatise on the epic. This approach has since informed a succession of articles, commentaries (e.g. Barchiesi 1992; Knox 1995; Casali 1995; Kenney 1996), and books (e.g. Spoth 1992; Fulkerson 2005), even as interpretation of the *Heroides* has begun to incorporate other critical methods, including Lacanian psychoanalysis (Lindheim 2003) and gender studies (Spentzou 2003). John Miller's brief study explores one component in the lexicon of intertextuality, the trope of memory. It is an example of how analysis of the formal aspects of Ovidian allusion then leads to broader interpretative conclusions in Ovid's relationship to other texts. In opening a vista on Lucretian presences in Ovid's tale of Narcissus, Philip Hardie deploys the tools of an intertextual reading to explore the play of sensory perception and illusion in this narrative. Readers of his subsequent study of the *Metamorphoses* (2002*a*) will recognize the ways in which this paper informs his broader interpretations of how Ovid creates illusions of presence and absence. Both Casali on Ovid's 'Aeneid' and O'Hara on Ovid's appropriations of Virgilian etymologies illustrate another aspect of Ovid's relationship to his great predecessor as a reader and critic. In these studies, and in the further work that they have informed and inspired, Ovid's manipulation of his literary sources is treated as an integral part of his poetic method, a means by which his own representations of human character are enriched by triggering the reader's recognition of the panoply of inherited associations.

Interpretations of Ovid that set his work in the cultural context of Augustan Rome are particularly insistent upon the primary position of Ovid's amatory elegies, which have proved particularly fertile ground for interpretations inspired by trends in contemporary criticism of the latter part of the last century. The four papers in the second section on 'Ideologies of Love and Poetry' illustrate how contemporary critics have located Ovid's poetics within the broader setting of post-revolutionary Rome under Augustus. Maria Wyke's paper explores some of the larger questions confronting the genre of elegy through an examination of one poem of Ovid, the programmatic introduction to the third book of the *Amores*, in which personifications of Elegy and Tragedy compete for Ovid's attention. Her reading of the poem's parodic treatment of the stereotypical mistress forms the basis of a reading of Propertian elegy and translates the body of the elegiac mistress, as represented in elegy, into a site for the expression of Callimachean poetics. Wyke's essay was integrated into a larger argument on the representation and reception of the elegiac mistress (2002), and is a significant component in the continuing reinterpretation of the genre by an important cadre of critics (e.g. Keith 1992*b*; 2000; Sharrock 1994). A reading of another poem from the *Amores* by Barbara Weiden Boyd reflects the continuing vitality of close philological reading in Ovidian criticism and the fruitful ways in which it interacts with critical reassessments of ancient poetics. Here Boyd situates the poem on Corinna's parrot as a commentary on the poet's claim to originality within the Alexandrian tradition. Boyd's work is an example of the reinvigorated line of philological criticism of Augustan poetry that traces its affiliation with the poetry of Callimachus and his successors. While much of the work in this field has focused on Catullus, Virgil, and Propertius, Boyd's detailed investigation demonstrates the applications available to Ovidian critics, later resumed in her major study of the *Amores* (1997), and reflected in a large number of studies by other scholars. Such investigations have not infrequently led to syntheses in the reading of parts of the Ovidian corpus, an instance of which is R. A. Smith's paper on intertextualized myth and the conflation of generic variants in the *Heroides*. As a group these papers may be taken to reflect a decisive shift in critical approaches to the amatory works of Ovid. Detailed observation of the text here intersects with theoretical speculation to construct a synthesis between epistle and elegy, between Ovid's heroines and Ovid. Where scholars once asked how it was possible to take Ovid seriously, these critics have posed the question rather differently, by assuming that a serious hermeneutics is essential to decoding Ovid's ludic verse. This reformulated question is posed all the more earnestly when analysis turns to the *Ars Amatoria*, the putative cause of Ovid's relegation by Augustus in 8 CE. In her investigation of the political dimensions of elegiac discourse in Ovid's mock didactic, Alison Sharrock well illustrates how Ovid's love elegies have been repositioned from the periphery of Augustan discourse to its uncomfortable centre.

Within the corpus of Ovid's own work, the centrality of the *Metamorphoses* is reflected in a continuing stream of books, articles, and translations of the poem, which, together with the *Fasti*, forms the focus of the next group of essays on 'Narrators and Narratives'. Perhaps the most influential work to appear during this period, in an appropriate paradox, is among the shortest: the paper on the proem to the *Metamorphoses* by E. J. Kenney, who surely ranks as the most important contributor to the prominence of Ovid in Latin literary studies of the late twentieth century. In 'Ovidius Prooemians', Kenney relocates the *Metamorphoses* in the critical dialogue about the relationship of the Roman poets to their Greek Hellenistic antecedents. His elegant defence of a neglected manuscript variant and explication of the Callimachean affiliations of Ovid's opening declaration paved the way for a new line of interpretations of the poem, in which it is not seen merely as a pale reflection of Virgilian epic narrative. The complex generic affiliations of the *Metamorphoses* had been an object of investigation early in the twentieth century (Heinze 1919), but in the intervening years this critical dimension was lost. Subsequent studies following on Kenney's observations (e.g. Knox 1986*a*, Hinds 1987*a*) have taken his reading of the proem as the starting point for investigations of the body of the poem within the discourses of genre and intertextuality. Kenney's paper reflects the mutually supportive relationship of close textual scholarship and literary analysis that has marked much Ovidian scholarship during this period.

This approach to the poem is also much influenced by the breakthroughs stemming from the broader dissemination of Italian scholarship such as Conte's seminal work on intertextuality (1986). In this critical conversation another influential voice has been that of Alessandro Barchiesi, who, in his many publications on Ovid, some of them recently assembled in one volume (2001), has advanced the discourse on Ovidian intertextuality well beyond the identification of specific models. One of his most important contributions, exemplified in the paper reproduced here, has been to combine narratological and intertextual approaches to identify the multiplicity of narrative voices in the text. Through close analysis of specific passages Barchiesi demonstrates the importance of situating Ovid's narrators in context. Together with Hinds's later monograph on intertextuality and allusion (1998) Barchiesi's work has exerted a powerful influence on the present generation of Ovid's critics.

Much work remains to be done in discovering and describing the sources of Ovid's mythological scholarship, particularly as it informs the narrative of the *Metamorphoses*. Important studies have focused on his engagement with surviving texts, but the vast array of stories in the poem is supported by a largely unknown body of literature, which was known to Ovid, but may remain largely lost to us. Papyrus

discoveries of the twentieth century have yielded substantial portions
of important authors such as Callimachus, whose influence on Ovid
was long known to be considerable and has not yet been fully assessed.
Other key texts remain lost, but their existence can sometimes be
teased out of other materials, as attempted by Knox in his survey
of the evidence for the pre-Ovidian existence of one of Ovid's most
celebrated tales, Pyramus and Thisbe. Unlike a previous generation's
concern with identifying potential sources for their own sake, on the
assumption that Ovid merely reproduces them, contemporary source
criticism seeks to incorporate new materials into the complex literary
texture of Ovidian intertextuality, recognizing that lost works figure
much in Ovid's work as felt presences. In current studies of ancient
mythography (Forbes Irving 1990; Lightfoot 1999; Cameron 2004),
we are learning that the relationship between source texts and Ovid's
poetic reconfigurations is not a matter of simple transference. Future
discoveries may yield new information about the Greek (and Roman)
material that Ovid knew and drew upon in fashioning his narratives
(Hutchinson 2006).

One of the distinctive contributions of recent scholarship on the
Metamorphoses has been an intense focus on the processes of narrative in Ovid's great poem. From the beginnings of the Ovidian
revival, critics have attempted to account for the multiple levels of
voice and interlocking structures (Wilkinson 1955: 169–89). Subsequent studies tended to deal primarily with the voice of the epic
narrator (Otis 1966; 1970), and while the complexity of the poem
gradually yielded to more subtle analyses (Galinsky 1975; Solodow
1988), these often tended to rely heavily upon the identification of a
single narrative voice identical with the historical personage known as
Ovid. But much of the most exciting work of recent years has drawn
its inspiration from narratological studies of the 1970s and 1980s (e.g.
Genette 1980; Bal 1985). Gianpiero Rosati's paper, like Barchiesi's, is
intensely focused upon the study of voice and modulations of voice
in inset or 'metadiegetic' narrative. His study begins with the tale
of the opposition of the Minyads to the cult of Bacchus introduced
in *Met.* 4.37–41 and its counterpart in the story of the competition
between Arachne and Minerva in the sixth book. Rosati traces the
levels of narrative voice through Ovid's deployment of the familiar
metaphor for poetry in descriptions of the spinning and weaving of

wool. In these scenes, the literal sense overlaps with metaphorical concepts associated with poetic composition. Much recent criticism of the poem employs similar techniques of narratological analysis (e.g. Wheeler 1999; 2000; Tissol 1997), while Rosati himself has also contributed an elegant work of synthesis (2002).

Critical enthusiasm for engaging with the narrator(s) of the *Metamorphoses* has had a salutary effect on readings of Ovid's other major narrative work, the elegiac calendar-poem, the *Fasti*. In her paper on the narrator in the *Fasti*, Carole Newlands extends the investigation of the Ovidian persona from the *Metamorphoses* to the antiquarian researcher in much the same vein as Barchiesi's approach to the *Metamorphoses*. The variant aetiologies explored in the poem invite the reader to participate in destabilizing the constructions of Augustan ideology in Roman religion. Newlands's work, which was carried forward in an influential monograph (1995), was in the vanguard of renewed scholarly interest in the *Fasti*. New investigations of the historical context (Herbert-Brown 1994), new commentaries (Fantham 1998; Green 2004), and new critical readings (Herbert-Brown 2002; Murgatroyd 2005) that have radically altered readers' perceptions of this poem may be traced to this stimulus.

One aspect of Ovid's poetry that has always proved particularly challenging for critics is the poet's situation within the political circumstances of his time. Ovid's literary output spans a period of at least forty years, during which the new imperial system matured—some might say 'hardened'—into the principate of the first-century CE. Ovid's works have proved especially fertile ground for scholars as the critical discourse about the politics in Augustan Rome has expanded beyond a simple interest in the relationship of the emperor to the poets to include contemporary constructions of power relationships that include gender, social status, sexual mores, and imperialism (Habinek 1998). Attention has naturally focused on the most overtly political of Ovid's works, the *Fasti* and the poetry from exile. The *Fasti* are no longer viewed now simply as a versified calendrical tribute to Augustus, but as a complex document that both reflects and reflects upon the dissemination of the Augustan programme (Zanker 1988; Galinsky 1996). A crucial factor in the revaluation of the poem has been scholars' recognition that 'Augustanism' was not a static phenomenon and that the political context in which the *Fasti* and the exile poetry took shape was very different from the high-water mark of Augustan poetry in the 20s and teens BCE. The last group of essays deals with this political dimension to Ovid's poetry as it is positioned 'On the Margins of Empire'. Elaine Fantham's paper on the shifting dynastic situation in the years following Tiberius' return from exile in 4 CE inaugurated a sea change in the criticism of Ovid's later poetry by compelling critics to focus on these changed circumstances, rather than evaluating the poetry against a fixed, anachronistic view of Augustanism (Knox 2004). This has generated a lively debate in subsequent scholarship on the *Fasti*, with some critics seeing the poem as a positive response to Augustus' interest in the calendar and religious institutions (e.g. Herbert-Brown 1994), and others advocating a reading of the poem as a critique of the *princeps* and the new imperial system (e.g. Newlands 1995; Barchiesi 1997).

With the recognition of a changing and complex political environment has come critical acknowledgement of concomitant shifts in the situation of literature under the early principate and the consequences for our reading of Ovid's late work. Early impetus for this shift came in E. J. Kenney's influential paper on the exile poetry (1965), the full impact of which was not felt until the 80s and 90s, in concert with the continuing reassessment of the political and cultural context. The article by Stephen Hinds reproduced here gives this problem a definitive formulation in his reading of the first book of the *Tristia* by figuring the literal journey made by Ovid's book from Tomi to Rome as it relates his literary present to the literary past. Much work on the exile poetry has been built on the foundations established by Kenney and Hinds, with Gareth Williams establishing himself as a notable voice in readings of the exile poetry (1994), including the difficult and seldom anthologized curse-poem, the *Ibis*. The paper included here introduces a theme developed at greater length in his monograph (1996), which reintegrates this obscure poem into the fabric of Ovid's poetic exile, showing it to be not simply a learned *jeu d'esprit* in the Callimachean vein, but an experiment in a new poetics of exile. Critical books and articles (e.g. Claassen 1999), new editions and new commentaries (e.g. Galasso 1995; Helzle 2003; Gaertner 2005) are changing our reading of the poems from exile, altering our perception of what Ovid himself meant when he described these works in derogatory terms. Yet, the reality of Ovid's exile remains a powerful factor in all readings of this poetry, a problem well described by Denis Feeney in his reading of the missing books of the *Fasti*, a monument of the shifting ambiguities in the relationship between political power and poetic expression.

While these four horizons in Ovidian scholarship may fairly be said to mark the major developments in the last thirty years, other perspectives on the poet and his works that lead out from them cannot be treated in this volume, even though they often represent some of the most fruitful approaches. Often a stimulus to criticism has come from the traditional fields of textual scholarship and commentary. And indeed, the period has witnessed the production of some of the first truly critical editions of Ovid's works since Burman's in the eighteenth century, with definitive texts produced for the amatory works (Kenney 1961; 2nd ed. 1994), the *Fasti* (Alton et al. 1978), the *Epistulae ex Ponto* (Richmond 1990) and most recently the first reliable edition of the *Metamorphoses* (Tarrant 2004). It has also been a time when commentaries on individual works have opened new vistas on Ovid's techniques: the progress of J. C. McKeown's magisterial commentary on the *Amores* (1987; 1989; 1998) has been a significant stimulus to reassessments of Ovid as an elegiac poet. And contributions in this genre by Adrian Hollis (1970; 1977), Elaine Fantham (1998), and Roy Gibson (2003) have had similar effects on other parts of the corpus, while the major German commentary on the *Metamorphoses* by Franz Bömer (1969–86) has become an indispensable reference work. It is likely that this activity will continue, perhaps accelerate, with important commentaries on other Ovidian works looming on the horizon. The curious symbiosis between philology and literary criticism is a largely unexplored territory in Latin literary studies, but the history of Ovidian criticism illustrates quite well how they function in tandem.

It has long been noted that Ovid has consistently held for poets, artists and writers a fascination that is occasionally lost on scholars, often manifested in new works of translation. The past decades too have been an age of translation (Martin 1998). A. D. Melville's version of the *Metamorphoses* reintroduced a generation of Latin-less readers to the swift pace and dazzling turns of phrase in Ovid's narrative. His other translations—the amatory elegies (1990) and the *Tristia* (1992)—have likewise brought Ovid's other works back into the ken of non-specialists. New translations of the *Metamorphoses* (Slavitt 1994; Martin 2003; Raeburn 2004) and other works (Boyle and Woodard 2004; Green 2005) herald a continuing interest in making Ovid new for the next generation of readers. Likewise, the intersection between translation and interpretation is a vast area of Ovidian studies just beginning to be explored, as scholars and critics increasingly recognize the significant role played by translation in the English literary tradition (Lyne 2001). Of course, the horizons of Ovid's influence extend far beyond the English-speaking world, which scholars of Ovidian reception will increasingly draw on in their assessments of his impact on western culture (Guthmüller 1981; Gallo and Nicastri 1995).

Ovid's continuing attraction to creative artists is also evident in the number of writers who find in the mystery of Ovid's exile not a historical problem to be solved, but a locus for exploring the experience of the artist on the margins. The novels of David Malouf (1978) and Christoph Ransmayr (1988) inscribe Ovid in the contemporary imagination as the iconic poet of exile, but the assessment of Ovid's vast impact on the literary imagination of the twentieth century is a task barely begun (Kennedy 2002; Ziolkowski 2005). The publication of Hofmann and Lasdun's anthology of new poetry (1994) inspired by Ovid took many in the world of classical scholarship by surprise, and it was soon followed by Ted Hughes's critical success with his *Tales from Ovid* (1997), which incorporated some extracts from the earlier anthology in a new version of Ovid's *Metamorphoses*. The ability of Ovid's poetry to take hold of the popular imagination is perhaps best illustrated by the success of Mary Zimmerman's Broadway production (2002) based on the *Metamorphoses*. Professional classicists responded to this renewed evidence of Ovid's hold on the artistic imagination (Brown 1999; Henderson 1999), and it is likely that reception studies may represent the next major horizon in Ovidian criticism. Still awaiting the attention of scholars is the study of Ovid as a source of inspiration in the visual arts (Allen 2002).

In looking ahead towards new contributions to our understanding of Ovid on the horizon, some familiar outlines emerge. New critical editions are still needed of several major works, including the *Heroides*, *Tristia*, and the *Ibis*, and it is only to be expected that scholars will fill these gaps as they also re-edit other texts. In spite of

Peter E. Knox

the production of several major commentaries on Ovid during these decades, there remains ample scope for detailed verbal scholarship in this format, since Ovid has generally been less thoroughly investigated than any other Augustan poet. In the near future we can look forward to the completion of McKeown's *Amores*, and a commentary on the *Metamorphoses* by an international team of scholars is also in the works. Even as fundamental research into constituting and explicating the text of Ovid continues, new criticism, new readings, new receptions of his work will proliferate. Ludwig Traube once famously dubbed the twelfth century an 'Ovidian age' (*aetas Ovidiana*) because of the renewed interest during that time for copying texts of Ovid and imitating his style in new literary productions (1911: 113). But from the vantage point of the present, it would probably be more appropriate to talk of a succession of Ovidian ages, for as each one recedes the contours of the next inevitably rise to meet us.

Part I

Contexts and Intertexts

1

Generalizing About Ovid

Stephen Hinds

The aim of this essay is to confront some ageing generalizations about Ovid which seem to have survived the latest close readings of his poetry intact. Most of the critics who have recently been casting new light on particular poems and passages have been too cautious to use their very specific findings to call explicitly into question long-established overviews of the Ovidian *oeuvre*. However, an attempt of some kind should be made. Today's generalization is nothing more than an accretion of yesterday's particular readings; and reassessment of it can come only when it is tested against a new generation of particular readings. My focus, therefore, will be on specifics, but with an untimid eye towards overviews.

A like absence of timidity will also be found in my specifics themselves. Writers of 'general' articles tend to eschew difficult or controversial interpretations of particular passages, lest some overall balance in their presentation of an author be upset. I shall have few such qualms: one of my aims is precisely to destabilize—however slightly—the terms of reference within which Ovidian poetry is usually read. Indeed, I shall risk beginning with what will probably be the most controversial reading in my essay.

1. 'THE SHALLOW AND OVER-EXPLICIT POET'

My inaugural poem is *Amores* 1.5. It seems an appropriate focus for my discussion, since two influential critics who espouse traditional overviews of Ovid have adopted it as a paradigm for their respective positions.

Ovid, we have been told for years, is an over-explicit poet. Where his predecessors hint and suggest, Ovid spells out and enumerates. Gordon Williams, in *Tradition and Originality in Roman Poetry*, turns to the beginning of *Amores* 1.5 to substantiate this long-standing charge (1–13):

aestus erat, mediamque dies exegerat horam;
    adposui medio membra levanda toro.
pars adaperta fuit, pars altera clausa fenestrae,
    quale fere silvae lumen habere solent,
qualia sublucent fugiente crepuscula Phoebo
    aut ubi nox abiit nec tamen orta dies.
illa verecundis lux est praebenda puellis,
    qua timidus latebras speret habere pudor.
ecce, Corinna venit tunica velata recincta,
    candida dividua colla tegente coma,
qualiter in thalamos formosa Semiramis isse
    dicitur et multis Lais amata viris.
deripui tunicam . . .

It was sultry, and the day had completed its mid hour; I laid my members to be refreshed on the middle of my couch. One part of my window was open, the other part closed: the light was such as oft in a woodland, or as the faint glow of the twilight when Phoebus is taking his leave, or when night has gone and yet the day is not sprung. That is the light to offer to coy maids, in which their timid modesty may hope to find a hiding-place. Lo! Corinna comes, draped in an ungirt tunic, with her divided hair covering her fair neck: just as lovely Semiramis is said to have been when passing to her bridal chamber, and Lais loved by many men. I tore away her tunic . . .

'This should be compared,' writes Williams (1968: 512), 'with the suggestiveness of Catullus 68 [lines 67–72], where a few details are selected and portrayed with precision, touching in outlines which the responsive reader can apprehend. Ovid indeed tries to convey feeling, but by exhaustive enumeration, and the weaknesses are clear. He lies in a room with one shutter closed, the other open, and the light is as in a great wood: this is excellent; but he must try to reach greater expansiveness, assist the reader to a more complete realisation of the exact nature of the light, so he adds in evening at sunset and then dawn before sunrise. By the addition all mystery is removed, and the way is paved for the clever, knowing advice about modest girls . . . The poetic technique is to exhaust all the possibilities, lest any escape the reader: it is a mistaken zeal and one avoided by both Catullus and Propertius—and also, in his idiosyncratic way, by Tibullus. There is no denying the cleverness and wit of it; what may be questioned is its implied assessment of the poet's activity.'

Let me shift to another, related generalization, and to another critic. Ovid, according to a widespread view, is a shallow poet. R. O. A. M. Lyne (1980: 259–64) puts it in the gentlest possible way in *The Latin Love Poets*, writing of Ovid's 'positive attitude to love—and love poetry. It is *fun* [his italics]. Not perhaps a profound view, but a valid one.' *Amores* 1.5, singled out for the way that it 'illuminates Ovidian thought and art', emerges from Lyne's essentially sympathetic reading as a stylish erotic romp. The first of his observations is excellent: 'Ovid describes how he was taking his siesta. Apparently he did not expect Corinna. That is the clear point of *medio . . . toro* in line 2. Those who sleep in the middle of their beds are sleeping alone: cf. *Am.* 2.10.18. What *is* implied however is that Ovid was very much in the mood for her. He was randy. He manages to communicate this in the siesta description . . . The half-light, which might have encouraged others to sleep, was to Ovid a stimulus to thoughts of sex. Corinna may not have been expected but she was certainly needed. Somewhat in the manner of Propertius 1.3 or Catullus 68 Ovid is using dramatic evocation ("reportorial technique") to suggest the feelings of the time. And he suggests more or more tastefully than he ever could explicitly tell.'

Note that where Williams saw over-explicitness, Lyne sees suggestiveness. Contrast the second half of *Amores* 1.5, where Lyne too finds the poet in explicit mode: in lines 13–26 Ovid 'revels in the attractive but *definable* [his italics] beauty of Corinna'. Lyne has here recognized an important feature of *Amores* 1.5, its marked *shift* in tone and tempo after Corinna's sudden arrival in lines 9–12.[1] (I draw attention to this partly to prepare for my own later discussion.) So far, so good.

---

[1] See the first half of line 13, which I have included in my quotation as an indicator of this shift. Limitations of space preclude full quotation of all the passages which I discuss in this essay: I am assuming a reader who has a complete text of Ovid to hand.

However, like many critics who are less than fully committed to Ovid, Lyne seems to have some difficulty in sustaining his awareness of this distinctively Ovidian world of tonal fluctuation. By the time that he comes to sum up *Amores* 1.5, he has strangely elided his reading of the first half of the poem into his reading of the second half—so that the poem *as a whole*, not just lines 13–24 of it, is now characterized by '. . . explicit, unmysterious, and splendid sensuality'. Barely perceptibly, Lyne has simplified his own originally complex account of the poem's movement.

My quibble may seem ungenerous. However, the reductive impulse just discernible here may be regarded as symptomatic of a broad tendency amongst critics to draw back at moments when they are about to treat Ovid as a complicated poet. Let me bring the charge of shallowness more into the open by quoting from Lyne's earlier, less sympathetic assessment of the *Amores* in a review article entitled 'Ways of Resurrecting Ovid'.[2] 'Ovid's *Amores* are basically verse of wit,' he writes, 'but they are not great poetry of wit; Horace's *Pyrrha* Ode or *donec gratus eram* . . . (for example) probably are. Reread these and the texture forms anew, the complexion of the wit changes—deepens if you like; indefinable resonances of words contribute to some always new aspect. Ovid in the *Amores* dazzles with the surface of words and presents us with a face of wit. Certainly we reread him and are amused again—but it is essentially the *same* amusement. Words are basically static in one function; the use of *words* is shallow and that matters.'

Two very dissimilar critics, then, make against Ovid two closely linked charges, each with a long pedigree in the annals of Ovidian scholarship: over-explicitness and shallowness. Let me now trace my own, rather different path into *Amores* 1.5.

In the rush to assess the great debt of Ovidian elegy to Propertius, the Catullan affinities of the *Amores* are often forgotten. The standard commentaries have long noticed the collection's most conspicuous Catullan echoes: the variations on *odi et amo* in 3.11b and 3.14; the associated near-quotation in 3.11a of the injunction from Catullus 8, *perfer, obdura*; and the version of Lesbia's *passer* in 2.6. To the

---

[2] In *Times Literary Supplement*, 7 March 1975. Once again, the italics in the passage quoted are his.

present-day reader of Ovid, more attuned than previous generations to the range and subtlety of Ovidian literary reference, what
perhaps stands out about these allusions is, precisely, their conspicuousness. Such clearly marked allusion seems designed to draw
attention to Catullus as an especially privileged model. Catullus is
indeed an important model. Ovid's stress in the *Amores* on the
need to observe rules in the game of love owes more (in its own
way) to the Catullan idea of a formal code of amatory commitment than to anything in the world of Propertian *furor*. And, significantly, in naming his mistress after the Greek poetess Corinna,
Ovid bypasses the Augustan elegiac procedure of choosing feminized
cult names of Apollo for this purpose (Lycoris, Cynthia, Delia) in
favour of a return to Catullan practice (Lesbia, from Sappho of
Lesbos).

In *Amores* 2.6, in fact, the conspicuousness of Ovid's allusion to
Catullus amounts to an extreme case of self-reference (*Am.* 2.6.1–2):
psittacus, Eois imitatrix ales ab Indis, | *occidit* ... 'The parrot, winged
imitator from the Eastern Ind, is dead...' Here we find a phenomenon to which I shall be returning later in this essay: the allusion
which is so constructed as to draw attention to its status as allusion.
Corinna's engaging *psittacus* is modelled on Lesbia's famous *passer*, or
'sparrow': and it is called an *imitatrix ales* by Ovid not just because,
as a parrot, its role in nature is to mimic; but because its role in the
Latin erotic tradition is to 'imitate' that particular bird celebrated by
Catullus.

Catullus is always present in the background of Ovid's *Amores*: and
elegy 1.5 covertly alludes to one of the most important moments in
the neoteric poet's *oeuvre*. Lyne and Williams both come close to
noticing this when (in the passages of their criticism quoted earlier) they compare and contrast Corinna's arrival in Ovid's chamber with the arrival of Lesbia at the trysting house of Catullus 68
(70–5):

> quo mea se molli candida diva pede
> intulit et trito fulgentem in limine plantam
>   innixa arguta constituit solea,
> coniugis ut quondam flagrans advenit amore
>   Protesilaeam Laudamia domum
> inceptam frustra ...

There with gentle foot my fair goddess made an entry, and set her shining step on the worn threshold, pressing on her sounding sandal: even as once burning with love for her husband came Laudamia to the house of Protesilaus, that house begun in vain . . .

The entry into the trysting house of Lesbia, strikingly idealized as a *candida diva,* is the pivotal moment of this celebrated Catullan elegy, a moment which will be arrested—quite literally on the threshold—for no less than 60 lines, as the associated mythological simile describing Laudamia's entry into her marriage home runs its course. It is also, on any terms, one of the key moments in Lesbia's poetic 'career' as a whole, and probably marks her first entry into a collection of Catullan elegiacs inaugurated at poem 65.[3]

What of *Amores* 1.5? The Ovidian elegy describes the arrival in Ovid's bedchamber of his mistress Corinna; an arrival which marks Corinna's first entry as a named figure into Ovid's elegiac collection. Two similes are associated with this moment, the first of which describes the entry of a legendary queen into her marriage chamber (1.5.11).

Two 'staged' arrivals in two elegiac affairs: but the circumstantial similarities are noteworthy only because of a remarkable verbal allusion which Ovid has executed at this juncture, an allusion which has been passed over by modern criticism because (one supposes) it is so wilfully and elementally verbal. Here, once again, is the moment of the mistress's arrival at the tryst in Catullus 68.70–1 (I give translations only under my first quotation of a passage):

> quo mea se molli candida diva pede
> intulit . . .

And here again is the equivalent moment in *Amores* 1.5.9–10:

ecce, Corinna venit tunica velata recincta,
    candida dividua colla tegente coma . . .

Does the echo make itself heard? Corinna again, this time with the inner ear tracing the rise and fall of the couplet more closely:

---

[3] See Wiseman (1969) 17–18 and (1985) 159 and 184, arguing a strong case for regarding the arrangement of poems 65 ff. as essentially Catullus' own.

ecce, Corinna venit tunica velata recincta,
  candida div—

The reference to the Catullan goddess is offered for an instant only, as
the pentameter opens—only to be withdrawn, as the syntax of the line
completes itself. Corinna is not, after all, a *candida diva*: the epiphany
fades. The adjective qualifies her *colla*, not herself; and *div-* emerges
as the first syllable of *dividua*, qualifying *coma*.

Critics hostile to recent demonstrations of the centrality of wordplay to Ovid's consciousness will bridle: but they should pause to
reflect. The poet's *docti lectores* will have been at their most attentive in the couplet under discussion, crucial as Corinna's arrival is
to the *mise en scène* of the *Amores*. Equally important to Catullus'
elegiac output, I have suggested, is Lesbia's strongly marked entry into
poem 68 in the idealized role of *candida diva*, the prototype of many
such idealizations in Augustan elegy. And we should begin to see the
point of the Ovidian wordplay if we think about the significance of
that Catullan idealization in its original context. The main progression of thought in Catullus 68 is towards a *failure* of the idealization of
Lesbia set up in lines 70–4—a 'step-by-step collapse of the romantic
vision', as Lyne (1980: 52–60) puts it in a sensitive discussion. By
the end of the poem, Catullus has realized that Lesbia is less than a
Laudamia (131); *candida* only in respect of the stone with which she
will mark her calendar for him (148); and, alas (as is unmistakably,
if somewhat obliquely, intimated), no *diva* (68.141): *atqui nec divis
homines componier aequum est* 'And yet to compare mortals with
gods is not right . . .' In the course of a long and vertiginous poetic
argument (which, however, represents a single moment of epiphany
in 'actual' time), Catullus has first offered, and then withdrawn, an
idealization of his mistress as a fair goddess coming to tryst with
him. Herein lies the precision of the Ovidian wordplay in *Am.* 1.5.10.
In a fleeting moment (no narrative suspension in this case), Ovid
salutes his predecessor's vision of epiphany—and, simultaneously,
the collapse of that vision. Like her prototype Lesbia, Corinna first
appears as, but cannot sustain an appearance as, her elegiac poet's
candida diva.

Is this a fair answer to a charge that in the *Amores* 'words are
basically static in one function'? Well, yes and no. The complaint is

that Ovid's use of language is shallow: and a virtuoso pun like the one just described, though in a way answering the charge, also lays itself open to disparagement, in isolation, as a mere piece of superficial showiness. However, such disparagement must needs subside if it can be shown that the pun does *not* exist in isolation in the texture of *Amores* 1.5. I believe that a closer look will reveal the wordplay of 1.5.10 to be at the centre of some wider adumbrations of divine epiphany in this apparently straightforward scene of erotic encounter.

Consider the catalogue of light-effects at the beginning of the elegy, which Williams found so over-explicit. By the criteria of naturalistic description he has a good case. It *is* oddly excessive in these terms for Ovid, having already compared the filtering of the sun through part-open, part-closed shutters (line 3) to the lighting in a wood (line 4), to go on to compare it to twilit dusk (line 5)—and then to the transitional time of dawn (line 6).

But what if criteria other than those of naturalistic description are relevant? Half-light in ancient poetry not infrequently carries a suggestion of the near presence of divinity. There is a good Ovidian example in *Metamorphoses* 4, where some very deliberate light-effects accompany the supernatural exercise of Bacchic power upon the unfortunate daughters of Minyas (*Met.* 4.399–401):

iamque dies exactus erat tempusque subibat,
quod tu nec tenebras nec posses dicere lucem,
sed cum luce tamen dubiae confinia noctis.

And now the day was ended, and the time was coming on which you could call neither darkness nor light; it was the borderland of dubious night, yet with some light.

Ovid may be a supremely rational poet; but that does not mean that we should deny to him (any more than we deny to, say, Euripides) an interest in the irrational. Through the half-light of *Am.* 1.5.3–6, and especially through the confusing *overdetermination* of that half-light, our poet can be argued to be hinting at something supernatural in the background of his elegy. *Pars adaperta . . ., pars . . . clausa* (line 3), *sublucent . . . crepuscula* (line 5), *aut ubi nox abiit nec tamen orta dies* (line 6): Ovid's catalogue, I suggest, almost incantatory in its tone, fleetingly threatens to transform the poem's early afternoon setting into a zone of boundaries and transitions, a time out of time in which normal human rules may cease to apply. A few bold believers in wordplay may wish to go further, and faster, here. Corinna, a divided *diva* (the allusion in *dividua* alludes to its own processes), aptly inhabits this highly patterned world of borderlines—and of midpoints (lines 1, 2, 26). She is like Catullus' *candida diva* in poem 68, poised on the threshold of definition (line 10); she is like *Semi*ramis, 'half' in name (line 11); and she is like Lais, whose etymologically marked name (line 12) makes her half of Catullus' *Lau*damia, half of his Protesi*laus*.[4]

Such strictly verbal matters are occult in their own way: but let me return to more orthodox symptoms of divinity in the poem's dramatic setting. I have yet to account for one element in the overdetermined description of half-light in *Am.* 1.5.3–6: the obscurely lit *silva* in line 4. Is it merely coincidental that this too seems to fit into the picture which is emerging? Woodland, more than any other setting, is associated with divine epiphany in Augustan poetry. One particular example stands out in the present context, viz. the setting in which Elegia herself (as opposed to Corinna, her representative) will stage an epiphany later in this very collection (*Am.* 3.1.1–2):

stat vetus et multos incaedua silva per annos;
   credibile est illi numen inesse loco.

There stands a wood, ancient and uncut through many years; it is worthy of belief that a deity inhabits that spot.

---

[4] Let me amplify the final item in this slightly vatic paragraph. Lais, as the commentaries remind us, was a famous courtesan; but in *Am.* 1.5.12 the main interest is in the purely verbal matter of the etymology of her name. Ovid's simile here for his quasi-*candida diva* reinforces his primary allusion to Catullus by picking up the beginning of Catullus' own simile for his *candida diva* at 68.73 f. On this reading, Lais, overtly etymologized (*multis Lais amata viris*, 'Lais loved by many men [= Greek *laos*]'), operates as a distillation of and learned gloss on the highly mannered juxtaposition of names in that first Catullan pentameter: *coniugis ut quondam flagrans advenit amore | Protesilaeam Laudamia domum*. The Catullan juxtaposition is probably itself implicitly etymological: allusion to the common etymological ground between Protesi-laos and Lao-dameia seems to be a long-established *topos* in Latin poetry, if we may judge from the title of Laevius' *Protesilaudamia*.

Another circumstantial hint may be felt in the *manner* of Corinna's arrival. No knock at the door, no explanation of her sudden presence, half-clothed (*tunica velata recincta*), in Ovid's chamber: just (1.5.9) *ecce Corinna venit.* Simple narrative economy—or a hint also of dreamlike epiphany? If the suggestion seems forced, compare the rhetorical device used by Ovid to begin an overt epiphany scene at the beginning of *Fasti* 6 (once again, in a wood): *ecce deas vidi,* 'Lo! I saw goddesses' (6.11).

All this aura of divinity (if such it be) is dispelled by the healthy erotic specificity of the elegy's second half, justly admired by Lyne. As I hinted earlier, it is probably because of the forthrightness of lines 13 ff. that the subtler shades of lines 1–12 have been missed: critics of the *Amores* are generally less sensitive to Ovidian tonal fluctuation than are critics of the *Metamorphoses.* Yet, even in this second half, lingering traces of the covert epiphany theme are discernible, in the perfection of Corinna's form as first seen whole (*Am.* 1.5.18)—*in toto nusquam corpore menda fuit* 'nowhere on all her body was a sign of fault'—and also, perhaps, in her magnificent stature (*Am.* 1.5.22): *quantum et quale latus* 'how great and how fair her flank!' The attributes of an idealized mistress, certainly; but also, more pointedly than in most elegiac idealizations, the attributes of a goddess.

None of the above nuances is inescapable in isolation; but together they form a significant pattern of suggestion in the poem, a pattern which deepens and complicates the reference of the punning allusion originally discerned in 1.5.10. At one level, the Corinna of *Amores* 1.5 is the accessible, definable *domina* beloved of (or despised by) the *communis opinio.* But at another level she is a Catullan *candida diva,* an adumbrated goddess: and in accordance with this her first entry into Ovid's elegiacs is charged with something of the numinousness of epiphany.

Scenes of divine initiation have dominated the beginning of Ovid's *Amores*: by Cupid in poem 1.1, by Cupid and a host of other gods and divinized figures in poems 1.2 and 1.3. Here in 1.5, where the poet finally introduces us to a named mistress for the first time, is it surprising if she arrives on the scene with a divine aura of her own?

It is time to take another look at the general charges against Ovid with which I began. First, shallowness. I suggested, half way through my discussion, that on its own the *candida diva* pun in *Am.* 1.5.10 might be felt to be an insufficient response to an accusation of verbal superficiality. However, the associated patterns of suggestion which I have been tracing since that point seem to me to answer any such reservations more than adequately. *Amores* 1.5 *does* show new aspects of itself as one reads and rereads it. As poetry, and as poetic language, it is as subtle and as profound as anything in Latin personal poetry—even (if that be the chosen standard) Horace's *Pyrrha* Ode.

Second, the related issue of over-explicitness. Williams is certainly right to see an interest in catalogues as an Ovidian trait. But what my analysis of *Am.* 1.5.3–6 perhaps shows is that increased enumeration does not necessarily imply increased explicitness. Catalogues are not inherently 'counter-poetic', and in this case Ovid's accumulation of light-effects serves to generate, not to disperse, an atmosphere of poetic suggestiveness and mystery.

2. 'THE EXCESSIVELY LITERARY POET'

Let me use my reading of *Amores* 1.5 to introduce another area of critical generalization. Corinna's quasi-divine epiphany in *Amores* 1.5 arguably hints at an alignment of the *Amores* with the *mise en scène* at the beginning of Propertius' *Monobiblos,* in which the elegiac mistress implicitly takes on some of the functions normally associated with a divine agent of poetic initiation. Ovid began the *Amores* in elegies 1.1–3 with a most un-Propertian stress[5] on *overtly* divine initiation (Cupid et al.: see my discussion just above): but here at the moment of his mistress's first named appearance in the collection, he seems to offer a belated acknowledgement of Propertius' more *covert* approach to the initiation scene.

I offer the above paragraph as a first step towards a more helpful way of looking at the relationship between Propertian and Ovidian erotic elegy. The picture which I have just painted of Propertius 1.1 is by no means the orthodox one. I write of a difference between *covert*

---

[5] Un-Propertian, that is, until Propertius' belated conversion in his third book to an overtly divine apparatus of inspiration: see especially poem 3.3.

literary programme and *overt* literary programme. But the established view of the difference between the beginning of Propertius' *Monobiblos* and the beginning of Ovid's *Amores* is, much more starkly, one between personal inspiration and literary inspiration; between 'a question of life' and 'a question of metre'.[6]

Important issues are at stake here. The purpose of this central section of my essay will be to come to grips with the charge of excessive literariness often levelled against Ovid's writing. Is Ovid more 'literary' than other poets? What is the role in Ovid, and in Latin poetry at large, of self-reference and of poetic programme?

The specific question with which I have begun is something of a throwback to previous decades of literary critical debate. At a time when Propertian criticism has in most respects shaken itself free of the biographical fallacy, it is odd to find the old opposition between 'sincerity' and 'literariness' still persisting in discussions of the difference between Propertian and Ovidian elegiac inspiration. That opposition may seem to offer the simplest way to deal with the undoubted fact that the tone of Propertius 1.1 is fundamentally serious, whereas the tone of *Amores* 1.1, with its tale of a stolen foot, is fundamentally whimsical: but it will not do, for all that. As we shall see if we take a careful look at the two couplets most commonly adduced when Propertian 'inspiration from life' is set up as something to be contrasted with Ovidian 'inspiration from literature', Propertius yields to no poet in his literary self-consciousness.

Like Gallus and Tibullus, Propertius has given his mistress a name which is a feminized cult title of Apollo: Cynthia.[7] No one disputes this. Yet, when contrasting Propertius with Ovid, critics still persist in taking at simple face value the earlier elegist's apparent rejection of the traditional apparatus of literary inspiration in a couplet at the beginning of his second book (Prop. 2.1.3–4):

non haec Calliope, non haec mihi cantat Apollo;
  ingenium nobis ipsa puella facit.

---

[6] This formulation of the traditional contrast comes from Lyne (1980: 260). However, in a discreet footnote (309 n. 33) he hints at the possibility of a less extreme emphasis in reading Propertius: 'we are entitled to infer ulterior artistic motives . . .'.

[7] I have already alluded to this circumstance in section 1 above.

It is not Calliope that gives me my songs, nor Apollo; it is my girl herself that inspires my wit.

What at first sight looks like a *disavowal* of Apolline influence in favour of a wholly personal inspiration is actually at an important level a *redefinition* of Apolline influence, Cynthius yields—but only to Cynthia. And so too in the other couplet customarily adduced, the very first in the *Monobiblos* (1.1.1–2):

Cynthia prima suis miserum me cepit ocellis,
    contactum nullis ante cupidinibus.

Cynthia first captured me with her eyes, poor unfortunate, previously touched by no passion.

Propertius begins his book with a plunge into obsessive love: let us give that primary level of meaning its due weight. But also, simultaneously, he uses his mistress's name to hint at his Apolline initiation into erotic elegy, an initiation not so very far removed from another poet's more overtly divinized change of life (Virgil, *Ecl.* 6.3–4):

cum canerem reges et proelia, Cynthius aurem
vellit et admonuit . . .

When I was for singing of kings and battles, Cynthius plucked my ear and urged me thus . . .

These two key personal avowals by Propertius, then, also constitute highly literary avowals.[8]

There is something reductive about an opposition which on the one hand denies to Propertius his interest in literary process, while on the other denying to Ovid his interest in anything other than literary process. Both poets stand to gain from a reformulation of the traditional contrast between the beginning of the *Monobiblos* and the beginning of the *Amores.* Once we have come to terms with the self-conscious interest in literary inspiration which underpins Propertius' highly personal approach, we can start to move away, on the other

---

[8] I should acknowledge a general debt in my reading of Propertius to the work of Maria Wyke. Also, I should draw the reader's attention to Keith (1992*b*), an important paper that appeared subsequent to mine, but to which I had prior access. I have not divulged here any of the contents of this paper; but it will be found to set on a new—and newly firm—basis some points which are merely adumbrated here.

side, from the impoverished view of the beginning of Ovid's *Amores*
as a simple conversion of a non-literary Propertian programme to
literariness. The sequence of elegies which opens the *Amores* is more
varied and wide-ranging in its themes than most analyses suggest.
Ovid does not 'debunk' or 'parody' Propertius. Rather, he interprets
him, he alters his emphases: often towards more overt discussion of
literary programme; but sometimes too (as my reading of *Amores* 1.5
may serve to suggest) in the direction of a vision which can be as
elusive and as mysterious as anything in Latin elegy.

It is always important to remember that we have inherited the
stereotype of an excessively literary Ovid from the English-speaking
Latinists of the first half of this century, who tended to look down
on Alexandrianism as a kind of intermittent disease afflicting Roman
poetry. Ovid was evidently incurable. Even the verse of Propertius,
with 'its abuse of mythological ornament and . . . the laboured and
artificial character of some of its passages', was redeemable only
because of the poet's expressions of 'sincerity . . . when he lays aside
his erudition'. Catullus invariably carried off the palm, because the
influence of Alexandria was perceived only in a few of his longer
productions. My quotations come from Sir Paul Harvey (1937: s.v.
'Propertius'), to whom few of us would now turn for explications of
Propertius, or of any other Roman poet; but who represents a mental
set which we still allow to dictate, more than we realize, the *terms of
reference* within which we make our assessments of Roman poetry. As
hundreds of detailed readings over the past thirty years or so have
shown, all the poets mentioned above are full-time Alexandrians,
all are self-conscious artificers of language. What distinguishes Ovid
from other *docti poetae* is not in any sense literariness *per se*; but,
perhaps, the greater vigour of Ovidian literariness.

Let me further test and explore this last point with the aid of
an extended illustration. Every learned poet obsessively triangulates
from his literary predecessors and contemporaries as he writes: but
only Ovid, perhaps, attempts the kind of sustained and obtrusive
tour de force represented by the 'versions' of Virgil's *Aeneid* in *Met.*
13.623–14.608 and in *Fasti* 3.545–656. The latter of these exercises is
perhaps the less well known. Ovid, explaining the festival of Anna
Perenna on the Ides of March, identifies that goddess with Anna,
sister of the Carthaginian queen Dido. The narrative explanation

of how Anna came to Italy after her sister's death is at one level a sequel to the *Aeneid,* 'completing' as it does a strand of Virgil's story; and is at another level a re-enactment of the *Aeneid,* in that Anna's voyages replay in miniature various key moments in the voyages of the Virgilian Aeneas.

Out of the many prominent echoes of the *Aeneid* in the episode (well catalogued in earlier critical discussions), let me single out for consideration one, near the beginning, which falls easily into the category of sequel to its particular model passage (*Fast.* 3.555–6):[9]

diffugiunt Tyrii quo quemque agit error, ut olim
    amisso dubiae rege vagantur apes.

The Tyrians scatter wherever each in his wandering is impelled, even as at times bees stray about unsettled, when their king has been lost.

The queen is dead *(Fast.* 3.545–50) and Iarbas has invaded (551–4): Ovid describes in the quoted couplet the collapse of Dido's Carthage. The use of the bee simile immediately identifies a specific Virgilian source: our poet is recalling the description of the *rise* of Dido's Carthage in *Aeneid* 1. Aeneas' (and our) very first sight of the city in Virgil's epic is of its new buildings being erected by ardent Tyrians, whose industry and organization is conveyed by an extended simile picturing a disciplined community of bees *(Aen.* 1.430–6), one of three bee similes in the *Aeneid.* Here in Ovid's sequel the city is falling, the Tyrians are scattering—and the bee simile has become illustrative of chaos.

The allusion is neat: but does it have anything to recommend it other than neatness? As I stated at the outset, the whole *Fasti* episode is something of a *tour de force* in its sustained and obtrusive echoing of the *Aeneid.* That is fine, as far as it goes: but is Ovid's procedure perhaps open to a charge of unsubtlety, when set beside the more oblique kind of reference to a model and to combinations of models generally characteristic of Augustan poetry?

I think not. First, such sustained *tours de force* are actually less than common in Ovid's *oeuvre.* Second, even here, where the poet's

---

[9] See Döpp (1969) 56–76; Littlewood (1980); McKeown (1984). However, my remarks here on Ovid's role as a reader of Virgil are more significantly indebted to research in this general area by Catherine Connors.

allusive strategy seems to be at its most facile, a closer look will reveal his debt to Virgil to be more complex and thoughtful than at first appears. Let me return to the two bee similes. Virgil's seven-line comparison applied to the hard-working Tyrians is one of a small group of striking near-quotations of the *Georgics* in the similes of the *Aeneid* (Austin 1971: ad 1.430 ff.): the lines *Aen.* 1.430–6 are taken almost *verbatim* from the description of an industrious bee-community at *Geo.* 4.162–9. And Ovid's sequel? At one level, he is probably acknowledging Virgilian procedure within the *Aeneid* itself, where the bee simile of 1.430–6 finds a kind of sequel in the last of the epic's three bee similes at 12.587–92: there the bees are chaotic, not disciplined; and there it is Latinus' city which falls, not Dido's which rises. We do seem to discern here a prefiguring of the pattern of Ovid's sequel to the *Aeneid* 1 passage. [10] But the principal inspiration for the behaviour of the Ovidian bees in *Fast.* 3.555–6, agitated at the loss of their king, lies not in *Aeneid* 12 (where the bees are upset for another reason), nor anywhere else in the *Aeneid:* the vignette is drawn from the *Georgics.* Again, Ovid's allusion to Virgil is also an acknowledgement of Virgilian procedure. Virgil found a simile for the rise of Carthage, as described in *Aeneid* 1, amongst the bees of the fourth *Georgic*; Ovid seeks a simile for his sequel to this scene just fifty lines further on in the same *Georgic* book. The esteem of bees for their king, writes Virgil there, surpasses even that shown by the peoples of the East (*Geo.* 4.210–12):

praeterea regem non sic Aegyptus et ingens
Lydia nec populi Parthorum aut Medus Hydaspes
observant . . .

Moreover not Egypt, nor great Lydia, nor the Parthian peoples, nor Median Hydaspes have such high regard for their king . . .

Therefore, the loss of the bee-king is something which provokes utter chaos (*Geo.* 4.212–14):

---

[10] Also, where Ovid's sequel illustrates a scene of chaos which immediately follows the suicide of a queen (Dido), Virgil's own sequel within the *Aeneid* illustrates a scene of chaos which immediately precedes the suicide of a queen (Amata). Does Ovid here show his awareness of the recurrent narrative parallelism between Dido and Amata in Virgil's epic?

... rege incolumi mens omnibus una est;
amisso rupere fidem, constructaque mella
diripuere ipsae et cratis solvere favorum.

...when their king is safe, there is one mind among all; when he has been
lost, they immediately sever their allegiance; they themselves tear to pieces
the fabric of their honey, and demolish the structure of their combs.

Here it is that Ovid has found the material for the simile which is his
sequel to the simile of *Aen.* 1.430–6 (*Fast.* 3.555–6):

diffugiunt Tyrii quo quemque agit error, ut olim
    amisso dubiae rege vagantur apes.

The debt to the *Georgic* passage is visible in the emphatic verbal echo
of *amisso* in initial line position, and in the completion of the implied
ablative absolute with *rege*.[11] Ovid's *quo quemque* clause in *Fast.* 3.555
is antithetical in sense to Virgil's *mens omnibus una* in *Geo.* 4.212. In
the *Georgic* passage bee-communities behave like Eastern peoples; in
the *Fasti* 3 passage an Eastern people (the Tyrii) behaves like a bee-
community.

The virtuosity of the *Fasti*'s 'miniature *Aeneid*', then, does not
preclude subtlety: even in this fairly extreme display-piece, there is
nothing superficial about Ovid's literariness. Here, as elsewhere in his
oeuvre, Ovid shows himself to be one of Virgil's most sympathetic
and perceptive readers. His interest is not just in Virgilian words and
themes, but in the very roots of Virgil's poetry. Through the allusion
just analysed, he enriches his microcosmic version of the *Aeneid* with
an evocation of a fundamental Virgilian technique: the self-conscious
reshaping of the world of the *Georgics* to fit the world of the *Aeneid*.
That technique, which is by no means confined to the few extended
'quotations' of the *Georgics* in the *Aeneid*, constitutes one of the most
personal aspects of Virgil's literariness (note, as earlier in the present
section, the inadequacy of any opposition here between 'personal'
and 'literary'); and the literariness of Ovid's response to it constitutes
a personal tribute from one self-conscious artist to another. To speak

---

[11] Note too perhaps, by way of reinforcement, that each of the lines beginning with
amisso is adjacent to a line which begins with a *di-* compound. McKeown (1984: 171)
recognizes Ovid's *Georgic* source in these lines, but offers no discussion.

of parody here would be worse than reductive: it would border on solecism.

What can be talked about without fear of reductiveness, however, is the delightful vigour of Ovidian literariness. Consider what happens immediately after our poet's complex allusion to Virgil's bees (*Fast.* 3.555–9):

>   ... ut olim
> amisso dubiae rege vagantur apes.
> tertia nudandas acceperat area messes,
>   inque cavos ierant tertia musta lacus:
> pellitur Anna domo ...

> ... even as at times bees stray about unsettled when their king has been lost. Thrice had the threshing floor received the harvest to be beaten out, and thrice had the grape-juice flowed into the hollow vats: Anna is driven from her home ...

Three years pass (557–8); and then Anna flees from Carthage. The description of the passage of years, conventional narrative 'prop' though it be, already carries a certain emphasis through the mere fact of its presence in the calendar-oriented action of the *Fasti* (Hinds 1987*a*: 69). But the specifically agricultural slant in the lines is surely evocative of something more immediately at hand. In lines 555–6 Ovid complicates his episode's sustained reference to the *Aeneid* with an allusion to the world of the fourth *Georgic*. Now, I suggest, in lines 557–8, he underlines that momentary switch of Virgilian model by evoking, in one line each, the central themes of two other *Georgic* books, the first and the second. The result is an internal 'gloss' which is very much in the spirit of the episode's general preoccupation with Virgilian microcosm. And (to take up a point made earlier in the paragraph) by using *Georgic* themes in lines 557–8 to measure, precisely, the passage of *years*, perhaps Ovid programmatically underlines the new literary destination reached by the *Georgic* bees in lines 555–6: not, as before, the world of the *Aeneid*; but (albeit in an *Aeneid*-like episode) the 'year-by-year' world of his own *Fasti*.

Fast. 3.557–8 functions, according to my argument, as a sort of commentary by our poet on the allusion to Virgil's *Georgics* in his previous couplet. The tendency of Ovid's allusions to take on additional layers of self-reference, though rarely noticed by critics, is both widespread and various. Let me attempt in an excursus over these next two or three pages to illustrate something of the range of this kind of self-commentary. The vigour of Ovid's literariness will continue thus to emerge.

An especially clear instance of self-referential elaboration of allusion, rather different in nature from the one just discussed, occurs in the account of the catasterism of Ariadne's crown—which, as it happens, immediately precedes the 'Virgilian' voyage of Anna in *Fasti* 3. There, on the beach, we find the unfortunate daughter of Minos, mourning her desertion by Bacchus, which has followed hard upon her desertion by Theseus (*Fast.* 3.471–6):

'en iterum, fluctus, similes audite querellas.
    en iterum lacrimas accipe, harena, meas.
dicebam, memini, "periure et perfide Theseu!"
    ille abiit, eadem crimina Bacchus habet.
nunc quoque "nulla viro" clamabo "femina credat";
    nomine mutato causa relata mea est.'

'Lo! once more, waves, hear a like complaint. Lo! once more, sands, receive these tears of mine. I used to say, I remember, "Perjured and faithless Theseus!" He has gone; Bacchus now incurs the same guilt. Now too I will exclaim, "Let no woman trust a man"; my case has been repeated, with only the name changed.'

The words recollected by Ariadne in the double quotes of lines 473 and 475 constitute, piquantly enough, a literary 'memory' of words which she has indeed spoken before—in her previous, Catullan identity in which she experienced that earlier desertion by Theseus (see Catullus 64.130–5, 143–4). *Memini* (473) can therefore be thought of as self-referentially drawing attention to, or commenting on, Ovid's allusion here to a celebrated poem by Catullus. I take this example from Gian Biagio Conte (1986: 60–2), whose discussion here of the different levels of Ariadne's complex 'memory' is one of the best moments in modern Ovidian criticism. We may note, incidentally, certain general affinities between this Ariadne episode and the immediately succeeding Anna episode: here, as there (though with different emphases), Ovid offers a sequel to a famous hexameter narrative which is also a kind of re-enactment of that narrative.

Ovid's, or Ariadne's, *memini* in *Fast.* 3.473 is in effect a refinement of the 'Alexandrian footnote' (D. O. Ross's term[12] for the signalling of allusion by a poet through seemingly general appeals to tradition and report, such as *dicitur* 'it is said', *ferunt* 'they relate', or *fama est* 'the story goes'). And allied too are those ingenious allusions which, rather than being signalled by 'added' comments, are actually so constructed as *through their own wording* to draw attention to their status as allusions. I have offered in the first part of this essay a textbook example, the *imitatrix ales* of *Amores* 2.6, which is not only a mimic *qua* parrot, but also a *literary* 'imitator' of Catullus' *passer*.[13]

Ovid's use of the succeeding couplet to 'gloss' his *Fast.* 3.555–6 allusion to the *Georgics*, the point of departure for my excursus here, represents a different way in which Ovid may comment on his own allusions: namely, by adding specific hints as to their source. I have commented elsewhere (1987*a*: 6–16, esp. 15–16) on a good example of this procedure at *Met.* 5.256–64, where the presence of the Muse Uranie ('the Heavenly one') signals an allusion to Aratus' astronomical poem, the *Phaenomena*.

Much more speculative in this area of hinted specification of a model is a suggestion which might be made about a couplet in *Heroides* 14. The poem's letter-writer, Hypermnestra, ends an extraordinary narrative digression on the story of Io (*Her.* 14.85–108) with these words (*Her.* 14.109–10):

ultima quid referam, quorum mihi cana senectus
    auctor? dant anni, quod querar, ecce, mei.

Why should I relate things of remote times, for which white-haired old age has been my authority? Behold! my own years give me matter for lament.

The slightly odd phrase[14] *quorum mihi cana senectus | auctor* looks like an 'Alexandrian footnote'. The story which Hypermnestra claims

---

[12] See Ross (1975*a*) 78, newly developing an observation by Norden (1926) ad *Aen.* 6.14.

[13] For another example see Hinds (1982) = Hinds (1987*a*) 38–40: *Fast.* 4.417 closely echoes Cicero, *Verr.* 2.4.107; *Fast.* 4.418 both *continues* the allusion and footnotes it *as* allusion.

[14] See Palmer (1898) ad loc.: '*cana senectus* ['white-haired old age'] can hardly be for *cana uetustas* ['hoary antiquity']: and if sound is probably abstract for *cani senes* ['white-haired old men']. Old men and women had told Hypermnestra these family legends.'

to have heard from *cana senectus* will presumably have been derived by Ovid from an *auctor* (note the word's suggestiveness: 'author' as well as 'authority') of the literary kind. But may Ovid also perhaps hint at the *identity* of this venerable *auctor*? The principal source in pre-Augustan Latin for the story of Io was the celebrated epyllion of that name by the poet Calvus, now sadly lost. In describing the *senectus* to which Hypermnestra owes the story of Io as *cana*, 'white-haired', could Ovid be using the Roman etymological technique of naming things *a contrariis*[15] to hint at the word which in Latin describes the condition of old age precisely opposite to *cana*: viz. *calva* 'bald'? There is some reason to think that the Romans were in the habit of setting these two words against each other in a jingle: Macrobius preserves an anecdote (*Sat.* 2.5.7) in which Augustus, teasing his daughter Julia for having some premature white hairs plucked from her head, asks 'whether she would prefer in later life to be white-haired or bald', *utrum post aliquot annos cana esse mallet an calva*. The suggestion is at every level unprovable. But such hinted specification of the literary model would have an especial point here, where Hypermnestra's strongly marked Io digression certainly represents some kind of interruption of the epistle's main source, Horace, *Odes* 3.11—whether or not that interruption is in favour of the older poet Calvus.

Interestingly, the previously mentioned 'Uranie' hint is analogously situated: Ovid's internally 'glossed' echo of Aratus' *Phaenomena* interrupts a wider pattern of allusion to Nicander's *Heteroioumena*. And such too is the situation of the 'glossed' allusion to the *Georgics* in *Fast.* 3.555–8, with its interruption of a pattern of sustained reference to the *Aeneid*.

For one last instance of hinted authorial specification of a model, a little different in its approach, we may turn to E. J. Kenney's felicitous observation about the Baucis and Philemon episode in *Metamorphoses* 8.[16] Much of the detail of this story-within-a-story derives from the *Hecale* of Callimachus: and Ovid self-referentially points to this by including one of the *Hecale's* two main characters, Theseus, in the audience of his enclosed tale. The 'nudge to

---

[15] See e.g. Quintilian, *Inst.* 1.6.34, commenting on this technique of etymologizing.

[16] The observation is made in Melville (1986) xxviii; the phrase 'nudge to the reader' comes from Kenney's associated note on *Met.* 8.726.

the reader' comes at the very moment when the internal narrator
has just finished his account of the old couple's hospitality (*Met.*
8.725–6):

desierat, cunctosque et res et moverat auctor,
Thesea praecipue...

He had ended: both the tale and the teller had moved them all, Theseus
especially...

Let me close this survey by briefly suggesting another kind of
specific information which may be conveyed when the poet elaborates the self-referentiality of his allusions, viz. commentary on the
manner of a literary borrowing. The enclosed narrative of the story of
Erysichthon in *Metamorphoses* 8 will furnish us with a good example.
As with the immediately preceding episode of Baucis and Philemon,
just discussed, Ovid's source is Callimachus, this time in the *Hymn
to Demeter*: and, as in the case of Baucis and Philemon, the reflexive
hint with which we are concerned lies in the narrative frame. Critics
have long agreed (albeit with differing emphases) that what Ovid
does here to Callimachus' version of the Erysichthon story, with its
'Alexandrian' interest in the details of domestic embarrassment, is,
essentially, to recast it in the style of grand epic. What seems to
have been overlooked is the relevance to this of the identity of the
story's internal narrator, Achelous, emphatically presented in the text
as the god of a river which is in flood—even as he tells his tale
(*Met.* 8.549–59; cf. 8.583–7, 9.94–6). It is indeed only because of the
swollen state of his waters that Achelous finds himself hosting this
story-telling symposium in *Metamorphoses* 8–9 at all. In a context
of allusion to Callimachus, the programmatic hint is unmistakable.
The metaphorical association of excessive flows of water with literary
bombast (see Callimachus, *Hymn* 2.105–13) is central to the tradition
of Callimachean water-symbolism transmitted to and refined by the
docti poetae of Augustan Rome (Wimmel 1960: 222–33). Our poet's
choice of a swollen river (of all things) to narrate his version of the tale
of Erysichthon operates as a self-referential comment on the grand
epic manner of his allusion. Ovid is wilfully imitating his model in
a style specifically condemned by his model: he is de-Callimachizing
Callimachus.

The above excursus on these Ovidian elaborations of literary allusion can perhaps be regarded as a kind of supplement to the stimulating typology of allusion described by Richard Thomas (1986).[17] That article implicitly raises an interesting methodological question concerning generalization which may be relevant here too. Thomas' examples are all drawn from Virgil's *Georgics,* and he offers his typology first and foremost as a description of the complexity of literary 'reference' in the *Georgics.* But he also suggests, quite rightly, that his conclusions are applicable in a greater or lesser degree to much other Latin poetry too. To what extent, then, should the art of the *Georgics* as elucidated in his article be regarded as exceptional, and to what extent paradigmatic? The question is not an easy one to answer.

Nor is it any easier in the present case. In cataloguing some instances of self-commentary in Ovidian allusion, my main purpose has been to reinforce points made earlier in this section about the remarkable vigour of Ovid's literariness. However, I should tread carefully. While I do incline to the view that he pursues such effects as these more, and with more *panache,* than do most poets, I also suspect that the area is one which has been insufficiently investigated in the criticism of Roman poetry as a whole. Perhaps Ovid's procedures are exceptional; but perhaps they will turn out to be no more (or no less) than typical of a literature whose profound self-consciousness we have not yet fully apprehended.

I have been focusing on one neglected aspect of Ovidian self-reference, viz. self-referential elaboration of allusion; but there are many other ways in which our poet comments, as he writes, on his poetic activity. The opening verses of one of the elegies from exile may serve to encapsulate for us this wider area of his art (*Trist.* 5.3.1–12):

illa dies haec est, qua te celebrare poetae,
    si modo non fallunt tempora, Bacche, solent,
festaque odoratis innectunt tempora sertis,
    et dicunt laudes ad tua vina tuas.
inter quos, memini, dum me mea fata sinebant,

[17] Thomas prefers to speak of 'reference' rather than of 'allusion'. The main drawback is his consequent appropriation of the already existing 'self-reference' to describe something narrower than is ordinarily meant by that term. In effect, Thomas's 'self-reference' is what others call, *faute de mieux,* 'self-echo' or 'self-imitation'.

non invisa tibi pars ego saepe fui,
quem nunc suppositum stellis Cynosuridos Ursae
   iuncta tenet crudis Sarmatis ora Getis.
quique prius mollem vacuamque laboribus egi
   in studiis vitam Pieridumque choro,
nunc procul a patria Geticis circumsonor armis
   multa prius pelago multaque passus humo.

This is the day on which poets are wont to celebrate you, Bacchus, if only the times do not mislead me; they bind their festal brows with fragrant garlands, and sing your praises over your own wine. Amongst their company, I remember, while my destiny allowed me, I was often a member not distasteful to you—I who am now confined on the Sarmatian shore, close to the ferocious Getae, under the stars of the Cynosurian Bear. I who before led a gentle life, free from toils, in pursuits associated with the Pierid Muses' band, now far from my country am surrounded by the clash of Getic arms, after many sufferings by sea, many by land.

The banished writer uses the occasion of the Liberalia to make an appeal to Bacchus as patron god of poetry. His nostalgic memory (5 *memini*) of his former participation in symposiastic celebrations of the Liberalia amongst Roman poets, a scene picked up again later in the elegy (5.3.47–52), is also a *literary* memory of his extended celebration of that day in his own calendar poem, the *Fasti*, a celebration which begins thus (*Fast.* 3.713–14):

tertia post Idus lux est celeberrima Baccho:
   Bacche, fave vati, dum tua festa cano.

The third day after the Ides is for the universal celebration of Bacchus: Bacchus, favour the poet, while I sing your festival.

In this couplet, as in the opening couplet of our elegy, the stress is explicitly on a *poet's* view of the Liberalia. There is even some verbal reminiscence, with *celebrare* in one hexameter recalling *celeberrima* in the other, and a vocative address to Bacchus positioned in each pentameter. More striking is the echo in the *Tristia* elegy's very first phrase of one of the *Fasti's* characteristic opening formulae (see *Fast.* 2.195, 4.379, 6.713): *illa dies haec est.* And most interesting of all is Ovid's self-referential comment on these 'memories' of the *Fasti*, adumbrated in *Trist.* 5.3.2. *Si modo non fallunt tempora:* not just 'if only the times do not mislead me'; but also, *tempora* being the opening and therefore titular word of the *Fasti*, 'if only my poem about "Times" does not mislead me'. The programmatic hint is all the more aptly placed in that it makes a quiet contribution to a central theme of the *Tristia*, Ovid's frequently advertised loss of confidence in his own poetic powers.

The third line of the elegy offers a new twist. After the *tempora*, 'times', of the immediately preceding verse, we now read of *tempora* again: but here, oddly, the meaning is 'brows', not 'times'. The switch between homonyms in the same sentence seems merely awkward—until we perceive its self-consciousness. Ovid's stipulation in line 2, *si modo non fallunt tempora*, has found here a new point. *Tempora* can in fact mislead—as the abrupt change in the word's meaning between lines 2 and 3 has just proceeded very precisely, and self-referentially, to demonstrate.

Moreover, by a common Ovidian ploy, this overt change in the sense of *tempora* between lines 2 and 3 serves to alert us to the more covert play in the word's meaning within line 2 itself. The transferred epithet *festa*, 'festal', associated with the 'brows' of line 3 may offer another sly reminder of the third, programmatic term in the ambiguity: no adjective could be more evocative of the *Fasti*'s particular brand of *tempora*.

In *Trist.* 5.3.9–11 we encounter an element of poetic self-reference associated with one of those rich seams of imagery in which Roman writers debate aesthetic principles derived (with many complications along the way) from Callimachus. The allusion to that imagery here may seem casual and off-hand: but it has something important to tell us about the place of literary self-consciousness in Ovid's life and experience.

Ovid's life was previously a gentle one: 9–10 *mollem . . . egi* | *. . . vitam*. Now, however, in exile on the Black Sea, he lives surrounded by the clash of arms: 11 *Geticis circumsonor armis*. A contrast between two ways of life, one pleasant and the other insupportable: but the vocabulary hints at a contrast between two ways of *writing*, one smooth and elegant, and the other (in its extreme form) harsh and intractable.

Let me make this point as starkly as possible. By the time of Ovid's arrival on the Roman poetic scene, the adjective *mollis* and the noun *arma* have by constant iteration become so loaded with programmatic connotation that it is virtually impossible for *any* antithesis between the two to be wholly free of the resonances and values of Callimachean literary debate.[18] It is irrelevant to the case that both words are common or garden items of vocabulary with many diverse senses in the Latin language at large. We are dealing with the formal discourse of Augustan poetry: and in that discourse the programmatic values in these words—especially where they are set in antithesis—can reasonably claim to be the dominant ones.

A short, polemical excursus is in order here. There has been a reactionary tendency in some recent scholarship to see the Callimachean vocabulary of self-reference as merely peripheral to central and enduring concerns of Augustan poetry such as life, death, and love. I find this tendency misguided: but the fault lies partly with the very critics who opened up this exciting area of programmatic imagery for us in the first place. In concentrating on certain poems, or parts of poems, where such imagery is especially pointed and prominent, they tended to underestimate the extent to which the vocabulary of Callimachean debate retains its programmatic connotation in other, less marked contexts; and in underestimating this, they left the way open for hostile critics to claim the interest of Augustan poets in this area to be merely intermittent, or even perfunctory. But the Callimachean vocabulary of self-reference is not an intermittent phenomenon. Rather, it constitutes a continuous stratum in the language of Augustan (and, I think, post-Augustan) poetry, sometimes more visible and sometimes less visible in its effects.

In our particular passage, the Callimachean nuances in the key adjective *mollem (Trist.* 5.3.9) are the more clearly operative because of the overt conflation of life and literary pursuit which completes the clause in which *mollem* is situated: *Trist.* 5.3.10 *in studiis vitam*

---

[18] In the context of such debate, the word *mollis* ('gentle, soft, smooth') naturally evokes the *carmen deductum* ('fine-spun song') favoured by 'Callimachean' poets: compare such adjectives as *tenuis, exiguus, levis* ('fine', 'slight', 'light'). *Arma* ('arms'), on the other hand, are suggestive of the *carmen perpetuum* ('continuous song') which sings of *reges et proelia* ('kings and battles'), widely characterized by such adjectives as *gravis, inflatus, durus* ('weighty', 'inflated', 'solid'). The 'Callimachean' poet conventionally praises the former kind of writing and denigrates the latter, offering by means of this contrast a succinct, if disingenuously simple, formulation of his artistic values.

Pieridumque choro. These nuances are in no sense detachable from
the central concerns of the passage. In its contrast with *circumsonor
armis* below, the phrase *mollem vitam* serves economically to conjure
up the whole *way of life* which Ovid has lost. Circles of literary friends,
elevation of private over public pursuits, ideas of elegance and beauty,
state-of-the-art poetry: these are all things which can be written about
in the Callimachean vocabulary of self-reference; but, more than
that, these are all things which constitute, and are constituted by,
the Callimachean vocabulary of self-reference. Let me make myself
clear: my claim is not that Callimachean values are central to Roman
consciousness at large; but rather that they are central to the atypical
consciousness which we inhabit when we read the work of Ovid or
one of his fellow poets.

So too, when Ovid describes Pontus in line 11 as a place clashing
with arms, the programmatic hint in *armis* offers a literary analogy
for his exile (the world of the Getae is like the world of strident epic);
but, more than that, it describes how his exile actually impinges on
Ovid's consciousness: as an absence of literary friends, as a separation
from congenial pursuits, as an impediment to poetic inspiration—
and, perhaps, as a feeling of resentment against the emperor whose
poor moral and artistic sense has put him there.

The Callimachean vocabulary of self-reference is nothing less than
a code through which the Augustan poet expresses his vision—his
atypical, poetic vision—of the world at large. If we are interested
in what is most personal to Ovid in his experience of exile; if, for
that manner, we are interested in what is most personal to Ovid,
or to Propertius, in his experience of love, we will do well to treat
as central this important area of vocabulary through which the self-
conscious poet discusses, more pervasively than is generally acknowledged, many of his most deeply felt values. [19]

A brief word must suffice on the twelfth line of Ovid's exile elegy,
multa prius pelago multaque passus humo. Ovid recalls his sufferings
en route to Pontus in AD 8; he recalls his account of his sufferings in
Tristia 1; and, more specifically, he recalls the Odyssean and Aenean
terms in which he presented his sufferings in that initial book of

[19] I have learned much in this connection from the work of Alison Sharrock and
Jamie Masters.

journeying.[20] His memory of his experience is a memory of the way in which he thought and wrote about his experience: and what, to a poet, could be more real than that?

3. 'THE PASSIVE PANEGYRICIST'

The above remarks on Ovid's exile bring me to the wider question of the poet's relationship with his emperor; and to my final discussion of an important area of critical generalization. The view to which I shall be reacting, like the views represented in my headings for sections 1 and 2, involves a negative value judgement on our poet; and, just as important, it offers this negative value judgement on Ovid as a prescription for negative value judgements on Ovid's successors in the so-called 'Silver Age' of Latin literature.

An especially bold formulation of these judgements can be found in Gordon Williams's *Change and Decline* (1978), his controversial sequel to *Tradition and Originality in Roman Poetry*. Williams, like many other literary historians, treats Ovid, to the poet's disadvantage, as a transitional figure between two sharply contrasted periods of literary production. We saw at the beginning of this essay an instance of his adverse verdict on Ovid's performance vis-à-vis his predecessors: now he measures the poet against his successors. Ovid, we read, 'was the first poet to fall a victim to the clash between republican ideals and the imperial system' (52). He was 'not only a poet of enormous, even paramount, influence on the writers of the early Empire, but also one whose own career foreshadowed the perils of their situation' (3). So far, so good. But next, crucially for our discussion here, the following question is posed: 'What sort of example did [Ovid] provide for later writers on the delicate question of treating political themes, and particularly on the question of the relationship between the writer and the emperor?' (53) And Williams's answer? Ovid devised 'three modes of escapism: into Greek mythology, into a safe antiquarianism, and into ingenious panegyric of the emperor. All involved, almost

---

[20] For the Odyssean and Aenean resonances in *Trist.* 5.3.12, see Luck (1967–77) ad loc., with (esp.) Homer, *Od.* 1.3–4, Virgil, *Aen.* 1.3–5. For the Odyssean and Aenean *color* in *Tristia* 1, see especially elegies 2–5.

inevitably, a retreat from reality. Most succeeding writers chose one, or a combination, of these modes.' (3)

It is on Williams's third 'mode of escapism' that I wish to focus in this last section of my essay. In effect, his formulation amounts to a charge of mild sycophancy against our poet. Ovid, we are told, 'gradually learnt to live easily with the necessity for panegyric [of the emperor]' (96)—and so did his successors.

Any work of critical reassessment here may at first seem superfluous, since the view of Ovid's politics thus expressed, prevalent though it was some years ago, is now falling from favour in most quarters. There are relatively few Ovidians (as Williams himself acknowledges) who still read Ovidian panegyric as passively acquiescent, and who deny the existence of traces of irony and deflation in the poet's rhetoric when he speaks of Augustus and his doings. Similarly, there are few who still seek, as does Williams, to amplify this verdict of mild sycophancy into a wider view of Ovid's poetry as somehow slightly tainted and debased in its thought when compared with the poetry of Horace, Virgil, or Propertius.

However, if current critical work is largely freeing Ovid himself from charges of political sycophancy, such charges still represent the orthodoxy of opinion on most of his 'Silver Age' successors. My aim in the brief remarks which follow, therefore, is twofold. First I shall make a small contribution to the already widespread reassessment of Ovidian panegyric; and then I shall consider whether this reassessment should be leading to a like reassessment in the case of other, later poets as well. It is customary to speak in wholesale terms of 'Silver Latin panegyric': but how confident can we be in the validity of this generalized label, when so few critics actually *read* the poets thus grouped with anything like the same care and attention to nuance that is now at last bestowed on Ovid?

First, let us examine an Ovidian passage. Here is a famous piece of panegyric from the episode of Julius Caesar's deification in the *Metamorphoses,* in which the poet offers praise to Julius so as to offer greater praise to Augustus (*Met.* 15.750–8):

neque enim de Caesaris actis
ullum maius opus quam quod pater exstitit huius.
scilicet aequoreos plus est domuisse Britannos

perque papyriferi septemflua flumina Nili
victrices egisse rates Numidasque rebelles
Cinyphiumque Iubam Mithridateisque tumentem
nominibus Pontum populo adiecisse Quirini
et multos meruisse, aliquos egisse triumphos,
quam tantum genuisse virum! . . .

For amongst [Julius] Caesar's achievements there is no work greater than
this, that he shone forth as father of this man [Augustus]. We should, doubtless, think it a greater thing to have subdued the sea-girt Britons, and to have
led victorious ships along the seven-mouthed streams of the papyrus-bearing
Nile, and to have added to the people of Quirinus the rebellious Numidians,
and Cinyphian Juba, and Pontus, swelling with the fame of Mithridates, to
have celebrated some triumphs and to have earned many more—than to
have begotten so great a man! . . .

No commentator on Ovidian panegyric can afford to ignore the
presence in line 752 of *scilicet,* that ambiguous particle which is used
in Latin to signal one of two opposite things: the evidently absurd
proposition; and the evidently true one. Ovid's assertion in lines
750–1 seems to require us to read 752–8 as a statement that it is
'absurd' to regard all Julius Caesar's military exploits as more important than the fathering of Augustus. Yet the sheer length and impressiveness of Ovid's catalogue in 752–8 may well lead us to feel that, in
fact, these exploits *are* the more important thing in Caesar's career.
Evident absurdity; or evident truth? The volatile *scilicet* is available
to point up the second interpretation, no less than the first one—
especially, perhaps, when we remember that Julius Caesar's fathering
of Augustus was done only belatedly, and by adoption.

The same question of tone continues to be a problem two lines
further on in the deification episode (*Met.* 15.760–1, where *hic* is
Augustus, and *ille* Julius):

ne foret hic igitur mortali semine cretus,
ille deus faciendus erat . . .

So, then, that the son might not be born of mortal seed, the father had to be
made a god . . .

No *scilicet* here; but nevertheless the interpretative problem might
be said to be, once again, of the '*scilicet*' kind. Is Ovid presenting an

evidently true argument—or an evidently absurd one? I believe, with the majority of recent critics, that Ovid intends a hint of irony here; but others, including Williams, are equally sure that the conceit is a piece of straightforward, if contrived, panegyric.

We could multiply examples of this sort of crux in Ovid's *oeuvre;* but in no instance would we ever be likely to persuade each last Ovidian critic to agree on a verdict of subversion. The real error, into which critics on both sides tend to fall, is to imagine that the matter is susceptible of final proof either way. It is not: how could it be? Ovid was a formal poet who wrote and recited publicly, under his own name, in a city where the emperor's word was law. If he *was* subversive in his writing (as I believe he was), how could he possibly proceed but by indirection and nuance? In any but the most powerful or the most reckless of Romans, publicly voiced anti-Augustanism must needs be a rhetoric of ambiguity and innuendo. Every passage ever written by Ovid about Augustus admits of a non-subversive reading: but that is not in itself a refutation of Ovidian subversion.

An allied point may be made. Just as modern critics are far from unanimous in finding subversion in passages like the one under discussion, so must it have been with Ovid's first listeners and readers. We should not fall into the trap of regarding 'the Augustan reading public' as a monolith. There were many different readers living in Rome in the early years AD, who had many different ways of interpreting Augustan politics, and of interpreting Augustan literature. Imagine that you are the sort of Roman (and who would deny that such Romans existed?) who finds something absurd in the idea of a deified Julius Caesar: then you will probably respond to nuances in Ovid's literary treatment of the deification which, on the view that I espouse, point up its absurdity. But now imagine yourself to be the sort of Roman who sees no absurdity in the idea itself: then it is entirely likely that you will find Ovid's description unexceptionable too. Indeed Ovid, if his intent *is* subversive here, will be relying on the existence of readers like you to give him what one may term his hermeneutic alibi: and, of course, your belief in Ovid's straightforwardness will make the joke all the better for those who have opted for the subversive reading.

Having thus considered how to approach Ovidian panegyric, let us examine a piece of panegyric by one of Ovid's 'Silver Age'

successors. As it happens, this passage too concerns the deification of a Caesar: the poet is Lucan, and the lines come from the
prominent invocation of Nero early in Book 1 of the *Bellum Civile*
(1.45–58):

>   te, cum statione peracta
> astra petes serus, praelati regia caeli
> excipiet gaudente polo: seu sceptra tenere
> seu te flammigeros Phoebi conscendere currus
> telluremque nihil mutato sole timentem
> igne vago lustrare iuvet, tibi numine ab omni
> cedetur, iurisque tui natura relinquet
> quis deus esse velis, ubi regnum ponere mundi.
> sed neque in Arctoo sedem tibi legeris orbe
> nec polus aversi calidus qua vergitur Austri,
> unde tuam videas obliquo sidere Romam.
> aetheris inmensi partem si presseris unam,
> sentiet axis onus. librati pondera caeli
> orbe tene medio . . .

When, your term of guard-duty done, late in time you shall seek the stars,
your preferred celestial palace will welcome you, and the skies will rejoice.
Whether it please you to wield the supreme sceptre, or to mount the fire-
bearing chariot of Phoebus and to circle with wandering flame an earth that
feels no fear at the changed sun—every deity will give way to you, and nature
will leave it in your power to choose what god you wish to be, where to establish your kingdom of the universe. But pray do not choose your seat either in
the Northern circle or where the hot skies of the opposing South decline: for
thence you would look upon your Rome with beam aslant. If you press upon
one side of the boundless heavens, the axis will feel the burden. By staying in
the centre of the system, keep the weight of the universe in balance . . .

To Williams (1978: 164), this is 'a seriously intended, but highly
stereotyped, tribute'. Lucan here acquiesces in the necessity for imperial panegyric, just as Ovid had had to do two generations earlier. These verses have not been debated as extensively in modern
times as have passages of Ovidian panegyric like *Met.* 15.750–61:
Lucan is only now beginning to emerge from years of undeserved
neglect by critics of Latin poetry. However among those who have
shown an interest in Lucan's invocation of Nero, we find vehement
disagreement on the question of tone—just as we did in our Ovidian

passage (Ahl 1976: 47–9 and n.54). Perhaps half of their number agree with Williams in interpreting the verses as sycophantic—including some who nevertheless countenance implicit subversion of Caesarian ideology in the main body of the poem's narrative. However, there is another view: and it can claim the support of the ancient Lucanian *scholia*.

The crux comes in lines 56–8, at the end of my quotation. Why does Lucan say that Nero will weigh down the side of heaven upon which he chooses to sit? Because weight is a traditional attribute of the divine—or because it is an attribute of the historical Nero? The author of the *Adnotationes super Lucanum* is in no doubt: *adlusit; fuit enim [Nero] corporis pinguis;* 'a playful allusion: for [Nero] was corpulent'. The obesity of the emperor is indeed widely attested; see e.g. Suetonius, *Nero* 51.

Suetonius also remarks in the passage just cited upon Nero's 'somewhat weak eyesight', *oculis . . . hebetioribus*. This perceived characteristic of the emperor prompts our scholiast to find further subversion in the phrase *obliquo sidere*, 'with beam aslant', in line 55: *adlusit: strabus enim Nero fuit*; 'a playful allusion: for Nero was squint-eyed'.

Williams dismisses the scholiast's comments here as absurd. It is no part of my brief to claim that any ancient reader has a monopoly on interpretative truth; but, as it happens, I find the suggestion offered on line 55 tempting, and the suggestion on lines 56–8 quite compelling. Evidently, critical unanimity here will remain as elusive as in the case of Ovidian panegyric. The essential methodological issue is the same. One does not much advance the question of the presence or absence of subversion in a passage like this by showing (as one can) that it admits of a non-subversive reading; for this will be as true of a subversive passage as of a genuinely panegyrical one. The anti-Neronian poet, if he exists, is an ironist, not an open denouncer: and he relies for his self-preservation on that very mental set which will allow certain of his readers to take his panegyric at face value.

In arguing that the matter of literary subversion is not susceptible of final proof, I may seem to be abandoning all hope of critical progress in this area. However, I do not mean to imply that it is impossible in any given case to tilt the balance of probability. A new reading is always capable of bringing fresh evidence to light: and, in the present Lucanian passage, at least one important nuance has had insufficient attention paid to it.

Consider this detail in the lines already quoted (Lucan 1.48–50):

seu te flammigeros Phoebi conscendere currus
telluremque nihil mutato sole timentem
igne vago lustrare iuvet . . .

A straightforwardly panegyrical reading, as always, is available. Lucan flatters the emperor by predicting for him a divine role which will neatly dovetail with his earthly self-image: see Suetonius, *Nero* 53 . . . *quia Apollinem cantu, Solem aurigando aequiperare existimaretur*; '. . . since he was acclaimed as the equal of Apollo in singing, and of the Sun in driving a chariot'.[21]

But the lines admit of another, less flattering construction too. If Nero takes over the chariot of the Sun from its usual driver, as envisaged here, in whose footsteps will he be following? Why, in those of Phaethon, the most spectacularly unsuccessful charioteer who ever rode. The point is not lost on the scholiast of the *Adnotationes*, who offers the following gloss on line 49: '*mutato sole timentem*': *propter Phaethontem dictum, qui patris currus male rexit*; '"fear at the changed sun": an allusion to Phaethon, who rode his father's chariot to ill effect'.

Nero, it seems, will do better than Phaethon—or will he? Once the spectre of Phaethon has been raised, the phrase *igne vago* in line 50 acquires a worrying connotation. If Nero is envisaged as steering the Sun's chariot 'with wandering flame', does that adjective *vagus* simply refer to the non-fixed position of the sun in the firmament (we are in the world of ancient astronomy, remember), or does it perhaps hint at the 'erratic' motion which is likely to characterize the chariot's course in the hands of this *Phaethon redivivus*?

The resonances of this evocation of Phaethon in lines 48–50 continue to be felt, I think, as the passage continues. In the canonical Ovidian version of the myth, Phaethon's driving of the Sun's chariot is disastrous not just to himself but to the whole fabric of the cosmos. Lucan's invocation of Nero culminates in a prediction that his deification will usher in an era of universal peace (1.60–2). Yet

---

[21] Cf. the remarks on the emperor's interests at Tacitus, *Ann.* 14.14.

the Phaethontic associations of the emperor's envisaged divine role seem to align him not with the forces of peace but with the forces of cosmic dissolution—as explicitly invoked a few lines later in Lucan's first full-scale analysis of his epic theme, the civil war between Caesar and Pompey (1.72–4):

> ... nec se Roma ferens. sic, cum compage soluta
> saecula tot mundi suprema coegerit hora
> antiquum repetens iterum Chaos...

> ... and Rome unable to support herself. Even so, when the last hour shall close all the many ages of the universe, its structure dissolved, reverting again to primeval Chaos...

This analysis of the civil war begins in line 67 with what looks like an echo of the titular opening of Ovid's *Metamorphoses (fert animus . . . ,* 'my mind moves me . . .'); and the words quoted in line 74, *antiquum repetens iterum Chaos,* seem to allude, remarkably enough, to a key line in Ovid's account in *Metamorphoses* 2 of the ride of Phaethon (298–9):

> si freta, si terrae pereunt, si regia caeli,
> in Chaos antiquum confundimur...

> If the sea, if the land, if the palace of heaven perish, we are all thrown together into primeval Chaos...

The speaker is Tellus, the Earth, warning Jupiter of the reversion to Chaos (in Ovid's terms, a reversion to the beginning of the *Metamorphoses*) which is threatened by Phaethon's erratic progress through the cosmos on the chariot of the Sun. Is Lucan's echo of these words in 1.74 a random one? Or, coming as the echo does so soon after the prediction of a second usurpation of the Sun's chariot by Nero, the new Phaethon (1.48–50), does it perhaps hint at an association between the present emperor's potential for destructiveness and the power to wreak cosmic dissolution already shown by his warring ancestors?[22] The above interpretation demands of the reader a small

---

[22] One might now be tempted, turning back to the original Phaethontic allusion in line 49, to read *mutato sole,* 'changed sun', as a self-referential 'gloss' by Lucan specifying a literary source: namely, Ovid's poem of *mutatas formas,* 'changed shapes' (*Met.* 1.1).

hermeneutic leap—but perhaps that is what constitutes Lucan's hermeneutic alibi.[23]

According to the view represented in my heading for this section, Ovid responds to the necessity to praise Augustus by developing a language of passively acquiescent panegyric; a language which he bequeaths to his poetic successors, including Lucan. On my own reading, however, what Ovid actually does is to turn elements of apparently inert panegyric into an effective rhetoric of subversion. Is it possible that *this* is his real legacy to the poets of the 'Silver Age'?

Having ventured a few remarks on seeming subversion in Lucan, I shall not seek any further to answer my own question. The criticism of post-Augustan poetry has already been sufficiently disabled by wholesale generalizations about 'Silver Latin panegyric' which lump together the works of different poets writing in different circumstances (and under different emperors), and treat them as symptoms of a collective 'Silver' way of handling encomium. This is the worst kind of generalization, which denies individuality to an author, and effectively shuts out the role of the reader. The art of generalization, rightly viewed, offers a challenge to read, to take stock, and then to read again: it should never be seen as a substitute for reading. Now that I have contributed my remarks on Ovid, the author I know best, and have sought in them to achieve a fair balance between reading, generalizing and reading, the next best contribution which I can make is to resist the temptation to use Ovid as a way to explain the whole century of poetry which follows him.

---

[23] Was there also a Virgilian idea behind Lucan's use here of the Phaethon myth? A quite compelling observation on *Geo.* 1.511–14 by R. O. A. M. Lyne suggests to me that my inquiry is far from over. Let me quote, without comment (1987: 140, n. 63): 'At *Geo.* 1.463 ff. the sun, "Sol", is associated with Julius Caesar (cf. Lyne 1974: 51–2). In the impotent *auriga* ["charioteer"] of 514 there is a whisper of the Sun's son Phaethon, figuring the "son" of the dictator, as yet ineffective in managing the chariot of State.'

2

Playing with his Life: Ovid's 'Autobiographical' References

Niklas Holzberg

We are told again and again that, of all Roman poets, Ovid is the one whose biography is by far the best known to us.[1] What we think we know is, in point of fact, drawn almost exclusively from references made by the first-person speaker in Ovid's works. Two other sources offer only the following information. Firstly, the manuscripts include in the titles the author's full name, Publius Ovidius Naso (whereas in the texts themselves only the one that is metrically convenient appears—Naso). Secondly, Seneca the Elder, who met Ovid personally when the latter was a student of rhetoric, reminisces more than half a century later in his *Controversiae* about the young man's particular leanings within the discipline that was to be so important for his writings (Fränkel 1945: 6–8; Davis 1989: 15–28; Döpp 1992: 24–8). These 'memoirs' are, however, of dubious historical value. In the years since the two men's encounter, Seneca has become acquainted with Ovid's now famous works and is clearly pro-, or rather retrojecting the opinion he has of them into his account of the poet's early rhetorical exercises; he even offers an example of these (*Contr.* 2.2.8). This is the deductive method typical of ancient biography: 'Just as the Twig is bent, the Tree's inclin'd.' It is, of course, the tree that Seneca is looking at here.

---

[1] Wheeler (1925: 1); Fränkel (1945: 4); Green (1982a: 15). Lefèvre (1980: 158) is even able to 'peek into the Black Sea workshop of the resigned poet'.

Now, are the details which Ovid himself, speaking in the first person, gives us any more reliable? Most of them are indeed presented
in a text which is commonly labelled 'autobiography', in the poem
Tristia 4.10. However, recent analyses of Ovid's works have made
it increasingly clear that we would be well advised to differentiate
between the person talking in the poems and the person of the poet
himself. We must, I think, now acknowledge that Ovid actually takes
on a different role in each of his works (and in his erotic elegies there
is even 'method' in it).[2] In the *Amores* he is the *poeta/amator*, in the
Epistulae Heroidum he embodies each of the mythical female (and
male) letter-writers, in the *Ars Amatoria* and the *Remedia Amoris* he is
the experienced *praeceptor amoris*, in the *Metamorphoses* a *mythologus*
(Graf 1988: 62–7), in the *Fasti* an *antiquarius* (Newlands 1992; Newlands 1995: 51 ff.), and in the exile poems the *relegatus* (Bretzigheimer
1991: 40). Yes, the banished poet is a *persona* too, as is, therefore, even
the speaker in the 'autobiography'.

Before we turn to this particular text, let us take a look at one
of those 'autobiographical' references that are scattered over Ovid's
entire oeuvre (with the exception, of course, of the *Epistulae Heroidum*). It will provide us with a first demonstration of how even in
such seemingly personal moments the literary game of playing roles
is continued. The example in question is *Ex Ponto* 2.10, an elegy in the
form of an epistle from the *relegatus* to the epic poet Macer, who had
already been the addressee of an erotic elegy, *Amores* 2.18. In both
cases Ovid uses the *personae* of the epic poet and the first-person
elegiac poet to confront the 'grand' with the 'little' genre, a variation then on the theme of *recusatio*. In *Ex Ponto* 2.10 this comprises
recollections of a journey the two friends had undertaken together at
some point in the past. First they had toured the *magnificae Asiae
urbes*, with Macer acting as guide here. Then, again with Macer
as guide, they had travelled to Sicily and, once there, to Etna and
the flame-belching giant buried beneath. Crossing the island, they

---

[2] The poet transforms himself from the *poeta/amator* in the *Amores* fifteen times
into a *puella* in the *Heroides* (and in 15 even into a *poetria/puella*), and in *Ars Amatoria*
and *Remedia Amoris* into the experienced teacher of both *amator* and *puella*. On
the *persona* of the *Amores* cf. esp. Gauly (1990: 24–8), who differentiates perhaps
unnecessarily between several *ego*'s; on that of the *Ars,* Wellmann-Bretzigheimer
(1981: 4–7).

had seen Henna, the pools of Palicus and the rivers linked with the mythical names Anapus, Cyane, Alpheus, and Arethusa. Two modes of transport are mentioned (33–4):

seu rate caeruleas picta sulcauimus undas,
  esseda nos agili siue tulere rota.

Either we ploughed in a painted boat through the blue waves, or a carriage took us with swift wheel.

A journey leaving no sight unseen, but one that could, considered more closely, also prove to be a literary journey, or perhaps even solely that, as Gareth Williams has shown in his *Banished Voices* (1994: 42–8). With Macer acting as cicerone in the cities of Asia Minor— presumably in Troy too, then—and on the way to Sicily, where fiery Etna is the first port of call, it is therefore the world of the *Iliad,* of the *Aeneid* (in which the hero also lands in Sicily and goes to Etna) and of a Gigantomachy that falls to the epic poet's lot. The other stops on the island, which, like Macer's part, take up four verses (21–4/25–8), belong to Ovid's poetical territory: they are mentioned in the same order in book 5 of the *Metamorphoses,* in the story of the abduction of Persephone. Likewise the transport. Not only is travelling by ship and chaise a metaphor which Augustan poets liked to use for the joint trip of author and reader through a poem (Lieberg 1969; Heydenreich 1970: 59–61), but the vehicles named here—in a distich with one line for each—also stand specifically for 'grand' and 'little' poetry. The 'painted' vessel of the hexameter, ploughing through the waves, has sister ships in Virgil's *Aeneid* (e.g. in 5.158 or 663), and an *esseda* is the same type of carriage that takes Cynthia to Tibur in Propertius (2.32.5) and would take the *puella* to Sulmo in Ovid's *Amores* (2.16.49).

Who could say now whether the literary journey was also one actually undertaken by the poets, and if it was, then when? Naturally, it is all quite feasible. However, for the poet the intertextuality of his verses is clearly more important than their 'autobiographical' content, which he could easily have presented in a more simple and precise form. Whatever the case may be, it is definitely carrying things too far when attempts are made to pinpoint the date of the trip—it must have been in Ovid's younger days, of course[3]—in order then to describe its significance for the poet's life in, for example, the following terms (Kraus 1968: 69): 'He returned home with a treasure-trove of impressions locked in his faithful memory, with which he was to sustain the wonderful graphic power of his poetry.'

This instance demonstrates the need for extreme caution in the evaluation of any autobiographical references made by a poet whose game of literary and other contexts also includes playing even 'with his life'. In any case, Ovid and other ancient authors often signal that the world of the poetic 'I' is not necessarily that of the poet himself.[4] The oldest such suggestion known to us is actually found as early as Catullus, who tells the two addressees of his *carmen* 16 that they should not conclude from the obscenity of his poems that he himself is not quite *castus*. Even in antiquity, then, readers of poetry could not automatically assume that the *ego* speaking in a poem was identical with the poet himself (Feichtinger 1989: 143–54). And when reading *Tristia* 4.10 we too must naturally consider very carefully which of the particulars about Ovid's *vita* offered there can be rated as historical facts and which look suspiciously like stylized literary usage (Fredericks 1976; Fairweather 1987).

Let us for the moment just recapitulate those biographical details gleaned from *Tristia* 4.10 and elsewhere in Ovid's writings that stand unshaken even in the face of the gravest doubts as to their historicity![5] The poet was born on March 20th, 43 BC in the Paelignian town of Sulmo. His family, landed gentry, was very old and in Rome they had equestrian rank. Ovid and his brother, who was exactly one year older and who died young, studied together in Rome under several outstanding rhetoricians. After completing his legal training Ovid seems to have had the option of embarking upon a senatorial *cursus,* which indicates that he was wealthy. His financial means were certainly ample enough to allow him to reject any thought of a political

---

[3] After a 'period of studying' in Athens (set forth in florid detail by, for example, Kraus 1968: 69), a deduction based on *Trist.* 1.2.77. It ought to be considered that this is a priamel with a clear allusion to Prop. 1.6.13 ff. (cf. 3.21.1).

[4] Cat. 16.5–6; Ov. *Trist.* 1.9.59–60; 2.353–6; 4.10.68; *Pont.* 2.7.47–50; Mart. 1.4.8; 11.15.13; Plin. *Epist.* 4.14.4–5; Apul. *Apol.* 11.

[5] All relevant passages conveniently collected in Wheeler (1925) and Kraus (1968).

or military career. At the age of about twenty, after holding various minor administrative positions in Rome (exactly which can no longer be ascertained) and just before reaching the quaestorship stage, Ovid dropped out, and could from then on devote himself entirely to his poetry. He led a carefree life in the capital, in constant discourse with his fellow-writers and his audience, until one autumn, probably that of the year 8 AD—his parents were already dead, he himself was living with his third wife and his only child, a daughter, had two children from two husbands—he was banished for life by Augustus to Tomi in the Dobridja on the Black Sea. He was, however, permitted to keep his citizenship and his property, banishment in his case taking the mild form of *relegatio*. He published several poetic works there— this too he was apparently still allowed to do—but in spite of his repeated appeals to the emperor for forgiveness, neither Augustus nor his successor Tiberius pardoned Ovid. He probably died in exile, perhaps soon after completing the fourth book of his *Ex Ponto*, which can be dated some time after 16/17 AD. This then the *curriculum vitae*; we shall come to the dating of his works later.

This is meagre indeed. So meagre that, if anyone actually wanted to interpret Ovid's works biographically, it could no more provide the basis for such an approach than could the known facts about other Roman poets. But what about the remaining 'autobiographical' references in *Tristia* 4.10? My decidedly cautious evaluation of such material in the elegy means that I would class, for example, the passage in which we are told that Ovid's father often declared his son's first poetic ventures void of prospects (21–2), as freehand improvisation to add colour to the 'autobiography'. And similarly the first public recitation of *Amores* poems by the poet, then a mere eighteen years old or thereabouts (57–8). Is this a fair assessment? And what about the picture of life in Tomi painted by the *relegatus* in this and other exile poems? Is it too of only very limited historical value?

The credibility of Ovid's 'autobiographical' sketches of his experiences as an exile on the Black Sea is not something I need delve into in great depth here, since it has recently been the subject of several studies (Claassen 1990; Williams 1994: 6 ff.; Chwalek 1996: 32–64). Suffice it to say that the impression created by the speaker in the *Tristia* and the *Ex Ponto*, who endures ills such as almost perpetual icy winters, a life in the society of the most primitive barbarians and the constant threat of the Scythian hordes attacking Tomi with their poisoned arrows, is in complete contradiction to the very convincing findings of modern studies on Black Sea history in ancient times. Ovid's descriptions of the region and people are not based on his own experiences there, but drawn from literary sources such as the Scythian passage in Virgil's *Georgics* (3.349–83). And as for the personal lot of the exile—its depiction gives us a new, playful variation of the 'elegiac system' developed by Gallus, Propertius, and Tibullus. Here too we have, for example, a paraclausithyron situation: the *relegatus*, like the elegiac lover lying before the door, is denied entry to a better existence, in this case life in a more pleasant place of exile.[6]

But back to the so-called 'autobiography' *Tristia* 4.10! This carefully composed elegy is, in terms of form and content, calculated to bring out certain antitheses in bold relief. The most important of these are the contrasting pairs 'carefree youth in Rome/wretched old age in exile' and 'political career/poetic *far niente*'. In the outer structure Ovid expresses this by using for his 'autobiography' the compositional pattern found in Greek encomia from the 4th century BC and then later again in encomia-influenced Latin biographies. The traditional tripartite arrangement, for us first perceptible in Nepos' *vita* of Atticus (Holzberg 1995), next in Tacitus' *Agricola*,[7] and then regularly in Suetonius' *Caesars*, looks in the last of these authors something like this: a relatively short Part One describes more or less chronologically the life of the later emperor up to the point where he assumes office; Part Two, which forms a broad centrepiece, deals under various rubrics with the individual virtues (and/or vices) and deeds of the emperor; Part Three, again shorter and again for the most part chronological, gives an account of the emperor's final days.[8]

---

[6] On the transformations of elegiac motifs in *Tristia* and *Ex Ponto* cf. esp. Nagle (1980); Williams (1994); Holzberg (1997: 181 ff.).

[7] Here significantly the place of the set of rubrics in the middle section is taken by an account of Agricola's exploits in Britain in the style of a historical monograph.

[8] Comparable also is, besides the structure of Pliny the Younger's *Panegyricus* on Trajan (where, of course, Part Three is missing), that of Augustus' *Res Gestae*. Perhaps Ovid knew an earlier version of this latter? That would also explain why

In Ovid, Part One takes up 40 verses and ends with the exile telling us, after a chronological account of the first twenty years of his life, that, instead of striving to become a senator, he let the Muses talk him into a life of *otia*. Thus he names here his way of 'assuming office', and it corresponds exactly to the alternative life chosen by the elegiac *poeta/amator* in Propertius and Tibullus. In the slightly longer centrepiece (41–90) there then follow two sections of almost equal length in which the remaining details of the exile's life are presented under various rubrics. In verses 41–64 he lists the Roman poets famous in his youth, some of whom he knew personally, and appoints himself Benjamin of their number at the end. In verses 65–90 he talks first about his three wives—what a rubric this!—about his daughter and two grandchildren, and then about the death of his parents. Part Three finally (91–132), which has roughly the same length as Part One, deals with his 'final days' in so far as the now—in his own words—grey-haired exile, after a chronological account of his sufferings to date in banishment, declares proudly that his Muse, his constant comforter, has already granted him the kind of fame normally only attained after death (121–2).[9]

The *relegatus*, then, paints a picture of himself as, on the one hand, a man tormented day and night since his enforced departure from Rome—and we have just seen briefly above that the author, given his real-life situation in Tomi, is laying it on thick here. On the other hand, he would also have himself seen as an 'elder poet', already immortal in his own day. It seems quite evident to me that when thus carving his own niche in the hall of fame, which is clearly what Ovid intended to do in *Tristia* 4.10, the author also needed to sculpt the portrayal of himself as a young poet accordingly. There, in complete contrast to the old man in exile, he presents himself as a typical elegiac poet with all the freshness of youth. As such he first distances himself expressly from the world of *negotium*, represented by his father and brother. In verses 17–20 the brother's early liking for the *fortia arma*

in *Trist.* 4.10 he evidently includes some details for the sake of the analogy to Augustus (the year 43, equestrian rank, three wives, one daughter; cf. Fairweather 1987: 193 ff.).

[9] *Musa* in 20 and 117 underlines the contrast and the correspondence between Parts One and Three.

fori are compared with his own poetic inclinations, then follows the passage about his father. Who is not automatically reminded here of the famous opening situation in *Amores* 1.1, where the *poeta* about to write of *arma* and *uiolenta bella* is prevented from doing so by Amor and is thus reprogrammed to become first an elegiac poet and then an *amator*?

The poetic 'I' of *Tristia* 4.10 is, so he tells us, persuaded by the Muses to write elegies. And when he then gives a public reading of his first poems, he naturally cannot be young enough to contrast with the sorely tried grey-headed poet. Only if we fail to recognize the deliberate antithesis here can we read that his beard had, as the exiled poet recalls, at the time of this recital been trimmed only twice at the most, and take this so literally as to calculate on the basis of ancient shaving practices—as described in a handbook—that this all took place in the year 25 BC and that therefore Ovid's work on the *Amores* dates from thence. The author's game with the elegiac system is such a strong element in this text too that the poem cannot simply be regarded as a data bank for historical reconstructions of a biography.

Let us just have a look at the *Amores* and see whether the work itself can give us any idea when and under what circumstances it was written. In the introductory epigram the three elegy books even talk to us personally, declaring:

Qui modo Nasonis fueramus quinque libelli,
    tres sumus; hoc illi praetulit auctor opus.
ut iam nulla tibi nos sit legisse uoluptas,
    at leuior demptis poena duobus erit.

We, who only recently were still five books of Naso, are now three; the author has chosen this opus rather than that other. Since reading us is no fun for you anyway, with two of us removed the punishment will at least be lighter.

Scholars are unanimous in their interpretation of these words: Ovid, they say, indicates here that the text following is the 'second edition' of the *Amores*, which, having originally been published in five books, is now reduced to three.[10] As to the approximate date of publication for this lost 'first edition', here the conclusions differ. Attempts to reconstruct it—and up until quite recently there have been almost as many of these as there have been interpretations of the existing texts—have not come up with a reliable answer on this point. The poem *Amores* 1.14 with its allusions to the Romans' capture of Sygambri (45–50) would seem to fit nicely into the time around 15 BC. If it can be assigned to the 'first edition', then that would be an approximate publication date. If not, an earlier date would have to be assumed, but for those who read the passage in *Tristia* 4.10 discussed above as historical information, then not before 25 BC.

The 'second edition', the *Amores* in its extant form, is generally dated to some time around the birth of Christ. A reference in the *Ars Amatoria* permits the assumption that this work was published not long after the first half of the year 1 BC (Kraus 1968: 99),[11] and the majority of scholars believe that the *Ars* itself is mentioned in *Amores* 2.18.[12] This elegy begins with the speaker giving the epic poet Macer his reason for continuing to write, unlike his friend, short poems, the reason being that his (repeated) attempt to leave his *puella* has failed. A failure too has been the outcome of his effort to change to 'grand' poetry. The *poeta/amator* describes this venture as follows:

sceptra tamen sumpsi curaque tragoedia nostra
    creuit, et huic operi quamlibet aptus eram.
risit Amor pallamque meam pictosque cothurnos
    sceptraque priuata tam cito sumpta manu;
hinc quoque me dominae numen deduxit iniquae,
    deque cothurnato uate triumphat Amor.
quod licet, aut artes teneri profitemur Amoris

---

[10] So too Holzberg (1990: 88). Of all the countless studies on the chronology of the early works I should like to pick out only Cameron (1968); Jacobson (1974: 300–18); Syme (1978: 1–20); Primmer (1982: 250–9); McKeown (1987: 74–89). A trace at least of doubt as to the second edition theory can to my knowledge so far only be found in Goold (1983: 97–8). But see now Barchiesi (1988).

[11] Syme (1978: 13–15) presents here too his case for a second edition. His arguments are as hard to swallow as many parts of his book, which completely ignores the literary character of Ovid's work.

[12] 2.18.19–20 is taken to refer to the *Amores* by, for example, Fränkel (1945: 175 n. 4) and Cameron (1968: 331–2).

(ei mihi, praeceptis urgeor ipse meis!),
aut quod Penelopes uerbis reddatur Vlixi
    scribimus et lacrimas, Phylli relicta, tuas...

Still, I took up the sceptre and through my effort a tragedy grew and I was not
even that unsuited to the task. Amor laughed at my cloak, brightly coloured
buskins and the sceptre which I had so lightly taken into my layman's hand;
from here too the divine power of my unfair mistress brought me down
and Amor triumphed over the sublime tragedian. What I may do is either
tell of the arts of tender Amor (woe is me, I am getting tangled in my own
teachings) or write of what Odysseus is told in Penelope's words, or of your
tears, abandoned Phyllis.

The last distich here is an allusion to the *Epistulae Heroidum* 1 and 2.
There follow further allusions to the *Epistulae* 5, 11, 6, 10, 4, 7, and
15, then a brief account of the answers penned by one Sabinus to six
of these letters; finally, the speaker suggests that Macer too likes to
join the 'camp' of the elegiac world.

So the speaker was not able to change to the 'grand' genre tragedy
either and now just continues to do what is sanctioned: either he
teaches the *artes Amoris*, but sees himself then ensnared in his own
teachings, or he writes letters from mythical women, of which he
has, apparently, already produced nine. Now, the words *artes Amoris*
and *praecepta* are interpreted by most scholars as an allusion to the
Ars Amatoria, which must, in that case, already have existed. In my
view, however, this distich refers both within the elegy 2.18 and in
the poem's wider context to the *Amores*. As current analyses of this
collection are making ever clearer, the elegies are meant to be read, in
the order we know, as an 'erotic novel' (Zimmermann 1994, Buchan
1995, Holzberg 1997: 55 ff.). And within the plot of this 'novel' the
wail let out by the *poeta/amator*, which is not a word in the ear of
literary historians, but as so often, a genuine outburst on the part of
the fictional 'I', is entirely appropriate to the given situation.

I can hardly present here a complete structural analysis of the
Amores, but I can outline briefly what I mean. The 'erotic novel'
begins in the first elegies of book 1 with the *poeta/amator* vowing
fidelity to his *puella*, but indicating at the same time that he is by
nature polygamous (1.3).[13] He encourages the *puella* to be unfaithful

---

[13] On the double entendres in 1.3 cf. Woytek (1995).

too, teaching her ways to deceive her *uir* (1.4). But once she has slept with him (1.5), he on the one hand worries and is constantly on his guard lest she deceive him—he talks about this in several elegies in book 1 (especially 6, 7, 8, 10; 14 must also be included here). On the other hand, he himself soon begins to show an interest in other women; the first mention of this is in 2.2. But then he finds out that the *puella* has used what he taught her in 1.4 against him, and from then on he has a number of unpleasant experiences with her. She has an abortion, for example, and the *poeta/amator* does not even know who would have been the father (2.13/14). There apparently follows a period of separation (2.15 and 16), and this results in the *poeta/amator* remembering now the power of his poetic talents. He reminds the *puella* that his elegies can make her immortal (2.17), and he even tries to change to the 'grand' genre, tragedy. And when this fails, he realizes for the first time the full extent of the unfortunate situation he has brought upon himself with his earlier *praecepta* for the *puella* (2.18). He does try to snap out of it with a little infidelity of his own (2.19). At the same time, however, he cynically encourages the *uir* of the new *puella* and the new *puella* herself not to make his erotic successes too easy for him. It is the same old mistake again— meting out *praecepta* that can cut two ways. Realizing this, he lets out an aside (2.19.34): *ei mihi, ne monitis torquear ipse meis!* 'Oh my, I only hope I won't suffer torture myself on account of my own teachings!' Scholars taking the biographical approach to the *Amores* have always been bothered by the fact that elegy 2.18, a poetological-programmatical one, is followed by this primarily erotic poem, while Books 1 and 3 end each with a programmatic elegy. It should be obvious now, however, that there is method in this. For Ovid the story line of his 'erotic novel' is more important at this point than a Propertian structural principle, even if he does apply this in the traditional position in books 1 and 3. The above-quoted verse pro- vides furthermore a transition to the novel's 'continuation' in book 3, where the *poeta/amator* will actually suffer 'torture', but this is not something we need pursue here. What we have seen so far ought to have made it clear why I believe that the much-debated *artes* distich 2.18.19–20 refers to the *Amores* themselves.

If my interpretation is correct, then the extant text of the *Amores* must have been written before the *Ars*. This would fit in perfectly

with the reference in book 3 of the latter to both the *Amores* and
the *Epistulae Heroidum* together (343–6).[14] And I can now also throw
doubt on the assertion that our *Amores* text is the 'second edition' of
a work that had already seen a 'first edition'. What is this 'unabridged'
version of the extant collection of elegies with its carefully designed
narrative structure supposed to have looked like? Was it too an 'erotic
novel', but with more episodes? For whom would the 'epitome' we
now possess have been written—for impatient readers? But then
the second distich of the epigram would have to be taken literally
and not understood as it is quite clearly meant to be—ironically,
that is.

I would interpret the two verses in which the reader is informed
that his 'punishment' has been reduced from five to three books as a
witty allusion to the famous words of Callimachus: 'great book, great
evil' (fr. 465 Pf.). The new *poeta doctus*, publishing his first work in
written form, wants to make it clear right from the start that he is, as
it were, writing himself into the Alexandrian tradition with this book.
And this he does by sifting through the vast quantity of compositions
he has kept as groundwork on a number of papyrus rolls—we shall
be asking directly why he names the number five—and compiling
from these an opus that conforms to the standard set by the critic
Callimachus. It is not hard to believe that in the years before publication of the *Amores*, when Ovid was giving the customary private
and public readings from his manuscripts (Starr 1987), he did indeed
earn himself a reputation for being a *nimium amator ingenii sui* ('all
too fond of his own talent'), as Quintilian was later to characterize
him (*Inst.* 10.1.88). Well, now he could put critical readers' minds at
rest, and herein lies the epigram's irony.

Why originally 'five' books? Perhaps we should bear in mind that
about the same time as Ovid was publishing his *Amores*, around 15 BC
then, or a little later, two of his great predecessors on the Roman
poetry scene—Horace and Propertius—each published the fourth
book of a collection of poems, and this in both cases after a conspicuous gap of several years between the appearance of the new book

---

[14] The old theory according to which *Ars* 3 was published later than *Ars*
1/2 can be considered invalidated in the light of arguments to the contrary put
forward by Wellmann-Bretzigheimer (1981) 3 n. 7; 7; 14 and Sharrock (1994)
18–20.

and the first three earlier ones.[15] Thus perhaps Ovid is alluding here to his two fellow-authors. If so, the epigram would once again have to be read ironically, with the talking books of the *Amores* declaring saucily: 'If our *auctor* had wanted, we would even have been one book longer than Horace's collected odes and Propertius' collected elegies now, and we would all have been published at one fell swoop to boot!'

It would seem, then, that the decades of debating about the chronology of Ovid's early works were much scholarly ado about nothing. The order of their composition, at any rate, now appears to be a very uncomplicated matter. Around 15 BC Ovid published the *Amores*; prior to this, over a period of time—exactly how long we cannot say—he read his erotic elegies to a variety of audiences, but then decided that not all of these poems were worthy of inclusion in the book which he now proposed to circulate, an 'erotic novel' passing muster as strictly Alexandrian. Before the first publication of his poetry 'in print', as it were, Ovid had already begun to write letters from mythical women and had presented some of them at readings.[16] This new variation of the genre 'elegy' apparently caused such a sensation that Sabinus immediately wrote the answering epistles mentioned in *Amores* 2.18 (Heldmann 1994). The 'printed' version of the various letters from heroines appeared between 15 and 1 BC. It now comprised a total of 15 elegies, probably divided into three books with five in each (Pulbrook 1977; Stroh 1991). Some time after the first half of the year 1 BC there then followed the *Ars Amatoria* and the *Remedia Amoris*.

But what about the tragedy mentioned in *Amores* 2.18? Well, this attempt on the part of the poetic 'I' to write a work of 'grand' poetry was not the first. As he tells us in *Amores* 1.1, he had already tried his hand at an epic in the style of Virgil's *Aeneid*, but Amor had laughed at that, just as he would later laugh at the idea of a tragedy,

---

[15] *Odes* 4 is generally thought to have been published around 13 BC, Propertius' fourth book not long after 16 BC. Barchiesi (1988: 103), on the other hand, points to Gallus, *Amores*, 1–4, 'the founding text of Roman elegy'.

[16] This would be the simplest interpretation of *Am.* 2.18.21–6. All *Epistulae* not named here are now, almost as a general rule, regarded as spurious amongst Anglo-American scholars (cf. most recently Knox 1995: 5–12), but this is to my mind a very dubious consequence of the biographical approach.

and had put a stop to it. In 2.1 he talks about having started a Gigantomachy, but its completion had been prevented by the *puella*, who denied him her favours. Both of these passages are generally interpreted not as Ovid's own autobiographical references, but as variations on the *recusatio* theme, and it would seem logical to suppose that the same applies to the tragedy story. Here the ground is being prepared for the end of the *Amores*, where the elegiac poet eventually will actually be turning into a tragedian. And this is the very metamorphosis that the *poeta/amator* promises in 3.1 to the personified Tragedy, after she has been arguing with the personified Elegy over him.

The verses in 2.18 could, then, be interpreted as a further variation on the *recusatio* theme. Ovid's choice of tragedy as the 'grand' genre to which the *poeta/amator* turns at the end could simply have been his only option for this very effective scene with the two female personifications of the 'grand' and the 'little' genre: he could hardly have used epic, at least not without disregarding gender. All the same, we are told by Quintilian (*Inst.* 8.5.6; 10.1.98) and Tacitus (*Dial.* 12) directly and indirectly by Seneca the Elder (*Suas.* 3.7) that Ovid wrote a Medea tragedy, and the two rhetoricians each even quote one verse from the work (Döpp 1992: 71–4). Was this drama really written by Ovid? This is a question that must certainly be asked, if only because the *relegatus* in the *Tristia* says (5.7.27–8):

nil equidem feci—tu scis hoc ipse—theatris,
    Musa nec in plausus ambitiosa mea est.

I have certainly written nothing for the theatre—you yourself know this—nor is my Muse desirous of applause.[17]

In *Tristia* 2, the letter to Augustus, however, the *relegatus* does try to prove what a serious poet he can be with the following (549–56):

sex ego Fastorum scripsi totidemque libellos,
    cumque suo finem mense libellus habet,

---

[17] How irritating these lines are for Ovid scholars becomes evident when the conclusion is drawn from them that *Medea* was meant to be read, not staged (e.g. Kraus 1968: 87).

idque tuo nuper scriptum sub nomine, Caesar,
   et tibi sacratum sors mea rupit opus;
et dedimus tragicis scriptum regale cothurnis,
   quaeque grauis debet uerba cothurnus habet;
dictaque sunt nobis, quamuis manus ultima coeptis
   defuit, in facies corpora uersa nouas.

Six books of *Fasti* I have written and as many again, and every roll ends with its own particular month; and this work too, just recently superscribed with your name, Caesar, and dedicated to you, has my fate interrupted; and I have given the buskins of tragedy a regal piece of writing, and the solemn buskin has the language owing to it; and sung by me were—although the finishing touches are lacking in this undertaking—the bodies turned into new forms.

So, a drama after all. But is it not odd that the actual title *Medea* is not mentioned here either, and that the distich 553–4 is not particularly good poetry, the ugly repetition being but one reason for this?[18] Furthermore, it separates the *Fasti* from the *Metamorphoses*, the text alluded to in verses 555–6, and both are referred to as unfinished. Could it be possible that someone understood the *Amores* speaker's description of his transformation into a tragedian as an autobiographical account of Ovid's own development, and deemed it appropriate to insert this distich here? And could it even be possible that this someone (or another someone) felt that a tragedy was needed to go with the tragedian and so published a Medea drama under the name of Ovid? A tragedy, then, which Seneca the Elder, Quintilian, and Tacitus presumed genuine, just as Pliny the Elder did not recognize the *Halieutica*, a text now generally considered spurious (Richmond 1981: 2746 ff.), as a Pseudo-Ovidianum? This latter didactic poem, the *Consolatio ad Liviam* (Schoonhoven 1992), and *Nux*[19] all show that in early imperial times there were already poets who could produce very exact imitations of Ovid (Lee 1958: 469). And if *Medea* was a forgery, it was a clever one in the selection

---

[18] Emendations have of course been proffered (cf. now Hall's edition, *app. crit.* on these lines). The wording is, however, the same in all manuscripts.

[19] Pulbrook (1985) now believes that this is genuine. To Richmond (1981: 2767) it seems 'very improbable, but not quite impossible' that Ovid wrote it.

of its subject, as this very theme is treated frequently by Ovid, twice
even at great length (*Her.* 12;[20] *Met.* 7.1–403).[21]

Naturally we can only speculate here. However, in the middle of the generic transformation which Ovid so carefully planned
and executed—from the *Amores* over the *Epistulae* to the *Ars* and
Remedia—a work of 'grand' poetry does seem downright out of
place. Earlier interpreters of Ovid were quite happy with this development of his from elegiac poet to tragedian, as documented for
them in *Amores* 2.18, 3.1 and 15, and they credited the author
with having undergone a very laudable process of artistic maturing.
Walther Kraus, for example, observed (1958: 141): 'Ovid is the typical precocious heir to an already fully developed art, writing verse
before really living himself. Deeper quality needs time to emerge.'
In 1982 E. J. Kenney remarked on *Amores* 3.15.17–18, where the
poeta | amator announces his final changeover to the 'grand' genre
(1982: 421): 'in retrospect it will be seen chiefly as having been a
stepping-stone to higher things'. In 1974 Howard Jacobsen had even
declared (1974: 109): 'The loss of his tragedy *Medea is* likely one of
the most significant gaps in our treasure of works from antiquity
and is but scarcely repaired by the relatively extensive treatments of
Medea in the *Heroides* and *Metamorphoses* and the numerous allusions to her in virtually every work Ovid wrote.' Assessments such as
these, of which many more could be cited, quite unmistakably arise
from the wishful thinking inherent in the biographical approach and
attributable to the influence of Romantic poetics. Such projections
entirely obscure the very clear purpose with which the *poeta doctus*
Ovid organized his life's work on the basis of the elegiac system—so
clear a purpose in fact, that one might in retrospect almost believe
that Ovid welcomed banishment because it even afforded him the
opportunity to create a new variation for his genre: the 'exile elegy'
(Spoth 1992: 142–56; 223–5; Holzberg 1997: 24 ff.).

The cliché of Ovid as a poet 'fulfilling his potential' can actually be traced back to Quintilian, who felt the need to note: 'Ovid's
Medea seems to me to demonstrate how much the man could have

[20] For Knox (1986*b*) one argument for classing this elegy as spurious is that it is
based on the Medea drama. Cf. in contrast Hinds (1993).
[21] It is also worth remembering that in *Trist.* 3.9 Tomi is named as the scene of
Medea's fratricide.

achieved had he chosen to bridle his talent rather than indulge it'
(*Inst.* 10.1.98). And precisely because the tragedy was, according to
Quintilian, so very different from Ovid's other works, I find it hard
to believe that he really was its author. Then again, he might have
been! But gone is gone. Perhaps I may at least be permitted to find
it rather peculiar that some books on Ovid's *Gesamt*output devote a
whole chapter to *Medea* and thus, proportionally speaking, give more
space to two measly verses[22] from a lost opus than they do to other
works that survive in their entirety (e.g. Fränkel 1945: 46–7).

As we come to the end of these deliberations, let us cast a glance at
a surviving Ovid text once again. At the beginning of the elegy *Amores*
3.15, the *poeta/amator* says (1–2):

Quaere nouum uatem, tenerorum mater Amorum:
  raditur haec elegis ultima meta meis.

Look for a new poet, mother of tender loves: this turning-post will be
scratched for the last time by my elegies.

A farewell to elegies? Yes. Does it actually also apply to the author
himself? Well, let's not go into that again. But does it even apply at all
to the elegiac 'I'? Anyone who has read the *Amores* from the beginning
to this point in one sitting will remember that only four elegies previously, in 3.11, the *poeta/amator* takes leave of his *puella* too, because
he cannot bear the *seruitium amoris* any longer. Amongst other things
he says there in v. 28: *quaere alium pro me qui uelit ista pati* 'Look
for another to take my place, one who will put up with this!' These
parting words are unmistakably echoed in the later farewell to elegy.
But here, in 3.11, there follow four verses later—some editors make
this the start of a new elegy (Keul 1989)—the clear retraction and
renewed submission to the yoke of elegiac love so much hated only a
moment before.[23] Given this sudden about-turn, what are we really
to think of the tear-jerking goodbye to elegy in 3.15? Is Ovid not just
trying to play a game with us once again? With all of us, that is—those
of us who interpret his verses as autobiography and those of us who

[22] The similarity between the verse quoted in Quint. *Inst.* 8.5.6 and Ov. *Her.* 12.73–
6, one attributed to the elegy's derivation from the tragedy (Döpp 1992: 72–3), could
naturally be reversed too.
[23] I am grateful to Herbert Neumaier for drawing my attention to this verbal echo.

don't. I think that he is. And this is why I have presented here some
examples of how the poet plays with the facts of his life and the facts
of the background of his poetry. And if we play the game with him,
then we must be more cautious than at any poker table.[24]

---

[24] Afterword 2005: Even if Richard Tarrant is not happy with my suggestion that
the tragedy heralded in *Am.* 3.1 and 3.15 cannot be *Medea*—he writes: 'The scepticism
of Holzberg...on this point is stimulating but not in my view persuasive' (2002:
16 n. 12)—I continue to find my own notion convincing. Support for it has also
been forthcoming in the form of Gerlinde Bretzigheimer's detailed discussion of
the problem (2001: 47; 79–83). To name just one important argument: Tragoedia's
exhortation '*cane facta uirorum*' (3.1.25) conveys up images of a historical drama,
not of a heroine cast in a tale of woe (cf. also now the completely revised edition of
Holzberg 1990 (2001: 110–11). Bretzigheimer (like Boyd 1997: 142–7) also confirms
my doubts that the epigram which opens the *Amores* should really be read as the
preface to a second edition of the elegies (11–12; 91–4; 153–4). And, in this same
context, Bretzigheimer is particularly persuasive when arguing that, in the words *artes
teneri profitemur Amoris* in 2.18.19, Ovid is speaking as the poet of the *Amores*, not
of the *Ars Amatoria* (273–82). Finally, a word on the authenticity of the *Medea*: I
now find myself variously placed in solitary Pseudo-Ovidianum confinement (e.g.
by Ulrich Schmitzer, *Gymnasium* 105 (1998): 358) and feel that I must protest. All I
am saying in this paper is that 'I find it hard to believe that he really was its author.'
After all, the 'authentication' offered by Seneca the Elder, Quintilian, and Tacitus can
scarcely be called an argument: did not Lucan (Suet. *vita Lucani* p. 50 Reiff.), Martial
(8.55.20; 14.185), and Statius (*Silv. praef.* I; 2.7.74) call the *Culex* a work written by
Virgil?

3

The Epistolary Mode and the First of Ovid's *Heroides*

Duncan F. Kennedy

In April 1741 there appeared a slim volume entitled *An Apology for the Life of Mrs Shamela Andrews* by a certain Mr Conny Keyber, whose name is generally supposed to conceal that of the novelist Henry Fielding. *Shamela,* to give the book its more familiar title, was a parody of Samuel Richardson's epistolary novel *Pamela: or Virtue Rewarded,* which had been published to great acclaim the previous year. In a series of letters purportedly sent to each other by the main characters, the story unfolds of the honest servant-girl Pamela, her efforts to avoid seduction by her master Mr B., and her eventual marriage to him. Fielding's chief target was the morality of the book (Pamela's virtue contains a disturbingly large element of self-interest), but in passing he drew cruel attention to some of the pitfalls of the epistolary form as a vehicle for narrative. One passage in particular deserves quotation, from Letter VI, which Shamela writes to her mother at (so we are duly informed at the top of the letter) twelve o'clock on Thursday night:

Mrs Jervis and I are just in Bed, and the Door unlocked; if my Master should come—Odsbods! I hear him just coming in at the Door. You see I write in the present Tense, as Parson Williams says. Well, he is in Bed between us, we both shamming a Sleep, he steals his Hand into my Bosom, which I, as if in my Sleep, press close to me with mine . . .

Decorum forbids the quotation of any more. Shamela's master clearly has his hands full, and if we are rash enough to ask what is in

Shamela's hand at this moment, in view of the epistolary form of this account, we can only conclude: a pen is.

Shamela's letter illustrates many of the difficulties that accompany the use of the epistolary mode. The restrictions it imposes are immense, and very few works which use it can claim to be successful in overcoming them, still less in turning them to advantage. I should like to concentrate upon two considerations whose observance or neglect can be of vital importance in any literary text which presents itself as a letter. The first is that a letter is the product of a specific time, the second is the motivation for the epistolary form from the dramatic context. Shamela is in bed at midnight about to receive the not unwelcome attentions of her master: it is implausible that she should even think of writing to her mother, let alone in the circumstances actually be doing so. If the epistolary form is to be adopted as the vehicle for telling a story without straining the reader's belief that what he is reading is a letter, then it is imperative that the motivation for the writing of a letter at any particular stage in that story should be felt to arise naturally out of the events depicted, and, ideally, the resulting letter should be seen to be itself an agent in the forward movement of those events. This is extremely difficult to sustain over a series of letters and is where many epistolary novels falter. Pamela's letters to her parents are largely first-person narratives punctuated periodically for the sake of the form by opening and closing epistolary conventions. The letters she writes play only a sporadic part in the development of the plot. By contrast, the epistolary form of Laclos' *Les Liaisons Dangereuses* (1782) is central to its plot. Every exchange of letters is subtly motivated by the progress of events it depicts and then provides its own impetus to the subsequent development of the plot, until finally the accumulated correspondence of the leading characters itself leads to their downfall.[1]

Ovid's paired epistles (*Heroides* 16–21), those in which hero writes a letter to heroine and receives a reply from her, clearly contain the potentiality for the kind of dramatic development that can be seen in the best epistolary novels, and Ovid pays careful attention

---

[1] On these considerations see in general Mylne (1981) 149–55, 234–6. Most recent research on the literary potentialities specific to the epistolary form has concentrated on the epistolary novel and on Laclos in particular; cf. Rousset (1962), Jost (1966), Todorov (1967), Altman (1982).

to the purported time of composition and the motivation for the writing of the letters from the dramatic context. In the absence of an omniscient third-person narrator, we the readers must reconstruct for ourselves the dramatic context of the exchange from details mentioned in passing by the two correspondents. The letter of Paris to Helen (*Her.* 16) and her reply to it (*Her.* 17) represent his declaration of love and her cautious encouragement of it, and so form the prelude to the most famous of all elopements. Paris, it appears, is writing to Helen actually within the palace of Menelaus in Sparta,[2] which stated baldly sounds implausible—in normal circumstances one rarely has cause to write to anyone staying under the same roof, but it emerges that Paris' covert attempts to declare his love in person have been rebuffed (Her. 17.75–92),[3] and he has also failed to suborn Helen's companions (16.259–62). Now that Menelaus has departed to Crete, Paris sees his best hope of winning Helen's heart as she lies in her solitary bed (16.317) in an account of the origins and growth of his passion for her. As he remarks at the outset (16.13–14), the very fact that she is reading his letter has given him the entrée he needs. In the specific dramatic context adroitly engineered by Ovid from the outlines of the traditional story, the exchange of letters we read seems to be a natural outcome of the story so far, and it also emerges as the agency which precipitates subsequent events.

---

[2] Cf. *Her.* 16.129–30, 217 ff., 275–6, 299–300, 17.7 ff., 159–60.

[3] *Les Liaisons Dangereuses* provides a close parallel to this successful transgression of the logical epistolary convention of separation of writer and addressee. The arch-seducer, the Vicomte de Valmont, does not address a letter to the virtuous object of his attentions, Madame de Tourvel, a fellow-guest staying under the same roof in the absence of her husband, until (Letter XXIV) she has rejected in horror his first approach to her, an event he describes in Letter XXIII. He thus loses the social intimacy he previously enjoyed and must henceforth press his suit by letter. Her reluctant willingness to reply (Letter XXVI), like that of Helen, marks the beginning of her downfall. A coincidence? I know of no treatment of Ovid's possible influence on Laclos (Laurent Versini's otherwise encyclopaedic treatment (1968: 242–6) mentions Ovid only in the most vague terms), but Valmont's description of his attempted seduction presents us with an unmistakably Ovidian scene and sentiment; cf. Letter XXIII: 'Aussi, en descendant de voiture, elle [Mme de Rosemonde] passa dans son appartement, et nous laissa tête à tête, ma belle et moi, dans un salon mal éclairé; obscurité douce, qui enhardit l'amour timide', and Ov. *Am.* 1.5.3–8, esp. 7–8 *illa verecundis lux est praebenda puellis | qua timidus latebras speret habere pudor.*

The exchange of letters between Acontius and Cydippe (*Her.* 20 and 21) is again plausibly embedded by Ovid in the details of the story he inherited from Callimachus (frr. 67–75Pf.). Acontius fell in love with Cydippe when he caught sight of her at a festival of Diana on the island of Delos. Inscribing 'I swear by Diana to marry Acontius' on an apple, he rolled it towards her, and she, reading the words aloud, bound herself by the oath. After her return home, her wedding to her formal fiancé had to be postponed three times, as she fell victim to a mysterious illness. Her parents consulted the Delphic oracle, which revealed the truth about the oath, and she duly married Acontius. Ovid sets the exchange of letters after the third postponement of the wedding (21.257) and just before the response from Delphi is received (21.231–4). As the languishing Cydippe is being kept under close surveillance (21.17–20; cf. 20.129–32), we can accept that the only way the eager Acontius can press his suit is by a smuggled letter (the obvious intermediary being the 'nurse in the know' (*conscia nutrix*) of 21.17), while Cydippe's reply, the epistolary form permitting the gradual revelation of her attraction to his brash and confident manner, gives psychological depth and complexity to the rather mechanical resolution of the problem by the Delphic oracle in the Callimachean version (fr. 75.20–37 Pf.).

Ovid's most effective use of purported time of composition and motivation of the epistolary form from the dramatic context occurs in the exchange between Leander and Hero (*Her.* 18 and 19), young lovers separated by the waters of the Hellespont. Every evening to see his beloved, Leander bravely swims across the dangerous straits until, inevitably, one stormy night he drowns. Within this general dramatic context, Ovid sets Leander's letter during a prolonged and violent storm. For seven days now (18.25) he has been unable to make his accustomed swim, and, although he would much sooner brave the waters, all he can do is to commit his love to a letter (18.21–4). Even getting this to Hero will prove difficult: only one seaman has been bold enough to put out on to the Hellespont, and he is the one who will deliver the letter (18.9–10). Hero is constantly looking out for similar opportunities to send her reply (19.29–30). Leander cannot travel with this sailor for fear of discovery, as the port is overlooked and the affair must be kept from his parents (18.11–14). In the circumstances depicted, the writing of his letter could hardly be better motivated. Hero longs to see him again, and her reply is deeply affectionate. She realizes, and is afraid of, the dangers the sea holds for him, but in her impatience she casts just a hint of suspicion on his motives for not attempting the swim (19.57–8, 95–6, 116). She can remember a time, she writes, when the sea was no less fierce— or at least not much less—and yet he made the swim (19.85–6). Where, she asks, is the great swimmer who scorned the waves (19.90)? That is all the information the letters give us. The correspondence cannot, of course, predict future events, though it does foreshadow them (18.191–200),[4] but we need little imagination to conjecture that Leander's reaction to Hero's imputation that his ardour is cooling will be to attempt the swim in spite of the conditions and against his better judgement. So, not only is the exchange of letters superbly motivated from the dramatic context, but it can also be felt to pre-cipitate the dénouement, and the direct revelation and interplay of character the epistolary form allows grants a tragic dimension to the sad accident which ends this tender love story (Anderson 1973: 70–4).

In the double *Heroides*, then, Ovid seems to have worked out the implications of his use of the epistolary form, and to have exploited it to good effect by making the exchange of letters an integral part of the three stories. In the single *Heroides* (1–15) such accommodation of the epistolary form to its dramatic context is harder to find. Within the confines of Ovid's treatment of the story of Phaedra (*Her.* 4), her letter to Hippolytus revealing her passion must be regarded as the motivation of ensuing events,[5] and Arthur Palmer (1898: 339) made the attractive suggestion that the timing of Dido's letter (Her. 7) was prompted in Ovid's mind by Virgil, *Aeneid* 4.408–15. Few of

---

[4] Cf. also the bad omens mentioned at *Her.* 18.81–2, 141–2, 19.195 ff. The outcome of the story would have been familiar to Ovid's readers at least from Verg. *G.* 3.258 ff., and probably also from Hellenistic antecedents; cf. Page (1941) 512–14.

[5] Cf. *Her.* 4.7–10 *ter tecum conata loqui ter inutilis haesit | lingua, ter in primo destitit ore sonus. | qua licet et sequitur, pudor est miscendus amori; | dicere quae puduit, scribere iussit amor* 'three times my tongue attempted speech with you, three times it vainly stopped, three times the sound stopped on the tip of my mouth. Wherever it is permitted and natural, love should be mingled with modesty; what modesty forbade me to say, love commanded me to write'. Whether this is Ovid's idea or is derived from one of his numerous possible sources for the story of Phaedra remains uncertain; cf. Jacobson (1974) 142 ff., esp. 146 n. 11.

the poems, however, draw much more than cursory attention to their epistolary status, and by and large it is the apparent inappropriateness of the epistolary form to the dramatic context that has time and time again drawn the critics' fire. In lines 3–4 of the tenth poem, when Ariadne, abandoned on the deserted shore of the island of Naxos, writes 'the words you are *reading*, Theseus, I *send* to you (*quae legis* . . . *tibi* . . . *mitto*) from that shore from which your sails carried off your ship without me', it is by no means unreasonable to wonder how Ariadne is going to have her letter delivered, and even where she has managed to find writing materials. At the opening of the third poem, the barbarian Briseis draws attention to the difficulty she has in writing to Achilles in Greek.[6] Incongruous though these situations may be, it is wrong to lay much emphasis on their absurdity. In epistolary fiction, the very implausibility of the circumstances of writing can be a commentary on the writer's character or situation. Thus in *Les Liaisons Dangereuses,* when Valmont writes a love letter to Mme de Tourvel in the bed of a favourite courtesan Emilie and uses her bare back as his writing desk (Letter XLVII introducing Letter XLVIII), we can hardly construe this as anything other than an expression of the utter depravity of his character. Ariadne's words emphasize her isolation and the complete helplessness of her situation, and her belief that her letter will reach Theseus and that he will read it may be the first of the numerous delusions induced by her isolation which we can detect her experiencing in the course of her letter (cf. especially 79–88). Briseis' reference to her linguistic shortcomings underlines the difficulty she has in establishing any sort of communication with her stubborn and aloof addressee. These last two cases might be dismissed as special pleading, and it might be concluded, perhaps correctly, that Ovid's realization of the implications of the epistolary form had not developed completely at this stage. Be that as it may, by ignoring the fact that the *Heroides* are meant to be letters—and Ovid quite

---

6 Paradoxically, the amusement that such a flirtation with verisimilitude arouses in exotic contexts seems to aid the suspension of disbelief by emphasizing the playful, literary quality of the text. Zilia, the heroine of Mme de Grafigny's *Lettres d'une Péruvienne* (1746), abducted from Peru, tells how she recorded her first seventeen letters to her betrothed Aza, a Peruvian prince, on *quipos,* knotted cords of various colours used by the Peruvians for sending messages, until her French was good enough to translate them; cf. Mylne (1981) 154.

categorically regarded them as such[7]—we are in danger of overlooking cases in which Ovid did manage to exploit the potentialities of the form. I have a specific instance in mind, Penelope's letter to Ulysses (*Her.* 1).

Writing of Ovid's adoption of the epistolary framework for the *Heroides,* W. S. Anderson (1973: 66) has remarked:

We are reading the letter, or, to be more accurate, we are peeking over the woman's shoulder as she is writing it. Sometimes the fiction is transparent, or even breaks down. Penelope's letter to Ulysses is apparently one of those she gives to almost every passing sailor, in the hope that it will reach her husband; but Ulysses never receives it.

Anderson is referring to lines 59–62 of the poem:

quisquis ad haec vertit peregrinam litora puppim,
    ille mihi de te multa rogatus abit,
quamque tibi reddat, si te modo viderit usquam,
    traditur huic digitis charta notata meis.

Whoever turns his foreign ship to these shores departs only when he has been asked many questions by me concerning you, and a letter written by my own fingers is handed over to him to give to you if only he should see you anywhere.

The proposed method of delivery might have sounded less strange to the ancients than it does to us. We may perhaps recall how Iphigeneia recognized her brother Orestes when she asked him to deliver a letter to Greece which was in fact destined for him (Eur. *IT* 727–33). At first sight, admittedly, these lines do look like a rather feeble attempt on Ovid's part to justify the existence, as it were, of this poem, but in that he could have glossed over the problem merely by not alluding to it, we should for this very reason take a closer look at the passage, bearing in mind as we do so the two considerations discussed earlier: the purported time of writing of the letter and the motivation for its writing at that point. Penelope claims that she writes a letter to give to each and every sailor who puts in at Ithaca in the hope that one day

---

[7] Cf. *Ars* 3.345 *vel tibi composita cantetur* epistula *voce* 'or let some *Epistle* be read by you with practised voice'; also *Am.* 2.18.21 ff. and Kirfel (1969) esp. 11–36.

he may be able to give it into Ulysses' hands. So, when is she writing *this* letter, and to whom is she going to give it?

First, the supposed occasion of composition. Surveying the poem for clues given in passing, we find that Troy has fallen (3), so it is the period of Ulysses' wanderings. This is confirmed in line 25 by the information that the Argolic chieftains have returned, though this is hardly very helpful in that Ulysses wandered for ten years. Much more interesting are lines 37–8. Penelope has to explain how she knows about the celebrations for the return of the Greek leaders to their cities which she has described in lines 25–36,[8] so she mentions in passing that she heard all this from Telemachus, who in turn got it from Nestor. This is very specific indeed: Telemachus relates what he heard on his mission to Pylos and Sparta to his mother on the day after his return in *Odyssey* 17.108–49. This would clearly seem to be the period Ovid has in mind, for there are two further apparent references to the mission of Telemachus in lines 63–5 and 99–100. In the *Odyssey*, Telemachus' interview with his mother takes place on the morning of the day before the suitors are killed. That is, Penelope must be writing this letter just before she is reunited with her husband. I am not aware that attention has been drawn before to the purported time of composition of this letter, but once we realize it, much of what Penelope says takes on considerable irony: her appeal to Ulysses not to write back, but to come in person (2), her complaints about how slowly time passes for her (7–8), about how she does not know where he is (57–8), and above all the closing couplet of the poem, in which she laments 'I, who was a girl when you left, though you should come home *immediately* (*protinus ut venias*, 116), will seem to have become an old woman'. Penelope will not have to wait very long to find out her husband's reaction to the physical changes the intervening twenty years have wrought in her.

So, the purported time of composition is the very eve of the slaying of the suitors. What prompts her to write *this* letter at *this* point? Returning to lines 59–62, we find that she claims to write a letter whenever a foreigner arrives who can carry it for her. It so happens that somebody does arrive in the palace on the day before the suitors

---

[8] All of Ulysses' men were, of course, killed at one stage or another on the journey home.

are killed who fits this description, a beggar who claims he is a Cretan who has fallen on hard times, and indeed, in *Od.* 19.123–63, Penelope does what she claims in line 60 of this epistle to do in such cases, she questions him at length about her husband. Presumably this particular letter she is now writing she intends to give to him. But we know that this Cretan beggar is actually Ulysses in disguise, so all unknowing, Penelope is about to deliver this letter into the hands of its addressee. *Her.* 1.59–62, then, far from being an embarrassingly feeble attempt on Ovid's part to convince his readers that what they are perusing is a letter, are an inspired example of motivation of the epistolary form from the dramatic context which infuse the poem with a most delicious irony.

Or are they? A number of considerations enjoin caution. If the situation I have depicted was in Ovid's mind, then his friend Sabinus did not catch on, for we learn from *Amores* 2.18.29 that among the replies he composed to Ovid's heroines' letters was one from Ulysses to Penelope; but Sabinus seems to have been oblivious to, or to have been prepared to overlook, the implausibility that any of Ovid's heroines should receive replies from their absent menfolk. More important, the purported time of composition of this letter on which this interpretation hangs is derived entirely from the three apparent references to Telemachus' mission to Pylos and Sparta in lines 37–8, 63–5, and 99–100. It is somewhat disconcerting to find, therefore, that so substantial a critic as Richard Bentley was in favour of ejecting lines 37–40 and 99–100 from the text, thus leaving only 63–5, which on closer inspection do not unequivocally refer to the mission of Telemachus.[9] Bentley's judgement is preserved only in the brackets he put round the lines in question in his copy of the text, but his condemnation of them will not have been based entirely

---

[9] *Nos Pylon, antiqui Neleia Nestoris arva,* | *misimus; incerta est fama remissa Pylo.* | *misimus et Sparten; Sparte quoque nescia veri* 'we have sent to Pylos, the land of ancient Nestor, Neleus' son; the word brought back from Pylos was uncertain. We have sent to Sparta, too; Sparta also did not know the truth'. If these lines refer to the mission of Telemachus, they contradict not only Homer but 99–100 *ille per insidias paene est mihi nuper ademptus,* | *dum parat* invitis omnibus *ire Pylon* 'Recently he was almost taken from me in an ambush, while preparing to go to Pylos *against the will of all of them*'. However, it is surely to complicate matters unduly to postulate a separate mission to these same places not attested in Homer.

on considerations of linguistic usage.[10] The interpretation I have aired presupposes that Ovid had, and expected his readers to have, a close acquaintance with the Odyssey, yet one of Bentley's reasons for wishing to excise 37–40 and 99–100 will undoubtedly have been the marked deviations in these lines from the Homeric account. In 37 (and cf. 63–5) Penelope claims that *she* sent Telemachus to Pylos and Sparta to enquire after Ulysses, whereas in Homer, Telemachus goes to Pylos without telling his mother,[11] and indeed he instructs the old nurse Eurycleia not to do so (*Od.* 3.373–6). In 99–100, Penelope says that the suitors plotted to ambush Telemachus on his way to Pylos, whereas in *Od.* 4.701, where she first hears of the plot, the herald Medon explicitly tells her that it has been laid to trap him 'travelling homewards' (οἴκαδε νισσόμενον).

These are not the only deviations from the Homeric account. In line 15, if the manuscript reading is correct,[12] Antilochus is said to

---

[10] Notably the infinitive of purpose *quaerere* after *misso* in 37; 39–40, linked in sense to 37–8, contain further difficulties. Excision is the path of least resistance, but leaves an impossible transition between 36 and 41. Cf. the next note.

[11] Indeed against her wishes, as she says to him on his return (ἐμεῦ ἀέκητι 'against my will', *Od.* 17.43). The editors have passed on to me the suggestion of reading *iusso* for *misso* in 37, comparing the variant readings at Juv. 3.78. This would immediately account for the infinitive *quaerere*. I would hesitate to alter the transmitted text on two grounds: (i) *misso* gains some support from Penelope's insistence (cf. the emphatic repetition of *misimus* at the beginning of 64 and 65) that it was *she* who initiated the journey of Telemachus. (ii) *iusso* immediately reminds us that Telemachus was indeed ordered to go to see Nestor and Menelaus by Athene disguised as Mentes (*Od.* 1.284–5), but when Penelope learns of his mission from Medon (4.701–2), she is puzzled at what impelled him to go (707 ff.), and she is nowhere told, not even by Telemachus on his return (17.108 ff.), of the divine instigation of his journey. If the *Odyssey* functions as an 'objective' account of the events which lie behind *Her.* 1 (the central interpretative problem of the poem which I discuss below), Ovid's Penelope, however deviously she may distort those events for her own purposes, strictly speaking should not have access to information which the *Odyssey* clearly indicates she has not been given.

[12] The transmitted text *Antilochum ... ab Hectore victum* 'Antilochus ... defeated by Hector' was questioned as early as 1489, by Politian (*Miscellanea*, i. 76), who suggested either *Amphimachum* (cf. *Il.* 13.185 ff.) for *Antilochum* (necessitating a similar change in line 16), or *Memnone* (cf. n. 13 below). Housman (1897: 102–3) suggested *ab hoste revictum* 'defeated by the enemy'. He adduced the two main arguments in favour of emendation: (i) the deviation from the canonical Homeric account; this is part of a larger question bearing on the poem as a whole which I shall deal with below; (ii) the inelegance of the repetition of Hector's name directly after *nomine in Hectoreo pallida semper eram* 'I was always pale at the mention of Hector's name' (14). It could be argued, however, that *sive ... sive ...* (15–18), with the death

have been killed by Hector, whereas it is stated in the *Odyssey* that he was killed by Memnon,[13] and in line 91 the herald Medon is included among those hostile to Penelope, whereas in the *Odyssey* he is generally presented as loyal to her, although there are two isolated references which suggest the contrary, one in which Telemachus numbers him among the suitors (16.252) and the other in which the poet describes him as a favourite of the suitors (17.172–3). Finally, in lines 41–4, in referring to how accounts of Ulysses' bravery during the Trojan war would fill her with fear, Penelope mentions the night attack made by Diomedes and Ulysses, giving to her husband the chief role in the slaughter of Rhesus and his men, whereas the Homeric version (*Il.* 10.488–94) clearly states that it was Diomedes who did the killing, while Odysseus merely dragged away the bodies. The total number of these discrepancies is disconcertingly large, so large that wholesale excision or emendation on these grounds alone is inconceivable. We might either conclude that Ovid has not been concerned to follow his source closely, and hence will not have expected his readers to bring an exact knowledge of the *Odyssey* to bear on this poem—in which case the interpretation I have suggested becomes less easy to defend—or we must seek an explanation or explanations for these deviations from Ovid's artistic purposes in the *Heroides*.

To ascertain which of these two conclusions is the correct one, we must examine Ovid's procedure in the two other epistles which seem similarly to be derived from a single major literary source, *Heroides* 3 and 7.

The letter of Briseis to Achilles is a very close adaptation of those parts of the *Iliad* in which she appears—in places, in fact, almost a translation.[14] None the less a couple of deviations are found. In

of Patroclus at the hands of Hector forming the second instance, should form *two* illustrations of Penelope's fear of Hector before she goes on to include all Greek deaths at the hands of Trojans as a cause of fear for her husband's safety (19–22).

[13] 4.187–8. This is the normal version; cf. Pind. *Pyth.* 6.28 ff., Dio Chrys. 11.352, Dict. 4.6, Quint. Smyrn. 2.244–5. I cannot satisfactorily account for the deviation in Ovid. Hector is found as the killer of Antilochus elsewhere only in Hyg. *Fab.* 113, but nothing can be inferred from this, as in *Fab.* 112 his killer is said to have been Memnon. Textual corruption in Hyginus has been suspected; cf. Housman (1897). Another variant, in which Paris killed Antilochus, is recorded in Dares of Phrygia, *De excidio Troiae historia* 34.

[14] Cf. *Her.* 3.30–6 and *Il.* 9.122–30; *Her.* 3.37–8 and *Il.* 9.144–7; *Her.* 3.47–50 and *Il.* 19.291–6.

Her. 3.147–8, Briseis cries out to be run through with the sword
with which, 'if the goddess had allowed it' (*si dea passa fuisset*),
Achilles would have killed Agamemnon. In *Il.* 1.198, Athena appears
to Achilles alone (οἴῳ φαινομένη), so strictly speaking Briseis should
be unaware of her intervention. It would be understandable if Ovid
had overlooked this small detail.[15] More significantly, in *Her.* 3.23–4,
Patroclus is represented as comforting Briseis as she is handed over
to Agamemnon. There is no corresponding scene in the *Iliad*, but
Ovid has clearly adapted a detail from Briseis' lament for Patroclus
in *Il.* 19.295–9, in which she recalls how Patroclus comforted her
after Achilles had killed her husband and sacked her city.[16] In this
case, a reason for the deviation can confidently be advanced, a reason connected with the epistolary form of Ovid's poem. Ovid had
a very limited amount of material at his disposal for the portrayal
of Briseis. Her letter had to be set before her return to Achilles (*Il.*
19.246), that is, before the event which brought this about, the death
of Patroclus, which prompted her lament for him in the *Iliad*. His
kind treatment of her after her original capture was not relevant
to her present predicament, Achilles' failure to reclaim her, so Ovid
devised a similar scene in which Patroclus promises a quick end to her
abduction by Agamemnon, which Briseis can then use to emphasize
Achilles' lack of concern for her, the motivating spirit of her letter
(21–2).

    In the seventh epistle, Dido refers to the shrine which she main-
tains to the memory of her dead husband Sychaeus, and she recounts
how she has heard a voice inviting her *Elissa, veni*, an invitation she
welcomes joyfully. This is clearly based on *Aeneid* 4.457–61, where
Virgil refers only to her seeming to hear 'the voice of her husband
as he called' (*verba vocantis . . . viri*, 460–1), and does not describe
the effect these words have upon her, though he does include this
among the incidents that are driving Dido to the edge of madness (*Aen.* 4.450–73). Ovid's Dido is trying, as always, to play on
the feelings of Aeneas, but Ovid himself has an ulterior purpose in
making his Dido *welcome* the ghostly voice of Sychaeus. His readers

---

[15] Unless Jacobson (1974: 36 n. 56) is correct in suggesting that Ovid meant us to
understand that Achilles had told Briseis of the incident.

[16] By contrast, Achilles is represented as addressing her at this point in Ovid
(*Her.* 3.54).

remember from the *Aeneid* that she will be reunited with Sychaeus in the Underworld (6.473–5), but Dido when she is writing this letter cannot, of course, know that. Ovid is trying to foreshadow future events for his readers through her words, a technique that is an important but neglected aspect of the *Heroides,* and one that must be dependent on the knowledge of the story the reader brings to Ovid's version.[17]

It may be granted, then, that while it is impossible to rule out oversight on Ovid's part, in principle an attempt should be made to explain deviations from a major source in terms of some artistic end or other. Recognition of such deviations implies, of course, a close knowledge of the source, and there are instances in Penelope's letter where the point of a passage seems to depend on a fairly exact knowledge of the *Odyssey*. In 75–7, Penelope remarks: 'perhaps, knowing you men and your desires, you could be in thrall to some exotic love, and perhaps you are telling her what a homely wife you have' (*quam sit tibi rustica coniunx,* 77). It is indeed the case in the *Odyssey* that not only does Odysseus spend a considerable time with Calypso, but in 5.215–18 he says that Penelope cannot compare with her, though he does not mean this as a criticism: Calypso, after all, is a goddess. The reader with this much knowledge of the *Odyssey* will see considerable irony in the Ovidian Penelope's remarks. Without

[17] It is possible that foreshadowing might help to account for the deviation from Homer in Penelope's description of the night attack in *Her.* 1.41–4 *ausus es, o nimium nimiumque oblite tuorum,* | *Thracia nocturno tangere castra dolo,* | *totque simul mactare viros, adiutus ab uno!* | *at bene cautus eras et memor ante mei!* 'You had the nerve—O too forgetful of your own—to set foot in the Thracian camp on a night-time raid and to slay so many men, assisted by only one! But, to be sure, you were cautious and took thought for me before!' Is Ovid inviting us to look ahead to events Penelope necessarily cannot know of at the time she is writing this letter, when against large odds Ulysses *will* play the major part in killing a great number of men at one and the same time, the suitors, and will keep Penelope totally in the dark as to what is to happen? The only snag is *adiutus ab uno* 'assisted by only one' (43). In *Od.* 22, Odysseus is helped in the slaying of the suitors not only by Telemachus but also by the swineherd Eumaeus, the cowherd Philoetius, and, at a later stage, Athene disguised as Mentor, as seems to be foreshadowed in 103–4 *hac faciunt custosque boum longaevaque nutrix,* | *tertius immundae cura fidelis harae* 'on our side are the cowherd, the aged nurse, and, third, the faithful warden of the unclean sty'. But if it is not to be obtrusive and spoil the epistolary illusion, foreshadowing must be partial and allusive. Foreshadowing was a recognized literary technique in the ancient world; cf. Duckworth (1931) 320–38, esp. 326 on foreshadowing by analogy and 328 on foreshadowing of action outside the narrative of the epic itself.

realizing it, she has innocently stumbled on the truth, though her interpretation of it is incorrect. The reader with a deeper knowledge of the *Odyssey* will see things in a different light, for if he recognizes the stage at which Penelope is writing this letter, he will realize that Penelope knows about Calypso, for Menelaus tells Telemachus in *Od.* 4.555–6 that she is holding Odysseus back against his will, and Telemachus recounts this news to Penelope on his return from Sparta in *Od.* 17.142–6. So, although Ovid's Penelope cannot know what her husband says about her to Calypso, and thus her remark *forsitan et narres quam sit tibi rustica coniunx* in 77 remains ironical, her character changes dramatically in our eyes. Far from being innocent, she is being somewhat disingenuous, and indeed is prevaricating in lines 64–5 when she says she has received no firm news of him from Pylos and Sparta. This is substantially the position Howard Jacobson (1974: 243–76) takes in his book on the *Heroides*:[18] a Penelope who mentions weaving to her husband, as Ovid's does in lines 9–10, without telling him of the ruse with which she kept the suitors at bay, we might reasonably suspect to have a motive for withholding this information, which is such eloquent testimony to her chastity. Viewed in this way, deviations from Homer serve to differentiate Ovid's characterization of Penelope. When in lines 37 and 63–5 she claims responsibility for initiating the mission to Pylos and Sparta, this is a deliberate lie on her part to impress upon Ulysses that she has gone to all reasonable lengths to find him before succumbing to the overwhelming pressure to remarry to which she alludes in 81–3. Desperate situations call for desperate arguments. Within the epistolary context, deviation from an established source allows the reader to recognize and penetrate the subjectivity of the 'writer's' viewpoint, which is a central feature of the form.[19] Inconsistency within a letter may perform the same function in the *Heroides*. Thus when Penelope falsely claims to have sent Telemachus to enquire after his father

---

[18] Jacobson traces in detail the freedom, not to say irreverence, with which the character of Penelope was treated by post-Homeric writers.

[19] That the epistle was the form which above all others revealed the character of its writer was recognized by Demetrius, *On Style* 227: 'an epistle should express character to a high degree, like a conversation; for the epistle a person writes is almost a likeness of his soul, and while it is possible to discern the character of the writer from every other composition, from none is it so clear as from an epistle'.

(37, 63–5), but then contradicts herself further on by saying that he
went, as was nearer the truth, 'against the will of all of them' (*invitis
omnibus*, 100), we should see this contradiction not as an oversight
on Ovid's part, nor as evidence of textual corruption or interpolation,
but as a clue planted by Ovid which will prompt us, with our supe-
rior knowledge through the *Odyssey* of what 'objectively' happened,
to question Penelope's state of mind and motives in writing this
letter.[20]

Reference to the *Odyssey* in reading Penelope's letter is unavoidable, and the resonance of the poem and the complexity of Penelope's character seem largely to arise from recognition of Ovid's
deviations from the canonical Homeric account. These deviations
thus need not be seen as an insuperable obstacle to the interpretation I have offered of the epistle's occasion and recipient. The exact
whereabouts of Ulysses are thrown into prominence by Penelope's
question in 57–8. Lines 59–62 are then very specific, and they are
clearly derived from Penelope's interview with her disguised husband in *Od.* 19.163 ff. It is impossible to say whether ancient readers
would have been attuned to the ironic possibilities afforded by the
epistolary form at this point. Ovid's chief claim for the *Heroides*
was that they were innovative (*ignotum hoc aliis ille novavit opus*
'he invented this work, unknown to others' *Ars* 3.346), so a priori
we might not expect a high level of 'competence' on the part of
Ovid's readership in dealing with these epistolary narrations. An
intriguing sidelight is cast on this problem, however, by the well-
documented response of ancient readers to Ovid's source for Penelope's letter. For Aristotle, the plot of the *Odyssey* was 'complex' precisely because it contained 'recognitions throughout' (ἡ δὲ Ὀδύσσεια
πεπλεγμένον (ἀναγνώρισις γὰρ διόλου) καὶ ἠθική, *Poetics* 1459 b14–
15). Aristotle's preoccupation with this aspect of the epic is reflected
in the scholia, which repeatedly remark upon the variety of means of

---

[20] Blatant inconsistency within a single poem occurs elsewhere in the *Heroides* and
must, I think, be seen as a function of characterization. Jacobson (1974: 148) draws
attention to *Her.* 4, where Phaedra describes herself as a married woman (17 ff.), yet
immediately afterwards presents herself to Hippolytus through images which suggest
virginity (21 ff.), a manifestation of her desire to see herself in relation to Hippolytus
as a *puella* (cf. 2), and not as the *noverca* (cf. 129) she really is. Cf. also Pearson (1980)
110 ff., esp. 113.

recognition employed in the *Odyssey*.[21] Interestingly, on a number of occasions, the scholiasts feel impelled to discuss at considerable length why Odysseus reveals his identity to several characters before the slaying of the suitors, but not to Penelope, as in Schol. N *Od*. 13 init. (Dindorf, p. 789):

Διὰ τί Ὀδυσσεὺς τῇ μὲν Πηνελόπῃ ἡλικίαν τε ἤδη ἐχούσῃ καὶ φιλούσῃ αὐτὸν οὐκ ἐδήλωσεν ὃς ἦν, τῷ δὲ Τηλεμάχῳ νέῳ ὄντι καὶ τοῖς οἰκέταις, τῷ μὲν συβώτῃ, τῷ δὲ βουκόλῳ ὄντι; οὐ γὰρ δήπου μὴ πεῖραν ἐκείνης εἰληφώς...[22]

Why did Odysseus not reveal his identity to Penelope, who was in the prime of life and loved him, while he did to Telemachus, a young man, and to his household slaves, the one a swineherd, the other a cowherd? Apparently because he had not tested her...'

The lengthy answers the scholiast gives to his question need not detain us. Whilst it would be foolhardy to suggest that Ovid was directly influenced by any of these comments, they do respect the typical preoccupations of a tradition of criticism with which he had at least a passing familiarity,[23] and which will have determined to some extent the way in which he and his readers approached the Odyssey. If the theme of recognition and its means was in Ovid's mind, we could do worse than recall Aristotle's pronouncements on the theme. For him the best kind of recognition-scene was one which arose naturally out of the development of the action, and his two favourite examples occur in the *Oedipus Rex* of Sophocles and the *Iphigeneia in Tauris* of Euripides: πασῶν δὲ βελτίστη ἀναγνώρισις ἡ ἐξ αὐτῶν τῶν πραγμάτων, τῆς ἐκπλήξεως γιγνομένης δι᾽ εἰκότων, οἷον ἐν τῷ Σοφοκλέους Οἰδίποδι καὶ τῇ Ἰφιγενείᾳ 'But, of all recognitions, the best is that which arises from the incidents themselves, where the startling discovery is made by natural means, as in the *Oedipus* of

---

[21] Cf. Schol. *Od*. 4.69, 113, 8.43, 489, Eust. 1487.15 ff., 1489.35 ff. I owe the references in this and the following note to the kindness of Dr N. J. Richardson. On Aristotle's influence on the scholia see his article (1980).

[22] Cf. Schol. Vd. *Od*. 21.208 (Schrader 1890: 123), Eust. 1873.45 ff.

[23] Cf. *Rem*. 364–5 *ingenium magni livor detractat Homeri;* | *quisquis es, ex illo, Zoile, nomen habes*. In spite of a number of attractive practical demonstrations of the relevance of the Homeric scholia to the criticism of Virgil by Heinze (1915) and Schlunk (1974), the methodology of their application to Roman poetry remains to be explored.

Sophocles, and in the *Iphigenia*' (*Poetics* 1455 a 16–18).[24] In the latter play, as we remarked in passing, recognition takes place when Iphigeneia gives to Orestes a letter intended for himself. *Mutatis mutandis* Penelope's letter fulfils the highest expectations of Aristotelian criticism.

---

[24] The recognition scene in the *IT* obviously made a deep impression on Aristotle, as he refers to it also in *Poetics* 1452b 5–8 and 1454a 7.

4

Ovidian Allusion and the Vocabulary of Memory

John F. Miller

Three recent discussions of the self-referential quality of Ovidian poetry draw attention to a technique that deserves to be recognized more clearly in its own right. I refer to Ovid's habit of signalling, or glossing, literary allusions with the vocabulary of memory (*memor, memini, recordor* and the like). The explicit notation of a character's, or the Ovidian narrative persona's, reminiscences is designed to correspond with, and therefore to comment upon, the text's recall of earlier literature in various interesting ways. In his anatomy of 'poetic memory' in Latin poetry, Gian Biagio Conte (1986: 57–63) adduces two Ovidian texts that exhibit the phenomenon in order to illustrate what he calls 'reflective allusion'. At *Fasti* 3.473–5, when Ariadne, lamenting her desertion by Bacchus, calls to mind (*memini*) her grieving words on the earlier occasion when Theseus abandoned her, the quoted words pointedly call to our minds through direct echoes the depiction of that latter lament in Catullus 64 (lines 132–3 and 143–4). Likewise, when, in Book 14 of the *Metamorphoses*, the concerned father Mars reminds Jupiter of his promise to elevate Romulus to divine status (14.812–15), recollected speech dovetails perfectly with literary reminiscence: Mars' quotation of Jupiter is at the same time a quotation of Ennius' *Annales* (fr. 54 Sk.).[1] And once again the allusion is highlighted by the speaker's parenthetical reference to his

---

[1] Actually, it is a virtual quotation. Ovid repeats an entire hexameter from Ennius, but treats the latter's adjective *caerula* (modifying *templa* in the next line) as a noun.

memory (14.813 *nam memoro memorique animo pia verba notavi,* 'for I remember these pious words and have marked them in my retentive mind').

Conte draws both of these examples from some brief remarks by Moritz Haupt (1876: 2.71–2) that first identified the Ovidian technique in question.[2] In turn, both examples recur in other recent studies which further enhance our appreciation of this technique in Ovid's poetry. Joseph Solodow (1988: 227–8) independently points to the latter text in his discussion of literary self-consciousness in the *Metamorphoses.* He then adds two other instances where mention of memory cleverly alerts us to poetic *imitatio,* both from the long speech of Pythagoras. The philosopher recalls—*nam memini* (15.160; again a parenthetical remark)—that during the Trojan War he was the hero Euphorbus, slain by Menelaus, in lines imitating Homer's description of that action (*Il.* 17.43–60). Some verses later Pythagoras notes his reminiscence (15.436 *quantumque recordor*) of another experience from his earlier life—hearing the seer Helenus' speech to Aeneas—, which is at the same time a creative reformulation of the event as told in Virgil's *Aeneid* 3.374–462. As in the two aforementioned examples, the speaker here allegedly quotes an earlier utterance. Finally, in a useful re-evaluation of Ovidian literariness, Stephen Hinds (1987: 17, see ch.1 above) puts forth Conte's Ariadne example as 'an especially clear instance of self-referential elaboration of allusion'.[3] A few pages later (20–1), he evinces another example of (parenthetical) *memini* as a gloss on literary memory: in the opening verses of *Tristia* 5.3, when Ovid nostalgically recollects his participation in poetic symposia at the Liberalia in Rome, he is also recalling (and playing upon) his own extended celebration of that festival in an earlier poem, the *Fasti.*

Even in the very unusual practice of borrowing an entire verse, Ovid characteristically changes something in the original.

[2] 'Hoc autem artificium, ut eorum quae apud antiquiorem poëtam aliqua carminis persona dixerat eandem aut aliam personam recordari fingeret nobilisque poesis memoriam excitaret.' Haupt illustrates his point with the aforementioned examples.

[3] On the importance of Conte's discussion for the study of Ovidian allusion in particular see also D. Feeney's review (1989: 206). J. F. Miller's characterization (1988: 118) of Conte's two Ovidian examples of allusion as 'unusual' is somewhat misleading. The suggestively titled collection of essays by Papponetti (1991) does not intersect significantly with the present topic.

In discussing the memory of Ovid's Ariadne, Hinds (1987: 17) remarks that the word *memini* in that passage is a refinement of what David Ross (1975*a*: 78) has termed the 'Alexandrian footnote', the use of words and phrases appealing to tradition and report (e.g. *dicitur, ferunt*) as means of signalling poetic allusion.[4] We may now add that all of the aforementioned references to memory demonstrate the same footnoting function. Furthermore, we may note that this lexical phenomenon is even more widespread in Ovidian poetry than even my collection here of these five examples might suggest. In what follows I discuss four other instances, which have not to my knowledge been pointed out by other scholars. Like Hinds's example, these four all involve allusion to Ovid's own earlier poetry.

Let us begin with a direct mention of earlier poetry which is enriched and complicated through an intertextual reference, once again signalled by parenthetical *memini*. In the programmatic introduction to *Fasti* 2, Ovid announces that this elegy on the Roman calendar is a 'greater' enterprise—in size, in theme, in stature—than the 'slender work' that characterized the genre in even the recent past (2.3–8):

nunc primum velis, elegi, maioribus itis:
    exiguum, memini, nuper eratis opus.
ipse ego vos habui faciles in amore ministros,
    cum lusit numeris prima iuventa suis.
idem sacra cano signataque tempora fastis:
    ecquis ad haec illinc crederet esse viam?

Now for the first time, my elegiacs, you proceed on more ample sails: just recently, as I recall, you were a slender work. Myself I have found you pliant ministers in love, when early youth toyed with verse appropriate to youth. Now I sing of sacred rites and the seasons marked on the calendar: who could think that the path led from there to here?

The poet's memory of that past (*memini*) of course includes his own love elegies, a point which he makes explicit in the second couplet quoted. That point is further underscored by the accompanying

---

[4] See also Hinds (1987*a*) 8–9, 40, and 58. For many perceptive comments on the self-reflexive quality in Ovidian narrative of words associated with speech and the like, see also Keith (1992*a*).

allusion to one of his *Amores*—not coincidentally, to another introductory, programmatic text (3.1.21–8):

fabula, nec sentis, tota iactaris in Vrbe,
  dum tua praeterito facta pudore refers.
tempus erat thyrso pulsum graviore moveri;
  cessatum satis est: incipe maius opus.
materia premis ingenium; cane facta virorum:
  'haec animo' dices 'area digna meo est.'
quod tenerae cantent *lusit* tua Musa puellae,
  *prima*que *per numeros* acta *iuventa suos.*

You are not aware of it, but you're the talk of the whole city, while you talk
about what you've done and show no shame. It's time you were stirred by
a greater thyrsus; you have loafed enough: begin some greater work. You
suppress your talent with this subject. Sing the deeds of heroes, and you
will say 'This field is worthy of my intellect.' Your Muse *has toyed* with song
appropriate for tender maidens, and your *early youth* was spent *on verse
appropriate to youth.*

Ovid's present address to elegiac couplets refers to the earlier occasion
when he himself was addressed by Elegia and her rival Tragoedia. In
that *recusatio*-scenario, the latter goddess had urged Ovid to 'begin
a greater work' and had accused him of scandalizing himself and
suppressing his talent by concentrating on love poetry. 'Your Muse
has (thus far) played at poetry for tender girls to sing, and your early
youth has been spent with verses appropriate to youth.' In *Fasti* 2 Ovid
takes up these very words in his own characterization of his youthful
poetic endeavours: *cum lusit numeris prima iuventa suis,* 'when early
youth toyed with verse appropriate to youth'. Now that, as the *vates* of
the Roman calendar, Ovid is writing not a tragedy but a *maius opus*
nonetheless, when he is, in other words, obeying the goddess who
berated him, he pointedly adopts her critical perspective on his past.
  However, this adoption of Tragoedia's perspective, this declared
break with his poetic past, is tinged with a delicate irony. And that
irony emerges not only against the background of the body of the
Fasti, which, despite its nobler theme than love, does share much with
Ovid's erotic elegy in the way of literary personality, techniques, and
occasionally even topic. As others have noted (Korzeniewski 1964:

196, 198; Le Bonniec 1969: on 2.7–8; Frécaut 1972: 272),[5] an ironic perspective also arises from these verses themselves. The closing question about the wondrous movement from past to present is playfully extravagant. The word *idem* seems to hint at a continuity of spirit as well as of style and genre from his earlier elegies to the present 'greater' work. And the word that signalled the coming allusion, *memini*, also evokes the same light-hearted tone. For Ovid to say that he 'remembers' the recent history of Roman elegy is to draw such attention to the obvious as to be downright silly.

One of the most famous examples of Ovidian self-imitation is the story of Procris' death, told in both *Ars Amatoria* 3 and *Metamorphoses* 7. The earlier, third-person narrative is poignantly retold in the *Metamorphoses* by the recollecting Cephalus,[6] the husband falsely suspected of adultery who accidentally killed his eavesdropping wife. In the many studies of these two versions of the tale, there has been almost no attention to Ovid's subtle but unmistakable comments

---

[5] For a full discussion of the ironic dimensions of the entire proem see Miller (1991) 23–8.

[6] William S. Anderson (1990) has challenged this, the traditional, chronology of the two versions. He entertains the idea that the simpler account in *Ars* 3 aims in part to improve upon the expansive narrative in *Metamorphoses* 7—actually three narratives told by Cephalus—by correcting certain of the latter's inconsistencies and other deficiencies. Anderson's paper has advanced our understanding of the relatively underrated exemplum in the *Ars* and has sharpened awareness of certain differences with the hexameter version. But his overall argument is unconvincing. It seems to me that Ovidian imitation, including self-imitation, is typically motivated by a desire to strike out in new direction—here the fuller, more ambitious, story in the *Metamorphoses*—, less so by the wish to tie up loose details into a neater package. Ovidian self-imitation no doubt has a significant measure of *aemulatio sui*, but 'improvement' could in the present instance be seen in the greater complexity and depth of the *Metamorphoses* version, in spite of a few inconsistencies of the sort found elsewhere in the poem. Moreover, some of the 'problems' in the hexameter version pointed to by Anderson are not as troublesome as he claims. For instance, on the passage discussed just below, he notes (136) that 'the odd way of tentatively adding three more hexameters in *Met.* 7 [i.e. 7.818–20] . . . would be a dubious poetic decision after the functional spareness of the other account'. But—quite apart from the metaliterary pointers for which I argue below—what of Ovid's well-known penchant for elaboration? Anderson (1990: 135) correctly remarks on the oddity of Cephalus' lack of assurance about his own earlier words (816 *forsitan*) in contrast with his confident insistence on fate's power over him on the same occasion (816 *sic me mea fata trahebant*). Yet this logical lapse need not be interpreted as an artistic defect; it is not inconsistent with Cephalus' character as narrator and the histrionic quality of his reminiscence.

on his *imitatio sui*.[7] Perhaps the most striking instance[8] involves yet
again a parenthetical reference to memory. Cephalus' report of his
fateful idle song to the breeze follows closely the version in the *Ars
Amatoria* (*Met.* 7.813–15; *Ars* 3.697–8):

'*aura*' (recordor enim) '*venias*' *cantare solebam*,
'meque iuves intresque *sinus*, gratissima, nostros,
utque facis, *relevare* velis, quibus urimur, *aestus*.'

'*Come, Aura*,' *I would call* (you see, I remember), 'soothe me and come to my
breast, most welcome; and as is your way, *relieve the heat* with which I burn.

'quae'que '*meos releves aestus*', *cantare solebat*
'accipienda *sinu*, mobilis *aura, veni*'.

And *he would call*, '*Come*, wandering *Aura*, and *relieve the heat*, come nestle
in my *breast*.'

This is imitation, not repetition. Note the elegantly reversed order
of the two commands verbally echoed, which is a common mark of

---

⁷ Although several scholars see Ovid in the *Metamorphoses* narrative alluding to
another (non-Ovidian) version of the tale: specifically, to the pederastic episode edited
out by Ovid (or by Cephalus): e.g. Otis (1966) 179–80, 383–4; Anderson (1972) on
7.751 'probably'; Mack (1988) 131–4; cf. Davis (1983) 138, n. 141. Major studies of
the Ovidian versions: Rohde (1929) 30–51, esp. 46–51; Pöschl (1959); Ruiz de Elvira
(1972); Labate (1975); Segal (1975); and Anderson (1990), with additional references
(144 n 2).

⁸ For another see the critical juncture when Procris hears from a busybody the
false report of her husband's infidelity. Cephalus begins to describe his wife's reaction
thus: *subito conlapsa dolore,* | *ut mihi narratur, cecidit . . .*, 'smitten with a sudden pain,
as the story was told to me, she fell . . .' (826–7). The phrase *ut mihi narratur,* besides
contributing a measure of verisimilitude to Cephalus' narrative, functions also as a
footnote or metaliterary pointer to the text from *Ars 3*, which is at this point emphatically echoed: *excidit et subito muta dolore fuit,* 'she fainted and was speechless with
sudden grief' (3.702). The immediately following verses then diverge sharply from
their 'model': Ovid's continued physical description of Procris' agitation—paleness,
tearing of clothes and cheeks, Bacchic raving—is replaced by Cephalus' meditation
on her mental state and her words, now lamenting, now trustfully denying the report.
Ut mihi narratur is not a deflating suggestion that Cephalus heard this part of the story
from Ovid, but the phrase does draw attention to the process of imitation, in this case
self-imitation. Occurring as it does in the company of strong echoes which are not
sustained in the following verses, the phrase nearly makes the echoing words a kind
of literary 'tag' like those opening some Horatian odes. As in the example discussed
below, our attention is directed both to a literary model and to a rather sharp deviation
from that model.

Ovidian imitative artistry.[9] At the same time, the echoes of course evoke the earlier context—this is, in fact, the first cluster of strong echoes of the elegiac version. What is more, the narrator's explicit reference to his memory insists on that evocation of the previous context. To some extent, the voice of Cephalus as recollecting narrator has been virtually superimposed on Ovid's own narrative voice in the *Ars*. For even the distinctive phrase of citation (*cantare solebat*) has been adapted. On the other hand, Cephalus here recollects what he himself has lived some time ago—in another Ovidian poem. The parenthetical remark points up the relationship of the two poetic worlds to one another. And lest we miss the point, there follows immediately another gloss on the process of imitation. Cephalus expands his account of his customary words to the breeze by next 'quoting' a hymnic praise of the *aura* (7.816–20):

forsitan addiderim (sic me mea fata trahebant)
blanditias plures et 'tu mihi magna voluptas'
dicere sim solitus, 'tu me reficisque fovesque,
tu facis, ut silvas, ut amem loca sola, meoque
spiritus iste tuus semper capiatur ab ore'.

And perhaps I might add (so my fates led me on) more blandishments and say, 'You are my great joy. You refresh me and comfort me; you are the reason I love the forests and the lonely places. Your breath I always seek on my lips.'

But he is careful to qualify this quotation from the start: *forsitan addiderim* ('perhaps I might add . . .'). Since readers of *Ars* 3 know that the tired huntsman did not in that version add such *blanditiae*, there is perhaps a playful comment here on the old man's over-active imagination. Be that as it may, on another level Cephalus'

---

⁹ e.g. *Fasti* 5.665–8 and the characteristics of the god Mercury verbally echoed from Horace, *Odes* 1.10 (see note 13 below): the latter's sequence *cultus . . . palaestrae . . . lyrae . . . superis deorum . . . et imis* becomes in Ovid *superis imisque deorum . . . lyrae . . . palaestra . . . culte*; and *Fast.* 1.663–8, which inverts the Tibullan model's order of ideas (Tib. 2.1.1–8): the latter's *lustramus . . . requiescat humus, requiescat arator . . . suspenso vomere cesset opus . . . ad praesepia . . . plena coronato stare boves capite* becomes in Ovid *state coronati plenum ad praesepe . . . opus . . . suspendat . . . aratrum . . . da requiem terrae . . . da requiem . . . viris . . . lustrate.* The technique is not peculiar to Ovid; see, for example, the echoing frame of *Aen.* 2–3: cf. 2.1–2 *conticuere omnes intentique . . . pater Aeneas sic* and 3.716–18 *sic pater Aeneas intentis omnibus . . . conticuit.*

qualification of his second quoted speech surely glosses that speech as an elaboration of Ovid's earlier version of the event. This further underscores the self-referential force of *recordor enim* just above. Confidence in memory coincides with, and points to, allusion to an earlier text; the lesser surety of *forsitan addiderim* points to an elaboration of the same text. Overall in Cephalus' long narrative, the theme of recollection adds a depth and poignancy that are absent from the version of *Ars* 3.[10] At least in the present instance, however, reference to the old man's memories has as well a metaliterary dimension.

All of the seven aforementioned examples somehow play upon a speaker's recollection. Nearly all of them feature parenthetical references. But two further instances from the *Fasti* show that neither of these aspects is necessary in the Ovidian footnoting of allusion with the vocabulary of memory. In the first instance the word expressing memory has multiple associations. On the occasion of the Megalensia in April, the curious antiquarian poet wishes to interrogate Cybele, as he does so many other deities in the *Fasti*, but he is intimidated by her procession's frightful din—the crashing cymbals, the tambourines, and shrill flute. Understanding Ovid's discomfort, the Magna Mater sends her granddaughters, the Muses, to help him out. He then addresses them in what would not inaccurately be called a mock invocation (4.193–4):

pandite mandati memores, Heliconis alumnae,
    gaudeat assiduo cur dea Magna sono.

The words framing the hexameter ('Reveal, nurslings of Helicon') are in grand epic style and in fact resemble a Virgilian epic invocation.[11] But the object of Ovid's query to the Muses, arising as it does from the immediate (and comic) situation before Cybele, hardly fits the lofty introduction: 'O unfold to me, Muses, why the Great Goddess

---

[10] On motifs of recollection deepening the tale see Segal (1975) *passim*, esp. 178 and 181. In the text note especially, in the introduction to the tale of Procris' death, 7.797–8 *iuvat o meminisse beati | temporis*. Here, too, there is an element of 'poetic memory'; cf. Virg. *Aen.* 1.203 *forsan et haec olim meminisse iuvabit*, pointed out by Segal (1975: 187). Note further that the echo of Virgil involves, as usual, a response as well. To the model's idea of a possible future delight in remembering Ovid seems to say 'yes, in this instance it is a delight to remember'.

[11] Virg. *Aen.* 7.641 (= 10.163) *Pandite nunc Helicona, deae, cantusque movete*. Cf. Ov. *Met.* 15.622 *pandite nunc, Musae, praesentia numina vatum*.

enjoys this constant racket'. The deflation is already underway, however, in the hexameter's phrase *mandati memores*. As the daughters of Mnemosyne, the Muses themselves are said to remember things and to remind their poets. Thus Virgil explains why he invokes them before his catalogue of warriors: *et meministis enim, divae, et memorare potestis*, 'for you both remember, goddesses, and have the power to remind' (7.645).[12] In Ovid's invocation, the Muses' association with memory has been mischievously twisted into a cheeky injunction to remember what Cybele commanded them to do, i.e. to assist the frightened antiquarian. As if the daughters of Memory might forget!

By now we should also expect that the word *memores* is alerting us to a poetic allusion. When the respondent to Ovid's speech, Erato, steps forth in the following couplet, our expectation is straight away fulfilled (4.195–6):

> sic ego. sic *Erato* (mensis *Cythereius* illi
> cessit, *quod* teneri *nomen amoris habet*):

> So I spoke and so *Erato* responded (the month of *Cytherea* fell to her *because her name derives from* tender *love*).

For the explanation of this Muse's appearance here—the connection between Erato's name and the tutelary goddess of April—echoes the justification of her mention in the introduction to *Ars Amatoria* 2 (15–16):

> nunc mihi, si quando, puer et *Cytherea*, favete;
> nunc *Erato, nam* tu *nomen Amoris habes*.

> Now, if ever, favour me, *Cytherea* and your boy, and you, *Erato, for your name derives from Love*.

Since that mention was, not coincidentally, in an invocation, the reference involves an elegant *oppositio in imitando*. Ovid's justification for invoking Erato becomes a justification for Erato's response to his invocation, or rather to his aetiological question closely resembling an invocation. Moreover, our recall of the inspirational role of Erato

---

[12] Cf. Virg. *Aen.* 1.8 *Musa, mihi causas memora*; 7.41 *tu vatem, tu diva mone* (and Fordyce ad loc.), and Horace's parody at *Sat.* 1.5.53.

in Ovid's earlier elegy, and perhaps of the fact that she was the only named Muse invoked in the *Ars Amatoria,* suggests that her appearance to the aetiological elegist has an additional relevance. Of all the Muses, she is the one with whom this poet, currently in need of help, would feel the most comfortable (Frécaut 1972: 276).

My final example involves a double reference, the simultaneous allusion to two separate and unrelated poetic texts. Ovid's entry on the merchants' festival in May (*Fasti* 5.663–92), which constitutes a carefully crafted elegy, opens with a hymnic address to the deity being honoured, Mercury, that is shot through with echoes of Horace's hymn to the same god (*Odes* 1.10).[13] Although Ovid's aretalogy of Mercury allusively ranges over the whole ode, he studiously— and noticeably to the informed reader—avoids any reference to that aspect of the god to which Horace devotes half of his poem, viz. Mercury's deceptiveness and thievery. In introducing an old Roman feast, the *vates sacrorum* wishes to strike a solemn note. That solemnity quickly dissolves, however, when, in the ensuing description of a merchant's purificatory ritual, we hear the worshipper utter a rather outrageous prayer to Mercury: he asks not only for cleansing and (as usual) for profit, but also for the joy of cheating his customers and for permissible perjuries in the future. The god himself then provides the crowning moment—a sort of punchline for the whole elegy—by favourably responding to this prayer (5.691–2):

talia Mercurius poscenti ridet ab alto,
    se memor Ortygias subripuisse boves.

At such prayers Mercury laughs from on high, remembering that he himself stole the Ortygian cattle.

Not the least significant aspect of this couplet's closural force is the renewed allusion to Horace's hymn. Ovid refers to the famous event featured in the central stanza of *Odes* 1.10, Mercury's theft of

---

[13] 5.663 *Clare nepos Atlantis* (cf. *Odes* 1.10.1 *Mercuri, facunde nepos Atlantis*); 665–6 *pacis et armorum superis imisque deorum | arbiter, alato qui pede carpis iter* (cf. 1.10.5–6 *magni Iovis et deorum nuntium* and 19–20 *superis deorum gratus et imis*); 667–8 *laete lyrae pulsu, nitida quoque laete palaestra, | quo didicit culte lingua docente loqui* (cf. 1.10.6 *lyrae parentem* and 1–4 *facunde . . . qui feros cultus . . . voce formasti . . . et more palaestrae*).

his brother Apollo's cattle. On the purely aural level, the hexameter's close (*ridet ab alto*) perhaps recalls the clinching phrase of the Horatian stanza (1.10.12 *risit Apollo*). This reference completes the pattern of allusion to *Odes* 1:10 in a climactic fashion. For we here finally find mention of the god's thievishness and guile, which were felt to be missing from the extensive imitation of the ode at the elegy's outset. And, once again, poetic allusion coincides with a reference to memory (*memor*): here the smiling reminiscence of the trickster god points to Horace's humorous lines commemorating his trickery.

At the same time that this distich alludes to Horace, it echoes as well an earlier Ovidian text. Mercury's response to the tradesman evokes a precedent of sorts set by the knavish god's father in his roguish aspect (*Ars Amatoria* 1.633–6):

Iuppiter *ex alto* periuria *ridet* amantum
    et iubet Aeolios inrita ferre Notos.
per Styga Iunoni falsum iurare solebat
    Iuppiter: exemplo nunc favet ipse suo.

At the perjuries of lovers Jupiter *laughs from on high* and commands the winds of Aeolus to carry them away unfulfilled. Jupiter used to swear falsely by the Styx to Juno: now he favours his own example.

Since the verbal echo is in this case slight, one might argue that the similarity is purely coincidental and should rather be classed with parallels or repetitions—of which there are surely many in Ovid with no particular resonance—than with (self-)allusions, which demand an evocation of the previous context. Is Ovid not here simply recycling a passage from his earlier work rather than referring to it?

The rareness of the verbal echo should give us pause: the collocation *alto . . . ridet* occurs in Ovidian poetry only in the two verses under discussion. So, too, should another striking similarity, which emerges when the two passages are considered against a generic background. The idea that the gods sweep away, or should sweep away, lover's perjuries with the winds is a topos of love elegy.[14] We have already been put in mind of this motif in the merchant's prayer just above (5.686–8). Thus we are in a sense prepared for the reminiscence

---

[14] Prop. 2.16.47–8; Tib. 1.4.21–6; Ov. *Am.* 1.8.86; 2.8.17–20; [Tib.] 3.6.49–50. Cf. Littlewood (1975*a*) 672–3.

at the entry's close of a specific elegiac text containing the topos, which is the only other instance where the god's action is motivated by his own past behaviour.

What clinches bona fide allusion here are two other aspects of the passage in question vis-à-vis its predecessor. First of all, in the verbal echo itself there is a significant difference from the passage in the *Ars*. We do not have here simply two male deities from on high making light of false oaths in memory of their own deceptive behaviour. Literally, only Jupiter does this, i.e. 'treats human perjuries as a laughing matter' (*ridere* + accusative in the *OLD*'s sense 5b) or, we might say, 'laughs them off'. Although the new situation in the *Fasti* resembles the earlier one closely, Ovid varies rather than exactly repeats the expression: Mercury 'laughs (or smiles) upon' the petitioner benevolently (*ridere* + dative; see *OLD* 2).[15] But that petitioner, the merchant, has asked, above all else, that the god overlook his perjuries, both those of the past and those of the future (5.681–2, 687–8):

'ablue praeteriti periuria temporis', inquit
  'ablue praeteritae perfida verba die . . .
et pateant veniente die periuria nobis,
  nec curent superi siqua locutus ero'.

'Wash away the perjuries of past time,' he said, 'wash away the treacherous words of the past day . . . and let tomorrow open the door to me to fresh perjuries and may the gods not care if I utter any!'

Thus, by smiling upon the tradesman and answering his requests, Mercury too, just like Jupiter, makes light of false oaths. The meaning of *ridet* in the earlier passage is reflected in the new situation at the same time that the word itself undergoes a transformation. The echo—and this is the second point in favour of allusion here—plays

---

[15] Some MSS have *poscentes*, which some editors have accepted—others print the singular *poscentem*. But the recent editors (Le Bonniec, Pighi, Alton-Wormell-Courtney) who adopt the reading *poscenti* are certainly correct. The meaning yielded by the dative, 'laughs as a sign of good will upon the petitioner', is what the context demands. Moreover, although *ridere* + accusative of the person with the meaning 'make light of' appears at Propertius 2.16.47 (*periuros ridet amantis*), the model for Ovid's verse *Ars* 1.633, the construction appears nowhere in Ovidian poetry. On the other hand, the construction with the dative occurs, as the recent Teubner edition notes in the apparatus, at *Ars* 3.513 (*ridenti mollia ride*).

upon the earlier context. All in all, then, Mercury's memory parallels (and glosses) two distinct poetic memories or intertextual strands.

This paper hardly exhausts all instances of the vocabulary of memory in Ovid with a metaliterary force. A comprehensive study would carefully consider, for example, the more direct sort of footnoting found at *Ars Amatoria* 3.659–69 *questus eram, memini, metuendos esse sodales;* | *non tangit solos ista querella viros*, 'once I lamented, I remember, that comrades were to be feared: it is not men only that my lament touches'. As he addresses his erotic instruction to women, the teacher's *memini* reinforces an already emphatic cross reference[16] to the admonitory lament of false friendship that he directed to the male pupils in book 1 (739–54). Similarly, when the professor of love notes his 'memory' of having himself once angrily mussed his girl's hair (2.169 *me memini iratum dominae turbasse capillos*, 'I remember that in my anger I disarranged my lady's hair'), not only do we behold the *praeceptor* illustrating the programmatic principle that his erotodidaxis derives from his own personal experience (1.29 *usus opus movet hoc*, 'experience prompts this work'); Ovid is also here pointing to an 'event' recorded in another of his poems, *Amores* 1.7. In both of these examples the literary self-reference is relatively simple and much closer to the surface of the text than in the passages explicated earlier.

The phenomenon to which I have drawn attention in this paper is, I think, larger in another sense as well. Sometimes, just a gesture of reminding or an appeal to memory, without any explicit reference to recollection, may similarly alert the reader to poetic allusion. There is another Ovidian occasion, at *Fasti* 2.487, when Mars quotes (from Ennius' *Annales*) Jupiter's promise to make Romulus a god. We noted above that the identical situation in *Metamorphoses* 14 was marked by Mars' emphatic reference to the fact that he recollected his father's words (14.813 *nam memoro memorique animo pia verba notavi*, 'for I remember these pious words and have marked them in my retentive mind'). Although such a comment is lacking in the *Fasti's* version of the scene, one might argue that the remindful thrust of the act of

---

[16] The reference is verbal as well as conceptual—with *questus eram . . . querella* compare the first word of the lesson to men in Book 1 (739 *conquerar an moneam mixtum fas omne nefasque?*).

quotation itself serves as a formal trigger—albeit a more subtle one—of poetic allusion. Likewise, if even more subtle, in *Metamorphoses* 1, Daphne's plaintive reminder to her father of Diana's perpetual virginity alludes to that goddess's request for perpetual virginity from her father, Zeus, in Callimachus' *Hymn to Artemis*.[17] In the light of Ovid's practice with explicit references to memory, it is difficult to deny the bare appeal to memory itself here the function of a metaliterary cue.

On the other hand, of course not all words and situations involving memory signal poetic reference. And even when they do, we should be alert to other associations as well. On one memorable occasion, such a word actually has the paradoxical effect of both confirming literary allusion and undercutting a direct statement about Ovid's poetic past. *Ausus eram, memini, caelestia dicere bella*, 'I had dared relate, as I recall, heaven's wars' (*Amores* 2.1.11). Ovid says that he had attempted a poetic Gigantomachy but was forced by his girlfriend to abandon the project. The situation immediately calls to mind the traditional scenario of the *recusatio* and Propertius 3.3 in particular. Again, Ovid's alleged memory awakens ours of earlier literature. Yet Ovid's version of the *recusatio* is to a large extent a spoof, which draws out the comic potential of the topos already present in Propertius 3.3 and heightens the motif's fictionality. In other words, Ovid strongly suggests, just as in *Amores* 1.1, that he never really made such an attempt at epic. And not the least of his winks at the reader is the parenthetical reference to his memory.[18] Here, after the movement's grandiloquent opening *ausus eram*, with its associations of originality,[19] the breezy informality of the colloquial-sounding paratactic *memini* (Knox 1986a: 61) comes as something of a jolt. As usual, Ovid's permutations on a technique are numerous.

---

[17] *Met.* 1.481–7 and Call. *H.* 3.4–8. See, besides the commentators, Williams (1981) 250.

[18] See Due (1974) 45. Santirocco (1969: 83–4 and 95) examines the irony here in the context of similar parenthetical phrases in the *Amores.*

[19] Enn. *Ann.* fr. 210 Sk., Lucr. 1.67, Hor. *Sat.* 2.1.62, Ov. *Fast.* 6.22; cf. Buchheit (1972) 22–3.

5

Vergil's Best Reader? Ovidian Commentary on Vergilian Etymological Wordplay

James J. O'Hara

In *True Names: Vergil and the Alexandrian Tradition of Etymological Wordplay* (Ann Arbor 1996), I discuss those many instances in which Vergil alludes to etymology, whether in order to make some thematic point, or to indicate allegiance to the Alexandrian tradition, or simply to increase the reader's pleasure. I regularly cite other ancient authors who mention or allude to the derivation to which Vergil seems to be alluding. Often I found myself adding references to Ovid, and at some point I became aware that there were many overlaps between Vergilian and Ovidian wordplay, and that in fact many Ovidian passages allude to and interact with instances of etymological wordplay in Vergil, in ways that are meant to be recognized,[1] and that should be a part of our understanding of each poet's goals and methods. I have literally dozens of examples or possible examples, of which this paper will cover some quickly, a few at greater length, and others only by the barest mention in a footnote. In the interest of brevity references to both ancient and modern sources will aim to be helpful rather than comprehensive. For many examples fuller information about the Vergilian wordplay is to be found in my monograph, while for others this paper may serve as incentive for further study, rather than the last word on a subject of considerable complexity.

---

[1] Cf. the familiar description in Sen. Rhet. *Suas.* 3.7 of one of Ovid's borrowings from Vergil: 'he did something he had done with many other lines of Vergil, not to plagiarize, but intending that his open borrowing should be noticed'.

It will be noted that some of my examples are uncertain, either because the wordplay in one or both poets is uncertain, or because Ovid's wordplay may be similar to but independent of Vergil. Scholars have long thought that the sources for Ovid's etymological wordplay were not other poets, but either simple schoolboy etymologies or the works of grammarians like Varro or Verrius Flaccus, who may be of particular importance because he may have written after Vergil, and before Ovid.[2] These sources may be important for Ovid's knowledge of etymology, but my research indicates that Ovid was directly and actively interested in Vergilian etymological wordplay. My claim is that he even offers, in the manner of the Alexandrian scholar-poet, learned 'commentary' on his predecessor,[3] and so can help us think about the difficult question of whether wordplay is taking place in Vergil, and make us a tiny bit more like ancient readers in terms of the 'competence' with which we approach the text (Culler 1975: 113–30; Slater 1990: 1–23, esp. 6). Thus my paper combines two recent trends in scholarship on Latin poets: that of seeing the importance of learned etymological wordplay,[4] and that of exploring how later poets read Vergil, in a way that casts light on both the earlier and later writers.[5]

The paper moves from examples where both Ovid and Vergil explicitly gloss a word, to some where both merely allude to etymology, then to passages where Vergil alludes and Ovid is more

---

[2] Cf. McKeown (1987: 61–2), who perhaps rightly suggests an Ovid less fully learned, and more influenced by the school, for the earlier *Amores*, and Porte (1985: 197–264), who provides a wealth of information on etymologies treated by Ovid, Varro, and Verrius.

[3] My notion of Ovid as 'commentator' was first inspired by Thomas (1982*b*) 152–3; Hinds (1987*a*) index s.v. 'allusion: as commentary' and esp. 153 n. 42: 'it is characteristic of Hellenistic poetry to use imitation to comment on and interpret the model'; and Boyd (1990). See further below n. 5.

[4] See e.g. Cairns (1979*a*), Boyd (1983), Ahl (1985), Porte (1985: 197–264), McKeown (1987), Ross (1987); O'Hara (1990*b*), (1990*c*), (1990*d*), and (1992), Keith (1991) and (1992*a*), Moskalew (1990), Myers (1992), Wheeler (1993).

[5] For poets' readings of Vergil see esp. Martindale (1993) and Hardie (1993); among the many other studies of Ovid and Vergil cf. Döpp (1991), Tissol (1993), and Smith (1994) on Vergil and the *Metamorphoses*, and Hardie (1991), Fantham (1992) and Brugnoli and Stok (1992) on Vergil and the *Fasti*. Each of these offers references to earlier work; cf. also above n. 3. For my notion of Ovid as commentator on earlier etymologizing cf. Courtney (1969: 80–2), who suggests that a gloss of the name Dipsas in *Am.* 1.8 points both to a gloss of Acanthis in Prop. 4.5 and to a likely Greek source for Propertius.

explicit. Finally I shall consider at greater length some complex examples in which Ovid calls attention to aspects of Vergil's text that many
have missed, or makes multiple suggestions about a word Vergil has
glossed, with extremely clear allusions to Vergil, that may serve to
lessen doubt about earlier examples.

1. BOTH VERGIL AND OVID EXPLAIN

At times both Vergil and Ovid refer explicitly to etymology. Vergil
does this mainly through the voices of his characters, while Ovid
can do it as the narrator of both the *Metamorphoses* and especially
the didactic *Fasti*, although in both of those poems Ovid also speaks
through other characters (Myers 1994: 67–73). Explicit etymologies
fit the aetiological nature of both the *Aeneid* and the *Metamorphoses*,
and are particularly at home in the *Fasti*, whose debt and generic
similarities to Callimachus' *Aetia* are even more extensive than are
those of the two hexameter poems.[6] Both Vergil and Ovid refer
explicitly, for example, to the derivation of the name Iulius Caesar
from that of Aeneas' son Iulus (Iulius, *a magno demissum nomen*
Iulo, '*Julius*, the name descended from great *Iulus*', *Aen.* 1.288, Jupiter
speaking; *nomen* Iuli, | *unde domus Teucros* Iulia *tangit avos*, 'the name
of *Iulus*, through which the *Julian* house reaches back to Teucrian
ancestors', *Fast.* 4.39–40). Both explain the connection of the name
Latium with the verb *lateo* (Latium*que vocari* | *maluit* [sc. *Saturnus*],
his quoniam latuisset *tutus in oris*, 'and he [sc. Saturnus] wanted it
to be called *Latium*, because he *had hidden* safely in this land', *Aen.*
8.322–3, Evander speaking; *mansit Saturnia nomen;* | *dicta quoque est*
Latium *terra*, latente *deo*, 'the name Saturnia remained; the country
was also called *Latium* from the *hiding* of the god', *Fast.* 1.237–8, Janus
speaking). Both explain the story that the Tiber was named for an
early king, although they differ on the question of just how early.
Vergil's Evander speaks of a king Thybris who lived before his time
(*Aen.* 8.330–2):

---

[6] Again Myers (1994) index s.v. '*Fasti*, and Callimachus' *Aetia*' offers fruitful
discussion and references to other recent work; on aetiology in Vergil cf. also Shechter
(1975), Horsfall (1991*a* and *b*), and O'Hara (1996*a*) 102–11.

tum reges asperque immani corpore *Thybris,*
a quo post Itali fluvium cognomine *Thybrim*
diximus; amisit verum vetus Albula nomen.

Then kings and *Thybris,* cruel and huge, from whom we Italians later called
the river *Thybris* by name; the former Albula lost its true name.

Ovid derives the river name from a Tiberinus in his list of Alban
kings, both in the 'Little *Aeneid*' of *Metamorphoses* 14 (*regnum Tiber-*
inus ab illis | *cepit et in Tusci demersus fluminis undis* | *nomina fecit*
aquae, 'Tiberinus received the kingdom after them and after drown-
ing in the waves of the Tuscan stream gave his name to the water',
14.614–16) and in the *Fasti* (*Albula, quem Tiberim mersus Tiberinus*
in undis | *reddidit,* 'Albula, which Tiberinus renamed Tiber after he
was drowned in its waves', 2.389–90; cf. too 4.47–48 *Tiberinus . . . in*
Tuscae gurgite mersus aquae, 'Tiburinus . . . who was drowned in the
whirlpool of the Tuscan water').[7]

2. BOTH ALLUDE

At other times both poets only allude to an etymology. Both link
the name of the god *Portunus* with the word *portus,* Vergil in *Aeneid*
5.241–3:

et pater ipse manu magna *Portunus* euntem
impulit: illa Noto citius volucrique sagitta
ad terram fugit et *portu* se condidit alto.

---

[7] Below in this note, and in the longer lists below in nn. 23 and 26, I offer additional examples, found in both Vergil and Ovid, of the type of etymologizing discussed
in the text. In the interests of brevity I offer little explanation of the wordplay, and only
rudimentary bibliography, but the etymologizing should be easy enough to discern.
See O'Hara (1996*a*) on each Vergilian passage for fuller explanations and references;
my debt to Maltby (1991) is also considerable. These lists are extensive, but probably
not comprehensive. More examples in which both Vergil and Ovid explicitly gloss
names: 1) *Aen.* 7.707–8 Clausus . . . | Claudia *nunc a quo diffunditur et tribus et gens,*
Fast. 4.305 Claudia *Quinta genus* Clauso *referebat ab alto;* 2) *Aen.* 8.357–8 hanc Ianus
pater, hanc Saturnus *condidit arcem;* | Ianiculum *huic,* illi fuerat Saturnia *nomen, Aen.*
8.319, 329 Saturnus . . . | *saepius et nomen posuit* Saturnia *tellus;* cf. *Fast.* 1.235–48,
esp. 237 Saturnia *nomen,* 246 Ianiculumque *vocat;* 3) *Aen.* 10.145 et Capys *hinc nomen*
Campanae *ducitur* urbi, *Fast.* 4.45 *ille dedit* Capyi *repetita vocabula Troiae.*

And father *Portunus* himself with his great hand drove it on: swifter than the south wind or a winged arrow she fled to land and settled in the deep *port*.

and Ovid in *Fasti* 6.546–7: *in* portus *nato ius erit omne tuo,* | *quem nos* Portunum, *sua lingua Palaemona dicet,* 'your son will have all authority over *ports*, he whom we call *Portunus* will in his own tongue be Palaemon'.[8] Both gloss the name Hippolytus, 'torn apart by his horses' (ἵππος, 'horse' + λύω, 'to loose, break up'). Vergil alludes to the etymology in *Aeneid* 7.765–7:

namque ferunt fama *Hippolytum*, postquam arte novercae
occiderit patriasque explerit sanguine poenas
turbatis *distractus equis*, ad sidera rursus . . .

For they say that in the story *Hippolytus*, after he died through his step-mother's trickery and paid with his blood the punishment inflicted by his father, *torn apart* by his terrified *horses*, to the stars again . . .

Ovid does so in three passages: *Hippolytus* loris direptus equorum, 'Hippolytus, *torn apart* by the reins of his horses' (*Fast.* 3.265); *Hippolyte,* . . . *diripereris equis* 'Hippolytus, . . . you were torn apart by your horses'(*Fast.* 5.309–10); nomenque simul, quod possit *equorum* | admonuisse, . . . | *Hippolytus* 'and the name too, which could remind one of the *horses*, . . . *Hippolytus*' (*Met.* 15.542–4).

Other examples need a little more explanation. On *aerias Alpis* 'high Alps' in *Georgics* 3.474, Servius says that *Alpes* is Gallic for 'high mountain,' and that *aerias* is thus a gloss or explanation of the etymology.[9] One might think that etymology was not required to call the Alps 'high,' but in a search of the word 'Alp' on the Packard Humanities Institute's Latin disk with the Ibycus Scholarly Computer, I have found no prose author who bothers to give the mountains this kind of epithet referring to height, while such phrases appear in

---

[8] Some sources link the name instead with *porta*, 'gate'; cf. Varro fr. 376 (*Grammatical Romanae Fragmenta* p. 345 = schol. Veron. *Aen.* 5.241); Paul.-Fest. p. 48 L; more in Pease and Frazer.

[9] Serv. on *Geo.* 3.474: *AERIAS ALPES: id est Galliam. et dicendo 'aerias' verbum expressit ex verbo: nam Gallorum lingua alti montes Alpes vocantur*; on *Aen.* 4.442 *ALPINI BOREAE flantes de Alpibus, quae Gallorum lingua alti montes vocantur*; on *Aen.* 10.13 *sane omnes altitudines montium licet a Gallis Alpes vocentur, proprie tamen iuga montium Gallicorum sunt* (then Serv. cites Varro on ways of crossing the Alps [Varro fr. 379, *GRF* p. 346]; did Varro explain the word Alps?). Similar information in Schol. Bern. Lucan 1.183, Isid. *Etym.* 14.8.18.

verse in Catullus (where Ellis (1889: 42) long ago suggested it was an etymological gloss), Ovid, Petronius (where Connors (1989: 108–9) has suggested etymologizing), and Silius Italicus: *altas . . . Alpes* (Catullus 11.9); *aeriaeque Alpes* (Ovid *Met.* 2.226); *Alpibus aeriis* (Petr. *Sat.* 122, *BC* verse 144); *celsae . . . Alpes* (Sil. Ital. 1.117), *Alpibus altis* (370), *aerias Alpis* (15.168). Possibly Vergil is imitating Catullus, and the others Vergil; possibly, however, each is signalling awareness of all those who came before him. I should add here that my suspicion is that what I am doing with Ovid and Vergil could be done with many poets of the first century AD (cf. Hardie 1993: 9, 64).

In his comment on *Aeneid* 4.302–3, *audito stimulant . . . Baccho | orgia nocturnusque vocat clamore Cithaeron* 'when Bacchus is heard and the mysteries arouse her and at night Cithaeron calls with a shout', Servius connects the word *nocturnus* with an epithet of Bacchus, Nyctelius, although we may start off being sceptical about whether Vergil's lines here (or at *Geo.* 4.521 *nocturnique orgia Bacchi*) allude to the epithet and its etymology.[10] A more likely example is found in Ovid, who, as André noted (1975: 194), presents the words *Nyctelius* and *nocturnus* in one line at *Ars* 1.567 Nyctelium*que patrem* nocturna*que sacra precare* 'pray to the *Nyctelian* father and nocturnal rites'. Ovid's verse may cause us to be more willing to see the allusion in Vergil, and possibly that is even Ovid's point, although admittedly little in his line points directly to Vergil.

Both Ovid and Vergil seem to allude to the derivation that links 'Saturnian' Juno to words like *satis* 'enough' and to notions of 'insatiability' (the connection is also mentioned in a discussion of Saturn in Cicero).[11] Vergil's wordplay in several passages has been noted by Anderson and Lyne (*Aen.* 5.606–8, 5.781–6, 7.297–312):

Irim de caelo misit *Saturnia* Iuno
Iliacam ad classem ventosque aspirat eunti,
multa movens necdum antiquum *saturata* dolorem.

---

[10] Serv. on *Aen.* 4.303: *NOCTVRNVSQVE nocte celebratus; unde ipsa sacra 'nyctelia' dicebantur* (sim. on *Geo.* 4.520).

[11] This would be etymology by opposites or κατ᾽ ἀντίφρασιν; see O'Hara (1996a) 66. For the etymology cf. Cic. *ND* 2.64 *Saturnus autem est appellatus quod saturaretur annis*; 3.62 *Saturnus quia se saturat annis*. I am indebted here to Anderson (1958: 519–32, esp. 522–5), Pease (1955) on Cic. *ND* 2.64, Lyne (1989: 173–7), Feeney (1991: 201).

Saturnian Juno sent Iris down from heaven to the Ilian fleet and caused the winds to speed her way, still causing much trouble, her ancient pain not yet *sated*.

Iunonis gravis ira neque *exsaturabile* pectus
cogunt me, Neptune, preces descendere in omnis . . .
non media de gente Phrygum exedisse nefandis
urbem odiis *satis* est . . .

Juno's grievous anger and *insatiable* heart compel me, Neptune, to descend to all manner of entreaty . . . It is not *enough* for her cursed hatred to have eaten away the city from the midst of the Phrygian people . . .

   at, credo, mea numina tandem
fessa iacent, odiis aut *exsaturata* quievi . . .
vincor ab Aenea. quod si mea numina non sunt
magna *satis*, dubitem haud equidem implorare quod usquam est:
flectere si nequeo superos, Acheronta movebo.

But, I suppose, at last my powers lie exhausted, or *sated* on hatred I have rested . . . I am defeated by Aeneas. But if my powers are not great *enough*, I would certainly not hesitate to call upon any power anywhere. If I can not bend the gods above, I will raise Hell.

Some of these same associations are exploited by Ovid in *Met.* 9.176–8 *Saturnia . . . | corque ferum satia* 'Saturnia . . . satisfy your savage hart', and perhaps also in the story of Diana and Actaeon at 3.249–72 (where the anger of Diana, unlike that of Juno, is able to be satisfied).[12] Both the etymology and thematic thread in the *Metamorphoses* seem borrowed from the *Aeneid*'s depiction of Juno; both poets' wordplay could be described as part of the long conversation about the gods carried out by numerous epic poets, as Denis Feeney, to whom I owe the example from Ovid, has shown.

   In *Aeneid* 4.402–5, as Aeneas' men prepare their ships to depart from Carthage, Vergil compares them to ants:

ac velut ingentem *formicae* farris acervum
cum populant hiemis memores tectoque reponunt,
it nigrum campis agmen praedamque per herbas
convectant calle angusto. . . .

---

[12] Feeney cites *Met.* 3.140 *canes satiatae sanguine erili*; 252 *ira . . . fertur satiata Dianae*, followed by the contrast with Juno at 271 *nec sum Saturnia, si non . . .*

And just as when *ants*, mindful of winter, raid a huge pile of grain and store it at home, a black line proceeds in the fields and they *carry* their plunder along a narrow path . . .

In a note on this passage, Servius derives the word for ant, *formica*, from the ant's 'carrying of crumbs' (*micas ferat* or *ore micas ferat*).[13] O. S. Due cites fairly clear allusions to this etymology in two passages in Ovid: formica . . . granifero *solitum cum* vehit ore *cibum*, 'the ant . . . when it *carries* in its *grain-bearing mouth* its usual food' (*Ars* 1.93–4); *grande onus exiguo* formicas ore gerentes '*ants carrying* in their tiny *mouths* a great load' (*Met.* 7.625). Due is understandably uncertain about whether there is etymologizing in the Vergilian passage. It is possible that Ovid is suggesting that etymologizing is taking place in Vergil, but it is hard to claim this with any conviction.[14]

At times etymologizing is more certain in Vergil than in Ovid. In *Aeneid* 6.810–11 *regis Romani primam qui* legibus *urbem | fundabit* 'the Roman king who first will establish the city with *laws*', Vergil glosses the name of the king Numa, which he does not mention here, as if from Greek *nomoi* 'laws', which Servius helpfully provides.[15] Suppression, or omission of one of the words involved in etymological wordplay, is also a technique typical of Vergil and Ovid; the result of this technique is that the reader must take a more active role in recognizing the etymologizing (O'Hara 1996a: 79–82). McKeown (1987: 53) suggests allusion to this etymology also in Ovid's phrase in *Amores* 2.17.18 *iusto . . . Numae*.[16] This would be the kind of gloss by epithet common in poetic etymologizing (O'Hara 1996a: 64–5), but without the Vergil, I would find this argument about Ovid less than compelling. With Vergil's precedent, the example from Ovid is plausible.

In *Aeneid* 3.271 *Dulichiumque Sameque et Neritos ardua saxis* 'Doulichion and Same and Neritos, steep with rocks', Vergil offers a gloss of the old Greek epic word or name *neritos*: his phrase *Neritos*

---

[13] Serv. on *Aen.* 4.402: *sane 'formica' dicta est ab eo, quod micas ferat* (Serv. Auct.: *quod ore micas ferat*).

[14] Neither of the Ovidian passages points with any specificity to Vergil, although the *Ars* couplet does occur in a simile, and shares a couple of words with Vergil's lines.

[15] Serv. on *Aen.* 6.808: *Numa dictus est ἀπὸ τῶν νόμων*; Serv. Auct.: *ab inventione et constitutione legis, nam proprium nomen Pompilius habuit.*

[16] Cf. too (?) *Fast.* 3.275ff. *Numa . . . iure . . . leges.*

ardua saxis calls attention to the meaning 'large, immense' (O'Hara 1990*d*).[17] In *Tristia* 1.5.57–8, Ovid uses the epithet to describe Odysseus:

pro duce *Neritio* docti mala nostra poetae
   scribite: *Neritio* nam mala *plura* tuli.

Write, learned poets, of my evils instead of the *Neritian* chief: for I have borne *more* evils than the *Neritian*.

Stephen Hinds will explain to us, in his forthcoming commentary on *Tristia* I, that Ovid alludes to *neritos* as meaning 'countless,' 'numerous.' Ovid points to etymology by his use of the word *plura*: more suffering than Neritian Odysseus would be much suffering indeed. One slightly uncertain example involves four poets. Sources connect the name Heracles with that of his stepmother Hera.[18] Similar and doubtless interrelated hexameters in Callimachus and Apollonius are framed with the words Hera and Heracles, possibly alluding to the derivation, although some might argue that sound play is enough: Ἥρης ἐννεσίῃσιν, ἀέθλιον Ἡρακλῆι 'Hera's devising, a task for *Heracles*'(Callim. *H*. 3.108); Ἥρη, Ζηνὸς ἄκοιτις, ἀέθλιον Ἡρακλῆι 'Hera, Zeus' mate, a task for *Heracles*'(Apoll. Rhod. *Arg*. 1.997). Framing of a line like this is common in poetic etymologizing (O'Hara 1996*a*: 82–6). Lines in Vergil and Ovid are framed by the name Hercules and not the word Hera, which I would describe as suppressed (like the name Numa above in *Aeneid* 6.810–11), but the word *noverca* 'stepmother', so that the wordplay only takes place when the reader supplies the name Hera: *qui carmine laudes | Herculeas et facta ferunt; ut prima* novercae 'who tell in song the praise of *Hercules* and his

---

[17] Cf. *Od*. 9.22 and *Il*. 2.632 Νήριτον εἰνοσίφυλλον, Hes. *Op*. 511 νήριος ὕλη =? 'forest of countless trees', μεγήριτα at *Theog*. 240, of 'numerous' Nereids, *Il*. 22.349 εἰκοσινήριτ'ἄποινα; Apoll. Rhod. *Arg*. 3.1288–9 **νήριτα** ταύρων | ἴχνια μαστεύων (glossed by scholia as τὰ **μεγάλα** καὶ ἀναρίθμητα, 'large,' and 'countless'), 4.158–9 περί τ'ἀμφί τε **νήριτος** ὀδμή | φαρμάκου ὕπνον ἔβαλλε.

[18] Cf. Schol. T on *Il*. 14.324 παρὰ τὸ ὑπὸ τῆς Ἥρας κληθῆναι Ἡρακλῆς λέγεται, Diod. Sic. 4.10.1 διόπερ Ἀργεῖοι πυθόμενοι τὸ γεγονὸς Ἡρακλέα προσηγόρευσαν, **ὅτι δι'Ἥραν** ἔσχε **κλέος**, Ἀλκαῖον πρότερον καλούμενον, Macrob. *Sat*. 1.20.10 Ἡρακλῆς *enim quid aliud est nisi* Ἥρας, *id est aeris*, κλέος? *quae porro alia aeris gloria est nisi solis illuminatio*, Prob. Verg. *E*. 7.61 *Pindarus initio Alciden nominatum, postea Herculem dicit ab* Ἥρα, *quam Iunonem dicimus, quod eius imperiis opinionem famamque virtutis sit consecutus*.

deeds; how first his *stepmother's*' (*Aen.* 8.287–8); Herculis *implerant terras odiumque* novercae '[the deeds] of *Hercules* had filled the lands and the hatred of his *stepmother*' (*Met.* 9.135).

In *Georgics* 1.62–3, Vergil's use of the phrase *durum genus* alludes to the aetiological pun, first made in treatments of the myth of Deucalion and Pyrrha in archaic Greek poetry, between λαός, 'people,' and λᾶας 'stone:'[19]

Deucalion vacuum *lapides* iactavit in orbem,
unde *homines* nati, *durum genus*.

Deucalion tossed *stones* into the vacant world, whence *men* were born, *the hard race*.

Vergil does not gloss any of the Latin words he is using; his words *lapides*, *homines*, and *durum genus* merely allude to the wordplay made in earlier Greek sources. Ovid twice alludes to the wordplay (*Am.* 2.14.11–12 *quique iterum iaceret generis primordia nostri* | *in vacuo lapides orbe, parandus erat* 'someone had to be found to cast in the vacant world the stones that were the first beginnings of our kind'; *Met.* 1.414, *inde genus durum sumus experiensque laborum* 'thence comes the hardness of our race and our endurance of toils'). The second passage even echoes Vergil's *durum genus*, and so acknowledges that the Deucalion and Pyrrha story he is telling at some length was mentioned briefly in the *Georgics*.

Later in *Georgics* 1, Vergil's mention of lightning, *fulmina*, offers a gloss on the name *Ceraunia*, which Apollonius of Rhodes had explicitly connected with κεραυνός, 'lightning' (*Geo.* 1.328–33):[20]

ipse pater media nimborum in nocte corusca
fulmina molitur dextra, quo maxima motu

---

[19] Cf. Hes. fr. 234 M-W, Pind. *O.* 9.45 κτισσάσθαν λίθινον γόνον | λαοὶ δ' ὀνόμαθεν; Callim. fr. 496 Pf. ΛΑΟΙ Δευκαλίωνος ὅσοι γενόμεσθα; Apollod. 1.48.7 καὶ Διὸς εἰπόντος ὑπὲρ κεφαλῆς ἔβαλλεν αἴρων λίθους,... ὅθεν καὶ λαοὶ μεταφορικῶς ὠνομάσθησαν ἀπὸ τοῦ λᾶας ὁ λίθος.

[20] Apoll. Rhod. *Arg.* 4.518–21 ἀνδράσιν Ἐγχελέεσσιν ἐφέστιοι· οἱ δ' ἐν ὄρεσσιν | ἐνναίουσιν ἄπερ τε Κεραύνια κικλήσκονται | ἐκ τόθεν ἐξότε τούσγε Διὸς Κρονίδαο κεραυνοί | νῆσον ἐς ἀντιπέραιαν ἀπέτραπον ὁρμηθῆναι. See O'Hara (1990c) 374–6, where I draw also on Serv. on *Aen.* 3.506: *Ceraunia sunt montes Epiri, a crebris fulminibus propter altitudinem nominati; Unde Horatius (C. 1.3.20) expressius dixit 'Acroceraunia' propter altitudinem et fulminum iactus*, and Isid. *Etym.* 14.8.12: *Ceraunii sunt montes Epiri, a crebris dicti fulminibus. Graece enim fulmen* κεραυνός *dicitur*.

terra tremit, fugere ferae et mortalia corda
per gentis humilis stravit pavor; ille flagranti
aut Atho aut Rhodopen aut *alta Ceraunia telo*
deicit;

The father himself in the midnight of clouds wields the thunderbolt with
his gleaming right hand. At this motion the great earth trembled, the beasts
fled and a cowering fear laid low mortal hearts throughout the world. With
flaming *weapon* he casts down Atho or Rhodope or *lofty Ceraunia*.

McKeown (1987: 47), citing Vergil, has suggested that 'in characterizing *Ceraunia* as *violenta* at [*Amores*] 2.11.19, Ovid is alluding to
the derivation of that name from κεραυνός,' but he is somewhat less
confident about the suggestion in his commentary on that passage
(1998: 243).

3. VERGIL ALLUDES, OVID EXPLAINS

At times Vergil merely implies wordplay, and Ovid is more explicit. In
Aeneid 6.763–5, Vergil links *Silvius* and the woods:

Silvius, Albanum nomen, tua postuma proles,
quem tibi longaevo serum Lavinia coniunx
educet *silvis* regem regumque parentem.

Silvius, an Alban name, your late-born offspring, whom your wife Lavinia
shall rear in the *woods* for you late in your old age, a king and the father of
kings

In *Fasti* 4.41–2, Ovid is explicit:

Postumus hinc, qui, quod *silvis* fuit ortus in altis,
Silvius in Latia gente vocatus erat.

Postumus, who, because he was born in the deep *woods*, was called *Silvius*
among the Latin people.

In *Aeneid* 8, Vergil links the name *Carmentis* with the verb *canere*
(337–41):

vix ea dicta, dehinc progressus monstrat et aram
et *Carmentalem* Romani nomine portam

quam memorant, nymphae priscum *Carmentis* honorem,
vatis fatidicae, *cecinit* quae prima futuros
Aeneadas magnos et nobile Pallanteum.

He had hardly finished speaking when he moved on and showed the altar
and the gate that the Romans call by the name of *Carmentalis*, an ancient
honour to the nymph *Carmentis*, a prophetic seer, who first *sang* of the great
sons of Aeneas to come and noble Pallanteum.

In *Fasti* 1.467, Ovid explains: *quae nomen habes a carmine ductum*
'you who have a name taken from song', although here Ovid suppresses the nymph's name.[21]

In *Aeneid* 8.663 *exsultantis Salios* 'dancing Salians', Vergil glosses
with an explanatory epithet. Ovid is overt in *Fasti* 3.387 *iam dederat*
Saliis a saltu nomina ducta 'he had already given to the *Salians a name
taken from dancing*'.[22]

At *Georgics* 1.406–9, Vergil describes the myth in which Nisus,
changed into a kind of sea-eagle, pursues his daughter Scylla, changed
into the bird *ciris*. Vergil does not mention the word *ciris*, but he
seems to allude, by his repeated use of the word *secat*, 'cut,' to the
derivation of the bird-name ciris from Greek κείρω 'cut':

apparet liquido sublimis in aere Nisus,
et pro purpureo poenas dat Scylla capillo:
quacumque illa levem fugiens *secat* aethera pennis,
ecce inimicus atrox magno stridore per auras
insequitur Nisus; qua se fert Nisus ad auras,
illa levem fugiens raptim *secat* aethera pennis.

Nisus appears high in the clear air and Scylla pays the penalty for the purple
lock of hair: wherever she *slices* the light air, with her wings as she flees, you
can see Nisus, her terrible foe, following through the air with a great shriek;
where Nisus rises to the airs, she *slices* the light air, fleeing hurriedly on wing.

In the original myth the 'cutting' would be that of Nisus' hair by
Scylla; here she 'cuts' through the air. Both Ovid and the pseudo-
Vergilian *Ciris*, as Thomas notes, explicitly refer to the derivation,

---

[21] See Le Bonniec (1965) ad *Fasti* 1.467 for brief comments of Ovid's rivalry with
Vergil in this whole passage.
[22] Porte (1985: 245) cites as Ovid's models not Vergil but Varro *LL* 5.85 and Verrius
Flaccus p. 438 L (cf. above n. 2).

which must have appeared in poetry before Vergil (*Met.* 8.150–1 *in avem mutata vocatur* | Ciris *et a* tonso *est hoc nomen adepta capillo* 'changed into a bird she is called *Ciris* and she acquired this name from the *cutting* of the lock': [Verg.] *Ciris* 488 *facti de nomine Ciris* 'Ciris named for the deed').[23]

---

[23] Cf. Thomas (1988) ad loc. Callimachus may have glossed the name at Aet. fr. 113.4 *K*]εῖριν..., or at *Hec.* fr. 288 Pf. = 90 H Σκύλλα γυνὴ κατακᾶσα καὶ οὐ ψύθος οὔνομ' ἔχουσα | πορφυρέην ἤμησε κρέκα, although the latter passage is usually understood to gloss the name Scylla as 'dog', 'bitch'; see O'Hara (1996a) on *Geo.* 1.404–9 and *Ecl.* 6.74-7, where I quote Pfeiffer (1949–53) ad *Hec.* fr. 288 and Shechter (1975: 358–9). More examples in which both Vergil and Ovid seem to allude to etymology (see above n. 7 for the nature of these lists; this list and the one below at n. 26 also contain some examples in which the etymologizing is uncertain, which I sometimes note with a question mark after the book and line reference; at times it will be unclear whether the passage offers etymologizing or simply paronomasia): 1) *Aen.* 1.87 *clamorque virum* strido*rque* rudentum, *Aen.* 3.561–2 *primusque* rudentem | *contorsit laevas proram Palinurus ad undas*, *Met.* 11.495 *quippe sonant clamore viri*, stridore rudentes—cf. *rudens*, 'rope' with *rudeo*, 'bellow, roar'; see Ahl (1985: 29); 2) *Aen.* 1.493 *bellatrix, audetque viris concurrere virgo*, *Met.* 4.681–8 *primo silet ilia nec audet* | *adpellare* virum virgo; 3) *Aen.* 2.682–94? *comas . . . stella facem ducens*, *Aen.* 8.681 *laeta vomunt* patrium*que aperitur vertice sidus*, *Aen.* 10.270–2 *ardet apex capiti . . . non secus ac liquida si quando nocte* cometae, *Met.* 15.746–50 *in sidus vertere novum stellamque comantem* (sc. *Caesarem*)—cf. κομήτης; see Knox (1982a: 76), Connors (1989: 104–5), and (less plausibly) Nadeau (1982); 4) *Aen.* 3.660–1 *lanigerae comitantur oves; ea* sola *voluptas* | solamen*que mali*, *Met.* 1.359–60 *quo sola timorem* | *ferre modo posses? quo* consolante *dolores*? (this common paronomasia might involve no suggestion of etymologizing); 5) *Aen.* 3.701–2? *campique* Geloi, | *immanisque* Gela fluvii *cognomine dicta*, *Fast.* 4.470 *et te, verticibus non* adeunde Gela—cf. Rehm (1932: 38); 6) *Aen.* 6.570–1 *continuo sontis* ultrix *accincta flagello* | Tisiphone *quatit insultans*, *Am.* 2.1.13 *ulta est (Titan)*—cf. τίσις; see McKeown (1987: 46); 7) *Aen.* 6.714–15 Lethaei *ad fluminis undam* | *securos latices et* longa oblivia potant, *Pont.* 2.4.23 securae *pocula* Lethes; 8) *Aen.* 6.842–3 *geminos, duo* fulmina belli, | *Scipiadas, cladem Libyae*, *Am.* 2.1.17–20 *clausit amica fores: ego cum Jove* fulmen *omisi;* | *excidit ingenio Iuppiter ipse meo.* | *Iuppiter, ignoscas: nil me tua tela iuvabant;* | *clausa tuo maius ianua* fulmen *habet*—cf. Skutsch (1968: 145–50), McKeown (1989: 132); 9) *Aen.* 7.30–1 Tiberinus . . . | *verticibus rapidis et multa* flavus *harena*, *Met.* 2.245 Xanthus flavusque Lycormas—cf. Trojan Xanthus; see O'Hara (1990a: 107 n. 37); 10) *Aen.* 7.411–12 *locus* Ardea *quondam* | *dictus avis, et nunc* magnum *manet* Ardea *nomen*, *Aen.* 7.623–31 ardet *inexcita Ausonia atque immobilis ante;* | *. . .* | Ardea *Crustumerique et turrigerae Antemnae*, *Met.* 14.573–80 (city burned, then *ardea* emerges)—cf. Ahl (1985: 265 n. 29); Hardie (1992: 77 n. 16 and 81 n. 81); 11) *Aen.* 7.720 *vel cum sole novo densae* torrentur aristae, *Her.* 5.111–12 *et minus est in te quam summa pondus* arista, | *quae levis adsiduis* solibus usta *riget*—cf. Ross (1987: 35); 12) *Aen.* 8.48 Ascanius clari *condet cognominis* Albam, *Met.* 14.612 clarus *subit* Alba Latinum; 13) *Aen.* 8.194 *semihominis* Caci (and in general throughout the passage), *Fast.* 1.551–2 Cacus, *Aventinae timor atque infamia silvae,* | *non leve finitimis hospitibusque* malum—cf. κακός; see Clausen (1994: 223); 14) *Aen.* 8.425 Brontesque Steropesque et nudus

I move now to gradually more complicated examples. The first is one of my favourites, and shows Ovid most clearly in the role of commentator. In *Aeneid* 8, Vergil offers two etymologies, one explicit and more or less put in the mouth of Evander, and one only implicit, for the cave known as the Lupercal.[24] Both connect it with the word *lupa*, 'wolf,' but when Evander is showing Aeneas the future site of Rome he links the Lupercal with the Arcadian Pan Lycaeus (*Aen.* 8.343–4):

> . . . et gelida monstrat sub rupe *Lupercal*
> Parrhasio dictum Panos de more *Lycaei*.

and he shows him the *Lupercal* under the cool crag, called after the Parrhasian custom the place of Pan *Lycaeus*.

On the shield of Aeneas, however, in a way that is easy to miss, Vergil seems to connect the Lupercal, the *antrum* 'cave' in 630, with the wolf that nourished Romulus and Remus, a myth of which Evander, of course, cannot know (*Aen.* 8.630–4):

> fecerat et viridi fetam Mavortis in *antro*
> procubuisse *lupam*, geminos huic ubera circum
> ludere pendentis pueros et lambere matrem
> impavidos, illam tereti cervice reflexa
> mulcere alternos et corpora fingere lingua.

And he had fashioned a pregnant *she-wolf* lying in the verdant *grotto* of Mars, and two boys playing as they hung about her udders and licked their mother

membra Pyracmon, *F.* 4.288 Brontes et Steropes Acmonidesque solent; 15) *Aen.* 9.128–9? his Iuppiter *ipse* | auxilium *solitum eripuit, Am.* 2.1.19 Iuppiter, *ignoscas: nil me tua tela* iuvabunt—see McKeown (1987: 49); 16) *Aen.* 12.521–8 *ac velut . . . ignes* | . . . | . . . *non* segnius, *Am.* 3.7.13–14 tacta tamen veluti gelida *mea membra cicuta* | segnia *propositum destituere meum*—see McKeown (1987: 50–1); 17) *Ecl.* 8.107 Hylax *in limine* latrat, *Met.* 3.224 acutae vocis Hylactor, 18) *Geo.* 1.308–9? tum figere dammas | stuppea torquentem Balearis *verbera* fundae, *Met.* 2.727–8 Balearica *plumbum* | funda iacit, 4.709–10 Balearica . . . | funda; 19) *Geo.* 1.500? hunc saltem everso iuvenem succurrere saeclo, *Am.* 3.6.23 *flumina debebant* iuvenes in amore iuvare—see Du Quesnay (1981: 133), McKeown (1987: 49); 20) *Geo.* 3.1–3 Te quoque, magna Pales, et te memorande canemus | pastor *ab Amphryso*; cf. *Geo.* 3.294, *Fast.* 4.723 alma Pales, faveas pastoria sacra canenti—see Ross (1987: 168).

24 On the Lupercal, cf. Ahl (1985: 85), who cites both Vergil and Ovid on the Arcadian roots of the name, Putnam (1994: 359), citing allusion to the connection *Lycaeus* | *lupus* | *Lupercal* in Horace *C.* 1.17 as well as *Aen.* 8, Horsfall (1991a: 112), citing Varro fr. 189, *GRF*, as source for *Aen.* 8.343–4.

without fear, while she bent her smooth neck backwards, licking each in turn, and shaped their bodies with her tongue.

Ovid, in a manner consistent with the *Fasti* narrator's fondness for multiple explanations or 'variant aetiologies,'[25] characteristically gives tentative endorsement to both theories, although his long passage concentrates on the derivation to which Vergil only alludes. Near the end of Ovid's discussion of the derivation of the name from the wolf that nourished Romulus and Remus, his language echoes that of the Vergilian shield: *Fasti* 2.418 *et* fingit lingua corpora *bina sua* 'and licks into shape their two bodies with her tongue' recalls *Aen.* 8.634 *mulcere alternos et* corpora fingere lingua. Then Ovid offers his open-minded endorsement of the rival theory, which derives the name from the Arcadian Lupercal (*Fasti* 2.421–4):

illa (sc. *lupa*) loco nomen fecit, locus ipse *Lupercis*;
    magna dati nutrix praemia lactis habet.
quid vetat Arcadio dictos de monte *Lupercos*?
    Faunus in Arcadia templa *Lycaeus* habet

She (sc. the *she-wolf*) gave her name to the place, the place gave their name to the *Luperci*. The nurse has a great reward for the milk she gave. What prevents the *Luperci* from having been named after the Arcadian mountain? *Lycaean* Faunus has temples in Arcadia.

While at line 418 Ovid echoed the Vergilian shield in the phrase *fingit lingua corpora*, here in lines 423–4 he echoes the Evander passage. Compare Ovid's *quid vetat Arcadio dictos de monte Lupercos?* | . . . *Lycaeus* with Vergil's (*Aen.* 8.343–4) . . . *Lupercal* | *Parrhasio dictum Panos de more Lycaei*. Here in addition to the shared words *Lupercal* | *Lupercos*, *dictum* | *dictos*, and *Lycaei* | *Lycaeus*, Ovid's *Arcadio* both reproduces the rhythm of and glosses Vergil's *Parrhasio*, while his *de monte Lupercos* echoes the sound at line-end of Vergil's *de more Lycaei* (McKeown 1994; O'Hara 1996a: 63). The words Lupercos and Lycaei at line-end also point to the relationship between Latin *lupa* and Greek λύκος that underlies the putative connection of the Lupercal with Arcadia. Just like a commentator, then, Ovid cites both Vergilian passages offering etymologies for the Lupercal; for the shield

[25] On Ovid's 'variant aetiologies' see Martin (1985), Porte (1985), Barchiesi (1991), Hardie (1991) 62–4, Newlands (1992), and esp. Miller (1992).

passage, he brings to the surface something only implicit, or easy to miss, in Vergil.[26]

At the start of *Aeneid* 7, Vergil offers an explicit etymological aetiology linking the port of Caieta with Aeneas' nurse (1–4):

Tu quoque litoribus nostris, Aeneia nutrix,
aeternam moriens famam, Caieta, dedisti;
et nunc servat honos sedem tuus, ossaque nomen
Hesperia in magna, si qua est ea gloria, signat.

You too, Caieta, nurse to Aeneas, by your death gave eternal fame to our shores; even now your honour guards the spot, and your name marks your bones in great Hesperia, if that is any glory.

Servius preserves a different explanation: Caieta is where the Trojan ships were burned, and so named from the Greek for 'burn,' καίω.[27] Ovid also handles the Caieta episode briefly, in *Metamorphoses* 14,

---

[26] A possible, though uncertain, parallel for what Ovid does with Vergil's glosses of *Lupercal* may be found in his discussion of the name *Quirinus* at *Fast.* 2.475–80: *proxima lux vacua est, at tertia* dicta Quirino | *qui tenet hoc nomen (Romulus ante fuit),* | *sive quod hasta* 'curis' *priscis est dicta Sabinis* | *(bellicus a telo venit in astra deus),* | *sive suum regi* nomen posuere Quirites, | *seu quia Romanis iunxerat ille* Cures. Ovid says that Romulus' name Quirinus may be derived from either a Sabine word for a weapon, or from the name Quirites, or from the Sabine city Cures (cf. Brugnoli and Stok 1992: 123–32). Vergil alludes to the connection between Quirites and Cures at *Aen.* 7.709–10 *... postquam in partem data Roma* Sabinis. | *una ingens Amiterna cohors priscique* Quirites, and may just possibly suggest a connection between the name Quirinus and weaponry in Aen. 6.859? *tertiaque* arma *patri suspendet capta* Quirino, and *Geo.* 3.27? *victorisque* arma Quirini.

More (and more certain) examples (cf. above nn. 7 and 23) in which Vergil alludes, Ovid is explicit: 1) *Aen.* 7.10–11 proxima Circaeae *raduntur litora terrae,* | *dives inaccessos ubi* Solis filia *lucos...,* Met. 14.348: *nomine dicta suo* Circaea *reliquerat arva,* Fast. 4.70 *et quod adhuc* Circes *nomina litus habet;* 2) Aen. 8.105 *una omnes* iuvenum *primi pauperque* senatus *habet,* Fast. 5.63–4 *nec nisi post annos patuit tunc curia* seros, | *nomen et* aetatis *mite* senatus; 3) *Aen.* 8.231–5 Aventini *montem... | dirarum nidis domus opportuna* volucrum (hill < *avis*), Aen. 7.657–8 pulcher Aventinus... | collis Aventini *silva quem* Rhea sacerdos... (man < hill), *Fast.* 4.51–2 *venit* Aventinus *post hos, locus unde vacatur,* | *mons quoque* (hill < man; perhaps also man <*adventus*—see Maltby s.v. Aventinus), *Met.* 14.620–1 *tradit* Aventino, *qui... eadem* | *monte iacet positus tribuitque vocabula monti*; 4) *Ecl.* 10.55–61? (Acontius), *Her.* 21.211–12 *mirabar quare tibi nomen* Acontius *esset;* | *quod faciat longe vulnus,* acumen *habes*—cf. Rosen and Farrell (1986); 5) *Geo.* 4.45–8 *cubilia* limo | *unge fovens...* | *... neve rubentis* | *ure* foco *cancros,* Fast. 6.301 focus *a* flammis *et quod* fovet *omnia dictus*—cf. Thomas (1982a: 91 n. 42).

[27] Servius on 7.1: *lectum tamen est in philologis in hoc loco classem Troianorum casu concrematam, unde* Caieta *dicta est,* ἀπὸ τοῦ καίειν.

where the geographical aetiology seems implicit, but Ovid also makes prominent mention of the burning of her pyre (443–4):

Hic me Caietam notae pietatis alumnus
ereptam Argolico quo debuit *igne cremavit*

Here me, *Caieta*, snatched from Argive flames, my nursling of celebrated piety burned with fitting fire.

Ovid probably is playing on the association of the name with καίω— and alluding to the derivation that Vergil omitted.[28]

A few lines later in *Aeneid* 7 comes Vergil's invocation of the muse Erato: *nunc age, qui reges, Erato, quae tempora, rerum . . .* 'come now, Erato, what kings, what circumstances, what state of events . . .' (*Aen.* 7.37). Apollonius, at the start of the second half of his epic, comments explicitly on the 'erotic' connotations of this Muse's name, as he is about to start telling of the love of Jason and Medea (*Arg.* 3.1–5):

Come now, Erato, stand beside me and relate to me how it was that Jason brought the fleece from Colchis to Iolkos through the power of Medea's *love*. I invoke you because you also have been allotted a share of Kypris' power, and you bewitch unmarried girls by the cares you bring; for this reason a *lovely name* has been attached to you.

Vergil certainly borrows from Apollonius here; does he, or perhaps must he, evoke the thematic and etymological associations of the name Erato as well? I think so, and many others do, for passions of various kinds will be important in *Aeneid* 7–12, but a number of scholars are sceptical. Ovid's two references to Erato, however, both make explicit the connection of her name with *eros* (Miller 1993: 159–60, see ch. 4 above): *sic* Erato (*mensis Cythereius illi | cessit, quod teneri* nomen Amoris *habet*), 'so *Erato* replied (the month of the Cytherean fell to her, because her name is derived from tender *love*' (*Fast.* 4.195–6); *nunc* Erato, *nam tu* nomen Amoris *habes* 'now *Erato*, for your name derives from *love*' (*Ars* 2.16). Nothing about these lines

---

[28] Cf. also Myers (1994: 104) on Ovid: 'When Aeneas reaches the shores of Italy, they are described with hyperchronological accuracy as *litora adit non nutricis haben-tia nomen* (14.157), thus correcting Vergil, who mentions the name of the shore at *Aen.* 6.900, before Caieta's burial, and then gives the *aetion* at the beginning of *Aen.* 7.1–5.' She cites Kenney (1986: 454), but her explanation is fuller than his. For Ovid's tracing of the Vergilian Aeneas' itinerary, cf. also Brugnoli and Stok (1992: 145–9).

points directly to Vergil; they nevertheless can serve, regardless of whether Ovid intended this, as a kind of commentary on Vergil, or at the very least as good evidence for how readily contemporary readers would have linked Erato and *eros*.

My last three examples are complicated instances of allusive etymologizing from the *Fasti*, about which I have written before, but they should profit from being considered in the context of this paper, plus I have some information I missed before.

The first involves epithets for Venus in Catullus, Vergil, and Ovid (O'Hara 1990*b*). In Catullus 64.72, Venus is called *Erycina*, 'lady of Sicilian Eryx,' as Catullus describes the erotic suffering of Ariadne: *spinosas Erycina serens in pectore curas* 'the lady of Eryx sowing thorny cares in the heart'. In *Aeneid* 1.720, Vergil refers to Venus by the rare epithet *Acidalia*, as Cupid begins to obey her command to make Dido fall for Aeneas. In *Metamorphoses* 5 Ovid refers to Venus as *Erycina* as she asks Cupid to shoot Pluto with an arrow so that he will love Persephone. Ovid's scene is directly modelled on *Aeneid* 1, but Ovid uses Catullus' epithet *Erycina* as he imitates the scene in which Vergil calls Venus *Acidalia*. Why? Perhaps simply because Ovid's Venus is in Sicily, but my suggestion is that Ovid has noticed that both Catullus and Vergil are engaging in wordplay linking epithets for Venus to 'thorny cares,' *spinosae curae*, Catullus by the resemblance between *Erycina* and the Latin word for the thorny hedgehog, *ericius*, and Vergil by allusion to a derivation, mentioned by Servius, of Acidalia from Greek ἀκίς: 'thorn,' 'dart,' 'care,' 'pang of love.'[29] Scholars have noted that when Ovid imitates Vergil he brings back the arrows of Cupid, which on the literal level are left aside in Vergil, although they figured prominently in Vergil's model in the Eros/Aphrodite/Medea scene in Apollonius' *Argonautica* 3. Ovid's story brings back the literal

---

[29] Hollis (1992) has offered what may be regarded either as a counter-explanation of the epithet Acidalia (making my suggestions unpersuasive), or as further motivation for Vergil's choice. The *Etymologicum Genuinum* explains the epithet Κιδαλία, in a fragment of verse without attribution but that may be Callimachean, as the poet's misreading (we might say, scholarly interpretation) of the words χείρ᾽ Ἀκιδαλίας in a fragment of Pindar as χείρα Κιδαλίας (cf. Callim. fr. inc. 751 Pf.). If Vergil were aware of the passages from Pindar and (?) Callimachus, he could be entering the scholarly debate to offer his support for the reading χείρ᾽ Ἀκιδαλίας. For more wordplay involving thorns (not cited in O'Hara 1990*b*) see McKeown (1989: 202) on *Amores* 1.8.2 and esp. Courtney (1969: 80–1) on Acanthis in Prop. 4.5.

arrows that were absent in Vergil, and Ovid's epithet *Erycina* alludes to the arrows or thorny cares of the epithets in both Catullus and Vergil: Ovid shows that he sees both what Vergil is doing, and that Catullus had done it before.

In *Georgics* 1.217–18 *candidus auratis* aperit *cum cornibus annum* | *Taurus*, 'when Taurus, bright with gilded horns, opens the year'. Vergil implicitly glosses the name *Aprilis*, as if from *aperio*, 'to open.'[30] At *Fasti* 4.87 and following, Ovid explicitly rejects the derivation of *Aprilis* from *aperio* implied by Vergil, favouring instead an etymology involving the name Aphrodite, to whom the start of *Fasti* 4 is dedicated (61–2, 85–90):

sed Veneris mensem Graio sermone notatum
    auguror: a *spumis* est dea dicta maris . . .
Quo non livor abit? sunt qui tibi mensis honorem
    eripuisse velint invideantque, Venus.
nam quia ver *aperit* tunc omnia, densaque cedit
    frigoris asperitas, fetaque terra patet,
Aprilem memorant ab *aperto* tempore dictum,
    quem Venus iniecta vindicat alma manu.

But I divine that the month of Venus is named from the Greek language: the goddess was named after the *foam* (cf. ἀφρός) of the sea . . . Where does envy not come in? Some would envy you, Venus, and want to pilfer the honour of the month. For they say that *April* was named from the *open* time, because spring then opens all things, and the dense, harsh cold departs, and the rich earth *opens*. Kindly Venus stakes her claim and lays her hand upon it.

Danielle Porte[31] has shown, however, that because Ovid's text has so many details about how things open up and bloom in the Spring, Ovid actually provides plenty of evidence for the etymology from *aperio*, especially in lines 125–8:

nec Veneri tempus quam ver erat aptius ullum:
    vere nitent terrae, vere *remissus* ager,

---

[30] See Thomas (1988) ad loc., and cf. McKeown (1987: 55) on Ovid and Hor. *C.* 4.11.14–16.

[31] Porte (1985: 229); her whole section on 'L'étymologie double' is important, especially in the context of discussions of Ovid's 'variant aetiologies' (above n. 25). See also O'Hara (1992), and for different views of this example Newlands (1992: 38 n. 13), and now Herbert-Brown (1994: 81–5).

nunc herbae rupta tellure cacumina tollunt,
  nunc *tumido gemmas cortice palmes agit.*

And no season was more fitting for Venus than spring. In spring the lands glisten; in spring the soil is *loose*; now the grasses raise their tops through the broken ground; now, the *shoot drives its buds from the swelling bark.*

In a sense he is at the same time arguing for the validity of both the derivation from *aperio* and that from Aphrodite. Alternately we might say that the narrator of the *Fasti* endorses the derivation from Aphrodite, while the more subtle poet of the *Fasti* endorses both possibilities.

Ovid's gloss of *Aprilis* does not point with any specificity to Vergil, but this is not the case with my last example, which begins with *Georgics* 1.137–8 (O'Hara 1992):

navita tum stellis numeros et nomina fecit
Pleiadas, Hyadas, claramque Lycaonis Arcton.

Then a *sailor* numbered the stars and named the *Pleiades, Hyades*, and bright Arctos daughter of Lycaon.

Vergil says that sailors first named the stars called Pleiades and Hyades. By saying that *sailors* were the name-givers, Vergil is arguing that, among the many etymologies suggested in antiquity, those having to do with sea-faring are correct: derive Pleiades from πλέω, 'to sail,' because their Spring rising marked the beginning of the sailing season, and Hyades from ὕω, 'to rain,' because their May rising marked the start of Spring rains. It is on the Hyades (which Vergil will gloss twice more in the *Aeneid*)[32] that Ovid offers comment,[33] mentioning at *Fasti* 5.163–6 the 'Hyades, which the Greek sailor calls after the rain,' in a line that resembles Vergil somewhat, but not too distinctively.[34]

at simul inducent obscura crepuscula noctem,
  pars Hyadum toto de grege nulla latet.

[32] Cf. *pluviasque Hyadas* at *Aen.* 1.744 = 3.516, where the adjective glosses the noun; see Brown (1990).
[33] For brief comment on the Pleiades, cf. *Fast.* 3.105–7, with the comments of Brugnoli and Stok (1992: 48–50).
[34] At first glance line 166 more resembles Cic. *Arat.* fr. 29 (quoted and discussed at *ND* 2.111.1) *has Graeci stellas Hyadas vocitare suerunt.* But other features of the passage make allusion to Vergil certain.

ora micant Tauri septem radiantia flammis,
  navita quas Hyadas Graius ab imbre vocat;

But no sooner shall the dusk of twilight lead on the night, than no part of
the whole flock of the Hyades shall be hidden. The head of the Bull sparkles
radiant with seven flames, *which the Greek sailor calls the Hyades after the
rain.*

But Ovid is rejecting this etymology: his story focuses on Hyas, the
brother of the Hyades killed while hunting, from whom Ovid says
they get their name (167–8, 179–82):

pars Bacchum nutrisse putat, pars credidit esse
  Tethyos has neptes Oceanique senis . . .
mater Hyan et Hyan maestae flevere sorores
  cervicemque polo subpositurus Atlas,
victus uterque parens tamen est pietate sororum:
  illa dedit caelum, *nomina fecit Hyas.*

Some think that they nursed Bacchus, some believed that they are the granddaughters of Tethys and old Oceanus . . . His mother wept for Hyas and for
Hyas his sad sisters wept, and Atlas, soon to place his neck under the pole.
And yet both parents were surpassed by the piety of his sisters: it gave them
a place in heaven, but *Hyas gave them their name.*

The phrase *nomina fecit* is noteworthy, for it appears also in *Georgics*
1.138. In fact, before Ovid, *nomina fecit* seems to appear only in
that *Georgics* passage: I believe there are no other examples outside
of Vergil and Ovid of the phrase *nomina fecit*. Ovid uses the phrase
five times, and each of the examples is an etymological aetiology
of a single name, where *nomen fecit* would be more appropriate (if
less metrically convenient).[35] Ovid's acknowledgement of Vergilian
precedent, even when he is disagreeing with Vergil, is unmistakable.

---

[35] The only other uses of *nomina fecit* (in any author) of which I am aware, all
etymological aetiologies: *Fast.* 3.869–70 *dicitur infirma cornu tenuisse sinistra | femina*
(sc. *Helle), cum de se* nomina fecit *aquae*, 4.283–4 *transit et Icarium, lapsas ubi perdidit
alas | Icarus et vastae* nomina fecit *aquae*, 5.149–50 *est moles nativa loco, res* nomina
fecit; | *appellant Saxum; pars bona mentis ea est, Met.* 14.614–16 *regnum Tiberinus ab
illis | cepit et in Tusci demersus fluminis undis |* nomina fecit *aquae.* Cf. O'Hara (1992:
59 n. 35); at that time I checked the Packard Humanities Institute Latin disk, a number
of concordances, and also Schumann (1979–83).

Ovid's passage does more than just reject one etymology in favour of another, however, for he subtly suggests two other possibilities. In 164 the word *grex* is an unusual term for a group of stars; Frazer suggests that Ovid 'alludes to the derivation [of the name Hyades] from ὗς,' 'pig,' which would correspond to the Latin name *suculae*.[36] Furthermore—and here is a detail that I think has not been noticed before—Ovid's reference in line 167 to Bacchus, and to the nymphs that nursed him, alludes to another etymology. A line of Euphorion, and the scholia to Aratus that preserve the line, tell us that Hyas was another name for Dionysus, and so the Hyades (who are mentioned in the Aratean lines being commented upon) were named for having nursed him (Schol. Aratus *Phaen.* 172):

They are named because they raised Dionysus. And Dionysus is (called) Hyas. So Euphorion's (fr. 14.1 Powell) 'angry at bull-horned Dionysus Hyas.'[37]

So here we have at least four possible etymologies: Ovid refers explicitly to, but does not endorse, the connection made by Vergil and others with ὕω 'to rain' (166). He also alludes to the etymologies from ὗς 'pig' (*toto de grege*, 164) and from Dionysus as Hyas (*pars Bacchum nutrisse putat*, 167). Finally he endorses the derivation from Hyas the hunter (*nomina fecit Hyas*, 182), but does so using the distinctly Vergilian phrase *nomina fecit*. Going even further than in the passage from *Fasti* 4 that seemed to endorse two derivations for *Aprilis*, Ovid here seems to suggest that all four possibilities are equally valid.

Close examination of Ovidian commentary on Vergilian etymological wordplay, then, even in this rather cursory survey, points to several conclusions. The first is that Ovid's wordplay is more genuinely learned than some have suggested, and not overly dependent on schoolboy etymologies or handbooks. The second is that Ovid read Vergil with meticulous care (a position to which many scholars have moved in recent years, of course), and enjoyed aspects of Vergil

[36] Aul. Gell. 13.9 = Tullius Tiro fr. 13, *GRF* p. 402: *Sed ὑάδες οὐκ ἀπὸ τῶν ὑῶν, id est non a subus ita ut nostri Opici putaverunt, sed ab eo, quod est ὕειν, appellantur* (cf. Cic. *ND* 2.111.1, Serv. Auct. on *Geo.* 1.138; more in O'Hara 1992).

[37] Cf. Hes. fr. 291 M-W, and also Hesych. s.v. ἔναστρος ὥστε μαινάς· Ἀχαιὸς Ἀλφεσιβοίᾳ (fr. 16) ἀντὶ Ὑάς· τὰς γὰρ Βάκχας Ὑάδας ἔλεγον. But for the latter Nauck-Snell *TGF* p. 750 endorses Valesius' emendation of Ὑάς and Ὑάδας to θυάς and θυάδας.

that some modern readers have neglected. The third goes somewhat beyond the evidence presented here, but both my other research and this paper suggest that it is true: that Ovid's fondness for variant etymologies exceeds that of Vergil, who has a few but not too many of these, and to whose variant explanations of the name *Lupercal* Ovid draws special attention. Ambiguity is hardly in short supply in Vergil in terms of countless thematic matters, but Ovid's etymologizing is more boundless, creative, open-minded, and even contradictory than Vergil's. My fourth and final conclusion: that in the *Fasti*, Ovid's combination of explicit and implicit etymologies in the same passage sometimes makes the poet of the *Fasti* more learned than the narrator of that poem.

6

Lucretius and the Delusions of Narcissus

Philip Hardie

Ever since Heinze's classic discussion (1919) the question of genre has been at the centre of criticism of the *Metamorphoses;* in his important book Stephen Hinds (1987*a*) has demonstrated that the first participant in the debate was none other than Ovid himself, sketching out the positions through the teasingly self-reflexive narrative of his *perpetuum carmen*. In this essay I discuss one episode, the story of Narcissus, which combines *imitatio* of high and low genres, of the lofty scientific didactic of Lucretius and the humble themes of love elegy. This is imitation that is highly alive in a number of ways to the imitative practice and pedagogic strategy of Lucretius himself. In the first place, Lucretius already points to the combination of genres, for the discussion of love at the end of *De Rerum Natura* 4 exploits the topics and clichés of erotic poetry in order to bring out an Epicurean *ratio*. Secondly, Lucretius' poem may be described as an epic in ways that extend beyond the ancient classification of didactic within the genre *epos* by virtue of the hexameter that it shares with the poems of Homer; Lucretius diverts to his own ends an association between heroic epic and natural-philosophical didactic that is deeply embedded in the Latin epic tradition from the time of Ennius, and that continues after Virgil into the hexameter poems of Ovid and Lucan—and beyond (Hardie 1986: 157–240). The *Metamorphoses* is Ovid's answer to the *Aeneid,* a poem that maps out the universal pretensions of Rome: Ovid will give us a poem of still greater scope, one that traces a universal 'history' of which the story of Rome is only a part, albeit a perhaps climactic part. Overt didacticism

frames the whole 'epic', in the philosophical cosmogony of book 1
and the Speech of Pythagoras of book 15; this lengthy philosophical
disquisition at almost the end of the poem looks back to the very
beginning of the Roman hexameter epic, to the Speech of Homer in
the first book of Ennius' *Annals*; the cosmogony and the Speech of
Pythagoras are also both shot through with Lucretian reminiscence.
Thirdly, Ovid's mythological narrative of Echo and Narcissus pointedly reverses the rationalism of Lucretius' materialist account of the
world; this reversal, or inversion, of the model in itself represents
a continuation of Lucretian imitative practice, but turned against
Lucretius.

1.

In book 4 of the *De Rerum Natura* Lucretius, having in the previous book given an account of the nature of the human soul in
terms of atoms and the void, turns to an explanation of the way
in which the soul receives information about the outside world.
Sense-perception, too, is the result of strictly materialist mechanisms, but although each and every sensation and mental image,
whether waking or sleeping, is to be traced to truly existing arrange-
ments of atoms, room for mistaken belief as to the nature of the
external world is opened up in the gap between sensation proper
and the mental judgements that we impose on our perceptions.
Lucretius' scientific account of sense-perception and imagination is
at the same time an exposure of certain powerful types of error that
prevent the attainment of 'calmness' ($\dot{\alpha}\tau\alpha\rho\alpha\xi\dot{\iota}\alpha$), just as the description of the soul in the previous book was directed specifically to
removing the fear of death that results from wrong notions about
the nature of the soul. A key word in book four is *simulacrum*;
indeed the term is the point of departure for the whole discussion
(33–4):

nunc agere incipiam tibi, quod uementer ad has res
attinet, esse ea quae rerum *simulacra* uocamus.

Now I will begin to deal with a topic extremely relevant to these matters, that
there exist what we call images of things.

The word is Janus-headed: like its root, *simulo,* it can refer both to the fitting likeness of image to model (cf. *similis*), a fit which is particularly close in the Epicurean explanation of sense-images as films of atoms which originate as physically part of the objects we perceive, and whose reliability as a record of those objects is guaranteed by their fine texture and by the speed at which they fly to our senses;[1] but it may also refer to the deceptiveness (cf. *simulatio*) of images, which may for various reasons correspond to no substantially existing objects, but nevertheless lead us to believe in the existence of such objects. The first example of such delusive images discussed in book 4 by Lucretius, one chosen to establish a link with the subject-matter of the previous book, is *simulacrum* as image of a dead person, or 'ghost';[2] Lucretius returns to this type of delusion briefly at 733–4 in a discussion of mental representations. In the course of the book he adverts to a much wider range of misleading simulacra: images that correspond to no originals, the result of spontaneously occurring configurations of atoms (129–42); images that distort the nature of their originals (e.g. ship-sterns appearing broken in water, 436–42); images that seem to lead an independent life of their own (e.g. shadows, 364–78); images that come to us in dreams as we sleep (962 ff.). The diatribe against love that concludes the book deals with a different type of *simulacrum*-based delusion, not one that mistakes the existence or shape of the original but one that falsely identifies an object of appetite; the insolidity of the *simulacrum* here teaches a lesson about the vanity of desire.

In the narrative of Narcissus and Echo in *Metamorphoses* 3 Lucretian psychology is transformed into Ovidian mythology. The extent of Ovid's originality in his handling of the stories of

---

[1] Lucretius stresses the speed of *simulacra* at 70–1 and esp. 143–229; with regard to Narcissus' delusion of the ideal responsiveness of his beloved it is worth noting that the phenomenon of reflection provides Lucretius with a useful argument for the speed of *simulacra*   (150 ff.). In a number of places Lucretius seems to hint at a derivation of *simulacrum* from *simul ac* (4.210–12 . . . *quam celeri motu rerum simulacra ferantur,* | *quod simul ac primum sub diu splendor aquai* | *ponitur* . . ., 344–6, 781–2.

[2] *simulacraque luce carentum* 4.39. *simulacrum* is not found in the sense 'ghost' before Lucretius (but may have been so used by Ennius: Skutsch 1985: 155); the pun is calqued on εἴδωλον, Epicurus' word for the atomic image of an object, but also a 'shade of the dead' (*Od.* 11.476 etc.).

Narcissus and Echo is difficult to gauge given the fragmentary state of our knowledge of Hellenistic poetry (S. Eitrem, *RE* xvi 1725.12 ff.; Castiglioni 1906: 215–19; Rosati 1983); the following discussion would tend to the conclusion that his reshaping of the material was very considerable, and that Lucretius' predominantly non-mythological poem was more important in the reworking of the legendary material than hypothetical Hellenistic treatments of the subject-matter. The final impression of Ovid's Echo and Narcissus narrative is almost one of a fantasy based on a dreamlike meditation on the Lucretian discussion of sense-perception and delusion, a subtle example of reflection and echo as mechanisms of literary *imitatio*. In particular Ovid dwells on three of the central concerns of Lucretius' fourth book: i) Auditory and visual illusion. ii) Obsession with ghosts. iii) The snares of love. Verbal echoes of Lucretius litter the surface of the Ovidian text, but it is the combination of these three themes that gives a decisively Lucretian flavour to the narrative, a recognition of Lucretius' imaginative power in forging a unity out of the separate themes of death, love, and delusion.[3]

2. ECHO AND REFLECTION; THE COMEDY
OF THE SENSES

There is no evidence for the conjunction of the stories of Echo and Narcissus before Ovid, though a Hellenistic predecessor is conceivable. In favour of Ovidian innovation it has been pointed out that the intricate parallelism between the stories of Echo and Narcissus in *Metamorphoses* 3 is helped by the linguistic chance that allows Latin to use *imago* to mean 'echo' as well as 'visual image, reflection', whereas in Greek εἰκών in this sense is very rare; Lucretius 4.570–1 (*pars solidis allisa locis reiecta sonorem* | *reddit et interdum frustratur* imagine *uerbi* 'some beating upon solid spots are cast back, and give back the sound, and at times mock us with the echo of a word') is cited as the first example of *imago* in the former

---

[3] For some interesting remarks on Ovid's use of Lucretius 4 see Hinds (1987*a*) 31. In general on Ovid's use of Lucretius see Due (1974) 29–33.

sense.[4] I would suggest that the Lucretian parallel extends further, and that Ovid has been led to the idea of combining echo and reflection by the parallel treatment of the two phenomena in *De Rerum Natura* 4.

The Epicurean explains reflected sound and reflected sight by the same atomist model that accounts for all sensation. In orthodox manner Lucretius makes sight the paradigm case in his discussion of the senses (230–521); next in importance is sound (522–614); finally come taste (615–72) and smell (673–721). At 689–94 we learn that sound and sight, as against smell, share the property of being able to travel long distances without being dissipated. Lucretius devotes much space to the subject of reflection in his treatments of both sight and sound: mirrors are used already at 98–109 to prove the hypothesis of streams of *simulacra* pouring from objects whose likeness they preserve (*similis* 104, 109), and at 150–67 in a demonstration of the great speed at which *simulacra* travel, and mirrors are made the subject of a special section at 269–323. The topic of echo occupies over a third of the discussion of sound (570–94). In detail there is a parallelism between Lucretius' discussion of multiple mirror-images (302–3):

fit quoque de speculo in speculum ut tradatur imago,
quinque etiam sexue ut fieri simulacra suerint.

It also happens that a reflection is relayed from mirror to mirror, so that up to five or six images are produced.

and of multiple echoes (577–8):

sex etiam aut septem loca uidi reddere voces,
unam cum iaceres.

I have seen places that reflect up to six or seven sounds, if you utter one.

A particular concern of Lucretius is the way in which visual and auditory reflection both lead to the illusion of non-existent presences

---

[4] *TLL* 7.1.408.45; the Lucretian usage is noted by Vinge (1967: 12); Rosati (1976: 85, n. 8); Stirrup (1976: 99, n. 5). Ovid points up the coincidence by his carefully balanced descriptions of Narcissus' aural and visual delusions: 3.385 *perstat et alternae* deceptus imagine uocis; 416 *dumque bibit, uisae* conreptus imagine formae.

and sentiences (part of his wider concern to empty the universe of malignant spirituality): the discussion of visual reflection ends with a passage on the tricks that mirrors play (318–21):

> indugredi porro pariter simulacra pedemque
> ponere nobiscum credas gestumque imitari
> propterea quia, de speculi qua parte recedas,
> continuo nequeunt illinc simulacra reuerti.

You would further believe that the images were walking in step with us and imitating our movements, the reason being that the second you move away from a part of the mirror, images cannot return from that part.

The mirror-image of oneself seems to be endowed with independent powers of motion, but it is shown up as in fact the prisoner of the laws of optics (*nequeunt*); there is no one else there. The discussion of echo is largely taken up with an account of how the deserted countryside (573 *loca sola*, 591 *loca deserta*) is peopled with imaginary divine presences as a result of misinterpretation of the acoustic phenomena. The same polemical point is made in the course of the main section on sensory illusion, in a description of the apparent animation of one's shadow, where Lucretius uses language earlier applied to mirror-images (364–9):

> umbra uidetur item nobis in sole moueri
> et uestigia nostra sequi gestumque imitari;
> aera si credis priuatum lumine posse
> indugredi, motus hominum gestumque sequentem.
> nam nil esse potest aliud nisi lumine cassus
> aer id quod nos umbram perhibere suemus.

Again our shadow seems to move in the sun and follow our steps and imitate our movements—if you believe that air devoid of light can walk, imitating the movements and gestures of men. For what we are used to calling a shadow can be nothing but air empty of light.

Lucretius seeks to explode the superstition that would see in the shadow an uncanny presence rather like one of the ghosts of the dead,[5] making instead of the shadow something as truly powerless

---

[5] With *priuatum lumine* and *lumine cassus* cf. 4.39 *simulacraque luce carentum*; the phrase *cassum lumine* is used of the dead Palamedes in *Aen.* 2.85; might it be Ennian in this sense? Cf. *lumen* of the 'light of life' at *Ann.* 109, 137 Skutsch.

as Homer's 'strengthless heads of the dead, souls' (νεκύων ἀμενηνὰ κάρηνα, ψυχαί) which exist only as pale shadows of the former individuals.

This credulity in the independent existence of his reflection is precisely the error of Narcissus (*Met.* 3.432–6):

credule,[6] quid frustra[7] simulacra fugacia captas?
quod petis, est nusquam; quod amas, auertere, perdes![8]
ista repercussae, quam cernis, imaginis umbra est:
nil habet ista sui: tecum uenitque manetque,
tecum discedet, si tu discedere possis.[9]

Gullible boy; why do you catch at fleeting phantoms in vain? What you chase is nowhere; if you turn away, you will lose/destroy what you love. What you see is the shadow of a reflected image; it has no substance of its own. With you it came and stays; with you it will go away; if you could go away.

At 457 ff. Narcissus speaks as the Lucretian fool wondering at the responsive gesturing of his reflection, but imprisoned in the text he is impervious to the Lucretian appeal to realize the *error*[10] of his ways.

For Lucretius the phenomena of sound are to be explained on the hypothesis that *vox* is *corporea* (4.524 ff.); Ovid plays with the paradox of a *corpus* that turns into a *vox* (359 *corpus adhuc Echo, non uox, erat* 'Echo was still a body, not a voice'). [11] The nymph Echo belongs to

---

[6] Cf. *credas* Lucr. 4.319, *credis* 4.366.

[7] Cf. 3.500 frustra *dilecte puer. frustra* and cognate words in Lucretius' discussion of delusion and of love: Lucr. 4.571, 817, 972, 1099.

[8] Narcissus will end up destroying what he loves: *quod amas, auertere, perdes* may mean *either* 'if you turn away you will lose what you love' *or* 'turn away, or else you will destroy what you love': with the latter sense cf. Lucr. 4,1082–3 *et stimuli subsunt qui instigant laedere id ipsum | quodcumque est, rabies unde illaec germina surgunt.*

[9] Narcissus' *umbra*, like the Lucretian shadow, has no substantial independent existence (*nil,* Lucr. 4.368); cf. also 4.320 *de speculi qua parte recedas.*

[10] *Error: Met.* 3.447 *tantus tenet error amantem,* which I take (contra Kenney 1970: 291 and cf. Vinge 1967: 334, n. 48), as words in the mouth of Narcissus which have more meanings than he realizes, playing on elegiac (e.g. Verg. *Ecl.* 8.41, Ov. *Am.* 1.2.35, 1.10.9) and Lucretian senses of *error* (Lucr. 4.824, 997, 1077).

[11] With the slightly strange use at *Met.* 3.357–8 *quae nec reticere loquenti | nec prius ipsa loqui* didicit, compare Lucr. 4.579 *uerba repulsantes iterabant* docta (Lachmann's conjecture) *referri*; see also 4.317, and perhaps Verg. *Ecl.* 1.6 *resonare doces Amaryllida siluas.*

a time before the truths of the Epicurean world are established: her wasting away is the *aition* of the phenomenon we know as echo. It is a time when the bodily presence of sound does indeed betray the presence of *somebody*; when the mythological fantasies that Lucretius dismisses are reality. Lucretius uses the example of wandering through the mountains and calling for straggling companions (4.575–6):

palantis comites cum montis inter opacos
quaerimus et magna dispersos voce ciemus.

When we search amidst the shady mountains for our straying and scattered companions, calling them in a loud voice.

The first person plural sounds incongruously in this romantic picture, which calls up mythical models like the story of Hercules calling in vain for Hylas, the beautiful boy who wanders until he stops at a fatal pool, a favourite neoteric subject which has undoubtedly helped to shape the Ovidian narrative of Echo and Narcissus.[12] Narcissus is another beautiful boy who wanders from his companions (3.379–80):

forte puer comitum seductus ab agmine fido
dixerat 'ecquis adest?', et 'adest!' responderat Echo.

---

[12] Prop. 1.20.49–50 *cui procul Alcides iterat responsa, sed illi | nomen ab extremis montibus aura refert* provides a concrete example of Lucretius' general picture at 4.573 ff.; Virgil gives a vivid impression of what was heard, *Ecl.* 6.43–4 *his adiungit, Hylan nautae quo fonte relictum | clamassent, ut litus 'Hyla, Hyla' omne sonaret*: the metrical effect is reproduced by Ovid in the last words of Narcissus and Echo, 3.501 *dictoque 'uale' 'uale' inquit et Echo.* Note also Propertius' picture of Hylas at the spring, 1.20.41–2 *et modo formosis incumbens nescius undis | errorem blandis tardat imaginibus*; with 35–6, apples on branches overhanging Hylas' pool, cf. *Met.* 3.483–4, the figurative apples over Narcissus' pool. There are also parallels with Valerius Flaccus' Hylas narrative: with *Met.* 3.421, *et dignos Baccho, dignos et Apolline crines* (cf. Val. Fl. 3.538 ff. Juno tells Dryope that Hylas is as good a catch as Bacchus or Apollo); and with *Met.* 3.420, *spectat humi positus geminum, sua lumina, sidus,* and the play on sunlight (see n. 16 below) cf. Val. Fl. 3.558–9, *stagna vaga sic luce micant ubi Cynthia caelo | prospicit aut medii transit rota candida Phoebi.* Is Valerius using Ovid, or a shared source? Gallus? (The enclosing apposition in *geminum, sua lumina, sidus* has been taken for a Gallan mannerism: Skutsch (1956) 198–9.) A different star image is found at Theocr. 13.49 ff., where Hylas falling into the pool is compared to a shooting star.

It happened that the boy had been separated from his faithful band of friends; he said 'Is anyone here?', and 'Here' answered Echo.

The *loca deserta* are full of voices that suggest presence and the possibility of meeting (*adest, coeamus, sit tibi copia nostri*). There is an illogicality in the Ovidian text in the words (385) 'deceived by the reflection of his voice', which imply the everyday, Lucretian world in which the echo has no substance but where we may be deluded into believing that it is the voice of another intelligence. It is true that Narcissus fails to realize that the words he hears are the words that he has just spoken, and to that extent he is 'deceived', but in another sense he is not deluded in his belief that what he hears are sounds expressing the thoughts of another person.[13] There is another tension between the real and the imaginary worlds in the coyness of the otherwise forward Echo, which defers her appearance until the (satisfyingly lascivious) word *coeamus*, when *adest* might have been an adequate cue; again this is how echoes behave in our world, whereas in the Ovidian world Narcissus' words have the effect of conjuring up one of those nymphs that for Lucretius are merely the fictional products of imagination (4.580 ff.).[14]

Ovid creates a mythological drama out of a psychological account of the delusions of the senses of sound and sight; he also plays with a third sense, touch. Narcissus is the untouched, *uirgo intacta,* in the reworking of Catullus (62.42–5) at 355:

nulli illum iuvenes, nullae *tetigere* puellae.

No youths touched him, no girls.

multi illum pueri, multae optauere puellae;
idem cum tenui carptus defloruit ungui,
nulli illum pueri, nullae optauere puellae;
sic uirgo, dum *intacta* manet, dum cara suis est.

[13] Ovid also plays on the paradoxical substantiality of this echo at 386 *libentius* and 388 *uerbis . . . suis.*

[14] But in another way Narcissus' experience corresponds to the physics of the Lucretian world: his inability to see Echo until she comes out of the woods (388) is in keeping with Lucretius' explanation of how it is that we can hear voices through closed doors but not see the bodies that produce them, 595–611. In 'remythologizing' this particular passage of Lucretius Ovid has a predecessor in Virgil: see Hardie (1986) 218–19.

Many boys desire it, many girls. But once a tender fingernail has picked it and it has withered, no boys desire it, no girls. Just so a maiden is dear to her friends, as long as she is untouched.

The punishment for Narcissus' pride and his refusal to be 'touched' in the sexual sense is his absolute inability to touch the object of his desire (*quod tangere non est*, 478), as he realizes his earlier error (*posse putes tangi*, 453). Of taste and smell, however, Ovid makes nothing.

3. GHOSTS AND THE UNDERWORLD

For Lucretius *simulacra* of sense may be as delusive as the traditional belief in ghosts; in the Epicurean system, indeed, ghosts are to be explained as atomic *eidola* ('images') of the same nature as sense-images. Ovid, too, mingles with his comedy of the senses a story of the Underworld. The narrative of Echo showed us a desert paradoxically full of presence; not thus inhabited is the mysterious fountain where Narcissus himself is doomed to dwindle away to nothing more than a small flower (509 *nusquam corpus erat*). Apart from Narcissus the only presences are the *simulacra* he sees in the pool. It is a deathlike place;[15] perhaps the pool itself is an upwelling of the waters of Hades, another Avernus. Like Virgil's Avernus shaded by a wood impervious to the sun (412; cf. *Aen.* 6.238)[16] the fountain is disturbed by no birds (409 f.), *quem nulla uolucris* | . . . *turbarat*—ἄ-ορνος.[17] It is an opening through which Narcissus sees into a world beneath his feet, and what stares back is an *umbra* (417 *spem sine corpore amat, corpus putat esse quod umbra est*).[18] As he stares at this pool, Narcissus' humanly

---

[15] So Vinge (1967) 17. On the further connections of the ναρκίσσος with the Underworld see: Rosati (1983) 13–14, Richardson (1974) on *Hom. Hymn. Dem.* 8.

[16] It is lit only by the 'stars' of Narcissus' eyes, 420 *spectat humi positus geminum, sua lumina, sidus*; cf. perhaps *Aen.* 6.641 *solemque suum, sua sidera norunt*. At *Met.* 3.412 in the ecphrasis of the pool we hear of *siluaque sole locum passura tepescere nullo*; in the final simile, 487–9, Narcissus melts away *ut intabescere . . . matutinaeque pruinae* | *sole tepente solent*: his 'own sun'? Lucretius also writes of stars reflected in water: Lucr. 4.213 *sidera respondent in aqua radiantia mundi*.

[17] Cf. Lucr. 6.738 ff.; Austin on *Aen.* 6.242.

[18] In line 417 I take *umbra* (cf. 434), not *unda*, to be the correct reading (Rosati 1983: 4): it is not true to say that the reflection 'is water'. For examples of

satiable thirst turns into one of those Hellishly insatiable thirsts or hungers, ever raging just out of reach of the objects that might satisfy it, *inops* amidst *copia* (466). The language of his vain attempts to reach the deceptive *simulacrum* is the language of Tantalus: *fallax* (427), *capto* (428), *fugio* (456), *refugio* (477).[19] At the end the image of thirst amidst the flood is replaced implicitly by that of hunger for forbidden fruits, in the simile comparing the blush on his beaten breast to ripening apples or grapes, a vision that precipitates his final evanescence; these apples he can no more reach out and pick than could Tantalus.[20] Narcissus' Tantalizing desire may be viewed as one

umbra = 'reflection' (in both water and mirrors) see Shackleton Bailey (1956) 86. Reflections and shadows are often thought of as analogous, scientifically in Lucretius, who further points up the *corpus/umbra* distinction in his discussion of shadows, 4.373–4 *propterea fit uti videatur, quae fuit* umbra | corporis, *e regione eadem nos usque secuta.* Lucretius fantasizes on reflections in water as offering a view into the Underworld: 4.416 ff. *despectum praebet sub terras impete tanto,* | *a terris quantum caeli patet altus hiatus;* | *nubila despicere et caelum ut videare uidere et* | *corpora mirando sub terras abdita caelo*, with the echoes of Hes. *Theog.* 720, *Il.* 8.16. Virgil's version of the topos at *Aen.* 6.577–9 echoes the language of Lucr. 4.414 ff.; cf. also the confusion of sky and Hades at Lucr. 4.168 ff. Ovid may also think of the belief that lies behind Prop. 4.1.106 *umbraue quae magicis mortua prodit aquis*; Butler and Barber compare Cic. *Tusc.* 1.37 *inde in uicinia nostra* Averni *lacus 'unde animae excitantur obscura umbra; aperto ex ostio* | *altae Acheruntis.'* The attempt to evoke an *umbra* from the lower world also recalls the story of Orpheus and Eurydice (so Schickel 1962: 487); cf. Verg. *Georg.* 4.501 *prensantem nequiquam umbras*. There is of course the ironic contrast that the 'presence' of Narcissus' beloved is wholly dependent on the lover's gaze. Narcissus' experience is also that of Aeneas trying to embrace the *simulacrum atque ipsius umbra Creusae* (*Aen.* 2.772): *ter frustra comprensa manus effugit imago* (2.793 = 6.701).

[19] e.g. Prop. 2.17.5–6 *vel tu Tantalea moveare ad flumina sorte,* | *ut liquor arenti fallat ab ore sitim*; 4.11.24; Hor. *Serm.* 1.68 *Tantalus a labris sitiens fugientia captat* | *flumina*; Ov. *Met.* 10.41–2 *nec Tantalus undam* | *captauit refugam; Her.* 18.173 ff. (Hero and Leander) runs closely parallel to the Narcissus story: *quid mihi, quod lato non separor aequore, prodest?* | *num minus haec nobis tam breuis obstat aqua?* | . . . *quo propius nunc es, flamma propiore calesco,* | *et res non semper, spes mihi semper adest.* | *paene manu, quod amo, tanta est vicinia, tango.* | . . . *velle quid est fugientia prendere poma* | *spemque suo refugi fluminis ore sequi?* Cf. also *Ibis* 177–8 *poma pater Pelopis praesentia quaerit et idem* | *semper eget liquidis semper abundat aquis.*

[20] Vinge (1967) takes the fruit simile as an image of Narcissus' hunger. Don Fowler points out the echo of the epithalamium topic of the bride as a flower or fruit to be plucked (note especially Sappho 105a L-P); Narcissus will never 'ripen' in a consummated relationship, like the *uua nondum matura* of 484–5 (on the erotic topos of unripe grapes see Nisbet and Hubbard on Hor. *Carm.* 2.5.10). The Narcissus episode began with allusion to the untouched flower image of Catullus 62, a marriage song, and ends with Narcissus as a literal flower, the only form in which he can be

of those self-inflicted Hells on Earth that Lucretius allegorizes out of the traditional stories about the Underworld at 3.978 ff.; but it is also a divinely imposed punishment for Narcissus' erotic *superbia* (406), one in a chain of such dooms that motivates the whole Echo and Narcissus narrative. The fatal pool is still in the world above, and Narcissus is still a living human being; in the nature of things his torment cannot be eternal, and a Tantalus on earth starves as a result of his deprivation. The story reaches its final conclusion only with the disembodiment of Narcissus, and with the transformation of his pains on earth into a literal Tartarean torture (504):

tum quoque se, postquam est inferna sede receptus,
in Stygia spectabat aqua.

Even then, after he was admitted to the Underworld, he gazed at himself in the waters of the Styx.

A love between *umbra* and *umbra*,[21] as well-matched as the 'responsive cares and equal love' of the shades of Sychaeus and Dido, but also the final horror of desire unfulfilled to eternity.[22]

4. THE SNARES OF LOVE

In book 3 of the *De Rerum Natura* Tantalus is taken as a figure of the superstitious man oppressed by imaginary terrors hanging over him (3.980–3); it is Tityos, eaten away by the cares of his passion (984–94), who symbolizes the lover. In book 4, developing a parallel between

plucked; at the end of his affair with Lesbia Catullus is a 'flower', 'deflowered' (*tactus*) by Lesbia's wickedness (Cat. 11.22 ff., a poem that plays with epithalamium imagery). Epithalamium and blushing: Lyne 1983: 59–60.

[21] 'A shade gazing at a shade', Brenkman (1976: 325). Cf. the pointedly paradoxical formulation of Underworld punishments at *Met.* 4.458 ff.

[22] There is a teasing similarity between the above 'infernal' interpretation of the Narcissus story and the allegorization by Plotinus, *Enn.* 1.6.8, of a version of the story in which Narcissus falls into the pool as the descent of the soul into the 'Hades' of the world of matter; is it possible that there was already before Ovid an interpretation (of whatever kind) of the myth as a story about the Underworld? Plotinus' image of grasping after the *eidolon* of bodily beauty alludes to Plato *Symp.* 212a1 ff., a dialogue that may also have been in Ovid's mind: see note 35 below.

the lover and the sleeper, Lucretius compares the futile attempts of the former to assuage his desire to a dreamer (4.1097–104):

ut bibere in somnis sitiens cum quaerit et umor
non datur, ardorem qui membris stinguere possit,
sed laticum simulacra petit frustraque laborat
in medioque sitit torrenti flumine potans,
sic in amore Venus simulacris ludit [23] amantis
nec satiare queunt spectando corpora coram
nec manibus quicquam teneris abradere membris
possunt errantes incerti corpore toto.

Just as in a dream when a thirsty man wants to drink and finds no water to slake his burning body, but strains after phantoms of water and toils in vain, and thirsts as he drinks in the middle of a raging river, so in love Venus tricks lovers with phantoms, and they cannot sate themselves by gazing at bodies face to face, nor can they scrape off anything from the soft limbs as their hands wander aimlessly all over the body.

Lucretius refers to the experience of drinking imaginary water in a dream without quenching a thirst, but he is also thinking of the slightly different situation of Tantalus.[24] Lucretius' argument has moved from an account of the *simulacra* responsible for dreams, through the particular case of wet dreams, to a general discussion of sexual desire, and so to the delusions and frustrations of the lover. The lover is at the mercy of *simulacra*, atomic film-images coming from the object of his desire; his sexual appetite has no other object than these flimsy phantoms, and hence there is no possibility of ever satisfying the appetite, unlike the appetites of hunger and thirst which can easily be assuaged by the ingestion of quantities of food and drink.[25] Ovid's story of Narcissus' self-infatuation begins with the

---

[23] Cf. *Met.* 3.366 *delusa*, 403 *luserat*.

[24] See R. D. Brown (1987) ad loc., who notes that Lucilius 140 M may use Tantalus as an image of unsatisfied sexual desire (Marx compares *AP* 5.235, 245, Paul the Silentiary). Cf. Prop. 1.9.15–16 *quid si non esset facilis tibi copia? nunc tu | insanus medio flumine quaeris aquam*, where allusion to Tantalus is made more likely by the reference to the wheel of Ixion in line 20; Ov. *Am.* 2.2.43–4 *quaerit aquas in aquis . . . | Tantalus*; Ach. Tat. 2.35, evanescent beauty of boys like τῷ τοῦ Ταντάλου πώματι.

[25] Lucr. 4.858–76. Lucretius' choice of vocabulary prepares the way for the discussion of the appetite of love: *amorem . . . edendi* 869, *ieiuna cupido* 876. Lucretius uses

contrast between a literal thirst, raised by exercise and heat, and a figurative thirst (3.413–17):

hic puer et studio uenandi lassus et aestu
procubuit faciemque loci fontemque secutus,
dumque sitim sedare cupit, sitis altera crevit,[26]
dumque bibit, uisae conreptus imagine formae
spem sine corpore amat, corpus putat esse quod umbra est.

Here the boy, exhausted by the exertions of the hunt and by the heat, threw himself down, attracted by the look of the place and the spring; and as he longed to slake his thirst, another thirst grew on him. As he drinks, enraptured by the image of the shape he sees, his hope of love is for something without a body, and he takes a shadow for a body.

Narcissus becomes the Lucretian lover, thirst raging in the midst of water. Ovid cleverly merges Lucretian simile and physics: Narcissus' 'thirst' is aroused by *simulacra* that literally come from water; the more he 'drinks in' the reflections from the pool the more his thirst burns him. Lucretius also plays with the opposites of fire and water, in the paradox of a thirst that is increased by drinking, 4.1100;[27] the fallacy lies in believing that the source of an appetite can also yield its satisfaction (1086–7):

namque in eo spes[28] est, unde est ardoris origo,[29]
restingui[30] quoque posse ab eodem corpore flammam.

For the hope is that the fire can be put out by the same body that is the source of the burning.

---

explere of the satisfaction of hunger and thirst, 4.876, 1093 (with Brown ad loc.): cf. *Met.* 3.439 *inexpleto … lumine.*

[26] The Lucretian parallel in this line is noted by Henderson ad loc., Stirrup (1976) 101 n.11.

[27] There is a pun in torrenti *flumine* (compare the related puns in Enn. *Ann.* 478 Skutsch, *rigidoque Calore*, and Verg. *Aen.* 11.659 *flumina* Thermodontis, if *pulsant* in the next line means that the river is frozen).

[28] *Met.* 3.417 *spem sine corpore amat*; Lucr. 4.1096 *quae vento spes raptast saepe misella.*

[29] *origo* is not in fact common of a source of water (e.g. Hor. *Carm.* 4.14.45), though *oriri* is frequently used of rivers.

[30] Narcissus' inability to 'extinguish' the flames of his passion leads to the 'extinction' of himself, 3.470 *extinguor.*

Ovid makes much of the paradoxes of fire and water: Narcissus' erotic thirst is aroused by a reflection in *water*; fire and liquefaction coincide in the final similes of the melting of wax and frost at 3.487–90, where there is again much Lucretian material.[31]

From the conceits of fire and water Lucretius turns to the moralizing topos of the impossibility of satisfying erotic appetite by increase in possession (1088–90):

quod fieri contra totum natura repugnat;[32]
unaque res haec est, cuius quam plurima habemus,
tam magis ardescit dira cuppedine pectus.

Nature protests that entirely the opposite happens: this is the one thing, the more of which we have, the more our breasts burn with terrible desire.

Narcissus puts it thus (3.466):

quod cupio mecum est: inopem[33] me copia fecit.[34]

What I desire is in my possession: my riches make me poor.

By the Lucretian paradox Narcissus' desire must be infinite, for he could not possess more of what it is that he desires. Furthermore

---

[31] Lucr. 6.515–16 (rain produced by the action of the sun on clouds) *quasi igni | cera super calida tabescens multa liquescat*; 4.1114 *liquescunt,* orgasm leading to a brief respite in *ardor*; 1120 *tabescunt: Met.* 3.445 *tabuerit.* Part of Ovid's game in the Narcissus story consists in the literal realization of *sermo amatorius:* e.g. Narcissus *does* perish (cf. 3.440 *perit*) of his love, he *does* destroy the object of his love (433 *perdes*: cf. Hor. *Carm.* 1.8.3, Ov. *Am.* 2.18.10), he *does* 'waste away to nothing', melted by the 'flame' of his love: this tactic coincides with the Lucretian ploy of revealing the literal truth hidden behind such clichés, which contributes to his brutal physical reduction of love. The double simile of melting frost and melting wax may owe something to the double simile of melting snow and melting wax doll of Erysichthon's wasting away from an insatiable appetite for literal food and drink, Call. *Hymn.* 6.91 f., a work very well known to Ovid and which shows other parallels with the latter's reworking of the Narcissus story, and note that in his Erysichthon narrative Ovid both uses the Lucretian motif of trying to satisfy a real appetite (here hunger) in a dream, 8.824–7, and also echoes his own Narcissus narrative.

[32] Cf. *Met.* 3.375–7 *o quotiens uoluit blandis accedere dictis | et molles adhibere preces!* natura repugnat | *nec sinit, incipiat*—a very unLucretian *natura! Flammam* occupies final position in the preceding line in Lucretius (1087); *flammas* the same position in *Met.* 3.374.

[33] Cf. Lucr. 4.1142 *in aduerso vero atque inopi [amore].*

[34] Cf. Prop. 1.9.15–16 *quid si non esset facilis tibi copia? nunc tu | insanus medio flumine quaeris aquam.*

he has already achieved the impossible wish of the Lucretian lover (4.1111) *penetrare et abire in corpus corpore toto* 'to penetrate and merge with the body with one's whole body';[35] but he finds that this absolute degree of possession is in fact absolute deprivation. Despite his privileged situation, Narcissus is condemned to the insatiable gazing of the Lucretian lover (cf. Lucr. 4.1102), who can never get past the surface, lured on by the *simulacra* that stream from the superficies of the body;[36] the surface of the pool is for him both a window on to perfect delight and the uncrossable barrier between him and the consummation of his desire. Indeed he is in an even worse plight than his Lucretian counterpart, for he cannot even *touch* the outside of the beloved body.

Narcissus eventually 'wakes up' from his delusion, at the point when he realizes that his reflection is soundless. But this sudden access of self-knowledge cannot free him, chained as he is to himself (3.467–8):

o utinam a nostro secedere corpore possem!
uotum in amante nouum: uellem quod amamus abesset.

Would that I could be separated from my body! Strange wish for a lover: I'd like the object of my love to be absent.

In a sense his wish is already fulfilled, for there is no real presence in the pool (433 *quod petis est nusquam,* unlike the self-presentation of Echo, with the word *adest,* 380); of Narcissus it can be said in the words of Lucretius, but with a different meaning (4.1061–2):

nam si abest quod ames, praesto simulacra tamen sunt
illius . . .

---

[35] Lucretius may remember the speech of Aristophanes in the *Symposium,* which tells of the ever-frustrated desire of the human individual to join up in the primal union with his or her other half. Ovid's Narcissus suffers the fate of the Aristophanic halved beings before Zeus turned round their genitals (*Symp.* 191a8), ἀπέθνῃσκον ὑπὸ λιμοῦ καὶ ἄλλης ἀργίας διὰ τὸ μηδὲν ἐθέλειν χωρὶς ἀλλήλων ποιεῖν. In the world of the *Metamorphoses* the lover's fantastic wish for the commingling of individuals is realized in the story of Hermaphroditus and Salmacis, 4.373–9. Suggestive for Ovid's Narcissus is also the language of *Symp.* 212a3 ff. (the vision of the Beautiful), ὁρῶντι ᾧ ὁρατὸν τὸ καλόν, τίκτειν οὐκ εἴδωλα ἀρετῆς, ἅτε οὐκ εἰδώλου ἐφαπτομένῳ, κτλ.

[36] Lucretius stresses the fact that the *simulacra* of sight come from the *surface* of bodies: 4.49 *mittier ab rebus summo de corpore rerum;* cf. also 72 ff., 90 ff.

For if the object of your love is absent, yet images of it are present.

Lucretius continues (1063–4):

sed fugitare decet simulacra et pabula amoris
absterrere sibi atque alio conuertere mentem.

But it is right to shun the images and keep the food of love away from oneself and turn one's mind elsewhere.

In the full awareness of what kind of food it is that he craves Narcissus persists in his demand (*Met.* 3.478–9):

liceat, quod tangere non est,
adspicere et misero praebere alimenta furori.

Let me look at what I may not touch, and supply food to my unhappy passion.

Narcissus knows that this is food that will fuel his *furor* but never satisfy the appetite, never yield him *fructus,* except of the Tantalean variety of the figurative fruits of 483–5.[37] Here too Ovid runs parallel with the Lucretian text. *Nec Veneris* fructu *caret is qui vitat amorem* (4.1073), whereas for the lover in the heat of his passion *nec constat quid primum oculis manibusque* fruantur 'they cannot decide what their eyes and hands should *enjoy* first' (1078); in these passages the image in *fructus, frui* may be primarily from the law of property,[38] but a little later *frui* recurs in a context where the language of vegetable growth is dominant, in the description of the lovers' approach to their final paroxysm at 1105–7:

denique cum membris collatis flore fruuntur
aetatis, iam cum praesagit gaudia corpus
atque in eost Venus ut muliebria conserat arua ...

At last when their limbs join and they enjoy the flower of youth, when the body has a foretaste of joy and Venus is on the point of sowing the field of the woman's body ...

---

[37] *Simulacrum* may also mean a 'comparison' (Lucr. 2.112); perhaps the ultimate fruitlessness of Narcissus' desire is signalled by his attempt to feed on a literary *simulacrum,* or simile.

[38] So Brown (1987) ad loc.

But of their love there is no final emotional fructification, in contrast
to the purely physiological fertility of the sexual act.[39]

5.

Ovid has made out of Lucretian psychology an endlessly fascinating
and provocative fable; does the story of Narcissus contain any
comment or judgment on Epicurean ethics? H. Fränkel (1945: 82 ff.)
saw in the story a moral allegory, but most modern interpreters
have denied any didactic seriousness to the story. But perhaps
there is a more earnest message underlying the tricks with mirrors,
and the point to grasp it is surely the crisis at which Narcissus
realizes his error and the impossibility of rectifying it. Ovid,
perhaps for the first time, combines two versions of the Narcissus
story, one in which the boy does not realize that it is himself he
loves, and another in which the self-infatuation is fully conscious
(Zanker 1966: 152; Rosati 1976: 98 ff.). There is thus engineered
an ἀναγνώρισις of a tragic kind; knowledge of the ἁμαρτία leads to
self-destruction. Behind the Narcissus story there hovers the figure
of the Sophoclean Oedipus, the glaring absence from the narrative
surface of Ovid's Theban books, *Metamorphoses* 3 and 4, but a
ghostly presence in much of the drama of blindness, sight, and
insight, particularly of the third book.[40] Narcissus' catastrophe is also
Oedipus': he comes to know himself, as Teiresias had warned long ago
(3.346–8):

> de quo consultus, an esset
> tempora maturae uisurus longa senectae,
> fatidicus uates 'si se non nouerit'[41] inquit.

[39] Cf. also 1083 *rabies unde illaec germina surgunt*; 1134 *surgit amari aliquid
quod in ipsis floribus angat;* note also 1093–5 *hoc facile expletur laticum* frugum*que
cupido.* | *ex homini vero facie pulchroque colore* | *nil datur in corpus praeter simulacra
fruendum.*

[40] For other tragic associations in the Narcissus story see Davis (1978).

[41] Note the philosophical topos of the mirror as an instrument of self-knowledge,
especially Sen. *Quaest. Nat.* 1.17.4 *inuenta sunt specula, ut homo ipse* se nosset ... (5)
fons cuique perlucidus aut leue saxum imaginem reddit; and see Oltramare (1926)
174.

When consulted whether he would live to see long years of a ripe old age, the prophetic seer said 'If he does not know himself.'

In tragedy obedience to the Delphic precept leads to knowledge but not to salvation; in the later stages of the genre the dilemmas of the tragic protagonist may become a deliberate challenge to the intellectualist ethics of a Socrates: Medea acts in full self-knowledge of what she does; Ovid made of the plight of the Euripidean heroine both another tragedy and a famous epigram, *uideo meliora proboque,* | *deteriora sequor* 'I see the better and approve it, but I follow the worse' (*Met.* 7.20–1). The story of Echo and Narcissus may be taken as an implied rebuke to the Epicurean version of Greek ethical intellectualism: it is not enough, as Lucretius will have us believe, to have knowledge of the universe and of oneself (and books 3 and 4 of the *De Rerum Natura* may be read as an extended essay on the theme of γνῶθι σεαυτόν 'know yourself'); there are events in the human world that lie outside our control. No more than Gallus could find in the pastoral world a cure for the wounds of the elegiac lover[42] can Narcissus find release from his erotic *error* by a Lucretian cultivation of self-awareness. *Iste ego sum! sensi, nec me mea fallit imago* (*Met.* 3.463): but the overcoming of fallacy in the Lucretian sense (cf. Lucr. 4.379, 464) does nothing to mitigate the despair caused by erotic deception; one of the two senses of *fallis* at 454 remains.[43] The gap between Ovidian and Lucretian psychologies is also forced on us by an ambiguity in the words *male sanus* at *Met.* 3.474, *dixit et ad faciem rediit male sanus eandem.* To quote Henderson ad loc.: '*male* often negatives laudatory or neutral epithets, whereas it intensifies pejorative ones'; the question is precisely whether Lucretian 'sanity' is a good or a bad thing for Narcissus. *Male sanus* may be taken both as 'insane' (the normal

---

[42] On the elegiac elements in the Narcissus story see Knox (1986*a*) 19–22; Rosati (1976) 93, n. 26; Tränkle (1963) 471; Galinsky (1974). The combination of natural philosophy and *sermo amatorius* is of course already central to Lucretius' treatment of love in book 4.

[43] *Fallo* in an erotic sense: *Ars* 1.346–7 The hexameter ending *fallit imago* echoes Verg. *Ecl.* 2.27 (Corydon viewing his reflection in water; *Eclogue* 2 is alluded to elsewhere in Ovid's Narcissus narrative); A. Traina (1965: 72) points out that Virgil in this line adds Epicurean, perhaps specifically Lucretian, physics to the Theocritean poetic model.

sense of the collocation, as of the infatuated Dido at *Aeneid* 4.8),[44] but also 'all too sane', in that the release from delusion brought by self-knowledge leads to an intolerable situation.[45] This is a world whose harsh truths are available not to the philosopher, but to that most anti-Lucretian of figures the *fatidicus uates* Teiresias (3.348).

6.

To be fair to Lucretius, he had recognized that, once trapped in the snares of love, escape is not easy, although he does sketch out a *Remedia Amoris* (1149–50):

et tamen implicitus quoque possis inque peditus
effugere infestum, *nisi tute tibi obuius obstes.*[46]

And yet even when trammelled and fettered you might escape the snare, *unless you still stand in your own way.*

That, of course, is precisely Narcissus' problem, although his special dilemma is obviously not what Lucretius has in mind. Nevertheless his words, detached from their context, will yield the Ovidian sense. I

---

[44] Narcissus is still in the grip of the *furor* of 350.

[45] The general point is made by Manuwald (1975: 361). Compare the *gratissimus error* of the Argive theatre-buff, Hor. *Epist.* 2.2.140. That unfortunate found no pleasure when *redit ad sese* (138); the common phrase (used by Lucretius at 4.997, 1023) may also lurk behind *Met.* 3.474 *dixit et ad faciem rediit male sanus eandem:* the same and yet not the same, for to the *simulacrum* has now been attached a different *opinatus animi* (Lucr. 4.465); Narcissus knows that he is 'coming to himself'. Note also Lucr. 4.1075–6 *nam certe purast* sanis *magis inde uoluptas | quam miseris;* Narcissus assigns himself to the latter category, *Met.* 3.479 misero *praebere alimenta furori*. The words *ad faciem eandem* (474) also play with the language of metamorphosis: *redire in/ad* may mean 'to turn back into', and see Hinds (1987a: 93) on the frequency of *facies* in transformation scenes. This is a change that operates through sameness, in the temporal gap between the two understandings of *eandem,* the reader's and Narcissus'.

[46] The identity of Narcissus with the object of his love, the feature that distinguishes Narcissism from other forms of desire, is of course the device which enables Ovid completely to transform the Lucretian discussions of love and delusion, but even here Ovid may play with Epicurean ideas of self-sufficiency and of happiness as the result of a correct relationship with the self: cf. in particular Lucr. 3.1068–70 on the discontents of the unenlightened, *hoc se quisque modo fugit, at quem scilicet, ut fit, | effugere haud potis est, ingratis haeret et odit | propterea, morbi quia causam non tenet aeger* (cf. Nisbet and Hubbard on Hor. *Carm.* 2.16.20).

want to suggest that reflection also provides a model for the *imitatio* practised on the Lucretian text by Ovid. It is clear that reflection in the Narcissus and Echo stories is not limited by the literal descriptions of echoing and mirroring; duplication also structures the narrative itself, above all in the exquisitely ironic parallelism between the Echo and Narcissus sections (Skinner 1965: 59–61; Stirrup 1976: 97–101). To this mirroring within the text may be added a third level of reflection, one that operates *between* the texts of Lucretius and Ovid. In this respect it is Echo rather than Narcissus who represents the later poet, picking up the words and themes of the earlier poet and making of them *sua uerba*,[47] but Ovid's narrative economy ensures that the distortions imposed on Narcissus' words by Echo are similar in kind to the ironic double meanings in Narcissus' later addresses to himself. One may finally note that Ovid's imitative practice is not unlike the distortions and inversions which Lucretius forced on *his* poetic predecessors.[48]

[47] For an interesting essay in applying the notion of echo to poetic influence see Hollander 1981. It has been common since the Romantics to see in Narcissus a figure of the artist or poet; Rosati (1983) argues vigorously for a self-referential reading of the Ovidian tale.

[48] See my discussion (1986: 223 ff.) of Virgil's imitation of Lucretius. The revenge taken on Lucretius by Ovid may be set beside the biographical fiction of Lucretius and the love-potion.

7

Other Voices in Ovid's 'Aeneid'

Sergio Casali

Dixit insipiens in corde suo 'Non est Deus'. *Psalms* 13.1

1. THE DEPARTURE FROM TROY: OTHER VOICES AND OTHER SILENCES

Aeneas is leaving Troy (*Met.* 13.623-6):[1]

Non tamen euersam Troiae cum moenibus esse
spem quoque fata sinunt: sacra et, sacra altera, patrem
fert umeris, uenerabile onus, Cythereius heros.
de tantis opibus praedam pius eligit illam
Ascaniumque suum . . .

And yet the fates do not permit Troy's hope to be overturned with her walls. The heroic son of Cytherea bears away upon his shoulders the sacred objects and, another sacred object, his father, a venerable burden. Of all his great possessions, the dutiful man chose that prize, and his son Ascanius . . .

In his introductory note to *Met.* 13.623 ff., Franz Bömer (1982: 363) prints a useful chart, summarizing the Virgilian and Ovidian versions of the journey of Aeneas from Troy to Sicily: in the left-hand column, the events of the *Aeneid*; in the right, those of the *Metamorphoses*.

---

[1] For a sketch of the critical debate on Ovid's 'Aeneid', see Baldo (1995) 29–37. Among the later contributions, see especially Hinds (1998) 104–22; Thomas (2001) 78–84.

The first point of comparison, then, is presentec
721–804: Flight from Troy; Creusa. Ovid: XIII 623–
Troy.' Obviously, Creusa is missing in Ovid. With ł
Ovid's reader will probably think that this absence
little account, in view of the fact that poor Creusa
disappear also from the following notes, which will b
the analysis of single verses. All the more so, since, on tł subject of
Aeneas' departure from Troy, we will be told (368) that 'an intentional
contrast with Virgil cannot be securely identified.'

Now it is clear that Ovid is alluding to another tradition about
Aeneas' departure from Troy, probably the one in which the
victorious Greeks allowed him to choose only one thing to take
away with him; and he chose his father. Impressed by this choice,
the Greeks granted him a second, and he chose the Penates. In
admiration the Greeks allowed him to take whatever he wanted.[2]
Certainly, Ovid's formulation does not exclude a presupposition
of the Virgilian version of events. But to be sure, it obviously
also does not rule out that things could have gone differently;
on the contrary, it makes it clear that Virgil is only *one of the
versions*, and there are others. There is one that the reader could
recall, in which Aeneas is positively guilty of treason.[3] Above all,
he could also recall that if Aeneas chose the Penates, his father,

---

[2] Thus Varro, *Rer. Hum.* fr. 9 Mirsch = Serv. Dan. *Aen.* 2.636, who suggests that the
formulation in *Aen.* 2.635–6 (*genitor, quem tollere in altos* | *optabam* primum *montis*
primumque *petebam*) alludes to Varro's version of the series of choices; cf. also Schol.
Ver. *Aen.* 2.717, pp. 106–7 Baschera. The same account is found in Diod. 7.4; cf. [Xen.]
Cyn. 1.15. The story that it was the Greeks who permitted Aeneas to leave Troy, with
some variants, was known since Hellanicus, *FGrHist* 4 F 31 = fr. 77 Ambaglio (in D.H.
1.47.4, the Achaeans permit Aeneas to leave Troy with the riches that they had saved
in their flight); cf. Lycophr. 1263–9 (the Achaeans allow Aeneas to take away the thing
he most desires: he chooses the Penates, neglecting wife and son, and leaves with
his father); Aelian, *Var. Hist.* 3.22; [Apollod.] *Epit.* 5.21; Quint. Smyrn. 13.334–49.
Cf. Barchiesi (1962) 349–52; Galinsky (1969*a*) 43–6; Càssola (1991) 276–85. Ovid's
allusion to this alternative tradition was first recognized by Stitz (1962) 25–6.

[3] Cf., e.g., Menecrates of Xanthos, *FGrHist* 769 F 3 (= D.H. 1.48.3); Dict. Cret.
4.22; Dares Phryg. 40–2; on this, see Ussani (1947) and (1952) vii–xviii; Galinsky
(1969*a*) 46–51, who, among other things, interprets Naev. fr. 23 Mor/Strz (*blande et
docte percontat, Aeneas quo pacto* | *Troiam liquerit*) in light of the versions of the flight
that are less honourable to Aeneas (50): 'the hero evidently had to justify himself';
Horsfall (1979) 383–8 and his summary in *Enc. Virg.* 2.223a; Gabba (1976) 91–2;
Braccesi (1984); Casali (1999) 206 n. 6; Thomas (2001) 71–3, 78–9, 109–10.

...id Ascanius, it was as *praeda*.[4] Now to characterize as *praeda* what Aeneas took away from Troy amounts to taking the point of view of the Greek conqueror rather than the conquered Trojan.[5] This is a bit risky, when we have accounts that Aeneas betrayed Priam: εἰς τῶν Ἀχαιῶν ἐγεγόνει, 'he became one of the Achaeans' (Menecrates of Xanthos, *FGrHist* 769 F 3 = D.H. 1.48.3). The juxtaposition *praedam pius* conceals a deep tension. Dictys Cretensis, in an altogether more appropriate use of the word *praeda*, will relate that the Greeks who were involved in Aeneas' betrayal decided that 'if he agreed to keep his word, part of the booty (*praeda*) and his whole household intact... would be granted to Aeneas' (4.22).

Let us return to Creusa. One point shared by the non-Virgilian versions of Aeneas' departure from Troy is a total lack of interest in the fate of Creusa, to the point where Lycophron can say that Aeneas, in his great *pietas* (cf. 1270 παρὰ ἐχθροῖς εὐσεβέστατος κριθείς, 'judged the most pious by his enemies'), had departed from Troy 'abandoning his wife, his children, and every other precious thing' (παρώσας καὶ δάμαρτα καὶ τέκνα | καὶ κτῆσιν ἄλλην, 1263–4). Evidently Virgil did not think it opportune for his hero to reserve his *pietas* for his father and the Penates, neglecting completely his wife. Creusa's absence was necessary for the sequence of the story, but it was necessary to *justify it*.

In Ovid's version of the departure from Troy, on the contrary, the silence about Creusa leaves open all possibilities. Perhaps Ovid wants to insinuate that things did not go just as Virgil recounted. Or perhaps he wants to insinuate that even in Virgil there are, in fact, many other possibilities, since it is not Virgil's voice that narrates the second book of the *Aeneid*. The justification for the disappearance of Creusa is entrusted to the voice of Aeneas: the narrative of Creusa's

[4] The Penates rescued by Aeneas from Troy are also called *praeda* at *Fast.* 3.423–4: there too Ovid alludes to the story that the Greeks let Aeneas leave Troy because they were impressed by his *pietas*: *di ueteris Troiae, dignissima praeda ferenti, | qua grauis Aeneas tutus ab hoste fuit.*

[5] Solodow (1988: 144) makes an allusion to this, but without quite hitting the nail on the head: 'the word *praeda* ("booty") strangely suggests that Aeneas was a victor of the Trojan War. Though contradicted by the text and plainly wrong, the suggestion misleads for a moment and does so on a crucial matter almost as if Ovid were indifferent to whether Aeneas was in fact victorious or vanquished.' Cf. also Stitz (1962) 26: 'Aeneas is able to choose, like a victor.'

fate on the last night of Troy belongs to him, and it is, we must admit, a somewhat confused narrative.[6]

Perhaps it is this that Ovid is inviting us to reflect upon with his version of the departure of Aeneas from Troy; that is, on the possibility that the version of the *Aeneid* is not so much the Virgilian version of the myth as it is the 'Aenean' version of the facts. And no one reassures us that Aeneas had told the truth, or all the truth. Clearly, by putting things in this perspective, Virgil's situation would become truly awkward, since he would be left with an unreliable hero and with the consequent uncertainty about what really happened on Troy's last night.

This is not the first time Ovid has suggested that the story of Creusa's disappearance in *Aen.* 2 is scarcely credible. But on the first occasion he had caused *Dido* to say it (in an absolutely explicit manner), in the elegiac voice of Dido in *Her.* 7.83–5:

Si quaeras ubi sit formosi mater Iuli—
occidit a duro sola relicta uiro.
Haec mihi narraras, at me mouere . . .[7]

If you should ask where the mother of handsome Iulus is—she fell, left behind alone by her hardhearted husband. This was the story you had told me, and it moved me . . .

In the *Metamorphoses*, his epic poem, the silence about Creusa transfers to the voice of the epic narrator the uncertainty about the veracity of Aeneas' account, which had been expressed by Dido in the *Heroides*. In the same way, and more explicitly, the openness of the version about the act of treason in *Met.* 13.626 (*praedam . . . eligit*, 'he chooses . . . his prize') constitutes an acceptance in epic objectivity of the point of view on book 2 expressed by Dido in *Virgil*, when she asserted that Aeneas' account of Troy's fatal night was false (a point of view eagerly adopted by the elegiac Dido: *Her.* 7.81 omnia *mentiris*,

[6] For a very negative evaluation of the story of Creusa in *Aeneid* 2, abandoned by Aeneas as Dido will subsequently be abandoned, see Perkell (1981). Ancient critics of Virgil had already regarded Aeneas' account of Creusa's fate with a certain suspicion; cf. Georgii (1891) 141–4 on the discussion by Serv. *Aen.* 1.711, 743, 746. On the problems raised by *longe* in *Aen.* 2.711, see Thomas (2001) 214–18.

[7] For the view that in *Her.* 7.83–4 Ovid anticipates the critical discussion developed by Perkell (1981) on Creusa as a foreshadowing of Dido, see Casali (2004–5). See too Desmond (1993) 61.

'everything you say is a lie'), and that he had been saved not in the manner recounted in *Aen.* 2, but thanks to *facta impia* (*Aen.* 4.596–9), the betrayal of his country (Casali 1999). This is the point of Ovid's strategy: in the *Metamorphoses* the 'other voices' in Virgil become the voice (or the silence) of the epic narrator.[8]

2. SCYLLA AND HELENUS

Aeneas' fleet docks at Zancle (*Met.* 13.730–4):

Scylla latus dextrum, laeuum inrequieta Charybdis
infestat; uorat haec raptas reuomitque carinas,

[8] For another voice that raises doubt about the credibility of Virgil's Aeneas, cf. Ahl (1989), esp. 24–31: 'Vergil's Aeneas convinced not only Dido, for a while, that he was not a perfidious traitor, but the majority of Vergil's readers from the Renaissance onwards' (30). Ahl's reading of the *Aeneid* is outrageously tendentious, but precisely for this reason it can be interesting to compare it with the no less tendentious reading that Ovid makes of the *Aeneid*. An example: we have seen that upon his departure, the Ovidian Aeneas takes as *praeda* only the Penates, his father, and Ascanius *de tantis opibus* (13.624–7). To be sure, it cannot be denied that the other Trojans could have taken some precious objects with them; nevertheless it is difficult not to detect a certain jarring, when, soon after, in the house of Anius it is disclosed that Aeneas and his companions are, in fact, loaded with riches: *nec leuiora datis Troiani dona remittunt | dantque sacerdoti custodem turis acerram, | dant pateram claramque auro gemmisque coronam* (13.702–4). It will be objected that also in Virgil Aeneas offers precious gifts to his hosts; for example, he offers Dido *munera . . . Iliacis erepta ruinis* (1.647), i.e. Helen's cloak and veil, and the sceptre, necklace, and the *duplicem gemmis auroque coronam* of Ilioneus (1.647–56); then he offers Latinus the sceptre, crown, and garments of Priam, *reliquias Troia ex ardente receptas* (7.243–8). Agreed, but is it not possible that *already in Virgil* a tendentious reader could notice some jarring? Especially when he contrasts the riches, of which the Trojans undoubtedly disposed, with the words Aeneas uses to ask Dido to receive in Carthage 'us, the leavings of the Greeks, with all the chances of sea and land now exhausted, *in need of everything*' (*nos, reliquias Danaum, terraeque marisque | omnibus exhaustis iam casibus,* omnium egenos . . . , 1.598–9)? Is it possible that that tendentious reader, Ovid, read it this way? What is certain is that another tendentious reader, Ahl, did. In commenting on *Aen.* 1.599, Horsfall (1986) 14–15 remarks: 'When Virgil describes the Trojans as *omnium egenos*, he intends primarily a contrast with the wealthy Dido, but we may also suspect a deliberate rejection of those stories in which Aeneas was permitted to carry off property and treasure from Troy, incurring thereby the suspicion of treason'. And Ahl (1989: 25) clarifies: 'The speaker who describes the Trojans as destitute of everything is, however, Aeneas. The authorial voice, in contrast, says the Trojans were carrying Trojan treasure (*gaza*) with them, some of which goes down with Orontes' ship: *Troia gaza per undas* (1.113–19).' Ovid picks up and develops this Virgilian point.

illa feris atram canibus succingitur aluum,
uirginis ora gerens, et, si non omnia uates
ficta reliquerunt, aliquo quoque tempore uirgo.

Scylla infests the right-hand coast, unresting Charybdis the left. The latter sucks down and vomits back the ships she has caught; the former's dark belly is girt with wild dogs though she has a maiden's face. And, if all the tales the poets have left are not false, in another time she too was a maiden.

And at this point the story of Scylla slips in, who first listens to Galatea, then is a protagonist in the story with Glaucus and Circe, which concludes with her transformation into a monster. But when the narrative returns to join the fleet of Aeneas after the conclusion of Scylla's tale, a surprise awaits us. We had left Aeneas (13.730–4) confronting a monster with the face of a maiden, girded about the waist with fierce dogs. But when the account of Ovid's 'Aeneid' resumes, we discover that in reality no monster awaits Aeneas (*Met.* 14.72–7):

mox eadem Teucras fuerat mersura carinas,
ni prius in scopulum, qui nunc quoque saxeus exstat,
transformata foret: scopulum quoque nauita uitat.
Hunc ubi Troianae remis auidamque Charybdin
euicere rates, cum iam prope litus adessent
Ausonium, Libycas uento referuntur ad oras.

She also would have drowned the Trojan ships had she not beforehand been transformed into a rock, which still now stands there: sailors avoid the rock too. When the Trojan ships had passed it and greedy Charybdis, and when they had almost reached the Ausonian shore, they were carried back by the wind to the coast of Libya.

Scylla would have sunk the Trojan ships if she had not previously been changed into a cliff, a cliff that exists even now. It is a cliff that Aeneas finds himself required to confront, not the mythological monster that the reader expected from the previous book. Why this surprise? As a perplexed Bömer asks (1986: 29), 'how should we understand the fact that Scylla is still in business at the time of Aeneas' landing, but at his departure has been turned to stone?'

Naturally we look for an answer in Virgil's *Aeneid*. This is the subject of the Ovidian 'Aeneid': Virgil tells us a story, Ovid a text—not (only) the journey of a character, but of a reader. And so let us see how things stand in the *Aeneid*.

In the *Aeneid* Scylla makes her first appearance in the prophecy of Helenus. And she is a monster, indeed she is precisely the monster of whom Ovid speaks in *Met.* 12.730–4 (*Aen.* 3.420–32):

dextrum Scylla latus, laeuum implacata Charybdis
obsidet . . .
  at Scyllam caecis cohibet spelunca latebris
ora exsertantem et nauis in saxa trahentem.
prima hominis facies et pulchro pectore uirgo
pube tenus, postrema immani corpore pistrix
delphinum caudas utero commissa luporum.
praestat Trinacrii metas lustrare Pachyni
cessantem, longos et circumflectere cursus,
quam semel informem uasto uidisse sub antro
Scyllam et caeruleis canibus resonantia saxa.

Now Scylla holds the right coast, insatiable Charybdis the left . . . But a cavern with blind retreats contains Scylla, who thrusts out her mouths and drags ships upon the rocks. Above she is a maiden with a human face and lovely breast down to her loins; underneath she is a monster with a huge body, joining dolphins' tails to her wolves' womb. It is better to go slow around the point of Trinacrian Pachynum and to bend your course around the long route than once to behold misshapen Scylla in her vast cavern and the rocks that echo with her sea-green dogs.

But matters are complicated when Aeneas then actually encounters her (*Aen.* 3.555–60):

et gemitum ingentem pelagi pulsataque saxa
audimus longe fractasque ad litora uoces,
exsultantque uada atque aestu miscentur harenae.
et pater Anchises 'nimirum hic illa Charybdis:
hos Helenus scopulos, haec saxa horrenda canebat.
eripite, o socii, pariterque insurgite remis'.

And far away we hear the mighty moan of the sea and pounded stones and voices broken at the shore; the shoals leap out and the sands mingle with the surge. And father Anchises cries, 'Surely here is Charybdis; these are the crags, these the fearful rocks that Helenus predicted. Save yourselves, comrades, and rise as one on the oars.'

To be sure, Helenus spoke also of cliffs, of 'Scylla ... who drags ships upon the rocks' (*Scyllam ... nauis in saxa trahentem*, 3.425), and of 'the rocks that echo with her sea-green dogs' (*caeruleis canibus resonantia saxa*, 3.432). Anchises can see these cliffs and understands, even through the great crashing, that they are the cliffs where Scylla nests: 'these the fearful rocks that Helenus predicted.' It might be so; that is, Virgil's reader is not bound to worry about it: Aeneas draws near to Scylla, but though he doesn't see her directly, realizes it, and steers away.

However, there are readers, and then there are readers. There could be a reader who would read Anchises' words and recall that the two monsters in question, Scylla and Charybdis, were nothing more than mythological personifications of two natural phenomena, a whirlpool and cliffs dangerous to those navigating the Strait of Messina.[9] This reader could think, then, that Aeneas' fleet is not in fact encountering either the monster Scylla or the monster Charybdis, but instead is encountering the cliffs called 'Scylla' and the whirlpool 'Charybdis': 'This whirlpool is what Helenus prophesized, calling it Charybdis; these cliffs are what Helenus prophesied, calling them Scylla'. This would be the sense of the words of Anchises, a good interpreter of Helenus' prophecy. Furthermore, an exegesis of this type is attested in Servius.[10]

Ovid wanted to read the Virgilian encounter of Aeneas with Scylla precisely in this way, somewhat mischievously. When Aeneas encounters Scylla in the *Metamorphoses*, she had already become a rock, the same rock that still exists today. She had already been 'transformed' into a rock. About this second metamorphosis Ovid says nothing,

[9] Cf. e.g. Sall. fr. 4.27 Maur.; Serv. *Aen.* 3.420.
[10] Serv. *Aen.* 3.559 HAEC SAXA HORRENDA CANEBAT *rettulit se ad historiam: nam pro Scylla 'saxa' dixit 'horrenda'*; similarly Pinotti (*Enc. Virg.* 4.726): 'Aeneas [in 200–1 *uos et Scyllaeam rabiem penitusque sonantis | accestis scopulos*] and his father [...] seem to become the spokespersons, so to speak, for the nationalistic explanations of the danger of Scylla'. The agreement between the ancient exegesis attested in Servius and the one suggested by Ovid fits into a pattern of analogies upon which I dwelt elsewhere (2003 and 2004).

which is a somewhat sly means of alluding to the fact that in reality no metamorphosis ever took place, neither of maiden into monster nor of monster into rock. The only thing that has happened is a poetic personification.

Exactly then as in the case of a mischievous reading of the *Aeneid*, in the *Metamorphoses* an expectation is created for an encounter of Aeneas with a monster that will never appear. After the description of the monster (*Aen.* 3.424–32, *Met.* 13.730–4), there follows the encounter of Aeneas with a rock. First the 'poetic' description, then the reality. Accordingly, it will not be by chance that the description of the monster in *Met.* 13.730–4 contains the following clarification (733–4): *si non omnia uates | ficta reliquerunt.* The allusion to the fact that the metamorphosis of Scylla could be nothing more than a poetic fiction sounds more appropriate than ever: what Aeneas will encounter will be nothing more than a simple rock.

But that is not all. In the *Aeneid* who took on the task of providing the poetic, mythical, and finally 'false' description of the monster Scylla? It was not Virgil's voice that uttered those phrases that Ovid, in his own 'false' description, cited practically word for word. It was the voice of Helenus, the seer Helenus. In other words, Helenus the *uates*. Immediately after completing his 'false' description, Helenus continued his speech (*Aen.* 3.433–4): *praeterea, si qua est Heleno prudentia uati, | si qua fides, animum si ueris implet Apollo . . .* 'Furthermore, if there be any prudence in Helenus the seer, if there be any trust, if Apollo fills his soul with truth . . .' For the mischievous (or attentive?) reader of the *Aeneid* there is no reason to place much trust in the truthfulness of this *uates*.

3. DIDO: OTHER VOICES

The story of Aeneas and Dido is dispatched in four verses, four verses in Carthage for four books of Virgil (*Met.* 14.78–81):

Excipit Aenean illic animoque domoque,
non bene discidium Phrygii latura mariti,

Sidonis, inque pyra sacri sub imagine facta
incubuit ferro, deceptaque decipit omnes.[11]

There the Sidonian woman received Aeneas in her heart and in her home,
doomed not to bear well the departure of her Phrygian husband. On a pyre
made under pretence of a sacred rite, she fell upon his sword and, herself
cheated, she cheated all.

I am not interested in discussing here the anti-Augustan Ovid or the
anti-Virgilian Ovid; I am interested in Ovid the (literary) critic of
Virgil. I am concerned to place Ovid in the stream of criticism that
eventually arrives at the *Further Voices* of Oliver Lyne (1987). It is
nevertheless a line of criticism that certainly has a political dimension,
which could easily be defined as 'anti-Augustan'. We could imagine that Virgil would have been a bit embarrassed if Lyne had had
Augustus read his study of *Further Voices in Vergil's Aeneid*. Likewise,
Ovid's version of the story of Aeneas does not aim so much at being
different from Virgil's, to show that Ovid has a different political
attitude, or that Virgil's approach was unacceptable. Ovid's version of
Aeneas' story is an unsettling reading of the *Aeneid*, an anti-Augustan
reading that aims at implicating Virgil himself in the charge of anti-
Augustanism.[12]

Ovid's 'Aeneid' is a critical reading of Virgil's, but an unsettling
one, unsettling for everyone, but above all for Virgil. That in the

---

[11] *Deceptaque decipit*: the polyptoton is pungent. For the suicide of Dido as deception, see, for example, *Aen.* 4.675 (Anna speaking) *me fraude petebas*? For the narrating voice of the *Metamorphoses* to describe Dido as *decepta* constitutes a startling
accommodation of Dido's point of view to the objectivity of epic; cf. *Aen.* 4.330 *non
equidem omnino capta ac deserta uiderer* and Ov. *Her.* 7.69 (Knox 1995: 105). In Dido's
speech to Anna at *Aen.* 4.17, *deceptam* referring to Dido 'cheated' by the death of
Sychaeus is tragically ironic. But perhaps in this case too Ovid wants to note that again
he has been preceded in this formulation by Virgil: the polyptoton *decepta decipit*
alludes to the fact that in Virgil's account 'deceptions' are attributed both to Aeneas
and Dido by means of the same word (*doli*): 296 *at regina dolos (quis fallere possit
amantem?) | praesensit . . .* (cf. also the problematic *doli* of Venus and Juno at 4.128);
and 563 (Mercury speaking) *illa dolos dirumque nefas in pectore uersat | certa mori.*
But actually Mercury's very words are a deception, for Dido is not planning to attack
Aeneas and, to be precise, the only 'deception' will be her suicide.

[12] See Knox (1995: 23–4) on *Her.* 7: 'The so-called "negative" reading of the *Aeneid*
associated with modern criticism began almost simultaneously with the release of the
poem . . . Ovid is not interested in re-creating a Dido of his own; he is interested in
Virgil's Dido.' On Ovid as a pessimistic critic of Virgil, see now Thomas (2001) 74–83.

Aeneid there were 'other voices' than the one we call 'Augustan', Ovid will argue explicitly and directly to Augustus in his handbook on reading, *Tristia* 2 (533–6):

et tamen ille tuae felix Aeneidos auctor
    contulit in Tyrios arma uirumque toros,
nec legitur pars ulla magis de corpore toto,
    quam non legitimo foedere iunctus amor.

And yet that fortunate author of your *Aeneid* brought his 'arms and the man' to a Tyrian couch, and no part of the whole work is read more than the love affair joined by an illicit bond.

It is not the epic voice alone: Dido is one of the scandals of the *Aeneid*. This is an extraneous section: it is anthologized and read separately, and so it distracts from the more Augustan parts. It violates the genre: *arma uirumque*, the epic, is contaminated with erotic poetry. As Barchiesi (1993: 169 = 2001: 93) puts it, 'these lines are a tendentious, but also meticulous, reading of the *Aeneid*; *arma uirumque* at once recalls both the proem—and hence, the epic poem in general—and the scene in which the hero and his arms are physically framed in Dido's bedroom (4.495 *arma uiri, thalamo*...)'.[13] A meticulous reading: in that case let's have another look at that love *non legitimo foedere iunctus*. Even a glance at the Virgilian bibliography reveals that a hotbed of 'other voices' resides precisely in this *foedus*, which is illegitimate to be sure, but is also betrayed by the pious Aeneas. When, in fact, does Virgil mention that those hero's arms were in Dido's bedchamber? When Dido takes them to commit suicide. And, if we want to be punctilious, there will indeed come a moment in which the arms of Aeneas, and Aeneas himself, in the form of a likeness, will in effect climb *in Tyrios...toros*: *Aen.* 4.507–8 *super exuuias ensemque relictum* | *effigiemque toro locat* 'on the couch above she sets the clothes and the sword he left and his effigy.'

By characterizing the love of Aeneas and Dido as *non legitimo foedere iunctus*, Ovid turns against Aeneas (and Augustus and Virgil) the essential point around which the 'Augustan' reading of *Aen.* 4 revolves: the marriage of Aeneas and Dido was not a true one (and

---

[13] See further Barchiesi (1993) 18–19, and on the sword of Aeneas see also Lyne (1987) 22.

so Aeneas is right, and with him the Augustan readers). But *precisely for this reason* Aeneas (and Virgil) have committed a scandalous fault. Here Ovid (unlike in *Her.* 7 and *Met.* 13, as we shall soon see) focalizes the narrative through the point of view of Aeneas, but the adoption of Aeneas' point of view serves to put in a bad light this thoroughly Augustan hero.

And so let us look at the Dido episode in Ovid's 'Aeneid': let us look at it as a chapter in Ovid's assessment of the unsettling voices of the *Aeneid*: excipit *Aenean illic animoque domoque*... Everyone recognizes here the echo of *Aen.* 4.373–4:

'Nusquam tuta fides. eiectum litore, egentem,
excepi et regni demens in parte locaui'.[14]

Nowhere is trust certain. When he was cast out on the shore, in want, I received him and in my madness placed him in a share of my kingdom.

Actually this is not simply an echo of the *Aeneid*, it is an echo of words that in the *Aeneid* belong not to the epic voice, but to the antagonistic voice of Dido. What in the *Aeneid* amounted to conceding a creditable point of view to a character, the possibility of seeing things from a different perspective, becomes the point of view of the epic text. Ovid says something unsettling, that to yield room to other voices, antagonistic to Aeneas, is risky. Because these voices can be more attractive and convincing than the Augustan voice; they can become the dominant voices. To say that *nec legitur pars ulla magis de corpore toto,* | *quam non legitimo foedere iunctus amor* (*Trist.* 2.535–6) also amounts to saying that more than any other section of the poem called the 'Aeneid', the public reads a section of which a large part is taken up by shameful insults directed at Aeneas.

In *Met.* 14.79 *non bene discidium* Phrygii *latura* mariti, even the expression *Phrygius maritus* to indicate Aeneas is taken directly from the fourth book of the *Aeneid*. But who uses it? Who utters the phrase? It is Juno's: *liceat* Phrygio *seruire* marito ... (*Aen.* 4.103). 'A venomous line, for *Phrygius* is often a term of contempt used by the enemies of Troy and *seruire* implies the abjectness of Dido's love' (Austin ad loc.). How can Bömer (1986: 31) so blandly assert that 'in Ovid there is no

---

[14] Compare Dido's words at *Her.* 7.89–90, *fluctibus eiectum tuta statione* recepi | *uixque bene audito nomine regna dedi.*

negative undertone'?[15] The voice of the principal opponent of Aeneas and his mission becomes the 'official' voice of the text.

Virgil has brought *arma uirumque*, the epic, *in Tyrios toros*: he has contaminated the epic. And to say that Dido is 'destined not to well endure the *discidium* of her Phrygian husband' is certainly not a very epic way of presenting the situation: the phrase *non bene... latura* recalls *moritura* which is repeatedly referred to Dido (*Aen.* 4.308, 415, 519, 604). On the contrary, *non* bene discidium... latura brings to mind the opening of an elegy: Tib. 1.5.1 bene discidium *me* ferre *loquebar*. And this could be more than a casual echo, for Tib. 1.5 is an elegy that could, for a malicious reader, present some traits similar to Dido's situation. Consider for example verses 9–18, in which Tibullus complains that by his prayers he snatched from death the sick woman who now reveals herself to be ungrateful, just as Dido reproaches Aeneas for the help she offered him. Not only an elegiac voice, then, but an unsettling voice. The *discidium* of Delia, in fact had little fatal consequence: 1.5.17–18 *omnia* (sc. *uota*) *persolui: fruitur nunc* alter amore, | *et precibus felix utitur ille meis* 'I paid them all, and now someone else enjoys my love and that lucky man profits from my prayers'. Delia has abandoned Tibullus for a new lover, a *diues amator*, an idea that is perhaps somehow evoked also in the elegiac voice of Dido: *Her.* 7.17 scilicet alter amor *tibi restat et altera Dido* 'evidently another love awaits you and another Dido'.[16]

Ovid devotes four verses to the fourth book of the *Aeneid* (14.78–81); then the summary of Aeneas' wanderings follows rapidly until he lands at Pithecusa. Here ten verses (91–100) are devoted to the account of the metamorphosis of the inhabitants of the island, the Cercopes, into monkeys, whence the name Pithecusa. Of course, the story is completely absent from Virgil's *Aeneid*, but, as Galinsky (1975: 223–4) rightly notes, Ovid does not limit himself to

[15] Lamacchia (1969) 7 is better: Ovid adopts the expression 'to express the point of view of the deluded Dido'. This is right; the entire verse is focalized through Dido: on *discidium* cf. *OLD* s.v. 2b in the sense of 'divorce'. This is how Dido sees her relationship with Aeneas. Therefore, if *discidium* signifies 'divorce', the termination of a marriage, it cries out the point of view of Dido; on the other hand, if *discidium* is a 'breaking off' in the elegiac sense, it recalls a too human precedent. Either Aeneas has married Dido, or he has abandoned her in the elegiac manner for an *alter amor*.

[16] The text is corrupt: with Rosati (1989) and Knox (1995), I print the reconstruction proposed by Diggle (1967) 138. See Knox's apparatus and his note ad loc.

emphasizing the theme of metamorphosis, he inserts into the story 'a moral note that is far more typical of Vergil than of the *Metamorphoses*'. In fact, in the version of the myth followed or invented by Ovid, the transformation of the Cercopes into monkeys is motivated by Jupiter's wish to punish them for perjuries and deceptions: 'he is a highly moral and awesome Jupiter at that'. Now why this metamorphosis and why this moral note, with a 'Virgilian Jupiter' who punishes those guilty of perjury and deception? If we recall that this is the first inserted narrative that follows on the summary of the book about Dido *decepta*, perhaps the answer is already grasped (*Met.* 14.91–2):

quippe deum genitor, fraudem et *periuria* quondam
Cercopum exosus *gentisque* admissa *dolosae* . . .

For the father of the gods, hating the fraud and the *perjuries* of the Cercopes and crimes of that *treacherous race* . . .

How can we not recall *Aen.* 4.296 *at regina dolos* . . . or the words of Dido (4.541–2), *necdum | Laomedonteae sentis* periuria *gentis* 'do you not yet understand the perjuries of Laomedon's race'? And another voice is added (*Met.* 14.98–9): *nec non prius abstulit usum | uerborum et natae dira in* periuria linguae 'and first he took away from them the use of words and a tongue made for dreadful perjuries'. It is the voice of the elegiac Dido (*Her.* 7.67): *protinus occurrent falsae* periuria linguae 'the perjuries of your lying tongue will immediately come to mind'.[17]

4. TURNUS: OTHER VOICES

Aeneas finally reaches Latium (*Met.* 14.449–51):

. . . Faunigenaeque domo *potitur* nataque Latini,
non sine Marte tamen: bellum cum gente feroci
suscipitur, *pacta*que furit *pro coniuge* Turnus.

---

[17] In light of the possible, implied analogy between the perjurious Aeneas and the Cercopes transformed into monkeys, I cannot refrain from thinking of the parodic representation of Aeneas, Anchises, and Ascanius as *monkeys* (or perhaps, dogs) in a famous Pompeian painting: cf. Galinsky (1969*a*) 32, fig. 30 and Canciani (1981), according to whom they are represented as dogs.

...and he takes possession of the house and daughter of Latinus, but not
without warfare. War with a fierce race is begun and Turnus rages *for his
promised bride.*

The phrase bellum *cum gente* feroci | *suscipitur* echoes a version of the
war in Latium that is very 'Augustan' and equally concise: Jupiter's
prophecy to Venus at *Aen.* 1.263–4 bellum *ingens geret Italia popu-
losque* ferocis | *contundet* 'he shall wage war tremendous in Italy and
crush *fierce* peoples'.[18] The voice of the epic narrator could, with
complete legitimacy, borrow from Jupiter's prophetic voice, as well
as taking it as a model of concision. But the problem is that alongside
this most authoritative borrowing are other borrowings from other
voices of a much different authority.

In the first place, *potitur*. Aeneas 'takes possession of the house and
daughter of Latinus'. Not only is this a somewhat abrupt manner of
presenting things.[19] Virgil uses the form *potitur* twice in the *Aeneid*.
The first time, the epic narrator is speaking about the infamous
Polymestor, who treacherously kills Polydorus and 'violently takes
possession (*potitur*) of the gold' (3.55–6). The second time *potitur*
occurs in reference to Aeneas, as here in Ovid, and in a reference to
Aeneas taking possession of a woman, in the words of another enemy
of the Trojans, Iarbas (*Aen.* 4.214–16):

et nunc ille Paris cum semiuiro comitatu,
Maeonia mentum mitra crinemque madentem
subnexus, rapto *potitur* . . .

And now that second Paris with his crew of half-men, binding his chin and
his dripping hair with a Maeonian ribbon, *takes possession* of his plunder . . .

The action of Aeneas in Latium, his 'taking possession' of Lavinia, is
described in the epic voice of the *Metamorphoses* borrowing the word
that Aeneas' enemy Iarbas used in the *Aeneid* to describe Aeneas'

---

[18] Here too *cum gente* could be an 'etymological' echo of *ingens*.
[19] *Faunigenae* 'refers also to the oracle so decisive for events in Latium' (Galasso
2000: 1529), but the reference to the fatal oracle clashes stridently with the action of
potiri: we expect Latinus, the son of Faunus, to *offer* his daughter to Aeneas, as in *Aen.*
7, not that Aeneas takes possession of her.

action at Carthage, his 'taking possession' of Dido in the guise of the new Paris.[20]

And as we know, in Virgil's *Aeneid*, Aeneas will again be identified in Latium with Paris the abductor of women: just as he took possession of Dido as a new Paris, so he takes possession of Lavinia, again as a new Paris and again, naturally, from the point of view of Aeneas' enemies. We come, then, to Turnus, who, in Ovid and according to the epic voice, 'rages for his promised bride'. In the *Aeneid* it is never said explicitly that Lavinia was officially promised to Turnus. Not by Virgil's voice, I mean to say, since we know that there is another voice, Juno's, which puts things in a different light (*Aen.* 10.77–9):

'quid face Troianos atra uim ferre Latinis,
arua aliena iugo premere atque auertere praedas?
quid soceros legere et gremiis abducere *pactas*...'[21]

What do you say of the Trojans' attack on the Latins with their dark torches, what of their pressing others' land with the plough, of their taking plunder? What of their choosing their fathers-in-law and kidnapping *betrothed* women from their mothers' bosom...?

The hostile voices of the *Aeneid* become the epic voice. Iarbas' point of view and Juno's, which agree in advancing an identification of Aeneas with Paris, the abductor of women, are assumed as its own by the narrating voice of the *Metamorphoses*.

5. THE END OF THE *AENEID*: ARDEA

After the episode of the ships of Aeneas (*Met.* 14.526–65), Ovid's 'Aeneid' swiftly draws to an end (*Met.* 14.572–80):

           tandemque Venus uictricia nati
arma uidet, Turnusque cadit: cadit Ardea, Turno
sospite dicta potens; quem postquam barbarus ensis
abstulit et tepida latuerunt tecta fauilla,

[20] In a wonderfully ironic piece of retaliation, in *Fast.* 3.552 it will be Iarbas himself who will formally take possession of Dido's house: *et potitur capta Maurus Iarba domo*.
[21] Lundström (1980) 57–8. As is known, Juno's version coincides with Livy's (1.2.1): *Turnus rex Rutulorum cui* pacta *Lauinia ante aduentum Aeneae fuerat...*

congerie e media tum primum cognita praepes
subuolat et cineres plausis euerberat alis.
et sonus et macies et pallor et omnia, captam
quae deceant urbem, nomen quoque mansit in illa
urbis, et ipsa suis deplangitur Ardea pennis.

And finally Venus sees her son's arms victorious and Turnus falls. Ardea falls,
called powerful when Turnus was safe. After the barbarian sword killed him
and his home lay hidden by warm ashes, from the midst of the pile a bird flew
forth, recognized then for the first time, and beat the ashes with its flapping
wings. Its sound, its thinness, its pallor, all things which become a captured
city, even the city's name remained in it, and Ardea is itself lamented by its
wings.

And so, immediately before the apotheosis of Aeneas (14.581–608),
ends the 'Aeneid' of Ovid. The pious Aeneas, forgetting his fated
mission, takes Ardea, the city of Turnus, and destroys it, burns it,
razes it to the ground. *Tepida latuerunt tecta fauilla* (575); of the
powerful city of Ardea there remain only ashes and shapeless ruins.
Since Ovid's poem does *not* end here, Ovid would have had an excellent opportunity to 'correct' the Virgilian scandal of the end of the
Aeneid with Turnus killed by Aeneas, by supplementing the *Aeneid*
with a more conciliatory conclusion. In effect, Ovid does supplement
the end of the *Aeneid* in a certain sense: Virgil's *Aeneid* ends, in the
text of the *Metamorphoses*, at 14.573–5 (the death of Turnus, on
which see below), but Ovid continues. He continues, indeed, with
the destruction of the Turnus' city, Ardea. A metamorphosis now
closes the 'Aeneid', appropriately, but the end point remains an act
of destruction. Ovid supplies a truly Virgilian sequel to the plot of
the *Aeneid*. In *Aen.* 12.930–8, Turnus, wounded and suppliant, had
begged Aeneas to spare him, invoking his old father Daunus, or at
least to restore his body to his people: 'do not press on your hatred'
(*ulterius ne tende odiis*, 938). Turnus suggested an Iliadic sequel to the
story: *Iliad* 24 and the meeting of Priam and Achilles. The Ovidian
Aeneas seems to act precisely on the basis of this prayer by Turnus,
by rejecting it. Aeneas' deadly anger is not satisfied with the death of
Turnus, Aeneas *ulterius tendit odiis*: he goes to Ardea, old Daunus'
city, and, far from humanely returning Turnus' corpse, he destroys
the city.

To annihilate a city is certainly a very debatable way of fulfilling the mandate that Virgil's Anchises had entrusted to the Augustan hero: *paci . . . imponere morem* (*Aen.* 6.852), just as killing the unarmed Turnus was a very debatable way of *parcere subiectis et debellare superbos.* In his note on *Aen.* 7.412, Servius commits a significant lapse when he remarks that in the *Metamorphoses* Ovid told of Ardea 'burned by Hannibal'.[22] But again what matters is not so much the Ovidian 'Aeneid' *per se*: Ovid's Aeneas is different from Virgil's, so Ovid has a different ideological vision from Virgil's. What matters is Ovid's 'Aeneid' as a *reading* of Virgil's. Now it would seem possible to assert that Virgil says nothing about the destruction of Ardea by Aeneas. But is it really so? Many things can be said even by saying nothing; or rather, even one who says nothing can be made to say many things.

Ovid's 'Aeneid' closes with the death of Turnus and the destruction of Ardea. Virgil's *Aeneid* spoke of Ardea just before introducing Turnus for the first time in the poem (*Aen.* 7.411–13): *locus Ardea quondam | dictus auis, et nunc magnum manet Ardea nomen, | sed fortuna fuit* 'There was once a place called Ardea by our ancestors, and still today Ardea remains a great name, but its power is gone'. Ovid's 'version' amounts to a critical reading of this passage, in which a comment is made on *sed fortuna fuit*: why? Why did Ardea's power disappear? Virgil doesn't say, but Ovid does: because Aeneas, pious Aeneas, destroyed it. Ovid's reading transforms *sed fortuna fuit* from 'a romantic poetic recollection of the glorious poetic past of a city among the most powerful of archaic Latium' (*Enc. Virg.* 1.301–2) into a sinister and ominous allusion. Ovid's reading suggests (or allows us to understand) that when Allecto goes to Turnus in Ardea, Virgil is already forecasting the destruction of Ardea *by Aeneas*. Ovid recovers the allusion to a 'glorious past', to faded power, but explains it: *cadit Ardea Turno | sospite dicta potens . . . | . . . tepida latuerunt tecta fauilla.* Virgil's silence on the reason for *fortuna fuit* becomes a noisy, unsettling *reticence.* The grammatical parallel, diligently cited by commentators, between *fortuna fuit* and the words of Aeneas in 2.325 (*fuimus*

---

[22] 'Rome is witness (rather it is practically always the cause) to the fall and sometimes the annihilation of numerous cities, great and small. But the cultural ideal of *humanitas* [. . .] ought to render ambiguous the spectacle of an enemy city in flames, injecting doubt into the ferocious joy of the conqueror' (Labate 1991: 168).

Troes, fuit Ilium) could become uncomfortably significant: the sudden destruction of Troy is destined to repeat itself through Ardea, and its agent will be the very exile whose story had moved us in the second book of the *Aeneid*.

In Ovid's 'Aeneid', from the ashes of Ardea is born a bird never seen before, which by its cry, by its leanness, and by its ashen colour is well adapted to the ruined city and preserves its name: it is the *ardea*, the heron (14.576–80). This miraculous birth is not attested elsewhere. Naturally, Virgil makes no reference to the heron, but he does allude to the etymology of *Ardea* from *ardua*, as already Servius explains: '*magnum manet*[23] *Ardea nomen*: a good allusion, for Ardea comes from *ardua*, i.e. great and noble'.[24] According to Virgil, for Ardea 'no longer powerful' (a euphemism for 'destroyed', according to Ovid's interpretation) *manet . . . nomen* of 'lofty'; according to Ovid, for the bird that rose from the ashes of the city, *nomen . . . mansit* of the city.

It's been said that Virgil makes no reference to the heron, but are we really sure of that? It would seem so: according to an orthodox reading, there is no mention of birds. But Ovid was not an orthodox reader and if we reread the passage of the *Aeneid* with eyes much less orthodox, perhaps a bird will appear (*Aen.* 7.411–12): *locus Ardea quondam | dictus AVIS . . .* 'There was once a place called Ardea by our ancestors', but also 'there was once a place called "Ardea the bird"'. I do not say that in Virgil's text *there is* this double sense of *auis*; I say that a 'perverse' reader, who leaves out the different quantity of the termination *-is*, could see it.

This is provable. Two examples. In his apparatus Heyne (1833: III, 59) asks: '*Locus Ardea quondam Dictus auis*; is *auis* here 'ancestors'? Or is *Ardea avis*? With the result that the city is called Ardea, a bird (cf. Ge. I, 364) by name'. Heyne inclines toward the first

---

[23] Thus MV: Servius reads *tenet* of M²R; note Ov. *Met.* 14.579 *mansit*.

[24] Perhaps it would be better to interpret simply 'lofty'; cf. also immediately after, 413 *tectis hic Turnus in altis* and above all *Geo.* 1.364 *altam supra uolat ardea nubem*, with Servius ad loc. In Ovid, *dicta potens* (574) alluded to the Virgilian etymology of Ardea from *ardua*. Then since for the heron the *nomen . . . mansit* of the city burned, the suspicion arises that Ovid wants to suggest a new etymological motivation: after *fauilla* (575), after *cineres* (577), ARDEa from ARDEo.

hypothesis and notes, 'In my opinion this second sense, that *Ardea avis* is connected, is somewhat silly'.[25]

In discussing *Aen.* 7.411–13, Frederick Ahl notes that *ardea* is also the name of a bird (which among other things Virgil knew well, as can be seen from *Geo.* 1.364), and, even without taking Ovid into account or the etymological connections that were made between Ardea and the *ardea*, he concludes, without excessive scruples (1985: 265, n. 29): 'As a result we should be a little suspicious of Vergil's reasons for describing Turnus' city of ARDea as *locus ... quondam | dictus AVIS* in *Aeneid* 7.411 f.: since *AVIS* (in Latin) means either "by one's forebears" or "a bird"'.[26]

We have tried to show that, in *Met.* 14.572–80, Ovid creates a critical discourse on *Aen.* 7.411–13, a rather unsettling one for Virgil. It is also quite probable that Ovid (like Heyne and Ahl) saw a bird in the Virgilian passage (Hardie 1992: 77, n. 16; Dyson 1997: 315, n. 3). In that case, what value, what meaning would he have given to this presence? In light of Ovid's discourse on the destruction of Ardea, the etymology of *ardea auis* that Virgil possibly suggests for the city comes to acquire a particular emphasis. At the same time as he alludes to the etymology of Ardea from *ardua*, Virgil would also be alluding to *another* etymology of the name of the city, of *Ardea* from *auis ardea*. But if the place had been called '*auis ardea*', that would mean that, according to Virgil, the bird was not born from the ashes of the ruined city, since clearly it existed already, having given its name to the place.

Servius attests for us that Hyginus (noted Virgilian critic and friend of Ovid)[27] gave a different explanation of the origin of the name Ardea: Ardea is so called because it is *ardua*, 'even if Hyginus, in his work on the cities of Italy (Hyg. fr. 15 Fun., fr. 11 P.) maintains that Ardea was so called following an augury provided by a heron'. Virgil could have known this etymology and alluded to it in 7.411–12; or alternatively, it might be possible that this etymology originated from

[25] Cf. Conington (1883) III, 43: 'some have fancied that "avis" here means a bird'.

[26] Cf. also O'Hara (1996a) 190; Dyson (1997) 314–15; and, more cautiously, Horsfall (2000) 282.

[27] For a coincidence between an exegesis of Virgil attested in Ovid and one in Hyginus, see Casali (2004) 45–8. On Hyginus, see Timpanaro (1986) 51–67, (2001) 13–23, and Kaster (1995) 205–14.

his own text. Given Hyginus' interest in Virgilian exegesis, it is in fact possible that his etymologizing of Ardea was suggested to him by an 'ornithological' exegesis of this passage on *Ardea . . . | auis* in *Aen.* 7.411–12.

In any case, at this point we may suggest that Ovid not only develops the ornithological etymology of Ardea suggested by Virgil's text, but makes a polemical *correction*. Ovid says that the bird is the product of the *destruction* of the city, and he is quite precise in this regard (576–7): *congerie e media* tum primum cognita *praepes | subuolat*. It was not the place that was named from the bird, but the bird from the place. Hyginus' explanation (certainly) and Virgil's (if interpreted 'perversely') is impossible, Ovid says, because the bird did not exist before the destruction of the city. This is a way of insinuating that Hyginus' (and Virgil's) version is nothing more than an 'accommodation', a version originated to cover up an uncomfortable and unsettling truth: the destruction of Ardea by the pious Aeneas.[28]

6. THE END OF THE *AENEID*: TURNUS

'Poetry is the foreknowledge of criticism.' Paul De Man

A final word on the ends of the two Aeneids. Aeneas' murder of Turnus, now a suppliant and unarmed, has been and remains one of the most debated interpretative problems of Virgilian criticism. In the finale of the *Aeneid* many have seen the failure and defeat of what Aeneas owed to *paci . . . imponere morem, | parcere subiectis et debellare superbos* (6.852–3). The non-Augustan reader who more than any other has framed this antagonistic mode of reading the ending of the *Aeneid* is Michael Putnam. At the end, Putnam asks (1972: 67), 'does Aeneas act the part of civilizer or *barbarian* (my emphasis)?' Ovid had already asked the same question, and had also given the same

---

[28] On Ovid as an interpreter of Virgilian etymologies, see O'Hara (1996*b*, = ch. 5 above). This would be an example of a category not envisioned by O'Hara: not 'Vergil alludes, Ovid explains' (1996*b*: 263–73), but 'Virgil alludes, Ovid denies'.

identical response (*Met.* 14.574–5): ... *quem* [sc. *Turnum*] *postquam barbarus ensis | abstulit* ...[29] The problem is not (only) whether with this Ovid was being anti-Augustan. What Ovid says is that this reading might be a *possible*, albeit unsettling, reading of the end of the *Aeneid*.[30] No one will deny that he was also a good prophet.[31]

[29] This is also an obvious reversal of Tibullus 2.5.48, where the Sibyl prophesies to Aeneas himself the death of Turnus with this apostrophe: *iam, tibi praedico*, barbare Turne, *necem*. Perhaps the Sibyl is speaking as a Greek, but the implications don't change: '*barbare*, i.e. "cruel, savage"' (Smith 1913: ad loc.). Cf. also Murgatroyd (1994) 198: 'Also possible is the translation "fierce, savage" (...) which (...) would imply that Aeneas brought civilization to Italy'.

[30] On attempts at 'textual cleansing' (for the concept, see Thomas 2001: 190–221) in *Met.* 14.573, cf. Bömer ad loc., who in turn tries to neutralize *barbarus ensis* by saying that 'here in epic poetry *barbarus* is morally indifferent'. Tarrant (2004) prints the variant quam *postquam barbarus* ignis, which is also possible, and has the merit of preserving *barbarus* against, e.g., *Dardanus* (Heinsius); in favour of *quem* ... *ensis*, see Junod (1991) 73–4; Galasso (2000) 1538–9; Thomas (2001) 83.

[31] This article has been revised and corrected, with an updated bibliography. I am grateful to Alessandro Barchiesi, Andrea Cucchiarelli, Luigi Galasso, Mario Labate, Oliver Lyne, and Gianpiero Rosati, who provided valuable assistance for the first version. Thereafter I have received fundamental encouragement and help from Peter Knox and Richard Thomas, to whom I am deeply grateful. Unfortunately, in the meantime, Oliver Lyne has left us: this paper, which owes so much to his teaching, is respectfully dedicated to his memory.

Part II

Ideologies of Love and Poetry

8

Reading Female Flesh: *Amores* 3.1

Maria Wyke

The Propertian lover poet itemizes the physical attractions of his mistress in poem 2.3 at the same time as he declares that it was her skills in dancing, singing, and poetic composition that captivated him more (2.3.9–16):

Nec me tam facies, quamuis sit candida, cepit
    (lilia non domina sint magis alba mea;
ut Maeotica nix minio si certet Hibero,
    utque rosae puro lacte natant folia),
nec de more comae per leuia colla fluentes,
    non oculi, geminae, sidera nostra, faces,
nec si qua Arabio lucet bombyce puella
    (non sum de nihilo blandus amator ego) . . .

It's not so much the face, although radiant, that captivated me
    (lilies could not be whiter than my mistress;
just as if Maeotian snow with Iberian vermilion contended,
    and just as on pure milk rose petals swim),
nor hair habitually over a smooth neck flowing,
    not eyes, twin torches (our stars),
nor if the girl glitters at all in Arabian silk
    (I am not a lover who flatters without cause) . . .

In order to materialize as an elegiac mistress, the female body is here fragmented into parts (face, hair, eyes) and metamorphosed into a catalogue of inhuman or inanimate metaphors (lilies, snow, vermilion, milk, rose petals, torches, stars). Reified in the extreme, woman enters the elegiac text with a body constructed for her by the poet that is in no way her own.[1]

The process of gathering such brief physical descriptions from their scattered locations in the Propertian corpus in order to assemble out of them a credible and singular portrait of an Augustan girlfriend has been essential to the project of romantic scholars. Yet the conventionality, textuality, and aesthetic ambitions of western love poetry's female flesh has long been recognized even within the tradition of that poetry's production. In the world of fourteenth-century Petrarchan love poetry (following that of Augustan elegy) woman dominates and man adores the codified perfection of her beauty. Yet later writers in the erotic tradition regularly parodied and undercut the conceits of such Petrarchan desire for golden hair, ivory hands, ebony eyes, rosy cheeks, lily-white skin, coral lips, or breasts like globes of alabaster (Forster 1969: 1–60 and Stapleton 1996).

In the preface to *Le berger extravagant* (1627), for example, Charles Sorel expressly declared his intention to entomb the absurdities of poetry, in this case, the amatory world of the Italian pastoral (Whitfield 1963: 37). The hero of his French novel (much like a romantic critic in the extreme) has read too many pastorals and taken them for truth. Having taken to the way of life of the fictional shepherd they depict, his friends first flatter and then shatter his unhealthy illusion. In the second book, the deluded hero commissions a visual portrait of his beloved Charité—just as Petrarch had represented himself in his sonnets commissioning a portrait of Laura (Miller 1997: 144–5)—but the outcome is most disturbing, as the engraving of beautiful Charité which accompanies Sorel's text vividly reveals (Fig. 8.1). For the painter

had in this business acted a piece of ingenious knavery; observing what the Shepherd had told him of the beauty of his Mistress, and imitating the extravagant descriptions of the Poets, he had painted a Face, which instead of being of a flesh-colour, was of a complexion white as snow. There were two branches of Coral at the opening of the Mouth; and upon each Cheek a Lilly and a Rose, crossing one another: where there should have been Eyes, there was neither white nor apple, but two Suns sending forth beams, among

---

[1] I borrow here for Propertian elegy the analysis by Flynn (1997) of the fragmented female body that can be found in medieval Latin lyrics.

Figure 8.1. 'La Belle Charité'. Engraving to illustrate Charles Sorel's novel *Le berger extravagant* (1627).

which were observed certain flames and darts... And to add perfection to the work, the Hair floted about all this in divers manners: some of it was made like Chains of Gold; other-some twisted, and made like networks; and in many places there hanged lines, with hooks ready baited.[2]

Taken literally, the metaphors of Petrarchan love delineate not a living mistress but the beautiful monstrosity that is erotic poetry.

Within the confines of this chapter, I shall argue that, as in Sorel's anti-Petrarchist novel, Ovid *Amores* 3.1 constitutes a point in the tradition of western love poetry where an amatory text itself signals demonstrably and humorously that such poetry's female flesh can bear a reading as fiction.[3] Like the painting described in Sorel's novel, *Amores* 3.1 is 'a piece of ingenious knavery' that picks up on and deconstructs the anatomy of the elegiac mistress that had been supplied in the earlier elegies of Propertius and Tibullus. And like the anti-romantic novel itself, *Amores* 3.1 is designed to mock and entomb the absurdity of reading amatory poetry as real. A close reading of *Amores* 3.1 can thus provide clues to the operations of female representation elsewhere in Augustan elegy, and (I shall argue further) teaches an important lesson in why and how we should read Cynthia, Delia, Nemesis, and Corinna as textual bodies bearing both poetic and political meanings.

FEMALE FLESH AS POETICS

The scene of *Amores* 3.1 is set in the vicinity of a cave. The narrator (as poet) recalls his encounter there with two writing practices in female form: Elegia and Tragoedia. He describes their appearance and comportment and a debate in which each woman advocates her own mode of poetic production, denigrating or dismissing the other. Eventually the narrator adopts Elegia (however temporarily) as his

---

[2] I quote from the translation of the French by John Davies (1653: 25). I am most grateful to David Constantine for having originally drawn my attention to this image and its implications for the female body in erotic poetry. All translations are the author's own unless otherwise indicated.

[3] Cf. Stapleton (1996) on Ovid's *Amores* as a model for such later subversions of conventional love poetry as Shakespeare's sonnets.

Muse. Thus the third and final book of Ovid's *Amores* gets under way.[4]

The manner in which Ovid has here depicted female flesh (as if poetic genres were proud possessors of a human anatomy) has been cited by a romantic critic as an example of how poets' encounters with naked prostitutes at Rome are raised to the level of art by the application of a thin brushstroke of mythology or allegory: 'the picture of a Roman man about town, running an eye over the girls on offer in some louche establishment' is often visible beneath a dignifying veneer of appropriate poetic devices (Griffin 1985: 105). Others have read the female flesh with which Elegia is endowed rather differently: 3.1 has readily been accepted by some commentators as depicting not a prostitute but an elegiac poetics. The poem is one of a whole series scattered throughout the corpus of Augustan elegy that map out a debate over styles of writing. On this occasion, however, the terrain is not Helicon's slopes, but female physiques.[5] It is worth dwelling for a moment on the second of these approaches to *Amores* 3.1, since critics are so rarely prepared to read female flesh as poetic fiction. Clearly that practice is acceptable here because the flesh is labelled 'Elegy'.

Amores 3.1 is viewed as principally concerned with a stylistic contrast first expounded in the polemical works of Callimachus as an opposition, in poetic practices, between the *lepton* and the *pachu*. The Latin literary-critical terminology for this *Stilkampf* was then established in neoteric poetry, further developed in Virgil's *Eclogues*, and frequently deployed in the Propertian corpus.[6] In the context of 3.1, the advocacy of Fine Poetry is constructed round the dramatic device of a contest between two women but, entitled Elegia and Tragoedia, these women have only a precarious signification as individuals, so

---

[4] The question of what relationship holds between the first and second editions of the *Amores* does not have a substantial bearing on my readings of 3.1. Cameron (1968) argues that the second edition constitutes little more than a shortened version of the first. Boyd (1997: 136 and 142–7) argues cogently that the second edition is packaged as a complete 'story' of the poet's conversion to, and control over, amatory elegy.

[5] See esp. Schrijvers (1976). Cf. Reitzenstein (1935); Wimmel (1960) 295–7; Berman (1975) 14–20.

[6] See Wimmel (1960) *passim*. On the Propertian corpus, cf. Quadlbauer (1968) and (1970), and Wyke (2002) 46–114.

that a catalogue of their physical features functions more importantly as a catalogue of stylistic practices. The attributes of poetic genres are made flesh, and women are displayed as choices of generic style for males, as Sir Joshua Reynolds understood when he borrowed from this poem (among other sources) to depict the actor David Garrick choosing between Tragedy and Comedy.[7] Critics have noted that in this famous painting, exhibited at the Society of Artists in 1762, Comedy is depicted in the style of Correggio and Tragedy in the style of Guido Reni, establishing a stylistic opposition that works to highlight the directions in which both the actor and the painter were torn: between types of dramatic performance in the case of Garrick, and types of portraiture (intimate or heroic) in the case of Reynolds himself (Fig. 8.2; Wendorf 1996: 147–51; Postle 1995: 20–32).

In the case of *Amores* 3.1, every aspect of Ovid's women (their shape, comportment, and speech) is constructed in accordance with a Callimachean apologetics, and everywhere the reader is required to unite these women with issues of poetic production: 'The point throughout depends on the simple device of treating these two personifications as human beings and at the same time as poetic genres' (Lee 1962: 169. Cf. Bertini 1983: 227). Thus even the cave before which the women come to play out their struggle for an author (whose sylvan setting Reynolds recalls in his painting) reproduces the topography of the poetic programme with which Propertius introduced *his* third poetry book, thereby setting out Ovid's work for comparison (Berman 1975: 15–16; Morgan 1977: 17–18).

The narrator describes the first woman's approach (7–10):

uenit odoratos Elegia nexa capillos,
    et, puto, pes illi longior alter erat.
forma decens, uestis tenuissima, uultus amantis,
    et pedibus uitium causa decoris erat.

She came—Elegy—her scented curls bound up,
    and, I suspect, one foot longer than the other:
well formed, finely dressed, a lover's look,
    imperfect movement occasioning elegance.

---

[7] E. J. Kenney's suggestion of *Amores* 3.1 as a source for the painting is discussed by Postle (1995) 25.

Figure 8.2. 'Garrick between Tragedy and Comedy'. E. Fisher, after original exhibited in 1762 by Sir Joshua Reynolds.

Elegia is endowed with the body of the elegiac mistress: 'Miss Elegy resembles in every detail the beloved sung by the elegiac poets' (Schrijvers 1976: 415). The hairstyle, outline, dress, and expression catalogued in the hexameter verses 7 and 9 all reproduce attributes ascribed elsewhere to elegy's beloveds. When Cynthia first makes a physical appearance in the Propertian corpus, her hair is elaborately styled and perfumed, her dress is of fine Coan silk, and she possesses an ornamented *forma* (1.2.1–8).[8] The affinity between Elegia and the elegiac mistress is disclosed, moreover, by the reappearance of Elegia's attributes in the two poems directly following *Amores* 3.1, where physical features are assembled for an Ovidian *puella*: her look is full of erotic promise (3.2.83), her dress is delicate (3.2.36), her body defined by *forma* and *decens* (3.3.7–8).

To the attributes of a beauty, however, the pentameter verses 8 and 10 attach an incongruous limp. Accustomed to the physical characteristics usually allotted to the elegiac beloved, a reader would expect this *puella* to possess feet which were snowy-white or slight: a reminder arrives at *Amores* 3.3.7 (*pes erat exiguus—pedis est artissima forma*). In this poem, however, the elegiac woman's body has been awkwardly reshaped to serve poetic concerns. Now entitled Elegia and supplied with elegiac feet to match the unevenness of elegiac verse, this comic representation of a female form has 'a completely fictive character' (Schrijvers 1976: 416). In particular, the allocation to this woman of unequal feet demonstrates that here at least a female body has been shaped to suit an elegiac poetic programme, because physically they constitute a defect (*uitium*), stylistically an asset (*decor*).

In the pentameter verses *pes* signals ambiguously both human and metrical feet, but some critics have observed that such ambiguities are also generated by the language of the hexameter verses. So *forma* and *tenuissima* are recognized to be as applicable to a collection of words as they are to a woman. Guy Lee, for example, retains the ambiguity of these terms with translations such as 'she had style' (Lee 1968: 119). The delicacy which *tenuissima* suggests is read as qualifying the clothing of a Callimachean discourse, since *tenuis* is a well-documented signifier of the writing

---

[8] In the first poem of the *Monobiblos*, nothing is ascribed to the name *Cynthia* except a pair of eyes and the capacity to captivate.

style which Callimachus had designated *lepton* (Bertini 1983: 227; Lee 1962: 169).[9]

The vocabulary in which Elegia is formulated as flesh is thus allowed to point to her as being also a way of speaking, a mode of poetic composition. Yet, elsewhere, part of that vocabulary delineates the elegiac mistress. So *Amores* 3.1 invites its readers to ask the question whether other love elegies also present the female body in ambiguous terms. In the second poem of the *Monobiblos* for example, where Propertius first sets out the features of his elegiac mistress, she too possesses clothing that is *tenuis*, and a body defined by *forma*. The Propertian *puella* is charged with an excessive use of ornament in a poem whose style is paradoxically ornate and whose central theme has been identified as artifice itself (e.g. Curran 1975). Since there is every reason to suppose that—as the subject of Propertian art—the female form is an appropriate site for the expression of artistic concerns, what theoretical justification is there for depriving Cynthia of literary-critical possibilities, when they are welcomed for Elegia?[10]

Thus, in *Amores* 3.1 the flesh of the elegiac mistress is reproduced and recalled in the hexameter verses 7 and 9. In the pentameters (8 and 10) it is provided additionally with unequal feet. The comic incongruity reveals that here the beloved's body has been placed openly at the service of poetic concerns. Since the elegiac metre requires that the stylistic asset of foot shortening be put into practice precisely at the two moments when Elegia's physical defect is being pronounced, at least at this point in the elegiac corpus the body of a woman may be read uncontentiously as the anatomy of a text.

Tragoedia has now arrived in hot pursuit (11–14):

uenit et ingenti uiolenta Tragoedia passu:
    fronte comae torua, palla iacebat humi;
laeua manus sceptrum late regale mouebat,
    Lydius alta pedum uincla cothurnus erat.

She came too in grand strides—impassioned Tragedy:
    braids draping a darksome brow, her gown the earth,

---

[9] On *tenuis*, see also Quadlbauer (1968) 95–6; Fedeli (1985) 54 and 59.
[10] Curran (1975), for example, distinguishes the 'real' woman of Prop. 1.2.1–8 from the artist's creation which he claims the remainder of that poem is advocating.

left hand wielding wide the princely sceptre,
a Lydian boot her foot's high prop.

The second party to the *Stilkampf* is not the recipient of the
favourable stylistic appraisal suggested earlier by *decens* and *tenuissima*, but once again the attributes of a writing practice are fleshed
out and a female figure constructed to suit a Callimachean polemic.
As symbols of a Graeco-Roman tragic tradition, *palla, sceptrum*, and
cothurnus have already made an appearance in *Amores* 2.18.15–16
(Brandt 1911: *ad loc*; Reitzenstein 1935: 83). There they were associated with the narrator (as producer of tragic discourse). Here they
are associated with a narrative practice personified. Thus *uiolenta* is
suggestive of both human behaviour and dramatic technique (Brandt
1911: on *Am*. 3.1.11). In every way, Tragoedia is shaped to compare and contrast with Elegia. While Elegia's limp mimics the movement of elegiac couplets, Tragoedia's enormous stride embodies the
grandeur of the tragic metres. Similarly her hairstyle (*fronte comae
torua*) characterizes the diction of a dignified writing style.[11] As with
the features of Comedy and Tragedy in the painting by Reynolds,
female flesh and its paraphernalia evidently operate here as a means
of differentiating one genre from another. If, however, Tragoedia
dramatizes the *pachu*, then the body of the elegiac mistress has
entered the Ovidian narrative here because it is a manifestation of the
lepton.

    After Tragoedia has advocated her own production in terms which
are both moralistic and appropriately passionate, the narrator next
recalls her comportment and that of her rival for an author's attentions (31–4):[12]

hactenus, et mouit pictis innixa cothurnis
    densum caesarie terque quaterque caput.
altera, si memini, limis subrisit ocellis;
    fallor, an in dextra myrtea uirga fuit?

Thus far, and propped on her ornamented boots she bowed
    three times and four her thick-fleeced head.

---

[11] For the tragic tone of *torua*, cf. Pacuvius *Trag*. 36 and 37, and Accius *Trag*. 223.

[12] Schrijvers (1976: 417–21) offers a detailed account of the speech as incorporating a parody of tragic diction.

The other (if I remember) stole a peek and giggled—
am I wrong, or in her right hand was there a myrtle twig?

Each woman is attired with an emblem of poetic practice (*cothurnis* and the *myrtea uirga*), and each behaves in a manner appropriate to her own literary production. Tragoedia nods majestically like an Homeric Zeus. Elegia flirts in the manner of the elegiac mistress at the races in *Amores* 3.2.83: *risit et argutis quiddam promisit ocellis.* Diction matches behaviour as a means of differentiating levels of discourse: *caesarie* is a highly poetic word, in Ovid's work found otherwise only in hexameter verse; *limis* does not usually belong in literary language (Brandt 1963: on *Am.* 3.1.33; Reitzenstein 1935: 83–4; Schrijvers 1976: 421). Thus two opposed poetic traditions are demarcated by the two different ways in which these fictive females move.

So far, in this reading of *Amores* 3.1, attention has been drawn to the poem as a narrative of conflicting literary interests in which female forms have been shaped to suit a poetic purpose. The body of the elegiac mistress then enters such a discourse as a device to signify one particular practice of writing. A similar strategy is in operation when, in the course of her plea for production, Elegia mentions Corinna and the ease with which her pupil learned to slip through front doors (43–52). For in the general context of that speech (35–60), Corinna functions demonstrably as a signifier of erotic (specifically Ovidian) discourse and, therefore, may be read as representative of elegiac fictions. Firstly, the doors through which Corinna once stole have already been identified as among the props of elegy's producers rather than as an obstacle facing Augustan lovers (35–42) and, secondly, the woman who taught Corinna is subsequently identified wholly as text (53–8).

In the first part of her speech Elegia concedes *non ego contulerim sublimia carmina nostris:* | *obruit exiguas regia uestra fores* (I would not set towering poetry beside my own; | your palace eclipses tiny doorways, 39–40). The contrast between palace entrances and house doors is set within another opposition: Tragoedia is accused of being perpetually *grauis* (36), while Elegia boldly confesses that she is *leuis* (41). The signification of the *grauis | leuis* opposition is drawn away from the level of female dispositions and towards the level of writing styles by frequent references in the course of the passage to poetic production: compare *carmina* here (39) with *uerbis* (35), *numeris* (37), and *uersibus* (38). Furthermore, the reader will recognize the *grauis | leuis* opposition within which the respective doorways are described as the terminology of a Callimachean polemic already so used in *Amores* 1.1. There weapons were to be narrated *graui numero* (1), but beloveds (either boy or girl) *numeris leuioribus* (19). Thus the doors are positioned in a literary-critical framework signalled in 39–40 by *sublimia* and *exiguas* (Lee 1962: 169–70; Schrijvers 1976: 422). The word *sublimia* is of particular interest. Its etymology is obscure but the possibility of its derivation from *sub limen* immediately connects it as a stylistic evaluation with the subsequent discussion of doors. In such a context, *regia* and *fores* signify majestic and modest arenas of discourse respectively, as do allusions to streams of Helicon elsewhere.[13] So, since the royal palace constitutes the scenic backdrop for a tragic performance with no status independently of a tragic text, the house door becomes merely a property employed in elegy's amatory production.

In the last part of her speech, Elegia offers three examples of how she has suffered for love (53–8). The personification is continued through the use of active verbs such as *non uerita* (54) and *memini* (55), but the circumstances suffered (being pinned to a door, hidden in the folds of a dress, or submerged in water as an unwelcome birthday present) are appropriate for a tablet of wax, ludicrous for a woman. In each case, a comic mismatch between *puella* and love poem arises in which Elegia's status as text is paramount.[14] The first of these examples, after all, identifies her clearly as a literary practice, a poetical scroll, because she is *legi* (54). Thus Elegia is first presented in *Amores* 3.1 as a living woman of flesh (although even that flesh is incongruously elegiac in its structure) but, by the poem's close, the woman of flesh has been playfully reshaped into a work of elegiac art.

The centrepiece of Elegia's speech, 43–52, recalls both her own success as a *magistra amoris* and her prize pupil Corinna but, as we have seen, this teacher is also a poetic text and her speech an avowal

---

[13] See e.g. Virgil *Ecl.* 6 and Prop. 2.10, and the discussion of them in Wyke (2002) 46–77.

[14] As Brandt (1963) on *Am.* 3.1.57: 'hat nun das Mädchen weiter nichts als ein liebesgedicht bekommen'.

of a Callimachean poetics. So Corinna and the *custos* she has deceived constitute past samples of the writing practice Elegia advocates and stand in opposition to the *facta uirorum* (25) for which Tragoedia has just now called. Both the demeanour and the circumstances of the elegiac mistress are fashioned in order to signal past poems of the elegiac corpus. Firstly, memories of her *tunica uelata soluta* (51) recall Corinna's negligent appearance at *Amores* 1.5.9 (*tunica uelata recincta*). Thus, in a poem which puts female flesh on the poetic genre Elegy, physical features ascribed elsewhere to the elegiac mistress (most notably the first detailed depictions of both Cynthia and Corinna) are constantly recalled. Secondly, the elegiac beloved's past circumstances are so articulated as to survey the elegiacs of Tibullus. For Elegia claims to have provided Corinna with the sort of protection offered by Venus in Tibullus 1.2 (Reitzenstein 1935: 84), and sets the scene for that claim by reproducing terms that featured prominently in the first and last poems of that Tibullan poetry book (namely *rusticus* from Tibullus 1.1.8 and *lasciuus Amor* from Tibullus 1.10.57). Similarly, Elegia's ability to render a *ianua laxa* (46) recalls poems by all three Augustan elegists. Centred on the mistress's closed door, these poems include Tibullus 1.2, Propertius 1.16, Ovid *Amores* 1.6 and 2.19. Thus Corinna and her front door are constructed to recall an array of elegiac poems and function as signifiers of a poetic tradition opposed to the tragic narration of kings and palace entrances.

Finally, to conclude the narrative of *Amores* 3.1 and introduce a third book of love elegies, the adoption of Elegia as a practice of writing is recounted (61–70). Now her attractions are described solely in terms of poetic production and a Callimachean poetics, for she is said to grant *nostro uicturum nomen amori* (65). Elegiac composition is chosen not as the result of a pressing, romantic commitment to a mistress, but out of a desire for lasting fame. In *Epigr.* 7(9) Pfeiffer, Callimachus had already suggested that, since Theaetetus followed a clear poetic path towards the composition of epigrams rather than tragedies, Greece would forever sing his skill.

The theme of great glory arising, paradoxically, out of slight poetry features frequently in Latin literature descended from the Callimachean tradition (Quadlbauer 1968: 96–7). Consequently, as a recipient of lasting acclaim, the Ovidian *amor* may be read as equivalent to a Callimachean *sophiê* or skill: love is literary eroticism and its artful composition. Thus, by the close of *Amores* 3.1, the encounter between two female figures has been clearly identified as a contest between styles of writing, and love is understood to be a poetic activity. The only respect in which Ovid has veered from the clear path of Callimachus' poetics is in his suggestion that he has some interest in, and will shortly embark upon, tragic composition. The elegiac mistress (as the embodiment of Callimachus' *lepton*) is only temporarily the poet's practice for, at some point, Ovid does produce a tragedy—the now lost *Medea*. Reynolds borrows this conceit too for his painting of Garrick's choice of performance styles: Garrick is posed glancing backwards at Tragedy with an apologetic expression. Like Ovid, the actor appears to be promising Tragedy that he won't be gone for long.[15]

Amores 3.1 provides poetic genres with female flesh in order to dramatize a Callimachean opposition between poetic practices. However, Corinna (along with her front door) enters the debate as an example of elegiac composition in the requisite Callimachean manner and, throughout the poem, the attributes and activities of the elegiac mistress are recalled and subsumed under personified Elegy. The text sets up a series of witty mismatches between what is appropriate to the depiction of an elegiac *puella* and to the description of an elegiac poem: supplied now with elegiac feet and subjected to a variety of indignities, the body of the elegiac mistress has become a site for the humorous expression of Callimachean concerns.[16]

FEMALE FLESH AS POLITICS

Amores 3.1 is not concerned exclusively, however, with issues of poetic practice and their articulation through representations of the female form. The account it provides of the narrator's choice between the relative attractions of Elegia and Tragoedia travesties the structure of another famous choice between female forms—namely the

---

[15] As Postle (1995) 25 on Kenney's Ovidian reading of the painting.
[16] Cf. Keith (1999) on the literary-critical terminology inherited from Callimachus (and mediated by Roman rhetorical theory) in which the body of the poet-lover is described in Augustan elegy.

allegorical presentation of Hercules' choice between Aretê (Virtue) and Kakia (Vice) first expounded by the sophist Prodicus, transmitted in Xenophon's *Memorabilia* 2.1.21–34, and then widely and repeatedly imitated in western literature and art. In Sebastian Brant's enormously popular late fifteenth-century German morality tale *Narrenschiff* (The Ship of Fools, 1494), for example, the fools who do not heed the right road in life are briefly contrasted with the Prodican Hercules who makes the correct choice of Wisdom over Joy, Virtue over vain Delight. The woodcut that accompanies this chapter of Brant's well illustrates his description of Wisdom as a pale, hard, sour, and joyless woman in contrast to the physical attractions of Delight (Fig. 8.3).[17]

A few commentators on Ovid's *Amores* 3.1 have observed the correspondence between the narrator's choice and that of Hercules (Reitzenstein 1935: 81–2; Brandt 1963 on *Am.* 3.1.11; Schrijvers 1976: 407–13), but its implications for reading elegy's female forms as playful signifiers of a moral or political position have not been fully explored. Only P. H. Schrijvers noted briefly that moral arguments are employed in *Amores* 3.1 and that the allocation of victory to Elegia involves 'the re-evaluation of values' (Schrijvers 1976: 422), but the article in which these valuable points were made appeared as part of a Festschrift for J. C. Kamerbeek and was therefore concerned primarily with issues centring on the practice of tragedy.

The narrative strategy of positioning the conflict between Elegia and Tragoedia in a direct line of descent from that between Aretê and Kakia discloses an important structural function of female flesh as signifier of male political and moral practices. The recollection and comic debasement of the earlier moral allegory assigns the Ovidian narrator the role of a latter-day Roman Hercules deciding not just between writing styles, but between lifestyles, and it is through the shape, comportment, and speech of the poem's two female constructs that conflicting moral and political ideologies are articulated and appraised.

---

[17] Zeydel (1944) conveniently provides a description and English translation of Brant's work. Panofsky (1930) and Galinsky (1972) discuss chapter 107 (and its dependency on both Xenophon and Ovid) in the context of their accounts of the choice of Hercules in western literature and art.

Figure 8.3. 'The Choice of Hercules'. Woodcut illustrating 1497 edition of *Narrenschiff* by Sebastian Brant.

In their appearance, their attire, and their pose, Elegia and Tragoedia are clearly differentiated as respectively *meretrix* and *matrona*.
As matron, Tragoedia is clothed in the concealing garments of
a respectable Roman wife (*palla iacebat humi*, 12), and adopts
highly dignified gestures (31–2; Schrijvers 1976: 416–17). As mistress, Elegia is provided with both a sexually provocative dress (*uestis
tenuissima*, 9) and expression (9 and 33). Yet the earlier, allegorical account of divergent modes of conduct had also been expressed
in terms of a choice between *meretrix* and *matrona*, and later

manifestations of Hercules' choice followed suit.[18] According to
Xenophon's account, Hercules had been faced with a choice between
Aretê as a woman wearing a modest look and the purity of white
or Kakia as a woman wearing a brazen expression and a dress that
revealed all (*Mem.* 2.1.22), while the fifteenth-century illustration of
the event hides the body of stern Wisdom in floor-length garments
and discloses all but the genitalia of smiling Joy.

In the features and in the dress of the Ovidian women, a counterpart for Elegia is to be found in Kakia, and for Tragoedia in Aretê.
By reproducing the features of female forms that are employed elsewhere to typify codes of conduct, the Ovidian text identifies its female
figures also as such types: in *Amores* 3.1, Tragoedia functions as an
Augustan embodiment of Virtue and Elegia as an embodiment of
Vice. The victory of Elegia as Vice, the preference for a *meretrix* over
a *matrona*, then constitutes a witty and provocative re-writing of the
mythic parable in which Hercules chooses Virtue.[19]

It is not just through female physiques that an ideologically
provocative position is established for the narrator of *Amores* 3.1.
Moral and political concerns are to the forefront of Tragoedia's plea
for authorship. Before advocating herself as a practice of writing,
Tragoedia condemns her opponent (17–22):

nequitiam uinosa tuam conuiuia narrant,
      narrant in multas compita secta uias.
saepe aliquis digito uatem designat euntem
      atque ait 'hic, hic est, quem ferus urit Amor'.
fabula, nec sentis, tota iactaris in Vrbe,
      dum tua praeterito facta pudore refers.

Your depravity tipsy parties tell,
      crossroads tell it—split into many streets.
Often someone with his finger points out the passing bard
      and says 'That's him, that's the one cruel Love burns!'
You're talk, you don't realize, spread round the whole city,
      while you report your own acts, shame abandoned.

---

[18] As e.g. Gigon (1956) 64. See Kuntz (1994).
[19] The same has been said for the painting by Reynolds who was known to have
read a version of Hercules' choice in the works of Lord Shaftesbury. See Postle (1995)
21–3.

The context of this passage and its central reference to a *uatem* and *Amor* (rather than to a lover and his girlfriend) identify it as an assault on erotic elegy, although that assault is expressed in terms of an author's actions and is enclosed by the terminology of moral conduct—namely *nequitiam* (17) and *pudore* (22). As an Augustan matron and embodiment of Virtue, Tragoedia gives voice to the values of the establishment and interprets the production of elegy as vice, for matrons would be expected to regret the passing of *pudor* and to denigrate the sexual licence that *nequitia* suggests. The practitioner of poetic eroticism is portrayed as isolated from the rest of the community at Rome and labelled as morally corrupt. Tragoedia thus ascribes to Augustan elegy an unorthodoxy boldly proclaimed by its authors elsewhere: the poet was introduced at the beginning of a second book of *Amores* as *ille ego nequitiae Naso poeta meae* (2.1.2; Brandt 1963: on *Am.* 3.1.17) and in the Propertian poem 2.24 (which *Amores* 3.1 here recalls) the scandal of *nequitia* is said to accrue to the creator of poems on Cynthia.[20] Once again, at this point in the corpus of Augustan elegy, its unorthodox nature is to be understood through the agency of a female form.

Tragoedia continues her case by commanding her immediate production (23–30):

tempus erat thyrso pulsum grauiore moueri;
    cessatum satis est: incipe maius opus.
materia premis ingenium; cane facta uirorum:
    'haec animo' dices 'area digna meo est'.
quod tenerae cantent lusit tua Musa puellae,
    primaque per numeros acta iuuenta suos.
nunc habeam per te Romana Tragoedia nomen:
    implebit leges spiritus iste meas.

Time, propelled by the weightier wand, to be moved—
    there's been ample idleness. Undertake a greater task.
Your material suppresses talent; celebrate the feats of heroes:
    'this arena', you'll say, 'suits my spirit'.
Ditties for delicate girls to sing your Muse has played,
    first youth driven by its proper rhythms.

---

[20] The language of 3.1.17–22 recalls that of Prop. 2.24.1–8 where *urere, fabula, tota urbs*, and *pudor* are also to be found.

Now, through you, let Roman Tragedy win fame;
  your energy will satisfy my demands.

Tragoedia offers not only the allurement of a grander writing style
but, following the mythic parable of Hercules, the attractions of work
and social responsibility. According to Prodicus' tale, there are no
thoughts of war or business in the pursuit of Kakia (Xen. *Mem.*
2.1.24). Similarly, in *Amores* 3.1, the rival of Elegia/Kakia describes
elegy's pursuit as unemployment, or an act of idleness; used of poetic
eroticism *cessare* suggests that it involves the absence of any adequate
political or social role for its author. Elegy is associated with girls,
delicacy, adolescence, and play; tragedy with men, deeds, and dignity.
Tragoedia concludes her speech by describing the result of her practice in the community: from elegy there arises gossip at Rome, but
from tragedy glory. *Romana* marks the different positions tragedy
and elegy hold in relation to the state, for drama may be read as a
national genre (a state institution) while erotic elegy is often associated with the history of struggles against Roman militarism. Thus
the *Amores* as a whole is rounded off by the location of its narrator
within the Paelignian (rather than the Roman) race, and then that
race is recorded as having fought against Roman oppression during the Social Wars (*cum timuit socias anxia Roma manus*, 3.15.10).
Propertius too had closed a collection of elegiac poems by linking
its author's birthplace with civil war and a period *cum Romana suos
egit discordia ciuis* (when Roman discord drove her own citizens,
1.22.5).

   While Tragoedia thus takes on the part of Aretê in denying moral
or social responsibility to the authorship of elegy, Elegia cleverly
appropriates the vocabulary of Virtue to express a different ideological position for her narrator. In Prodicus' parable, Aretê talks
to Hercules about the necessity of suffering to achieve the good life
awarded by the gods (Xen. *Mem.* 2.1.28), a suffering that manifests
itself in the fifteenth-century woodcut as thorn bushes and a dark
night sky around Wisdom (in contrast to the flowers and sunlight
surrounding Joy). In the Ovidian poem, Elegia redefines what is to be
thought of as the good achieved through *ponos* for the world of erotic
discourses (Schrijvers 1976: 422); the end of some rather ludicrous
ordeals becomes sexual access (43–58).

In *Amores* 3.1, therefore, Aretê and Kakia have been reproduced in the flesh and speech of Tragoedia and Elegia respectively. The written women of this elegy are also to be read as signifiers of moral and political ideologies. However, in allowing his narrator to be won over by the attractions of the *meretrix*, rather than the *matrona*, Ovid has radically rewritten the mythic parable (as Reynolds will much later).[21] Pursuit of Virtue is still depicted here as a hard task—the Ovidian *labor aeternus* of writing tragedies (68) parallels the Prodican long, hard road to Aretê (Schrijvers 1976: 424), but the glory that was once its reward is no longer Virtue's to bestow. According to Prodicus, the friends of Virtue are not forgotten and dishonoured, but remembered and celebrated (Xen. *Mem.* 2.1.33). In the morally perverse world of literary eroticism it is the awkward figure of limping Elegia/Vice who bestows on her poets everlasting fame (*nostro uicturum nomen amori*, 65) and not the swift death which, in the fifteenth-century woodcut, is envisaged as Delight's hidden companion.

The female forms Elegia and Tragoedia have clearly been constructed to suit a playful Ovidian narrative of moral and political difference, but the extent of the political unorthodoxy which the choice of Elegia articulates is best understood in the historical context of elegy's production as an ideological discourse. For the presentation of an Augustan 'Hercules' choosing Vice rather than Virtue, a *meretrix* rather than a *matrona*, actively conflicts with the contemporary, institutionalized role of Hercules as symbol of the Roman state and its *princeps*. In Roman culture, as Karl Galinsky has observed, Hercules had become idealized as the perfect embodiment of Stoic virtue and was so closely conjoined with Augustus as 'to be considered an Augustan symbol' (Galinsky 1972: 153). Both through Augustus' own efforts (such as in timing his triple triumph of 29 BC to coincide with the official festival of Hercules on 13 August) and through such notable literary representations as those in Virgil's *Aeneid*, Hercules became a symbol of political orthodoxy, of the hegemony of the Augustan state in the post-Actium period (Galinsky 1972: 126–66; 1996: 222–4). Thus comic debasements of the Hercules mythology, such as the conversion of hero into clumsy suitor in Propertius 4.9 and in *Heroides* 9, are read as narrative strategies for the expression of anti-Augustan sentiment.[22] Here, in *Amores* 3.1, when faced with the same dilemma as Hercules in the shape of *meretrix* or *matrona*, the elegiac narrator rejects the expected response institutionalized in myth and opts for a female form openly dissociated from social and political responsibility.

Through the flippant association of Ovid's female forms Elegia and Tragoedia with the mythic parable of Kakia and Aretê, *Amores* 3.1 signals that its written women articulate a political, as well as a poetic, heterodoxy for their narrator. Here women enter elegy's fictive world to formulate an amusing manifesto of both literary and political difference, and their bodies are clearly shaped to suit that manifesto. In particular, the asymmetric body with which Elegia is endowed functions as a signifier both of a Callimachean poetics (the advocacy of what is *lepton*) and an anti-Augustan politics (the advocacy of *nequitia*). Since, however, Elegia's body has already been identified in all respects (except its unequal feet) with the body assigned elsewhere to the elegiac mistress, the question immediately arises as to whether Elegia's narrative function in *Amores* 3.1 has any implications for the function of the mistress elsewhere in the corpus of Augustan love poetry.

THE ELEGIAC MISTRESS

It is not possible, in fact, to confine a reading of female flesh as political fiction to *Amores* 3.1 and thereby safeguard the identification of elegy's female subjects with specific individuals living in Augustan Rome. For, at the same time as *Amores* 3.1 incorporates many features of the elegiac *puella*, it encourages its readers to look both outwards to other modes of representing the female form and backwards at the role of the *puella* in articulating elegy's poetic and political concerns.

The narrative structure of *Amores* 3.1 locates its female figures firmly in a tradition for representing women that stretches back to Prodicus' parable and on beyond Ovidian elegy. Although the story of

---

[22] On Prop. 4.9, see Anderson (1964) 11 and Pillinger (1969) 189; and DeBrohun (1994), Lindheim (1998), and Janan (1998) and (2001) 128–45. On *Heroides* 9, see Galinsky (1972) 153–60.

Hercules in Biuio has been represented in numerous and diverse ways
in the accounts of philosophers, poets, and painters (Panofsky 1930),
the allocation of attributes to the female embodiments of man's moral
or political choices falls into a set pattern: the features of Ovid's
Elegia and the elegiac beloved she recalls are thus also those commonly possessed by such figures as *Kakia, Hêdonê, Tyrannis, Pseudo-
doxia, Adulatio,* or *Voluptas* (Alpers 1912: 51–8). In his epic poem
on the second Punic War, Silius Italicus (especially close to Ovid
in the chronology of representations of Hercules' choice) presents
P. Cornelius Scipio with a dilemma. He structures his account to
match the mythic dilemma of Hercules by depicting a contest for
the soldier's allegiance between the divine figures *Voluptas* and *Virtus*.
The physiques of his goddesses closely resemble those of Elegia and
Tragoedia (*Punica* 15.23–31):

alter Achaemenium spirabat uertice odorem,
ambrosias diffusa comas et ueste refulgens,
ostrum qua fuluo Tyrium suffuderat auro;
fronte decor quaesitus acu, lasciuaque crebras
ancipiti motu iaciebant lumina flammas.
alterius dispar habitus: frons hirta nec umquam
composita mutata coma; stans uultus, et ore
incessuque uiro proprior laetique pudoris,
celsa umeros niueae fulgebat stamine pallae.

One from her crown breathed Persian scent,
spilling her ambrosial curls, and brilliant in a dress
Tyrian purple had traced with rosy gold;
elegance on her brow acquired with a pin, her desirous eyes
darted left and right repeated flames.
Far different the other's look: a shaggy brow never by
styled hair altered, a firm gaze,
both face and pace nearer to a man's and joyfully modest;
towering, her shoulders gleamed with thread of snowy robe.

From Ovid's Elegia, *Voluptas* has inherited scented hair, expensive
clothes, and a provocative look. From Tragoedia, *Virtus* has inherited
a mannish stride, dishevelled hair, a stern expression, and matronly
gown (Bruére 1959: 240–2). The same grouping of physical features,
the same *meretrix/matrona* dichotomy for female flesh, is to be found

in Silius' hexameters as in Ovid's elegiacs because those features bring with them a whole constellation of cultural values through which to articulate the moral and political choices men face. The *meretrix* figure again acts as a signifier of social irresponsibility and idleness, the *matrona* of state duties and military pursuits. It is because everywhere such female types may have ideological repercussions that Silius is able to deploy the same *meretrix/matrona* dichotomy in order to dramatize Scipio's Stoic pursuit of a command in Spain.[23]

The employment of such archetypes for female flesh has not of course been confined to variations on the theme of *Hercules in Biuio*.[24] The opposition between Innocent and Seductress has subsequently played a crucial role in shaping the Christian Church's models for female behaviour (the Virgin Mary and Eve)[25] while, for instance, 'the two most common types of women in film noir are the exciting, childless whores, or the boring, potentially childbearing sweethearts'.[26] For images of women, and the values attached to them, arise out of both the social relation between the sexes and concepts of gender in a given culture. In patriarchal cultures, the central measurement of women, the way women enter cultural forms, is through sexuality. Patriarchy's familial ideology then associates the sexually unrestrained, childless woman with social disruption and locates her on the margins of society. Marriage and motherhood, being concerned with the ordering of female sexuality in terms which will be socially effective for patriarchy, restore women to a central position, while still withholding full economic or political power.[27]

[23] For Scipio as built in the image of the Stoic Hercules, see Bassett (1966).
[24] See now McGinn (1998) 147–71 and 208–9, who argues that the distinction between *matrona* or *mater familias* and *meretrix* was deeply rooted in Roman ideas about social status and sexual morality. The Augustan legislation of 18 BC then gave legal force to what was before a social and moral contrast.
[25] See e.g. Warner (1976); Cameron (1989).
[26] Harvey (1980) 25. On the cultural polarization of Woman into either demonized whore or exalted goddess as used to depict conflicting facets of Latin love poetry's beloved, see now Janan (1994) esp. 71. She uses this polarization specifically to compare Catullus' Lesbia in poems 11 and 51. Cf. Greene (1998) 62–6 on the duality of Propertius' Cynthia and 80–1 on Ovid's Corinna. Fredrick (1997) also argues that the elegiac mistress oscillates between a representation as virgin and as whore.
[27] See e.g. Berger (1972); Lipshitz (1978); Kaplan (1980). For the prevalence of this mode of structuring femininity in antiquity, see Lefkowitz (1981), Dixon (1988), Edwards (1993) 34–62, Skinner (1997) 9–11, McGinn (1998) esp. 17, and Dixon (2001) chs. 3 and 5. See also Wyke (2002: 78–114) on the women of Propertius book 4,

In the case of the theme *Hercules in Biuio*, women enter cultural discourse to define male moral and political choices and their physiques are shaped accordingly and appropriately labelled *meretrix* or *matrona*.

Thus the similarities between the *meretrix* figures of Prodicus' tale, Ovid's elegies, and Silius' epic demonstrate that the flesh of the elegiac mistress has a history beyond the physical features of any Augustan girlfriend and belongs, rather, to an archetypal dichotomy whore/matron through which are expressed male political and moral conflicts. It is the silks and scents, the coiffure, and the provocative look borrowed from the elegiac mistress that link Elegia with symbols of pleasure and the absence of virtue. Silius' *Voluptas* owes more to the features of an elegiac *puella* than to a personification of elegiac poetry since only the evident attributes of writing styles have been carefully avoided in his version; elegy's limp, tragedy's boots.

Ovid's Elegia identifies her component parts as belonging to a pervasive tradition in which female flesh functions as a signifier of male ideological positions. In her flimsy dresses and adorned to lure lovers (Prop. 1.2, 1.15.1–8), the elegiac mistress is differentiated from the Roman *matrona* who wears the long gown of respectability (Tib. 1.6.67–8) and is said to have no place in elegiac discourse (*Ars* 1.31–2). Not the narrator's wife, she is a *meretrix* in the broadest sense of the word: a symbol of *nequitia* and the absence of *pudor* (Prop. 2.24.1–8). Thus by claiming to be entrapped by an unrestrained female sexuality, by the figure of 'une irrégulière' (Veyne 1983: 15), the writers of elegiac poetry are able to portray themselves as abandoning traditional social responsibilities: not soldier, lawyer, or politician, but poet of love (*Am.* 1.15).

There is a second, pressing reason why it is not possible to view the function of female flesh in *Amores* 3.1 as unique to this particular point in the corpus of Augustan love poetry, but necessary instead to view the poem as having important implications for reading the flesh of the elegiac mistress elsewhere. As a narrative openly expressing poetic concerns (the rejection of a higher form of writing in

and (2002: 195–243 and 321–51) on Roman constructions of (respectively) Cleopatra and Messalina.

favour of elegy), *Amores* 3.1 belongs to a group of Augustan elegies ultimately indebted to the rejection of epic that Callimachus had expressed in the elegiacs of the *Aetia*. Often to be found at the opening or close of poetry books, these poems have been grouped together under various headings, such as the *recusatio* or the *apologetischen form* (Wimmel 1960). Poem 3.1 cannot easily be isolated from other such programmatic poems within the *Amores* since they have been read as offering a unifying movement to the collection, from an initial acceptance of elegy to its ultimate rejection (Du Quesnay 1973: 5–6).

In particular, references within *Amores* 3.1 to a pressing demand for tragic composition bind it tightly to an earlier *recusatio* (2.18.13–18):

sceptra tamen sumpsi curaque tragoedia nostra
    creuit, et huic operi quamlibet aptus eram:
risit Amor pallamque meam pictosque cothurnos
    sceptraque priuata tam cito sumpta manu;
hinc quoque me dominae numen deduxit iniquae,
    deque cothurnato uate triumphat Amor.

Still I seized sceptres, and tragedy, thanks to my pains,
    grew. But, however suited I was to this labour,
Love laughed at my gown and ornamented boots
    and the sceptres so quickly seized by a humble hand.
From this also a cruel lady's sway fetched me back,
    and over a booted bard triumphs Love.

In this version of the *apologetischen Form* (Wimmel 1960: 305–6; Morgan 1977: 15–17; Fedeli 1980: 186), it is the narrator who plays Tragoedia's role as advocate of a grander writing style. Here the symbols of tragic discourse (the sceptre, the gown, and the painted boots) adorn the figure of a poet not a personified genre (Brandt 1963: on *Am.* 2.18.15 and 3.1.11). The narrator is already equipped with the regalia Tragoedia offers him at *Amores* 3.1.63.

If it is the narrator who plays Tragoedia's role, it is *Amor* and a *domina* who play Elegia's and orchestrate the retreat from the production of tragedy. It is also *Amor* and a *puella* who orchestrate a retreat from epic earlier in the poem, as *quoque* recalls (2.18.3–12):

nos, Macer, ignaua Veneris cessamus in umbra,
    et tener ausuros grandia frangit Amor.
saepe meae 'tandem' dixi 'discede' puellae:
    in gremio sedit protinus illa meo;
saepe 'pudet' dixi: lacrimis uix illa retentis
    'me miseram, iam te' dixit 'amare pudet?'
implicuitque suos circum mea colla lacertos
    et, quae me perdunt, oscula mille dedit.
uincor, et ingenium sumptis reuocatur ab armis,
    resque domi gestas et mea bella cano.

I idle, Macer, in Venus' lazy shade
    and delicate Love shatters my grandiose ventures.
'At last', I've often said to my girl, 'leave':
    she's sat on my lap immediately.
'I'm ashamed', I've often said: with tears scarcely checked
    'poor me', she's said, 'are you ashamed to love already?'
She's wrapped her arms around my neck
    and kisses that kill me, she's given a thousand.
I'm beaten: my talent is recalled from the armour it seized,
    I celebrate domestic action and my personal battles.

Just as Elegia lures the poet away from tragedy with a lover's look and a provocative smile, so an elegiac mistress lures him away from epic with an erotic embrace.

This *puella*, however, is only as relevant to the real life of a love poet as armour to an epic poet or painted boots and a sceptre to a tragedian. In *Amores* 2.18 weapons, stage properties, and a girl function as material symbols of poetic production in a *Stilkampf* where elegy always gains ultimate ascendancy.[28] Thus elegy is humorously identified as already incorporating elements of epic when military metaphors are applied to erotic activity (11–12; Quadlbauer 1968: 94 n. 5): overpowered by a woman (*uincor*), a poet must summon his talent back from the front (*reuocatur ab armis*) and write instead militant elegies on bedroom battles (*resque domi gestas et mea bella*). Similarly, the contrast between *tener* and *grandia* with which the epic poet Macer is confronted recalls the stylistic

[28] For *arma* as a symbol of epic, see Fedeli (1985) 57–8. For the actor's costume of gown and boots as a symbol of tragedy, see Brandt (1963) on *Am.* 2.18.5.

contrast between *lepton* and *pachu* set out in the *Aetia*. Yet the elegiac *puella* is also implicated in the victory of delicacy, since her physical prevention of epic composition (5–12) enacts and elaborates the destruction by delicate *Amor* of a poet's ambitious schemes (4). So, in submitting to the attractions of an elegiac mistress, the narrator also embraces an embodiment of Callimachus' *lepton*.

Positioned at the opening of a third book of erotic elegies, *Amores* 3.1 also invites comparison with the introduction to the second book of the collection. Following the pattern for the *apologetischen Form*, *Amores* 2.1 rejects a higher form of poetic discourse in favour of elegiacs.[29] The poet first declares that he had ventured on the production of a Gigantomachy (11–16). As material symbols of such an exalted practice, the Ovidian narrator is depicted playfully clutching clouds, a thunderbolt, and, most irreverently, Jupiter himself (*in manibus nimbos et cum Ioue fulmen habebam* 15). The poet confesses that he then dropped poor Jupiter and his thunderbolt to resume the production of elegiacs (17–22). Once again it is a Callimachean poetics that is expressed through such a bizarre evocation: Jupiter's thunderbolt marks the 'thundering' style which Callimachus had opposed to his own in *Aetia* fr. 120 (Innes 1979: 166–7), while production of elegies which are *leuis* (21) obeys the Callimachean call for *leptotês* (Giangrande 1981:38). But what instigates the retreat into Callimachean elegiacs? As in *Amores* 2.18, epic composition is disrupted by the elegiac mistress who this time slams her front door (*clausit amica fores: ego cum Ioue fulmen omisi*, 17). Just as Elegia institutes the third book of the *Amores*, so an elegiac *puella* institutes the second.

Thus, within the *Amores*, a succession of humorous programmatic poems deploys female forms to articulate a Callimachean apologetics. Elegia opens a third poetry book playing the role already undertaken by the elegiac mistress in the second, and the association between personification and realistically constructed beloved is sustained by a reduplication of physical features. The ungainly figure of asymmetric Elegia then challenges any romantic reading of the elegiac mistress

---

[29] See Wimmel (1960) 303–5; Morgan (1977) 12–14; Giangrande (1981) 33–40; Boyd (1997) 191–4; and Keith (1999) 51–2.

because it incorporates many of her attributes, and replays her part in the elegiac narrative, at the same time as it embodies political and poetic concerns. It is, moreover, her reproduction of the elegiac figure of the *meretrix* that enables Elegia to symbolize an anti-establishment politics while, in symbolizing a Callimachean poetics, Elegia plays with the beloved's function in earlier versions of the *apologetischen Form*.

So the physique of the Ovidian *puella* appears to be as much a travesty of love elegy's conventions as the text in which she figures. The series of programmatic poems that culminate in *Amores* 3.1 first ridicule and then decode elegy's own romantic convention that love poets begin to write because they are in love, that a frustrating passion for a woman who exists outside the confines of the text instigates its production, that her physical features are beautiful beyond compare. Comic circumstances surround the renewal of elegiac composition in *Amores* 2.1 (a girl's door slams, the poet drops Jupiter in surprise), and in *Amores* 2.18 the poet is forced to abandon his ambitious schemes when pinned down by a girl in his lap. As the last poem in the series to institute elegiacs through a female form, *Amores* 3.1 even abandons realism and, by providing its *puella* additionally with a limp and the title 'Elegy', reduces the romantic convention to an amusing conceit that finally exposes elegy's female subjects as fictions.[30]

CYNTHIA REVISITED

Amores 3.1 recalls the earlier fictive practices of Tibullus and Propertius, belongs to a cycle of *Apologien* that extends back beyond the Ovidian corpus, and is even set in the landscape of Propertius' programmatic poetry. The poetic text, therefore, encourages its readers to locate it squarely within the corpus of Augustan elegy, and to associate it with a particular pattern of narrative strategies deployed throughout the *Amores* to probe Propertian erotic discourse. Does the

---

[30] See Keith (1994), who analyses the *puellae* in some of the non-programmatic poems of the *Amores* in terms of the relationship between their 'style' and the aesthetic principles of elegy.

poem's playful warning (that elegiac *puellae* are simply textual bodies) then apply even to Cynthia?

Critics recognize that the narrative of the *Amores* is constructed within the framework of a general critical strategy they variously describe as a burlesque of elegiac conventions, a *reductio ad absurdum* of elegiac practices, a breaking of elegy's rules, a parody of Propertian poetry, a demystification of elegy's romanticism and its fiction of male erotic enslavement to one dominating mistress.[31] Ovid is seen to be decoding the romantic and realistic practice of writing associated most notably with the Propertian corpus. In this way, the strategy of recalling earlier Propertian poems has been called one of the most significant aspects of the *Amores*, and the programmatic poems identified as important stages in its execution.[32]

As an example of this process, the first poem of *Amores* 1 reveals a rich seam of 'demystification'. There the first logical step is taken to construct a literary eroticism: the adoption of the elegiac metre. The poet was planning to write epic in solemn hexameters, when Cupid stole a foot from the second line and thus converted the poetry into elegiacs. At this point the narrator is not yet in love. He does not make the declaration of love for a specific woman that his audience might expect from a poet continuing the tradition established in Augustan elegy by Gallus, Tibullus, and Propertius (*nec mihi materia est numeris leuioribus apta*, 1.1.19). The role of poet is given priority over that of lover and the Ovidian narrator expresses his metrical (rather than emotional) concerns. The poem demands comparison with the beginning of Propertius' *Monobiblos*.[33] There the narrator makes no such overt reference to poetic preferences: Cynthia is the cause of his being in love. The reader understands that the *Monobiblos* has been written in an autobiographical mode and that, at least on the narrative's surface, the Cynthia of the text is to be read as if a real woman. Ovid's poem, however, by drawing attention to the creative process,

---

[31] See e.g. Otis (1938); Du Quesnay (1973); Lyne (1980) 239–87; Davis (1981); Conte (1989) 449–56; Greene (1998) 67–113 and O'Neill (1999).

[32] Respectively Du Quesnay (1973) 6 and Morgan (1977) 7–26. See too Boyd (1997) esp. 1–18. While Boyd concedes that the *Amores* reverse the illusion of sincerity central to the poetry of Propertius and Tibullus, she does not consider that reversal to be the overriding concern of the Ovidian poems.

[33] As e.g. Gross (1975–6) 153–4. See Keith (1992*b*) and Boyd (1997) 136–8 and 147–9.

warns that realism is merely a property of the text. By describing the poet's mastery over his own material, Ovid exposes the conventions of elegiac romanticism and the fictionality of its mistress (Greene 1998: 68–73). Similarly, the programmatic poems of Ovid's second book have been thought to imply a playful criticism of Propertian arguments in favour of elegiac production that were addressed to the epic poet Ponticus in poems 7 and 9 of the *Monobiblos* (Morgan 1977: 12–17; Du Quesnay 1973: 25–7).

If *Amores* 3.1 is not commonly read as forming part of this general Ovidian strategy to expose realism's romantic conventions, it is precisely because here elegy's realistic representation of female flesh undergoes demystification and exposure as a poetic convention. The crooked contours of Elegia (the *puella* as a practice of writing) mark the culmination of a series of three programmatic poems (2.1, 2.18, 3.1) that first burlesque and then decipher the realistically constructed Propertian *puella* and her part in the expression of poetic and political concerns.

Furthermore, the sequence of poems makes its own operations manifest by commencing with an account of how a mistress's antics thwarted the composition of a grand Gigantomachy (2.1.11–16). This isolated reference in the *Amores* to a failed Gigantomachy, its position in the first poem of a second book, its language and line structure, are all designed to recall the Gigantomachy rejected by Propertius in favour of elegiac composition in the introduction to his own second poetry book (2.1.17–20; Morgan 1977: 16 and Boyd 1997: 197). The first poem in Ovid's series indicates clearly that, on this occasion, the physique of the Propertian *puella* has been taken as starting point for the process of demystification. For, among all the programmatic poems of the Propertian corpus, it is 2.1 that employs the body of the elegiac mistress most openly and most extensively to trace its author's poetic and political heterodoxy (2.1.5–16):[34]

siue illam Cois fulgentem incedere <cogis>,
    hac totum e Coa ueste uolumen erit;
seu uidi ad frontem sparsos errare capillos,
    gaudet laudatis ire superba comis;

---

[34] Cf. Keith (1999) 52–3 on the analogous use of the poet lover's body in 2.1 to describe a Callimachean corpus.

siue lyrae carmen digitis percussit eburnis,
  miramur, facilis ut premat arte manus;
seu cum poscentis somnum declinat ocellos,
  inuenio causas mille poeta nouas;
seu nuda erepto mecum luctatur amictu,
  tum uero longas condimus Iliadas;
seu quidquid fecit siue est quodcumque locuta,
  maxima de nihilo nascitur historia.

If gleaming in Coan silks you make her go,
  of that Coan dress the whole book will be composed;
or if on her brow I have seen scattered curls stray,
  she delights to walk with pride in praised hair;
or if the lyre's song with ivory fingers she's struck,
  we wonder at the quick hands she presses with skill;
or when she lowers eyes that desire sleep,
  I discover causes, a thousand new ones for a poet;
or if naked she grapple with me, her robe stripped off,
  surely then we construct lengthy Iliads;
or whatever she's done, or whatever she's said,
  from nothing the grandest history is born.

The context makes it clear that this *puella*, who instigates a second book of love elegies, forms part of a serious polemic on literary and political choices. The first line of the poem introduces the elegiac mistress as the answer to a literary question that concerns only the narrator and his readership (*quaeritis, unde mihi totiens scribantur amores,* 2.1.1). After her appearance, Callimachus is called upon openly as a model for the production of alternatives to the epic writing style (39–42), and the subject of Cynthia is presented as occupying the space of an unorthodox account of the birth of the Augustan state: the unwritten poem on Caesar's *bellaque resque* that a *puella* replaces locates Actium in a catalogue of bloody civil wars (25–34). Poetic and political concerns thus enclose and inform a serious and realistic depiction of the second book's heroine.[35]

[35] On the overt Callimachean polemic of 17–46, see Wimmel (1960) 13–43, but contrast Fredrick (1997) who finds Callimachean polemic here undercut by epic parody. Cf. Greene (2000) and Miller (2001) 135–41. For the unorthodox perspective on Roman history in 25–34, see Galinsky (1969b) 81–2; Hubbard (1974) 100–2; Putnam (1976) 121–3; Nethercut (1983) 1839–40; and Miller (2001) 135–41.

The series of *Apologien* that culminates in *Amores* 3.1 has led its readers back to this earlier Propertian poem. With the playful warning offered by Elegia in mind, a re-reading of the Propertian *puella* here underscores some disturbing features of the text that jeopardize even the status of Cynthia as a living Augustan girlfriend and declare the textuality of her body. Firstly, Cynthia's attributes and activities (which are said to precede and excite elegiac production) are already set in a tradition for erotic writing before they become the material of Propertian fiction. For a beloved's appearance and skills, her sleep, and erotic battles, are far more frequently the themes of Hellenistic erotic epigrams than the love elegies of the Propertian corpus (Boucher 1965: 210–11). Even Cynthia's clothing assists the identification of elegiac *puella* with elegiac practice, since *Cous* is used elsewhere in the Propertian corpus to signal the Hellenistic poet Philitas. Just as Elegia is adorned in a Callimachean delicacy, so Cynthia is decked in the poetic discourse of Philitas (Miller 2001: 135–41). Cynthia's attributes and activities are implicated yet further in a Callimachean apologetics: as inspirer of poetic *causas* the elegiac mistress becomes the key to a new version of Callimachus' *Aetia*, one that looks into the origins of a mistress's behaviour, rather than the workings of myth and ritual. This Propertian *Aetia* is then set against the higher genres of epic and history through the agency of a female form. The erotic struggles of Propertius' *puella* match the battles of Homeric heroes, and accounts of her every word and deed surpass all previous histories (11–16).[36] At the very moment that the elegiac mistress is realistically and physically depicted as existing prior to elegiac discourse, a rejection of higher forms of writing in favour of a Callimachean practice takes place through her agency.

Secondly, the vocabulary in which Cynthia is formulated as a creator of art also points to her as being an artistic creation. Momentarily Cynthia's physique is said to be manufactured out of ivory (9), suggesting a *puella* who is herself an art form rather than an instigator of art (Wiggers 1976–7: 335). Since, however, the epithet is transferred from a musical instrument to its player, and is not incongruous with the features of a beauty, the Propertian attribution of ivory

---

[36] King (1980) 63 and cf. Wiggers (1976–7) 336. See Greene (2000) on the comparable construction of the male lover in Prop. 2.1 as a kind of epic hero.

fingers is far less disturbing than the Ovidian attribution of unequal feet.

Finally, the entire depiction of elegy's female subject is enclosed by two terms that undermine even further Cynthia's superficial status as a woman who exists prior to the production of an elegiac text. Precisely because it does not give the beloved her expected independence, many commentators have queried the MS tradition's *cogis* (you make her, 5);[37] while *de nihilo* (from nothing, 16) suggests that the history of a mistress is being composed that has no firm basis in reality. Thus even a Propertian poem itself argues against the attribution of an independent identity to its female subject and for her status (even at the level of her flesh) as political and poetic polemic. Nor is it the only Propertian poem to do so.

It is precisely from the material of poems such as 2.2 (as well as 2.3 quoted at the opening of this chapter) that critics have built a living partner—an intelligent blonde—for its author Propertius, since 2.2 overtly describes the power of a look to restore its narrator to his occupation as lover. Yet the poem which immediately precedes it presents elegiac poetry (and, therefore, the *entire* second book) as an alternative to epic—an erotic *Aetia*—when it calls openly on Callimachus as a model for Fine Poetry. So the same critics who have read the text of 2.2 transparently in order to construct a fleshly mistress for Propertius have also conceded the presence in the poem of literary concerns: the poem has been interpreted as an immediate demonstration of the claim of Propertius, in 2.1, to his Callimachean heritage, while a real woman is retained to read her own conversion into a Callimachean literary practice. That poetic practice is observed at work in the physical shape of the poem (its epigrammatic brevity), its esoteric narrative style, and its revision of epic motifs. Even the figurative presentation of Cynthia in 2.2.6–14 (her comparison with Juno, Pallas, Ischomache, and Brimo, and her victory in a recast judgement of Paris) is read as a manifestation of a Callimachean writing practice: the revision of epic material in slight poetry, the delineation of Cynthia in epic proportions (King 1981).

Not all of the poem can be thus decoded, however, if the notion is still to be sustained that Cynthia is the pseudonym of an extratextual

---

[37] See e.g. Camps (1967) 66 for the substitution of *uidi.*

addressee. After all, if Cynthia is to signify a woman of flesh she must be provided with some. So there occurs a noticeable silence, an absence of comment, on the point in the poem where the elegiac mistress is provided with physical properties: *fulua coma est longaeque manus, et maxima toto | corpore* (tawny hair, and long hands, and vast entirely in body, 5–6). What justification is there for thus preserving by omission a referentiality for these lines? Can they be said to sketch the unique physical characteristics of one Augustan woman?

The documented popularity of the Junoesque blonde in classical literature suggests rather that Propertius has assembled here a selection from a repertoire of archetypal features for the female beauties of fiction. For example, the catalogue of feminine physical assets possessed and absent in Catullus 86 and 43 respectively provides an obvious parallel for the features of this Propertian woman.[38] Moreover, since the Homeric poems, tall stature (*megethos*) had been a characteristic of literary representations of the ideal woman and yellow hair (*xanthotês*) a set feature of the beauty in the Greek novel (Lilja 1965a: 123–4, 128–9). A reading of the list of feminine qualities which occur at 2.2.5–6 as detached from the physique of any one Roman woman is aided by the syntax of the passage and the narrative mode adopted for the poem as a whole. A dative of the (human) possessor is provided neither for *fulua coma* nor *longaeque manus*, and *maxima* has no immediate noun to qualify. The whole may therefore be considered as loosely attached to the impersonal *facies* with which the poem opens and closes. The qualities of a body are allotted to an abstract Look, not to an individuated and realistically constructed mistress.

If the textual characteristics of Cynthia do not amount to the unique features of an Augustan girlfriend, could they have been chosen to suit the poetic context (the narration of a Callimachean literary practice) as a reading of *Amores* 3.1 has suggested? Interesting parallels for the delineation of Cynthia at 2.2.5–6 may be found outside the realms of erotic discourse, in the literary construction of the warrior (the epic man). The adjective *fuluus* signals the area

---

[38] Quinn (1963) 66–73. See also Richlin (1983) who argues that a prescribed list of ideal female features can readily be compiled from Roman epic, lyric, and elegy (32–3 and 44–56 in the 1992 edition of her book on Roman sexuality and aggression).

for comparison, for yellow hair is far more frequently identified by *flauus* in the discourses of Roman fictive eroticism. *Fuluus*, however, is employed in the *Aeneid* as an epithet of ferocious animals (such as the eagle or the lion) or of ferocious warriors. At *Aeneid* 10.562, for example, the bravery of Aeneas is matched by the resistance of his opponents: *fortemque Numam fuluumque Camertem*. The other physical properties with which the elegiac mistress is provided evoke particularly the large-limbed Homeric warrior. The more delicate build customarily devised for the female Beauty would be more read-ily suggested by the application of *longus* to fingers rather than the whole hand. The transference allows a parallel to be drawn from an attribute of the epic man: the Homeric *cheiri pacheiêi*, the *manu magna* or *dextra ingenti* of the Virgilian *bellator* (Virg. *Aen.* 5.241 and 11.556). Similarly, the tall stature of the ideal beloved is often signified by *longa* in erotic poetry. The wording here, however, com-pares with the description at *Aeneid* 11.690–1 of two opponents wor-thy of Camilla's military prowess: *Orsilochum et Buten, duo maxima Teucrum | corpora.*

  It appears then that at 2.2.5–6 a selection has been made from among the standard features of the female Beauty that produces a sketch of an elegiac woman in epic proportions. But, in the previous poem, Propertius had illustrated his obedience to the Callimachean call for *leptotês* by emphasizing that his erotic *Aetia* would incorporate and thus subvert epic material: *Iliads* would be transformed into ele-giac narratives of erotic battles (2.1.11–14). Book 2 takes as its project a paradoxical version of the Callimachean polemic: the revision of epic in elegy (King 1981). Poem 2.2 then contributes to that project by presenting a woman of epic proportions in a short poem, incor-porating into poetry which is *kata lepton* the *megalê gynê* opposed to it and rejected by Callimachus in the preface to the *Aetia* (fr.11–12).[39] Thus even the flesh of Cynthia is moulded to fit a poetic purpose. Furthermore, a political (as well as a poetic) context is supplied for this project in 2.1. That poem contains not just one, but two tables

[39] I am grateful to Professor Kenney for this suggestion. See Kennedy (1993) 31–3, Greene (2000), and Miller (2001: 135–41) on the characterization of the beloved elsewhere as *dura*. They argue that such an attribute breaks down the boundaries between elegy and epic, and turns the beloved into an adversary worthy of her elegiac 'hero'.

of contents for the second book; one erotic (5–16) and one political (17–38), of which the first is formulated as substitute for the second, a sexual instead of a military *historia* (13–16). Cynthia replaces Caesar as the subject of poetic discourse. One anti-epic speaks for another.

The flesh with which the elegiac mistress is endowed in Propertius 2.2 is moulded to suit the politics and poetics of its author: Cynthia's body is built out of the bones buried at Perugia and yet signifies a style of writing that is *lepton*. A brief study of some of Cynthia's textual characteristics thus demonstrates again that useful lessons are to be learned from reading *Amores* 3.1. The awkward figure of Elegia operates in a direct line of descent from the massively proportioned Cynthia of Propertius' second book. Her title, her limp, and her comic plight all contribute to a humorous demystification of elegy's female flesh and its exposure as everywhere a site for the expression of poetic and political concerns.

Like the painting described and illustrated in the anti-romantic novel which demonstrates ingeniously the absurdities latent in Petrarch's codification of his beloved's beauty, Ovid's *Amores* 3.1 discloses that the Propertian beloved is a textual body clothed in ideological and aesthetic ambitions. Ovid's *Amores* also suggest that clues to such a reading of elegy's female flesh are already there in the Propertian corpus, just as they were considered to be in the love poetry of Petrarch. Even contemporary readers of Petrarch's Laura identified her with the ambitions of his poetry; we should do no less for Propertius' Cynthia.[40]

---

[40] On this reading of Laura, see e.g. Miller (1997) and Stapleton (1996) 115–32. See too McNamee (1993) for such a reading of Cynthia's attributes in the *Monobiblos*, and Keith (1994) for a comparable analysis of the *puellae* to be found elsewhere in Ovid's *Amores*.

9

The Death of Corinna's Parrot Reconsidered: Poetry and Ovid's Amores

Barbara Weiden Boyd

From the very opening of the first book of *Amores*, it is *Ovidius poeta* who dominates the elegies, first in the prefatory epigram (*Qui modo Nasonis fueramus quinque libelli,* | *tres sumus: hoc illi praetulit auctor opus* 'We who before were Ovid's five slim volumes are three: the author preferred this to its previous form', 1–2), and then in 1.1 (*Arma gravi numero violentaque bella parabam* | *edere* 'Arms and the violent deeds of war I was preparing to sound forth', 1–2). He invites us to watch as, over the course of the first three elegies, he assumes the character of *amator*; but it is the character and development of the *poeta* in which, throughout the *Amores*, Ovid is in fact most interested. To investigate this *poeta*-persona, I intend to examine in some detail *Am.* 2.6, which together with 3.9 has recently received attention: Leslie Cahoon (1984), emphasizing the centrality of the 'obtuse' *amator*, has argued that the funeral elegies for Corinna's parrot and for Tibullus present 'conflicting ethical attitudes' for lovers.[1] This

---

[1] Cahoon is not the first to observe that the two elegies invite comparison; she in fact takes as the basis for much of her argument Thomas (1965); cf. also Wilkinson (1956) 242. Cahoon adopts in particular Thomas's view that 'in many ways the affectations or conceits of II.6 are more appropriate, or at least less offensive, than those which sometimes mar III.9' (Thomas 1965: 599). Cahoon chides Thomas for 'not develop[ing] these central questions, but confin[ing] herself to the *safer ground* of the structure of ancient funeral elegies for both animals and people' (Cahoon 1984: 29; italics mine); Cahoon then proceeds to develop her own interpretation of these two elegies. In her view, both elegies reflect the 'obtuseness' of the *amator*, who finds the death of the parrot 'genuinely moving', although this bird in fact embodies the virtues

paper will suggest an alternate reading of *Am.* 2.6 and, tangentially, 3.9, as expressions of poetic rather than ethical values. My vantage point will be the conventional motifs that are the stock-in-trade of the ancient poet, particularly motifs of an Alexandrian character. It is my contention that *Am.* 2.6 has far less to do with amatory *fides* than it does with the paradox of poetic originality within the Alexandrian tradition, and with the humorous self-consciousness of the Ovidian *poeta*.

In *Am.* 2.6, Ovid mourns the passing of Corinna's pet parrot. In order to demonstrate that Ovid and the poet share similar ethical values, Cahoon points to the fact that the bird is described in terms applicable to a poet: *vox... ingeniosa* 'a gifted voice', 18; *garrulus* 'talkative', 26; *sermonis amore* 'love of speech', 29; *loquax humanae vocis imago* 'the loquacious image of human voice', 38; *ora... docta loqui* 'a mouth skilled in speech', 62. In other words, 'Ovid identifies with the parrot' (1984: 34). Two points should be observed here: first, the basis for the identification between poet and parrot might best be described as linguistic emulation. The similarities between the two are expressed in terms of language and its use, not in terms of ethical values. Secondly, while Ovid's emphasis on the bird's most outstanding characteristic, its *vox ingeniosa*, is striking, this emphasis is itself a cliché: the parrot's 'human voice' ($\phi\omega\nu\grave{\eta}$ $\mathring{a}\nu\theta\rho\omega\pi\acute{\iota}\nu\eta$) is, understandably, the focal point of all ancient descriptions of this exotic and curious bird, noted also for its colour, breadth of tongue, and hardness of beak.[2] It is not in fact until the close of the elegy, with Ovid's

---

most antithetical to his own *urbanitas* (30); conversely, the lover's *urbanitas* compels him to make his reaction to Tibullus' death 'a *gauche* travesty of the sorrow he felt in II.6' (31). Cahoon suggests that the two poems may be seen as Ovid's challenge to his readers 'either to sink to the lover's level of obtuseness or else to make a choice between the conflicting ethical attitudes that the funeral elegies present. Through comparison with III.9,... II.6 emerges as a corrective to the lover's programmatic poems in general as well as to the elegy for Tibullus' (33). For the application of ethical values to the *Amores*, see also Cahoon's discussion of *Am.* 3.13 (1983: 1–8).

[2] The *psittacus* is first mentioned in Ctesias' *Indica*, *FGrHist* 688 F 45: see also Arist. *HA* 8.597*b*25; Paus. 2.28; Arrian *Ind.* 1.15.8; Solin. 53; Pliny *NH* 10.117; Apul. *Fl.* 12; and elsewhere: see Thompson 1936: 335–8, and Wotke, 'Papagei', *RE* 36.2 (1949) 926–32. Ctesias remarks upon the parrot's 'human tongue... and speech' ($\gamma\lambda\hat{\omega}\sigma\sigma\alpha\nu$ $\mathring{a}\nu\theta\rho\omega\pi\acute{\iota}\nu\eta\nu$... $\kappa\alpha\grave{\iota}$ $\phi\omega\nu\acute{\eta}\nu$); Aristotle uses the epithet 'human-tongued' ($\mathring{a}\nu\theta\rho\omega\pi\acute{o}\gamma\lambda\omega\tau\tau\sigma\nu$); Arrian cites the bird's 'human speech' ($\phi\omega\nu\grave{\eta}\nu$... $\mathring{a}\nu\theta\rho\omega\pi\acute{\iota}\nu\eta\nu$); Pliny's expression is *humanas voces*.

description of the bird's last words, afterlife, tomb, and epitaph, that the parallel between parrot and poet becomes explicit. Ovid means us to find his exploitation of a cliché amusing, as the very choice of a *psittacus* as a focal character would suggest; most of the humour derives, however, from the fact that Ovid transforms the cliché— turns a frog into a prince, as it were—before our eyes. Corinna's parrot hardly represents 'the natural order of things' (Cahoon 1984: 34).

The parrot as Ovid describes it, then, is indeed much like a poet, but never more so than in death. Its last words are those of a poet; its afterlife is that of a poet; its tomb and epitaph might very suitably be accorded a poet. But that the *psittacus* is not to be seen simply as any kind of poet, but as a specifically Alexandrian poet, becomes clear from numerous details in this passage. Let us consider the last four lines, in which Ovid first remarks upon the size of the parrot's tumulus and monument, and then puts the parrot's epitaph in the first person, so that the bird may speak even from the grave:

ossa tegit tumulus, tumulus pro corpore magnus,
    quo lapis exiguus par sibi carmen habet:
colligor ex ipso dominae placuisse sepulcro.
    ora fuere mihi plus ave docta loqui.

A mound covers his bones, a mound appropriate to his stature; on it, a small stone displays a couplet just its size: 'From my very monument you may gather that I pleased my mistress. My skill at speech far surpassed the learning of a bird.'

A description of the funeral is a standard element in the *epicedion*;[3] Ovid's description, however, is not standard. First of all, Ovid uses

Ovid makes at least oblique references to each of the parrot's traditional character-istics in his description: exotic origins, 1 (*Eois . . . ab Indis* 'from Indian land of dawn') and 38 (*extremo munus ab orbe datum* 'gift brought from the limit of the world'); colour and beak, 17 (*rari forma coloris* 'the beauty of that rare colouring'), and 21–2 (*tu poteras fragiles pinnis hebetare zmaragdos | tincta gerens rubro Punica rostra croco* 'you could dim with your wings the fragile emerald, and your beak was Punic-red with ruddy saffron tinge'); tongue, 24 (*blaeso . . . sono* 'with broken sound') and 48 (*clamavit . . . lingua* 'the tongue cried').

[3] The best general discussion of the *epicedion* is by Norden (1927) ad 868–86. See also Vollmer 1891: esp. 449–78; Nisbet and Hubbard (1970) 280-1 (ad *Od.* 1.24); and Thomas (1965).

the periphrasis *tumulus pro corpore magnus* to emphasize the slight size of the tomb. The appropriateness of the tumulus' size to the bird's stature is complemented by the fact that the site is marked with a small stone, on which is a suitably slender epitaph (*lapis exiguus par sibi carmen habet*). An appreciation of the unusual character of this elaborate though brief description can be gained by comparison with one of the numerous Hellenistic pet-epitaphs which are likely to have provided a general precedent for *Am.* 2.6: *AP* 7.198 (Leonidas of Tarentum).[4] In this poem, a deceased cricket (ἀκρίς) remarks that the slight size of its monument is not meant to suggest that the creature was little loved by its mistress; Philaenis is rather to be commended (αἰνοίης) for not disowning (οὐδὲ... ἀπανήνατο) the creature after death. The pathos of this epigram is underlined by the reference not once but twice to the smallness of the monument, in the first and last couplets: μικρός ἰδεῖν... | ... λᾶας ὁ τυμβίτης 'the tombstone is small in appearance' and τὠλίγον... σᾶμα 'the little monument'. In the parrot's case, on the other hand, a small tomb is not something demanding apology or explanation; although the bird, like the ἀκρίς, interprets its burial as a sign of its mistress's fondness (*colligor ex ipso dominae placuisse sepulcro*), there is no suggestion in *Am.* 2.6 that the smallness of mound, tomb, and epitaph may be interpreted as a slight upon the *psittacus*.

For Corinna's parrot, then, smallness has not a pathetic but a positive connotation; this unusual twist is but one of the numerous factors

---

[4] Approximately twenty-five epigrams on the deaths of beloved pets are to be found in book 7 of the Palatine Anthology: *AP* 7.189–92, 194, 197–209, 211–16. *AP* 7.193, 195, and 196, although about an ἀκρίς, are not funerary; neither is 7.210, on the death of a swallow's brood. *AP* 7.200, on a cicada (τέττιξ), is also probably not funerary; see Gow and Page (1965) 2.90–1 and on the specific epigrams. On the influence of Hellenistic epigrams on Ovid generally, see Day (1938) 134: 'But far exceeding in importance the evidence of direct translation or of borrowed themes or of verbal echoes, there remains to be noticed Ovid's peculiar use of Hellenistic epigrams as a thematic base for enlargement into erotic elegies, in accordance with the rules of formal rhetoric...'

For the opinion that *Am.* 2.6 is simply an imitation—and an inferior imitation, at that—of Catullus 3, see e.g. Brandt (1911) 25; Fordyce 1961: ad Cat. 3. Ferguson 1960: 353 remarks: 'The whole thing [*Am.* 2.6] is amusing and utterly unfeeling. He has taken nothing from Catullus except the idea... Ovid is amusing, but he draws out his humour to the point of tediousness.' As will become apparent in what follows, *Am.* 2.6 and Cat. 3 are probably equally indebted to Hellenistic epigram, but with quite different results in each case.

contributing to the literary character of the *psittacus*. A particularly noteworthy parallel appears in Propertius 2.13b, where throughout his funerary fantasy the poet expresses his preference for the small and simple (19–26, 31–6). While it is conventional in funerary poetry to describe the tumulus or grave as small, sometimes too small for the person buried within (Nisbet and Hubbard 1970: 321–2), small-ness is a desirable characteristic in Propertius' fantasy. He aims not to evoke pathos, but, as Wilkinson has suggested (1966: 142–3), to describe a funeral in keeping with the Alexandrian character of his work. Propertius has adapted Callimachean literary terminology to the metaphor of poetry as monument; his most lasting memorial is to be not a grave but his elegies.[5] When Ovid describes the parrot's last resting place in similar terms, it is reasonable to suppose that Ovid expects us to recall Hellenistic pet epitaphs on the one hand, and the Alexandrian connotation of smallness (τὸ κατὰ λεπτόν) as part of an artistic creed on the other.[6] In other words, this parrot is much more like an Alexandrian poet than like the typical pets of Hellenistic epigram.

The suggestion of a similarity between parrot and poet is rein-forced by the bird's epitaph. A literary epitaph is itself a cliché of Roman elegy; both Propertius and Tibullus, in imagining their own deaths, provide their own sepulchral addresses to passers-by (Prop. 2.13b.35–6; Tib. 1.3.55–6). Even more telling, however, are the diction and style of the parrot's epitaph. As I noted earlier, the *psittacus* addresses us in the first person (*colligor; ora fuere mihi*). The first-person address tends to add to the mock-pathos of the elegy: the bird which spoke in life speaks also in death, and expresses its deathless devotion to Corinna. The words in which it does so are an odd mixture of the exotic and the clichéd, the pompous and the punning: *colligor* with the infinitive (*placuisse*), for example, is a nov-elty here; in classifying this occurrence of *colligere* among instances where the verb connotes *ratiocinari* (= *ratiocinatione percipere*), the *Thesaurus* indicates that this is a unique example of the verb used

[5] In Latin poetry we first find a positive connotation for smallness in a funerary metaphor in Catullus, who refers to the works of a good poet as *parva monimenta* (95b.1); see also, of course, Hor. *Od.* 3.30.

[6] See Reitzenstein (1931) 31–5. Cf. Hor. *AP* 77 and Prop. 3.9.36 for *exiguus* used with Callimachean overtones.

in a construction *nominativus cum infinitivo*.[7] *Placuisse*, meanwhile, is a *double entendre*: in addition to its standard meaning, this verb frequently assumes an erotic connotation in comedy and elegy.[8] This *double entendre* is further reinforced by the juxtaposition of *placuisse* with *dominae*—the ubiquitous presence of the *domina* in Roman amatory poetry, especially elegy, needs no elaboration here.[9] In other words, the *psittacus* describes its behaviour with a word we would normally expect, in elegy, to be used by a lover, and calls its owner by a name normally indicative, in elegy, of a lover's mistress.[10]

In the pentameter, *docta loqui*, like the infinitival construction in the previous line, is a Graecism; *doctus* with an infinitive is exclusively poetic diction (Tränkle 1960: 73), not appearing in prose until Tacitus (*ThLL* vol. 5.1, cols. 1760–1). The parrot thus suggests, by its choice of words, that it is a neoteric bird; *docta* itself of course evokes the learning of an Alexandrian poet. The literary pretensions of the *psittacus* culminate in its use of the phrase *plus ave*: as Lee has noticed (1968: 189),[11] we have here another play on words, in which *ave* may be understood either as the ablative of *avis* or as the greeting *ave*. In other words, Corinna's parrot had the training of a more than average bird, *or* Corinna's parrot was trained to say more than 'hello'.

This play on words brings us to consider what in fact is said by the parrot in *Am.* 2.6. Aside from its first-person epitaph, the *psittacus* itself utters only two words in this elegy: its last words are 'farewell, Corinna' (*clamavit moriens lingua 'Corinna, vale'*, 48). This closing address has been noted for its 'high, splendid absurdity' (Lyne 1980:

---

[7] See *ThLL* vol. 3, col. 1617.10–11 and col. 1618.23–4 (s.v. *colligo*). Cf. also Herrlinger (1930) 86 n.54: '*colligor* with the inf. is new here,' and the translation by Brandt 1911 ad loc.: '. . . man darf von mir annehmen, dass ich gefallen habe'.

[8] See e.g. Preston (1916) 28; Pichon (1902) 234. Cf. also e.g. Prop. 1.7.11, 2.7.19, 2.22a.1; Tib. 1.8.15; Hor. *Epist.* 1.14.33. *Placeo* never appears in an erotic context in Virgil.

[9] Pichon (1902) 134 remarks '. . . more often *domina* is nothing more than a trite and familiar appellation used by lovers to address their girlfriends.'

[10] Note the ambiguity of the possessive adjective in verse 19, *nostrae placuisse puellae*. Cf. the remarks of Sauvage (1975) 276: 'Ovid's poem evokes Corinna, the poet's *puella* and the parrot's *domina*: we might ask ourselves if the last verse of the epitaph (*Am.* ii, 6, 61) is not intentionally ambiguous and implicates the lover and the bird at the same time.'

[11] An anonymous reader for *CJ* has suggested to me 'the possibility of another (bad) Ovidian joke' here: 'The bird says *plus ave*; that is, it also says *vale* (48)'.

265);[12] we must imagine these words in parrot tones to appreciate their full effect. Nonetheless, the full impact of their absurdity is felt only in comparison with the vocal training of other birds. We find in ancient literature several references to talking birds, known in Rome at least by the time of the battle of Actium. Macrobius (*Sat.* 2.4.29–30) records that several birds, including a *psittacus*, were brought before Octavian to praise him as victor. Pliny, perhaps aware of the same or a similar anecdote, reports that hailing the emperor is a common parrot pastime: *imperatores salutat* (*NH* 10.117).[13] This motif receives verse treatment in the Anthology (*AP* 9.562), when Crinagoras[14] describes a pet parrot which escapes into the woods and there, like Orpheus, instructs the other birds to cry 'hail, Caesar'. In comparison, the pun at the close of *Am.* 2.6 suggests that Corinna's parrot is not a typical talking *psittacus*, renowned for its civic pride; 'hail, Caesar' is not the high point of this bird's repertoire. The parrot's favoured audience is not public, but private; not the Emperor, but its mistress. To the last, this bird behaves like the lover poet of elegy.

The parrot's journey to the underworld completes its characteriza-tion as poet. In death, the *psittacus* presides over an Elysium inhabited exclusively by birds, a *Vogelparadies*[15] (49–58):

---

[12] See also Herrlinger (1930), who calls the parrot's farewell 'the style of authentic *epicedion*' (85).

[13] See also Persius Prol. 8; Martial 14.73; and Weinreich (1928) 113–25. In his discussion of talking birds, Pliny also reports on a *corvus* which lived at Rome during Tiberius' reign. For several years this bird flew every day to the forum, where it greeted Tiberius, Germanicus and Drusus Caesar, and finally the Roman people. When this bird was murdered, the murderer, a Roman citizen, was punished, and the *corvus* was honoured with an elaborate funeral: two Ethiopians to carry the bier, a flute player, wreaths, and a pyre on the Via Appia. Pliny even gives a date for the funeral, 28 March, CE 36: *NH* 10.121–3. Further on animal funerals, cf. also Theophr. *Char.* 21.9; Diod. Sic. 13.82; Pliny *NH* 8.155; Galletier 1922: 329–33; and Herrlinger 1930: 11–12.

[14] Or Philippus; see Gow and Page (1968) 2.232. Gow and Page prefer the ascrip-tion to Philippus on the basis of style and contents, but leave it among the epigrams of Crinagoras. Weinreich (1928) argues convincingly for Augustan dating and prefers the ascription to Crinagoras. If Crinagoras is the author, it is possible that Ovid knew his epigram, or that he knew Ovid's elegy; I do not think, however, that either poet can be shown to imitate the other.

[15] The exclusively avian frame of reference for *Am.* 2.6 is discussed at some length by Herrlinger (1930: 83–5). Unlike most critics of this elegy (above, n. 4), Herrlinger judges it an accomplished and successful parody of the pet-*epicedion*: 'In der Haupt-sache muss man . . . Ovid als Verskünstler bewundern . . .' (86). It is also worth noting

colle sub Elysia nigra nemus ilice frondet
  udaque perpetuo gramine terra viret.
si qua fides dubiis, volucrum locus ille piarum
  dicitur, obscenae quo prohibentur aves:
illic innocui late pascuntur olores
  et vivax phoenix, unica semper avis;
explicat ipsa suas ales Iunonia pinnas,
  oscula dat cupido blanda columba mari.
psittacus has inter nemorali sede receptus
  convertit volucres in sua verba pias.

At the foot of the Elysian hill there is a grove leafy with black oak, and
the moist earth flourishes with grass that never fades. If we may have
any faith in doubtful things, that place, it is said, is the home of faithful birds, a place from which ill-omened fowl are kept away. There feed
far and wide harmless swans and the long-lived phoenix, ever alone of
its kind; there Juno's bird herself, the peacock, spreads her feathers, and
the winsome dove gives kisses to her eager mate. Welcomed among these
birds in their shady home, the parrot attracts to his words the feathered
faithful.

Several elements in this description deserve special note. As befits
an *epicedion*, Ovid emphasizes the *pietas* of the dead by using the
phrase *piae volucres* three times (at 3, 51, and 58), once in contrast
with *aves obscenae* (52).[16] Cahoon makes much of the fact that the
psittacus is one of only two characters in the *Amores* representative

in comparison that the Elysium through which the pseudo-Virgilian *culex* passes is
populated by traditionally heroic figures: *Culex* 258–371.

[16] Norden (1927) ad *Aen.* 6.878–81 (p. 343) notes the remarks of Menander
Rhetor (420.12) that, in an *epicedion*, a twofold description of the deceased's nature
($\phi\acute{v}\sigma\iota\varsigma$), is standard: $\epsilon\H{\iota}\tau\epsilon\ \tau\grave{o}\ \tau o\hat{v}\ \sigma\acute{\omega}\mu\alpha\tau o\varsigma\ \kappa\acute{\alpha}\lambda\lambda o\varsigma\ldots\epsilon\H{\iota}\varsigma\ \tau\epsilon\ \tau\grave{\eta}\nu\ \tau\hat{\eta}\varsigma\ \psi\upsilon\chi\hat{\eta}\varsigma\ \epsilon\mathring{v}\phi\upsilon\acute{\iota}\alpha\nu$
'[such a description takes into account] both physical beauty and the character's
natural goodness'. Norden identifies the first of these in Virgil's description of Marcellus as *egregium forma iuvenem* (*Aen.* 6.861), the second in the lament *heu pietas,*
heu prisca fides invictaque bello | dextera! (6.878–9). As Norden comments ad loc.,
'dafür setzt Vergil die spezifisch römischen Tugenden: *pietas* und *fides*.' The $\phi\acute{v}\sigma\iota\varsigma$ of
Corinna's parrot is succinctly summarized in one verse, *quid tamen ista fides, quid*
rari forma coloris | . . . ? (*Am.* 2.6.17). This exotic bird might well be a naturalized
Roman!
  Ovid may have had the Virgilian underworld in mind in his emphasis on
pietas. At *Aen.* 5.734–5, Anchises describes Elysium as *amoena piorum | concilia*
Elysiumque, after characterizing its opposite as *impius* (*impia . . . | Tartara*, 733–4;
cf. *Aen.* 6.543).

of *fides* (*Am.* 2.6.14; 17; 51) and *pietas*; she includes in this count the husband of 3.13 but discounts the Tibullus of 3.9. In fact, however, the *psittacus* and Tibullus are not so very different from each other in death. Tibullus too is to be counted among *numeri pii*; in his case, however, this select group is limited to poets, including Calvus, Catullus, and Gallus (*Am.* 3.9.59–66):

> si tamen e nobis aliquid nisi nomen et umbra
> restat, in Elysia valle Tibullus erit.
> obvius huic venies hedera iuvenalia cinctus
> tempora cum Calvo, docte Catulle, tuo;
> tu quoque, si falsum est temerati crimen amici,
> sanguinis atque animae prodige Galle tuae.
> his comes umbra tua est, si qua est modo corporis umbra;
> auxisti numeros, culte Tibulle, pios.

Yet, if any part of us survives besides reputation and shade, Tibullus will be in the Elysian vale. You will come to meet him, learned Catullus, your temples entwined with youthful ivy, and in company with your dear Calvus; and you, too, Gallus, if the charge of having insulted your friend is false, wasteful as you have been of your blood and your life. Your shade is a companion to these, refined Tibullus, if any shade survives the body; you have enlarged the numbers of the faithful.

In describing the poets as *pii* 'blessed', Ovid accords to Tibullus, as to the parrot, conventional funeral praise; neither the parrot nor Tibullus, however, has gained Elysium through heroism. Instead, Tibullus has done so through his conduct as *Elegiae vates*, while it is for the parrot's verbal talent that the deceased bird is rewarded. We have, then, the central characters of Ovid's two *epicedia* descending to similarly exclusive Elysia, and the suggestion that the two have, if not identical, at least parallel fates; in other words, Ovid makes an equation of sorts between Corinna's parrot and the elegist Tibullus. That the parrot has entered a poet's realm becomes an even greater likelihood when we consider the likely source for both the poet-Elysium of 3.9 and the *Vogelparadies* of 2.6—the Elysium Tibullus himself describes in his elegy 1.3.57–66:

> sed me, quod facilis tenero sum semper Amori,
> ipsa Venus campos ducet in Elysios.
> hic choreae cantusque vigent, passimque vagantes

> dulce sonant tenui gutture carmen aves;
> fert casiam non culta seges, totosque per agros
>   floret odoratis terra benigna rosis;
> ac iuvenum series teneris immixta puellis
>   ludit, et adsidue proelia miscet amor.
> illic est, cuicumque rapax Mors venit amanti,
>   et gerit insigni myrtea serta coma.

My spirit, though, as I have always welcomed tender love, Venus herself will lead to the Elysian fields. Here dances and songs flourish, and birds wandering here and there produce sweet song from their slender throats; the crop, though untended, bears wild cinnamon, and through all the fields the beneficent earth blooms with fragrant roses; a row of youths mixed with tender girls makes sport, and Love repeatedly joins in battle. There is every lover to whom rapacious Death has come, and all wear myrtle wreaths as tokens in their hair.

As Tibullus is himself a lover (*quod facilis tenero sum semper Amori*), it is appropriate that he spend his afterlife among similar creatures; conversely, those who have sinned against love (1.3.81–2) are condemned to Tartarus (*scelerata sedes*, 67–80). As has been frequently noted,[17] Tibullus is apparently the first not only to introduce erotic motifs to the underworld, but also to create an Elysium for lovers alone.[18]

Ovid's portrait of the parrot is now complete; it is entirely derivative, but nonetheless delightful in its execution. The parrot of *Am.* 2.6 sees itself as an elegiac lover; its words at death and its epitaph cast Corinna into the role of the bird's elegiac *domina*. That the *psittacus* is suited for this role Ovid suggests by describing the bird's death in terms appropriate to the depiction of an elegiac poet's death; the parrot's last resting place is fittingly described in Alexandrian terms. Even the diction of the epitaph reflects the literary concerns of the *psittacus*. The potential for humour inherent in the conceit of an *epicedion* for a parrot comes alive through Ovid's deft exploitation of convention.

---

[17] On Tibullus' innovation, see e.g. Solmsen (1961: 283), who suggests that the Elysium of Prop. 4.7 is also inspired by Tibullus; Henderson 1969: 649–53; Bright 1978: 28–9; and Cairns 1979*a*: 52: a 'concept unparalleled in surviving earlier literature'.

[18] The latter point is denied by Smith (1913: 254); on Smith see Cairns (1979*a*) 51.

Let us conclude by considering briefly how the parrot-turned-poet contributes to our understanding of the Ovidian *poeta* persona. Ovid uses the character (if I may call it that) of the *psittacus* to undermine the sincerity of the elegiac *poeta*. It is useful to remember that Ovid has chosen in *Am.* 2.6 to immortalize neither swan nor nightingale,[19] nor even the unassuming *passer*, but rather the large, clumsy, unmusical, and occasionally dirty parrot. The reason for this choice, as the *poeta* himself tells us several times, is that the parrot was his gift to Corinna (*ut datus es*, 19; *extremo munus ab orbe datum*, 38); and, as anyone familiar with this novelty pet would realize, the *psittacus* can only mimic what it has learned from the *poeta*. The poet himself, then, provides the model for the bird's vocal output; accordingly, its farewell to Corinna blurs the distinction between elegiac poetry and parrotry.[20]

Much in the *Amores* is humorous primarily because these elegies exist as heirs to the best—and worst—that Alexandrian poetry contains. Ovid brings the *poeta* to the fore in these poems; although the *amator* persona serves as a recognizable and useful convention, Ovid's real concern is the creative process as it is understood and undertaken by an Alexandrian poet at Rome. Emulation is, from Hesiod onwards, basic to the character of ancient poetry; in *Am.* 2.6, Ovid explores the limits and the excesses of this character. His use of the *epicedion* as the framework and of Alexandrian, particularly elegiac, conventions as the substance for *Am.* 2.6 typifies Ovid's emulative technique: applied to so incongruous a central character, these devices serve to highlight

[19] Both swans and nightingales are frequently associated with poets and their poetry: see e.g. Virg. *Ecl.* 9.36 (and Serv. ad loc.); Call. *Epig.* 2 (= *AP* 7.80: on the poetry of Heraclitus of Halicarnassus); and Call. *Aet.* 1, fr. 1 Pf. 16 (and Pfeiffer ad loc.).
   The voice of the *psittacus* appears, tantalizingly, in a derogatory context in Call. *Iamb.* 2 fr. 192 Pf. 10–13: καὶ κ[υ]νὸς [μ]ὲ[ν] [Εὔ]δημος, | ὄ[νο]υ δὲ Φίλτων, ψιττακοῦ δὲ[| οἱ δὲ τραγῳδοὶ τῶν θάλασσαν οἰ[κεύντων | ἔχο[υ]σι φωνήν· 'Eudemus [has] the voice of a dog, Philton that of an ass, and [...] that of a parrot; and the tragedians have the voice of those dwelling in the sea'; on the last, see Bing (1981) 33–6.
[20] In his edition of the *Silvae*, Vollmer (1898: ad *Silv.* 2.4.16) comments upon a similar scenario in Statius, probably suggested by Ovid *Am.* 2.6: 'Die Vögelversammlung auch bei Ovid, doch nach andern Gesichtspunkten zusammengestellt; die Aufforderung an die *doctae aues* parodiert den Appell an die *poetae docti* v 3.89–103'.

not only the hybrid nature of the parrot, but also the activity of a poet at work. Through the self-consciousness of the *poeta* persona, Ovid is able simultaneously to exhibit his credentials as Alexandrian elegist at Rome and to assert his own place in the tradition.[21]

[21] For a useful discussion of the *poeta* persona in the *Ars Amatoria* and *Remedia Amoris*, see Durling (1958). Much of the paper reprinted here was incorporated, in revised form, into my discussion of poetic immortality in Ovid's *Amores* (Boyd 1997). Since this article first appeared, several other discussions of the literary affiliations of Ovid's *psittacus* have been published; chief among them are Myers 1990 and Schmitzer 1997; cf. also Houghton 2000 and McKeown's comprehensive and rewarding commentary (1998). Growing interest in post-Augustan Latin poetry has also drawn attention to Statius' parrot poem and its intertextual relationship to earlier poetic birds: see Myers 2002. Finally, I note that Paula James and Julia Courtney of the Open University (Milton Keynes, UK) recently organized a day-long conference entitled 'Parrot Play: The Trickster in the Text' (held 10 February 2005), the papers from which are now being assembled for publication; James's essay provides an overview of recent interpretations of Ovid's and Statius' parrot poems.

10

Fantasy, Myth, and Love Letters: Text and Tale in Ovid's *Heroides*

R. Alden Smith

In the *Epistulae Heroidum*, Ovid presents us with many poetic strata, the synthesis of which produces unique, and uniquely beautiful, literature.[1] This essay will focus principally on the interplay of three levels of that text, the first of which could be called mythical or intertextual, for myth, by Ovid's time, or at least in Ovid's text, is not an expression of a religious faith but a part of a poetic tradition. One might regard the second level as the fantastic or psychological, for the writers of these letters serve as affective filters, both in terms of processing the 'influences' they have experienced in their previous literary loci and in terms of presenting the material in this new context in an emotional and fantasizing manner. The third level that will be considered here could be termed 'contextual' or generic, i.e., the literary vehicle by which the newly created, fully psychological, mythical character has access to the literate audience. All three of these levels function together to create the various poetic personae that Ovid adopts in these letters. Consideration of the tension between these three elements will be the focus of this brief study which, it is hoped, may

---

[1] For the sake of limiting the field of this study, I will follow Jacobson (1974: ix) in excluding the last six epistles from consideration. Jacobson regards the double epistles as a distinctly different work. See also Anderson (1973) 68–81; this is now the consensus opinion. Dörrie (1971: 287–90) accepts *Her.* 15 as Ovidian, but attributes its strange manuscript history to Ovid's having removed it in preparation for a second edition which included the double epistles. See also Dörrie (1975) 224–6.

shed some light on Ovid's boast to have created, with his *Heroides*, a new genre.[2]

Intertextuality provides the mythical dimension of the *Heroides*, a feature not at all unique to that collection or to Ovid in general,[3] though perhaps even more apparent here than elsewhere in his other early works.[4] Indeed, it has long been recognized that intertextuality is created through what Giorgio Pasquali called 'arte allusiva'[5] and that poetic allusion is a prominent aspect of Augustan poetry. Gian Biagio Conte (1986: 61–3) has analysed a poignant allusion to Catullus in Ovid's *Fasti*, where the mythological heroine Ariadne receives life anew within the Roman poetic tradition, referring explicitly to her previous poetic locus. Before turning to the text of the *Heroides*, it will be useful to consider this parallel example of intertextuality in the *Fasti* (3.473–5):

dicebam, memini, 'periure et perfide Theseu!'
  ille abiit; eadem crimina Bacchus habet.
nunc quoque 'nulla uiro' clamabo 'femina credat!'

As I remember it, I kept saying 'Perjurous and perfidious Theseus!' He departed; Bacchus commits the same crime. Now again, I will exclaim, 'Let no woman trust a man!'

Here Ariadne alludes to the poetic tradition whence she is drawn and thus signals that she has a personal knowledge of Catullus' poem (64.132–7):[6]

sicine me patriis auectam, *perfide*, ab aris,
perfide, deserto liquisti in litore, Theseu?

---

[2] *Ars* 3.345–6. On this topic, cf. Steinmetz (1987). For more on Steinmetz's conclusions, see n. 25, below. See also Spoth (1992: 26–7).

[3] Cf. the comments of Barchiesi (1984) 66: 'The *Heroides* are ... intertextual formations, developed in association with other texts.'

[4] The date of the *Heroides* is generally assumed to be sometime between 25 and 1 BC; Jacobson (1974) 312–13 collates the various views and offers his own opinion of 10–3 BC on pp. 316–17. See also, among others, McKeown (1987) 86–8.

[5] For use of the word 'allusion', see Pasquali (1942) 185–7. For Ovidian allusion to Virgil generally, see Bömer (1968) 175.

[6] Conte 1986: 61–3. In the *Metamorphoses*, in particular, Ovid uses literary allusion to establish a 'poetic mythology' for his characters. For Ovid's use of allusion to suggest a generic program, see Hinds (1987a) 21–4.

sicine discedens neglecto numine diuum,
immemor a! deuota domum periuria portas?
nullane res potuit crudelis flectere mentis
consilium?

Thus, *perfidious Theseus, perfidious, have you left me,* carried away from my paternal home, *on the deserted shore?* Thus, departing, neglecting the will of the gods, *unmindful (alas!), do you carry home your accursed broken oaths?* Could nothing change the purpose of your cruel mind?

and further on at 143, though here applied just to Theseus:

nunc iam nulla uiro iuranti femina credat,

From now on let no woman trust a man; even one under oath . . .

Bömer (1957: 176) cites this parallel and Conte (1986: 61) rightly draws attention to the fact that Ovid's Ariadne 'recalls' (*memini, Fasti* 3.473) her lamentation from when she was formerly the Ariadne in the text of Catullus 64. While Conte's discussion does, on the one side, establish for us a model for Ovidian allusion, it will also be useful at this juncture to go beyond Conte's analysis and consider another Ariadne, that of *Heroides* 10.

Howard Jacobson (1974: 213–27) has, if chiefly as a matter of *Quellenforschung*, presented in some detail the parallelism of *Heroides* 10 with Catullus 64, and Verducci (1985: 244–6) has even gone so far as to suggest that Ovid deliberately reverses Horace's advice against poor writing in the *Ars Poetica* (131–5).[7] The result for Verducci is, in contrast to the Catullan piece, a 'rococo description' of which the mood is a 'universal travesty' (1985: 246). Yet when Ovid recreates Ariadne in the *Heroides*, one finds imitation similar to that of the *Fasti*, for an echo of Catullus 64 can clearly be sensed in the words of Ariadne in *Heroides* 10 (21–3, 35–6, 55–8):

Interea toto clamanti litore '*Theseu*'!
    reddebant nomen concaua saxa tuum
et quotiens ego te, totiens locus ipse uocabat;

---

[7] As in Galinsky's suggestion (1975: 81) that, by putting dolphins in trees *in fluvio* at *Met.* 1.302–3, Ovid flouts the Horatian precept of *AP* 30–1.

Meanwhile, the whole shore was crying out '*Theseus!*' and the hollowed out rocks were returning your name and as often as I called you, so often did that very place do so;

'Quo fugis?' exclamo 'scelerate revertere Theseu!
    Flecte ratem! Numerum non habet illa suum!'

'Where are you fleeing?' I cry out, 'Return, O wicked Theseus! *Turn back* your ship! It doesn't have its full payload!'

Incumbo lacrimisque toro manante profusis
    'Pressimus' exclamo 'te duo, redde duos!
Venimus huc ambo; cur non *discedimus* ambo?
    Perfide, pars nostri, *lectule*, maior ubi est?'

I lie down and the whole couch is dripping wet with my tears. I cry, 'Two of us made an impression on you, so return two of us! We came here two, why don't *we depart* as two? *Perfidious little bed*, where is the bigger part of us?'

One can see from the italicized text the obvious parallels with Catullus' presentation, particularly in the words of Ariadne there.[8] It is the bed, however, that Ariadne now addresses as 'perfidious,' for it cheats her of her lover (*Her.* 10.58; Cat. 64.132–3): this is the politic thing to do, since the objective of the letter is to persuade Theseus to come back, whereas the point of the address in Catullus 64 is to denounce him after his departure. Note, too, the close proximity of the verb *discedere* with the vocative *perfide* in both texts (*Her.* 10.57–8; Cat. 64.132-4), by which Ariadne clearly evokes her previous poetic situation. Moreover, one should not fail to notice the line termination *litore Theseu*, which also occurs in each piece (*Her.* 10.21 and Cat. 64.133), though with a difference: in Catullus it is part of Ariadne's direct address to Theseus, whereas in the *Heroides* one finds that it is the beckoning of nature, merely an echo of Ariadne's own speech, just as *Heroides* 10 echoes the text of Catullus 64.

Whether or not one accepts Verducci's assessment that Ovid's version is a travesty of that of his predecessor, it is nevertheless clear that

---

[8] At this point some distinction should be made between 'quoted' allusion found in the mouth or, in the case of the *Heroides*, the written text of the characters and general poetic allusion by an author to the text of a predecessor. In the case of Ovid's Ariadne, cited above, it is clear that the character herself is referring to her own words spoken in the same context but in a previous poetic text.

in the *Heroides* Ariadne invokes the tradition whence she comes, not so much expressing her 'debt' to it but rather establishing herself in a kind of intertextual mythology that gives life to literary characters. My view, then, would be that the seemingly tongue-in-cheek references to Catullus are not parodic but indicative of the character's personal growth, as it were, from text to text. Indeed Jacobson (1974: 225) seems a little surprised by the fact that Ariadne does *not* appeal to Theseus' former love for her or to renewing it. Yet this does not seem strange when considered in light of Ariadne's 'maturation' over the course of time since she had last appeared in literature: she will not try again what didn't work last time. Indeed, as Jacobson rightly observes (1974: 226), she is more concerned with her personal survival than with her perfidious lover, for she knows that while her 'former' appeal to love failed, perhaps this time a more universal human appeal will work.

Alessandro Barchiesi (1984: 66) has suggested that it is not so much the case that the traditional story offered Ovid a world of possibilities to work with, but rather that he opened a new window in an already existing story, as we saw in the case of Ariadne. In some instances, however, Ovid goes beyond expansion. When Dido writes to Aeneas in *Heroides* 7, her plea is one very much set against the backdrop of and in the context of *Aeneid* 1–6. Even a glance at Palmer's commentary on this poem (1898: 339–50) reveals just how abundant these references are, and it is not necessary to detail them all here; but let us briefly consider one or two examples. When Dido begins to draw heavily on the Virgilian account, she synecdochically recreates the Virgilian atmosphere by numerous references to the *Aeneid*.[9] At *Heroides* 7.81–4, Dido accuses Aeneas of lying about his wife:

Omnia mentiris; neque enim tua *fallere* lingua
   incipit a nobis primaque plector ego:
Si quaeras ubi sit formosi mater Iuli—
   occidit a duro sola relicta uiro.

You lie about everything; nor indeed does your tongue begin its cheating with me and I am not the first to be struck by you: if you want to know

---

[9] These examples are abundant in Palmer's commentary. On the notion of creating an atmosphere by alluding to an author, see Knauer (1981) 870–918; here, 876.

where the mother of handsome Iulus is, she perished, alone and abandoned by her harsh husband.

This remark cannot exist apart from the textual/mythical context which is the unseen counterpart to it, for Dido's charges only make sense when viewed in light of the myth as it would be familiar to the reader. The second book of the *Aeneid*, of course, is the source to which Dido alludes (736–44):

> namque auia cursu
> dum sequor et nota excedo regione uiarum,
> heu misero coniunx fatone erepta Creusa
> substitit, errauitne uia seu lapsa resedit,
> incertum; nec post oculis est reddita nostris.
> nec prius amissam respexi animumue reflexi
> quam tumulum antiquae Cereris sedemque sacratam
> uenimus: hic demum collectis omnibus una
> defuit, et comites natumque uirumque fefellit.

For while I follow the trackless places in my running and I depart from the section of the road that I know, alas, my wife Creusa, taken away—whether by a wretched fate she checked her step or she wandered from the path, or she sat down because she had fallen—I just don't know; nor did she appear to my eyes again, and I didn't look back for her when she was lost, nor did I pay any attention before we got to the mound of ancient Ceres and her sacred seat. Here, at long last, when all had been gathered, she alone was missing, and she cheated her friends, her son, and her husband.

Both authors employ passive participles of Creusa in order to indicate her fate (*erepta, Aen.* 2.738; *lapsa, Aen.* 2.739; *amissam, Aen.* 2.741; *relicta, Her.* 7.84): Ovid, however, specifies an agent, *a duro...uiro* (7.84). Furthermore, the manner in which Dido turns the verb around in his passage is remarkable: according to Aeneas, it is Creusa who 'cheated (*fefellit*) her friends, son, and husband' (*Aen.* 2.744), but now, as seen from the vantage point of Dido when she composes her epistle, it is Aeneas and his words that cheat her (*fallere, Her.* 7.81), just as he had previously cheated his Creusa by abandoning her at Troy. Because she has already heard Aeneas' story in *Aeneid* 2, Dido is familiar with Aeneas' allegations that Creusa is to blame and she does not accept his account. Rather than simply opening a new window in an old story (Barchiesi: 1984: 66), she 'sets him straight,' using against him the very verb he had used to describe his wife's disappearance. [10]

Yet, as Palmer notes in his commentary, it is when Dido refers to the marriage in the cave that the allusion to Virgil's text becomes most pointed. The passage that Dido has in mind, of course, is that of *Aeneid* 4 (161–72):

interea magno misceri murmure caelum
incipit, insequitur commixta grandine nimbus,
et Tyrii comites passim et Troiana iuuentus
Dardaniusque nepos Veneris diuersa per agros
tecta metu petiere; ruunt de montibus amnes.
speluncam Dido dux et Troianus eandem
deueniunt. prima et Tellus et pronuba Iuno
dant signum; fulsere ignes et conscius aether
conubiis summoque ulularunt uertice Nymphae.
ille dies primus leti primusque malorum
causa fuit; neque enim specie famaue mouetur
nec iam furtiuum Dido meditatur amorem:
coniugium uocat, hoc praetexit nomine culpam.

Meanwhile the sky grows threatening with peals of thunder, and rain follows, with hail mixed in. The scattered Tyrian company and the Trojan youth, as well as the Dardanian grandson of Venus, in fear sought out different places for shelter through the fields; now torrents are rushing down from the hills. Dido and the Trojan leader come into the same cave, Primal Earth and Juno of the marriage rites give the signal; the torch-fires flashed and the air was a witness to the nuptials, and on the mountain top the Nymphs did wail. That day first was of death and of ills the cause; in fact Dido is no longer moved by appearances or reputation, no more is she fixated upon a secret love: she calls it marriage and with this name hides her fault!

This scene is a third-person description of an event that, here in the *Aeneid*, Dido clearly considers marriage (172). Gordon Williams (1968: 381–2) has gone so far as to regard this wedding scene as

---

[10] In light of Ovid's clever manipulation of Virgil's text here, it is interesting to recall the comment (cited by Anderson 1973: 56) of John Dryden who was once quoted by Joseph Addison (*Spectator* 1710, v.62): 'I think I may be judge of this [the difference between Ovid's and Virgil's account of Dido], because I have translated both. The famous author of the Art of Love has nothing of his own; he borrows all from a greater master in his own profession, and, which is worse, improves nothing which he finds.' On the idea of 'correction,' cf. Thomas (1986) 185–9.

evocative of the ancient form of common law marriage (*affectio maritalis*). Later in *Heroides* 7, however, Dido's desperation leads her to reconsider the marriage scene and she is willing to compromise (169–70):[11]

si pudet uxoris, non nupta, sed hospita dicar;
    dum *tua* sit Dido, quodlibet esse feret.

If it shames you that I be your wife, let me not be called your bride, but your hostess, provided only that Dido be *yours*, she will tolerate being whatever you want.

Here the Virgilian event is, as it were, perceived through the psychological filter of Dido: it is now presented in the first person and we understand that she backs away from her Virgilian position of 'marriage' in an effort to preserve the relationship. Similarly, if we turn to her words elsewhere in this epistle, we find that, while clearly referring to her previous poetic context, Dido presents us with a new perspective of the event, namely a first-person perspective (93–6):

illa dies nocuit, qua nos decliue sub antrum
    caeruleus subitis compulit imber aquis.
audieram voces, nymphas ululasse putaui:
    Eumenides fatis signa dedere meis.

That day did me harm, the day on which rain of the blue sky with a sudden downpour drove us into the sloping cave. I had heard voices: I thought it the nymphs wailing: it was the Furies that gave signals for my doom!

Dido's words in *Heroides* 7 more than merely echo Virgil's description of the encounter in the cave. Rather, as Gordon Williams has suggested (1968: 381), Dido refers to that scene directly and she does so in a unique way. As a participant in that text, Dido's 'interpretation' of Virgil is perceptibly different from the reader's. While she agrees with Virgil that in fact that was a fateful day when she and Aeneas entered the cave (93), Dido recalls the acoustical effects differently: what she thought was the cry of nymphs (as is stated in *Aen.* 4.168), turns out to be the signals of the Furies. Palmer suggests that this change amounts to a correction of Virgil's view (1898: 344); but it

---

[11] Cf. also the words of Briseis 3.69–70.

is not Ovid who changes Virgil's account here—it is Dido.[12] Indeed, this is not strictly a correction, but simply a different perception of events described in Virgil's text by a character within that text; in this regard note the pluperfect *audieram* in line 95: 'I had heard (when I was in the *Aeneid*).' Virgil specifies that Juno and Tellus gave the signal, but from Dido's perspective of forlorn lover, she remembers it as the signal of the Furies: she *feels* differently and so she 'recalls' *Aeneid* 4 differently.[13]

Like Ariadne and Dido, the other composers of these letters (and other Ovidian characters generally) have a Pirandello-like quality about them. Ovid's heroines possess a certain autonomy within their mythical contexts and the mythical context is itself moulded by the tradition of which the characters are a part. A further example can be seen in the case of Penelope, whose letter, for obvious reasons, is rich in references to the *Odyssey*. She reveals that she has been 'reading' the *Odyssey* in several instances when she purposely deviates from Homer's text, the most poignant of which, perhaps, is her statement that she sent Telemachus to Pylos to inquire after Odysseus (*omnia namque tuo senior te quaerere misso | rettulerat nato Nestor, at ille mihi*, *Her.* 1.37–8). This has presented a great problem for commentators on this poem. Many, and Jacobson among them, assume that Ovid had not read his Homer carefully enough. Yet it can be seen from Jacobson's review of this poem (1974: 267) that even he has a very difficult time believing that Ovid could have been careless. If one assumes that Penelope, like Ariadne or Dido, has 'read' the *Odyssey* and now presents her case in light of it, she can be viewed as justifying the account of her actions there—not Ovid correcting Homer, but rather Penelope altering, or distorting, her place in intertextualized mythology, for now she gets the opportunity to tell her side of the story (Barchiesi 1984: 70–1; Kennedy 1984: 419–21). It wasn't *really* Athene who sent Telemachus, it was Penelope herself (37–8). On this reading, Jacobson's contention that Ovid is 'slipshod' in presenting the material from the *Odyssey* regarding Penelope and Telemachus

---

[12] My view of allusion here contrasts with the more traditional view of Lamacchia (1960) 310–30, and, more recently, Boyd (1990) 82–5.

[13] Cf. Alessandro Barchiesi's discussion (1984: 71–4) of Penelope in *Her.* 1, where Penelope's different perspective on events in the *Odyssey* is related to her subjective elegiac (specifically non-epic) point of view.

can be discarded, replaced by consideration of a richer, more complex Penelope, whose misrepresentation of the Homeric facts can be explained by her power as a character given new life by the poet very much within—and here distorting—the poetic tradition (Viarre 1987: 2–11). In sum, the mythical character presents us with a kind of psychological filter, which brings a heightened pathos to the new context. The first-person perspective in which Ovid's heroines write makes private and personalizes what had been public about them in their previous contexts.[14]

Ovid's other heroines, too, reveal in their new settings knowledge of their previous locations in the poetic tradition.[15] According to Simone Viarre (1987: 6) references to the Homeric poems are defined by their 'couleur psychologique ... ainsi que par l'attitude mentale attribuée à l'épistolière élégiaque.' As Viarre points out for these poems, and as we have already seen in the epistle of Dido in particular, the fantasizing quality of a love letter functions on a psychological level, evoking the most basic human emotions of longing, anger, hope, and despair (Steinmetz 1987: 134). Such qualities have been viewed by T. E. Apter as a general feature of fantasy literature (1982: 3–4): 'fantasy is unconscious, uncontrolled, highly personal, and its products lack integration or generality or balance.' Indeed, in his preface to the translation that he published to some of the Heroides, John Dryden mentions that the passion embodied in these poems seems to conflict with the eloquence of these heroines (Kinsley 1958: 180):

---

[14] For a similar observation on Dido, cf. Anderson (1973: 68): 'Ovid ... moves right out of the [sc. Virgil's] heroic framework. His Dido emerges simply as a woman, a famous woman, but otherwise not to be distinguished from any woman about to be abandoned by the typically selfish male.'

[15] Aside from Ariadne (Her. 10), Dido (Her. 7), and Penelope (Her. 1) discussed here, intertextual precedents include Homer Il. 9 for Her. 3 (Briseis to Achilles), Euripides' Hippolytus for Her. 4 (Phaedra to Hippolytus) and his Aeolus for Her. 11 (Canace to Macareus), Apollonius Rhodius Arg. 1.609 ff. for Her. 6 (Hypsipyle to Jason) and Arg. 3 (along with Euripides' Medea) for Her. 12 (Medea to Jason), Sophocles' Hermione and Euripides' Andromache and possibly Pacuvius' adaptation of Sophocles' play for Her. 8 (Hermione to Orestes), Sophocles' Trachiniae and Apollodorus 2.7.7 for Her. 9 (Deianira to Hercules), Euripides' Protesilaus and Catullus 68 for Her. 13 (Laodamia to Protesilaus), Horace's Odes 3.11 and Aeschylus' trilogy of Supplices, Aegyptii, and Danaides for Her. 14, and Sappho (along with the Attic comedies of Ameipsias and Diphilos) for Her. 15 (Sappho to Phaon; cf. Dörrie 1975: 14–18).

His thoughts which are the Pictures and results of those Passions, are generally such as naturally arise from those disorderly Motions of our Spirits. Yet not to speak too partially in his behalf, I will confess that the Copiousness of his Wit was such, that he often writ too pointedly for his Subject, and made his persons speak more Eloquently than the violence of their Passion would admit: so that he is frequently witty out of season: leaving the imitation of Nature and the cooler dictates of his Judgment for the false applause of Fancy.

Yet even if to some Ovid's wit may occasionally seem out of season (as apparently, regarding the *Ars Amatoria*, it later did to the emperor Augustus), in the case of these epistles this should be excused since these poems are not meant to be historically 'accurate' representations of letters, but rather the embodiment of the passion of mythical characters in the context of a love letter. Accordingly, it is no surprise to find that Dryden himself here refers to Ovid's presentation of the passion in these poems as engendered by spiritual disorder (Verducci 1985: 5, 25). Verducci has also discussed the disintegrating quality of these epistles; she notes that each of the letters embodies a disorder apparent to the reader but not to the heroines themselves (1985: 28). While clear examples of this can be found in the words of Phyllis (2.131 ff.) or Penelope (1.71 ff.), perhaps Briseis provides the best example (3.5–8):

si mihi pauca queri de te dominoque uiroque
    fas est, de domino pauca uiroque querar.
non, ego poscenti quod sum cito tradita regi,
    culpa tua est—quamuis haec quoque culpa tua est.

If it is right for me to complain a few things about you, my lord and my husband, about you, lord and husband, a few things will I complain. Just because I was quickly handed over to the king when he demanded, it is not your fault—yet *it is too* your fault.

On the one hand, one might view the epanalepsis found in lines 5–6 and the chiastic arrangement of line 8 as indicative of more eloquence 'than the violence of... Passion' should admit, to use Dryden's phrase. Indeed, commentators have been so troubled by the lines that they have proposed excising them[16]and, at one point, these lines led one scholar to suggest that the whole of *Heroides* 3 is spurious (Lachmann

---

[16] See Palmer (1898) ad loc., who with Merkel, wishes to excise lines 7–8.

1969: 58). On the other hand, notions of rhetoric and passion should not be considered contradictory: the rhetorical repetition here surely is indicative of a desperate tone and the design of line 8 should be regarded as suggestive of a moment of confusion on Briseis' part. Such a quality can also be seen in the love letters of Elizabeth Barrett and Robert Browning, e.g., E.B. to R.B.:

it is for you, I fear, whenever I fear:—and if you were less to me, should I fear do you think?—if you were to me only what I am to myself, for instance, if your happiness were only as precious as my own in my own eyes, should I fear, do you think, then? Think, and do not blame me.[17]

The disorder is a logic to itself and, in the case of Ovid's heroines, such fantasizing should perhaps sometimes be viewed as produced by the sexual frustration that arises from the suppression of erotic impulses produced by the prolonged separation of the lovers (Jacobson 1974: 268–74); one will recall Apter's (1982: 3–4) definition of fantasy as being 'unconscious, uncontrolled,' and lacking 'integration or . . . balance'. The words of Ariadne in *Heroides* 10.56 ff. reveal this as do the impassioned statements of Penelope in *Heroides* 1 (5–10):[18]

o utinam tum, cum Lacedaemona classe petebat,
      obrutus insanis esset adulter aquis!
non ego deserto iacuissem frigida lecto,
      non quererer tardos ire relicta dies
nec mihi quaerenti spatiosam fallere noctem
      lassaret uiduas pendula tela manus.

O would that then, when he was sailing for Sparta in his ship, that adulterer had been overcome by raging waters. Had it been so, I would not have lain here cold in a deserted bed, I, abandoned, would not be complaining that the days go slowly nor would the hanging woof weary my widow's hands, I who am trying to cheat the long and empty night.

I am not the first to suggest that Penelope's words are erotically charged. John Henderson remarks generally about this poem that ' "characterization" is caught up in the problematic of sexuality'

---

[17] Dec. 13, 1845, in Stack (1969) 68. Cf. also Henderson (1986) 7–10, 37–40, 67–70, 81–5, 113–20, who (p. 9) cites Barthes (1979: 157), 'I have nothing to tell you, save that it is to you that I tell this nothing.'

[18] Cf. also 1.50 and 1.75–6.

(1986: 7) and later (1986: 9) he states, ' "writing at once represses and reveals desire" (Wright 1984: 133). Yet the letter is exemplary Writing-as-the-dissimulation-of-its-status-as-Writing precisely because it is "addressed" to a "destination," as if desire is portable, postable...'
Howard Jacobson has gone so far as to see many references in *Heroides* 1, in particular, as sexually suggestive, including the seemingly innocent use of such phrases as *sine uiribus uxor* (97) and the epic reference *sanguine... tepefecerat hastam* (19); for Jacobson these indicate that Penelope is a 'sex-starved, sex-obsessed woman' (1974: 273).[19]
Yet, whether one accepts Henderson's more general post-structuralist reading or Jacobson's highly specific philological position, it is perhaps most telling that Penelope here refers rather forthrightly to her suppressed sexuality in spite of the fact that she was a proverbial symbol of chastity in the ancient world (as can also be inferred from line 10).

Similarly, when Oenone recalls for Paris their former rustic love-making, she points out that she would be even better in a bed (*Her.* 5.87–8):

nec me, faginea quod tecum fronde iacebam,
   despice; purpureo sum magis apta toro.

Just because I once used to lie with you on the leaves of a beech tree, don't despise me. I am more suited to the royal marriage bed.

Oenone's reference to the bed is indicative not only of her claim to royalty, but of her lovemaking generally. While Oenone's statement does not comport the same degree of sexual frustration that we saw in Penelope's words above, it is certainly not merely a reference to sexual contentment: rather it stands as a challenge to Paris to turn from the adulteress (*adultera certe est*, 125) to a more homespun love (79 ff.). But Sappho provides us with an even more graphic example (*Her.* 15.123–34):

tu mihi cura, Phaon, te somnia nostra reducunt,
   somnia formosa candidiora die.
illic te inuenio, quamuis regionibus absis;

---

[19] In general, Jacobson seems to me to take these 'erotic' words out of context. I do, however, agree that the general backdrop of the *Heroides* is clearly informed by erotic suppression.

sed non longa satis gaudia somnus habet.
saepe tuos nostra ceruice onerare lacertos,
    saepe tuae uideor supposuisse meos.
oscula cognosco, quae tu committere lingua
    aptaque consueras accipere, apta dare.
blandior interdum uerisque simillima uerba
    eloquor, et uigilant sensibus ora meis;
ulteriora pudet narrare, sed omnia fiunt,
    et iuuat, et siccae non licet esse mihi.

You are my care, Phaon. My dreams recall you, dreams brighter than the fairest day. I find you there, although you are gone from these regions; but sleep does not hold onto its delights long enough. Often I dream that your arms are pressing on my neck, often that my arms are around your neck. I can recognize your kisses that you used to give and take with your tongue—you were a great kisser. Sometimes I fondle you and I speak words so real they're true, and my lips keep watch for all my senses; I'm ashamed to mention the things that happen beyond this...But we go all the way, it's pure pleasure, and I get all wet.

This very rare literary specimen of an erotic dream further evidences that sexual suppression stands out as a leitmotif for these poems. In sharing her dream with Phaon in such a vivid manner, Sappho demonstrates the extreme to which the sexual fantasizing may go, a component of these poems that we have also seen presented in the other, less explicit, examples considered here.

Romantic fantasy, however, is not couched in strictly erotic terms in these poems. When Paris returns to the Trojan shore with Helen, Oenone reconstructs the scene of *anagnorisis* (*Her.* 5.63, 67–74):

hinc ego uela tuae cognoui prima carinae...
fit propior terrasque cita ratis attigit aura:
    femineas uidi corde tremente genas.
non satis id fuerat—quid enim furiosa morabar?—
    haerebat gremio turpis amica tuo!
tunc uero rupique sinus et pectora planxi
    et secui madidas ungue rigente genas
impleuique sacram querulis ululatibus Iden;
    illuc has lacrimas in mea saxa tuli.

Thence I recognized the first sails of your ship ... The ship gets closer and closer and, with a sudden breeze, it touches the shore: with trembling heart I saw a female face. And that wasn't enough—for what was I waiting for, I in my madness?—that shameless girlfriend was hanging all over your chest! But then I ripped at my bosom and beat my breast, and with my hard nails I cut into my streaming cheeks, and I filled sacred Ida with complaining cries; just there did I bear these tears upon my rocks.

The emotional quality of this passage amply demonstrates the high passion of these epistles. While Oenone retains her composure in recounting the incident, her portrait here is nevertheless the worst kind of lover's fantasy, namely to see one's paramour in the arms of another. Nor is this an isolated example: Medea's description of the wedding procession of Jason and Creusa (*Her.* 12.137 ff.) has similar effect, leaving her with only a desperate response (157–8): *Vix me continui, quin sic laniata capillos | clamarem 'meus est' iniceremque manus.*

That these heroines describe their worst fears for their romantic fantasies and lament their sexual separation is suited to these epistles, for as such they are documents of a highly personal nature. Yet it is also fitting on another level, specifically that of genre, for the elegiac meter had, of course, been long recognized as the meter of lament and had recently been described as such by Horace.[20] Furthermore, elegiac couplets were, of course, also known as the meter of love and thus it is not surprising that when Phaedra portrays herself as a spurned lover, she writes under the direction of the god Amor (*Her.* 4.9–20):

qua licet et †sequitur, pudor est miscendus amori;
   dicere quae puduit, scribere iussit amor.
quidquid Amor iussit, non est contemnere tutum;
   regnat et in dominos ius habet ille deos.
ille mihi primo dubitanti scribere dixit:
   'scribe! dabit uictas ferreus ille manus.'
adsit et, ut nostras auido fouet igne medullas,
   figat sic animos in mea uota tuos.
non ego nequitia socialia foedera rumpam;

---

[20] Horace's description is well known (*AP* 75–8): *uersibus inpariter iunctis querimonia primum, | post etiam inclusa est uoti sententia compos; | quis tamen exiguos elegos emiserit auctor, | grammatici certant et adhuc sub iudice lis est.* Cf. also Viarre (1987) 6.

fama—uelim quaeras—crimine nostra uacat.
uenit amor grauius, quo serior. urimur intus,
    urimur et caecum pectora uulnus habent...

Wherever it is right that modesty be mixed with love, love also follows; whatever I have been ashamed to say, Love has ordered me to write. It is not safe to despise whatever Love has ordered; he reigns and holds sway over the gods who themselves are lords. That one spoke to me when I was first hesitating to write: 'Write; the iron-hearted one will yield conquered hands.' Let him attend me and, just as he warms my marrow with his greedy flame, so let him pierce your heart in answer to my prayers. Not with wickedness will I break my marriage vows; go ahead and ask me and I'll tell you that my reputation is free from reproach. Love has come more gravely just as he has come later. I am burning within, I am burned and my breast has an unseen wound...

While Phaedra's romantic situation with Hippolytus is certainly unique to her, her artistic situation is the same as the other heroines who struggle to commit their emotions to writing. Her psychological state is, as we saw in the case of Dido and Ariadne, not set in the chronologically remote, mythical past but is thoroughly contemporary, for she is a lover with whom the reader can identify emotionally. Moreover, her act of writing here is one with which Ovid himself can identify, for he had recently been in a similar predicament when embarking on his career as an elegiac poet (*Am.* 1.1.21–30):

questus eram, pharetra cum protinus ille soluta
    legit in exitium spicula facta meum
lunauitque genu sinuosum fortiter arcum
    'quod' que 'canas, uates, accipe' dixit 'opus.'
me miserum! certas habuit puer ille sagittas:
    uror, et in uacuo pectore regnat Amor.
sex mihi surgat opus numeris, in quinque residat;
    ferrea cum uestris bella ualete modis.
cingere litorea flauentia tempora myrto,
    Musa per undenos emodulanda pedes.

I had made my complaint, when he straightway, having opened his quiver, chose arrows made for my destruction, bravely arching his sinuous bow on his knee. He said 'Receive the kind of poetry, bard, that you will sing.' Woe is me! that boy had accurate arrows: I burn, and Love rules in my empty breast. Six times does my kind of poetry rise up in its measures, and ebbs in five;

farewell iron battles together with your meter. Gird your blond temples with myrtle that grows by the beach, O Muse that must be sung in eleven-foot measures.

One can see from these lines not only that Ovid alleges originally to have contemplated writing epic but he also draws attention to the association of meter and content for both epic and elegy. She may not herself be debating over generic preference, as Ovid did, but by alluding to the predicament of the elegiac poet, Phaedra brings that text into play with her own in *Heroides* 4. Thus, on one level at least, Phaedra reveals that although she is a mythical persona, she is nevertheless writing in the manner of a Roman elegiac poet. As a woman and as a poet, Phaedra is part and parcel of the Roman world.[21]

By introducing the strict rules of genre into the generally fantastic complexion of these heroines' sentiments, Ovid could very well create an impossible tension between the spontaneity of the fantasy and the form of the literary genre. Yet ironically it is within the constraints of genre that Ovid's poetic genius has freest reign, for he defies traditional notions associated with the epistolary mode of expression: as was suggested above, the epistolary format of the *Heroides* cloaks another genre, namely Roman elegy (Barchiesi 1984: 69–71; Spoth 1992: 85–8, 107–8, 221–3). When Phaedra alludes to Ovid's programmatic poem on his choice of elegy, she brings a generic tension into the text of her epistle.[22] The genre of the epistle has an earlier tradition of both prose (obvious examples are Cicero, Plato, and Epicurus) and poetry (e.g., the hexameter tradition of Lucilius and Horace).

---

[21] In his preface to the *Heroides*, Dryden suggests that Ovid may have 'Romanized' these heroines too much. Ovid's use of fantasy within the Romanized context, then, does not offer his audience an escape, but rather brings the reality of the reader's situation to bear upon the fantasy of these women. This, Apter (1982: 2) has observed, is a normal feature of fantasy literature: 'fantasy is essential to the authors' various purposes, which must be understood not as an escape from reality but as an investigation of it.' This, however, runs counter to the view of Manlove (1982). For more on 'Romanization,' cf. Verducci (1985) 5 and, more recently, Solodow (1988) 55.

[22] The text of Horace, *AP* 75 ff. clearly suggests that in the Augustan period the genre of elegy was distinctly linked with the concepts of lament and love, suitable on both counts for these letters, as does Sappho herself, who says in *Her.* 15.7 ff.: 'my love must be wept over; the song of lament belongs to elegy . . .'

Recently Propertius had even cast one of his elegies in the form of an epistle (4.3), though not in a mythical setting (Cunningham 1949: 100). The Roman elegiac tradition is, of course, at the time of the *Heroides*, vibrantly represented by Ovid himself in his *Amores*. While the reader who has 'intercepted' this letter before it reaches Hippolytus barely senses the clever integration of the chronologically incongruous elements in the 'Romanization' of the mythical heroine, it is nevertheless likely that the tension of elegy-within-epistle is a feature that Ovid wishes to be prominent in this corpus of poems.[23] Still, the elegiac and the epistolary elements of these poems do not collide violently, but combine gracefully, as do the mythical and the Roman.

Such graceful combination can also be seen in the general constitution of the *Heroides*. Just as genre cloaks genre, so the author of these poems (Ovid) is cloaked by another author—the heroine (Steinmetz 1987: 141, section 5); and, as befits such a sexual reversal, in each case she writes to a male. I would suggest that this is why Ovid makes the recipient of Sappho's letter a man instead of a woman— not because Ovid enjoys engaging in 'transvestite ventriloquization,' as E. D. Harvey has argued (1989: 120). In fact, Harvey suggests that Ovid engages in sexual and poetic 'subjugation' and goes on to say that by preempting Sappho's voice in this epistle Ovid commits a Philomela-like 'linguistic rape.' Yet Harvey does not seem to consider adequately the textual dynamic of the relationship that Ovid, as heir of the literary tradition, establishes with the texts that he inherits—a relationship that strangely parallels the intimate relationship that the reader of an epistle has with the author of the epistle (Altman 1982: 117 ff.).

In contrast to Harvey's interpretation it should be noted that, as I suggested just above, the inversion of female/male for the author uniformly supposes a male recipient, no matter who the actual reader is, of course. Ovid does not 'ventriloquize' Sappho by having her write to Phaon, but allows her, as informed by the poetic tradition, to speak once more. Here, as elsewhere in the *corpus Ovidianum*, the characters speak because they live within the tradition; their rebirth

---

[23] See Steinmetz (1987) 143–4, Jacobson (1974) 331–4. For further discussion of reader as recipient for epistolary composition generally, cf. Altman (1982) 117 ff.

in the Ovidian text is obliged to that tradition and shapes their role in subsequent literature. Indeed, perhaps it would not be going too far to say that, as I have suggested in the case of other heroines, if anyone ventriloquizes anyone, it is Sappho who ventriloquizes Ovid.

But let us now bring some of these strands together. We have noted that the tension of author within author itself presents an interesting parallel to that of text (of the letter) within the text (of elegy).[24] In the midst of this combination of distinctly different generic ideas which inform the surface of the text, Ovid also performs the further internal synthesis of the opposing strands of intertextualized myth and personal fantasy. Disparate elements are so uniquely combined that the reader is rarely aware of the fleshing out of this dynamic. Could this be the new genre, a genre of conflict and synthesis, to which Ovid refers in his *Ars* (3.345–6)?[25] Such synthesis is, after all, elsewhere characteristic of Ovid's poetry (*Met.* 1.1–4):

in nova fert animus mutatas dicere formas corpora:
di, coeptis (nam vos mutastis et illa)[26]
adspirate meis primaque ab origine mundi
ad mea perpetuum deducite tempora carmen.

My mind carries me to speak of forms changed into new bodies; ye gods, breathe upon my undertakings (for you changed them, too) and spin forth a perpetual song from the first origin of the world to my own times.

One facet of his poetic programme, Ovid suggests at the beginning of his *Metamorphoses* is the integration and dichotomization of two major strands of the poetic tradition, the *carmen deductum* and the *carmen perpetuum* (Mack 1988: 107–8). By making *perpetuum ...*

---

[24] Or vice versa; or, perhaps, even a triple layer of elegy (the aspect of the content containing the heroine's love/lament), within the letter (of the heroine), itself within the elegiac couplets (of Ovid).

[25] Steinmetz (1987: 143–4) suggests that single aspects of various different literary forms, such as elegy, drama, and epistle combine in the *Heroides* to form a new genre, in a manner similar to Virgil's adaptation of previous poetic forms for the *Eclogues*. While Steinmetz is surely right that there is a conflation of elements that goes into the formulation of the *Heroides*, his tenfold schematization seems to me to be an oversimplification of a wider (inter-)textual dynamic, one that Barchiesi comes closer to defining. See Barchiesi (1984) 66, for a more sensitive, if less fully documented, approach to this question.

[26] Anderson (1977) has *illas*. For the reading of *illa* for *illas* here see Kenney (1976, ch. 12 below) 46–50 and Tarrant (1982) 350–1. See also Knox (1986a) 9.

carmen the object of *deducite*, Ovid reveals that he intends to bring these two kinds of poetic expression together in the *Metamorphoses*. Again, in the comments on this prologue that he makes in his exile poetry, Ovid reveals that such combination of tension and harmony is one of his poetic goals when he appeals to Caesar on the basis of the prologue to the *Metamorphoses* (*Trist.* 2.555–60):

dictaque sunt nobis, quamuis manus ultima coeptis
   defuit, in facies corpora uersa novas.
atque utinam reuoces animum paulisper ab ira,
   et uacuo iubeas hinc tibi pauca legi,
pauca, quibus prima surgens ab origine mundi
   in tua deduxi tempora, Caesar, opus!

I also told—though my efforts lacked the final touch—of bodies turned into new appearances. And I pray that you would tone down your anger a bit and bid that these few things be read to you, at your leisure, few things, by which, rising up from the first origin of the world, I spun the work down to your times, Caesar!

While the times have changed—specifically from Ovid's (*ad mea... tempora*, *Met.* 1.4) to Caesar's (*in tua... tempora*, *Trist.* 2.560)—the poetic objective, it seems, has not. Indeed, the participle *surgens* (559) here, as Stephen Hinds has demonstrated elsewhere, suggests generic tension:[27] in the *Metamorphoses*, Ovid, like a line of elegiac verse (cf. *Am.* 1.1.17), rises up in the epic tradition but winds up spinning out his work (*deduxi*) in a neoteric, elegiac manner. It is not surprising, then, to find him pursuing this same goal of generic synthesis at an earlier stage in his career, when he designs and executes this most interesting genre of amatory epistles, love letters set in elegiac couplets.

These three components, then,—intertextualized myth, psychological fantasy, and the conflation of generic variants—though different, are thematically inseparable in these poems and actually work together to create a uniquely Ovidian textual dynamic. The reader is drawn into the experience of the text by the very artificiality which

---

[27] On *surgo*, cf. Hinds (1987a) 166, n. 39. For the association of *deduco* with Ovid's elegiac poetry, cf. *Am.* 2.18.18–19, where Ovid is called back from writing tragedy to elegy: *hinc quoque me dominae numen deduxit iniquae, | deque cothurnato vate triumphat Amor.* Cf. also *Am.* 2.1.21 ff. and, as Hinds notes, Virgil *Ecl.* 10.75–6.

would seemingly conflict with the spontaneity of fantasy. As we have seen, conflict and synthesis exist at several levels in the work: epistle and elegy, Romanized fantasy and ancient myth, reader and recipient, heroine and Ovid. The result is a kind of incongruous harmony, which should not work, but does and does so elegantly. Just as Keats's Grecian urn comes to life through his portrait of the vessel's stiffness, the fantasy of these lovers is unencumbered for the reader by the very mechanisms of genre and text that would appear to encumber it.

11

Ovid and the Politics of Reading

Alison R. Sharrock

What did Ovid think of Augustus? Did he offend the emperor? Did he intend to? Why was he exiled (assuming that he was!)? These are questions which haunt modern (and not so modern) scholars, fascinated as we are by the biography of those we consider great (Thibault 1964). This will be no new investigation, in that I shall be addressing a question as old as the work it concerns: rather, it seeks to offer a fresh look at the issue, with the aid of some modern theory. Throughout this paper, in the manner of academic discourse, I appropriate the first person plural for rhetorical purposes, imposing my readings on you. But not because I'm a rotten cheat: rather because any use of the term 'we' involves such appropriation, and indeed because the act of reading my text involves you (and me) in playing the role of my reader, whatever other roles—such as that of a dissenting reader—you may wish to play as well (Martindale 1993: esp. 2–10). The question is: was the *Ars Amatoria* 'anti-Augustan'? Now, as is becoming increasingly realized, this question is not as simple as it seems.[1] One of the difficulties with discussions of this nature is that they necessitate confrontation with the rhetoric of 'parody' and 'irony'. A text can (always?) be appropriated into a reading opposite to some other reading by being declared 'ironic'. This, moreover, is only one of many ways in which texts may be appropriated to various readings. One might, for example, say that text x displays something y

---

[1] See, for example, the essays, particularly that by Duncan Kennedy, in Powell (1992).

which 'we' all agree is bad, and that although x seems to condone y, it must in fact have the effect of condemning it, because it exposes it as bad. But how can an author be sure to escape complicity with the thing supposedly parodied? One point should be clarified: by saying that 'texts can be appropriated to particular readings', I may seem to imply that those readings are wrong, that violence is being done to the text, and that there is a real, right, and true reading from which the appropriation has taken place. In practice, that may well represent my personal feelings on the matter, but it should be stressed that all readings are appropriations and that in the end a *text* of itself cannot be either 'pro-' or 'anti-' 'Augustan', only readings can be.

The debate over the political orientation of the *Ars Amatoria* has to a very considerable extent revolved around two questions. Firstly: is the *Ars* teaching? Is it really (intended to be) didactic? Secondly: is the *Ars* about adultery? Does it have anything to do with respectable women: that is, is the *puella* to be envisaged as married? (If not— sigh of relief—not adultery, not politically subversive, just the lads having a good time—and reinforcing their aristocratic superiority at the same time . . .) This paper seeks to offer some reflections on these questions.[2]

Further to the questions with which I began, we might also want to consider whether we mean 'did Ovid intend it to offend Augustus?'— and that question might refer to the emperor either 'officially' or 'personally'[3]—or do we mean 'were those who supported the regime in fact offended, and/or were those who were ambivalent about the regime amused by it and reinforced in their political sentiments?' This is probably not the place for a major discussion of authorial intention: suffice it to say that if Ovid intended it as an innocent joke (or even a text in positive support of the emperor) but everyone who responded to it read it as subversive—that is, if Ovid boobed—then it seems to me to stretch the credible bounds of the authority of intention to claim that the text is not anti-Augustan. Not that they did, of course,

---

[2] I have deliberately avoided attempting an exhaustive study of the possible source passages for discussion of the poem's politics, in order to try and focus on the politics of *reading* from which any individual readings must arise.

[3] Throughout this paper I must refer to Augustus. Let it be said that this signifies not simply the man, but also the concept of 'Augustus' as a focus for the new ideology.

and it is the variety of reactions to the political nature of the poem in the modern scholars which I shall now consider.

A glance at the literature on the *Ars Amatoria* in this century will show that there has been a marked (although not absolute) shift in the nature (or at least the formulation) of the question (Holzberg 1981). Much of the discussion has surrounded the question as to whether the *Ars* is really a didactic poem. Earlier scholars were concerned with the poet's intention and sincerity, whereas more recent critics (particularly outside the UK), perhaps reacting against the previous methodology, have tended to concentrate on formal didactic elements. The antithesis of intentionalism might perhaps be called the 'literary fallacy', meaning that in the obsession with features which signify the didactic genre, the significance of didacticism is lost. The force of both responses—to claim that the poem is only pseudo-didactic or to study its formal didactic properties—is to disconnect the poem from the contemporary political actualities. A dominant strain in the tradition of reading the *Ars*, particularly in Britain, has been to read Ovid as essentially apolitical and his early poetry as 'literary wit' unconnected with the serious business of Roman society. Undeniable examples of 'irreverence' merely create a 'pleasing atmosphere of burlesque', in Wilkinson's (1955: 120) phrase.[4] There has been a challenge to this quietist interpretation as early as Otis (1938: 211 and 1966: 20). Among 'anti-Augustan' readings are Rudd's interpretation (1976) of the *Ars* as deliberately setting out to poke fun at the monuments of Roman and Augustan achievement, and Stroh's discussion (1979) of the relationship between Ovid's amatory poetry and the *lex Iulia de adulteriis*, which shows how Ovid was able to make a joke at the expense of the marriage laws.[5]

A moment ago I referred to 'the Roman and Augustan achievement'. That 'and' is an ideologically charged conjunction which serves to create a propagandist link between Rome and Augustus (and one from which the possibility of acting disjunctively has been effectively removed, even by the recognition of its propagandist effect). That almost inevitable link between Rome and Augustus informs a

---

[4] Similar views are espoused by Hollis (1973); and McKeown (1984).

[5] See also Blodgett (1973) 330, Abbot (1966), Holleman (1971), Scivoletto (1976) esp. 71–2, Pianezzola (1972).

problem which arises with the *laudes Romae*, around which much discussion of the poem's political status has focused. Do Ovid's praise of Rome (like Vergil's praise of Italy in the *Georgics*) and his encomium of the Emperor and his family indicate a genuine patriotism and loyalty to the leader, or an attempt to veil immorality with flattery?—or, of course, our old friend irony! Augustus has successfully appropriated patriotism, to the extent that anything good one might say about Rome can potentially be read as praise of Augustus. Since 'official Roman', or even just 'Roman' has come to be equated with 'Augustan', the Augustan part in the significance of statements about Rome should always be borne in mind. The success of that appropriation at one level denies Ovid the possibility of producing a subversive text, since, whatever he means, the audience cannot escape the equation Rome = Augustus. With the other hand, however, it necessitates a subversive text, in that even sincerely intended praise of Rome in the context of a poem about adultery cannot avoid a subversive reading with regard to Augustus.

Focusing on the *laudes Romae*, Sciveletto (1976: 71–2) takes up the question in terms of the opposition between *rusticitas* and *urbanitas*.[6] Set in the society of the 'urbane' city, the *Ars* is in opposition to the *Georgics* and to the Augustan propaganda that 'farming' is the secret of Rome's power (68–70). The contrast might be described as not so much that between city and countryside as between *urbanitas* (the sophisticated and immoral society of the *Ars*) and the *Urbs* (the moral and political centre of Roman power, based on *mos maiorum*).

Among the most stimulating of modern discussions of Ovid's relationship to his contemporary political situation is that of Labate. His introduction is particularly useful in admitting to the personal stake of the critic in attempting to decide on a text's political flavour, an involvement always significant but rarely acknowledged.[7] As I

---

[6] This opposition receives its fullest treatment from Myerowitz (1985).

[7] M. Labate (1984) 14–15: 'il quadro però non e privo di fascino: un poeta anti-conformista, ribelle alle ragioni comuni dell'impegno civile, demistificatore giocoso dell'etica tradizionale; ci si sente tentati dall'immagine di un antagonista al progetto augusteo di restaurazione morale, di un intellettuale d'opposizione'. Naturally, the acknowledgement would have to apply to Labate (and me) as much as anyone else. Martindale (1993) 4 ff. has helpfully formulated the involvement of the critic's 'prejudices', or 'fore-understandings' as essential to and inevitable in any act of reading.

understand him, Labate seeks to confront the question of the relationship between literature and life. While I cannot agree with his
conclusions, the project is an important one. Labate claims to expose
an Ovidian paradox, that in so far as his poetry is anti-realistic, it
contests the 'tyranny of life on literature' (42), while at the same
time Ovid constructs a poetry able to maintain a rapport with reality.
On this view, (for example) the description of the naval battle in
book 1 is a harmonious conjugation of public ceremony and erotic
opportunity (55); literature and life are harmonized as the public and
private (an antithesis which becomes equated with one consisting of
'Augustan' and 'erotic'—questionably) are not mixed or juxtaposed
but merged as two sides of the same thing (50); this conflation of
love poetry and civic poetry finds its inspiration in Hellenistic court
poetry (55–7). Quite *how* Ovid would effect this harmonization is not
at all clear to me. It would be difficult for him to stop people reading
his 'conflation' as a subversive (parodic?) juxtaposition. Labate offers
us an opposing hierarchy which places Augustus, politics, and reality
on one side, with Ovid, love, and literature on the other, in the subordinate position. But these are oppositions which will not stay separate
(nor indeed will they in Labate's own text), for love in Augustan Rome
is a political matter; Ovid is an Augustan poet; Augustus is an Ovidian
construction.

   I propose to approach the two questions posed above through a
consideration of the 'reader'. In the past seventy years or so there
have been in literary studies many varied critical practices which
can be called reader-response criticism.[8] Many of these involve making distinctions between real readers and ideal readers, and many
shades within the latter term in particular. The distinction between
'real' and 'ideal' readers is a dichotomy which is ripe for deconstruc-
tion (Martindale 1993: 1–34). There cannot be a real reader who is
immune to other readings, because if you can read you have learned
something about reading, from readings. The use of other readings,
indeed the very act of reading, involves trying out the positions of
all sorts of readers, ideal ones both in the sense of imaginary, and
also in the sense of desired or perfected. Therefore a real reader is

---

[8] For an accessible survey see Tompkins (1980). The best work by a classicist
dealing with these issues is Martindale (1993).

also an ideal reader—and is not, since we do in practice have a sense of the difference between the 'me' who is reading and the 'roles' my reading plays, however false that sense might be. We cannot actually read texts without—at least implicitly—considering readers, for the pleasures of reading involve the activity of readers. That is a truism: my justification for stating it is that the focus on the readers is by no means universally accepted. One important pleasure in reading consists in the construction of meaning. Any primary-school teacher will tell you that you are not 'really reading' unless you 'understand' what you are reading: and to understand is to construct meaning, not idiosyncratically, randomly, chaotically, but—with greater and lesser degrees of subjectivity—in accordance with the practice of readers.[9] This is a point about reading generally: it is foregrounded in didactic literature by the text's own emphasis on a reader to whom the instruction is addressed.

I suggest that we should consider what it might be like to be a reader of the *Ars*, and what sort of political intimations it might involve. All the strategies involved in reading the *Ars Amatoria* today, as critics, students, and teachers, as twentieth-century women and men, are highly pertinent to our study. While being primarily concerned with ancient readers, that is, with my hypothetical construction of the original situation of reception, I must note the extent to which my construction is formed by my own situation. I once wrote that the original intended audience of the *Ars* was 'very broadly, educated Roman men of a detached and mildly subversive frame of mind, contemporary with Ovid'. So it may be, but does this not sound suspiciously like the self-image of modern university academics? My 'contemporary actual reader' is constructed in my own image.[10] To that proviso should be added another: while I am considering the situation of ancient readers, I suggest it be borne in mind that it is in practice difficult to distinguish clearly between an ancient reader and a modern reading (however much one/some might wish to do so in theory). Everything one can say about ancient readers is of necessity

---

[9] A pleasure in reading which does not involve the construction of meaning would be that taken in the sound of the literary work, which again involves the activity of a reader. It is one which on its own is unlikely to maintain sustained interest.

[10] I, the writer of this paper, am female, but, as is well known, the cultural ambience in which I am working is largely male.

a modern reading of them, for just as real and ideal readers cannot be kept separate, so ancient and modern readers can never be entirely distinct.

What was it like to read the *Ars*? What was it like to read a didactic poem? Literature was normally read aloud in antiquity, probably even when the reader was alone.[11] Further to that, however, I would claim that reading in antiquity is normally or rather, *normatively*—a group activity. From the primitive tribes sitting around the campfire listening to proto-Homer, through performance in the theatre of Dionysus in Athens, to the lazy city sophisticates invited to a formal *recitatio* as related by the Younger Pliny (*Epist.* 1.13), an ancient reader is a member of an audience. The Roman is often subordinated to the Greek in this regard: the *Aeneid* is called 'literary' as opposed to 'heroic' epic; we are taught that most of Horace's odes were 'not written for performance' as were their Greek models; Seneca's tragedy was 'not written for the stage' unlike its illustrious Greek predecessor. All this is probably true: it does not, however, mean that a reader of Roman literature perceived himself (*not*, in this case, 'herself') as a lone, individual reader. Rather, whether an actual reader is alone or part of a group, it is the group situation which is normative. Literature was read in *recitationes*, at private dinner parties—and so this literature *is* written for a type of performance—and by individuals. The *recitatio* should be privileged: the dinner party is a private version of the *recitatio*, while personal reading is simply at one remove further away, especially (as is normally the case with a literary text) if the reading is aloud, in which situation the reader becomes two people—speaker and listener.[12] The audience of the ancient Lives of Vergil clearly appreciated the role of performance in literature, whether or not the anecdotes are precisely true: that Vergil read the *Georgics* to Augustus (and others), Maecenas taking over when the poet's voice gave out, and that Octavia fainted at the mention of the young Marcellus when Vergil was reading Books 2, 4, and 6 of the *Aeneid* to an Imperial

---

[11] See Knox (1968). The point of his article is to argue that the ancients were perfectly capable of reading silently, but he also shows that, for literature, reading aloud was the norm. See also the discussion of the *recitatio* in McKeown's (1987: 63–73) introduction to the *Amores*. I am grateful to Gerry Nussbaum for his suggestions on this subject.

[12] I am grateful to Richard Wallace for the formulation of this point.

gathering (*Vita Donati* 27–34). From the same source we hear that Vergil read his work to many people. Even a supposedly shy and retiring poet is assumed to present his poetry personally. If another reader actually gives the performance, he is simply standing in for the author and making up for his absence (or incapacity). I suspect that there is in antiquity a strong sense of literature as an essentially oral activity, with writing as a (Derrideanly 'inferior') aid to memory.[13] In the *Tristia*, where the interplays of presence and absence are foregrounded, Ovid anxiously sends his book/slave/child off to Rome, away from the author/master/father's control and protection. The anxiety caused by the absence and loss of author(ial control) is witness (by contrast) to the norm in which the author at least poses as being present. I suggest that reading an ancient poem involves playing the role of an ideal reader who is a member of a *recitatio* audience.

But what was it like to read a didactic poem? Reading didactic poetry involves (at some level) being a member of a seminar group, for all didactic poems pose as being lessons. Not only is reading an oral and a group activity in antiquity, but so also is learning. Students sit at the feet of the speaking teacher, as readers do of poets (or their substitutes). Didactic poetry subscribes in particularly effective manner to the myth of the mutual presence of the author and audience by means of its frequent use of second person address—'you should do it like this'; first person singular advice—'I suggest . . .'; and first person plural invitations—'let us consider . . .'.[14] My claim, that didactic poems pose as lessons, does not imply that it is all a sham and no didactic poem really either intends to teach or has the effect of doing so: rather, that any didactic poem is always already a self-conscious 'imitation' of something else—a lesson. Or perhaps I should say it is consciously working in the genre 'lesson' (and so

[13] The work of Derrida's which is most accessible and relevant to Classicists in this regard is 'Plato's Pharmacy' (in Derrida 1981). His contention is that the Western philosophical tradition has always privileged the spoken over the written, with an implication of authority given to authorial control, but that it has done so in terms which undermine the clear hierarchical distinction.

[14] It will probably not have escaped your notice that the academic paper makes similar moves. I have deliberately not edited out the first and second person verbs in my text (as one is sometimes advised to do), in order to play with the myth of presence.

indeed are lessons). Whatever might be said about the pedagogic nature of didactic poetry generally cannot be excluded from the *Ars*, for it is not possible to make clear distinctions about intention— and by implication 'realness' (with added value)—within the didactic genre.[15] All didactic poems pose as teaching: the audience must play the role of being students.

But what does that pose have to do with Augustus and political realities? My answer is: everything. Let me return to Labate. I might perhaps focus my problem with Labate's reading on his analysis of Augustus and *otium* (43 ff.), in which he claims that Augustus sought not to abolish aristocratic leisure—the famous *otium*—but to absorb it. Lax behaviour, then, is acceptable when all the jobs are done. No problems here, for this is a well-known aspect of Roman morality: the light side of the great aristocratic heroes of the republic. Even Cato enjoyed a drink at the appropriate moment, according to Horace (*Carm.* 3.21.11). If Ovid writes light or obscene poetry in the evenings, then he is no different from Q. Lutatius Catulus, for example, or Cicero, or Augustus himself, composing epigrams in the bath, according to Suetonius (*Div. Aug.* 85).[16] I am sure that Labate is right that Augustus sought to absorb and appropriate this culture for his own ends: as a means of accommodating the aristocracy, of defining more clearly the seriousness ethic (by opposition), and so on.[17] So far, so good. The trouble with Ovid, however, is that the *Ars* is not spare-time poetry written when the jobs are done. Rather, it poses as *being* the job—it is *otium* as *negotium*. This is primarily because the poem must be read under the shadow of Vergil's *Georgics*.[18]

[15] It would be clear that I cannot accept the thesis of Heath (1985) that some poems are 'finally' didactic, while others are only (!) 'formally' so.

[16] See also Plin. *Epist.* 4.14 and 5.3, who says that many highly respectable men write light, obscene poetry.

[17] It seems likely that Augustus took measures to reinforce social distinctions among the classes, in order to produce a stable society and one in which the upper class is something for which it is worth striving (both to maintain and also to achieve—and therefore something for which one may be grateful to the emperor . . .). See Levick (1983) 114–15.

[18] An extensive and illuminating study of the effect on writing of the predecessor's shadow can be found in Bloom (1973). Classic works on the relationship between the *Ars Amatoria* and the *Georgics* are Kenney (1958) and Leach (1964). The broader subject of the intertextual relationship of Vergil and Ovid is a field awaiting reapers. [Workers have been busy in this field since the original comment was made, producing

That the *Ars Amatoria* consciously imitates the *Georgics* hardly needs to be argued. When as a contemporary Roman you read the *Ars*, you necessarily insert yourself into a certain image. You *must* go along with the poet's pretence to be repeating and correcting Vergil's *Georgics*.[19] Now, the *Georgics* uses the metaphor of farming to 'teach' good citizenship. Vergil's text contributes to the social discourse of farming as the restructuring of society, collectively assigned to Augustus as a focus for the new reality. The *Georgics* tell you 'how to run a farm': 'how', that is, cosmically, socially, morally, rather than at a purely mechanical level. Most readers of the *Georgics* presumably did not read the poem in order to discover how to run a farm in the simple sense; nor indeed in order to learn to be good (and pro-Augustan) citizens. Vergil may have hoped (I have no idea) that they would leave his text better people, better Romans—and perhaps better disposed towards Augustus. But that is not really the sense in which this is a didactic poem which really does teach. Rather, what happens here is that the readers insert themselves into the image of student (at one level, even of *colonus*—an actual farmer-on-the-ground) in which they play out the role of one learning farming = good morals. That individuals incidentally learned something I have no doubt (since all reading is didactic), but that is not the point. The point is that playing the role of Vergil's reader is a political act, or rather a socio-political act which Augustus was very skilled at manipulating for his own ends. It was no doubt possible to make reading the *Georgics* a political act of a very different nature: a reading that says 'this is not true' or 'this is true about farmers being the backbone of society, but Augustus has no right to monopolize that truth'. What would be difficult, it seems to me, would be to remove the political dimension from the reading altogether. It would be a perverse and blinkered

works notable among which are Smith (1997) and Barchiesi (2001). Indeed, Ovid is now widely acknowledged as 'Virgil's best reader'; see O'Hara (1996*b*, = ch. 5 above).]

[19] I might have to concede that to some extent it is always possible for an individual reader either not to know enough about Vergil to follow Ovid's instruction about how to read the *Ars* or simply to refuse to do so. The readings of the individual ignorant reader (and this would demand a remarkable level of ignorance for a contemporary reader) can fairly safely be ignored, relevant though they may be for him/her. The recalcitrant reader is another matter. On the one hand, refusal is always a possibility; but again on the other hand it isn't because even refusal of a reading necessarily involves recognition of it. In this regard see Freund (1987), and Fetterley (1978).

reading which simply ignored the cultural (and hence political) status of farming at Rome, and in fact, few critics try to read the *Georgics* apolitically.

After Vergil, it becomes impossible to read didactic poetry apolitically. Whereas the *Georgics* inculcates good morals (appropriated by Augustus), the *Ars* inculcates bad morals. This is not to say that people read the *Ars Amatoria* 'as a practical guide to ensnaring the other sex',[20] or in order to learn how to commit adultery (although some may have done so!), or even in order to learn how to oppose Augustus (albeit privately). Ovid may have hoped (I have no idea) that they would leave his text worse people, worse Romans, less well disposed towards Augustus, but that is not the point. I shall shortly argue that the *Ars Amatoria* poses as teaching adultery. The point is that by posing as learning how to commit adultery (and get away with it!) readers are performing a political act. It was no doubt possible to make reading the *Ars* a political act of a very different nature: a reading that says 'this is bad behaviour' or 'what a good thing we have Augustus to sort this sort of thing out'. What would be difficult, it seems to me, would be to remove the political dimension altogether. The only way of doing so is the modern way—to say it is all a joke. But sex is no joke in Augustan Rome. The apolitical reading is a (political) appropriation of the text, and one that I do not find persuasive. This is not to imply that I think Ovid really thought that the way to right citizenship was by committing adultery—nor the way to wrong citizenship for that matter, since I am claiming that the *Ars* 'teaches bad morals'. So in that sense, the 'literary joke' school is right. Of course it's all a joke. But at the same time it isn't. The very fact that we need to say 'of course, it is all a joke' shows that it isn't. My point is that the poem is as really didactic as anything else, and that reading it is a political act. When in the early 80s my husband was an engineering undergraduate, he was sponsored by the Ministry of Defence. Working for them in the summer vacation, he would go on trips in an MoD minibus reading *Das Kapital* and *Teach Yourself Russian*. It was not that he was really learning Russian (although he may have picked up a bit on the side), but nor was it 'only a joke'—it was, rather, reading as a political act.

---

[20] So Hollis (1973) 85. He is saying that the *Ars* is *not* such a guide.

I have said that writing didactic poetry after Vergil is necessarily political. It might, then, be questioned why the *Ars* is political when other didactic poems enumerated by Ovid in his self-defence are not (*Trist.* 2.471 ff.). In *Tristia* 2, while posing as excusing and defending his *Ars*, Ovid is in fact extolling it and displaying its subversive nature. His arguments 'fail'; his logic is specious. These unknown or hypothetical poems about swimming and dice-playing are not subversive because they have failed to attract attention—unlike the *Ars*, they are not great poems. (That is, assuming that they are *not* political. It seems possible to imagine a subversive poem on dice-playing.) They are also not teaching subjects explicitly proscribed by the new regime. And why is Ovid's work political when obscene mime is not? My answer is: the *Georgics*. Obscenity is not politically sensitive: rather, it is the undermining of authority which might be so. The *Ars* imitates the *Georgics* as a 'joke', but just a bit too 'seriously' to be ignored.

Let us return to *otium*. The indulgence of *otium* is made acceptable, even positively good, by context: it comes after *negotium*. A poem extolling lax and decadent aristocratic leisure in a way in keeping with the 'good Roman' work ethic says things like *nunc est bibendum* ('now is the time to drink', Hor. *Carm.* 1.37.1) not *hoc opus, hic labor est, primo sine munere iungi* ('this is the job, this the task, to be joined without a gift in the first place', *Ars* 1.453). The line just quoted is, as is well known, a direct allusion to *Aen.* 6.129. It is quite valid to read this 'parody' as 'mocking one's own pretensions' (Hollis 1977: ad loc.), but self-mockery may display as much as it 'excuses' those pretensions. The allusion is to Vergil. In the context, it may remind us not only of the *Aeneid* and Aeneas' journey to the Underworld, but also of the *opus* and *labor* of the *Georgics*. Evidence is plentiful for Ovidian appropriation of didactic expressions from the *Georgics*. For example, in the second book he plays around with moral and physical turpitude, when he tells his pupil not to be ashamed to bear the curses and lashes of his mistress and to bring kisses to her feet (*Ars* 2.533–4). The formula 'do not be ashamed to . . .' accords with Vergil's didactic diction. Early in the first book, Vergil encourages the farmer not to be ashamed to fertilize his fields: that is, to do something which, although unpleasant in itself, will further his cause (*Georg.* 1.79–81). Ovid amusingly, ironically (ab)uses the Vergilian formula. Muck-spreading is physically *turpis* ('foul') but spiritually noble and ennobling. Ovid appropriates and inverts Vergil's moral language to apply it to behaviour at which moral repugnance might indeed be expected, if this work belonged to the discourse of Roman moral philosophy, rather than (as it does) to its anti-discourse. In writing the *Ars Amatoria*, in close and conscious imitation of the *Georgics*, Ovid is pretending that catching and keeping a girl is a worthwhile pursuit on a level with the august occupation of farming. He is claiming that it *is* the job.

I have so far argued that the *Ars Amatoria* is 'really didactic' in the sense that its didactic form is a decisive factor in the meaning of the act of reading it. The next question to consider relates to the subject the poem teaches. To some extent this is up to the reader—it may be adultery, it may be courtly courtship, it may be political subversion, it may even be political quietism, it may be poetry: it will differ for different readers at different times (and need not be confined to one 'lesson'). I submit that for the Augustan reader (ambiguity intended) one of those lessons has to be adultery. The convenient escape route by which scholars find Ovid not guilty of subversion is to say that he is talking only about courtesans (which is largely a euphemism for prostitutes), not about respectable women, therefore not about adultery, therefore nothing to do with Augustus' celebrated public concern with (other people's) morals as displayed in his marriage reforms (Watson 1967: 32 ff.). The usual supportive texts for this argument are the various disclaimers which Ovid makes against the adulterous reading.[21] But surely the disclaimers are disingenuous. Here we must invoke irony, an element of communication which is particularly obviously open to appropriation. I offer you an ironic reading of the disclaimers (as have others).

The first disclaimer comes at the end of the prologue to Book 1 (31–4):

este procul, uittae tenues, insigne pudoris,
    quaeque tegis medios instita longa pedes:

---

[21] See for example McKeown (1984) 176: 'Ovid showed clearly in the *Ars Amatoria* that he was already aware of, and anxious to obviate, the danger of incurring Augustus' displeasure'. See Otis (1938) 20 on this.

nos Venerem tutam concessaque furta canemus
  inque meo nullum carmine crimen erit.

Keep away, slender bands, the sign of honour, and you, the long dress who
cover to the middle of the feet: We will sing of safe Venus and allowed thefts
and in my song there will be no grounds for accusation.

Ovid makes his poem safe by sending respectable women away. That's
alright then: now the virgins and matrons have gone we can get on
with the fun. But real and implied readers are not so easily divisible.
Do the critics who accept these disclaimers at face value really think
that any respectable women reading the poem would now put it down
as instructed? Of course not: they know that isn't the point, and they
know that in any case the audience of this book is male—don't they,
isn't it? But the argument seems to proceed as if Ovid could just send
respectable women, Augustus, and the whole political culture away
with his magic wand.[22] In his generally useful discussion of the *Ars*
and the marriage reforms, Stroh comments that although respectable
women are excluded from the poem it is 'not precisely as reading
public' (1979: 323 n. 2). But, as I have argued, reading the *Ars* implies
playing a certain political role: respectable women simply cannot be
admitted as readers but excluded as students and therefore they are
inevitably drawn into the subversive culture. To attempt to exclude
them would be to ignore the functioning of reading generally and
reading didactic in particular. It is not really a question, however, of

---

[22] Let us be pedantic: it is not respectability but its signifiers which are to be
removed. Women are encouraged to throw off their *pudor* along with its trappings?
A similar point could be made of the disclaimer in the prologue to the third book:
in order to prove that not all women are bad, Ovid claims that the feminine gender
of *uirtus* is part of the reason it is so pleasing to the people (with all the erotic
associations of 'pleasing'). Not that his poem has anything to do with virtue: *nec
tamen hae mentes nostra poscuntur ab arte;* | *conueniunt cumbae uela minora meae* | *nil
nisi lasciui per me discuntur amores;* | *femina praecipiam quo sit amanda* (*Ars* 3.25–8).
This is 'a disclaimer', and so usually taken to mean that his poem is not adulterous
and has nothing to do with the marriage reforms. But what he actually says is that
virtuous minds are not demanded by his Art. Well, no, we never thought they were. I
am grateful to Alessandro Barchiesi for an addition to this point, with respect to the
disclaimer arising from the Mars and Venus episode which will be discussed below.
The claim that no *instita* belongs in this poem is taken by metonymy to mean that no
'real wife' belongs there. Perhaps also, however, it means 'no formal dress': Venus is in
fact a real wife, but she is caught naked.

whether respectable women read the poem, but whether men reading
it thought it applied to respectable women: we will come back to this.

The (perceived, contrived) 'need' to make a disclaimer like this
itself serves the function of *reminding* us of the moral legislation.
And just in case we should forget about it, Ovid keeps jogging our
memory at intervals through the text. While posing as displaying his
innocence, Ovid effects the placement of his poem firmly within the
context of Augustan morals. Furthermore, he chooses words which
undermine his apparent meaning: for what are *concessa . . . furta*
('allowed thefts') but an oxymoron? Certainly, *furtum* is a standard
term in erotic discourse, meaning little more than 'affair' or 'night
together'. In a legal context such as we have here, however, the legal
and moral sense of *furtum* as 'theft', and therefore a crime, must be
highlighted, especially when it is placed in absurd juxtaposition with
concessa. We are forced to remember that an erotic theft is a theft
from someone, be it husband, father, or *leno*. The undermining is
reinforced in the pentameter, for, as Stephen Hinds has pointed out
to me (in conversation), the line contradicts itself. Ovid claims that
there is no *crimen* in his *carmen*, but the letters of *crimen* fit into those
of *carmine*—so there *is crimen* in the *carmen*.

But what 'grounds for accusation'? It is often implied that Ovid's
work could only have been justifiably offensive to Augustus if it is
about adultery: that is, sex with another citizen's wife or daughter.
No adultery, no problem. And so considerable effort in the critical
discourse on elegy is expended in an attempt to ascertain the social
status of the *puella* (Sullivan 1961; Sabot 1976: 459–64; Wyke 1987).
But not only is this question unanswerable: its very unanswerability
is its answer, for the debate is its own solution. You can't tell; Ovid
knew you couldn't tell, and so did everyone else. If it is impossible
for us to decide in any instance whether *uir* means 'husband' or
'lover', then it was impossible for Ovid's readers to decide either: so
they, along with Augustus, could decide how they liked—or didn't
like.[23] I do not believe that Ovid knew perfectly well whether he

---

[23] It is not an adequate answer to say that they knew the language better. Although
at one level a truism, on another it is not exactly true, for they did not have the
advantage (?) of historical perspective and concordances. The point is that the word is
ambiguous. It is, it seems to me, an oddity of Latin that a culture which was very
concerned about whether there was a husband's honour (more than any intrinsic

meant husband or lover but the ambiguity of the word stopped him telling us. Rather, whatever his intention, the result is that the poem refers to adultery, for the girl has, not a husband *or* a lover—but a *uir*. Furthermore, while there is indeed contrast drawn between the *puella* and a *matrona* or 'respectable woman', there is also contrast with a *scortum* (prostitute). Ovid will not let us see what the *puella* is, because she does not have a simple, straightforward social status. It is not so much that she is an inaccurate representation of a real social type, but that social types themselves are complex entities, involving ambiguity in their self-construction and construction by society.

All poems about sexual behaviour written in Augustan Rome inevitably relate to the moral legislation: including even those whose composition predates the legislation itself, for it was an issue long before it became law, and moreover earlier poems take on a further nuance in the light of the legislation, particularly when they come from mainline Augustan poets. That does not necessarily make the poems subversive, but it does make them political. Let us take further this question of the marital status of the *puella*. If you want to avoid the 'political' (apparently equalling 'politically subversive' for those who would suppress it) reading, the story goes that the girl is some sort of a free agent, who has lovers, or perhaps one formal 'keeper'.[24] The poet or the student lover is then a rival to this other lover (or lovers), and must find ways of deceiving him and encouraging his beloved to cheat her *uir*. The second half of book 2 of the *Ars Amatoria*, which deals with how to keep a girl once she has been caught, is largely taken up with variations on the artful manipulation of infidelity—your own and hers. No one can seriously pretend that this has nothing to do with adultery. Of course it *could* be applied as well to married women as to those with semi-permanent 'keepers'. But it's not Ovid's fault if people take it that way, is it? This is what he tries to claim at *Trist.* 2.253 ff., adding (with characteristic

morality) to be offended in a sexual act should commonly use terms which leave the exact social relationship vague. In modern Britain, even now, when the legal and still more social distinctions between married and unmarried sex are being dissolved, the terminology remains quite precise.

[24] The very incoherence of the girl's status, and its tendency to vary, should warn us that a straightforward reading is not possible.

non sequitur—or perhaps we should call it a specious sequitur) that if *matronae* will be corrupted by his poem they ought also to be banned from Ennius' *Annals*. But he knows perfectly well that there is all the difference between a story which happens to involve some unmarried sex and a lecture which teaches adultery.

I should like now to look in a bit more detail at a passage which illustrates some of the points of this paper: which are that identification of the reader as student makes a difference to the political effect, and that the vagueness about exact social relationships is an indication of the potentially adulterous nature of the poem. The passage is the *exemplum* in book 2 about the affair of Mars and Venus. I have made a plea elsewhere (1994) for closer reading of the mythological and other *exempla* in didactic poetry and the *Ars* in particular (and I do not claim a monopoly on the subject). I shall not repeat the general arguments here. The *exemplum* comes in the second half of book 2, when Ovid is encouraging his trainee lover to put up with rivals and not to try and catch out an unfaithful *puella*. This, he claims, is the great climax of his work (*Ars* 2.535–42):

quid moror in paruis? animus maioribus instat;
    magna cano: toto pectore, uulgus, ades.
ardua molimur, sed nulla, nisi ardua, uirtus;
    difficilis nostra poscitur arte labor.
riualem patienter habe: uictoria tecum
    stabit, eris magni uictor in Arce Iouis.
haec tibi non hominem sed quercus crede Pelasgas
    dicere; nil istis ars mea maius habet.

Why do I delay in trifles? My mind is eager for greater things; great is my song: attend, ye people, with full heart. We strive for arduous things; but there is no virtue which is not arduous; a difficult task is demanded from my Art. Bear a rival patiently: victory will stand with you, and you will be a victor in the temple of Jupiter. Believe that not a man but the Pelasgian oaks are telling you this; than this my Art has nothing greater.

The climax of his work is advice to offend against the laws against *lenocinium*! It is an ironic climax, of course, in which the humorous deflation serves also to deflate the legislation. The quasi-elevated tone makes an appropriate introduction to the *exemplum*, belonging as it does to epic—the story is told in *Odyssey* 8.266–366. Mars and Venus were observed in their affair by the Sun, who whispered to Venus' husband Vulcan.[25]

The fire god then fashioned a net, so fine it was hardly visible, to catch the lovers in bed. The other gods were allowed in to laugh . . . at the exposed couple, of course, but Vulcan had reckoned without the social effect of being exposed as cuckolded, for it is he who has been the butt of Venus' laughter overtly, and perhaps, by implication, that of the other gods. He had also misjudged the effect of his action on his wife. The lovers now do openly what previously they hid, and so the husband is still more exposed to shame, still rejected by his wife, but more openly and completely (*Ars* 2.591–2):

saepe tamen demens stulte fecisse fateris,
    teque ferunt artis paenituisse tuae.

But, in a frenzy, you often confess that you acted foolishly, and they say that you repented of your Art.

The moral of this story is: be warned, you lovers, and do not try to catch your mistress in her infidelity, or you will simply increase her power and lose your own (*Ars* 2.597–8):

ista uiri captent, si iam captanda putabunt,
    quos faciet iustos ignis et unda uiros.

Let men/husbands catch at those things, if they think them worth catching now, those whom fire and water makes true men/husbands.

It is at this point that Ovid makes another of those ironic disclaimers (*Ars* 2.599–600):

en iterum testor: nihil hic nisi lege remissum
    luditur; in nostris instita nulla iocis.

See, again I bear witness: here nothing except what is allowed by law is played; there is no matron's band in my jokes.

---

[25] Alessandro Barchiesi helpfully pointed out to me that *Ars* 2.573 *quis solem fallere possit* ('who could deceive the Sun') echoes and parodies *Georgics* 1.463 *quis solem dicere falsum | audeat* ('who would dare to say that the Sun was false'). Vergil is talking about how the sun gives the farmer signs as indications of the right moment for various agricultural activities: Ovid subverts the proverbial omniscience of the sun to turn its truthfulness into the surveillance of the mind police.

Oh good! Nothing against the law; the lovers are not real husbands. But just a minute—we never thought they were. The question is, whether *the rival* is a real husband.[26] Moreover, Vulcan most certainly is. In the Homeric rendering, which must be borne in mind here, he makes a considerable fuss about the presents he brought to Zeus as bride price.[27] But with whom are we being encouraged to identify, when as audience we play out the role of Ovid's students? On the simple line of correlation between *exemplum* and *illustrandum*, it is with Vulcan, the real husband. We are told *not* to copy his behaviour, but we *are* equated with him. That's okay, because it is explicitly stated that 'we' are not real husbands. But the condemned behaviour on the part of the husband is precisely that imposed by the legislation about *lenocinium*.[28] To put it simply: Ovid is advising his readers to be compliant husbands. The legislation imposed penalties on husbands who were aware of their wives' infidelity and did nothing to prevent it (such as divorce the wife). This is part of Augustus' personally favoured legislation: that he himself probably did not adhere to the moral principles of his laws is irrelevant. The point is that he—or perhaps we should say the Augustan consensus—staked his authority on myths about Roman greatness in which the stability of marriage plays an important part. Ovid undermines that stability and the authority which rests on it and on which it rests. I have no idea whether Ovid really thought it was a good idea for husbands or lovers to be indulgent of their beloved's affairs (if I frankly doubt it then that may tell you more about me than about Ovid): but the result

[26] A case in point of the ambiguity of *uir* is that it is used for Ovid's rival (*uir . . . suus* 1.551), other men to be allowed access to one's woman (1.554), and the real husbands of the disclaimer in 1.598. It is not that it means 'lover' in some of those contexts and 'husband' in others, but that Ovid is deliberately fudging the distinction.

[27] That we should have the Homeric story in mind here, and that the Ovidian re-telling is a passage which requires defence from the charge of adultery, is shown by the reference to the story in *Trist.* 2.377 ff. When 'proving' that all poetry is about illicit sex, Ovid reminds us that the story comes from Homer: *quis, nisi Maeonides, Venerem Martemque ligatos | narrat in obsceno corpora prensa toro?*—to which the answer would presumably be 'you'! The Homeric story of Ares and Aphrodite was a cause of great concern to the ancient commentators on Homer, provoking criticism, defence, and rationalization. See Feeney (1991) 30, 369 n. 181.

[28] See Labate (1984) 105–6 for Ovid's use of the comic character 'compliant husband' for the tolerant lover. I cannot accept the absence of conflict which his discourse seems to imply. See also Stroh (1979) esp. 324, nn. 3 and 4, for further bibliography.

of the *exemplum* is that we, the audience, are placed in the position of learning how to offend against the legislation. It would perhaps have been possible for Augustus to attempt to disarm the political bite of this passage and the Ovidian project as a whole by laughing at it, but the very fact that he would need to say 'very funny, Ovid, what a good joke' would immediately expose the political nature of the 'joke'. The fact that he did *not* laugh at the *Ars* may in the first place show his political *nous* (in ignoring the barbs), and also display the real political force of the poem when Ovid was finally condemned (assuming that he was exiled 'for' the *Ars*, which seems likely, whether or not there were other reasons, official or unofficial).

On the other hand, although the official (so to speak) identification of the student is with Vulcan, it is very tempting for us, in our role as 'young rakes', to identify with Mars. It is surely the god of war who comes out of this story with his virility intact and his erotic credentials proven. To the extent, then, that we are allowed—tempted—to identify with Mars, we are placed in a situation almost as close as possible to open advocation of adultery.

In keeping with the oracular nature of much of this part of the *Ars*, Ovid becomes even more cryptic after his disclaimer (*Ars* 2.601–2):

quis Cereris ritus ausit uulgare profanis
   magnaque Threicia sacra reperta Samo?

Who would dare to promulgate the rites of Ceres to the profane, and the great holy things found in Samothrace?

What exactly he is talking about is left deliberately—oracularly— vague. It appears later that he is referring to keeping quiet about your amorous activities (he can talk!), but for the moment I think we must refer the line back to the disclaimer which precedes it. There is some subliminal suggestion lurking here, to do with keeping quiet about things, something which I suspect has important Augustan connotations. The passage continues: *exigua est uirtus praestare silentia rebus* ('it is a small virtue to proffer silence for things', 603). Ovid will *not* tell us what is going on—because this is all about keeping quiet—but he fails to tell us in such a way that we are encouraged to guess.

The lines must allude to a central locus for Augustan poetry, Horace *Odes* 3.2. Here at the heart of Horace's construction of Roman poetry in terms of Augustan ideology, he too praises silence (*Odes* 3.2.25–30):

est et fideli tuta silentio
merces: uetabo, qui Cereris sacrum
    uulgarit arcanae, sub isdem
        sit trabibus fragilemque mecum

soluat phaselon: saepe Diespiter
neglectus incesto addidit integrum:

There is also safe reward for faithful silence: whoever promulgates the rites of secret Ceres I will forbid to be under the same beams as me or to cast off in a fragile yacht with me. Often Jupiter neglected has added the innocent to the guilty.

That we are justified in recalling the *Ode* here is clear not only from the close reminiscence of the thought of *Odes* 3.2.25 in *Ars* 2.603, but also from the comparison between good silence and sacrilegious promulgation of mystery rites, not obviously relevant to the wider context in either poem. It would be worth adding that Ovid's formulation of the maxim with *uirtus* evokes the previous two Horatian stanzas, each opening with a semi-personified *Virtus*, narrowly disguising Augustus (*Odes* 3.2.17–24):

Virtus repulsae nescia sordidae
intaminatis fulget honoribus,
    nec sumit aut ponit securis
        arbitrio popularis aurae;

Virtus, recludens immeritis mori
caelum, negata temptat iter uia,
    coetusque uulgaris et udam
spernit humum fugiente penna.

Virtue, knowing no sordid repulse, shines with virgin honours,
And does not take up or put down the axes at the whim of the people's breeze;
Virtue, opening heaven to those undeserving to die, essays a journey on a forbidden path, and spurns the vulgar crowd and the wet earth with fleeing wing.

Williams, in his commentary on the Ode, says of the maxim that it 'is based on ἔστι καὶ σιγᾶς ἀκίνδυνον γέρας (Simonides fr. 19 Page) which is reported by Plutarch (*reg. et imp. apophth.* 207c) as a favourite saying of Augustus' (1969: 36). To make the saying even more 'Augustan', Horace adds *fideli*: this is silence which is committed to supporting a particular cause.

There is a further strand to this story of Augustan silence to add before we consider its impact in Ovid's poem. Suetonius says that Augustus manifested his liking for 'faithful silence' in annoyance at his lieutenant Maecenas' failure in it: *desiderauit enim nonnumquam . . . Maecenatis taciturnitatem, cum . . . hic secretum de comperta Murenae coniuratione uxori Terentiae prodidisset* (Suet. *div. Aug.* 66: 'for he sometimes missed silence in Maecenas, when he betrayed to his wife Terentia the secret that the conspiracy of Murena had been found out').[29]

So Ovid has appropriated an Augustan phrase and used it for his own purposes. But appropriation is rarely complete: the saying comes to Ovid's text loaded with ideological baggage which cannot simply be ditched in its new context. Ovid's appropriation cannot erase the associations which 'faithful silence' has for an Augustan audience, and indeed the recognition of those associations is essential to the force of Ovid's reinterpretation of the maxim.[30] On the establishment reading, which must still be present, at least in trace, the maxim recommends keeping silent about matters on which the establishment wanted silence.[31] Ovid for a moment poses as following that reading. 'I'm following the Augustan rules', he claims, 'you won't find me talking about forbidden things like adultery, because look, I make it clear that my audience are not true husbands!' (This fudges the point that in the accusation of adultery it is the marital status of the woman which is at issue.) The sequel, however, rereads the maxim to make it refer to silence about sex, giving Venus the status of the

---

[29] Might this 'faithful silence' also lie behind Horace's apology to Maecenas for being 'a little too talkative', the apology representing a perceived need to construct Maecenas in keeping with the ideology of those who (with Augustus) value 'faithful silence'?

[30] For one type of reader, I suppose Ovid might be condemning himself.

[31] Williams (1969) 37: '[t]he older generation were far from silent when Augustus tried to introduce moral reforms and they succeeded in getting them rejected.'

goddess of a mystery cult, whose 'rites' should not be divulged.[32] The proclamation of silence draws paradoxical attention to itself: 'look what I'm *not* saying!' And what is he (not) saying (that is, saying)? By turning an Augustan maxim about political 'faithful silence' into a 'joke' about sex, he is saying something like this: adultery (acting as a metaphor for opposition to Augustus) is a good thing; the moral reforms are intrusive and hypocritical; the Augustan demand for 'faithful silence' compromises great poets.

Ovid's disquisition on silence in erotic matters (however ambivalent and ironic within his own discourse it may be) constitutes, I suggest, a commentary on Augustan intrusion into the lives of Romans, focused on the moral reforms. Sex should be done *medio... in usu* (611), but hidden. Even Venus, as a naked statue, covers her *pudenda* with her hand (a hand which displays as much as it disguises, of course). Sex—now perhaps a metaphor for private lives in general— is a private matter for humans. Only animals copulate in public (615); humans have bedrooms; even in the Golden Age, so often appropriated by Augustan discourse as a model for the new society, they made love in groves and caves, *non sub Ioue* (623). Then there is a complaint about the gulf between actual sexual acts and claims about them (perhaps hinting at the potential for false accusations of adultery which are politically or otherwise motivated), culminating in the enigmatic statement (*Ars* 2.639–40) that

nos etiam ueros parce profitemur amores,
tectaque sunt solida mystica furta fide.

I sparingly publish even true affairs and my mystic thefts are buried under solid faithfulness.

Again the mystery cult, again 'faithfulness'. At one level Ovid is deeply compromised in his diatribe, but that need not undermine its effect. The implication is that Augustan social control makes people metaphorically have sex in public.

In the light of this reading, I wonder whether there may be a further subliminal dimension to the story of Mars and Venus. In the

[32] Note how lines 609 ff., which say that even if Venus does not have the trappings of mystery cult, nevertheless her rites ought to be secret, echo various disclaimers about the status of the elegiac *puella*, to the effect that even though she lacks the trappings of a matron she should still behave respectably, that is be faithful to the poet.

'primary' reading, Vulcan is the wronged husband, forced by Augustus' legislation to act against his adulterous wife as soon as some third party removes the possibility of ignoring the situation. But, as we know, in elegiac discourse the husband is the blocking character in the way of the erotic relationship (albeit sometimes as such performing a necessary role in the relationship). In this story, even while we are being overtly compared with Vulcan, it is with Mars, as lover, that we identify. Now the blocking character to the erotic relationship *par excellence* is Augustus himself. Could Vulcan be made to stand for Augustus, laying his traps for lovers? If that is valid, then perhaps Venus could suggest a particular adulterous woman—what about the elder Julia, banished to an island (Pandateria) in 2 BC (very close to the time of publication) on the charge of adultery? Relegation was also the punishment of four of the five nobles accused with her (Syme 1939: 426). Venus and Mars depart, Venus to an island (Paphos), as a result of their exposure. The connection can only be tenuous, if it is 'there' at all, and would no doubt have been risky if someone played the role of Sol and whispered the reading to Augustus. Whether or not Ovid intended any reference to a particular act of adultery, it seems to me by no means impossible that some members of his audience may have inferred it. Has Ovid kept 'faithful silence' about the adultery of Julia and the conspiracy (real or imaginary) for which it may be a cover or a pretext?—or not?

That might be called a 'strong' reading of the story. A weaker one would ignore the direct connection with Julia, but keep a hint of Augustus in Vulcan. On this reading, the 'moral' for Augustus would be the effective impotence of his legislation, since—it is claimed—exposure only serves to make lovers more brazen. That lesson is perhaps itself undermined by Ovid's eventual exile, and also by the very presence of the reference to the legislation here. Augustus always wins.[33]

I am offering you here a committedly anti-Augustan reading of the *Ars Amatoria*. It should be said, however, that my appropriation cannot be complete. At one level, I cannot help but play into Augustus' hands: for, while I read Ovid in such a way as to undermine Augustan authority staked on the moral legislation, I necessarily accord that authority status and so in a sense legitimize it.

---

[33] Or does he? There are different ways of winning.

Part III

Narrators and Narratives

12

Ovidius Prooemians

E. J. Kenney

In noua fert animus mutatas dicere formas
corpora: di, coeptis (nam uos mutastis et illa)
adspirate meis primaque ab origine mundi
ad mea perpetuum deducite tempora carmen.

illa P. Lejay ex Erfurtano Amploniano f. 1 saec. xii: *illas* codd.[1]

My mind carries me on to tell of bodies changed into new shapes: you
gods, favour my undertaking (for this too you changed), and bring down
a continuous song from the first beginning of the world to my own times.

In spite of several valuable contributions to the understanding of this
proem that have appeared in the last few years (Herter 1948; Fleischer
1957; von Albrecht 1961), it does not seem to me that modern exegesis has as yet taken all the points that Ovid has contrived to pack
into it. This is an astonishingly brief introduction to an epos over
12,000 lines long; and that very brevity ought to put us on our guard
(Fleischer 1957: 32). We should expect that not a word will be wasted;
and with so little sea room we should further expect that the reader,
though he may be playfully tantalized, will not be actually misled.
That was a risk Ovid could not afford to take. Unfortunately his
editors have taken it for him by printing and justifying the nonsense
which his copyists have made of the second verse of the poem. By so
doing they have set a stumbling block before the feet of the reader on
the very threshold, just where the going should be smooth and the

---

[1] See Tarrant (2004) ad loc.

omens fair. Ovid's own lines might have been written to the address of the next edition of the *Metamorphoses*:

missa foras iterum limen transire memento
  cautius atque alte sobria ferre pedem.

Next time you are sent abroad, remember to cross the threshold more cautiously, and take care to step high.

Von Albrecht's careful analysis of the vocabulary of the passage and its literary implications has shown that it is pitched at a stylistic level appropriate to epos. The structure of the verse period is also formal and emphatic. Ovid indeed begins by playing a little trick on the reader. The words *in noua fert animus*, as has more than once been pointed out, can be read autonomously: 'my inspiration carries (me) on to new things'.[2] As we shall find to be the case with other phrases in the proem, this can be taken in more than one sense. On the most obvious level it is a claim to originality: here is a work the like of which the world has never seen. That claim is certainly true and worth making. But the words also apply to the poet himself: Ovid's genius summons him to essay a kind of writing that is new for him. This point, as will be seen, is taken up and developed in what follows. However, as we read on we discover that *noua* after all does not stand alone, but has a syntactical complement in *corpora* at the beginning of v. 2; and we reinterpret the sentence. In doing so we do not discard our first interpretation; rather a new vista of meaning opens up. That this ambiguity is planned and not casual is probable a priori, for the reasons advanced above, but it is also suggested by the word order: Ovid could quite well have written *in noua mutatas animus fert dicere formas*.

The enjambment of *corpora* seems designed to throw emphasis less on that word than on what follows: the invocation, not of the Muse or a single deity but of the pantheon—all the gods indeed whose activities, irresponsible where they are not actually disreputable, Ovid is about to chronicle with such unsparing relish. But what was it that they 'also' changed? All attempts to retain the transmitted text are shipwrecked on the indefensible (though stoutly defended) placing

---

[2] The phrase contains all five vowels, as does the first hemistich of *Aen.* 1.1 (Bömer ad loc.). Cf. on *Am.* 1.1.1, Stroh (1971) 145 n. 19.

of *et*. It is possible to keep *illas* only, as Housman observed (Lee 1953: ad loc.), if *et* refers back to *mutastis*: 'Inspire me to tell of transformations, for you were also the cause of them', in Mr Lee's rendering.[3] But as Hartman long ago remarked, in a contribution to the discussion that has been too little heeded, we surely have a right to expect something a little more pointed from this poet (1905: 83): 'It is my belief at any rate (and who would disagree?) that Ovid attached a preface to his *Metamorphoses* that would be appropriate to them— and that would certainly have a bit of point as well.' Point, however, quite apart, the transmitted text is linguistically unacceptable unless it can be shown, not merely that the retrospective use of *et* is possible for Ovid, but that it is possible *in this context*. On the face of it *et* modifies *illas*, a fact of which Ovid could hardly be unaware. In this brief proem, where every word is to tell, how likely is it that he would have invited this obvious but, we are told, mistaken inference? And what was the literary gain in such an ambiguity? Or are we to suppose that this was the best he could do? We are discussing Ovid, not the poet of the *Culex* or *Ciris*.

It would be different if the defenders of the transmitted text were able to show that this trajection is not only characteristic of Ovid but is on occasion employed by him, with apparent perversity, to create just the kind of misunderstanding which the commentators on this verse so painstakingly endeavour to dispel. But this is not the case, and the 'parallels' collected by Bömer (1969: ad loc.) and the others prove no such thing. In the first place only three are from Ovid himself, and it is on these that the case for the transmitted text must stand or fall. First, a passage that must be totally disallowed:

(1) spes quoque lenta fuit: tarde, quae credita laedunt,
   credimus; inuita nunc es amante nocens. (*Her.* 2.9–10)

Hope too has been slow to depart; we are reluctant to believe what it hurts to believe. Even now your lover is unwilling to think you guilty.

---

[3] Which is to be preferred to that of Haupt et al. (1966: ad loc.): 'denn wie alle anderen (die kosmischen und physischen...), so sind auch diese Verwandlungen euer Werk'. Cf. von Albrecht (1961) 277.

That this is what Ovid wrote was first formally demonstrated in print
by M.D. Reeve (1973: 324–5); the reading for which he argues was in
fact approved by Housman many years before (1899: 175). This leaves
us with two Ovidian examples of postponed *et*:

(2) ... pertimuitque sonos propriaque exterrita uoce est.
uenit et ad ripas ubi ludere saepe solebat... (*Met.* 1.638–9)

... and she was terrified by the sounds (she made) and panic-stricken by
her own voice. She came too to the banks where she had often been used to
play...

Here *et* refers forward to *ripas* rather than back to *uenit*: 'she came
also/even to the banks of her own father's stream' (cf. Bömer, 'sie kam
auch'); but, what is crucial, *there is no ambiguity*.

(3) ... traxit in exemplum ferroque incidit acuto
perpetuos dentes et serrae repperit usum
primus et ex uno duo ferrea bracchia nodo
uinxit... (*Met.* 8. 245–8)

... he took (this) as his pattern, and cut a row of teeth in sharpened iron,
and (so) invented the saw, and he was also the first to join two strips of iron
at one end (sc. for a compass)...

I transcribe the text from Ehwald's revision (1915) of Merkel; the
vulgate punctuation, on which Bömer apparently relies, with a full
stop after v. 246, is not self-evidently correct.[4] However, let us accept
it for the sake of argument: the postponement of *et* is not in any
way unusual, and since the word can in this case refer to nothing but
primus, there is again *no ambiguity*.

I do not assert that nowhere in the works of Ovid is there a trajection of *et* analogous to that postulated by the defenders of the
transmitted text of *Met.* 1.2; but I do assert that I have not yet seen it
produced. Unless it is to be argued that Ovid is actually copying one
of his predecessors for some special effect, the usage of other poets
seems to me irrelevant. Nevertheless we may as well dispose of the
other alleged 'parallels':

---

[4] It seems to be due to N. Heinsius; his father's text reads '& serrae repperit
vsum | Primus, & ex vno' eqs. 'Repperit... primus', as Dr Diggle reminds me, recalls
Greek πρῶτος εὑρετής.

(4) dicendum et quae sint duris agrestibus arma. (Virg. *G*. 1.160)

and I must also tell of the equipment that hardy countrymen use.

More than one rendering is possible: 'I must also sing' or 'I must sing also'; but the emphasis falls on the new subject rather than on the word *dicendum* (cf. (2) above). More important: *there is no ambiguity*.

(5) quattuor hinc rapimur uiginti et milia raedis. (Hor. *Sat*.1.5.86)

From this place we are whirled four and twenty miles in carriages.

An undeniable and striking case of trajection, but: (i) this is satire, not a 'high' poetic genre; (ii) even for Horace this is a licentious postponement (cf. P. Lejay ad loc.), not in the least like our Ovidian passage or indeed any of the other passages cited by Bömer; (iii) there is no possibility of referring *et* to *milia* or to anything else but the two numerals. How this line sounded to the Roman ear I cannot guess, but *it cannot have been ambiguous*.

(6) tunc etiam felix inter et arma pudor. (Prop. 2.9.18)

Then even in wartime there was blessed chastity.

This example is again in a different category, since the words 'inter et arma' form a single phrase; and—for the last time—*there is no ambiguity*.

It has been convincingly shown by Hartman (1905: 83–4) and Luck (1958: 499–500), and should not need to be shown all over again by me, that the only reading that satisfies the demands of both sense and latinity is Lejay's *illa*. The persistent preference shown for the transmitted *illas* by recent editors and commentators strikes me as not merely unaccountable but disconcerting and depressing, for it reveals the low expectations that they apparently entertain of their chosen poet. As with the first four words of v. 1, the conceit, thus re-established in the teeth of copyists, editors, and interpreters, yields sense on more than one level. Obviously, as Luck points out, it glances at the change in Ovid himself, from *poeta nequitiae suae* to the creator of a *maius opus* that will for ever preserve his name and memory. But it is his *coepta* that the gods are actually said to have changed, and the word is ambiguous. Commonly it means 'undertaking'; but the literal sense of something begun can never be wholly unfelt. Ovid then may be making a point about the character and quality of the poem itself. If the literal sense of *coeptis* is pressed, the words imply that he had actually embarked upon another kind of poem but the gods had deflected his purpose. We have, that is to say, the adumbration, faint but in the context unmistakable, of the now classical theophany and divine admonition. Just as Apollo had intervened to turn Callimachus and Virgil from epic to a different kind of poetry (Virg. *Ecl.* 6. 3–5; Callim. fr. 1. 21–8 Pf.), so the gods—not only Apollo on this occasion but the whole of Olympus (perhaps, as Mr J. C. Bramble has suggested to me, a deliberate programmatic perversion of the topos: an implicit denial of the exclusive right of Apollo or a Muse to dictate the poet's course?)—have saved Ovid from setting his hand to some less auspicious plan. What might that have been? The implication is perhaps that Ovid might have exploited some hackneyed formula analogous to the Gigantomachy rejected in the *Amores* (2.1.11 ff.), a mythological epic à la Apollonius or a catalogue poem in the manner of Aratus or Nicander (Fleischer 1957: 47–8). It has indeed been ingeniously suggested that he went so far as to include in the *Metamorphoses* a specimen of the kind of epos that he wisely chose not to write, and that the monologue of Pythagoras in book XV was projected and composed expressly to show the public, by boring it, what it had been spared: what, in less accomplished hands, the whole poem might have been like (Galinsky 1975: 103–7). Be that particular point (highly improbable in my view) as it may, the implication of the phrase that we are considering is that the *Metamorphoses* itself exists in consequence of a metamorphosis. This is not cleverness for its own sake; it makes a perfectly serious point about the poem. It is, he tells us, not only original but (to strip Ovid's meaning of the polite fiction of divine assistance) the product of very careful thought and planning directed towards avoidance of all the possible pitfalls that lay in wait for the would-be writer of epic in the generation after Virgil. Ovid was here, in terms of the literary schema involved, traversing familiar ground. In the first three poems of the first book of the *Amores*, which form a unified programmatic sequence (with the theophany motif employed explicitly but in an unexpected way), he had already drawn attention to the quality of the strategical planning, so to call it, that he brought to his poetry. In the proem to the *Metamorphoses* he has refined and compressed to an almost incredible degree the scheme which in his first work had been developed through three entire elegies. The conventional apparatus—theophany and admonition, the poet's reaction, resistance, compliance—is taken for granted; the merest suggestion, three words, *mutastis et illa*, suffices to convey the point. It is an agreeable paradox, surely intended to be understood and enjoyed, that the complexity and elaboration of the means employed is in inverse proportion to the significance of the point to be conveyed. The *Metamorphoses* was Ovid's *chef-d'oeuvre*; this was the work on which he staked his posthumous reputation. In the coda to the poem (15.871–9) he is more expansive but not more explicit. The *doctus poeta* has the right to expect a *doctus lector*.

The sentence which extends from *di* to the end of v. 4 and of the proem moves fast and smoothly, with full enjambment of vv. 2–3 and quasi-enjambment of vv. 3–4 (Kenney 1973: 138 and n. 116). The effect is achieved with the assistance of a technical device which Ovid was to make peculiarly his own: the important point that we have just discussed is communicated not merely allusively but in parenthesis (von Albrecht 1963). The last verse of the period is a Golden Line of the abAB type, conferring dignity and emphasis and rounding the proem off. Even on this miniature scale the architecture is managed so as to impress. The interpreters have rightly stressed the implications of the word *perpetuum*. Read predicatively it has a purely chronological reference: 'assist me to tell a story that shall be continuous from the creation to my own day'. But in a programmatic context such as this *perpetuum carmen* must inevitably have recalled for Ovid's readers the 'single continuous song', ἓν ἄεισμα διηνεκές (fr. 1.3 Pf.), which Callimachus had been criticized for declining to write (Herter 1948: 139–44; Nisbet and Hubbard 1970: 97). In announcing the epic pretensions of the *Metamorphoses* Ovid does so in language that implicitly but clearly draws attention to its un-Callimachean character. On the face of it the poem may resemble the *Aetia*, consisting as it does of a series of more or less discrete episodes strung together on an often slender thread of ingenious and sometimes far-fetched transitions; but, hints Ovid, don't let that fool you—it does possess a real unity. The suggestion of theophany and admonition in v. 2 has helped to prepare the way for this discreet evocation of Callimachus, who was, so far as the Augustans were concerned, the *fons et origo* of the motif (Wimmel 1960: 132 ff.). But paradox now begins to verge on the disingenuous. 'When all is said and done, the resemblance to the *Aetia*, metre apart, is immediately obvious; and whatever thematic architecture Ovid's ingenuity might devise or the percipience of modern critics detect, the poem is bound to appeal to most readers as a collection of stories' (Kenney 1973: 116–17). Though the *Metamorphoses* no doubt ought to be read continuously for full effect, it need not be; the story of Acis and Galatea can be enjoyed without reference to the story of Narcissus and Echo, whereas no major episode of the *Aeneid* really makes sense in isolation (Otis 1970: 334). To evoke Callimachus in making this claim is a good example of the sort of inspired cheek at which Ovid excelled.

In conclusion I wish to suggest that Ovid may have gone out of his way to underline quietly the impudence of what he was saying. The innocent-seeming word *deducite* may itself be part of the intended paradox. With reference to the chronology of the poem it means simply 'bring down' or 'carry through' (*de-* of motion towards a goal). With reference to the poem itself it takes on another connotation altogether. Bömer has pointed out that when Horace and Propertius use *deduco* with poetry as object, the subject is the poet; in making the gods the subject Ovid is innovating, and the innovation may have been designed to assist a witty ambiguity.[5] For supposing that the gods comply with his request, what will be the literal result? Why, a *deductum carmen*: precisely that 'fine-spun song' enjoined on Virgil by the Virgilian-Callimachean Apollo (*Ecl.* 6.5).[6] That, however, is a contradiction in terms, for a poem cannot be both *deductum* and *perpetuum*, both Callimachean and un-Callimachean; but that, if we press the word *deducite*, is the implication. Whether we are right to press it of course admits of argument; two considerations suggest that we are. The first is based on the point that has already been emphasized more than once, the brevity of the proem and the consequent likelihood that every word in it is pulling its weight; could Ovid conceivably have overlooked the programmatic nuance now possessed by the word *deduco*? If he did, it is at least odd that he should have

---

[5] Yet another sense of *deduco* may be in play here, that of ceremonially escorting (*OLD* s.v. 8b; cf. 10e).

[6] Cf. Ross (1975*a*) 134–5. That Ovid uses *deducere* here in an unusual sense is remarked by W. Eisenhut (1961: 91), but he detects no double meaning.

introduced it in this slightly unusual new sense. The second is even more fundamental. The more one thinks about the poem itself the more probable it becomes that the implication suggested above was intended by Ovid; for the simple reason that it is true. *In noua fert animus*: of all the remarkable features of this highly original poem, not the least remarkable is indeed the way in which it manages to get the best of both worlds. If Propertius is the Roman Callimachus, Ovid is Super-Callimachus. *Naso magister erat*; not least, as he here demonstrates to the reader who is alert to take his point, in the Gentle Art of Puffing.[7]

[7] My confidence in the suggestion put forward in the last paragraph of this article is strengthened by the fact that it has also been made independently by Mr C. D. Gilbert (1976).

13

Voices and Narrative 'Instances' in the *Metamorphoses*

Alessandro Barchiesi

Readers of the *Metamorphoses* experience a continuous fluctuation of voices, addressees, levels, and narrative frames. But there is a growing tendency in criticism of Ovid's poem not to take this phenomenon seriously. It might be profitable (and I propose to do so in another context)[1] to undertake a comprehensive treatment of the act of narrating, of metadiegesis as fundamental to the *Metamorphoses*. But a work of this sort would be devoid of any interest if one were to accept the credo of a recent critic: 'I believe there is basically a single narrator throughout, who is Ovid himself' (Solodow 1988: 38).[2] The goal of this chapter is to suggest that we have gone too

---

[1] Namely, in an essay on Ovid's poetics, of which the present work is an approximation. I will deal with two aspects to which I cannot do justice here, that is, the use of narrativity as a theme for narrative, and the relationship between literary genres and the act of narration. See Barchiesi (1999) and (2002.)

[2] I cite him without polemic because he has the merit of expressing with the highest clarity the position that is implicitly dominant in Ovidian studies (cf. *contra* Hinds 1987*a*: 126). On the other hand, I will investigate in the essay promised in n. 1 a problem somewhat connected with the concept of a single narrator, that is, Ovid's tendency to demotivate metadiegetic procedures and reveal their arbitrariness. I follow here Genette's terminology (as in Genette 1976 and 1983), and therefore by 'metadiegesis' I mean a narrative within a narrative. So also the term 'instance', in the chapter's title and throughout the text, is used in the particular sense attributed to it by Genette's translator Jane E. Lewin: 'The narrating instance, then, refers to something like the narrating situation, the narrative matrix—the entire set of conditions (human, temporal, spatial) out of which a narrative statement is produced' (Genette 1980: 31).

far in this direction, and that something precious might thereby be lost.

A minor distinction is necessary. Ovid's narrative style is not truly polyphonic. The poet of the *Metamorphoses* is not concerned to characterize by stylistic means, in order to contrast the individual narrative voices he employs one with another. Thus the difference between the individual voices is to some degree neutralized. When one reasons in terms of style, the definition of 'single narrator' might be convincing. The polyphony of the *Metamorphoses* does not consist in a separation of narrative voices, but in an alternation among registers directly controlled by the single narrator's voice, according to an exhibitionary logic. This is a mimetic quality that more or less affects Ovid's entire corpus—'our poet excels in dropping just momentarily into a given style' (Hollis 1977: 123)—but this becomes predominant in the *Metamorphoses* where the very project of the work is 'an anthology of genres' (Kenney 1986: xviii, a very good definition, even if a bit static). More than polyphony, one should speak of *polyeideia*, of multiformity, a term that seems to be foreshadowed by the 'changed ... forms' (*mutatae ... formae*) of *Met.* 1.1.[3]

One should not therefore expect the voices of single narrators (as is the case sometimes in Petronius) to have recognizably distinct stylistic features or even to be separable one from another. Nor should one think that a plurality of narrators might have a primarily *informative* function. Ovid, on the contrary, works hard to demotivate his metadiegetic procedures. A flux of unstable narrative material flows through the *Metamorphoses*, a flux similar to Nature in Pythagoras' speech, and Ovid presents himself as its sole possible arbiter. The attribution of certain features of narrative to individual narrators is often arbitrary, and functionalist critics might search in vain for an explanation that would account for the interchangeability of direct and of metadiegetic narrations.

But the foregoing does not seem to me to warrant us speaking of a Single Narrator, if this implies denying the presence and the significance of the individual metadiegetic narrators. The insertion of secondary narratives into the main narrative involves for Ovid elaborate

---

[3] In the Greek of Ovid's age *polyeideia* has two distinct meanings: 'metamorphic capability' and 'plurality of literary forms and genres'.

and expensive narrative frames. A certain logic of expenditure and of luxury, of conspicuous consumption, is intrinsic to Ovid's poetics. But I cannot bring myself to believe that all these narrators and narratees are brought into the narrative *only* to display their singular irrelevance. On the contrary, experience of other narrative works suggests that between frames and inserted stories mutual implications may arise, interconnections only hinted at, but integral to the creation of meaning. For example, an internal audience's reception of a story can suggest to the reader a model of interpretation (which in turn may be adopted or dismissed). In other cases, the identity of the narrator can have an implicit relation to a theme, or even to the style of the narrative entrusted to him or her.[4] These are general guidelines to be kept in mind, even if our discussion will focus almost entirely upon specific examples.

A RIVER AS NARRATOR

The stories narrated at a banquet that Achelous the river god hosts, with Theseus and other heroes as his guests, occupy the central portion of the poem (the second part of book 8 and the beginning of book 9). Lelex, a hero with an archaizing name, tells the story of Baucis and Philemon (8.618–724). Achelous responds with the tale of impious Erysichthon's punishment (8.728–878), and with the autobiographical account of his duel with Heracles (8.879–9.88). Two recent observations shed some light on the connection between these stories and the narrative situation that frames them.

On the literary level, *Baucis and Philemon* and *Erysichthon* have a certain affinity: taken together, they are the most outstanding 'nest' of Callimachean influence in Ovid's works (and for that matter, in any other Latin poet known to us). The principal model for *Baucis and Philemon* is the short poem *Hecale* (the fragments of this work, however limited, still offer remarkable potential for comparison), and

---

[4] These are all problems familiar to readers of Petronius; on the interaction between metadiegesis, narrative frames, and the structure of the novel, see Fedeli-Dimundo (1988) 16–42.

Erysichthon echoes the central nucleus of Callimachus' *Hymn* VI.[5] Incidentally, we have here two Callimachean models in hexameters—that is, technically speaking, epic, like the *Metamorphoses*. Let us turn now to the narrative frame in Ovid.[6] The first story is narrated by Theseus' maternal uncle, and Ovid points out that among the listeners Theseus is the most impressed (8.725-6): *Desierat, cunctosque et res et mouerat auctor | Thesea praecipue* 'He made an end: both the tale and the teller had moved them all, Theseus especially.' Theseus' reaction, as Kenney observes, must have a subtle metaliterary motivation: the story so strikes him because Theseus himself is the hero of the Callimachean model for this account. The simple hospitality of Baucis and Philemon corresponds perfectly to the humble welcoming of the old Hecale that so moves the hero in Callimachus' *Hecale*.[7] There is also somewhat of a contrastive implication: in the narrative frame a god hosts mortals, whereas in the metadiegesis gods are hosted in a human abode.

But as Hinds has observed (1987*b*: 19, see ch. 1 above), the character of Achelous, the master of the house and narrator of the *Erysichthon*, also merits consideration. In reality he is a very peculiar figure, since he is at once a god and a river in flood. An interesting coincidence: in the poem's endless variety of narrators, the very one who offers the setting and the voice for Callimachean narrations is a wide river laden with debris—a most blatant negative symbol according to the poetics of Callimachus.

---

[5] The comparisons, obviously more problematic for the fragmentary *Hecale*, receive systematic treatment in Hollis (1983) in his commentary on book 8. In the *Met.*, Theseus' victory over the bull, the mythic situation of the *Hecale*, had already been recalled in the celebration at 7.433 ff. (cf. Call. fr. 290 Pf.).

[6] The banquet and hospitality as sites of narrative exchange are a common situation in Callimachus, as can be seen in both the fragments of *Hecale* and, even more so, in the *Aitia*. To be sure, the banquet as a metadiegetic device is widespread in all genres and at all levels of narrative.

[7] See Kenney (1986) xxviii. One might compare from the *Satyricon* the reaction of Lichas in the inset story of the Lady of Ephesus. There too one narratee of the story is struck more than others because he sees himself reflected in a certain feature of the plot (Fedeli-Dimundo 1988: 23). The difference is that for Petronius' reader the relation between the story and narratee is mediated and clarified by the preceding narrative of the novel (which presented Lichas, as far as we can gather, as a cuckolded husband); in Ovid this mediating function is supplied not by the context but by the intertext with the Callimachean model.

This suggestion deserves further amplification. The narrative situation of the banquet begins with Achelous' introduction of himself (8.549–59):

clausit iter fecitque moras Achelous eunti
imbre tumens. 'succede meis' ait 'inclite, tectis
Cecropide, nec te committe rapacibus undis!
ferre trabes solidas obliquaque uoluere magno
murmure saxa solent. uidi contermina ripae
cum gregibus stabula alta trahi, nec fortibus illic
profuit armentis nec equis uelocibus esse.
multa quoque hic torrens niuibus de monte solutis
corpora turbineo iuuenalia uertice mersit.
tutior est requies, solito dum flumina currant
limite, dum tenues capiat suus alueus undas.'

But Achelous, swollen with rain, blocked his way and delayed his journey. 'Enter my house, illustrious descendant of Cecrops,' he said, 'and do not entrust yourself to the greedy waters. They often carry along solid tree trunks and roll boulders headlong in a mighty roar. I have seen great stables that stood near the bank swept away, cattle and all, and in that current neither strength availed the ox nor speed the horse. This torrent has drowned many a strong man in its whirling pools when the snow in the mountains has melted. It is safer to rest until the waters run within their bounds, until its own bed contains the slender flow.'

It is good to stay put, he tells them, and wait for the waves to become *tenues* once again—a common theme both in *recusationes* (cf. Prop. 3.3.24; 3.9.36) and in literary theory (cf. Hor. *Ars* 28).

The swell of the river (853: *intumui*) continues until the end of the narrative situation (9.94–6):

discedunt iuuenes: neque enim, dum flumina pacem
et placidos habeant lapsus totaeque residant
opperiuntur aquae.

The youths depart, for they did not wait until the river had a peaceful flow and all the flood had subsided.

A great river, 'swollen' (*tumens*), roaring and laden with debris, is an image bearing a curious resemblance to the great Assyrian river in Callimachus' *Hymn to Apollo* (2.108–9), for generations of poets a

symbol of the 'grand' poetry to be rejected. Achelous' violent sweep-
ing force is also reminiscent of an important predecessor of Callimachus' Euphrates: Cratinus the poet is in Aristophanes figured as
a torrent that swept away every obstacle and carried away logs and
boulders in its path (Ar. *Eq.* 526 ff.). From this perspective, the figure
of Achelous operates somewhat as an emblem. The great river, while
he describes himself, 'speaks' a lofty style: his first words are epicisms,
such as the vocative *inclite ... Cecropide*, and his descriptive style itself
is accordingly tumid and overflowing. His account of the destructive
effects of his flood resembles well-known similes proper to epic. The
river's high tide, the occasion for the narrative, also influences his
style.

The story narrated by Achelous is in a certain sense coherent
with these premises. Comparisons between Ovid's and Callimachus'
Erysichthon have all agreed on one point: Ovid rewrites his model by
exaggerating its style.[8] Many humorous and realistic bourgeois features of the original are lost. To make up for this, Erysichthon takes on
a sinister and superhuman stature. The divine apparatus grows over-
powering, and the demonic personification of Hunger (*Fames*) towers
over the account. Ovid's transcription 'epicizes' Callimachus, and the
'tumid' identity of the narrator Achelous is, in the end, the signal
of this awareness. Greedy and insatiable, Erysichthon is an excessive
hero, fitting for the context. His hunger is a self-propelling force, it
grows 'unreduced' (*inattenuata*, 8.844). This unusual epithet (a *hapax*
in Latin) seems to play upon a literary register: *attenuatus* ('reduced')
is a technical term of literary criticism for a 'slender' and reduced
style, as opposed to an exuberant *redundantia* ('excess').[9] Unable
to curb his hunger, Erysichthon greedily consumes any available

---

[8] See especially Diller (1934) 25 ff.; Büchner (1957) 205 ff.; both end up underestimating the comic elements in Ovid's narration, which arise from the high pitch he
imposes on his model and are inseparable from this. If it is true, as we are observing,
that Ovid 'epicizes' Callimachus, this does not mean that Ovid is somehow 'more
serious' than Callimachus.

[9] Thus, for example, *attenuate* is the opposite of *sublate ampleque* (Cic. *Brut.*
201) and of *redundantia* (Cic. *Orat.* 108). On the *genus adtenuatum* and *adtenuatio*,
see in general *Rhet. Her.* 4.10–11. Cicero defines as 'attenuated' the oratorical style
of Licinius Calvus: bloodless, controlled, and accessible to only a few connoisseurs
(see *Brut.* 283). As is known, the Roman followers of Callimachus delineate the
stylistic ideal of *lepton* by relying upon the rhetorical terminology for the *genus tenue*
(Reitzenstein 1931: 25 ff., esp. 39 ff.).

resource until he consumes himself. Meanwhile, by imitating Callimachus in terms that suggest an inflation and crisis of the Callimachean programme, Ovid dilates the style of his model and creates a
field of contradictory tensions.[10] A similar field of tensions (as is now
commonly thought) affects the very proem of the *Metamorphoses*,
where opposing connotations are conjoined in an almost provocative
manner: *deducere* a *carmen perpetuum* is, in Callimachean terms, an
undeniable contradiction.[11]

   To claim that Achelous ought to be viewed in light of the Euphrates
in Callimachus, a point on which my whole analysis rests, might
seem unwarranted. But it is hard to overstate the importance of this
symbol of 'tumidity' in Roman poetry. Ovid's river can be added to
a list that includes the Euphrates (not only in Callimachus, but also
in Propertius 2.10.13), the Simois and Scamander (Prop. 3.1.26–7),
and the Rhine, both muddy (Hor. *Sat.* 1.10.37, 62) and polluted with
blood (Prop. 3.3.45).[12] The Achelous is the largest and most ancient
of the rivers in Greece, and figures as a symbol of the kind of elevated
and grandiose poetry one should reject (linked to the poetry of Antimachus?)[13] in the first 'Callimachean' elegy of Propertius (2.34.31–4):

   [10] Erysichthon's insatiability appears to be connected to an almost bombastic style
that goes beyond the usual level of epic elevation. We catch a hint of this in 8.855,
where the hero, who should be simply saying 'o fisherman', displays a periphrasis like
o qui pendentia paruo | aera cibo celas, moderator harundinis. (On the 'pomposity' of
Achelous' style see also Hollis on *Met.* 8.549 ff.). An amusing parallel in Plautus *Rud.*
311–12.: *saluete, fures maritumi ... famelica hominum natio.*
   [11] The force of *deducite* in opposition to *perpetuum* has been noted independently
by Due (1974) 95, n. 8, Gilbert (1976), and Kenney (1976, ch. 12 above) 51–3. See
also Hinds (1987a) 18–20. Of course, one should not forget that *deducite* already has
one satisfactory meaning: the narrative is 'brought down' from the origin to its final
destination (cf. Dion. Hal. *Ant.* 1.8: *katabibazo ... ten diegesin*).
   [12] The topos is analysed and well documented by Wimmel (1960) 222–5, 227–33.
See also Thomas-Scodel (1984) 339, and Clauss (1988) 309–20. Worth noting also is
Ov. *Fast.* 5.662: *leues cursum sustinuistis aquae*; in the *Fasti* the Tiber has *leues* waters,
but in the epic model for this passage (*Aen.* 8.66) the flow of the river is *tumens*.
   [13] Antimachus is cited with great emphasis on v. 45, and is the most probable
candidate for the negative examples in vv. 36–40 (the horse of Adrastus, Archemorus,
Amphiaraus, Capaneus), in addition to appearing as a typical antagonist of the Callimachean tendency towards the *lepton*. As a matter of pure curiosity, I mention that
Achelous is cited in a text of Antimachus (*POxy.* 2516 = *Supplementum Hellenisticum*
62.4): the editors suspect, but with great uncertainty, that it is part of a proem.
   The context of 2.34 is extremely complex, and this probably influences the choice of
examples. The struggle between Heracles and Achelous is undoubtedly an epic theme,
which Propertius pits against 'slender' love poetry, but one also gets the impression

tu satius leuiorem Musis imitere Philitan
  et non inflati somnia Callimachi.
Nam cursus licet Aetoli referas Acheloi,
  fluxerit ut magno fractus amore liquor ...

Better that you should imitate the slighter muse of Philitas and the dream of unpretentious Callimachus. For though you should tell of the course of Aetolian Achelous, how its waters flowed shattered by a great love ...

The myth that Propertius evokes, the defeat of Achelous in the battle with Heracles, is narrated by Ovid's Achelous at the beginning of Book 9, directly after the story of Erysichthon.

Before we leave this insidious terrain, I would like to mention two other possible applications of this image to narrative contexts; I mean certain sequences of narrative in which the image of a muddy river, certainly coherent and motivated by the context, might retain some literary-critical connotation.

We know that the *Fasti* is a work pervaded by an anxious question (Hinds 1987*a*). This text, while it develops according to the implicit norms of elegiac narrative, also confronts the limits of these norms and delimits its own territory in a dynamic confrontation with other poetic genres. The poem is written in the metre of elegy, and on the horizon can be glimpsed the competition of 'light' love poetry composed in couplets. On the other hand, the narrative themes of the *Fasti* are often a bit higher, or heavier, than the elegiac form can bear. So too with respect to epic, there is a problem of contiguity and of trespassing. In order to guarantee its own autonomy, the *Fasti* avoids some themes belonging quintessentially to heroic epos (and which instead are more suitable to the *Met.*). It is significant, for example, that Ovid abstains from battle scenes.

This rule is confirmed by a single exception, well noted by Heinze (1960: 339): 'If Ovid avoided battle reports ... then the reason is cer-

---

that behind this choice lies an agenda. The Achelous is presented as 'shattered by love' (*fractus ... amore*), which, on the one hand, may allude to the defeat he has just suffered (Heracles vanquishes him and breaks off one of his horns, as Ovid reminds us in *Met.* 9), but on the other hand, it reintroduces into the field of epic the theme of love, which ought to remain, in programmatic terms, in the opposite camp. The effect is subtle: Propertius offers Lynceus choice examples of poetry to be avoided since they do not serve love, but at the same time implies that even there, in the epic genre Lynceus obstinately practices, love makes its weight felt.

tainly that elegiac poetry always avoided such descriptions...Ovid makes *one* (Heinze's italics) exception only.' The reference is to the battle of the Fabii along the river Cremera (*Fast.* 2.195–241). In this scene, which according to Heinze ought to be viewed as the extreme point of 'epic' excursion granted to the *Fasti*, a great emphasis is placed upon a flooding river. The Cremera impedes the march of the Fabii and sets the stage for the battle (*Fast.* 2.205 ff.):

ut celeri passu Cremeram tetigere rapacem
    (turbidus hibernis ille fluebat aquis)...

When at a quick pace they reached the rushing Cremera (it flowed turbid with winter rain)...

Without a doubt this scenario is well suited for the most epic scene in the *Fasti*. The description of the bloody battle includes three epic similes, one of which is the image of a rushing torrent (it overflows its usual banks and invades everything, 2.219–22), concluding with an echo of a famous line of Ennius (v. 242 = Enn. *Ann.* 370 V^2). The detail of the swollen river is absent from historical sources (as far as we know) and I suspect that in Ovid it plays a precise role. The Fabii halt at the edge of a river, *rapax* and *turbidus*, as if to mark the farthest point of extension of the world of the *Fasti* with respect to epic grandeur, the limit beyond which the elegiac Ovid of the *Fasti* would be a trespasser.

Something similar might be observed in a 'pure' elegiac text, antipodal to epic, such as *Amores* 3.6. This elegy is a long appeal addressed to an obstinate little stream obstructing Ovid's path to his love. The erotic situation lies completely in the background, abstract and vague; Ovid turns his whole attention to the obstacle and to the strategies aimed at overcoming it. The river is described in essentially 'anti-Callimachean' terms: it has muddy banks (3.6.1), abundant and even filthy waters (*et turpi crassas gurgite uoluis aquas* 'and you roll gross waters in filthy whirls', 8). These features accord well with the narrative function of the stream that obstructs the amorous quest of the elegiac poet. But what is intriguing are the arguments Ovid uses to appease the flood. To honour the unnamed stream, the poet lists lofty examples of great rivers which have felt the power of love (among whom are Achelous with his horn broken during his duel with Heracles, v. 35–8). He then goes on to develop a long narrative example, the story of a river in love, but, significantly, the story is of *epic* provenance: Mars' rape of Ilia, who afterward was offered consolation by the Anio. The entire story, not only the meeting with Mars but also the final union with the Anio, appeared in a prominent position at the beginning of Ennius' *Annales*.[14] This episode, though transcribed by Ovid in his own manner and in the style of elegy, is indeed an unforeseen guest in a poem of the *Amores*. The outcome of Ovid's effort is rather ironic when seen in this light. While the poet speaks, that is, as he retells the Ennian epic, rather than being calmed, the river swells even more (3.6.85–8):

dum loquor, increuit latis spatiosus in undis,
    nec capit admissas alueus altus aquas.
quid mecum, furiose, tibi? quid mutua differs
    gaudia, quid coeptum, rustice, rumpis iter?

Even as I speak, your waters have grown more deep and wide, and your deep bed can't contain the headlong waters. What have I to do with you, wild river? Why do you delay the joys I am to share? Why do you break off the journey I have begun, you churl?

Once all hope has been lost, Ovid upbraids the river with appropriate epithets: *lutulentus* (95), *non candide* (105). The elegy as a whole is much more amusing if a specific part of Ovid's audience, namely the small circle familiar with debates concerning poetics, recognized the reciprocal relevance of several narrative features: the rustic, sullen, and untamed character of the muddy river, its opposition to love, the overflowing effect of the allusion to Ennius.[15]

Many of the observations made so far must remain conjectural. After all, there are not many perspectives from which to describe a flooding river, and the Callimachean symbolism, though well known in Ovid's time and even a bit commonplace, did not have exclusive copyright on the image.[16] I think, however, that it may be healthy

---

[14] For the encounter, see fr. XXIX, and for the union with the Anio see fr. XXXIX, but also XXXIV, XXXVI, XXXVII in Skutsch (1985) 206–13.

[15] On *Amores* 3.6, Suter (1989). She pursues the reference to Callimachus in a different direction than the one taken here.

[16] I believe this is an important point. Ovid's literary generation had by now been saturated with appeals to the *lepton*, refusals of epic, and the entire paraphernalia of Callimachean poetics. Beginning with his spectacular entrance upon the literary stage

to keep open this connotative dimension. The literary public of late Augustan Rome, a significant portion of it at least, was certainly able to appreciate manipulations of concepts and literary symbols of this sort. But this is a secondary level in the *Metamorphoses* (luckily for it) and the poem is perfectly enjoyable and interesting even for those who do not ask of it such questions. But even so, we are not obliged to ignore, while reading the poem, the presence of individual narrators and particular narrative settings. The hypothesis that between metadiegetic 'voices', stories, narrative settings, and narratees, implications may arise, reciprocal references in the text, deserves in each case at least our serious consideration. All the more so, since from now on we will not move from an allusive dimension—admittedly always conjectural and secondary—but will concern ourselves with concrete problems of interpretation, cases in which the identity of the narrating voice and its relevance to the narrative poses difficulties, suggesting not only poetic implications, but also differences of meaning.

ORPHEUS AND OVID

By ignoring the spectrum of narrative levels in the *Metamorphoses*, many Ovidian critics tend to flatten out internal narrators and conflate their voices with the voice of the primary narrator. The characters who narrate thus become transparent functions and fail to grab our attention. This habit of 'transparent' reading has some justification. In the *Metamorphoses*, the act of narration is constantly a spectacle, and the audience's attention is at each moment focused upon the virtuosity of the conductor. The primary narrator's voice is omnipresent and it will have the privilege of rounding out the lengthy narrative with the word *VIVAM* 'I SHALL LIVE'. No other

with *Amores* 1.1, Ovid brings with him a new breeze and ironically shuffles traditional dichotomies. Using a swollen river as a narrator seems integral to this ironic tendency; the image, by now worn out in its 'defensive' use against epic, now provokes instead a certain aversion, tempting one to regard the situation for once from the opposite point of view. For the somewhat 'dialectical' and problematic approach to Callimachean imagery, Horace's *Ars Poetica* offers important insights (fine observations in Brink 1985: 208 ff., 345 ff.).

poet (before Ariosto in the Renaissance) is able to maintain such an uninterrupted perception of a 'central' narrative voice against which the whole is measured. We are a bit like Orpheus' audience, the *theatrum* surrounding, and held mesmerized by, the magnetic singer.

But if Orpheus somewhat resembles Ovid, perhaps he too ought to be taken seriously. Among all the poem's narrators, he is the one who most evidently presents himself as a poet. The other, more esteemed practitioners of poetry in the poem are gods, Apollo and Calliope (incidentally, the parents of Orpheus). More so than a usual narrator, as a poet Orpheus has the right to open his stories with proemial formulas (10.147–8, 301–3):

ab Ioue, Musa parens—cedunt Iouis omnia regno—,
carmina nostra moue...

From Jove, O Muse my mother—for all things yield to the rule of Jove— inspire my song...

dira canam: procul hinc natae, procul este parentes,
aut, mea si uestras mulcebant carmina mentes,
desit in hac mihi parte fides, nec credite factum...

I shall sing of terrible things! Away, daughters! Away, parents! Or if my songs charm your minds, do not give me credence in this part: believe that it never happened.

These two introductions correspond to two separate story sequences: the pederastic loves of the gods (10.152–3), and the criminal passions of maidens (10.153–4). The first of these two overtures leaves no room for controversy. Only an absent-minded reading (still found however in some commentators) can separate the proem from Orpheus' personality and from the themes of the song it introduces. It is clearly not enough simply to recall the formula *ek Dios arkhomestha | Ab Ioue principium*.[17] Orpheus is not merely reciting a stock phrase (like those who say, 'let us begin from Jupiter,' only to move immediately to another topic). Orpheus begins from Jupiter *because* he is going to speak about Jupiter. The god will be the first

---

[17] The history of this motif is traced by Fantuzzi (1980: 163–72). It may be worth recalling that the formula, famous as the incipit for Aratus' *Phaenomena*, was attributed by ancient interpreters of Aratus to an Orphic source (163 n. 1). Callimachus does not use the formula, but begins his first hymn with the name of Zeus.

protagonist of the new song that consists of a catalogue of divine loves for human boys, and Orpheus rightly puts in the first line the most important god of all. The trite traditional motif is taken in a literal sense—a characteristically Ovidian move—and becomes, at the same time, mercilessly blasphemous. Given that Orpheus is about to sing how Jupiter overcame Ganymede, a very ambiguous light is cast on the traditional attribution of omnipotence (*cedunt Iouis omnia regno*). He thus shows how it is possible to rewrite an old repertoire of hymnological formulas into the unexpected register of *Mousa paidikê*.[18]

This is indeed Orpheus' new Muse, not his mother Calliope formally invoked at line 148—Calliope, as we know from the hymn to Ceres at 5.341 ff., is a god-fearing and unsuitably traditional poetess. Orpheus, on the contrary, is innovating here. His new poetics is dictated by a personal choice, caused by the loss of his wife Eurydice (10.83–5):

ille etiam Thracum populis fuit auctor, amorem
in teneros transferre mares, citraque iuuentam
aetatis breue uer et primos carpere flores.

He it was that taught the people of Thrace to shift their love to tender males, to enjoy the brief springtime of life before manhood and pluck first flowers.

The idea of associating Orpheus with pederastic love comes directly from a famous passage of Phanocles, a fragment of a long poem dedicated to the Muse of pretty boys. Ovid's Orpheus is viewing himself in the mirror of this model of homoerotic poetry (Phan. fr. 1.9–10 Powell):

... Πρῶτος ἔδειξεν ἐνὶ Θρήκεσσιν ἔρωτας
ἄρρενας οὐδὲ πόθους ἤνεσε θηλυτέρων

He was the first to make male love known among the Thracians, nor did he praise the desire for women.

---

[18] By curious coincidence, *ek Dios archomestha* occurs at the beginning of one of the most infamous and blasphemous pederastic epigrams of antiquity, one by Strato that became the proem to Book XII of the *Anthologia Palatina* (Fantuzzi 1980: 165, 168). Note also that Orpheus has just come from singing a *Gigantomachia* (10.149–51), the most elevated of all poetic genres, in which Zeus is the absolute protagonist responsible for super-epic deeds.

The connection between the two themes sung by Ovid's Orpheus, ephebic love affairs and the illicit passions of women, has been much discussed. The logical connection—praise for male love, denunciation of female perversion (cf. 10.152 ff.)—is fairly clear, and as in Phanocles it is well harmonized with the Maenads' revenge (cf. fr. 1.7 ff. Powell, with *Met.* 10.7). Homoerotic love is described as a *diligere*; that of women for men as lust (cf. 10.153 ff.). It might also be the case that Ovid has been inspired by the passage of Phanocles, pressing and altering its meaning a bit: *pothous theluteron* clearly signifies 'desire *for* women' (*theluteron* being simply an elegant variation on the adjectival construction *arrenas*), but in theory it could be interpreted as a subjective genitive (the lusts *of* women).

We thus have Orpheus as a singer of *paidika*, deriving from the model of Phanocles and, at the same time, composing poetry *in the style* of Phanocles.[19] The *Amores* of Phanocles were, according to the available evidence, in catalogue form, a point-by-point homosexual version of Hesiod's *Catalogue of Women*, perfectly comparable to Orpheus' song on the gods' love for ephebes. Orpheus' homoerotic mission needs to be read within the context not only of Ovid's Alexandrian culture and his interest in lesser-known poetic genres, but also in the context of Augustan culture. The most authoritative manifesto of Augustan poetics had chosen Orpheus as exemplar for the *civilizing uates* ('poet-seer'). According to Horace, Orpheus had established the prestige of poetry through a constructive programme of legislation: his Orpheus taught lawful and civil love, and corrected wild and promiscuous sexuality (Hor. *Ars* 391–8):

siluestris homines sacer interpresque deorum
caedibus et uictu foedo deterruit Orpheus …
 … fuit haec sapientia quondam,

[19] Phanocles' version of the Orpheus myth contains several *aitia* (Hopkinson 1988: 178), among which is an explanation of why Lesbos is a 'musical' island, filled with and renowned for song. This explanation is picked up by Ovid in *Met.* 11.50: Orpheus' head and lyre travel towards Lesbos, emitting a feeble lament (see 52–3: *flebile … flebile … flebile*). It seems plausible to me that both Phanocles and Ovid intend to suggest some continuity between the songs of Orpheus and the great love lyrics of Lesbos, which can be seen in some sense as their heir. Alcaeus, for example, might be cited as evidence for this poetic genealogy, in as much as he was a renowned singer of *Paidika* (see Hor. *Carm.* 1.32.10–12).

publica priuatis secernere, sacra profanis,
concubitu prohibere uago, dare iura maritis.

Orpheus, priest and intepreter of the gods, deterred early man from killings
and a revolting diet...This, once, was wisdom, to separate public from
private, sacred from profane, to bar people from promiscuous intercourse,
to lay down laws for married people.

This edifying Orpheus had fought in favour of marriage and against
a primitive sexuality, performed (as Horace explains in a parallel
passage, *Sat.* 1.3.109) *more ferarum*. Now we meet him again singing
of frivolous loves for boys and, in an aggressive reversal, women with
incestuous and bestial passions. Myrrha argues with herself and justifies her incest with the argument that the animals do it too (*coeunt
animalia nullo | cetera dilectu*, 10.324).

Given this, the second 'proem' quoted above also appears problematic and ambiguous, or at least it should. Still, modern interpreters
of Ovid are accustomed to ironing out the difficulty with a simple
interpretive move: *dira canam*, and what follows, is a direct intrusion
of the primary narrator, or better yet, of Ovid himself, since here the
author, more than the primary narrator, has more to fear should his
text come across as too immoral. In other words, we ought to forget
for a while the voice of Orpheus. In this case the *Metamorphoses*'
intrusive primary narrator is bending the rules of the game a bit. But
modern critics know how to account for his intrusion. The immorality of Myrrha's story, they say, is truly excessive, even for the libertine
Ovid, and this makes the author's precaution necessary in order to
limit his liability. (But would it not have been easier to insinuate, as
Callimachus had, that 'this myth is not mine, it belongs to someone
else?' After all, Cinna's *Zmyrna* had been around for a couple of
generations, with a retinue of admirers and even professional commentators, and to Ovid's tastes it had already become passé.)[20]

It is natural to turn, by analogy, to the story of Byblis, the other
narration on incest in the poem. There, as the primary narrator,

---

[20] Notwithstanding the scarcity of our knowledge of the *Zmyrna*, a weighty presence of Cinna's epyllion in Orpheus' epyllion seems a probable hypothesis. The only
certain point of departure is that fr. 7 M (see Haupt-Korn-Ehwald-von Albrecht
[1966] on 10.298 ff.) is echoed in the situation of 503 and in the tone of moral
condemnation in 469 (see also 474).

Ovid expresses a direct caveat on the scandalous content of the story about to begin (9.454): *Byblis in exemplo est, ut ament concessa puellae* 'Byblis exemplifies the principle that girls should love as law allows'. But before becoming a negative example, Byblis takes pains to provide herself with the best examples in an opposite sense, that is, those exhorting *towards* incest: Saturnus, Oceanus, Jove, the children of Aeolus (9.498 ff.), with the amusing addition (9.508), 'But from where do I know these? Why did I prepare these examples?' The entire story of Byblis is developed in a paradoxical mode, as a salacious contrast between the amorality of the ends and a cool-headed technical analysis of the means. The problem of incest, exorcized by the poet with a single verse, dissolves into questions of seductive techniques, highly concrete problems of amorous strategy. The heroine behaves as if she were an ideal reader of the *Ars amatoria*. I would agree, in general, with Kenney (1986: 429 ff.): Ovid broadcasts his morals very 'tongue in cheek'.

The case of Orpheus is made peculiar by the presence of an intermediary narrator, whose prerogatives we would be forced to violate if we overlook his presence. Almost all critics agree that Ovid 'is peeking through the figure of Orpheus' (Solodow 1988: 40), and by this is meant, surprisingly, that the moralizing proem should be taken seriously. The uneasiness that makes this solution attractive has various causes. Some (Galinsky 1975: 90), in order to save the role and the voice of Orpheus, appeal to the contrast between the pure and idealized love for his wife Eurydice, on the one hand, and the sinister transgression of Myrrha, on the other. But the shifting of Orpheus to free homosexual love makes this dichotomy rather doubtful. To this some have objected (Solodow 1988: 40) that Orpheus' puritanism would be too hypocritical: the discrepancy is an invitation for the reader to hear the 'authorial' voice. Others (Haupt-Korn-Ehwald-von Albrecht [1966] ad loc.; Fränkel 1945: 220 n. 70) do not accept that the mythical singer is contrasting the luxury and redolence of the Orient with his native Thrace, in terms clearly alluding to traditional praise of Italy. Rather than admitting an Orpheus who speaks like Virgil in the *Georgics*, they prefer to think that the metadiegetic narrator is for a while eclipsed. In this way, for those who accept that the voice of the proem is Ovid's own, any difficulty and contradiction is thus resolved.

But all the ironic effects of the situation are lost by this move. I will turn now to examine these point by point (10.301):

dira canam: procul hinc natae, procul este parentes!

I shall sing of terrible things! Away, daughters! Away, parents!

The implications here are very similar to those of *ab Ioue princip-ium*, the only difference being that here the pious formula is not denaturalized but inverted. The true poet-seer should avoid impure persons, and it is indeed a traditional feature of Orphism to begin singing with a solemn expulsion of the uninitiated. 'I will speak to whom it is allowed to speak: shut the doors, profane ones!' is the typical beginning of an Orphic *hieros logos*, from which derives Horace's *arceo* (*Carm.* 3.1.1).[21] Instead of continuing with a *uirginibus puerisque canto* ('I sing to maidens and boys'), Ovid's Orpheus, who announces 'terrible things' (*dira*) and not 'sacred things' (*sacra*), has to exclude from his audience parents and daughters. The conven-tional formula of chasing away is already present as an ironically inverted subtext in Ovidian passages such as *Amores* 2.1.3: *procul hinc, procul este seuerae!*; *Ars* 1.31: *este procul, uittae tenues, insigne pudoris* (cf. Verg. *Aen.* 6.258: *procul, o procul este, profani*). But another impor-tant aspect will appear, as we will see shortly, if we take into account the real audience of Orpheus' song (10.301-4):

aut, mea si uestras mulcebunt carmina mentes,
desit in hac mihi parte fides, nec credite factum;
uel si credetis, facti quoque credite poenam.
si tamen admissum sinit hoc natura uideri...

Or if my songs charm your minds, do not give me credence in this part: believe that it never happened; or if you do believe, believe also in the pun-ishment of the deed. If, however, nature allows this crime to show itself...

These lines clearly assume the narrative voice of Orpheus. The soothing power typical of his poetry (*mulcebunt*) has now become a danger against which he has to warn his audience, and it is therefore emphasized in this context (Segal 1989: 93). The tone of the warning is once again ironic. Orpheus asks his audience either not to believe in the reality of the incest, or to believe the crime *and* its necessary

---

[21] See Kiessling-Heinze 1968: ad loc.; Orph. fr. 245 K.

punishment. The division between the two events, transgression and punishment, is in no way innocent. The punishment itself, the seal of divine justice for Myrrha's story, is clearly the least plausible element in the story. The transformation of the pregnant Myrrha into a perfumed tree, one able nonetheless to give birth to a child, is a typical example of a 'metamorphosis not to be believed'. In strictly Ovidian terms, we have here a case of 'bodies changed in unbelievable ways' (*in non credendos corpora uersa modos,* as the *Met.* is defined in *Trist.* 2.64). The transgression is realistic, the expiation pure fantasy. The suspension of disbelief asked of the reader applies not to the moral nucleus of the story, but to the concluding moral—or at least the two themes are coupled in an ambiguous light (10.305–7):

gentibus Ismariis et nostro gratulor orbi,
gratulor huic terrae, quod abest regionibus illis
quae tantum genuere nefas.

I congratulate the Ismarian people and this our world, I congratulate this land on being far away from those regions which produced such a crime.

The contrast with faraway lands of the East, rich in spices and incense, but marked by other disadvantages, is central to the ideology of Virgilian *laudes Italiae* (*Geo.* 2.136–9; cf. also 117):

sed neque Medorum siluae, ditissima terra,
nec pulcher Ganges atque auro turbidus Hermus
laudibus Italiae certent, non Bactra neque Indi
totaque turiferis Panchaia pinguis harenis.

But neither the forests of the Medes, a rich land, nor the beautiful Ganges and the Hermus, muddied with gold-dust, may compete with the praises of Italy; not Bactra, not India, not the whole of Panchaia rich with incense-laden sands.

This correspondence is the source of irony.[22] Orpheus is obviously not speaking about Italy; but he shows that it is possible to compose, with conventional rhetorical material, highly improbable *laudes Thraciae*. The situation bears some similarity to the episode of Baucis

---

[22] The rhetorical matrix, resolved on a higher poetic register by Virgil, is made more evident by the repeated use of *gratulor*, probably a stylistic feature of declamation (see Sen. *Con.* 9.2.4: *gratulor sorti tuae, prouincia, quod…*; 10.4.9: *gratulor tibi, Roma, quod in conditores tuos homo non incidit*).

and Philemon (8.618 ff.), where the description of country life, simple and idealized, intentionally recalls the classic praise of country life found in Virgil and Horace. Reading these passages one feels transported into the traditional world of the Italian countryside, as seen through the nostalgic and austere eyes of the first generation of the Augustan period. But the concrete localization of the ideal peasants produces a slight dissonance. Baucis and Philemon live 'in the Phrygian hill country' (8.621), and thus belong to a people associated mostly with luxury and vice, a distillation of oriental delicacy. The effect is to relativize the ideological restrictions and nationalistic conventions on which the *laudes uitae agrestis* ('encomia of country life') are based.[23] As far as concerns the story's narrator, might it not be significant that while he tells about a frugal meal he is enjoying a luxurious banquet (cf. 8.573 with 8.678 ff. and Verg. *Geo.* 2.506)?

In our passage, Orpheus contrasts the Thracians with the East, full of perfumes but also of aberrant passions—which together form an indivisible unity, since Myrrha will become an Oriental perfume, an imported luxury. In this framework the choice of *Ismariis* is noteworthy, and very peculiar if Ovid was interested in having us forget the narrative setting, and wanted instead to project us into the familiar dimension of praise for Italy. The Thracian emphasis is embarrassing for more than one reason. Orpheus, as we have seen, is busy disseminating pederasty among the Thracians. *Ismariis* is an epithet that makes one think of wine and Bacchic cults much more than of moderation and simplicity of habits. Very soon, Orpheus will become the victim of a bloody bacchanal unleashed by his disdain for female orgies. Certainly the Thracians do not produce perfumes and ointments, but is it also the case that they are unfamiliar with criminal desires and passions? Common sense, well represented by Cornelius Nepos, revolts against this idea: *Thraecas, homines uinolentos rebusque*

---

[23] For a similar contrast between localization and characterization, see Fedeli (1986) 10 ff., who discusses how the modesty of the lady of Ephesus in Petronius is at odds with the connotations of the toponym Ephesus, a seaport associated with loose standards of morality. Some degree of ironic relativizing should be seen also in *Met.* 10.331 ff., where Myrrha envies the fortune of faraway peoples among whom incest is allowed. It is not said what regions these people inhabit, but readers used to the polarities of ancient ethnography would be tempted to answer 'in the Far East'— the only problem is that, with respect to Orpheus, the heroine is already an oriental character.

ueneriis deditos 'Thracians, drunkards addicted to sex' (*Alc.* 11.4). The main episode of the *Metamorphoses* staged in Thrace, the tragedy of Tereus and Philomela, explains the shameful passion of Tereus for his sister-in-law as a typical Thracian phenomenon, linked to the libidinous nature of the entire race (6.458–60):

> Sed et hunc innata libido
> exstimulat, pronumque genus regionibus illis
> in Venerem est: flagrat uitio gentisque suoque.

But inborn lust goaded him too, and the people in those regions are eager for sex: he was on fire with his own wicked impulse and his people's.

The raped Philomela will afterwards say to Tereus, 'you have confused everything' (*omnia turbasti*, 6.537), a standard reproach for incest, suitable to the enormity of the crime. The echo of *regionibus illis* (10.306 with 6.459) undermines the nationalistic emphasis of Orpheus.[24]

One last point remains, valuable for our analysis. The entire context invites us to take Orpheus seriously as the speaker of the 'proem'; this is the only way the text becomes coherent with its implications, i.e., ironical. We often find Ovid dull and superficial because we do not take him literally enough. We should also think seriously about the presence of an audience.[25] There is no longer any reason to believe that 'go away, daughters, go away, fathers', ought to refer to Ovid's audience. But of whom is Orpheus' audience composed? We find basically three categories, well known from the mythical tradition: (a) walking trees (10.88 ff.); (b) animated rocks (11.2); (c) mesmerized animals.[26] Trees and rocks are clearly in no great danger of being led down the path to incest. The case of animals is even

[24] For the proverbial lack of sexual restraint among Thracians, see also *Her.* 5.5; Men. fr. 794 Sandbach. The *Met.* also offers the parallel case of Boreas, featured as an unrestrained rapist of young girls (6.685 ff.), and of Pyreneus, a Thracian king who has the disconcerting goal of raping the Muses (5.269 ff.).

[25] It should not be passed over in silence that also in another of Orpheus' performances, his song that persuades the residents of Hades, the role of the audience is much emphasized (10.40 ff.), much more so than in the corresponding Virgilian model (Segal 1989: 24).

[26] See 10. 143 ff. *inque ferarum | concilio medius turba uolucrumque sedebat*; 11.1 *animosque ferarum*; 11.20 ff. *attonitas ... innumeras uolucres anguesque agmenque ferarum*; 11.42 ff. *auditum saxis intellectumque ferarum | sensibus*.

more symptomatic. In accordance with a known philosophical topos, Myrrha will soon make it clear that incest is the most natural of practices among beasts and birds (10.324–9):[27]

> coeunt animalia nullo
> cetera dilectu, nec habetur turpe iuuencae
> ferre patrem tergo: fit equo sua filia coniunx,
> quasque creauit init pecudes caper; ipsaque, cuius
> semine concepta est, ex illo concipit ales.
> Felices, quibus ista licent!

Other animals mate as they will, and it is not considered base for a heifer to be mounted by her father; his own offspring becomes the horse's mate and the goat penetrates the kids he has sired; and even the birds conceive from the seed that fathered them. Blest are those that have such licence!

Natae and *parentes* are out of the picture here; Orpheus is preaching against incest to an exceptional audience (the only one imaginable with these prerequisites) for whom incest is a natural and legitimate practice. The civilizing mission to which Horace devoted Orpheus—barring human beings from promiscuity and intercourse *more ferarum*—has been displaced by a relentless parody. Orpheus sings to his audience of animals a theme which *to them* cannot possibly be of any harm. (In the very same way, Ovid points out that the *Ars Amatoria* is innocuous and beyond reproach: it is addressed to those who already practise free love, certainly not to upright matrons.)

PYTHAGORAS AND OVID

The example of Orpheus has shown that it is dangerous to neglect the individuality of narratees and internal narrators as well as the specific circumstances attending each narrative act. Before posing questions about the narrating voice of the author, or Single Narrator, one should take seriously, and also very literally, the narrative instance, or level, in which the metadiegetic narrators are positioned. In a poet like Ovid, one should never lose sight of the potential for irony, and

---

[27] Note also 7.386 ff. *cum matre* | ... *concubiturus erat saeuarum more ferarum.*

the metadiegetic structure is precisely the most fitting site, as we have been observing, for these ironic 'dub-overs' of the primary narrator's voice.

This perspective is difficult to reach, however, for those inclined to view internal narrators as possible mouthpieces of the author. A real contradiction exists between an ironic reading, like the one developed here, and the temptation to read 'through' subordinate narrators in search of a genuine authorial voice. I believe a discussion of the episode of Pythagoras (*Met.* 15.60–480) can shed some light on this dichotomy, even if some digression is required in order to discuss it, as well as a slight bending of terminology. After all, Pythagoras is not a narrator, strictly speaking, even if he is in fact an internal narrative voice and, for that matter, among the most important and most fully developed. I am led to choose this field of analysis because Kenney—an important reader of Ovid close to my own point of view, and very interested in the ironic depths of Ovidian narration—selects Pythagoras as the most plausible candidate for the role of direct authorial voice. Pythagoras is the only truly historical character in a poem which otherwise stars gods, demigods, gods 'in waiting' (Aeneas, Romulus, Caesar, and Augustus himself), heroes and legendary characters, or personalities insubstantial to say the least, such as Numa, or the uncanny praetor Cipus with his horns displayed. The content of Pythagoras' doctrine—metempsychosis and the eternal flux of souls—seems to have a definite connection with the main theme of the poem, transformation. The precise modalities of this connection are heavily debated, and rightly so, since the *Metamorphoses* do not seem to me to display a clear integration between mythical and scientific levels, between the realm of transformation tales and that of Pythagorean doctrine. The identity of the speaker and the content of the episode are nonetheless an appealing argument for those who think Pythagoras is voicing Ovid's most deeply held beliefs (Kenney 1986: 460), or even a universal theodicy.

It is also true that Pythagoras could reinforce his role as a mouthpiece, or 'voice-over', since he has a certain aura of being a teacher of truth. Still, the experience we have had with the 'civilizing' Orpheus problematizes this type of credential, to say the least. Moreover, in antiquity—and in Roman culture in particular—Pythagoras' status as a teacher is a highly resisted one. Hence, for example, one of the most visible features of Pythagorean doctrine, namely vegetarianism, in Ovid's time rarely failed to elicit ironic responses. This example is significant, since Ovid's Pythagoras delivers a discourse—although its attendant themes are multiform and often grandiose—written entirely to advance a rather limited and surprisingly modest proposal: 'don't eat meat'. It has been noted, with a certain amount of radicalism, that Pythagoras offers Ovid's readers an eloquent speech *de rerum natura* framed by the precept 'strive for five!'[28] This dietary precept, a subordinate element of the Pythagorean tradition deriving from the desire for radical reform of life, sees its rank and function changed; it becomes the source, end, and didactic goal of *physiologia*. This shift of level might hide an agenda. Those who find in the discourse of Pythagoras the 'deep convictions' of the author do not think, obviously, that Ovid was a fanatical vegetarian. Instead, the fascinating nucleus of Pythagoras' revelation is his image of nature as a universal flux, as well as the instability and transformation that marks both the entire digression and its style of exposition. But these interpreters pay a high price: in order to bring the author's voice to the surface they are forced to disregard the context, and sharply divide the doctrinal nucleus from its bizarre 'vegetarian' framework.

This brings us back to a familiar problem. The search for an authorial voice conflicts with the specific features of the context and with the qualities of the metadiegetic voice. It is fitting again to begin from the narrative context and the problems it poses. Ovid reaches Pythagoras through Numa. It is Numa, his disciple, who introduces us to the world of Croton and Pythagorean doctrine. This connection had been historically discredited in Augustan Age culture, and it is impossible that Ovid was not aware of this fact. On the basis of the chronology that most ancient historians adopt, the disciple Numa was almost two hundred years older than his teacher: 'four generations', as Dionysius of Halicarnassus says, who together with Cicero and Livy is one of the harshest critics of the belief that Numa and

---

[28] [Translators' note: In the US the expression 'strive for five' is a slogan referring to the recommended daily number of servings of vegetables.] Aggressive, but in the end healthy, is the position of Solodow (1988: 164ff). My only reservation is that I do not consider valid any generalizing argument based on the unpopularity, or rather the popularity, of Pythagoreanism in Rome.

Pythagoras were contemporaries.[29] But Ovid makes no attempt to overcome the obstacle; on the contrary, the narrative bridge uniting Numa and Pythagoras is constructed in such a way as to highlight the contradiction. Numa arrives in Croton and asks an old man about the *aition* of the city. He receives a rather intricate answer: the city has an eponymous hero, a guardian hero, and an 'historical' founder. While a guest in ancient Croton, Heracles had foretold the founding of the city; then, in a following, but still ancient, era (cf. 15.20 *illius...aeui*), he compelled a certain Myscelus to cross the sea and colonize that land. Thus, the city's remote history already had many layers by the time of Numa. But Dionysius is particularly sceptical on this point, since in Numa's time Croton did not even exist and its founder Myscelus is connected with a later period. In Ovid, therefore, Numa arrives in a non-existent city and asks about the achievements of someone yet to be born.

This is the framework for Pythagoras' teachings. Numa is temporarily out of the picture, but implicitly present as an auditor, such that at the end of the episode he leaves Croton full of wisdom (15.479 ff. *talibus atque aliis instructum pectora dictis | in patriam remeasse ferunt...*). Meanwhile, the introduction to the didactic discourse offers at least a couple of points of critical tension. Here is how the audience of disciples is described (15.66–8):

> coetusque silentum
> dictaque mirantum magni primordia mundi
> et rerum causas et, quid natura, docebat.

and he would teach the crowds of silent people, wondering at his telling of the beginnings of the great universe, the causes of things and their nature.

---

[29] Dion. Hal. 2.59 ff. (cf. Cic. *Tusc.* 4.1; *Rep.* 2.28; Liv. 1.18.2–3). For the history of the coupling of Numa and Pythagoras and on its decline in the Augustan age, see Gabba (1967) 158 ff. Skutsch (1985: 263 ff.) dismisses the idea (for which Ovid scholars are mostly accountable) that Numa's Pythagoreanism may have had a model in the *Annales* of Ennius. Note also that the other two places in Ovid where Pythagoras is Numa's teacher are rather uncertain. In *Fast.* 3.153 ff. it is explicitly stated that Egeria, Numa's wife, is a source alternative to Pythagoras. In *Pont.* 3.3.44, the account is introduced with *ferunt* 'people say', which gives it a sense of distancing, especially when nothing of this kind is found with the other teacher-student couplings cited in that context (though they too are endowed with little historical weight: Eumolpus | Orpheus, Olympus | Marsyas, Chiron | Achilles).

An attentive and admiring audience is naturally an important acces-
sory for any didactic text. The Pythagoreans, moreover, are famed
for the stress they place upon listening ('acusmatic' is one of their
current labels), upon silence taken as a rule, and upon unconditional
reverence ('as the Master said'). *Coetusque silentum*, placed at the end
of the line, draws immediate attention to itself. It is important for the
pupils to pay attention in hushed silence, but the use of *silentes* as a
noun (as when in general *silentum* falls at the end of the hexameter)
occurs elsewhere in Latin only with the metaphorical meaning 'the
deceased'.[30] We catch a glimpse of the absurd image of Pythagoras
holding class for a gathering of the dead—and indeed, as we have
seen, one of the disciples ought to have been dead for generations.

A second element of surprise arises in the final line of the introduction (15.73–5):

> primus quoque talibus ora
> docta quidem soluit, sed non et credita, uerbis:
> 'parcite, mortales, dapibus temerare nefandis …'

He was the first to open his lips, learned indeed but not believed, in words
such as these: 'Mortals, do not pollute with feasts of sin … '

The framework for didactic communication has very precise, but
simple, rules: one needs only an addressee, and an attempt to persuade him or her. Didactic texts nurture and control the figure of the
recipients, goad them to attention, guide them, anticipate objections,
and counter resistances. The focal point of the discourse, as Lucretius
shows, rests on its credibility, on the capacity of the didactic voice
to make itself understood and to induce belief. I am not referring
to an abstract ideal. Ovid stylizes the entire speech of Pythagoras as
a didactic text, or better yet, with its extreme density of the stylistic
markers for this genre, as a hyperdidactic exhibition (see below). Such
a text focuses on the figure of the addressee and the issue of credibility.
We have seen that Pythagoras has a proper audience (even if there is
room for ambiguity, on which more later). But Ovid points out, at
the last possible moment before ceding the floor to the teacher, that

---

[30] For *silentes* in the sense of 'the dead', see Hor. *Epod.* 5.51; Ov. *Met.* 13.25; Sen.
Med. 740; for the use of *silentum* at line end, see Prop. 3.12.33; Verg. *Aen.* 6.432 ff.:
silentum | consilium (the *silentum* at Mat. 8 Mor. comes from the adjective *silentus*;
this is not clarified by Norden ad *Aen.* 6.432).

all his effort will be in vain: granted, Pythagoras has a *learned* voice, but he is not *believed*. The didactic rules are invoked only to signal their inefficacy and failure.

The notion that Pythagoras' teaching may not work could seem like a merely casual ironic jab, but it is not hard to imagine what is lurking behind the scenes. Lucretius, the great conceptual and stylistic model influencing the whole episode, is a textbook case of 'disbelieved' poetry. The *doctus Lucretius* lavished treasures of science and eloquence without being able to leave a lasting impression on either Memmius or the Roman audience whom Memmius represented. The case of Pythagoras is similar in outcome and style, but antipodal in content. Like Lucretius, Pythagoras too fights against the fear of death, but with opposite arguments. The former's dictum 'the soul is mortal, matter transforms', becomes 'the soul transmigrates and is immortal, all else perishes'. From this point of view, the solemn apostrophes *mortales* (15.75), *genus o mortale* (139 [*genus immortale*, Lachmann!]) sound out of place, if abstinence from meat depends on the idea that *morte carent animae* and *nihil interit*.[31] The concept of fluid universal change is brusquely shifted from matter to spirit. The effectiveness of the new message depends on one's point of view. Many readers of the third book of Lucretius feel that the mortality of the soul is, after all, not a very good antidote for the fear of death. Pythagoras, coming from the opposite direction, can play his hand: it might be that reincarnation is much more effective on this score than Epicurean materialism. On the other hand, Ovid and his readers know that they do not live in a Pythagorean culture; Pythagoras' great efforts, like those of Lucretius, have produced only marginal results and have lost the great battle for a receptive audience.

---

[31] This contrast is due to the fact that the apostrophe to mortals is an outworn and required feature of the repertoire of didactic diatribe. Lucretius had powerfully remotivated the cliché with dramatic effect, when he introduced Nature addressing a man (as Everyman) with the word *mortalis* (3.933). After the poet's long analysis dedicated to death and its dread, the term is stripped of its inertia and becomes the emotional keynote of the entire argument. The use of the apostrophe in the mouth of Pythagoras has an opposite effect: the didactic marker is demotivated by its unsuitability to the context, or else (a more troubling hypothesis), it works to dismantle the logical premises of the context. (Those who believe the seriousness of Pythagoras' consolatory message in Ovid would do well to reflect upon the sarcastic message of the extraterrestrials in Kurt Vonnegut's *Slaughterhouse Five*: 'we will all live forever—no matter how dead we may sometimes seem to be'.)

But there is a pivotal point that still eludes us. The struggle against the fear of death is only a secondary element in the message Ovid relates. The text hammers obstinately—and probably with a loss of seriousness—upon a completely different and much more limited theme. Animals should not be killed for any reason. They should not be eaten nor sacrificed. Even here, naturally enough, Pythagoras' mission anticipates its own failure: Roman society is not a world of vegetarians. But we have lost sight of Numa, whom Ovid presents as the main addressee for the Pythagorean doctrine. Is it possible that Pythagoras' failure affects him too?

We know that Numa, chosen king of Rome, leaves in search of new knowledge; his Sabine heritage was not enough for him (cf. 15.4 ff.). He later leaves Croton suffused with doctrine, returns home and fulfils his mission as a wise and peaceful civilizing king (15.482–4):

coniuge qui felix nympha ducibusque Camenis
sacrificos docuit ritus gentemque feroci
adsuetam bello pacis traduxit ad artes.

Blessed with a nymph for wife and the Muses as guides, he taught the rites of sacrifice and led a race accustomed to fierce war to the arts of peace.

According to the didactic model that Ovid presupposes, Numa has gone from being student to teacher, by putting into practice the teaching he received. One can observe that the mention of Egeria and the Camenae sounds a slightly dissonant note, since in the antiquarian tradition such local influences connected with the lore of archaic Latium are for the most part *alternatives* to the claim for Pythagorean origins. If Numa has been schooled by the nymphs, perhaps there is no need to connect him with Pythagoras; or has there maybe been a fusion of the two cultures? Ovid does not say, but in what Numa does at Rome we find a specific answer: *sacrificos docuit ritus*. This is a solid and incontestable tradition. Numa founded practically all the sacerdotal colleges upon which Roman state religion was based. Without Numa there would be no *Flamines* or Salii, no Vestal Virgins and no Pontifex, no rites of the Argei, no *Agonalia*, no *Fordicidia*, and so on: all the auguries, colleges, rites, and annual festivals bound to and connected with the art of sacrifice that unfolds (like a crimson thread of blood) from the age of kings down to Ovid's own time. In sum, Numa is responsible for the fact that the backbone of Roman religion is animal sacrifice. In *Fasti* 4.652, we see the king at work. He asks, while slitting the throat of two ewes, how to stop a famine, and in thanks for the answer he founds the annual rite of *Fordicidia*. Thirty pregnant cows must be slaughtered each year, drenching the *curia* in blood, and their foetuses are to be extracted by the priests and burned by a Vestal. Ennius' *Annales* provide a good witness for this practice: the first merit of Numa (fr. 114 Skutsch) is *mensas constituit*: 'he instituted the tables of sacrifice'.

Sacrifice is the culmination of Numa's activity as king, but it was also, as we have suggested, the focal point of Pythagorean doctrine as staged by Ovid. The prohibition against killing animals and eating meat culminates in a ban on slaughter for religious and sacral purposes (15.111–12, 116–42; cf. 463–9):

longius inde nefas abiit, et prima putatur
hostia sus meruisse mori . . .

From that wickedness spread further, and it is thought that the pig first deserved to die as a sacrificial victim

quid meruistis, oues . . .
quid meruere boues? . . .
immemor est demum nec frugum munere dignus,
qui potuit . . .
ruricolam mactare suum . . .
nec satis est, quod tale nefas committitur: ipsos
inscripsere deos sceleri numenque supernum
caede laboriferi credunt gaudere iuuenci!
uictima labe carens et praestantissima forma
(nam placuisse nocet) uittis insignia et auro
sistitur ante aras auditque ignara precantem
imponique suae uidet inter cornua fronti,
quas coluit, fruges, percussaque sanguine cultros
inficit in liquida praeuisos forsitan unda.
protinus ereptas uiuenti pectore fibras
inspiciunt mentesque deum scrutantur in illis.
unde (fames homini uetitorum tanta ciborum est!)
audetis uesci, genus o mortale! quod, oro,
ne facite et monitis animos aduertite nostris . . .

What guilt have the sheep...? What guilt have oxen...? How short of
memory and unworthy of the gift of grain is he who could...slaughter his
husbandman...And it is not enough that such crime is committed: they
enrolled the gods in this crime and believe that the powers of heaven take
pleasure in the blood of the labouring bullock! A victim without blemish and
of perfect form (for beauty is his bane), marked off with garlands and gold, is
set before the altar and hears the prayers he does not understand, watches the
grain, which he cultivated, sprinkled upon his brow between his horns, and
then when struck he stains with blood the knife that he saw perhaps reflected
in the clear water. Straightway they tear his entrails from his living breast
and inspect them, and probe the purposes of the gods in them. On this (so
great is humankind's hunger for forbidden food) you dare to feed, you race
of mortals! Do not do this, I beg you, and turn your minds to my words of
warning...

Ovid gives the impression of having done his research on the
Pythagoreans.[32] To give but one example, consider the winged
words with which Pythagoras introduces his cosmological revelation
(15.143–5):

> sequar ora mouentem
> rite deum Delphosque meos ipsumque recludam
> aethera et augustae reserabo oracula mentis...

I will dutifully follow the god who inspires my lips and reveal my Delphi and
heaven itself; I will unlock the oracles of the sublime intellect.

These lines contain a subtle reference to the etymology of the name
Pythagoras, from *puthios* (the Sybil at the Delphic oracle), and
agoreuein ('to proclaim'; cf. *recludam, reserabo*) attested by Aristip-
pus in Diog. Laert. 8.21 (cf. also Lucr. 1.734 ff.; 5.110 ff.). One can
thus infer that the choice of this line of argument is a conscious
restriction, indeed, one which Ovid states explicitly: 'with these and
other...precepts' (*talibus atque aliis...dictis*, 15.479). As usual, the
narrator of the *Metamorphoses* does not hide the fact that the actual

---

[32] The term should be taken in the widest possible sense, to include the entire
growing mass of *pseudo-Pythagorica*, as well as autonomous figures, such as Empedocles and Epicharmus and their Roman successors, who contributed in varying degrees.
The progress of knowledge in this field makes attempts—such as that of Georges
Lafaye—to connect Ovid with specific sources ever more improbable.

narration is the result of a process of selection: his act of storytelling is also an act of suppressing some narrative material.[33]

The result is paradoxical, and it should be appreciated not so much on the level of philosophical implications (as a battle 'for' or 'against' Pythagoreanism), as on the level of communicative form. As already noted above, Pythagoras' speech presents itself as a hyperdidactic text. It contains an unprecedented density of appeals to the reader— 'turn your minds' (*animos aduertite*, 140), 'apply your minds' (*animos adhibete*, 238), 'believe me' (*mihi credite*, 254)[34] —and a varied series of five imperatives and five hortatory subjunctives that emphatically close the entire sequence (473–8). It is marked by typically didactic formulas, such as *nonne uides* (361 and 382),[35] by topics and images used as expository transitions—such as the flight of mind (146 ff.: *magna...canam...*), lifting sails to the wind (176 ff.), horses and the turning post (453 ff.)—and by metalinguistic formulas that direct the discourse within the constraints of didactic communication (172 *doceo*; 174 *uaticinor*, 238 *docebo*). All of the above, together with the insistent usage of the second person, assure the connection not only to a communicative function, but also to the tradition of a literary genre. It is only natural that in this connection Lucretius is given the leading role. The will to overturn the ideology of the *De Rerum Natura* is evident in both the philosophical theme (the immortality of the soul) and in the programmatic choice of the *mirum*. When Pythagoras pursues and catalogues *mirabilia* and *paradoxa*, in the spirit of Pliny the Elder, it is hard not to think that the attitude of Lucretius is diametrically opposed to his own. 'Don't be amazed that', and 'what is so strange about?' are the ligaments of thought and the appeals to the addressee that oppose Lucretian science to eclectic

[33] Ovid is one among those narrators who could be called 'suppressive', because they frequently allow us to perceive that their narratives rest upon a selection of information, and that they do not cover 'everything' that might be said at any given moment of the story. The term 'suppressive' is used in a slightly different sense by Sternberg (1978).

[34] At least for a didactic text of around 400 lines. The process by which the markers of a particular literary style are 'densified' with respect to normal practice corresponds to what we usually call parody. However, as is known, it is not easy to draw a definite line between parody and intertextuality when the quoted text is itself so 'over-coded'.

[35] For the tradition of this peculiarly didactic formula, see Schiesaro (1984) 150. See also *Hal.* 69; in the entire corpus of Ovid there are only three other instances of *nonne*.

curiosity and dilettante polymathy (Conte 1990). With his ideology and mentality overturned, Lucretius is represented solely as a formal constraint and generic model.

On this point, one should understand and interpret the problematic relationship between Pythagoras and Numa as a sudden degeneration of the didactic genre. The lack of real communication between teacher and student undermines the basis of didactic discourse. After having sat in that proverbially attentive audience, Numa returns home and does the exact opposite of the precepts he has received. The leading 'didactic' hero of Roman poetry, Aristaeus in the *Georgics*, was a model of respectful compliance. His obedience to the sacrificial precepts constituted a clear model of successful didactic communication. His willingness to learn, and to translate learning into action, confirmed *sub specie narrationis* is the didactic status of the entire Virgilian poem.[36] To this confirmation Ovid's didactic model opposes an image of frustrated expectation and failure.

We can also offer an exact precedent for the idea of Pythagoras being 'learned but still not believed'. In Callimachus' *Iamb.* 1, the narrator Hipponax tells of Thales, who uses geometric figures 'invented by the Phrygian Euphorbus' (fr. 191.59 ff. Pf.). The context is highly ironic. Hipponax and Thales himself are a little older than Pythagoras, but the difficulty of chronology can be ironed out—with a wink—given that Pythagoras himself claimed to have already lived once, about six hundred years before, as the Trojan hero Euphorbus. Simply call him 'Euphorbus' and Pythagoras can now be the teacher of his predecessors. The discrepancy in time recalls the chronological difficulties involved in the link between Pythagoras and Numa. But Callimachus focuses his attention on the vegetarian message and on its inefficacy (61–2): 'and he taught men to abstain from living things, but they did not obey...' ($κ\mathring{η}δ\acute{\iota}δαξε\ νηστεύειν\ |\ τ\mathring{ω}ν\ \dot{ε}μπνεόντων\cdot\ οἱ\ δ'\ \mathring{α}ρ'\ οὐχ\ ὑπήκουσαν\dots$). Even if only by the working of an adverse

---

[36] The line uniting Aristaeus to the context of the *Georgics* is drawn by Conte (1984) 52: '[Virgil's Aristaeus] is not only the ideal model *of* a person who receives and applies those teachings but also a complete model *for* a person who will receive and apply [the teachings of the *Georgics*] ... the fable of Aristaeus is nothing other than the translation, into the dynamic form of a story, of the literary didacticism that underlies the whole poem and foreshadows its reception.' Like Numa, Aristaeus is a civilizer and an antecedent for religious and sacrificial practice. For an attempt to resolve the contradiction by attributing bloodless sacrifice to Numa, see Plut. *Num.*8.15.

daimon, people did not obey him; just like Ovid's Numa who becomes a wise and peaceful king, but also a slaughterer of animals.

Our discussion of Pythagoras and his addressees might end here, but there is still more to be drawn from that episode of Petronius' *Satyricon*, which too is set in Croton. According to Porphyry (*VP* 18, cf. Dicaearchus fr. 33 Wehrli), as soon as Pythagoras arrives in Croton he is appreciated for his experience and natural talents. His eloquence gains him the sympathy of the elders and he takes an active part in the education of the youth. The elders are pleased that the young converse with him (Isocr. *Busir*. 28). His 'conquest' of Croton finds an interesting counterpart in the analogous successes of Eumolpus in the *Satyricon*. Eumolpus (who has a portentous name, that of the founder of the Eleusinian Mysteries) acquires a reputation for being wise and concerns himself, for personal advantage, with the education of youths. Pythagoras' conquest culminated, as we know, in the victory of precepts such as the immortality of the soul and its corollary, abstinence from meat and from killing animals. Eumolpus, on the contrary, promulgates a will that becomes an invitation to cannibalism. The Crotonians take him seriously, and display their eloquence in demonstrating that anthropophagy is right. Their leader, Gorgias, bears the name of a sophist also renowned for his Pythagorean affiliations. Between these two narratives, one could say, there is a relationship of parodic inversion. But our analysis suggests that in a certain sense Ovid's irony paves the way for Petronius' parody.

The clues collected so far undermine somewhat the traditional idea that Pythagoras is principally a mouthpiece for the author. But we have so far avoided the deepest level of Pythagoras' discourse: that in which the universal principle of change is revealed (*sic omnia uerti | cernimus*, 15.420 ff.). This principle impinges upon the entire world of the *Metamorphoses* and in some sense the narrative style of the poem as well. Perhaps we have encountered, at last, an 'unmediated' voice. The idea that things are in flux is pure Ovid, it is the ideological basis of the poem and the source of the perpetual motion of its style and subject matter. We can grant that here more than elsewhere the figure of Pythagoras becomes transparent, a thin veil between the reader and the subject dearest to the poet. All the more so, since in this eulogy of change and disorder Ovid has nested his grandest prophecy of Roman greatness. The urgency of this theme can explain, according to some scholars, even the genesis of the character of Pythagoras: he is a wise man and a singer of truth introduced at the right moment to combine prophetically the origin of Rome and the triumph of Augustan order.

THE AUGUSTAN VOICE: THE PROPHECY

Thanks to Pythagoras, the *Metamorphoses* crosses paths with Rome as *domina rerum* and the Julian dynasty, and reaches, at last, the *telos* towards which a grand Augustan poem should tend if it wants to be a worthy companion of the *Aeneid*. The notion of a prophetic bridge between remote antiquity and the Augustan present is certainly to be measured against Virgil. Prophecy (through Jove, Anchises, and the shield of Vulcan) is the device by which the epic poet is able to break through into the present. This is also true for Ovid, but with a difference in motivation. The *Metamorphoses* is not bound, like the *Aeneid*, to a chronicle of events more than ten centuries in the past, and its programme (from the origin of the cosmos down to modern times) does not need to resort to prophecy as a *strictly necessary* device. We will return to this problem later on.

Pythagoras, with his universal knowledge and his Delphic connections, might seem the ideal candidate to be mediator of past and future. His chronological situation, more or less halfway between Troy and Rome, is a detail worth bearing in mind. But Ovid's original move is to present Pythagoras' prophecy as an act not of foretelling but of *memory*. The old man from Samos has already heard, as is likely, news about the rise of Rome, but his prophecy is based upon a gaze into the past. He remembers what he has heard said centuries before, in a previous life (15.436–8):

> quantumque recordor,
> dixerat Aeneae, cum res Troiana labaret,
> Priamides Helenus flenti dubioque salutis ...

And, as I recall, when Troy was tottering, Priam's son Helenus said to Aeneas, who was weeping and doubtful of his safety ...

Quantumque recordor is a poignant detail: what makes Pythagoras exceptional in ancient tradition is his prodigious memory, reaching back to previous reincarnations. The name of his father, Mnesarchus (the one who 'remembers his own beginning'), must fit in here somewhere. The best known avatar of Pythagoras is his existence as the Trojan warrior Euphorbus ('Good Food'?).[37] Callimachus, as we have seen, has already toyed a little with the potential for this exchange between different ages. As a former Trojan, Pythagoras is favourable to Rome. His extraordinary memory (160: *nam memini*) gives him access to the era of the Trojan War, and would allow him to remember valuable details. Lucian portrays a cock who, having been Euphorbus (via Pythagoras), transmits previously unpublished details about the Trojan War. But Ovid's Pythagoras possesses a memory that one could call intertextual. His recollection of the war (15.161 ff.) coincides very literally with a scene in the *Iliad* (the death of Euphorbus, *Il.* 17.43 ff.). His punctilious *memini* can be compared with the *memini* of Ariadne in Catullus 64, and with the *memoro* of Mars who recalls Ennius' *Annales*:[38] these are, in the true sense of the word, textual memories.

The prophecy on the future of Rome has an even more sophisticated background. Euphorbus recalls a prophecy that the prophet Helenus had given to Aeneas when the fortunes of Troy were in decline. The memory takes us back to the intersection between the *Iliad* and the *Aeneid*. Euphorbus is a Homeric character, Helenus and Aeneas are carried over into the *Aeneid*, and the prophecy resembles something that Helenus tells Aeneas in *Aeneid* book 3 (starting from the exordium *nate dea...*, 15.439 = *Aen.* 3.374). The nexus between Euphorbus and Helenus is implicitly but very carefully prepared: Helenus is the greatest Trojan augur and a character strictly connected both to Apollo and with Delphi. Euphorbus has very similar affinities, not only through Pythagoras' 'Pythian voice', but also as the son of Panthus, the Trojan priest of Apollo who has Delphic

---

[37] The allegorical function of the two names seems almost inevitable, and it is surprising that this exegesis gained no favour before Skutsch (1959) 114.

[38] The *Iliad* parallels are listed by Ovid commentators ad loc. For the memory of Mars (*Met.* 14.812 ff.; cf. *Fast.* 2.483 ff.), and of Ariadne (*Fast.* 3.469 ff.), see Conte (1986) 57–63.

connections.[39] The link has ironic consequences with respect to the *Aeneid*. If the prophecy can be given so early, we are led to think that Virgil might have dispensed with the entire toilsome quest, with its ambiguous prophecies, misleading clues, and its deferrals from one site to another. Already before the fall of Troy, Aeneas would have known all that he needed and could have taken solace beforehand in the promise of a great kingdom overseas[40] There follows then a more general ironic inference. If Pythagoras' prophetic knowledge turns out to be bookish expertise (accessible to any reader of Homer and Virgil), would one not be allowed to think that every prophecy, almost by definition, is pronounced *after the fact*?

But Pythagoras' historical knowledge is not limited to Troy and Rome. Before he announces the rise of Rome, he has to record the decline of illustrious Greek cities (15.426–31):

clara fuit Sparte; magnae uiguere Mycenae;
nec non et Cecropis, nec non Amphionis arces:
uile solum Sparte est, altae cecidere Mycenae.
Oedipodioniae quid sunt, nisi fabula, Thebae?
quid Pandioniae restant, nisi nomen, Athenae?
nunc quoque Dardaniam fama est consurgere Romam ...

Sparta was famous; great Mycenae flourished, and the citadels of Cecrops and Amphion as well. Sparta is now worthless countryside, lofty Mycenae has fallen. What is the Thebes of Oedipus but a story? What remains of Pandion's Athens but a name? Now too fame has it that Dardanian Rome is rising...

The whole passage, up to the first signs of Rome's greatness, has been since the time of Heinsius highly suspect and considered worthy of deletion (Bömer 1986: ad loc.); the reason being that one gets the sense of a blatant anachronism which clashes with the 'voice' of Pythagoras. The decadence of Greek cities is a typical theme of

[39] On Panthus, see e.g. *Aen.* 2.318 cum Serv. auct. ad loc.; schol. *Il.* [AB] 12.211; [T] 15.521; Pind. *Pae.* 6.74. On Helenus, see *Aen.* 3.359 ff.; Williams ad *Aen.* 3.295; *Il.* 6.76. With regards to the oracle at Delphi, Virgil and Ovid take opposite stands (Paschalis 1986: 47 n. 18).

[40] A similar question arises in the *Aeneid*, when Anchises remembers that Cassandra had already said the right thing, but had not been believed (3.184 ff.: *nunc repeto ... sed quis ... crederet? aut quem tum uates Cassandra moueret?*). In any case, an optimistic prophecy for Aeneas occurs already in Homer, *Il.* 20.302–8, and Creusa is extremely explicit in *Aen.* 2.781 ff.; see also the *Trojan* Sibyl of Tib. 2.5.19 ff.

late-Republican and Augustan sensibilities. In a letter of Sulpicius to Cicero (*Fam.* 4.5.4) one hears the romantic emotions of a Roman traveller on his Grand Tour. His gaze embraces names of flourishing cities of the past, Aegina, Megara, the Piraeus, Corinth; today the educated traveller sees (with some understandable exaggeration) mere ruins. The contrast between extinct grandeur and present ruins is a noble and sober theme of Augustan poetry. Take for example Propertius (naturally in his own voice): 'all things change...even Thebes is destroyed and lofty Troy has ceased to be' (*omnia uertuntur...et Thebae steterant altaque Troia fuit*, 2.8.7–10). But can we allow this point of view in the ancient Pythagoras? If one wants to salvage these lines, not suspect on the matter of style, one should accept the idea of intentional anachronism. Pythagoras, while illustrating the theme of transience, lets himself be carried away, and when he reaches the theme of Rome and Augustus, he speaks in the voice of Ovid.[41] (Two other possible alternatives—namely that Pythagoras in his omniscience might be indifferent to chronology, or that Ovid himself is—seem to me hardly worth consideration.)

But Augustan poetry knows how to regard the theme of transience from more complex, less linear, perspectives. A fine example occurs in Anchises' revelation in *Aeneid* book 6. His is a vision of the future, like that of Pythagoras, culminating with the destiny of Rome. But before this point it touches upon the greatness of the cities of Latium (*Aen.* 6.773–6):

hi tibi Nomentum et Gabios urbemque Fidenam,
hi Collatinas imponent montibus arces,
Pometios Castrumque Inui Bolamque Coramque.
haec tum nomina erunt, nunc sunt sine nomine terrae.

---

[41] Critics usually explain this intrusion of the author as an 'Augustan' commentary. Solodow (1988: 168) thinks, on the contrary, that Ovid's point of view is pessimistic about the destiny of Rome, since *quoque* in line 431 seems to connect strictly the ascent of Rome to the decadence of the other powers. Interestingly, Hollis vacillates between seeing in this passage a deep patriotic impulse (1970: xix), and later, an incidental comment with respect to the poem's structure (1983: 160). One might escape this set of alternatives by dropping the 'authorial' voice and instead taking the narrative situation at face value. Once again, we note that in the *Met.* the 'literal' interpretation, as suggested by the narrative contexts, turns out in the long run to be also the most ironic, relativized, and rich in implications.

They will found Nomentum and Gabii and the city of Fidenae; they will set the citadel of Collatina on the mountains, and Pometii, Castrum Inui, Bola, and Cora. Then they will be famous, now they are lands without name.

At first sight, Anchises is merely foreseeing a development that anticipates the expansion of Rome and paves the way for it. Now—about four centuries before the founding of Rome, according to the chronology accepted and made famous by Virgil—these cities are still to come, they are lands without names. Anchises foretells the names they will have (*haec tum nomina erunt*). But Virgil and his readers already know these names, and they connect them with contemporary reality. Now—in the age of Virgil and Augustus (or of Horace, Strabo, and Lucan)[42]—the cities of Latium in this catalogue are ghost towns, extinct, depopulated, or regressed to countryside, quite often countryside infested with malaria. Speaking of a place of this sort, Horace describes it as more depopulated than Gabii or Fidenae (*Sat.* 1.11.7 ff.). The line of development that Anchises announces is shadowed by the spectre of impermanence. In the readers' own time these cities yet to be named will be *nothing but* names and ancient ruins (*nomina erunt*; cf. *Aen.* 7.412: *nunc magnum manet Ardea nomen*).

This perspective can enrich our understanding of Pythagoras' speech. Paradoxically, Pythagoras more than Anchises has some chronological uncertainties. It is unclear whether Ovid wishes to anchor him to the time of Numa or to the philosopher's own traditional *floruit*. But for our purposes, a difference of a century or two should not cause us too much worry. In this span of time, Rome is growing, we are told, and this is true; and Sparta, Athens, etc., are pure names, ruins, literary topoi. If we read these accounts in context, and not as an aside of the author, a problem arises. Many readers rebel against the idea that Athens, Sparta, and even Thebes, are presented as archaeology. What would Pericles or Epaminondas think of this? But the names of Ovid's characters are very different: Cecrops and Amphion, the remotest founders; Oedipus and Pandion, lords and leaders of Thebes and Athens in mythology and tragedy. These are all characters whom the poem's chronology have long since left behind. The temporal distance is emphasized by heavy epithets like *Oedipodioniae*, *Pandioniae* (both *hapax legomena* in Ovid's works),

---

[42] For the parallels, one should see the subtle reading of Feeney (1986).

their resonance evoking *magni duces* or *tyranni* of the past (to return to Propertius 2.8.9). Pythagoras is speaking, with every right, about the original flourishing of these cities, the only one he could know in accordance with the chronology. The grandeur of Athens under its founding kings goes back a long way in time—back to book 2 of the *Metamorphoses*, in fact, for those who follow Ovid (2.794–5): *Tritonida conspicit arcem | ingeniis opibusque et festa pace uirentem* 'she sees Tritonia's city, thriving with intellects, wealth, and festive peace'. As any cultured Roman knew, a dark and decadent middle age falls between the Greek origins, exalted in myth and literature, and the florescence begun during the Persian wars. In this intervening void (Pythagoras speaks in the golden age of Ionia and Magna Graecia), Athens and the other cities are at the nadir of their fortunes. Thus Pythagoras speaks exactly as a contemporary of Ovid would, unaware that a new cycle of ascent and decline will bring these places to the acme of historical and cultural importance, and then again to the verge of nonentity. His theory of universal flux is truer than he himself could show; it is not liable to verification even by its author.

If we allow the discourse on Greek cities to be joined to the voice of Pythagoras, an interesting consequence emerges concerning Rome.[43] Let us assume that the prophecy of Rome's ascent is only what it claims to be, namely, an extrapolation by Pythagoras, and not an intrusion of Ovid the omnipresent narrator (15.431): *nunc quoque Dardaniam fama est consurgere Romam*. Pythagoras contemplates the decadence of Athens without being able to presage Pericles or Euripides. He foresees (through Homer and Virgil, as we have seen) Rome's trajectory of ascent up to Caesar and Augustus. But then what? How can we be sure? The poet has taught us that prophecies, inasmuch as they are given *ex euentu*, are always inseparable from their end point. In *Fast.* 1.509-36, Ovid ventures into the most interminable prophetic glimpse that any Roman poet ever dared sketch (cf. *Aen.* 8.340 ff.). Carmentis the soothsayer sets foot with Evander upon the soil of the future Rome, and immediately, well before Aeneas in the *Aeneid*, she foretells all that will happen up to the furthest point foreseeable by Ovid. Augustus' successor, son and grandson of a god, will come into

---

[43] On Ovid and the eternity of Rome, Galinsky (1975) 44 and 254 is balanced and convincing.

power, and Livia (whom Carmentis sees as her heir) will ascend to heaven. Ovid, with a touch of cruelty, remarks that from this point on Carmentis can say no more (*Fast.* 1.537–8):

talibus ut dictis nostros descendit in annos
  substitit in medio praescia lingua sono.

When with this words she came down to our years, her prophetic tongue stopped short in the middle of its utterance.

This is truly a sore point for epic prophecy. Poets are able to motivate the prophetic point of departure well enough. Virgil's Jupiter, for example, when forced to address the anxieties of Venus, also takes pains to justify the extraordinary span of his foresight: *fabor enim, quando haec te cura remordet, | longius, et uoluens fatorum arcana mouebo* 'For I will speak at greater length, since this care gnaws at you, and as I unroll the secrets of the fates I shall start' (*Aen.* 1.261 ff.). But this careful narrative justification conceals an inevitable inconsistency: the prophecy has its goal already fixed, and it moves from the narrative present to reach, with a rather suspicious degree of exactness, the present of the author and his text.

The future of Rome beyond Augustus is still a mystery, and the poet of *cuncta fluunt* (15.177) takes no chances on the crucial point of Rome's *eternity*. After Pythagoras has declared that change rules the world, there can be no confidence on this score. Now at last it is the author's turn to speak. At the end of the poem Ovid finally has a direct word, in the voice of the author, and connects, like a well-mannered official poet, the success of his poetry to the greatness of Rome (15.877–9):

quaque patet domitis Romana potentia terris,
ore legar populi, perque omnia saecula fama,
siquid habent ueri uatum praesagia, uiuam.

Where Rome's power extends in conquered lands, I shall be read by the lips of men, and, if the prophecies of bards have any truth, through all the ages in fame I shall live.

The poet expects for himself eternal life and immortal fame—vast fame, because it will be as wide as the universal confines of the Empire. It has been noted, however, that Rome offers only a spatial, geographic measure. Perhaps trained by Pythagoras, Ovid does not link his immortality to the destiny of empires; he does not conflate the dimensions of space and time, nor does he weave together the endurance *per saecula* of his *carmen* with the durability of Rome. He tactfully marks out his difference from the author of the *Carmen Saeculare*, who had identified his own literary glory with the glorious perseverance of Rome.[44]

What Ovid has to say about the *imperium* of Augustus had already been exhausted a little before this point. As in the first book of the *Aeneid*, Jupiter calms Venus in her anxieties with a prophecy about the destiny of the Julian line culminating in the peaceful rule of Augustus. The coincidence has a contrastive effect that deserves emphasis. Through Jupiter's prophecy the *Aeneid*, which narrates a brief span of time during an age already a millennium in the past, is able to reach out and touch the Augustan present. This use of prophecy is clearly a guarantee for Augustus: a story of the distant past which the narrator contorts so as to include the glorification of the present. But the structure of the *Metamorphoses* is diametrically opposed to this point of view. The plan of the poem unfolds from the origin of things down to modern times. Employing Jupiter's prophecy in this programme is a little arbitrary. It is not motivated by the narrative structure out of a lack of other means. The *Metamorphoses* come to a sudden halt with the death of Caesar, and the prophecy, instead of guaranteeing Augustus an otherwise unthinkable presence, ends up rather underlining his *absence* from the poem. The temporal span of the prophecy is in tune with this choice. In the *Aeneid*, Venus hears about the outcome of a millenarian history. But Ovid's Jupiter exerts much less effort: if Venus could be patient for just a couple more years, there would be no need for the prophecy. If the poet had not resolved to end precisely here, a narration of the glory and successes of the Princeps would be unavoidable.

In the *Tristia* (2.560), Ovid chose to represent his poem as a work culminating with Augustus: *in tua deduxi tempora, Caesar, opus* 'to your own time, Caesar, I have brought down my work'. The obvious

---

[44] In truth, Horace's statements about the eternity of Rome need to be evaluated with great care (La Penna 1963: 66–8). But Ovid's omission of any temporal reference in his *sphragis*, written with *Carm.* 3.30 in mind, is surprising, and suggests a conscious choice on Ovid's part (Galinsky 1975).

echo of *Met.* 1.4 reminds us most of all that the proem speaks in a slightly different way: *ad mea ... deducite tempora carmen*. This is a bold move, highly egocentric, which not all translators of the *Metamorphoses* give proper force.[45] When he addresses the Princeps, Ovid describes the plan of his work as 'from origins to Caesar Augustus'. But to his own audience he had already clearly said 'down to *my* times'. Depending on the circumstances, he might have also claimed that Augustus' empire, among all the ages of the universe, is given the *least* consideration in the poem. It is true that the latest event the poem recounts, the death of Caesar (15 March 44 BCE) with his transformation into a star and apotheosis (after July 44 BCE), is an obvious eulogizing concession to Augustus. Ovid could have said, 'from the origins down to your coming'—but he did not do so, and the chronology plays clever tricks. Since he was born on 20 March 43 BCE, Ovid has succeeded in the egotistical endeavour of telling a story from the creation of the world down to his own conception.

In perfect coherence with the poem's thematic system, the concluding event is viewed as a catasterism. The continuous and repetitive structure gives the reader an impression of duplication and seriality. The weight of the authorial voice announcing this new miracle cannot be separated from the work's overall narrative context. This is still the same voice that has led the readers from chaotic beginnings, and the metamorphosis of Caesar cannot be separated from the fabulous fabric of preceding metamorphoses. It is the last and closest, certainly, but the principle regulating it is no different than what transformed the Minyeiades into bats or the Cercopes into monkeys. The aura of incredibility that suffuses the entire poem seems to envelop this final miracle as well. The only difference being that this time, as Ovid warns his readers, at the last moment but firmly, things are a bit different—*we must believe* (15.760–1):

Ne foret hic igitur mortali semine cretus,
ille deus faciendus erat.

So then, that he might not be created of mortal seed, that one must be made a god.

---

[45] e.g. Melville (1986) 1: 'to our modern times'. For an author writing around the end of Augustus' Principate, the closing of a work is problematic; Livy might offer us an instructive point of comparison.

Caesar's transformation into a god in fact conceals a final movement, a metamorphosis not to be told, more serious and terrifying than any other: that which makes Octavian the first being of a species never seen before.

These lines seem to me of the utmost importance for our discussion of the *Metamorphoses'* Augustanism. In fact, a large part of our discussion rests on highly controversial allusions, which moreover will probably remain controversial forever. We are dealing with cases in which Ovid, according to 'anti-Augustan' critics, sends out signals while remaining, so to speak, below deck. These are ironic allusions, disenchanted and defeatist, critical, blasphemous or even subversive, smuggled beneath the fabric of an impeccable courtier's discourse. Supporters of Augustanism observe that these allusions are not necessary for our comprehension of the text, or that Ovid was in no position to afford them. Or even (depending upon their personal attitudes towards Augustus) these critics object that Augustus' power was neither repressive nor totalitarian, and that Ovid had no need to adopt a secret code if he wanted to lead some sort of literary opposition. Interpreters from the opposite camp counter this by objecting that the audience of the time was not monolithic, and that Ovid—under the authoritarian and repressive rule of Augustus—had no choice but to proceed by means of 'a rhetoric of ambiguity and innuendo' (Hinds 1987*b*: 25 ff., see ch. 1 above). 'Augustans' ask the other side for proof, unambiguous expressions to this effect, and receive the answer that the nature of the phenomenon is such that it does not allow for readings that are not ambiguous. The truth is that the question so posed only allows for solutions that are too subjective, both depending on our image of Ovid and, even more, on our image of Augustus and his regime. We are coming dangerously close to the 'circular' controversies opened up by the allusions to the Emperor in Senecan tragedy or, better yet, to the praise of Nero in the *Pharsalia*. Personally, I have tried to read with the eyes of a partisan such verses as Lucan 1.40–2:

ultima funesta concurrant proelia Munda.
his, Caesar, Perusina fames Mutinaeque labores
accedant fatis...

Let the last battle be joined at fatal Munda; and though to these be added the famine of Perusia and the horrors of Mutina...

If we take into account the fact that classical poetry places importance on the position of the vocative in its context, the effect here is striking. It is hard to avoid the impression that Caesar, that is Nero, is one of the disasters listed by the poet, a deadly catastrophe like Munda, Perugia, and Modena. But the effect works only if we look from the start with the eyes of an anti-Neronian partisan. Lucan's own position and the internal history of the *Pharsalia* continue to be uncertain data on which to ground our interpretation.

The phenomenon that we are discussing in Ovid is different. The authorial voice is not sending out encrypted messages or subterranean allusions. There is no subversive sense running between the lines. We would like, on the contrary, to apply to Ovid's voice the prerequisite that has been important in our reading thus far: every narrative expression is to be viewed in context, taking into account the audience, the speaker, and the temporal frame set up by the text.

Ovid is clearly stating—with an extreme clarity that no other Augustan author possesses—a blatantly evident truth. Caesar had to be made a god because Octavian *could not be a mortal* (or even 'for fear that' he was a mortal). This hindsight motivation for Caesar's deification is by no means as absurd as it seems to some modern critics.[46] In the terms imposed by Augustan propaganda, Caesar is precisely the projection of his son. His apotheosis comes from the future, not from the origin, as was the case in the obvious parallels of Heracles and Romulus (cf. *Fast.* 2.144). Augustus moulds Caesar into a 'double' of himself. The two characters are mirror images: they bear the same name (a fact obscured by our modern habits of onomastics, and a source of problems for Virgilian critics), and they are modelled upon one another in official iconography, at first the young upon the old, but then vice versa (Zanker 1989: 180). Let us imagine a modern historian called upon to re-evaluate Caesar's position in Augustan

---

[46] e.g. Hinds (1987*b*, ch. 1 above) 26, in a different train of thought. For a surreal version of the same theme, cf. instead Prop. 4.6.60: *sum deus; est nostri sanguinis ista fides*. Caesar, looking upon the victory at Actium, finds self-affirmation of his own divinity. Cairns (1984: 167) appropriately reminds us that an offspring can confer retrospective glory on his ancestors. But his proposal of reading *sum deus* as a formula for epiphany has no connection with Propertius' text, in which Caesar is not appearing to anyone. If one accepts *sum deus* (instead of a *facilior* emendation such as *tu deus*) it must be admitted that Propertius is playing with Augustan propaganda, and is pushing to its breaking point the machinery of retroactive deification.

ideology and literature. It is likely that her analysis, disenchanted, distanced, endowed with complex tools, would arrive at one crucial point: Caesar is important (and continues to be so) as the father of Octavian Augustus. His role as model for the Principate can be, for various reasons, problematic or exposed to winds of hostility, but his function is essential and permanent. The main reason for this delicate function is among the simplest, and has more to do with biology than with ideology: *Augustus too will die someday*. If he does not want his power to be revocable, it has to rest upon some form of continuity, and only the continuity of a family can ensure the permanence of the regime. In this sense, the idea that Augustus is the first and only example of a new species has its own dangers. The key to this continuity, in religious and ideological terms, is the expectation of Augustus' apotheosis. But this is an expectation that must be prepared for, cultivated even with a kind of pedagogy. Augustus' chosen mode for this preparation is to exploit the exemplary role of an analogous past event. The apotheosis of Caesar, the sign of Octavian's victory in the Civil Wars, is the symbolic threshold for the transfer of power, but also—a very significant point—the pledge and anticipatory reflex of what awaits the Romans when Augustus begins to wane.[47] Our modern historian could not but agree with Ovid: Caesar has been made a god because Augustus cannot be mortal.

This is why it is not correct to interpret Caesar's apotheosis as a relic of the early Augustan Age, an outworn legacy left to Ovid by Virgil and Horace. Too many Ovidian scholars view the end of the *Metamorphoses* as a triumph of rhetoric, of courtier language severed from all reality.[48] In particular, it is easy to put one's finger on certain themes that seem to 'show up late', because our literary-historical

[47] A glimpse into iconographic propaganda (Zanker 1989: 39, 180, 206, 235 ff.) shows that the presence of the *sidus Iulium* is strictly linked to a dynastic point of view. On an ideal diagram the high points would coincide with the Civil Wars (particularly up to Naulochus) and, after a dormant period, with the politics of adoption. The star reappears in order to shine on the young princes, Gaius and Lucius Caesar.

[48] An exception is Galinsky (1975) 258 ff., who is clear-minded and precise in comparing Ovid with Horace and Virgil, but in my view does not go far enough in accepting the 'realistic' implication of Ovid's position. Galinsky considers the rhetorical feel of the praise of Augustus to be justified and inevitable, for the reason that formulas grow old and are hard to update. But leaders grow old as well, and the problem of succession for Augustus casts a shadow over the entire finale of the *Met.* (a poem where persistent tensions between order and chaos, repression and disorder

categories associate them with other seasons and other situations. Caesar's apotheosis feels more natural in the context of the difficult years between the rise of Octavian and the battle of Actium. What then was a symbol of crisis, unrest within a void of power, and with messianic expectations, appears now as an empty compliment. But things are not exactly this simple. Around 8 CE, the problem of what happens when a leader dies is more urgent than ever. Similarly, the wish that the Princeps will not tire of the earth (15.868–70):

tarda sit illa dies et nostro serior aeuo,
qua caput Augustum, quem temperat, orbe relicto
accedat caelo faueatque precantibus absens!

Slow to come may that day be and later than our time, when Augustus' soul, leaving the world that he rules, comes to heaven and favours our prayers from afar.

To many this sounds empty and rhetorical. It seems particularly so in comparison with Virgil's *Georgics*, and with Horace in his first civil lyrics:

serus in caelum redeas diuque
laetus intersis populo Quirini ... (Hor. *Carm.* 1.2.45 ff.)

late may you return to heaven and long may you remain happily among the people of Quirinus

tuque adeo, quem mox quae sint habitura deorum
concilia incertum est ... (*Georg.* 1.24–5)

Yes, and you, whom it is still unclear which councils of the gods will include ...

hunc saltem euerso iuuenem succurrere saeclo
ne prohibete! ... (*Georg.* 1.500 ff.)

At least do not prevent this young man from coming to the aid of this ruined age ...

iam pridem nobis caeli te regia, Caesar,
inuidet ... (*Georg.* 1.503–4)

run from one end to the other, and the whole is pervaded by a sharp and objective perception of power relations and of hierarchies).

For a long time heaven's palace has begrudged us you, Caesar . . .

But the confrontation is unavoidable, and Ovid himself has antic-ipated it. Many years have passed, and the fashion of calling the Princeps *iuuenis* would now sound ridiculous. Horace's lyrics and Virgil's *Georgics* were addressing their passionate appeal 'don't leave us!' to a leader in his early thirties. The *Metamorphoses*, on the other hand, is written for an audience familiar with these poets, but who can also not ignore the fact that Augustus is now over seventy.[49] For this audience, the civil rhetoric of the first Augustan poets posed an insidious question. Before taking his leave, Ovid reminds us that a new transformation is inevitable, and it too will have to be faced.

---

[49] In *Met.* 12.542 ff., Nestor begins his speech with the famous topos of *renouare dolorem*: '*quid me meminisse malorum | cogis*'. He tells of an event in his early youth, and the reader cannot avoid the feeling that the narrator is over two hundred years old, and thus there is no chance, like Aeneas in Carthage, that he will reopen a wound still fresh. So too, in our passage, the reader is forced to notice that the topos '*serus in caelum redeas*' fits the actual age of Augustus *all too well*.

14

Pyramus and Thisbe in Cyprus

Peter E. Knox

In 1962 excavations of an extensive villa at Nea Paphos on Cyprus unearthed figured mosaic pavements of remarkably high quality. In the largest room of the villa a pavement was found portraying the 'Triumph of Dionysus,' showing the god crowned with ivy, riding in a chariot drawn by panthers and flanked by Pan, maenads, satyrs, and musicians; from this representation the villa, now known as the 'House of Dionysus,' derives its name (Nikolaou 1963 and 1966; Karageorghis 1963*a* and 1963*b*). The mosaics of this building have been attributed to the second or third century AD on stylistic grounds, and surely antedate the earthquakes of AD 332 and 342 that levelled the site. The pavement of the portico on the west side of the peristyle of the villa contains four panels which depict less familiar scenes from mythology, revealing something perhaps of the esoteric tastes of the villa's owner: Pyramus and Thisbe; Dionysus, Acme, Icarius, and the first wine drinkers; Poseidon and Amymone; Daphne and Apollo. Although the discovery has been well reported, the mosaics of the 'House of Dionysus' have yet to be fully published as a group, and individual scenes still require the attention of scholars.[1] In particular, the first panel of this mythological sequence, identified as the story of Pyramus and Thisbe by inscriptions above the two figures, stands

---

[1] Some scenes have become very well known; cf. Vermeule (1976) 95 n. 19: 'The Paphos mosaic of Pyramus and Thisbe ... best known from a color postcard sold all over the island.' I am grateful to my colleague, Alan Cameron, for sending me a sample. Since the first appearance of this article, these mosaics have received a detailed examination in Kondoleon (1995).

in need of fuller explanation than it has yet received. The myth that it represents is rarely attested in art or literature, and the form that it takes on this panel is extraordinary.

The mosaic (fig. 14.1) brings together separate elements of the story without combining them to provide a realistic representation of a single scene. Thisbe is depicted fleeing left, with a leopardess portrayed on a higher plane in the centre background holding Thisbe's veil in its jaws. Pyramus occupies the lower right-hand corner of the panel, where he reclines in the pose of a river god. Most discussions of this mosaic assume as background the most familiar form of the story, as it was first recounted by Ovid in the fourth book of the *Metamorphoses* (55–166).[2] No earlier narrative survives, and all later references to the story in Latin literature clearly rely upon Ovid, deriving from his account the familiar elements of the tale: the secret tryst between the young lovers at the tomb of Ninus, Thisbe's encounter with a lioness, and the mangled veil that convinces a tardy Pyramus that his beloved is dead.[3] It is highly unlikely, however, that any knowledge of Ovid's *Metamorphoses* can be attributed either to the craftsman who executed this panel or to the patron who commissioned it. Latin literature was little known in the East and did not much interest the Greeks, few of whom, even among the elite, acquired more than a smattering of the language for legal or administrative purposes (Marrou 1956: 255–64). In particular, there is no evidence of familiarity with Ovid's *Metamorphoses* before the thirteenth century (Maas 1935: 385).[4] A pictorial representation of a scene from Ovid's poem discovered in the East would therefore represent a striking discovery.

---

[2] e.g., Eliades (1982: 22–4), who retells Ovid's version, then describes Pyramus' representation as a river god without noticing the contradiction. Cf. too Vermeule (1976) 104.

[3] Of the references to the story in Latin literature, only Serv. Auct. on *Ecl.* 6.22, a summary of Ovid's account, provides any details. Other references suggest only the briefest acquaintance with the myth: Hyg. *Fab.* 242 includes Pyramus in a list of suicides (*Pyramus in Babylonia ob amorem Thisbes ipse se occidit*); *Anth. Lat.* 61 ShB is a muddled couplet confusing Thisbe with Themisto; *Anth. Lat.* 715.7 R contains a vague allusion to the origins of the colour of the mulberry tree; likewise, Ser. Samm. 548 (= *Poetae Latini Minores* 3.132 Baehrens) simply refers to the mulberry as *Pyramea arbor*. A badly preserved Greek inscription from Ostia of imperial date is the only other evidence for the story in the West: *IG* 14.930.12 οὐ φιλία Θίσβης καί Π[υράμου.

[4] The question of whether Nonnus knew Ovid is still open, although it now appears more likely that he did not: cf. Knox (1988).

Figure 14.1. Pyramus and Thisbe, 'House of Dionysus': Nea Paphos, Cyprus. (Courtesy of the Department of Antiquities, Cyprus Museum.)

But there are significant variations from Ovid's outline of the story reflected in the iconography of the Paphian mosaic which preclude direct acquaintance with Ovid's narrative. First, the setting of the mosaic has none of the topographical detail of the scene in the *Metamorphoses* (4.88–90):

conueniant ad busta Nini lateantque sub umbra
arboris: arbor ibi niueis uberrima pomis,
ardua morus, erat, gelido contermina fonti.

They were to meet at Ninus' tomb and hide in the shade of a tree. A tree was there, hanging full with snow-white berries, a tall mulberry, adjacent to a cool spring.

Two particularly distinctive landmarks described by Ovid are not portrayed in the Paphian mosaic: the tomb of Ninus (4.88) and the spring (4.90); but more significant is the omission of the third, the mulberry tree in the shade of which the two were to meet. It has been suggested that the mulberry tree is indeed represented on the rock behind Thisbe (Vermeule 1976: 104), but comparison with other mosaics in the House of Dionysus reveals this unimposing shrub as a standard landscape motif from the mosaicist's copybook. The absence of this element is a certain indication that the mosaicist was working without knowledge of Ovid's account: the role of the mulberry tree as meeting place and its transformation from white to red, stained by the blood of the young lovers, constitute the distinguishing features of Ovid's tale. Further, Ovid's narrative can in no way be reconciled with the representation of Pyramus in the mosaic: here, he plays no role in the drama and is portrayed instead as a river god, reclining on an overturned urn, facing right with a reed in his left hand, a cornucopia in his right, and his hair entwined with reeds. This aspect of the mosaic clearly represents a variant version of the myth which concludes with the metamorphosis of Pyramus and Thisbe into a river and a spring respectively. This metamorphosis is attested only in Greek sources, which have long been thought to bear little or no relationship to the Ovidian account. But an examination of this evidence may yield some information about the origin of the myth and the form in which Ovid and the artist who executed the Paphian mosaic found it.

References to the story of Pyramus and Thisbe in Greek literature are lamentably few and late. In contrast with the references in
Latin literature, which all derive from Ovid, they invariably identify the story with the Cilician river Pyramus; however, no Greek
author provides a full narrative of the events. The only reference
to the myth in Greek poetry occurs in the sixth book of Nonnus'
Dionysiaka, where he relates how Zeus extinguished the worldwide
conflagration that followed the death of Zagreus by unleashing a
flood of equal proportions. In the confusion of rivers attendant
upon the flood Alpheus addresses the river Pyramus (Nonn. *D.*
6.347–55):

Pyramos, why this haste? You have left your comrade Thisbe—to whom?
Happy Euphrates! He has not felt the sting of Love. Jealousy and fear possess
me together. Perhaps Cronos' watery son has slept with lovely Arethusa! I fear
he may have wooed your Thisbe in his flowings! Pyramos is a consolation
for Alpheios. The rain of Zeus has not stirred us so much as the arrow of the
Foamborn. Follow me the lover, I will seek the tracks of Syracusan Arethusa,
and do you, Pyramos, hunt for Thisbe.

That the background to this dialogue is a story of metamorphosis
is indicated by Nonnus in a later book, where he includes Pyramus
and Thisbe among the metamorphoses viewed by one of the Horae
in the tablets of Harmonia (*D.* 12.84–5): 'Thisbe shall be running
water along with Pyramos, both of an age, each desiring the other'.
We learn nothing from Nonnus about the details of the story, but on
the evidence of these two passages O. Immisch assumed that the story
referred to here constituted a parallel to the relationship of Alpheus
with Arethusa in Sicily, and further postulated that there was a spring
called Thisbe in Cyprus.[5] But there is no evidence for a spring of this
name on Cyprus (Duke 1971: 321), and in fact other references to
the story adduced by Immisch suggest a spring in close proximity to
the river. The fourth-century rhetor Himerius is quite explicit on this
point (*Or.* 1.11):

---

[5] Roscher(1884–1937) 3.3336–40 s.v. 'Pyramos und Thisbe.' For Cyprus as the
location of this spring Immisch adduces Strabo 536, where an oracle is quoted referring to the silting at the mouth of the river Pyramus: ἔσσεται ἐσσομένοις, ὅτε Πύραμος
ἀργυροδίνης | ἠιόνα προχέων ἱερὴν ἐς Κύπρον ἵκηται (= *Orac. Sibyl.* 4.97). See too G.
Türk, *Paulys Real-Encyclopädie* (hereafter *RE*) 6A.286–7 s.v, 'Thisbe,' who adopts the
interpretation of Immisch.

To the neighbouring river Marriage grants his neighbour Thisbe, whom he changes from a girl into water; and he watches over their love even to the springs, drawing together the streams of the groom and his beloved.

It is impossible to draw any conclusions about the location of the spring or the details of the story from the nearly contemporary reference to Thisbe by Themistius, which was adduced by Immisch in support of his hypothesis of an underground affair (*Or.* 11.151c–d, p. 180 Dind.): 'and you would call Peirene useless, and Thisbe; and you would say that in loving Arethusa, Alpheus brought trouble on himself in vain.' Although Alpheus and Arethusa are also mentioned by Themistius in the same context as Thisbe, the rhetorical structure of the phrase seems to associate her name more closely with Peirene, said to have produced the spring that bears her name by her tears of mourning for the death of her son (Paus. 2.3.2). Immisch' s 'Alpheus variant' is a ghost; all that can be concluded from these texts is that in a story associated with the Cilician river of the same name, Pyramus and Thisbe were paired as faithful lovers and transformed into streams.

The mosaicist who executed the Pyramus and Thisbe panel at Paphos, it thus appears, incorporated some details known to us separately from Ovid and Nonnus: a secret tryst, a chance encounter with a leopardess, the torn veil, and subsequent suicide and metamorphosis. The question then arises whether this sequence represents the prevalent form of the myth in the Greek East, which was followed by the mosaicist. A story which in its main outlines resembled Ovid's but concluded with the metamorphosis of the protagonists instead of the transformation of the mulberry tree would be consistent with virtually all references to Pyramus and Thisbe in Greek literature. An isolated divergence is found in the *Progymnasmata* attributed to Nicolaus of Myra, which, even if it is not authentic,[6] probably constitutes the latest independent witness to the story of Pyramus and Thisbe. It forms part of a series of twelve *diegeseis*

---

[6] Now ascribed to Aphthonius (or an imitator), whose views they reflect, these *Progymnasmata* conflict at several points with theories certainly attributed to Nicolaus; see W. Stegemann, *RE* 17.451–7.

from mythology not otherwise marked by acuteness or learning (*Rhet.Gr.* 1.271 Walz):[7]

Thisbe and Pyramus developed an equal passion for each other, so they fell in love and had intercourse. When the girl became pregnant, she tried to conceal the infant and killed herself, while the young man undertook the same fate when he found out. The gods were moved to pity by the event and changed both of them into water. Pyramus became the river that flows through Cilicia, while Thisbe became a spring with its outlet by him.

Although there is no evidence to suggest that the version reported here antedates either Ovid or the Paphian mosaic, the possibility cannot be ruled out; but when the tragic accident that led to the double suicide of the lovers is eliminated the metamorphosis is deprived of real motivation. The story appears rather to have undergone major adjustments. Moreover, the context in which Nicolaus records this summary, *exempla* from myth to be used in declamations, suggests that it represents a substantially later reduction of the story within the rhetorical tradition, emphasizing the social aspects of the lovers' behaviour rather than the aetiological aspect of the myth.

It has long been known that a local variant of the story of Pyramus and Thisbe circulated in the vicinity of Cilicia; the possibility that the Paphian mosaic represents independent testimony to this tradition ought therefore to be seriously entertained. It would then appear that in its broad outlines this local myth resembled the account in Ovid's *Metamorphoses* a great deal more than had been thought. A final obstacle to this interpretation is the possibility, recently raised by I. Baldassarre, that while the mosaicist may not have been familiar with Ovid, he may have known representations of Ovid's account in art and simply conflated elements of the story from an iconographical tradition deriving ultimately from Ovid (1981: 346).[8] While it

---

[7] The author of this treatise usually draws his material at second hand from earlier rhetorical tracts: cf. Jacobs (1890) *passim* for examples of parallel phrasing in earlier rhetorical texts. See too W. Stegemann, *RE* 17.448–9.

[8] The only attempt thus far to account for the apparent discrepancies in the mosaic: 'the mosaicist has unconsciously inserted here an element apparently drawn from the iconography of the Ovidian tale: the lioness, which is here a leopard instead.' The same interpretation is adopted without argument by Balty (1982) 419 n. 470. Both

cannot be ruled entirely out of account, this appears a very unlikely explanation. The only illustrations of the myth surviving from Antiquity are a series of related wall paintings from Pompeii, all apparently derived from the same model and clearly depicting the account described by Ovid. Unlike the mosaic, these paintings depict a single moment in the story, Thisbe kneeling over the dying Pyramus. In the accompanying example from the *Casa di Lucrezio Frontone* (fig. 14.2)[9] several characteristic details of Ovid's version are clearly depicted: the tomb of Ninus on the left, the mulberry tree which dominates the scene of the suicide, and the lioness moving off in the background.[10] No single element of this scheme is reproduced in the Paphian mosaic, which draws on different artistic conventions with a strong regional association. Antioch has been suggested as the home of the master craftsman who produced this panel,[11] a suggestion which offers many attractions. Indeed, two mosaics depicting Pyramus as a river god had been discovered previously at Antioch. In one of these mosaics, two corner medallions of an original four representing rivers surround a central panel in which only one female figure, representing Cilicia, is preserved from what was certainly a larger group. The figures in the two medallions are identified by lettering as Pyramus, portrayed as a beardless youth, and Tigris (Levi 1947: 57–9, pl. 9 b–d). A mosaic in another house contains four busts of rivers and streams, identified by lettering as Alpheus, Arethusa, Pyramus,

---

Baldassarre and Balty would limit the borrowing to the figure of the leopardess, since the figures of both Thisbe and Pyramus are of obvious eastern inspiration. But the pose of Thisbe, in flight, presupposes a version of the story with the lioness/leopardess and cannot be segregated from it.

[9] For this painting, see Herrmann and Bruckmann (1906) 225–6, pl. 162(a), who argue convincingly for direct dependence on Ovid; cf. also Rizzo (1929) 64, pl. 134.

[10] Three other paintings from Pompeii represent the same scene: Napoli, Mus. Nazionale, inv. no. 111483 (cf. Herrmann and Bruckmann 1906: pl. l62(b); *Casa di Ottavio Quartione* (cf. Spinazzola (1953) 404–5, fig. 458); and an unpublished painting from the *Casa della 'Venere in bikini'* (Baldassarre 1981: 349, fig. 3). In addition, another much later painting, which also seems to be derived from this composition, was discovered in the necropolis of the Isola Sacra (Calza 1940: 117, pl. 49).

[11] Vermeule (1976) 104 compares an *emblema* from the 'House of the Boat of Psyches' at Antioch with the Paphos Pyramus and Thisbe, and suggests an Antiochene origin for the workshop that created this panel.

Figure 14.2. Pyramus and Thisbe, 'Casa di Lucrezio Frontone': Pompeii. (After Rizzo.)

and Thisbe (fig. 14.3).[12] This mosaic is perhaps the only surviving representation of the transformed Thisbe.

---

[12] See Levi (1947) 109–10, pl. 18 a–d. Had this mosaic been known to Immisch, it would certainly have been adduced as evidence for his 'Alpheus variant.' Both Antioch mosaics are dated to the late second or early third century AD. It is surely not a coincidence that the story of Pyramus and Thisbe is also referred to in pseudo-Clementinus, *Recognitiones* 10.26 p. 234 Gersdorf: *Thysben apud Ciliciam in fontem et Pyramum inibi in fluuium.* The original Greek version, now lost, was perhaps composed in Antioch; cf. B. Rehm, *RAC* 3.198.

Figure 14.3. Alpheus, Arethusa, Thisbe, and Pyramus, 'House of the Porticoes': Antioch. (After Levi.)

Figure 14.3. *Continued.*

The identification of Pyramus as a young river god clearly had strong regional associations, a situation which is also reflected in the coinage of Cilicia. Pyramus appears as early as the first century BC on the reverse of coins minted at Hierapolis-Kastabala,[13] certain evidence that the personified river-god enjoyed a life before Ovid. Pyramus continues to be represented on the coinage of Hierapolis and other cities in Cilicia during the imperial period.[14] The two most common poses portray the river god swimming or reclining, as in the Paphian mosaic, his left arm resting on an overturned urn, and holding a river reed (Imhoof-Blumer 1924: 183). But there is a rare type represented only by two coins of the early third century AD from Mopsus,[15] which includes with the reclining Pyramus a female figure seated before him on the left (fig. 14.4). This figure, nude to the waist, perhaps represents a nymph, whose identity invites speculation, although only one scholar has made the plausible guess that she might be Thisbe (Duke 1971: 321).[16] With such evidence for an abundant local iconographical tradition the hypothesis of an Italian import appears even less likely.[17]

It is profitless to engage in prolonged speculation about Ovid's source: he may have found this pair of lovers in a mythographical compendium,[18] but we may never know for certain. The Paphian mosaic, which seems to have eluded the notice of Ovid's

[13] Cf. *Sylloge Nummorum Graecorum* (hereafter *SNG*) *Levante Cilicia* 1569–70; *A catalogue of the Greek Coins in the British Museum* (hereafter *BMC*) *Cilicia* p. 82, no. 2.

[14] For Hierapolis-Kastabala cf. *SNG Levante Cilicia* 1585, 1597, 1599; *BMC Cilicia* p. 83, no. 5; for Anazarbus cf. *SNG Levante Cilicia* 1388–9, 1394, 1396, 1405, 1437; *BMC Cilicia* p. 35, no. 22; for Mopsus cf. *SNG Levante Cilicia* 1319, 1330, 1346, 1348, 1352, 1359; for Flaviupolis cf. *SNG Levante Cilicia* 1550.

[15] *SNG Levante Cilicia* 1346, dated AD 216/17, and *BMC Cilicia* p. 107, no. 21, dated AD 219/20. For the rarity of this type see von Aulock (1963) 238.

[16] His other speculations, however, including the identification of Thisbe with Atargatis, are far less persuasive.

[17] The panel of Apollo and Daphne, also found in the 'House of Dionysus,' is a similar case. As Vermeule (1976: 109) notes, it has nothing in common with representations of the story at Pompeii, for which see Reinach (1922) 26 ff., nos. 2–7. The myth had strong local associations in Asia Minor (Levi 1947: 211–12), where it developed its own iconographical conventions.

[18] For this familiar hypothesis see Bömer (1976) 33: 'einer sonst unbekannten hellenistischen Sammlung vorderasiatischer Erzählungen verdankt.' Cf. Castiglioni (1906) 262; Vollgraff (1909) 138–9; Perdrizet (1932) 193–5; Wilkinson (1955) 203–4.

Figure 14.4. Pyramus and a female figure: reverse, *BMC Cilicia* 21. (© Copyright the Trustees of the British Museum.)

commentators, opens the possibility that Ovid learned of a local Cilician myth which he adapted to his own purposes.[19] In the *Metamorphoses* Pyramus and Thisbe have been transported to Babylon, but the earliest form of the story clearly belongs where the names are at home and must be identified with the metamorphosis of the two protagonists into the streams that bear their names. Ovid's reasons for

[19] The mosaic was not known to Bömer, although he does register the suspicion (1976: 34) that a Hellenistic narrative not unlike Ovid's was associated with this river. It is perhaps worth recalling at this point that the *Suda* includes among the works of Callimachus a treatise Περὶ τῶν ἐν τῇ οἰκουμένῃ ποταμῶν.

shifting the locale are clearly related to his rejection of the metamorphosis of the Cilician version in favour of the transformed mulberry tree, which he has taken from an unknown source: *uulgaris fabula non est*, 'the story is not commonly known'(*Met.* 4.53). Nonetheless, it is possible that Ovid alludes to the metamorphosis of the local myth when he describes Thisbe's reaction to the sight of Pyramus lying near death (*Met.* 4.134–6):

> retroque pedem tulit, oraque buxo
> pallidiora gerens exhorruit aequoris instar,
> quod tremit, exigua cum summum stringitur aura.

she started back and, paler than boxwood, shivered like the surface of the sea, which trembles when it is ruffled by a light breeze.

Such innovation is characteristic of Ovid in the *Metamorphoses*. In retelling the story of the two young lovers whose carefully planned tryst ended so tragically, Ovid has introduced a different conclusion. But for the learned reader familiar with the version not followed, Ovid's comparison of the trembling Thisbe to the surface of water disturbed by the breeze must surely have provoked a smile.

15

Form in Motion: Weaving the Text in the *Metamorphoses*

Gianpiero Rosati

> The role of the hand in production has become more modest, and the place it filled in storytelling lies waste. (W. Benjamin)

The thread of my discussion unwinds across two episodes of the *Metamorphoses*, the opposition of the Minyeids to the cult of Bacchus in the fourth book, and the competition between Arachne and Minerva in the sixth. They share the theme of conflict between gods and mortals (the mortals refuse to recognize the superiority of the gods, leading inevitably to divine punishment of hubris), and at the level of narrative structure, in each case Ovid employs the technique of *mise en abyme* (in the first case by metadiegesis, that is the 'tale within a tale' with internal narrators; in the second case, by ecphrasis, the description of the tapestries woven by the two contenders). But my immediate reason for considering the two episodes is that they are also connected by the detailed description of two techniques which are closely linked, or better of two phases of the same process, namely the spinning and weaving of wool. It is well known that in the Greek and Latin languages and cultures (and also in other Indo-European and non-Indo-European languages and cultures) the semantic field of spinning and weaving provides a large reservoir of metaphors for concepts associated with poetic writing and composition (Durante 1976: 173–5). My concern is with Ovid's use of this field of imagery, and with the way in which literal and metaphorical senses overlap

and interfere with each other. The *Metamorphoses* as a history of the
world, and therefore also of civilization, tells us something about the
history of language, about its figurativeness and its traps, about its
metamorphosis.

The tendency to expose the ambiguities of language, to discover the
proper sense behind a figure and restore it to its literal sense in order
to show the paradoxes to which it can give rise, or to reconstruct the
aetiology of a metaphor, is abundantly active within the poem: often
the metamorphosis itself is nothing but a metaphor in narrative form
(telling a metamorphosis, says Barkan (1986: 23), 'is to make flesh
of metaphors'),[1] the tale that explains the origins of an idiom. For
example, at 1.450 *in frondem crines, in ramos bracchia crescunt* ('her
hair grows into leaves, her arms into branches'), in the description of
how Daphne changes herself to laurel, the metamorphosis only serves
to 'realize' the widespread metaphors according to which the leaves of
a tree are its hair and the branches are its arms.

But now let us take a closer look at the first of the two episodes,
the section of the fourth book which narrates the hostility of the
daughters of Minyas, the king of Orchomenus in Boeotia, towards
the new cult of Bacchus, to which they oppose the veneration of Minerva. While all the women of the city are occupied with the orgiastic
rituals of Bacchus, they, in the privacy of their own home, scorn
those *commenta sacra* ('feigned rites', 37) and dedicate themselves to
the feminine arts patronized by Minerva, that is to say, to spinning
and weaving. To kill time, the Minyeids decide to accompany their
work by telling each other stories (39–41 *utile opus manuum uario
sermone leuemus | perque uices aliquid, quod tempora longa uideri | non
sinat, in medium uacuas referamus ad aures*, 'let us lighten our useful
handiwork with varied conversation, and let us take it in turns to
tell a tale for idle ears that will make the time seem to go quickly').
Ovid thus takes up the old theme, going back to Homer's Circe, of
the spinners who sing their stories while they work, and employs it
as a framing scene in which to set the erotic tales of this section. In
line with a general technique of the poem, he keeps active a semantic
relationship between the framing scene (the hostility towards the cult
of Bacchus) and the stories that are framed within it (for example, the

---

[1] But cf. already Pianezzola (1979).

words of Salmacis to Hermaphroditus at 4.320–1 *puer o dignissime
credi* | *esse deus* ('O boy most worthy to be believed a god') clearly
suggest, behind the erotic topos, a reminder of the storytellers' disbelief in the divine nature of Bacchus, the *puer aeternus* ('eternal boy',
4.18)), but Ovid is above all concerned to activate the relationship
between the two functions of the spinners/storytellers, the action of
spinning-and-weaving and the simultaneous action of storytelling.

   Already in Catullus 64 the Parcae accompany their work as spinners with their song of the destiny of Achilles: in the emphasized
simultaneity of the two processes has been noted the intention to
suggest a connection 'between speaking and weaving', in keeping
with a widespread 'interest in weaving and textiles . . . throughout the
poem' (Laird 1993: 28).[2] But, above all, Virgil, in the scene setting of
the Aristaeus episode in *Georgics* 4, had created a situation similar
to Ovid's: at the centre is seated Cyrene, the mother of Aristaeus,
and around her, like so many maids around the *mater familias*, the
nymphs spin the precious and widely renowned Milesian wool, while
one of their number, Clymene, recounts charming tales of love, the
loves of gods, beginning with the primitive chaos, and including the
affair of Venus and Mars made famous by Homer (*Geo.* 4.333–4,
345–9):

. . . eam circum Milesia uellera Nymphae
carpebant hyali saturo fucata colore . . .
inter quas curam Clymene narrabat inanem
Volcani, Martisque dolos et dulcia furta,
aque Chao densos diuum numerabat amores.
carmine quo captae dum fusis mollia pensa
deuoluunt . . .

Around her the Nymphs carded the Milesian fleeces, dyed with the rich hue
of glass . . . Among whom Clymene told of Vulcan's futile care and the tricks
and stolen joys of Mars, and listed the crowds of divine loves since Chaos.
While the nymphs, captivated by the song, twist down the soft coils with
their spindles . . .

   [2] In Seneca's *Apocol.* (4.1.1 ff.) instead it is Apollo who accompanies the Parcae's
work with his song (15–17; there is a 'contamination' of functions at v. 4, where Lach-
esis is crowned with Pierian laurel, i.e. is similar to a poet). In Ovid it is noteworthy
that at *Ibis* 241–6 (Hinds 1999: 63–4) the spinning Fate turns the job over to the poet,
to his poetic spinning of Ibis' destiny.

Scholars continue to argue over the meaning and function of the scene: 'it is not clear why these nymphs are engaged in wool-working' confesses R. Thomas (1988: ad 334–5). But if we reflect on the precious Alexandrian character of the scene—the catalogue of nymphs is followed at 363–73 by a catalogue of rivers, and it is well known that Callimachus wrote works on both nymphs and rivers (Thomas 1988: 207)—the connection between spinning the valuable Milesian wool and the seductive (*captae*) tales of erotic adventures of the gods, between the *mollia pensa* and the *dulcia furta* (which in the sequence of the Virgilian text are a prelude to the Aristaeus-Orpheus epyllion) may appear less obscure.[3] Further it is well known that Clymene's tale, which unfolds as the nymphs spin, is a sketch of the Ovidian *Metamorphoses* (*a ... Chao densos diuum ... amores*); from this perspective the analogy between Virgil's programme and Ovid's Minyeids episode becomes clearer: to the analogous framing situation (tales accompanying spinning) corresponds at the centre of the episode, in the mouth of Leuconoe, the story of the 'stolen joys' of Mars and Venus (171–89) which acts as a prelude to the loves of the Sun.[4] The episode of the Minyeids thus seems to develop what the Virgilian text merely adumbrates as a subject of Clymene's song of the nymphs; the hint of a possible poetic programme to tantalize the reader, but left on the margins of the georgic poem as it moves past the incipient erotic epyllion towards its proper conclusion. Ovid takes up the Virgilian invitation and in the *chansons de toile* of the Minyeids offers his reader a fuller version of that programme, but at the same time also develops and makes explicit the relationship between the simultaneous actions of spinning/weaving and narrating. A relationship that is very likely implicit in Virgil himself: suffice it to recall that the metaphor of poetic weaving is used transparently (as Servius already noted) in the closing image of the *Eclogues* (10.70–1): *haec sat erit, diuae, uestrum cecinisse poetam, | dum sedet et gracili fiscellam texit hibisco*, 'this will

---

[3] We may also think of 'Milesian tales' to go with the Milesian wool, risqué erotic stories.

[4] Note also that Clymene, etymologically connected with *fama*, is one of the Sun's lovers at 4.204; there may be another allusion to the model in the description of Leucothoe, who spins in the midst of twelve maids (4.220), the same number as the nymphs who surround Cyrene (*Geo.* 4.334 ff.).

be enough, goddesses, for your poet to have sung, while he sits and
weaves a basket from slender mallow' (Pöschl 1964: 12).

   Unlike the Virgilian nymphs in the *Georgics* (where the sole narrator is Clymene who does not herself spin, while her twelve listening
companions do), the Minyeids unite the two functions of spinners
and narrators; further, they do not limit themselves to the task of
spinning (*deducere filum*), but bring to completion the entire process
(*aut ducunt lanas aut stamina pollice uersant | aut haerent telae*... | *e
quibus una leui deducens pollice filum*... , 'they either draw out the
wool, or spin the threads with their thumbs, or concentrate on the
loom... one of them, drawing down the thread with a light touch of
the thumb, ...' 4.34–6): first they tend to carding the wool, then they
spin it and then they attend to weaving at the loom, thus completing
the entire process from the unrefined wool to the finished cloth. The
ascription of this double function to the three sisters highlights the
parallelism between the two actions, the simultaneous processes of
spinning/weaving and narrating; Ovid emphasizes the simultaneity
in the case of the first, anonymous sister, who after a long hesitation
in her choice of subject, sets out to narrate the story of Pyramus and
Thisbe (53–4):

hoc placet; haec, quoniam uulgaris fabula non est,
talibus orsa modis lana sua fila sequente

She decides on this; since this is no vulgar tale, *she begins in this way, as the
wools follows her threads.*

The unwinding of the *fila* of wool suggests the simultaneous unwinding of the narrative thread. The tale of Alcithoe is introduced with a
similar hesitation over subject matter, also with recourse to the technique of *praeteritio* (in this instance spoken by the narrator herself,
rather than related in indirect discourse), and in Alcithoe's case likewise attention is drawn to the simultaneity of the actions of weaving
and narrating (274–6):

poscitur Alcithoe, postquam siluere sorores.
quae *radio stantis percurrens stamina telae*
'uulgatos taceo' *dixit* 'pastoris amores...'

Alcithoe is called upon, after her sisters fell silent. As she *ran the shuttle through the threads of the loom standing before her* 'I pass over the well-known loves of the shepherd', *she said.*

The parallelism between the 'running' of Alcithoe's words (remembering that Alcithoe means 'swift, fast-racing', 'vigorous in the race')[5] and the 'running' of the shuttle, which in its continuous coming and going grafts the threads of the weft upon those of the warp, suggests the idea of the narrative text as *textus*, as the interlacing of a vertical and a horizontal series of threads, like a shuttling between weft and warp.

Even the structure of the episode, the 'fabric' of the framed narratives, may tell us something: within the overall framework of the opposition of the Minyeids to the cult of Bacchus and their ensuing metamorphosis (32–415), are inserted, in perfectly symmetrical arrangement, the consecutive tales performed by the three sisters (these tales occupy the space between an introduction (32–54) and an epilogue of comparable length (389–41)). The tale of the first, anonymous sister (Pyramus and Thisbe: 55–166, i.e. 112 lines) is balanced by the tale of the third sister, Alcithoe (Hermaphroditus: 276–388, i.e. 113 lines); between these two panels is set the tale of Leuconoe on the loves of the Sun (which is barely shorter (169–270, i.e. 102 lines) but with a more complex narrative articulation). This series of three tales, told by the three narrators, is punctuated by two brief connecting passages (167–8 and 271–5) which, on the 'vertical' axis, the *ordo* of the narration controlled by the narrator (that is the frame reaching from 32 to 415), permit the 'horizontal' insertion of the three interlaced narrative voices which graft the weft onto the warp.

The image of the narrative 'fabric' woven by the three sisters, who match the action of spinning and weaving to the action of narrating, is suggested in the words of the proposal made by the first narrator to the others: *utile opus manuum uario sermone leuemus* ('let us lighten our useful handiwork with varied conversation' 39); the ancients were conscious that *sermo* comes from *sero*, 'to link together, interlace' (Varro, *Ling.* 6.64), as demonstrated by the common etymological figure *sermonem serere* (Brink 1971: ad Hor. *Ars* 46). Note further that the idea of narrative 'fabric' is repeated at each of the junctions of the

---

[5] Cf. Gildenhard and Zissos (1999) 45–6 on the name of Ocyrhoe.

text, in its 'knots', each time that one of the three storytellers takes up
the narrating, in other words at the points where the weft is grafted
on to the warp: at line 54 the first sister begins the tale of Pyramus
and Thisbe with *talibus orsa modis*; *orsa est dicere* introduces the tale
of Leuconoe at 167–8; while at 275 Alcithoe begins to narrate *radio
stantis percurrens stamina telae*. The epicism *orsa est* is, moreover, rare
in the *Metamorphoses*, and it is noteworthy that with the exception of
5.300 (referring suitably to a Muse), two of the other three instances
occur in the episode of the Minyeids, and the third within the episode
of Arachne (6.28), both contexts in which the theme of weaving is
central. The literal sense of *ordior* is 'lay the warp of a web, begin
weaving' (Blümner 1872: i. 144);[6] although the metaphor is usually
a faded one, the original sense of *ordiri* when used of 'composing'
a speech or text is often reactivated (e.g. Plin. *Nat.* 25.132 *singulis
corporum morbis remedia subtexemus, orsi a capite*, 'we will add (lit.
'weave as an appendage') the remedies for the individual diseases of
bodies, beginning from the top of the list'). The metaphorical use
of *ordiri* of literary texts is often exploited in later Latin poetry: for
example in Ausonius (*Technop.* praef.): *ludicrum opusculum texui,
ordiri maiuscula solitus* ('I have woven a playful little work, although
I am used to setting about larger projects'), or Venantius Fortunatus
(*Carm.* 5.6.7, in the preface of a figured poem): *ut ordiretur una tela
simul poesis et pictura* ('so that at the same time both poem and
picture should begin on the same loom').[7]

It is common knowledge that the linked metaphors of spinning and
weaving are among the most widely diffused in the Greek and Latin
vocabulary for literary activities, and there is no need to compile an
exhaustive list. Homer already uses the image of 'weaving thoughts
and words' (*Iliad* 3.212) to refer to a conceptually elaborate and
rhetorically effective speech (Scheid and Svenbro 1996: 112 ff.), but
it is above all in Greek lyric poetry that the image of 'weaving poetry'
is widely found (Snyder 1981). It is here that is born one of the most
widespread metaphors of everyday language, one no longer noticed

---

[6] Cf. Plin. *Nat.* 11.22 *struunt* (sc. *apes*) *exorsae a concameratione alui textumque
uelut a summa tela deducunt*; 11.80 the spider *orditur telas*.

[7] The same is true for *exordium* and for *ordo*, a term of wide application in literary
contexts, especially in narrative texts: e.g. Ov. *Met.* 5.335; 7.520; 9.5; 14.473; and esp.
15.249 *idemque retexitur ordo*.

as metaphor, a dead metaphor, the metaphor of *textus*, text as textile. There are many examples from Pindar and Bacchylides, through to the 'woven tale' (μῦθον ὑφαινόμενον) of Callimachus (fr. 26.5 Pf.). Besides the specific image of weaving (ὑφαίνω), that of interlacing (πλέκειν, καταπλέκειν) also appears in Pindar to express the idea of the elaborated composition, of the art of placing words together; while μυθόπλοκος is the epithet attributed by Sappho to Eros (fr. 188 V.).

In Latin the most common image for writing poetry is *deducere (carmen)*, drawn as is well known from the technique of spinning (Eisenhut 1961; Deremetz 1995: 289ff); the most famous example is in the programmatic proem of the sixth *Eclogue*, where Apollo dissuades the poet Virgil from singing of epic *reges et proelia* ('kings and battles'), and exhorts him instead to a *tenuis* ('slender'), less ambitious poetic genre (4–5 *pastorem, Tityre, pinguis | pascere oportet ouis, deductum dicere carmen*, 'Tityrus, the shepherd should fatten up his sheep, but sing a slender song.'). Servius comments ad loc.: *translatio a lana, quae deducitur in tenuitatem* ('the metaphor is from wool, which is spun out into a fine thread'). The action of *deducere filum* (in Greek κατάγειν τὸν στήμονα) consists of drawing down the thread from the mass of carded wool, which is wrapped around the distaff (*colus*); the spinner then draws it, giving it form by the twisting and the pressure of the fingers, and wrapping it on the spindle. Thus from the shapeless mass of the fibre the patient and accurate spinner extracts something, the thread, which has form and continuity, and constitutes the necessary material for the *tela*, the fabric, the end product of the entire process.

In rhetorical terms one could say that spinning corresponds to the *inuentio* ('invention, devising'), weaving to the *dispositio* ('arrangement') and *elocutio* ('style'). Cicero glosses *inuentio* as *argumentationum expolitio* ('elaboration of arguments', *Inv.* 1.78), while *dispositio* is closely connected with *ordo* (on which see below): *dispositio est rerum inuentarum in ordinem distributio* ('arrangement is the putting in order of the matter that has been devised') says Cicero himself (ibid. 1.9; cf. *Rhet. Her.* 1.3, 3.16), and according to Quintilian *dispositio* is nothing but *rerum ordine quam optimo conlocatio* ('the placing of the subject matter in the best possible order', *Inst.* 3.3.8). Even *elocutio* is connected to *ordo* (Quint. *Inst.* 3.3.9; cf. *TLL* v ii. 399.83–400.2), but more often it is discussed in terms of *orna-menta* (Cic. *Inv.* 2.49; *TLL* v ii.399.75 ff.). Quintilian compares it to a variegated cloth: *illa translucida et uersicolor quorundam elocutio res ipsas effeminat quae illo uerborum habitu uestiuntur* ('that translucent and iridescent style of some authors renders effeminate the subject matter that is cloaked in that verbal costume', *Inst.* 8 pr. 20); it can display the fascinating iridescence of a beautiful cloth, precisely what Ovid admires in the tapestries of Arachne and Minerva (*Met.* 6.63– 6 *qualis ab imbre solet percussis solibus arcus* | *inficere ingenti longum curuamine caelum;* | *in quo diuersi niteant cum mille colores,* | *transitus ipse tamen spectantia lumina fallit,* 'just like the rainbow, when rain strikes sunlight, that stains the wide sky with a huge bow; although a thousand different colours shine in it, the transition from one to the other deceives the onlooker's eye'). In short, an imagery of clothing provides a wide semantic field for a rhetoric of literary discourse.[8]

The author of *On the sublime* (15.5) speaks of 'unworked ideas, all woolly, as it were, and tangled' (πoκoειδεῖs ... καὶ ἀμαλάκτουs); this concept Latin commonly expresses with *rudis*, a term of wide literary-critical application: *rudis* can refer to the unelaborated arte-fact, the unrefined work of art, but also frequently to an unfinished or unpolished poetic work (according to Festus, p. 322 L. *rudis* applies to *omnis fere materia non deformata, sicut uestimentum rude, non perpolitum,* 'almost any material that has not been given shape, such as a rough-spun, unfinished garment'), and is used especially of wool that has not yet been spun nor carded (Ov. *Her.* 3.78; *Met.* 6.19). The first operation on unrefined wool is that of carding (*carpere, trahere,* or the poetic *mollire;* Blümner 1872: i. 108–12); this is the operation of *carminare* (Isid. *Orig.* 1.39.4 *lanam, quam purgantes discerpunt, carminare dicimus,* '*carminare* is the word we use of wool that is cleaned and pulled apart'), performed with the tool known as a *carmen,* which allows the moistening of the wool and its preparation

---

[8] Cf. e.g. Petr. 118.1 *ut quisque uersum pedibus instruxit sensumque teneriore uer-borum ambitu intexuit,* and 5 *praeterea curandum est ne sententiae emineant extra corpus orationis expressae, sed intexto uestibus colore niteant,* but also 2 *controuersiam sententiolis uibrantibus pictam.* Cf. also the use of '*πέπλοs*' as a title of literary works (Lyne 1978: 109), and note the famous proem of the *Ciris,* where the poet wants to weave a *peplos* poem (*te... magno intexens... peplo,* 18–21) with the deeds of his addressee.

for spinning (it is curious that Uguccione of Pisa, a lexicographer of the twelfth century, in his *Deriuationes* glosses *carminare* as *carmina facere* 'make poems').

The metaphor of *deducere carmen* seems to take root in the Augustan age to denote both the elaboration of light, refined poetry (in opposition to ambitious and high-sounding genres: cf. above all the proem of the sixth *Eclogue*), and the composition of poetry in general;[9] even more frequently *deducere carmen* refers to the composition of narrative texts. This sense is easy to understand: if on the one hand the image of spinning, as a careful task, implies the idea of a precise, meticulous, and refined task (frequently noted is the *leuitas* ('lightness') of the thumb that handles the wool), on the other hand the length of the thread that flows from the spinner's hands suggests the idea of continuity and extension, of a product that is progressively given substance as long as the labour is continued. The notion of sequence is particularly appropriate for epic and narrative poetry, as in Statius' proposal at the beginning of the *Achilleid* (1.7) to *tota iuuenem deducere Troia* ('to lead the youth through the whole tale of Troy'), where Statius alludes to Ovid's request to the gods in the proem of the *Metamorphoses* to *deducere* a *carmen perpetuum* ('spin out a continuous song', 1.4).

Metaphors derived from the crafts of spinning and weaving are, in sum, ancient and widespread in literary contexts;[10] an entire semantic field is constructed around the idea of the text (written or verbal) as an interlacement, as *textus*.[11] For the most part it is clear that we are dealing with largely dead metaphors; but it is not uncommon (as we

---

[9] Besides the many Horatian and Propertian examples, cf. Ov. *Trist.* 1.1.39; even in Hor. *Epist.* 2.1.225 *tenui deducta poemata filo*, it is the epithet, *tenui*, that qualifies the refinement of the poetry, while *deducta* simply indicates the composition.

[10] A special interest in weaving, doubtless connected with its metaphorical potential, has been suggested in Callimachus by Thomas (1983) 106–11.

[11] One must therefore correct Gorni (1979: 21), who speaks of 'realizzazioni sporadiche e affatto individuali' of that metaphor in the ancient world, and indicates instead its zenith at the origins of the Romance literatures. Scheid and Svenbro (1996), on the contrary, rightly point out the pervasiveness of the imagery of weaving in the Greek and Roman world: but their interpretation of this cultural 'myth' (built on the idea of 'conjugation' between opposite principles: and thus totally disregarding spinning) is in my opinion very debatable (and sometimes it is based on false arguments: e.g. at Catull. 64.334 *contexit* has nothing to do with weaving ('has woven', 104), but comes from *contego*). Cf. also Deremetz (1995) 51 ff. and *passim*.

have seen) for authors to take the opportunity of rediscovering and
reviving such metaphors. Cicero, for example, often uses the image of
weaving of the construction of a speech, and sometimes clearly does
it with a view to revitalize the metaphor, as at *De orat.* 2.145 *pertexe
modo..., Antoni, quod exorsus est* ('finish weaving..., Antony, what
he has started'); 158 *ante exorsa et potius detexta prope retexantur,*
'let what has been started, or rather woven to the end, be unravelled'
(Fantham 1972: 159–60).[12] A yet more striking example from a Latin
writer fond of etymologies and of reviving dead metaphors occurs
in Apuleius, when Psyche's sisters plot her ruin (*Met.* 5.16.5): *exordio
sermonis huius quam concolores fallacias adtexamus* ('let us weave on
to the exordium of our speech tricks of as similar a hue as possible').[13]
(In this case it is the faded metaphor of weaving plots that is revived.)

However, Ovid goes beyond the simple 'rediscovery' of metaphor
that we can observe in many authors: in the Minyeids episode he
wishes not only to revive a dead metaphor, but also to illustrate its
aition and give it a narrative form. The *Metamorphoses* is in its way a
history of the world and of civilization (there is no hint at spinning
or weaving in the poem up to this point), and it contains a series of
foundation myths, not only of external reality, but also of language,
of figurative language. The Minyeids episode is thus an illustration
of the metaphor of *deducere carmen* (1.4), of the correspondence
between the thread of continuous narration and the thread which
flows uninterruptedly from the hands of the spinner; but it is also
an illustration of the metaphor of *textus*, of the text as weaving. The
process which parallels the Minyeids' narration extends from carding
the wool to spinning and weaving, the elaboration of a raw and
shapeless material into an artistically refined product. The reader is
asked to follow the analogies that run between the two simultaneous
processes, to see how the arts of spinning/weaving and poetic writing
are both an exercise in patience, in meticulousness, in lightness and in
exactness of detail. The episode is a fable about the art of narration as
weaving, on the analogies between two techniques, of such a kind as

---

[12] Cf. also *Pro Cael.* 18 *contexere... carmen.* Cf. Lucr. 1.418 (= 6.42) *pertexere dictis*; in Quintilian cf. e.g. *dicendi textum tenue* (9.4.17) and the doubly metaphorical
connection *sermonis contextus* (8.2.14; 3.38; 6.22; 10.7.13).

[13] Kenney (1990) puts it well ad loc.: 'their metaphor exploits the literal and figurative senses of *exordium, concolor* and *adtexo*' (but, I would add, also of *sermo*).

to give life to several metaphors in the literary-critical lexicon which originate in the textile crafts. In the Minyeids episode we have one of the archetypal scenes of storytelling.

I perceive a similar intention in the story of Arachne, another 'metaphor' of the metaphor of writing poetry. The metamorphosis into a spider of Arachne, the weaver so skilled as to appear not inferior to Minerva, is the dramatization of a whole repertory of images which associate the art of making poetry with the meticulous and refined art of the spider. The spider is the animal which *pede... gracili... deducit... filum* ('spins out a thread with its slender foot', Ov. *Am.* 1.14.7; cf. Plin. *Nat.* 11.83 *subitque pariter ac fila deducit*, 'it approaches at the same time and spins out threads'), which arouses astonishment and admiration at the refinement of the web it weaves (Catull. 68.49 *tenuem texens... telam*, 'weaving a slender web'; Plin. *Nat.* 11.80 *tam tereti filo et tam aequali deducit stamina*, 'it spins out the filaments with such a smooth and even thread'). Arachne, first in the narrator's description of her skill (6.18–23) and then in the tapestry produced by her fingers (which will become the spider's *exiles digiti*, 'thin fingers', 142), gives us an essay of refined art, of Alexandrian aesthetics (the Callimachean implications in the reference to *Liuor* at 129 are also clear: Hofmann (1986) 233, Harries (1990) 75). In the case of Arachne, as in that of the Minyeids, the entire process of working wool, from carding (19–21) to spinning (22), to weaving (23 and esp. 54–69), is described; but in this case the admiration of the narrator, as well as of the people who run to see the spectacle of her skill, relates to the *tenuitas*, the grace and refinement of the cloth that flows from Arachne's hands (*Met.* 6.17–23; 53–60):

nec factas solum uestes, spectare iuuabat
tum quoque, cum fierent: tantus decor adfuit arti,
siue *rudem* primos lanam glomerabat in orbes,
seu digitis subigebat opus repetitaque longo
uellera *mollibat* nebulas aequantia tractu,
siue *leui teretem* uersabat pollice fusum,
seu pingebat acu; scires a Pallade *doctam*...
haud mora, constituunt diuersis partibus ambae
et *gracili* geminas intendunt stamine telas:
tela iugo uincta est, stamen secernit harundo,

inseritur medium radiis subtemen acutis,
quod digiti expediunt, atque inter stamina ductum
percusso pauiunt insecti pectine dentes.
utraque festinant cinctaeque ad pectora uestes
bracchia *docta* mouent, studio fallente laborem.

Not only did they delight in looking at the finished robes, but also in watching them being made (such charm her art held), whether she was first gathering the *raw* wool into balls, or whether she was working it with her fingers and through repeated pulling *made* the pieces of wool as *soft* as cloud, or whether she turned the *smooth* spindle with her *light* thumb, or whether she was embroidering with her needle; you would know that she had been *taught* by Pallas... Without delay, they each take up their different positions and stretch the *slender* thread of their two warps; the warp is attached to the cross-beam, a rod separates the threads, and the weft is drawn through the middle with sharp shuttles, sped by their fingers, and when it is drawn through the warp the comb's teeth tap it and press it down. Both hurry and, their dresses tied up round their breasts, they move their *skilled* arms, as their eagerness beguiles their toil.

The activities of Arachne-*aranea* and the poet are associated through the metaphor of spinning/weaving; terms such as *tenuis*, 'slender' (62 *tenues parui discriminis umbrae*, 'slender shades difficult to tell apart'; 127 *tenui circumdata limbo*, 'surrounded by a slender border', in the 'author's signature' on her tapestry), *gracilis*, 'thin' (54), *leuis*, 'light' (22), *mollis*, 'soft' (21) are well-known Latin equivalents of the Callimachean aesthetics of λεπτότης, and from the same area comes the verb which points out the skill in telling an ancient story (69 *et uetus in tela deducitur argumentum*, 'an old subject is spun out on the web'). In Arachne's story Ovid does not limit himself to realizing an inert 'all-pervading identification of weaving with poetic composition' (Harries 1990: 74), but returns the metaphorical field of λεπτότης to its distant origins, which, as E. Reitzenstein (1931: 25–40) demonstrated, are to be located in the terminology within the linguistic sphere of textile craft (as well as, it appears, the Latin equivalent *tenuis*).

The Ovidian story of Arachne is thus the most complete narrative illustration of the metaphor of *textus*, indeed the *aition* of the metaphor itself. The story shows how from the clever weaver-artist is born, once and for all, the spider; but also how, from the spider, from its exemplary skill, the metaphor of spinning and weaving a text is born; the spider's activity thus becomes the emblem of *gracili conectere carmina filo* ('binding together songs with a slender thread', Colum. 10.227), of the refinement necessary for poetic composition. But as well as the art of refinement and lightness, the spider's art is also the art of patience and meticulousness (Front. *Laudes neglegentiae*, p. 219.6–8 van den Hout 'spiders are more diligent in weaving than any Penelope or Andromache'), and perhaps the most *docta* and admired art in the whole animal world (Sen. *Epist.* 121.22–3; Sauvage 1970: 270 n. 7). The spider's web is, in fact, an emblem of perfection in the weaver's art: ἔργον ἀραχνάων is how Callimachus describes the fine cloth of a cloak (*Hec.* 42.6 H.); and Plutarch affirms that a spider's web, admirable for its refined thread, is a model of perfection for the weavers themselves (*Mor.* 966e); according to Democritus, it is the spider that taught mankind to weave.

Ovid did not invent the story of Arachne, but it was he who out of that story created a foundation myth for the metaphor of poetic spinning/weaving, and for the connected image which associates the poet with the spider. It is not certain that this image was current in Greek culture, but it is probable, if we recognize the metapoetic value of Theocritus 16.96–7 (see below), and of Philostratus, *Imagines* 2.28 (Bryson 1994: 266 ff.; cf. also Plut. *Mor.* 358f). At all events there is an emphatic example of it in the programmatic proem of the author of the *Culex* (1–4):

Lusimus, Octaui, *gracili* modulante Thalia
atque ut araneoli *tenuem* formauimus *orsum*;
lusimus: haec propter culicis sint carmina docta,
omnis et historiae per ludum consonet *ordo*.

We have sported, Octavius, while my *slim* Muse made music, and like spiders we have shaped a *slender web*; we have sported: on this account may the song of the gnat be a learned one, and may the whole *thread* of my story sound harmoniously in my sport.

A metaphorical web of absolutely prodigious skill that the poet-spider interweaves in this proem, and certainly the most appropriate as a programme to trap a *culex*, a gnat. But if the author of the *Culex* can present himself as the poet-spider, he can do so, above all, thanks to

Ovid,[14] who had illustrated the metaphor in narrative form, and re-
endowed its metaphorical field, by then worn and inert, with a new
vitality, rediscovering its origins and its motivations.

I shall not here analyse at length the structural, aesthetic, and
ideological motivations of the two tapestries, which have already been
widely discussed. The episode of the artistic competition between
Minerva and Arachne is also, like the singing contest between the
Muses and the Pierides in the fifth book and the sequence of stories told by the Minyeids in the fourth, an essay on the relativism
of the work of art, and on the techniques used by the author to
affirm his ideology. In the aggressive anti-theological polemics which
inspire her tapestry, Arachne weaves a sarcastic representation of the
unrestrained eroticism of the gods at the expense of innocent mortal
women—a subject surely distasteful for a goddess whose chastity is
proverbial; above all, she does not forgo the recording of the rape of
Medusa by Neptune (6.119–20): and the reader knows, because he
has read it in the fourth book (798 ff.), that the rape had occurred in
a temple of Minerva herself, provoking her indignation: it is evident
that Arachne wants to offend the goddess by mentioning an episode
which is particularly odious to her.

The episode of Arachne and Minerva is, in short, an essay on narrative technique, a discourse on the partiality and ideology of the point
of view of the producer of a text. Moreover it is, as it is well known,
a fable about the problematic relationship between artist and power
(a fable which ironically acts as a sinister omen for the fate of Ovid
himself), on the brutality with which power exercises its authority
over the artist's ambitions for autonomy. Minerva, the *belli metuenda
uirago* ('fearsome maiden of war', 2.765) who likes to represent herself
with all her military attributes (*at sibi dat clipeum, dat acutae cus-
pidis hastam,* | *dat galeam capiti; defenditur aegide pectus*, 'she gives
herself a shield, a sharp-pointed spear, a helmet for her head; her
breast is protected by the aegis', 6.78–9), rends the masterpiece of
her competitor (I am tempted to see in *caelestia crimina*, 'a reproach
against the gods', of 6.131 also a comment of the narrator on the

---

[14] It therefore seems false to say that 'it was our poet [sc. the author of the *Culex*],
with no little wit, who put together for the first time the finest of spinners, the spider,
and the Callimachean-neoteric concept of the finely spun (*deductum*) poem' (Ross
1975a: 252), a view echoed by Zetzel (1996) 78.

gesture of the goddess). Minerva strikes Arachne on the forehead, the symbol of her pride and of her intelligence, the seat of her competence as an artist (note the relevance of *Idmonia*, from the root of 'know', at 6.133, the epithet which highlights the special feature of Arachne's personality), and condemns her and her offspring to weave delicate cobwebs exposed to the outrage and the destructive violence of power. The spider is a peaceful animal ('this creature loves to weave its web in quiet', Philostr. *Im.* 2.28.24–5), which weaves its *leue opus* ('light work', Ov. *Am.* 1.14.8) in tranquil and isolated places (*deserta sub trabe*, 'under a deserted beam'); and the image of the spider's web woven on weapons (an ancient image, already present in Bacchylides but known above all from Theocritus 16.96–7 'and as for the weapons of war, [I pray] may spiders weave over them their slender webs, and of the war cry the very name be forgotten') may be seen as the symbol of the Arachne's revenge on Minerva, of the secular rights of art over the authoritarian rights of power.

If the artistic competition between Arachne and Minerva is, as we know, 'an allegorical complement' to that between the Pierides and the Muses in the fifth book (Harries 1990: 64), it is also a complement to the Minyeids episode in the fourth book. Just as the Minyeids episode illustrates the metaphor of *deducere carmen* in its 'narrative' sense, the Arachne episode illustrates that same metaphor in its Callimachean sense (as the *deductum … carmen* of the sixth *Eclogue*), that is, as refined, *tenuis*, poetry. In the whole narrative section of books 4 to 6, the theme of literary creation, with its repertoire of images and metaphors, is thus widely explored and illustrated.

Thanks to the technique of *mise en abyme* the Minyeids episode also clearly displays its metaliterary, self-reflexive, character (the work of spinners/weavers who are at the same time narrators makes of the three women an obvious figure of the poet, just like Helen in the *Iliad* when she weaves a web showing the war between Greeks and Trojans (*Il.* 3.125 ff.), or like Achilles who sings to the lyre of 'the famous deeds of heroes' (9.186 ff.)); the clearest clue is in the two *praeteritiones* at 4.43 ff. and 276 ff., both stamped by the declaration of an openly Callimachean poetics (i.e. the rejection of 'vulgar' subjects), that alludes to a famous Virgilian programmatic passage, the 'proem in the middle' in the *Georgics* (cf. 3.4 *omnia iam uulgata*, and also 3.3 *uacuas … mentes*, echoed at *Met.* 4.41 *uacuas … aures*). But the self-reflexive nature of the episode is also marked by a series of mirroring effects between the framing scene and the framed narrative: I think not only of the frequent mention of the *radii* ('rays') of the Sun (193, 241, 247) in a context where the action of the *radius* ('shuttle') is central, but also of the story of Leucothoe (narrated by the almost homonymous Leuconoe), within which the beloved of the Sun is shown while she spins amidst her maids (220–1)—just like Leuconoe—and above all of the celebration of the net-making art of Vulcan, whose result is finer than *tenuissima...stamina* ('the finest threads', 178–9)[15] and than the spider's web itself (at *Odyssey* 8.280 the *aoidos* speaks only of chains 'as fine as the spider's threads', without reference to spinning). The λεπτότης that, thanks to the work of the file (178 *elimat*), characterizes the work of Vulcan (176 *graciles*) suggests a stylistic register appropriate for the story of erotic *furta* (174) of which it is a part, and thus very different from, or rather an alternative to, another famous work of the god's, the epic forging that he had executed, *haud uatum ignarus* ('not unaware of the prophets', *Aen.* 8.627), in the Shield of Aeneas (Hardie 1998: 259).

The mention of the spider as an emblem of skill in spinning within an episode about spinners/weavers who, as they narrate, make reference to the subtlety of the threads, not only anticipates the story of the weaver Arachne and of her metamorphosis (at the cost of an obvious anachronism in the poem's 'history of the world'),[16] but also connects the two narrative complexes of the fourth and sixth books, assimilating them both thematically and functionally (Arachne too is obviously a figure of the poet, and her tapestry a *mise en abyme* of the Ovidian poem). The episodes of the Minyeids and of Arachne are then two myths about poetics which explore the whole semantic field of textuality and at the same time give us a picture of the process of the construction of the text, of its mechanism, and of its sense. That the artists of these texts, both the Minyeids and Arachne, end as victims of the anger of the gods, this too is a part of the meaning of the *Metamorphoses*.

---

[15] Note also, in the context of textiles, the part played in the story of Pyramus and Thisbe by *uelamina* (101, 115; cf. 104 *tenues...amictus*).

[16] Even if not as striking as the anachronism by which the previous narrator refers to the art of Roman aqueducts (4.122–4).

16

Ovid's Narrator in the *Fasti*

Carole Newlands

In talking of the 'narrator' in Ovid's *Fasti*, I am making the assumption that the narrator who attempts to unfold the obscurities of
Roman religion is a creation of its author, and is not to be identified with Ovid, an elusive poet whose personal identity and beliefs
cannot be recovered from his sole legacy, teasing, skilfully wrought,
and deceptive language.[1] The purpose of this paper will be twofold,
first to describe the characteristic traits of the Ovidian narrator in
the *Fasti*, and second to examine the function of this narrator within
the poem as an element that destabilizes the text by calling into
question the value of his research into the origins of the festivals
and customs commemorated by the Roman calendar. Such antiquarian research was generally conceived as serving the programme of
religious reforms inaugurated by Augustus. Richard Gordon points
out that the writings of researchers such as Varro did not necessarily
clarify the obscurities of the religious system but rather mystified it.

---

[1] *Pace* Solodow (1988: 38) who, on debating the idea of an Ovidian persona in
the *Metamorphoses*, argues that 'there is basically a single narrator throughout, who
is Ovid himself.' Such a statement of course raises the unanswerable question of who
exactly the person Ovid was and of how we can tell nearly two thousand years later.
Recent work, for instance, shows that we should not treat Ovid's exile poetry as strictly
autobiographical; see for instance Nagle (1980). Robert Elliott (1982: 58) has argued
that even twentieth-century poets who write avowedly autobiographical poetry and
about whom we know a good deal thanks to audio-visual aids as well as the literary
medium nonetheless cannot appear in their poetry *in propria persona*: 'The "I" of the
poem can never be identical with the actual author who has a local habitation and
a Social Security number and duties and debts and a thousand involvements remote
from any particular poem.'

Access to its mysteries was the privilege of the élite only: 'In short, the growing significance of writing in Roman religion was one of the most important means of turning that religion into ideology, into a means of maintaining the social domination of the élite' (Gordon 1990: 191). Rather than using his writings to mystify his readers, however, the Ovidian narrator democratically invites them to share in his ongoing researches and indeed to make their own judgements. If both he and they nevertheless end up perplexed, the problem lies with the subject, not with its ideological manipulation.

In his two major didactic works, the *Ars Amatoria* and the *Fasti*, Ovid adopts two quite different narratorial stances. In the former work the narrator appears as a boastful, overconfident *praeceptor amoris* who thinks he knows it all.[2] From the start he dispenses with the help of the Muses and Apollo (*Ars* 1.25–30):

> non ego, Phoebe, datas a te mihi mentiar artes,
>   nec nos aeriae uoce monemur auis,
> nec mihi sunt uisae Clio Cliusque sorores
>   seruanti pecudes uallibus, Ascra, tuis;
> usus opus mouet hoc: uati parete perito;
>   uera canam. coeptis, mater Amoris, ades.

Apollo, I will not lie that you bestowed these arts on me, and I was not directed by the voice of a bird in flight, nor did I see Clio and her sister Muses as I was pasturing my flock in your valleys, Ascra; experience inspires this work; obey the skilled poet; I shall sing the truth; mother of Love, attend my undertaking.

He claims that his knowledge and inspiration derive from personal experience—*usus opus mouet hoc*, 'experience inspires this work' (29)—and he proudly describes himself as *uati perito*, 'a skilled poet' (29). Almost as an afterthought he invokes the presence of Venus (30), not as an inspirer of his theme, which he has already anyway begun (*coeptis*), but as a benign audience. The succeeding lines banish unsuitable readers (31–4).

The proem to *Fasti* 1 reveals a narrator quite different in demeanour from the bluffing, overly confident teacher of love (1.1–6):

---

[2] On the narrator in the *Ars Amatoria* see Durling (1958) and Fyler (1971). The latter argues that the *praeceptor*'s pose of absolute control is in fact subtly undermined throughout the work, for love is a passion which cannot ultimately be tamed.

Tempora cum causis Latium digesta per annum
  lapsaque sub terras ortaque signa canam.
excipe pacato, Caesar Germanice, uoltu
  hoc opus et timidae derige nauis iter,
officioque, leuem non auersatus honorem,
  en tibi deuoto numine dexter ades.

I shall sing of the events arranged throughout the Latin year along with their
origins, and also of the constellations that rise from the earth and glide below
it. Germanicus Caesar, accept this work with a face at peace and guide the
course of the timid ship. Do not scorn this slight honour, but come as a god
propitious to the homage vowed to you.

Whereas the teacher in the *Ars Amatoria* has only a general audience,
marked by a casual *si quis…*, 'if anyone…' (1) at the poem's start,
in the opening line of the *Fasti* the narrator addresses his work to
a specific person, Germanicus. Whereas the teacher of love claims
he has no need of a helping Muse or Apollo—his own experience
is sufficient—in the *Fasti* the narrator asks Germanicus not only to
accept his work, but to guide it, *derige* (4), and he invokes him as
a god (6). That Germanicus is in fact a substitute for the Muse or
Apollo is made clear later on in the proem when Germanicus as a
critic is compared to Apollo (19–20): *pagina iudicium docti subitura
mouetur | principis, ut Clario missa legenda deo*, 'my page, about to
undergo the judgement of a learned prince, trembles, as if it were
sent to Apollo to read' (Fantham 1985: 249, see ch. 17 below). Thus
the narrator of the *Fasti* does not rely on *usus*, 'experience'; he is
much more tentative about his project. When he describes his work as
timidae (4), he expresses his humility in invoking the august presence
of Germanicus as literary critic and writer as well as imperial leader.
The epithet succinctly expresses the narrator's fears for the success of
his work, which will be an investigation of the customs and festivals
of the Roman calendar.
    The narrator of the *Fasti* then lacks the supreme confidence and the
experience of his earlier counterpart. He is twice presented as *uates
operose dierum*, 'painstaking poet of the days' (1.101 and 3.177). Not
he himself but the gods Janus and Mars pay him this compliment
and it is a rather ambiguous one. In *Odes* 4.2.31 Horace describes his
poetry as *operosa*, intricately crafted and small scale in contrast to the

grandiloquent style of Pindar. When applied to the narrator instead of to his song the word *operose* also suggests how hard he has to labour. The narrator of the *Fasti* is not the *uates peritus*, the slick dispenser of widely varied personal knowledge. He is not versed in the field of religion as the *praeceptor*, the teacher of love, was in the erotic field. He does not have a vast fund of knowledge or experience on which to draw, for he is not omniscient in his field as the teacher of the *Ars* claims to be.

He still, however, exhibits a lot of the humour we associate with his earlier narratorial stance. Teasingly in the proem to the second book of the *Fasti* the narrator says, *idem sacra cano*, 'the same poet (as ever), I sing of sacred rites' (7).[3] The narrator is the 'same' only by underlying means that reveal a characteristically irreverent attitude to Augustan themes.[4] His lack of complete mastery of his subject, his tentativeness about his project, increases as the poem progresses and opens it up to doubt and questioning. His narrative control is undermined by his development in the poem not to greater self-confidence but to less. By the end of the extant poem, we see his few claims to authority, and his humour, wear thin.

Since the narrator in the *Fasti* does not sit on a lofty pedestal like the *praeceptor*, he sometimes defers to higher, more informed authorities for help with his subject. His characteristic technique in the *Fasti* is to interview these outside informants so that they speak in their own voices. The *Fasti* is thus a work with multiple narrators, and hence also multiple addressees. It is part of the personal tone of this poem that the narrator addresses himself directly to a variety of people who are not solely informants but sometimes are celebrants he invokes to worship or even characters in the narrative he

---

[3] On the relationship of the second proem to the first see Fantham (1985, = ch. 17 below) 257–66.

[4] In his work on Ovid's proems, Korzeniewski (1964:198) has interpreted the phrase *idem sacra cano*, 'I sing of sacred rites, the same as ever,' to mean that the narrator here will be the same as in his previous elegiac works, that is, he will bring his typically irreverent, jaunty wit to bear on his new subject. Certainly the narrator often takes a lighthearted view of his subject. However, Korzeniewski's interpretation ignores the different relation that the narrator has here to his new subject, a difficult one full of obscurities for which the narrator has little expertise and which, as he says later in the proem, he has to pursue with diligence, *studioso ... pectore* (15). As a sign of his need for patronage and guidance, in this second proem the narrator again has a political addressee, Augustus.

is telling.[5] When he addresses no such audience directly, the narrator uses the second person singular to indicate an implied reader.[6] He thus engages his readers closely in the text and in his ongoing researches into Roman religion. Since the narrator of the *Fasti* is not presented as omniscient, a substantial interpretive burden is placed upon us, the readers.

The narrator of the *Fasti* is different too from that of his influential predecessor in aetiological poetry, Callimachus. John Miller has argued that in the *Fasti* Ovid offers a more muted, less personal, and more didactic version of the scholarly persona in the *Aetia* (1982: 400–13). But the frequent use of the second person singular address to his reader, as well as the conversational tone he often strikes in his interviews with outside informants, establishes a very personal relationship between the narrator and his audience in the *Fasti*. The Ovidian narrator seems to lack the scholarly authority of his influential predecessor, of whom Heinze comments, 'in Callimachus the reader is not to forget that the learned and witty master Callimachus is narrating' (1960: 376). The Ovidian narrator is less a teacher than a researcher, and a rather naive, unsystematic, and casual one at that.

First of all, although his subject is a written document, the Roman calendar, the narrator rarely refers to any written sources. He four times mentions having consulted ancient calendars (1.7, 1.657, 3.87–96, 4.11), and once an ancient inscription (3.844), but these references are vague and unspecified.[7] More frequently he refers to his sources in an offhand way as *fama*, 'rumour,' or *fabula*, 'a story,' or even as old men's or boyhood tales (2.584 and 6.417–18), and he relies a good deal on the vague formulae *ferunt*, 'people say,' *memorant*, 'people mention,' and *putant*, 'people think.'[8] In *de Lingua Latina*

---

[5] e.g. at 4.133ff., adopting a Callimachean hymnic pose, he summons the worshippers of Venus *Verticordia*: see Miller (1982). The narrator frequently involves himself with the characters in a narrative; e.g. the story of Lucretia (2.685ff.) is punctuated by second person addresses to characters or even towns. On such narratorial interventions as an aspect of Ovidian art see Frécaut (1972) 135–71.

[6] When no named person is addressed, the narrator generally refers to the reader in the second personal singular, and only rarely in the second person plural, perhaps for metrical reasons.

[7] The first and last of these (1.7 and 4.11) occur within programmatic contexts and are not related to any particular subject of investigation.

[8] Thus in introducing the second *causa* for the goddess Anna Perenna the narrator tells us that *haec quoque, quam referam, nostras peruenit ad aures | fama nec a ueri*

Varro often documents or supports his alternative etymologies by reference to specific authors.[9] The Callimachean narrator adopts a scholarly approach when in *Aetia* fr. 75.53–77 he tells us that he learnt the story of Acontius and Cydippe from the history of Xenomades. The Ovidian narrator never cites any specific literary sources. Instead, he draws much of his information from supposed encounters with personal informants; his own personal experience, to which he refers occasionally, seems to have been limited. [10]

Secondly, although he is true to antiquarian methodology in providing alternative etymologies of a name and alternative versions of a myth, he rarely makes a choice among them, and when he does make a choice, it often seems arbitrary, not informed. For instance, he gives five derivations for the name of the festival 'Agonalia' (*F*. 1.317–32); Varro economically gives only two (*L*. 6.12). The first reason, the derivation from *ago, agonis*, 'sacrificial priest,' which Varro rightly seems to privilege, is the right one, but the narrator wades through the rest to fasten for no particular reason on the last and unlikely one: *et pecus antiquus dicebat agonia sermo;* | *ueraque iudicio est ultima causa meo*, 'the language of long ago used to call sheep "*agonia*", and in my judgment this final reason is the true one' (331–2).[11] As Bömer

dissidet illa fide, 'this story too which I shall tell has come to my ears, and it is not far from what we take as the truth' (3.661–2). He has already referred to the first *causa* as a *fabula* which he must disclose free from error (3.544). Yet despite his claim for authority, he typically does not impose it.

[9] It is illuminating to compare Varro's discussion of the etymology of April with the Ovidian account. In *L*. 6.4 Varro cites two scholars for the view that the name of the month derives from Aphrodite; then, because his own research in earlier literature gives no support for this derivation, he offers his own, from *aperire*, 'to open,' the derivation offered in the *Fasti Praenestini*. The Ovidian account, however, although the longest etymological discussion in the poem, makes no concessions to earlier or current scholarship in its insistence that the correct derivation is from Aphrodite (4.61–132); typically the supporters of *aperire* are referred to through the formula *memorant* (89). Varro's is a cool, reasoned account; the Ovidian narrator's is an emotional, partisan account, based on his loyalty to Venus.

[10] For instance he tells us he has participated in the Palilia (4.725–8). His repetition here of *certe ego* (725 and 727) gives comic emphasis to the (improbable) picture of our narrator (toga-clad?) leaping over a bonfire. Cf. also 2.27, 3.274, 3.541, 4.985ff., 6.237–8, 6.395.

[11] In deriving April from Aphrodite, however, the narrator defends the etymology at length, giving several supporting arguments and demolishing the main counter one (4.61–132). It is surely characteristic that the narrator will argue at length only for Venus.

comments on this passage, apart from the first definition, 'everything else is play' (39).

Thirdly, Ovid's narrator prefers human or divine contacts to book learning, and his approach to his informants is rather naive, or casually humorous. The method of the personal interview is borrowed from Callimachus. In the first two books of the *Aetia* Callimachus discusses *aetia* through a fictive dialogue with the Muses, and in books 3 and 4 with some other informants, human and divine. This device of interviewing the Muses does not suggest lack of confidence on the narrator's part. Rather, Callimachus thereby suggests that his inspiration and knowledge will be of the highest kind. As John Miller has shown (1983; also Rutledge 1980), Ovid greatly expands the Callimachean method of the personal interview. However, the narrator interviews the Muses collectively only once towards the end of his work, at the start of book 5, and summons individual Muses only twice elsewhere (1.657ff. and 4.195ff.). The work therefore lacks the stamp of the Muses' authority.

Instead, the narrator relies on a variety of informants, human as well as divine. Most of the Ovidian narrator's human informants are in fact old, 'antiquated old men' he calls them at one point (2.584). Such a situation is familiar enough to field workers today working with oral tradition, yet these informants are sometimes clearly unreliable, and the narrator is uncritical of the information they provide. For instance, he tells us that he derives a lot of the information in the *Fasti* from an old country friend: *is mihi multa quidem, sed et haec narrare solebat | unde meum praesens instrueretur opus*, 'he used to tell me many things, but especially these things which inform my current work' (4.689–90). But the one tale which he directly accredits to this old friend provides such an odd, ill-matched explanation for a strange rite at the Cerealia that we must doubt the wisdom of the narrator's reliance on him (4.679–712). First of all, the custom at the Cerealia of sending foxes into the Circus with burning torches tied to their backs is nowhere else attested; Bömer (1957–8 ii. 269) thinks this is sheer invention on Ovid's part.[12] The tale told to explain this unlikely custom is even more unlikely. A boy who captured a fox set it alight;

---

[12] He informs us that there is no evidence for any such custom at the Cerealia as is described here, and no known antecedent for the tale.

as it ran off in terror it burned the farmers' crops. The strange rite at the Cerealia is supposedly a reminder of this obscure event.

Other sources are equally problematic, for often the narrator's meetings with human informants are not deliberately planned but happen by chance. As he returns one day from Nomentum to Rome, he comes upon a procession celebrating the Robigalia and interviews the priest about the rites (4.905–42); he records the conversation of an old veteran beside whom he chances to sit at the Megalensian games (4.377–86); by chance he sees a matron walking barefoot on the Via Sacra and finds an old woman there to explain the custom (6.395–416). She tells him with trembling voice that the name of the god Vertumnus derives from *auerso amne*, 'the diverted stream' (6.410). Although she acknowledges that his name is appropriate for his ability to change shapes, and furthermore that the stream was dammed *after* the god first took up residence there (409), she seems unaware of this contradiction in her etymology. So too does the narrator. In *Metamorphoses* 14.641ff. Ovid connects the god with change of shapes and seasons; his Roman predecessor in aetiological elegy, Propertius, constructed *Elegy* 4.2 around the god's personal and full discussion of his name and makes Vertumnus specifically condemn the etymology from the damming of the stream. Without acknowledging the other etymologies of which his readers would surely be aware, the narrator of the *Fasti* concludes his interview with the old woman by simply wishing her well (6.415–16). Both Ovid and Propertius use first-person accounts to explain the etymology of Vertumnus' name, but unlike Propertius' Vertumnus, the old woman scarcely does justice to the task. Through this contrast the narrator's rather naive, unscholarly attitude to his sources is made quite marked, and the reliability of these sources is put in question.

Ovid's narrator thus reveals himself as less circumspect in his treatment of his sources than is Callimachus' scholar-poet in the *Aetia*. To cite one example from the *Aetia*, fr. 178, at a dinner party Callimachus' narrator asks a fellow diner from Icos the reason for the worship of Peleus on that island. Since the banquet celebrates a religious festival, all the guests are presumably interested in religious customs. This particular guest's name, Theogenes, suggests that he shares this interest. Moreover, the narrator here has the chance to sound his fellow diner out first by general conversation. He also takes care to note that Theogenes is only a moderate drinker, an important criterion of reliability.[13] The human informants of the *Fasti* do little to inspire either reverence for the rites they describe, or indeed complete credence, except on the part of such uncritical listeners as Ovid's narrator.

The narrator of the *Fasti* does not convey the impression of meticulous scholarship which we glean from the fragmentary role of the narrator in the *Aetia*. Instead, the Ovidian narrator's informal approach to his subject and his refusal, more marked as the poem progresses, to take authoritative positions, opens the poem up to different interpretive possibilities that can undermine its ostensible intent, to honour the Augustan household through the new, reformed calendar (*F*. 1.9–14). For example, the narrator's method of providing alternative possibilities in a seemingly undiscriminating fashion can in fact conceal an artful, subversive selectivity. When the narrator discusses the Lupercalia, for instance, he gives three lengthy reasons for the nudity of the Luperci without choosing among them (2.283–380). As A. W. J. Holleman has argued (1973), nudity seems to have been the one aspect of the Lupercalia that Augustus abolished when he revived and cleaned up the festival. At any rate, this particular aspect of the festival appears to have been a particularly sensitive one ever since Antony as one of the Luperci appeared, according to Cicero, *nudus, unctus, ebrius*, 'naked, perfumed, drunk' (*Philippics* 3.12), to offer the crown to Julius Caesar. Yet of all the different aspects of this important festival, this is the one to which the narrator devotes the most attention in the guise of reviewing different explanations. Indeed, although this ancient festival was a complicated and obscure one, he shows little interest in its other features apart from the name Lupercal (381–424) and the fertility rite (425–52), neither of which questions engages as much of his attention as does the topic of nudity.

Moreover, the narrator's central explanation for the nudity is an irreverent, and largely irrelevant, transvestite farce concerning two important Roman gods, Faunus, the god honoured in the Lupercalia,

---

[13] The priestess of the goddess Tacita, whose rites the narrator observes and reports, becomes inebriated due to the large share of ritual wine she drinks (2.571–82). In book 6.785–90 the narrator notes that the anonymous stargazer, whose reports he sometimes uses, cannot give a full account of the state of the heavens because he is drunk.

and Hercules (303–58). The former appears here as a frustrated seducer, the latter as an elegiac lover, whose slavery to Omphale has been transformed into a *seruitium amoris* (Fantham 1983). Although the narrator is careful to make the story of Hercules, Omphale, and Faunus only one of four explanations, it is the longest and most entertaining one. With this type of lascivious tale the narrator ensures that the nudity of the Lupercalia will be the one aspect of the festival that we will certainly remember (Littlewood 1975*a*: 1071–2). The story's exuberance and sheer irrelevance to the topic make gentle mockery of the aetiological method the narrator seemingly espouses. His lack of restraint contrasts markedly with the decorum of Callimachus (*Aetia* fr. 75.8–9), who checks himself from revealing divine secrets and claims that knowledge without discretion is a dangerous weapon. Yet the narrator of the Fasti can absolve himself from any blame deriving from his tales; he is after all only a reporter, or so he presents himself.[14]

This distancing of the narrator from the interpretive possibilities of his research is brought out by a brief, witty allusion to his earlier elegiac works in the first narrative of Anna Perenna (3.545–656). In this story the old Roman goddess Anna Perenna is identified as Anna, the sister of Queen Dido, and Aeneas appears as a wishy-washy, inept hero who is married to a jealous virago—Ovid's version of the sweetly blushing Lavinia of the *Aeneid*. In this sequel to *Aeneid* 4 the cards are stacked against Aeneas from the start, for the narrative begins with exactly the same epitaph that concludes Dido's accusatory and suicidal letter to Aeneas in the *Heroides*, *praebuit Aeneas et causam mortis et ensem.* | *ipsa sua Dido concidit usa manu*, 'Aeneas provided a reason for death and the sword which Dido used to kill herself' (7.195–6; *F.* 3.549–50). However, in the *Fasti* the narrator distances himself from the judgement resident in this couplet by telling us

---

[14] Echoing Callimachus perhaps, the narrator says at 3.325: *nobis concessa canentur* | *quaeque pio dici uatis ab ore licet*, 'I shall sing of lawful things that are allowed to be spoken by the pious lips of a bard.' This is probably a tongue-in-cheek remark, for later in the poem he tells us, *fas mihi praecipue uoltus uidisse deorum* | *uel quia sum uates, uel quia sacra cano*, 'it is right that I particularly should have seen the faces of the gods, either because I am a poet or because I sing of sacred things' (6.7–8). He then privileges his position as *uates* by reporting not just the appearance but the conversation of three goddesses, a conversation that puts all of them in a rather discreditable light.

that Dido wrote these words herself on her tombstone, *tumulique in marmore carmen | hoc breue, quod moriens ipsa reliquit, erat*, 'this short inscription, which she left as she was dying, was on the marble of her tomb' (547–8); these are not his own incriminatory words, therefore. Moreover, in addition to evoking *Heroides* 7 the couplet also echoes the couplet which appears in the *praeceptor*'s list of forsaken heroines in *Ars* 3.39–40: *et famam pietatis habet, tamen hospes et ensem | praebuit et causam mortis, Elissa, tuae*, 'He has the reputation for *pietas*, but all the same, Dido, as guest he offered you a sword and a reason for your death.' The *praeceptor amoris* here adopts a sympathetic stance to Dido, for he is writing book 3 specifically for women. Only in the *Fasti* does the narrator distance himself from the incriminatory view of Aeneas provided by the *Heroides* and *Ars Amatoria*. Subtly Ovid has adapted his own lines from two earlier elegiac poems to a different narrator. Unlike the *praeceptor*, the narrator of the *Fasti* typically cannot be identified with the point of view expressed in the epitaph; he only reports the words that another is imagined to have written here. He thus establishes from the start his distance from the events he goes on to describe, events in which Aeneas is represented as a henpecked husband who makes the mistake of bringing a beautifully dressed foreign lady home.[15]

This last example suggests that the narrator's removal from a controversial, authoritative stance can serve as a self-protective device, for irreverent or unusual views of the past can be included in a seemingly indiscriminate list of alternative explanations or can be attributed to

[15] Anna encounters Aeneas as he paces along the shore of Latium with his faithful companion Achates. The scene recalls the famous one in book 1 of the *Aeneid* when Aeneas and Achates explore the Carthaginian shore. Here in the *Fasti*, however, the shore is called *dotali* (603), an adjective that suggests Aeneas is not entirely his own master; there is something furtive about his walk for it is described, without any apparent reason, as *secretum* (604); and Aeneas is oddly barefoot—a condition more appropriate for a sorrowing elegiac lover than for a military hero, unless we are to assume that in his impoverished kingdom Aeneas cannot afford decent footwear. The similarities between Aeneas and Ariadne, whose story has just been told (*F.* 3.459–516), particularly hint at his unhappiness in love. In his discussion of this tale Ahl (1985: 309–15), points out that an alternative version of the Dido and Aeneas myth, one known to Varro, made Anna rather than Dido Aeneas' mistress. Such a tradition would help explain the ambiguous language in which Aeneas introduces Anna to his court (3.628–32), as well as Lavinia's subsequent jealousy. McKeown (1984) reaches a different conclusion from Ahl's, namely that Ovid's treatment is devoid of political implications. For a critique of McKeown see Wallace-Hadrill (1987).

other authorities. In the *Fasti* Ovid does not expose himself defiantly to the emperor's displeasure, as he did in the *Ars Amatoria*. He is writing his aetiological poem in a different political climate, in the sombre later years of the Augustan principate, and he must have recognized from the exile of Julia in 2 BC that Augustus' moral and religious reforms were not to be taken lightly (Wiedemann 1975). Ovid's mask as an earnest, innocent reporter and his use of multiple narrators are effective devices that hand over the responsibility of interpretation to the reader.

If we are to look for convincing, authoritative stances in the poem, we should, following Callimachean precedent, look to the divinities that the narrator interviews; they should carry more authority than his human informants, we might expect. However they too are not necessarily omniscient or correct in their beliefs. For example, Mars' explanation of the Matronalia involves a lengthy story about the women's peacemaking between the Sabines and the Romans (*F*. 3.179–232). However Mars follows it unexpectedly with three other *causae* (3.233–58). When Mars chooses the last of these as providing the correct etymology, the question is thereby raised of why he told the first story at such length, or indeed at all. *Quid moror et uariis onero tua pectora causis?* 'Why do I delay and burden your breast with different reasons?' (3.249), the god finally asks the narrator before he hits on his final choice. Mars is characterized as rather slow, a warrior ill at ease in an elegiac poem in which, reluctant to abandon his martial role, he keeps a grip on his spear (3.172). His treatment of various *causae* thus reflects his gaucherie. Other gods have their own axes to grind. For instance, in *Fasti* 4 (807–62) the murder of Remus is presented as the work of a guard, Celer, not of Romulus. This departure from the traditional version has often been interpreted as a sign that Ovid wrote the poem to support Augustus' revisionary view of Roman history and religion. Yet who does the narrator call upon for aid in telling this story? Quirinus, Romulus in his deified form (4.808)—scarcely a disinterested party.

The Muses, too, are not authoritative guides. Conventionally we would expect that if the Muses encounter a poet on Mount Helicon, they will provide him with divine authority and insight. The Muse whom the narrator interviews in book 4 backs up her miraculous story of Claudia by referring to the stage: *mira, sed et scaena testificata loquar*, 'my story is amazing, but a stage play proves its truth' (*F*. 4.326). She characterizes herself and others as biased towards untruth—*sed nos in uitium credula turba sumus*, 'but we are a group inclined to think the worse' (*F*. 4.312)—a statement hardly calculated to inspire confidence in a Muse. In book 5 the narrator's interview of all three Heliconian Muses follows the precedent set by Hesiod in the *Theogony* and Callimachus in the *Aetia*. These poets, however, introduced the Muses at the start of their works, thus providing their poems with the seal of divine authority. At this late point in the researches of the Ovidian narrator, the Muses are of little help. It comes as a shock when, after the narrator's question about the derivation of the name of the month of May, we are told that Hesiod's harmonious goddesses—'of one mind,' as that poet says in *Theogony* 60—here in the *Fasti* disagree among themselves, *dissensere deae* (5.9). The unusual word *dissensere*, used only here in Ovid's corpus, as well as the initial position of this alliterative phrase in the line, emphasizes the disruption of the reader's expectations for a lucid, unambiguous answer. Three of the Muses offer three different answers, and each Muse has two supporters for her view. Characteristically the narrator refuses to cast a decisive vote, not just because he lacks powers of judgement but because he fears to offend them (5.107–10).

The breakdown in the Muses' harmony is all the more evident as the scene in several ways corresponds to the scene in *Metamorphoses* 5.294ff. in which the Muses engage in a dispute on Helicon, this time not among themselves but against their human doublets, the Pierides. In the *Metamorphoses*, however, the Muses present a united front. Calliope is described in almost similar terms in both poems, with ivy binding her hair, but in the *Fasti* her hair is specifically called *neglectos*, 'neglected' (79), a further sign perhaps of breakdown in order.[16]

At the start of book 6 three goddesses again appear to offer different explanations for the name of the month of June. The contest occurs

---

[16] Of course she conforms too to the ideal of artless beauty found throughout Ovid's poetry; thus Daphne in *Metamorphoses* 1.477 is commended for *positos sine lege capillos*, 'hair arranged without art.' In *Metamorphoses* 5 Calliope's hair is *inmissos* (338), flowing and ordered. On the programmatic significance of Calliope in this scene in the *Metamorphoses* see Hinds (1987a) 121–33.

in a symbolic, numinous grove of the type that appears elsewhere in Ovid's poetry, notably in the contest between Elegy and Tragedy in *Amores* 3.1. Here in the *Fasti* we are told that the grove is secluded from every voice apart from the prattle or brawl of the brook. The use of *obstrepere*, 'to make a harsh grating sound' (10) to describe the *uox*, 'voice' (10) of the water, normally associated with sweet, smooth-flowing poetry, surely anticipates the dissonant voices of the goddesses to come. First Juno (21–64) and then her daughter Hebe (65–88) indulge in some warm special pleading, for each is certain that the month is named after her. Their explanations, of course, are highly emotional, and mother and daughter almost come to blows. We might expect Concordia, the goddess who next appears and who was particularly associated with the Augustan peace, to heal the breach and resolve the dispute (91–6).[17] Instead she simply adds to it by providing yet another etymology, one that in this case honours her. As in so many other human affairs, self-interest is the controlling factor in conditioning belief—a conclusion that was not likely to please Augustus. And characteristically, the narrator dare not choose among these alternate possibilities.

The narrator's heavy reliance on variant explanations and stories and his frequent refusal to choose among them calls attention to the multiplicity and ambiguity of tradition and challenges the authoritarian view of Rome's history and its heroes promulgated by current Augustan propaganda. At the same time the narrator's unscholarly approach to his material can mask an artful selectivity of treatment and theme by which the gravity of his subject is often undermined. But the process of destabilizing the subject leads inevitably to the destabilizing of the narrator. In the second half of the *Fasti*, the narrator seems to have increasing difficulty in presenting his material in a clear, interesting, and lively fashion. He appears as weary and confused with a subject whose complexities seemingly begin to lie beyond his control.

The narrator's weariness with his subject manifests itself particularly in two ways. First of all, his growing confusion is compounded

---

[17] *uenit Apollinea longas Concordia lauro | nexa comas, placidi numen opusque ducis*, 'Concordia came with Apollo's laurel woven through her long hair, the divinity and work of the peaceful leader' (*F.* 6.91–2). Cf. *F.* 1.645–50 and Bömer (1957–8 ii.71).

by a marked increase in the number of his informants in the second half of the poem.[18] Some of his informants are indirect; that is, he sometimes asks a deity for inspiration but reports in his own voice what the god said. If for simplicity's sake, we consider the number of informants he asks and who respond directly, what Genette calls intradiegetic narrators, we can see the clear difference between the two halves of the poem. In book 1 the narrator interviews directly two informants, in book 2 none, in book 3 one. This pattern fits in with the fairly confident demeanour of the narrator in these books. But in book 4 he interviews directly three informants; in book 5 the number doubles to six; and in book 6 he interviews eight.[19]

Moreover, the major informants of Ovid's narrator are noticeably unreliable in these last two books. At the start of book 5, he compares himself to a wayfarer stranded at the crossroads (3–6). When Plato likewise uses the metaphor of the crossroads in *Laws* 7.799c, he recommends that the traveller question himself and others and not proceed further until he has made sure which is the right path. The narrator's self-questioning fails, however, and so he turns to the Muses for help. Surprisingly, they leave him in the same state of perplexity as before. The warring goddesses at the start of book 6, although major deities, are likewise little help.

Secondly, starting with the second half of book 4, the narrator begins to make clear to the reader how confusing and difficult his subject is. Not, of course, that the narrator has ever presented himself as omniscient. But lack of knowledge is quite a different thing from the confusion he now begins to show. In a few but significant places he makes explicit to the reader that he is at a loss with how to proceed. His first complaint occurs in the middle of his explanation of the Palilia. Although he claims that he himself has often participated in the festival (725–8), he has no idea of the rationale behind the rites he describes: *turba facit dubium coeptaque nostra tenet*, 'the great number of explanations bewilders me and holds up my undertaking' (785). He then proceeds to give seven possible explanations for the

---

[18] I am grateful to Georgia Nugent who, in an unpublished paper, pointed this out to me.

[19] If one includes indirect informants, sources the narrator turns to for advice or inspiration but who do not speak directly, then the number of informants increases from three in *Fasti* 1 to ten in *Fasti* 6.

presence of fire at the Palilia (785–806). While he has often before provided a list of possible *causae*, what is new here is his frank acknowledgment that the obscurity of the subject has a detrimental effect on his work.

The programmatic introductions to these last two books make it clear that the narrator is increasingly at a loss with how to proceed with his subject. At the start of book 5 he addresses his readers who, he pretends, have asked him a question about the origin of the word May (1–6):

Quaeritis, unde putem Maio data nomina mensi?
  non satis est liquido cognita causa mihi.
ut stat et incertus qua sit sibi nescit eundum,
  cum videt ex omni parte, viator, iter,
sic, quia posse datur diversas reddere causas,
  qua ferar ignoro, copiaque ipsa nocet.

You ask what I believe is the origin of the name for the month of May? I don't know the explanation clearly enough. Like a traveller who stands still when he sees the road go in all directions and does not know which fork he should take, so because different reasons can be given, I do not know which way to go, and the very abundance of choice is harmful.

Although his readers turn to him for help, the narrator freely admits that he is almost as ignorant as they are in this matter, for there are many possible derivations. The analogy with the wayfarer standing perplexed at crossroads, drawn from Theognis 1.911ff., as well as Plato *Laws* 7.799c, underscores the narrator's confusion. Whereas Theognis refers to only two roads from which to choose, in the *Fasti* there are several roads, and the lack of precise specification adds to the impression of bewilderment. As with the line referring to the Palilia discussed above, the narrator finds the confusion of the subject harmful to his work, *copiaque ipsa nocet*, 'the very abundance of choice is harmful' (6). The scene here is emblematic of a crisis within the narrator. If the Muses themselves cannot agree on the answer, then the subject the narrator has chosen for his poem must be virtually impossible to explicate in rationally consistent terms. By this point it has become clear that the narrator must proceed through the mazes of obscure aetiology without the kind of guidance Callimachus had found. The alternative approach, mystification of his obscure subject, the narrator rejects by his refusal to deceive the reader about his own perplexities. The abandonment of his project surely now looms on the horizon.

His state of perplexity here at the start of book 5 is perhaps reflected in his muddled invocation to the Muses for help (7–8):

dicite, quae fontes Aganippidos Hippocrenes
    grata Medusaei signa tenetis equi.

Speak, you who possess the fountains of Aganippean Hippocrene, the pleasing marks of the horse that Medusa engendered.

The narrator here confuses the two springs on Mount Helicon, for Aganippe was further down than the Hippocrene, which can alone be properly called *Medusaei signa . . . equi*. Just as the narrator cannot distinguish the right path from the wrong, so he cannot distinguish these two springs; his poetic topography has gone awry.[20]

The preface of book 6 emblematizes this final loss of narrative control. Again the narrator avoids incriminating himself and refuses to make a choice from among different explanations, for he wittily recalls the disastrous consequences of the judgement of Paris (97–100). He has in fact already shifted the responsibility of choice to the reader, for he prefaces the goddesses' debate in book 6 with these opening lines (1–2):

Hic quoque mensis habet dubias in nomine causas:
    quae placeat, positis omnibus ipse leges.

This month too has controversial explanations for its name:
you yourself choose one you like and discard all the rest.

With the mandate to the reader of *ipse leges*, 'you yourself choose,' the Ovidian narrator abandons his putative role of guide through the mazy paths of ancient custom. His new subject has largely defeated his comprehension and that of his informants, for the Roman past emerges in the poem as too complex, obscure, and contradictory to admit of rational understanding or simple answers. Although the narrator has ultimately failed in making Roman religion accessible to his readers, he has succeeded in stripping the veil from antiquarian

---

[20] In *Metamorphoses* 5.312 the Pierides have no trouble distinguishing the two springs.

research—anyone, it seems, can try to make sense of his subject. The Ovidian narrator essentially demystifies the processes of antiquarian research. In the end it seems to matter little which *aetion* or etymology we choose to believe, as long as we are aware of the multiplicity of Roman tradition and of the many faces of its heroes and heroines.

We can look in vain in the *Fasti*, then, for any sort of canonical or authoritative view of the Roman past such as we find in Vergil's *Aeneid*. As an open-ended poem, the *Fasti* is hardly the sort of definitive, scholarly work that might have brought Ovid back from exile. Rather, both the multiplicity of voices and the narrator's lack of authority serve to destabilize his subject, the investigation of Roman rites and festivals, and provide an implicit challenge to the monolithic ideology of the Augustan regime.

It is significant that the narrator's expressions of doubt and requests for information from outsiders are confined largely to the Roman material. Although the Greek star myths he tells often had several variants, the narrator generally ignores them. Five times in the poem (2.81–2, 4.175–8, 4.717–20, 5.165–8, 5.617–20) he acknowledges some doubt about the origin of a constellation, never in a serious fashion. When for instance he does acknowledge that the constellation of Taurus could represent either the bull or Io metamorphosed, he does so in a joking fashion; the problem would be solved if he could see the hindquarters (4.717–20).

Joseph Solodow has pointed out that in the *Metamorphoses* the narrator frequently adopts a sceptical attitude towards his mythical material (1988: 68–73). In the *Fasti*, however, Greek myth poses few problems for the narrator; its subject matter is congenial to the elegiac poet committed to Callimachean ideals of sophisticated, skilfully wrought poetry. Here he can properly bring lightness of touch and subtlety to an aetiological subject. By contrast, Roman myth and rites emerge as intractable and often uncongenial.

The narrator's struggles with his Roman material, compared to the ease with which he treats Greek myth, serve to highlight the obscurity and *rusticitas* of much of Roman religion and myth. In throwing up his hands at the start of book 6 the narrator inevitably brings into question the value of the subject he investigates, much of which has obviously become meaningless in the course of time, since even Roman deities cannot always provide explanations for customs and rites. The failure of the *Fasti* to continue beyond six months of the year is not only understandable; it is skilfully engineered through a narrator whose growing confusion—compounded by the unreliability of many of his informants—cannot help but suggest the obscurity of the rites and festivals he describes. Perhaps too, since Ovid leaves us to draw our own conclusions, such a failure suggests the pointlessness of much of their revival. Since the narrator comes to approach the level of his uninformed readers, as he never does in the *Ars Amatoria*, his confusions increasingly convince us that they are endemic in his subject.

As Dr Johnson wisely observes in chapter 48 of *Rasselas*, 'the original of ancient customs is commonly unknown, for the practice often continues after the cause has ceased; and concerning superstitious ceremonies it is vain to conjecture; for what reason did not dictate, reason cannot explain.' Or, as one of the informants of Ovid's narrator more succinctly puts it, in almost the exact centre of the final book, *mos tamen ille manet* (6.414): the custom remains, but not its rationale or, necessarily, the religious spirit that once inspired it.

Part IV

On the Margins of Empire

17

Ovid, Germanicus, and the Composition of the *Fasti*

Elaine Fantham

I

Ovid's *Fasti* has always attracted more interest as a source for Roman religion than as a poetic composition or even as evidence for the poet's development. So it is not surprising that Bömer's great commentary is strongest on cult and antiquarian elements: but this bias may also explain why the *Fasti* has not shared in the current revival of Ovidian scholarship. Yet new and important techniques applicable to the *Fasti* have recently become available: a better insight into the dynastic tensions of the period after 6 BC and the gradual emergence of Tiberius,[1] a more perceptive evaluation of Ovid's exile poetry (Kenney 1965 and 1982), and for the *Fasti* itself a method of structural analysis which reveals different layers of composition in books 1 and 2 and so reopens the question of its chronology.[2] Our understanding of Ovid's relationship to Callimachus has gained from the

---

[1] From Seager (1972); Levick (1976a); Woodman (1977); from the articles on the dynastic conflict by Levick (1975); (1976b); Sumner (1967); and above all from Syme (1978) and the papers listed in the bibliography, p. 233.

[2] See Lefèvre (1976) and (1980); also Fantham (1983) 205–6, 210 ff. Note that Syme (1978: 34, 146) is convinced Ovid did no significant work on the *Fasti* after AD 4, apart from the obvious adjustments to honour Germanicus in book 1. Williams (1978: 85) suggests that the *Fasti* 'reflects the Ovid of AD 2–8, the years between the *Ars Amatoria* and exile', a dating endorsed by Littlewood (1981) 382 and n.8.

further study of Callimachean elements in his Roman predecessors[3] and been radically advanced by the publication in 1977 of the Victoria Berenices papyri representing the opening of *Aitia* book 3.[4]

Whether we talk of ideology, panegyric, or emperor worship, this aspect of Ovid's later poetry, particularly the final sequence of *Metamorphoses* and the exile poems, has also been illuminated by recent criticism and I should single out as examples of this approach to the *Fasti* the papers of Littlewood (1981; cf. also 1980) and McKeown (1984).[5] But so far interest in ideology has been separate from issues of composition and chronology, both relative and absolute. This discussion takes as its starting point Ovid's late prooemium to the whole poem, addressed to Germanicus, and will try to draw these threads together by considering Ovid's opening dedication of the poem to Germanicus from many angles: examining its programmatic and political functions, relating it to Germanicus' career and dynastic position following his adoption by Tiberius in AD 4 and to the evidence for Ovid's acquaintance with the prince and approaches to him as potential patron. A separate examination of *Ex Ponto* 4.8, one of Ovid's last poems, shows affinities with the dedicatory proem so close that I will argue for assigning the composition of both passages to the same short period. The firm dating this offers gives a point of reference to which less chronologically determinate sections of the *Fasti* and other works can be tethered.

Firstly Germanicus' own *Phaenomena*. Ovid honours the prince as a fellow poet. The *Phaenomena* and its much-disputed dedication have usually been dated, without absolute grounds, to the years just after Ovid's death. But it is worth questioning this dating, and asking whether Ovid could have known the prince's version of Aratus, perhaps imitating some features from the proem of that work in his own rededication of the *Fasti*.

---

[3] See especially Wimmel (1960); Clausen (1964) 181–95 and (1982) 310–19. Wimmel touches only briefly on the proem of the *Fasti* itself (314). On imitation of Callimachus' *Aitia* in Propertius book 4 and Ovid's *Fasti* see Miller (1982).

[4] By Parsons (1977). See now Thomas (1983), who brings out the contribution of the papyri to our understanding of Verg. *Georg.* 3.1–48 and Prop. 3.1.

[5] We owe these and other papers on Ovid's formal attitude to Augustan ideology to the stimulus of Williams (1978), ch. 2, but it should be noted that Williams' perceptive analysis is focused on the *Metamorphoses* and the exile poetry rather than the *Fasti*, and on the *princeps* rather than his family.

Then I turn to the main body of the *Fasti* to consider passages whose later composition is suggested by the ideology or associations of the Germanicus proem. A short section explores the relationship Ovid has set up between this proem and other dedicatory passages introducing books or marking off sections within the work, then moves to the reworked first book to illustrate from it dynastic and ideological leitmotifs which develop themes from the dedication. Finally, I will argue from affinities of diction and content with the datable elegy *Ex Ponto* 4.8, that the strongly ideological introductory panel of *Fasti* 5.1–110 was either composed or more probably reworked by Ovid to match the renewed republican tone favoured by Tiberius when he took over the principate on the death of Augustus and in the last years of Ovid's life.

My investigation has an interest beyond immediate concern with the composition process of the *Fasti* because this work, together with the exile poetry, represents the crucial period in which Augustus' personal supremacy was hardening into dynasty.[6] The accumulated blows of his grandsons' deaths, the Pannonian revolt, flood and famine of AD 5, the disgrace of Julia minor and the disaster of Varus in Germany had given the old man a fright which led to suspicion and flattery, the heightening of language akin to worship and the extension of imperial *maiestas* as a tool of autocratic control. Tiberius' republican hankerings could not reverse this trend and Ovid's later poetry offers the first filtered image of this Tacitean climate of mutual dis-ease between *princeps*, senate, and court.

In its present form the 26-line introduction to *Fasti* 1 divides into three sections: an introductory couplet defining Ovid's subject matter, and two units of twelve lines marked off by opening imperatives (*excipe* 'accept', 3: *adnue* 'approve', 15) addressed to Germanicus first as prince and heir to the imperial house (3–14) then as poet and man of letters (15–26). As we shall see, the two sections are linked by common encomiastic material: 9–14 presents as part of Ovid's

---

[6] Compare Syme (1974: 484), a study of Tiberius in literature prompted by reading Seager (1972): 'Not AD 14 but AD 4, that was the decisive year. Both foreign and domestic, the main themes ran back into the last decade of Augustus' reign: the German wars, the eastern question, prosecutions for high treason and the whole relationship between *princeps* and Senate ... above all the strains and discords in the dynastic group.'

contents feast days honouring Germanicus' family, while 15–16 argues that because Ovid's theme is these honours—*laudes... tuorum* 'praises of your kin'—he needs and deserves the prince's support and inspiration.

Does anything in the opening couplet presuppose that it was composed with the late Germanicus dedication, rather than preserved from Ovid's first attempt to dedicate his poem? The first line announces his intention to sing of occasions distributed over the Latin year with their *causae*. Each word is pointed: unlike Propertius, his predecessor in Latin aetiological poetry, Ovid will articulate his poem by times, *tempora*, that will be Latin and not simply Roman. Callimachus had presented highly selective origins of customs and rituals from many different Greek communities, but Ovid's *causae* are determined by the national calendar,[7] and he will attempt to give, if not full, at least representative coverage of the formal year. Propertius had dealt with *sacra diesque... et cognomina prisca locorum* 'rites and dates...and the ancient names of places' (4.1.69) but these were associated with Roman sites, and the element of *dies*, commemorated by feasts, is minimal, implicit rather than dominant in 4.1 on the Palatine,[8] omitted from 4.2 on the Vicus Tuscus, 4.4 on the Mons Tarpeius, or 4.9 and 10 on the Ara Maxima and the temple of Bona Dea subsaxana, and on the Capitoline temple of Jupiter Feretrius.

Ovid commits himself from the beginning to move through the seasons. The hexameter covers artificial dates, determined by human ordinance, the pentameter natural time, defined by the sequential rising and setting of constellations (*lapsa sub terras ortaque signa*). These marked the seasons for farmers and had been a subject of poetry from the time of Hesiod, just as they were used to indicate the seasons and identify points of the compass by sailors. Aratus' didactic hexameter poem, the *Phaenomena*, and its continuation, the *Prognostica*,

[7] On Ovid's use of Verrius Flaccus, *Fasti Praenestini* see Bömer (1957–8) i.23, and the reproduction of these *Fasti* for January. Bömer (1957–8) i.33–4. However the inscribed *Fasti* and commentary represent only a selection from a more comprehensive work *de fastis Romanis* on which Ovid must have based his poem, as both date and location of the inscription would suggest. For evidence that he also knew the earlier work of Fulvius Nobilior see below, p. 409.

[8] Propertius names the *Parilia* (4.1.19–20) and alludes to the *Lupercalia* (4.1.26) but his other elegies neither name nor allude to a dated annual festival. On the topography see Butler and Barber (1933) 333, 343, 370–1 and 375–6.

had immense influence in Rome, from Cicero's boyhood translation to echoes and adaptations in Lucretius, in Vergil's *Georgics*, to the *Astronomica* of Manilius (not a translation) and the paraphrase by Germanicus Caesar, all composed before the second quarter of the first century AD.[9]

There was good reason to include allusions to the constellations in a calendar poem, but they are in fact relatively marginal in the early books of the *Fasti*, becoming more frequent in books 5 and 6 (Fantham 1983: 212–13). There are tales of their origin in myth, but otherwise astronomy is most prominent in two passages of encomium, at 1.297–310, where Ovid turns aside to praise astronomers for their heavenly aspirations and services to men, and more briefly at 3.105–14.[10]

If it is neat and systematic that Ovid should divide his programmatic couplet between artificial and natural time, it is particularly apposite in the present preface, since it is addressed to Germanicus, the poet of the *Phaenomena*. But was he already, by the time of Ovid's proem, the adapter of Aratus? Syme assumes so[11] without comment on the usual dating of the poem to the prince's last three years (AD 17–19) and I will later put the case for assigning Germanicus' work on the poem, and even its completion, to an earlier time. But let us first follow the proem for the terms in which Ovid addresses his prince.

He asks him to accept the poem 'with peaceful countenance' and direct the course of his hesitant ship. The ship is the poem, an equation that will continue throughout the six books, for example at 1.465–6 (*unde petam causas horum moremque sacrorum?* | *deriget in medio quis mea uela freto?* 'Where shall I seek the causes and the manner of these rites? Who will guide my sails in mid ocean?'), where he answers his own question by appealing to the native prophetess, Evander's mother Carmenta, to foster his enterprise (468). Carmenta

---

[9] See Mair's (1921: 371–2) introduction to the *Phaenomena*. On Cicero's *Aratea* see Ewbank (1933) 23–4. Cicero was *admodum adulescentulus* (*ND* 2.104) when he translated the *Phaenomena*: Mayor suggests as young as 17. On the connotations of *admodum adulescens*, see now Badian (1984: 301 n.50).

[10] *Fast.* 3.105 ff. has clear echoes of *Georg.* 1.137–8 and recalls the argument of Lucretius 5.1183–93.

[11] Syme (1978) 46: 'after an interval he took a further step. Was not Germanicus himself a master of verse, the author of the *Aratea*? Ovid reverted to his *Fasti*...and equipped the work with a new preface.'

acts as his Muse in the Hesiodic sense, as a source of information.
By the same token Germanicus is acting as a surrogate for the Muse
in this proem, but in the more sophisticated sense of a source of
inspiration. The proem conceives the work as about to begin, not
yet *in medio...freto*, and does not ask Germanicus to accept the
completed poem, but to take up or sponsor the enterprise: yet the
word *excipere* is more appropriate to taking up the poet. So in *Ex
Ponto* 1.1.3–4 Ovid appeals to Brutus, asking him to give shelter to
his book: *si uacat, hospitio peregrinos, Brute, libellos | excipe* 'If you
have the time, Brutus, receive these foreign books with hospitality'.[12]
Another oddity of diction is the epithet *pacato* 'appeased' replacing
the conventional *placido...uultu* 'with a kindly look' in the appeal
for a propitious reaction from the god or patron.[13] Ovid is surely
not adopting this rare usage *metri gratia* to preserve the short final
syllable of *excipe*: he does not use inappropriate words to solve metrical problems. Rather he chose *pacato* in the rare sense of 'appeased',
'peaceful', to foreshadow his emphasis of *pax* and *pacare* reflected in
this proem by the rejection or allegorizing of *arma* (1.13 and 23) and
by the recurring celebration of *pax* in book 1 and later in the *Fasti*.
The word suggests a warrior who has imposed peace by conquest,
enjoying the leisure to attend to his petitioner, as in *si uacat* (*Ex Ponto*
1.3) and *Fasti* 2.18 *si quid ab hoste uacas*.

Next Ovid incites Germanicus to stand by him on the right, a good
omen which he also requests from Janus at 1.67 and 69 (*dexter ades
ducibus*), and favour his *officium*, the homage due from a client to
his patron.[14] He could be recalling the special control over auspices
for the beginning of an enterprise which Germanicus enjoyed as an

---

[12] There are Ovidian instances of *excipere* in two potentially relevant senses: 'to
take under one's care or protection...give shelter to' (as in *Pont.* 1.1.3–4; *OLD* s.v.
7); and 'to receive (a speech etc.) in a specified manner, greet', as in *Ars* 1.710 *excipiat
blandas comiter illa preces* (*OLD* s.v. 9a).

[13] Cf. *placido...uultu* at *Fast.* 2.17 (Augustus); 4.161 (Venus); 5.23 (Reuerentia);
and the synonymous *placato...ore* (*Met.* 14.593). In *Met.* 4.31 *placatus mitisque adsis*
addressed to Bacchus is probably the model for Statius *Silu.* 3.1.139 *pacatus mitisque
ueni*, the earliest parallel for this application of *pacatus*.

[14] On the history of this motif in such invocations, see Bennett (1968) 337, citing
Prop. 4.1.67–8, *date candida ciues | omina, et inceptis dextera cantet auis*, and *Aetna* 4
(to Apollo), *dexter uenias mihi carminis auctor*. For its role in the cletic hymn cf. *Aen.*
8.301–2 *salue uera Iouis proles, decus addite diuis, | et nos et tua dexter adi pede sacra
secundo*.

augur[15]—a neat personal compliment—but both the epithet *deuoto* and the associations of Germanicus with his *numen* raise the princely patron to the level of a divine protector, and one implication of *deuoueo* is surely that the offering is a *uotum* in return for a blessing unspecified. This will be the nearest Ovid comes in the proem to declaring his *uotum pro reditu* (the most common type of vow whether before a campaign or a voyage), though an intrusive outcry in book 4 will link Germanicus openly with his longing to escape from Tomis.[16]

Line 7 passes on to the contents of the poem, conceiving Germanicus now not as its source but as its reader. Germanicus will not discover, but rediscover[17] the rites Ovid has unearthed from ancient archives, a hint at the prince's erudition and antiquarian interests. Ovid mentions only dates of good omen (*quo merito* implies the white pebble) and reaches his panegyric theme, the *festa domestica*, celebrations of and by the family of the Augustan house. This will be a new element beyond the rare incidence in older Roman *Fasti* of days honouring the victory of a Cornelius Scipio or a Fabius Maximus, for the Augustan *Fasti* are crowded with official anniversaries of titles and victories won by the Julian house. Ovid honours Germanicus' *pater* (Tiberius, by adoption) and *auus* (Augustus, by double adoption) and rounds off the section with a complimentary prophecy of future celebration for the victories of the prince himself and his brother (Drusus, by adoption).[18] When Tiberius was given equal *imperium* with the 75-year-old Augustus in AD 13, he remained in Italy, leaving Germanicus in command of the Rhine armies to earn his first salutation in that year,[19] and

[15] Germanicus' augurate, attested by Tac. *Ann.* 1.62 and 83, can now be dated from *ILS* 107 before AD 7/8. See Sumner (1967) 432.

[16] *Fast.* 4.81–4 *Sulmonis gelidi, patriae, Germanice, nostrae.* | *me miserum Scythico quam procul illa solo est.* | *ergo ego tam longe—sed supprime, Musa, querellas:* | *non tibi sunt maesta sacra canenda lyra.*

[17] On this implication of *recognoscere* cf. Cic. *Tusc.* 1.57 (contrasted with *discere*) and the other two instances in Ov. *Met.* 11.62 and *Fast.* 4.418 *plura recognosces, pauca docendus eris.*

[18] For the double adoption see Suet. *Tib.* 15.1; Syme (1978) 45; and on the ensuing changes in family nomenclature and structure see Levick (1975) 29–38, and (1976*b*) 313–14.

[19] On Tiberius' equal *imperium* see Suet. *Tib.* 21.1; *Aug.* 27.5; Vell. 2.121; and Levick (1976*a*) 63 with n. 60. On Germanicus' first salutation in 13, see Barnes (1974)

Drusus Caesar as commander in Pannonia. By the time that Ovid revised book 1 of the *Fasti* Germanicus had erased the memory of the mutiny with some inconclusive raiding on the Cherusci in 14 and further campaigning in 15, earning the senatorial decree of a triumph either at the beginning or towards the end of that year.

Ovid honours this triumph at 1.285 ff., praising Germanicus with more tact than accuracy for having established peace in Germany and made possible the closing of Janus' temple. There is no conflict between celebration of peace and pride in warfare and the repudiation of *arma* as theme for his poetry in 1.13 should be understood primarily as a *recusatio* of epic, reaffirming his vocation as an elegiac poet. At the same time it provides a neat antithesis of symbols, balancing weapons against altars to mark religious celebrations. But the antithesis is only apparent, since the combination of *dies* and *Caesaris arae* evokes occasions when the altars burned sacrifices to honour victory; it stresses the commemoration without excluding the victories commemorated. Important sections of book 1 will recall sacrifices to honour Augustus and Germanicus' natural father Drusus[20] and the most famous of Augustan altars, the *ara pacis Augustae*, which introduces the coda of the whole book.

In the second half of the invocation (15–26) Ovid renews his equation of Germanicus with divine inspiration by the imperatives *adnue...da mihi te placidum* 'approve...show yourself favourable to me'. But more immediate than the divine associations is the allusion to Ovid's and Germanicus' predecessors, Vergil and Octavian, in the great proem to *Georgics* 1. The *Georgics* indeed open with an impressive list of rural gods, but reach a climax in the invocation of the *praesens deus* Octavian (1.40–2):

da facilem cursum, atque audacibus adnue coeptis...
ingredere, et uotis iam nunc adsuesce uocari.[21]

25–6, citing Crinagoras *AP* 9.283 and a recent inscription published by G. E. Bean in Cook (1973) 412: 'The inscription alone suggests a joint salutation for all three men for fighting under Augustus.'

[20] With *Fast.* 1.596–7 on Drusus, compare *Pont.* 2.8.47–50 *sic quem dira tibi rapuit Germania Drusum | pars fuerit partus sola caduca tui. | sic tibi mature fraterni funeris ultor | purpureus niueis filius instet equis.*

[21] So also *Georg.* 2.39–44 to Maecenas: *tuque ades inceptumque una decurre laborem |..., Maecenas, pelagoque uolans da uela patenti...* (44) *ades et primi lege litoris oram.* Vergil is also Ovid's model in marking the end of the book by the voyage

Grant me an easy course, and approve my bold enterprise...enter and already now become accustomed to being invoked in prayer.

Ovid like Vergil speaks of a poetic voyage (*Georgics* 1.25–6), asks the prince's blessing and substitutes for Vergil's *coepta* the personal *conanti ire*. Octavian was in his early thirties when Vergil composed the *Georgics*: Germanicus, born May 24th 15 BC, was about thirty in Ovid's last years. In adapting his proem from Vergil Ovid was making both a literary and a political statement: if he saw Germanicus as the rising new Octavian, heir to his adoptive father Tiberius (some 25 years older), he was also making a claim for himself and his poem. Despite its elegiac form and Callimachean ancestry, he presents it as *poésie engagée*, serious didactic with the elevation fitting to Roman reverence for the head of state and the gods or to the wonders of nature praised and explained by Aratus, Lucretius, and Vergil. He is presenting it as a patriotic alternative to military epic, celebrating the national hero as a civilian religious leader who has brought peace through victory.

I said that Ovid put Germanicus in place of his muse, but in this section he explicitly compares him to Apollo, god of Claros. The *doctus princeps* has unerring critical judgement and eloquence in prose and verse. Just as *dexter ades* deftly complimented the prince as Augur, so the allusion to Claros seems to be a personal reference, for Tacitus, describing Germanicus' journey to Asia after Ovid's death, lingers over his special visit to Claros and goes into detail about his consultation of the oracle.[22] Since the epithet is so rare in both Callimachus and Augustan poetry, we must surely infer that Ovid knew from personal contact of Germanicus' long-held devotion to the shrine at Claros. He rounds off the appeal with a figured request for Germanicus' guidance as a *uates* and his good augury for the

and race-metaphors: *Georg.* 2.541–2 *sed nos immensum spatiis confecimus aequor | et iam tempus equum fumantia soluere colla.* On Vergil's initiative in transferring his appeal for inspiration from the traditional Muse to his patrons see Bennett (1968), who gives a complete survey of these motifs from Lucretius to Ovid (327–33) but mentions the *Fasti*-proem only incidentally (338). See now Zetzel (1982) 87–102.

[22] On Germanicus' visit to Claros, see Tac. *Ann.* 2.54, with Goodyear (1981) 358–9. Apollo is only once associated with Claros in extant Callimachus, at *Hymn* 2.70, as one of a list of cult titles. Of the Augustans only Vergil (*Aen.* 3.360) mentions Claros before Ovid. Ovid calls Antimachus of Colophon the Clarian poet at *Tr.* 1.6.1, and alludes to Apollo of Claros at *Ars* 2.80; *Met.* 1.516; 11.413.

completion of Ovid's year. If the figure of the patron taking the reins recalls Propertius,[23] the plea for professional solidarity between poets is Ovid's own compliment, and one he will repeat in the parallel couplet at *Ex Ponto* 4.8.67–8:

non potes officium uatis contemnere uates:
  iudicio pretium res habet ista tuo.

As a poet, you cannot despise the service of a poet: that activity has a value in your judgement.

How could Ovid have known Germanicus in the years since he turned to the *Fasti*, perhaps as early as 2 BC? The prince lost his father at the age of 6 when he acquired Drusus' posthumous cognomen Germanicus and we do not know in whose household he was reared. At 18, in AD 4, he was adopted by his uncle Tiberius at his great-uncle's request, and must have married Agrippina, daughter of Agrippa and Julia, during AD 5: he was given the right to become quaestor five years ahead of the normal age and held that office in AD 7, serving on the Dalmatian front. In AD 8 he was sent to Rome with news of the Dalmatian surrender and probably remained there until he joined his adoptive father in celebrating games in memory of his father Drusus in AD 9.[24] Ovid was at Rome until the fall of Julia the younger and the disgrace of her set brought on his own relegation to Tomis in AD 8.[25] If Germanicus associated with his wife's sister and her friends he will have had the opportunity to know the poet at least until his quaestorship took him to Dalmatia; the disgrace of Julia minor and exile of Ovid may well have taken place before Germanicus' return. Germanicus continued to serve with Tiberius, and when a triumph

[23] Prop. 3.9.57–8 *mollia tu coeptae fautor cape lora iuuentae | dexteraque immissis da mihi signa rotis.*
[24] This summary of Germanicus' career is based on Gelzer, *RE* x 435–58, modified from Sumner (1967) 413–35; Levick (1976b) 315–20; and Syme (1978) 56–65, discussing Germanicus' salutations and triumph. Even if Levick is right that he was born in 16 BC he cannot have held the quaestorship before AD 7 and his public career began in that year. On Germanicus' movements at the time of Tiberius' accession, see Levick (1976a) 73–4.
[25] For the most recent discussions see Syme (1978) 219–21, Levick (1976b) 336 ff., and Green (1982b) 210 ff. Levick notes that Sidonius Apollinaris is the first source to associate Ovid with Julia, obliquely named as *Caesarea puella*. All three modern discussions attribute Ovid's disgrace to involvement with Julia, whether as witness to adultery or to marriage or to conspiracy.

was decreed to Tiberius (and of course Augustus) for the Dalmatian victories, Germanicus rode with his adoptive father in the triumphal procession of October 23rd, AD 12, the year of his first consulship. This is the occasion of Ovid's first published tribute to the prince, written from exile in the second book *Ex Ponto*. Throughout that year Germanicus, now 26 years old, was in Rome, active in the courts, exercising the consulship and basking in his immense popularity with the Roman people (*mirus apud populum fauor*, Tac. *Ann.* 1.7.9). But in 13 he left for the Rhine frontier to replace Tiberius as commander and was conducting a census in Gaul when he was called away to deal with the mutiny of the legions. He was still trying to restore discipline when the news came of Augustus' death and Tiberius' assumption of sole responsibility for the empire. Tacitus' subtle portrait of Germanicus shows that although he remained loyal to Tiberius he lacked dignity and judgement in calming the legions and his campaigns were extravagant in manpower;[26] they also violated Augustus' injunction against extending the limits of empire, and in Tacitus' interpretation Tiberius was glad to accelerate the decree of a triumph in 15, in order to justify his recall from the dangerous German front and transfer to a diplomatic role in the East. Though Ovid celebrates, and indeed anticipates Tiberius' Dalmatian triumph in which Germanicus shared the glory, and though he also anticipates Germanicus' German triumph in his last letters from Pontus and the *Fasti* proem, he did not live to record its celebration in May, AD 17, which is described for us by Strabo and (more briefly) Velleius.[27]

Ovid starts to honour Tiberius' triumph some time before Tiberius returned to celebrate it, and mentions Germanicus as one of the two heirs of Tiberius in the anticipatory descriptions of *Tristia* 3.12 and 4.2.[28] Only when he records the occasion in the opening poem of

---

[26] See Shotter (1968) and Ross (1973) for Tacitus' ambiguous presentation of the young commander, but note that the new Germanicus Edicts from Alexandria (printed in Goodyear 1981: 458–60) confirm the impression of immaturity.

[27] On Tacitus' dating of the Senatorial decree of the triumph to early 15 see Syme (1978) 59–61, Goodyear (1981) 68–9 and 315–16.

[28] Tiberius followed his suppression of the rebellions in Pannonia and Dalmatia by an urgent transfer to the German front to restore morale after the ambush of Quintilius Varus in AD 9. His campaigns in Germany in the years 10, 11, and probably 12 explain why Ovid anticipates Tiberius' triumph in terms not of his successes in Pannonia but of his recent and prospective victories in Germany. References to a

Ex Ponto 2 does he address the young prince by name. The poem
starts in terms of family glory; it is *Caesareus triumphus* (*Ex Ponto*
2.1.1) celebrated by *illa domus* (2.1.18). Tiberius himself is simply
victor (2.1.29). After paying respect to Augustus and the new temple
of Iustitia Augusta (2.1.33–4) dedicated in AD 13 Ovid reports the
procession and turns to Germanicus (2.1.49), wishing him a glorious
future as conqueror and *triumphator*, watched by his father Tiberius,
who will rejoice in due course at his son's honours with the same
delight which he now feels at his own (59–60):

maturosque pater nati spectabit honores,
  gaudia percipiens quae dedit ipse suis.

Your father will see the mature honours of his son, feeling the joy which has
given to his own.

While Ovid is at pains to stress Germanicus' junior status as *princeps iuuentutis* (*iuuenum . . . maxime*, 61–2) and the distant timing
(*maturos*) of these honours to come, the elegy risks invidious glorification of the rising young prince at the cost of the elderly Tiberius. *Ex
Ponto* 2.5 is scarcely more tactful. It is addressed to a Cassius Salanus
who is said to have been moved at Ovid's plight. From Pliny (*Nat.*
34.47) we know that Salanus was uncle of the governor of Narbo-
nensis and praeceptor of Germanicus, who presented him—perhaps
as a retirement gift—with two precious Hellenistic silver cups. Ovid
depicts Salanus more as an intellectual associate and childhood companion of the prince (2.5.41–2):

te iuuenum princeps, cui dat Germania nomen,
  participem studii Caesar habere solet.

The leader of youth, to whom Germany gives a name, Caesar has you as
partner in his intellectual pursuits.

He also shows him as a sort of pacemaker in declamation for the
young orator, whose performance he describes in adulatory terms
(49–56). Ovid mentions his triumph poem, hoping it may have been

German triumph in Ovid's exile poetry up to *Pont.* 2 should be related to the triumph of AD 12 correctly reported in *Pont.* 2.2.75–8: *adde triumphatos modo Paeonas,
adde quieti | subdita montanae bracchia Dalmatiae. | nec dedignata est abiectis Illyris
armis | Caesareum famulo uertice ferre pedem.*

recited in Salanus' hearing, and while deprecating his power to do justice to the occasion, he asks for Salanus' continued support for Ovid's poetry, ending with the pious claim that Salanus may enjoy Germanicus' friendship to the end of his life, and the prince succeed as ruler to the governing of the world, as is the wish of the people (*Ex Ponto* 2.5.75–6):

succedatque suis orbis moderator habenis:
   quod mecum populi uota precantur idem.

May he come to control of the world with his own reins, which is at once my prayer and the people's.

While he no doubt had in mind only the prince's role as successor to Tiberius, some 25 years his senior, the political wish at a time when Tiberius himself had still to establish his sole power risks the implication of bypassing the immediate heir to impose a more glamorous and popular figure from the next generation. However the main stress of the poem is on the literary interests that link Salanus both to his prince and to Ovid. Ideas appear for the first time which we also meet in the Germanicus proem of the *Fasti*, such as the *impetus* of the *princeps'* talent (*Ex Ponto* 2.5.45 = *Fasti* 1.24), the affinity of fellow writers (*ingeniis aliqua est concordia iunctis*, 2.5.59), and the sanctity of poetry (*commilitii sacra tuenda*, 2.5.72), despite the inconvenient fact that Salanus' speciality was prose, not verse. On this topic Ovid brings out some new and characteristically silver Latin ideas about the relationship between the genres (oratory provides poetry with *nerui* while verse lends *nitor* to eloquence), but the feature which will become the tenor of Ovid's communications with Germanicus and his circle is that of understanding and support between artists (2.5.63–4):

tu quoque Pieridum studio, studiose, teneris
   ingenioque faues, ingeniose, meo.

You too are an enthusiast in the grip of the enthusiasm for the Muses, and a talented man who favours my talent.

The addressee is still only an intermediary, but Ovid will soon address the prince himself. There is no reference to Germanicus in book 3 of *Ex Ponto*, which was probably arranged and published in a triad with

1 and 2, but the last collection contains many letters to the prince's associates, and 4.5, the second letter to Pompeius, consul of AD 14, and the letters 4.12 and 13 to Tuticanus and to Carus, tutor of Germanicus' children, offer tribute to the prince. The main vehicle, however is the eighth letter, ostensibly to Ovid's stepdaughter's husband Suillius Rufus,[29] the quaestor of Germanicus. We should note the position of 4.8. Along with 4.9, addressed to Pomponius Graecinus, suffect consul of 16, it is the longest poem and stands at the centre of the collection. The letter to Graecinus pays Ovid's due to the dead Augustus, describing his domestic shrine in honour of the imperial family and celebration of the *princeps'* birthday (4.9.105–16). Finally it apostrophizes the dead *princeps* with a résumé of Ovid's hymn on his apotheosis. Balancing the tribute to Augustus in 4.9, the pretext, as in *Ex Ponto* 2.5, is a message of sympathy Ovid has received from Suillius. Like other letters of the period it explains their relationship for the uninitiated and pleads Ovid's respectability and innocence (4.8.15–18, cf. e.g. 2.2.9–18). Ovid urges Suillius to supplicate for him the gods he worships, continuing: *di tibi sunt Caesar iuuenis; tua numina placa* (4.8.23). We see Germanicus as the young Caesar, equivalent to a god; here too Ovid may be borrowing from the young Vergil, echoing Tityrus in *Eclogue* 1.6–8:

> deus nobis haec otia fecit,
> namque erit ille mihi semper deus, illius aram
> saepe tener nostris ab ouilibus imbuet agnus…

A god created this peace for me; for that one will always be a god to me: his altar will often be stained by a tender lamb from my fold.

and 42–3:

> hic illum uidi iuuenem…quotannis
> bis senos cui nostra dies altaria fumant.

Here I saw that young man…for whom our altar will smoke twelve days each year.

---

[29] For the connection of these figures with Germanicus see Syme (1978). Tacitus summarizes Suillius Rufus' career at *Ann.* 13.42 when he was banished for the second and last time for his vicious record as a *delator*. He was Germanicus' quaestor, most probably at the time of this letter, since Ovid assumes he has access to Germanicus in the field.

Ovid drops Suillius, and in addressing the prince directly evokes earlier homage to Augustus; like Propertius he can only offer *parua munera* (incense 4.8.29–40) which should be as valuable an offering as any rich man's wealth. With some tendency to pastiche Ovid combines the self-deprecation of Propertius and the humble sacrifice of Vergil's Tityrus (4.8.41–2): *agnaque tam lactens quam gramine pasta Falisco | uictima* 'and the nursing lamb as well as the victim fed on Faliscan grass'.

But Ovid comes closest to the proem of the *Fasti* in the section on the homage of poetry (43–67). Like the proem Ovid's elegy stresses the *officium uatum | uatis* (43, 67) and his *laudes* (45, 61, 87; cf. *Fasti* 1.15). *Laudes* have unique power to immortalize *uirtus* (46 and 63) and the services of *carmina* to *uirtus* occupy the centre of the poem (45–47). Common also to the proem and the elegy is emphasis on Germanicus as critic and fellow poet. In the elegy Ovid advances a relatively intricate argument. Poetry immortalizes virtues, keeping memory green; it even creates gods (55), as Ovid illustrates from his own recent consecration of Germanicus' grandfather Augustus. So now Ovid will dedicate his talent to the prince, who as a poet will recognize the value of his art. Particularly close to the *Fasti* proem is the appeal, *non potes officium uatis contemnere uates* (67) asking Germanicus in the name of their *communia sacra* to arrange for his transfer to a nearer place *unde tuas possim laudes celebrare recentes*; finally Ovid returns to Suillius, commissioning him to petition Germanicus (89–90): *tangat ut hoc uotum caelestia... | numina pro socero paene precare tuo* 'that this vow may touch the heavenly... powers, offer a prayer for him who is practically the father of your wife'.

In the elegy we have a balance between exaltation of poetry and exaltation of its princely subject matter, not flattery but a confident claim by the inheritor of a great tradition that he has something to offer whose own immortality guarantees that of those it celebrates; at the centre of the poem stand ideas from Horace's *exegi monumentum* (*Odes* 3.30); from *ne forte credas* and *donarem pateras* (4.8 and 4.9— surely the numbering is a calculated gesture by Ovid?) and from Propertius' exaltation of *ingenium* and its commemorative power in 3.1 and 3.2. These are themes of major importance for Ovid's justification of his past life. But the elegy like the proem must subordinate its pride in the value of poetry to another purpose, since its goal is to justify Ovid's plea for relief from this place of exile.

It would be almost a violation of genre for the proem of a major work—didactic or epic—to ask for any help except in undertaking that work, or to seek a favourable verdict on the poet's life rather than his poem. So the *Fasti* proem must subordinate the theme to its programmatic function: the poet-prince is still judge of Ovid's work, but it is more important to appeal to him for inspiration. By its position *ingenium uoltu statque caditque tuo* can offer either sense, at first completing the meaning of 17 'my talent will succeed or fail in response to your countenance', then reinterpreted in the light of 19–20 as 'the product of my talent will succeed or fail according to your critical reaction.' Ovid oscillates between the literary fiction of a work needing the patron's inspiration to get under way and the reality of a finished work whose fate will be determined by the patron's verdict. Finally he takes refuge from the embarrassment of supplicating for himself or his poem by taking the prince inside the world of the poem, as augur presiding over the Roman year, for which he will of course desire success.

When did Germanicus become a poet? It is more important to ask when he began work on the *Phaenomena* than when it is likely to have been 'published'. Suetonius reports his literary interests in the *Life of Gaius* (3.3; cf. *Claud.* 11.2), mentioning an elegy and the composition of a Greek comedy, but we have no ancient evidence for the *Phaenomena*. Since the poem was substantially a free translation it may have been seen as something less than a real composition, justifying the indifference of later sources. Other works of the first century are similarly ignored, like Phaedrus' fables and Seneca's tragedies which do not reach Quintilian's selective survey, though Domitian, the other Germanicus Caesar, earns a place by virtue of being the ruling monarch (*Inst.* 10.1.91).

Editors, pointing to Germanicus' busy career from the age of 21 and the scholarly work behind the corrections of Aratus' astronomy, have urged dating the poem to his last years, after the period in Rome in AD 16 when Tiberius recalled him from Germany and before he went to the East (le Boeuffle 1975: vii–x). But this kind of enterprise is commonly associated with young men, as it was in the case of Cicero, who composed his *Aratea* when *admodum adulescentulus*.

Germanicus is far more likely to have begun work in his 'student phase' before his campaigns and Ovid's exile in AD 8; he had tutors and slaves to consult Hipparchus for him and prepare a corrected scheme for versification. He could also have devoted more time to this work in his consulship, since public business at Rome was largely prepared for its smooth passage by the *consilium principis* without effort on his part. Not only would this hypothesis give point to Ovid's choice of Germanicus as patron and his stress on the astronomical component in the *Fasti*, it would also explain some unremarked affinities between Germanicus' own proem and Ovid's more skilful verse.

One of Germanicus' modifications of Aratus was the personal dedication to his *genitor*, whom I understand as Tiberius, his adoptive father (1–4):

ab Ioue principium magno deduxit Aratus
carminis, at nobis, genitor, tu maximus auctor,
te ueneror, tibi sacra fero, doctique laboris
primitias.

Aratus took the beginning of his poem with great Jupiter, but you, father, are my chief authority. It is you that I reverence, to you that I bring sacred offerings and the first fruits of my learned labour.

Beginning with this displacement, he ends by appealing for his father's inspiration (15–16):

haec ego dum Latiis conor praedicere Musis
pax tua tuque adsis nato, numenque secundes.

As I attempt to tell of this in Latin verse, may your peace and your presence aid your son: grant your divine power.

Germanicus is clearly influenced by the *Georgics*, from which he derives *sacra fero* (*Georgics* 2.476) and the agricultural *color* of *laboris* and *primitias*, and indeed the whole spirit of his insertion from 5–14. So too he appeals to his father's help, invoking his *numen* and his peace to aid his undertaking, adapting Vergil's *coepta* in the form *haec ego dum conor* and his appeal for support in which *adnue* becomes *adsis*.

Germanicus has been seen as echoing these features from the *Fasti* proem, with Ovid's stress on *pax*, his *adnue conanti* and the appeal *numine dexter ades*; but his language can be explained by reference to Vergil, and its modifications are weaker and less effective than Ovid's words. One indeed is less daring, for the attribution of *numen* to his father Tiberius seems to conform to the growing association of *numen* with the emperor and his heirs, whereas Ovid's evocation of the *numen* of the 30-year-old Germanicus goes a step further in flattery. There will be additional argument for Germanicus' priority if we see *ab Ioue surgat opus* in Ovid's transition at *Fasti* 5.111 as imitation of Germanicus' opening line, but this would seem unnecessary when Pindar, Callimachus, Theocritus, and Aratus all offered precedents.[30]

Of course there are obstacles to an Augustan dating for Germanicus' work, the most important of which are lines 558–60, reporting Augustus' apotheosis, and the echo between *Phaenomena* 2, *tu maximus auctor*, and Manilius *Astronomica* 1.386, *Caesar, nunc terris, post caelo maximus auctor* 'Caesar, now on earth, later in heaven the chief authority'. The situation is made more complex because the *Astronomica*, like the *Phaenomena* and the *Fasti* itself, seems to contain conflicting indications of date; thus Goold concludes that books 1 and 2 were written during Augustus' lifetime, but 4 and 5 after his death (Goold 1977: xii);[31] Germanicus could have read Manilius 1.386 and transferred the phrase and its application in his poem to Tiberius and the lesser role of personal inspiration. Lines 558–60 are a bigger problem; some scholars, like Maurach, have rejected them as

---

[30] On the fine distinction between the living Caesar and his *numen* in cult see Fishwick (1969) 356–67. Poetry was less fastidious; compare Ovid's equation of Augustus' *numen* with the *princeps*; from *Tristia* we have *Augusti numen* (3.8.13), *Caesareum numen* (5.3.46 and 11.20), *Caesaris numen* (5.10.52), *tua numina* (2.573), and phrases such as *laeso numine* (2.108 and 3.6.23), *numinis ira* (1.5.44; 4.8.50; 5.4.17). *Ex Ponto* adds *Augustum numen* (3.1.163; 4.6.10), and after Augustus' death even transfers the divine aspect to Livia and Tiberius (4.9.108 *numina iam facto non leuiora deo*), while the transference of *numina* to Germanicus, self-conscious and assertive in *Pont.* 4.8.23, is stepped up to *caelestia numina* in 4.8.90; in 4.15.26 also, *numina* most probably means Germanicus.

[31] Goold notes that Manilius may have influenced Germanicus, citing a line from the Tiberian fifth book of Manilius (5.237 = Germ. 184). If the imitation were certain it would exclude the possibility of early composition.

interpolated.[32] I would prefer to see the poem as left unfinished like the *Fasti*, and incompletely revised as a result of the author's death. It is not essential to my arguments about the extended composition of the *Fasti* that Ovid should have known this proem, but I find it easier to see in Ovid's proem a courtly compliment to his dedicatee, transferring to the prince some of the Vergilian homage which Germanicus bestowed on his *genitor*. The theory both eases the boldness of Ovid's quasi-deification of his prince and explains the motivation of his choice of Germanicus as his new patron. The greater poet need not have been the model, for one distinguishing feature of Ovid's art and the poetry of the first century AD was the desire to remodel a predecessor, using his verse as a challenge to go one better—*aemulatio*.[33] To quote Seneca's comment on a similar sequence of echoes (*Epist. Mor.* 79.5–6): 'The fact that Vergil had already fully treated it did not prevent Ovid from dealing with it... and past discoveries don't stand in the way of future ones. Furthermore, the situation of the last one is best: he finds the words ready, which have a new aspect when arranged differently.' The question cannot be decided, but we may think the second coincidence of *Fasti* 5.111 and *Phaenomena* 1 increases the likelihood that the professional poet indulged in allusive imitation of the prince and amateur.

II

Although Ovid composed the opening address to Germanicus in his last years, he took pains to relate it to other prooemiac passages in the *Fasti*, just as he related them in turn to each other. Book 4, beginning the second group of three month-books, opens with an address to Venus, patroness of the month of April, then devotes lines 3–10 to a

---

[32] Maurach (1978: 17–20) oddly inclines to reject 558–60 as spurious, while concluding that 1) the proem is addressed to Tiberius *as princeps* and 2) Germanicus could have begun the poem in AD 10 or more likely 12, and worked on it in the winter between campaigns. These contradictory conclusions seem to depend on his assumption that Germanicus must have composed his proem after that of Ovid (cf. p. 33).

[33] See also Seneca Rhetor *Contr.* 7.1.27 for Ovidian *aemulatio*, and Fantham (1982) 25 ff.

poetic reminder of his rejection of love elegy (mirroring elements in
the proem of book 2) and lines 11–18 to recalling elements known to
us from the Germanicus proem, though our order of reading reverses
the order in which Ovid composed the two proems. Thus 4.11–12
repeats the opening couplet of *Fasti* 1, but replaces the second half
of the hexameter with the same half-line, *annalibus eruta priscis*,
that we find in *Fasti* 1.7. Venus' language in her reply to the poet,
coeptum perfice opus (4.16) resumes *excipe... hoc opus* from 1.3–4,
and *causae... dierum* (4.17) recalls elements in *Fasti* 1.1 and 1.8 *quo
sit merito quaeque notata dies*. Finally the provisional *dum licet* and
nautical image[34] *et spirant flamina, nauis eat* of 4.18 are matched in
Fasti 1.25 *si licet et fas est* and the opening nautical allusion *derige
nauis iter* (1.4).

If Ovid reworked his opening address so as to share these elements
with the proem of book 4, we should not exclude the probability
that lines 1–2, 7–8, and 25 were already in this form. But the composition of his opening to book 4 required far greater skill; besides
its evocation of echoes from the first two prooemiac passages, it has
been designed, as Braun has shown, to mark a parallel between this
address to Venus and the simpler address to Mars of book 3; thus
the introductory sections of books 3 and 4, apostrophizing the two
ancestral deities of Rome, are bound together as a pair (Braun 1981:
2347–8). So too we may see the proem addressed to Augustus in
book 2 as stressing the pairing of books 1 and 2, provided that we
also recognize Ovid's continuation of the imperial theme from 2.3–
18 on to 2.63–66 and 112–44 (Braun 1981: 2351 and n. 33; Kraus
1968: 125). There is perhaps a further structural parallel between the
invocation to Augustus at 2.63 ff. and that to Germanicus and Janus
which serves as a secondary invocation at 1.3–70.

Let us examine the proem to book 2, the lines which countless
editors have explained as the original proem to the entire *Fasti*. On
their theory Ovid replaced it with the new dedication to Germanicus
after Augustus' death. Either the poet or a posthumous editor could

---

[34] For the poetic voyage see Bömer on 1.4. It recurs midway through book 1 (466),
at the beginning and end of book 2 (3 and 863–4), at the end of book 3 (790), in
the proem of 4, discussed here, and before the Parilia-sequence (a point of great
importance for the *urbis origo*) at 4.729–30 but not thereafter. See also S. Hinds, *LCM*
9.5 (May 1984) 79.

not bear to discard the old proem, and so placed it at the beginning of book 2. Against this claim Braun rightly argues that this proem is needed in its present position, just as the further self-exhortation of 2.119–26 is needed to prepare the readers for the climactic panegyric that begins at 127. Whereas *nunc primum uelis... maioribus itis* could have been used to mark the new nationalistic theme of the *Fasti* from the beginning of the poem, the line in fact presupposes a voyage in progress; *itis*, like *signa cano* in 4.12, is present continuous, as opposed to the future or jussive of *canam* in 1.2; and the full sails mark a time when the ship is well out of harbour and ready to sail at full speed on the open sea.[35] In a poem so punctuated by nautical commentary editors should never have assigned this phrase to the moment of setting out. What 2.3–18 does provide is a second intensification of dignity from the elevation appropriate to reporting national legends to the even greater exaltation required for the praise of the *pater patriae*. Thus the proem of book 2 uses the theme of *militia* to look back on Ovid's old preoccupation with love elegy. The *exiguum opus* of 2.4 composed *cum lusit prima iuuenta* (2.6) makes the same point as 4.3–10, in which Ovid contrasts *maiora canebas* (4.3) and *nunc teritur nostris area maior equis* (4.10) with the love poetry: *quae decuit primis sine crimine lusimus annis* (4.9). Book 2 looks back with *sacra signataque tempora fastis* to his promise in book 1 of *sacra* (1.7) and *pictos signantia fastos... praemia* (1.11–12) and reinterprets Ovid's homage as a *munus* in contrast to other men's service in warfare (11–14) or his own old warfare in service of love. His new *munus* is to be service after the event, following in escort Augustus Caesar's honorific names and titles earned in warfare just as soldiers escort their triumphant general.

Ovid is in fact already following this sequence of titles; he has dealt with the name Augustus at 1.589–616 and will cover the titles *imperator* (4.673–4) and *pontifex maximus* (4.949 ff.), but at the beginning of book 2 he is leading up to Augustus' last and most treasured title, which he so valued that he postponed its acceptance

---

[35] See Tarrant (1975) 258 on 442 ff.: 'The men first row with the sails up, to reach the open sea (cf. Sen. *Tro.* 1045 ff.), then allow the stronger winds to carry the ships.' Tarrant compares Vergil's two stages in *Aen.* 5.778 (oars) and 796–7 *liceat dare tuta per undas | uela*, Aeneas' prayer for safe sailing in open sea.

until 2 BC and made it the climax of his *Res Gestae*.[36] The final appeal *ades et...* | *respice pacando si quid ab hoste uacat*, like the appeal to Germanicus, takes its colour from the assumption that the *princeps'* main activity has been the establishment of peace through victory; this might seem inappropriate to Augustus, who had not left Italy since 8 BC, and fought his last campaign in Spain in the 20s; but he remained titular commander while he lived, and the peace which is honoured by the *ara pacis Augustae* was won under his auspices. The proviso *si quid ab hoste uacat* might have seemed tactless during the Pannonian rising and downright painful after the ambush of Varus' legions in AD 9, from which Augustus never recovered confidence. Why did Ovid not remodel this passage even before Augustus' death? As with 2.63–6, so 2.15–18 required more than a change of tense or addressee; both apostrophe and blessing would need to be replaced by a quite different development.[37]

But book 1, reworked after Tiberius' accession, is saturated with allusions to peace and peacemaking, especially near its beginning and end. The word (or deity) Pax alone occurs 10 times in book 1, against 9 in the rest of the *Fasti*. Janus, origin of the year, is praised for the *otia* over which he presides, explains his power to release lasting peace to wander free among men (121–2), rejects war in favour of peace at 253, and links his safekeeping of peace with hopes for a long closure under Caesar's divine protection: *Caesareoque diu numine clusus ero* (282). Thanks to Germanicus, peace is now worldwide (284–5). Syme scolds Ovid for his imprecision in not recording the three times during Augustus' principate in which the gates were closed in peace;[38] certainly Augustus was proud of this record, but if there was peace at the time when Ovid returned to book 1 (as implied by 277, 282, and 698–703), it was more complimentary to the new Emperor to anticipate his future record (*diu clusus ero*) than to look back to the

[36] Braun (1981) 2363; see also his diagrammatic reconstruction of the linked Augustan passages in books 1 and 2, pp. 2370–1. For the occasion in 2 BC see *Res Gestae* 35 and Suet. *Aug.* 58, citing excerpts from the speeches of Messalla and Augustus.

[37] I agree with Kraus (1968) that Ovid must have expected to change at least the end of the address after the death of Augustus. For what might have been, compare *Pont.* 4.9.127 ff., and the late insertion to Germanicus at *Fast.* 4.81–4.

[38] Syme (1978) 24, *Res Gestae* 13, Suet. *Aug.* 22. But as Syme points out, Velleius writing in the time of Tiberius has omitted the details: perhaps he knew omissions would be appreciated.

Augustan past. Since the imposition of peace was the prerequisite of a triumph, Germanicus' triumph can be cited as proof of peace; the ministers of peace that Janus is to safeguard are Germanicus and his brother Drusus, heirs of the house of Augustus. This is confirmed by the twice-repeated allusion to the *domus Augusta* in 701 (*gratia dis domuique tuae*) and 721, where he ends the month with the pious prayer *ut... domus quae praestat eam cum pace perennet* 'that the house that proffers peace may last forever in peace'. It is not for Ovid to worry about the conflict between the high valuation of peace we know to have been Tiberius' policy (as well as that of Augustus' later years) and the youthful ambitions of Germanicus to win glamour by heroic warfare—the *principis artes* which Ovid recognized as Germanicus' own taste in the letter from Pontus (4.8.77).[39]

The theme of peace returns in the last two sections of the book. Ovid has gone out of his way to stress it, not only by choosing the January dedication of the *Ara Pacis* in 9 BC rather than waiting to commemorate Augustus' original vow of July 4th 13 BC, but also by postponing the *feriae sementiuae* with their celebration of rustic *otium* to a point after January 23rd, when only the imperial foundation of the temple of Castor and Pollux intervened[40] before the celebration of the Altar. And this foundation is itself highly significant for Tiberius' policy, sharing with his concern for the temple of Concord the political message of family harmony.[41] The Dioscuri themselves could be seen as prototypes for Tiberius and his brother Drusus, and were used to this effect when Tiberius dedicated their temple in his dead brother's name in March, AD 7; they could also serve as counterpart of the two brothers created by the adoptions of AD 4, Germanicus and Drusus Caesar. Finally when Peace comes to her altar she is wearing not simply triumphal laurels, nor German laurels, as she might to match the triumphs of 7 BC or AD 17, but the laurels of

---

[39] *Sic tibi nec... desunt principis artes* in 77 picks up *modo bella geris*, 73. The actual argument of 4.8.69 ff. is a commonplace adapted from e.g. Cicero's tactful praise of Pompey's oratory in *Brut.* 239: *uir ad omnia summa natus maiorem dicendi gloriam habuisset* (*Pont.* 4.8.70) *nisi eum maioris gloriae cupiditas ad bellicas laudes abstraxisset.*

[40] Bömer (1957–8) on 658 (cf. p. 37) states that the *feriae sementiuae* were determined by the *pontifices* and occurred on two days seven days apart.

[41] See Levick (1976a) 118: as Bömer notes (on 706) Ovid's allusion to *fratres de gente deorum* would then evoke Germanicus and Drusus Caesar, with further suggestion of brotherly concord.

Actium (*Fast.* 1.711): *frondibus Actiacis comptos redimita capillos* 'with
hair arranged and wreathed with Actian laurels'. The epithet does
more than recall Augustus' first, multiple, triumph; it assigns credit
for the present peace to that distant victory in the civil war. If 1.709–
13 was composed during the long interval between Tiberius' triumph
of 7 BC and the next triumph, also celebrated by Tiberius, in AD 12,
it was tactful to deprecate immediate triumphs, as Ovid does in 713–
14, and emphasize the original victory. Like Horace in the Augustan
odes of book 4, he could stress instead the awe with which barbarians
revered the *Aeneadae*,[42] a name aptly chosen to suggest either the *gens
Julia* or the *gens togata*.

Book 1 maintains this theme of peace to the end as the priests
are invited in 719 to offer incense to the *pacales flammae* (a rare
usage)[43] and pray for the eternal duration of the Augustan dynasty
that guarantees this peace.

Thus both the Germanicus proem, with its *domestica festa*, and the
final panel of book 1 are filled with allusions to the *domus Augusta*;
yet, as Bömer has shown, this concept first acquires public status in
the *Fasti*, and the allusions can be shown to arise in late sections of
the poem.[44] Here Ovid goes far beyond anything in the later poems
of Horace. From Suetonius' second-century viewpoint it is natural
that Augustus should value above all 'his own dignity and that of his
house' (*Aug.* 25). In the *Fasti* I believe Ovid adopts the concept at least

---

[42] *Aeneadae*, used by Lucretius for the Roman nation, is first given this wider
sense by Vergil in book 8 after repeated use for Aeneas' followers (1.153 etc.). But
while Carmenta's prophetic allusion in 8.341, *cecinit quae prima futuros | Aeneadas
magnos*, can be understood both of Aeneas' men and their later descendants, 8.648
is part of the history of Rome depicted on the shield of Aeneas. Ovid makes the
same transition from the followers of Aeneas at *Met.* 15.695, through *Aeneae genetrix*
15.761 to *Aeneaden* for Julius Caesar at 15.804. Note that in *Tr.* 2.261–2, Ovid echoes
Lucretius' solemn *Aeneadum genetrix*.

[43] The word first appears in Ovid; cf. *Met.* 6.101 and 15.591 *pacali cornua
lauro | uelat*.

[44] Bömer on *Fast.* 1.701 reports that Ovid is the first source for the term *domus
Augusta* and notes that all instances (*Fast.* 1.10; *Pont.* 1.5.31; 2.2.73 ff.; 3.1.135; 4.6.19–
20) date from his exile except *Fast.* 6.810. He adduces this as further support for
the claim that *Fast.* 6.797 ff. were not composed until the period of exile. Ovid's
application of *domesticus* to dynastic matters is also an Augustan innovation: cf. Livy
2.20.1 *domestica gloria accensus* with *Met.* 13.578 *luctus domesticus*. The only other
instance of the epithet in Ovid associates Apollo of Actium with Augustus as *Phoebus
domesticus, Met.* 15.865.

in part as a way of imposing surface unity on what we know to have been a tension-ridden family: Julians and Claudians can be tactfully merged. This merging was eased by the change of gentile names after Augustus required Tiberius to adopt his nephew Germanicus prior to his own adoption. By the two adoptions Augustus made Tiberius, Germanicus, and Tiberius' natural son Drusus into *Iulii Caesares*, and we can observe the happy verbal consequences in *Tristia* 4.2, where Ovid assimilates the aging Augustus with his active son, the commander Tiberius, to celebrate the victory of *Caesar uterque* (*Tristia* 4.2.8), adding the next generation of Germanicus and Drusus as promise of continuity (4.2.9–10):[45]

et qui *Caesareo* iuuenes sub *nomine* crescunt
  perpetuo terras ut domus illa regat.

and by the youths who are growing up under *Caesar's name* so that house may rule the world forever.

Livia is close behind; as in Horace's *Herculis ritu* (*Odes* 3.14) she is honoured as leader of womanhood (11–12): *cumque bonis nuribus pro sospite Liuia nato | munera det meritis . . . deis* 'and with her good daughters Livia for the safety of her son may offer gifts to the deserving gods'.[46] The expected triumph was delayed until late in AD 12 and the poem could have been written at any time after Ovid received news of the original decree for the Pannonian victory. Ovid reports the actual triumph to Messalinus in *Ex Ponto* 2.2, listing the imperial house, with Augustus (no longer represented as combatant, *Ex Ponto* 2.2.67–8) followed by Livia and Tiberius (*promouet Ausonium filius imperium*, 2.2.70), Germanicus and Drusus (2.2.71–2), and the unnamed granddaughters and wives of the two, a neat way of subsuming Agrippina and Livia under both categories. Most dynastic

---

[45] Compare Seager (1972) 46: 'The structure of the dynasty in Augustus' last years is repeatedly affirmed in the complaints of the exiled poet Ovid. At the head stands Augustus with Tiberius beside him: below them are the young men Germanicus and Drusus: Livia is regularly associated with her husband and son: the princes' wives Agrippina and Livia Julia are also sometimes mentioned along with their husbands.' The *domus* of this period is well illustrated on the *Gemma Augustea* (though the young prince may be Gaius, not Germanicus) and *Grand Camée de France*, reproduced facing p. 95 of Seager (1972).

[46] *Odes* 3.14.5–10 *unico gaudens mulier marito | prodeat iustis operata sacris | et soror clari ducis et decorae | supplice uitta | uirginum matres iuuenumque nuper | sospitum.*

allusions in the *Fasti* reflect this family grouping; the late dedication
to Germanicus differs only in bringing his father Tiberius forward
and letting Augustus recede. Both are included as founders of the
family festivals, but lines 13–14 are more easily understood of Augustus' religious foundations. Yet *Caesar* is happily ambiguous. We have
already noted one Tiberian dedication from this book and will meet
another shortly.

However, I believe we can also recover an earlier phase within the
Fasti where references to Augustus' *domus* were local allusions to the
Palatine residence; a house in space, not time. Twice it is associated
with the new title of Pontifex Maximus assumed by Augustus in 12 BC
when he absorbed the public cult of Vesta into his household worship:
compare the prayer that ends book 4 (949–54):[47]

> cognati Vesta recepta est
> limine: sic iusti constituere patres.
> Phoebus habet partem, Vestae pars altera cessit:
> quod superest illis tertius ipse tenet.
> state Palatinae laurus, praetextaque quercu
> stet domus: aeternos tres habet una deos.

Vesta has been received on the threshold of her kinsman: so have the just
fathers decreed. Phoebus has a share; another part has yielded to Vesta; what
remains he possesses himself. Long live the laurels of the Palatine, long live
the house wreathed with oaken boughs: a single house holds three eternal
gods.

Carmenta's prophecy in book 1 starts from the same associations.
Vesta is asked to welcome the Penates of Troy and anticipate the
time when one being will protect the world and a god perform
her ritual (1.529–30). Then Ovid introduces the dynasty (531–2): *et
penes Augustos patriae tutela manebit:* | *hanc fas imperii frena tenere
domum* 'the guardianship of the fatherland shall remain in the line
of Augustus: it is ordained that this house hold the reins of empire'.

---

[47] Several of these compliments to the residence of the *princeps* occur already in
Met. 1; at 1.175–6 the Palatine house is a counterpart of Olympus: *hic locus est quem,
si uerbis audacia detur,* | *haud timeam magni dixisse Palatia caeli*; for the laurel trees
note *Met.* 1.560–3, *tu ducibus Latiis aderis cum laeta triumphum* | *uox canet et uisens
longas Capitolia pompas,* | *postibus Augustis eadem fidissima custos* | *ante fores stabis.* In
the finale of *Met.* 15. Apollo and Vesta have become household gods: *et cum Caesarea
tu, Phoebe domestice, Vesta* (15.865).

Lines 533–4 carry on to events after Augustus' death: the god's son and grandson is Tiberius, as grandson of Julius and son of the newly deified Augustus unwillingly taking on his father's burden; and 535–6 end the prophecy with the new title and future consecration of Livia as Julia Augusta.[48] To my mind 529–30, equally applicable to the god Julius or to the deified Augustus in their role as Pontifex Maximus, form a natural climax, and could have been the last couplet of the original version. What follows, including the claims of the *domus Augusta*, belongs with 533–6 to the Tiberian remodelling.

Book 6 too ends with an allusion to the *domus*. It is the last word of Clio's speech in praise of Atia, aunt of Augustus and wife of Philippus; and Hercules with all the Muses assents to her words: *o decus, o sacra femina digna domo* (6.810). Ovid has prepared the ground for this consecration of the house in the account given at 6.455–6 of the transfer of Vesta's fire from the temple in the forum: *nunc bene lucetis sacrae sub Caesare flammae;* | *ignis in Iliacis nunc erit estque focis*. It is the cult of Vesta that entitles the *domus* to the epithet *sacra*. But in 6.799 ff. the pointed compliment to Marcia, wife of Ovid's patron Fabius Maximus, dates this last section of the poem to the period of Ovid's attentions to Fabius, the time of *Ex Ponto* 1–3, just before Augustus' death.[49] It is in keeping with the late composition that *domus* here should include Atia's role as ancestress of Augustus' line, at the same time that it plays on the sacred status of the physical house of the Pontifex-emperor.

One other concept that is prominent in book 1 and throughout the *Fasti* has links with both Pax and the *domus Augusta*. As Barbara Levick has pointed out in her study of Tiberian ideology, *pax* is simply 'the equivalent abroad of domestic *Concordia*,' and Concordia was the deity chosen by Tiberius as consul in 7 BC to symbolize his policy of reconciliation. Concordia at Rome bound the orders, or was invoked in hope of binding them by uniting the ambitions of the Equites

---

[48] Compare with 533–6 one of Ovid's latest elegies: *Pont.* 4.13.27–30: *esse parem uirtute patri qui frena rogatus* | *saepe recusati ceperit imperii,* | *esse pudicarum te Vestam, Liuia matrum,* | *ambiguum, nato dignior anne uiro*. Bömer believes only 533–6 were added after Augustus' death, but I support le Bonniec's argument that the plural *Augustos* presupposes that Tiberius had already succeeded.

[49] On the Fabian allusions as later additions to *Fasti* made in exile, see Lefèvre (1980) 154 and n. 14, developing the thesis of Heinze (1919) 399 n. 51. On the variant accounts of Fabius' death see Syme (1978) pp. 149–51.

with those of the Senate; in her temple both Opimius and Cicero had
affirmed the primacy of the senate by passing the *senatus consultum
ultimum*; later this deity was used to mark reconciliations between
the triumvirs, and was honoured by Augustus with an altar in 11 BC.
Levick comments 'to proclaim Concordia was to acknowledge that
opposition existed.'[50] No other personification is commemorated so
often in the *Fasti*, and the allusions are strategically distributed, starting with the commemoration on January 16th of Tiberius' dedication
in AD 10 of the new temple of Concordia Augusta[51] on the site in
the north-west corner of the Forum of the old Republican temple.
Ovid's panel begins with the original dedication by Camillus to commemorate the reconciliation of the orders and passes to Tiberius'
new building, financed from the spoils of his recent victories over
Germany. Here, then, is a reference dating from the reworking in
exile. But there is an ambiguity which has led Bömer into interpreting the addressee (*dux uenerande*[52]) of 646 as Germanicus, whose
triumph Ovid could anticipate in his last years. The final couplet,
to which I will return, makes it clear that Livia's son Tiberius must
be the addressee. If his triumph over Germany was hardly *recens* by
the time of the dedication in AD 10, he had achieved considerable
success in the campaigns with which he restored Roman control on
the Rhine frontier after the disaster of Varus' legions in AD 9. Thus his
recent spoils could be called *triumphatae munera gentis* (647). Since
Tiberius' second triumph did not formally include his victories in
Germany, Ovid refers to the German submission in informal terms

---

[50] Levick (1976*a*) 36 and n. 27; cf. Weinstock (1971) 260–6 for the history of
Concordia and Concordia Augusta, and Fears (1981) 886 and 891–3. For the close link
of Pax and Concordia in Augustan thinking, compare Livy 9.19.17: *modo sit perpetuus
huius, qua uiuimus, pacis amor et ciuilis cura concordiae*. Jal (1961) cites this and many
other references linking the two concepts.

[51] Fears (1981: 886) comments on the significance of the privileged epithet; after
Pax Augusta, dated by the Ara Pacis Augustae in 9 BC, Concordia is the next personification so honoured (AD 10) followed by Iustitia Augusta in AD 13, then Tiberius'
deification of Providentia Augusta and Salus Augusta during his principate. See also
Levick (1976*a*) 84–6, and Velleius 2.123.3 on Tiberius and Pax Augusta.

[52] *Venerandus* occurs only twice in Ovid; the other instance is in apostrophe of
Bacchus at Met. 4.22. Its synonym *uenerabilis* is applied only to abstractions or once
(*Tr.* 3.3.91) to the Palatine temple. Both words can be seen as substitutes for Augus-
tus/Sebastos, a neat way of honouring the new *princeps* Tiberius without prematurely
awarding him the title of his predecessor as *princeps*. As Bömer notes *dux* is most often
addressed to Augustus, as in *Fast.* 1.613, but is not a title with an exclusive application.

(645–6); indeed *auspiciis tuis* will enable him to praise Tiberius not only for his own campaigns but for the salutation accorded after Germanicus' successes in AD 13. In what sense are these occasions for homage to Concordia? Because, I would suggest, Germany had been perceived as a *prouincia* and part of the Roman *imperium* by the time of Varus' governorship; Arminius' action was rebellion, and the partial submission of Germany could thus be represented as her reconciliation to Rome.[53]

The last couplet of this panel (649–50), associates with Tiberius' temple a dedication by his mother Livia of an altar and furnishings to Concordia. But when and where was this dedication? There is no evidence for such a shrine in Tiberius' forum temple, nor indeed for dating any dedication by Livia to this occasion, January 16, AD 10. Before Bömer editors followed the text *hanc tua constituit genetrix* offered by one branch of the manuscript tradition, and Bömer is alone in adopting the alternative *haec* offered by the other branches, which relates Livia's dedication to Tiberius' forum temple. As Marleen Flory has recently argued (1984: 310, 323–4), there is, instead, good archaeological evidence for a shrine in the form of a monumental altar in the Porticus Liviae, where Ovid himself tells us (*Fasti* 6.637–8) that Livia dedicated a shrine to Concordia on June 11th of an unspecified year. The dedication may have been simultaneous with the joint formal dedication of the Porticus Liviae by mother and son which Dio 55.8.2 reports (without naming the date) for 7 BC. But, whenever it occurred, Ovid's connection of thought in book 1 will be neither local nor temporal: if we return, as the Teubner editors have done, to *hanc tua constituit genetrix*, the connection is through the Personification herself (*deae*, 648, the immediate antecedent of *hanc*) and Tiberius' kinship and cooperation with Livia.

Marleen Flory has argued on good grounds[54] that Livia's dedication was to marital rather than civic or political *concordia*, and Ovid's

---

[53] The best evidence for this association of *concordia* with peace in the provinces, or between the provinces and government at Rome, comes from the civil wars of AD 69–70: cf. the coin legends cited by Jal (1961) 230, *pax orbis terrarum, salus generis humani, concordia prouinciarum, concordia exercituum*; and Tac. *Hist.* 1.56.6; 2.20.4; 3.70; and 3.80.4 (Jal p. 221 n.9).

[54] Flory (1984) 313 for the women's festival of the *Matralia*, and the *dies* of *Fortuna uirgo* on Livia's dedication date June 11th; 314–22 on Livia's association with women's charities and with marriage. I am less convinced by the claim that the shrine, which

language reflects this both in 1.650, *sola toro magni digna reperta Iouis* 'she who alone was found worthy to share the bed of great Jupiter', and 6.638–9, *aede… quam caro praestitit ipsa uiro* 'a shrine which she presented to her dear husband'; yet the fact that Ovid has imported this allusion to Livia's shrine into book 1, creating a symmetrical and parallel structure in the opening and closing books of the set, shows the importance he gave to Concordia as an embodiment of the family cohesion of Augustus, Livia, and her son, his adopted heir. If Livia's act was in support of Augustus' moral reforms, Ovid's presentation of it is dynastic and political.

Ovid brings back Concordia on four more occasions. In book 2.631–8 he includes her in the feast of the Caristia in honour of kinsmen, as if she were one of the *di generis* (631). This passage belongs in the lifetime of Augustus who is toasted along with the family as *patriae pater optime Caesar* (637). Augustus' dedications of March 30th 11 BC occasion the next reference, at 3.881–2:

Ianus adorandus, cumque hoc Concordia mitis
    et Romana Salus, araque Pacis erit.

It will be time to worship Janus and gentle Concord with him, and Roman safety, and the altar of Peace.

Ideologically a recall of deities celebrated in book 1, Ovid's notice of the triple dedication coincides with the divine abstractions particularly cultivated by Tiberius: Concordia, Salus, and Pax.

The remaining instances of Concordia are set conspicuously near the beginning and end of the last book. In book 6 as in book 5 Ovid has provided a choice of three etymologies for the month, deriving *mensis Iunius* successively from Juno and the *iuniores* whom Juventas-Hebe sponsors against her mother's claims. Bömer believes that Ovid's third derivation, from *iungere*, is without precedent and contrived by the poet to bring out his theme of cooperation and harmony. Certainly it is Concordia who resolves this family conflict by offering the non-partisan derivation, but she is described in Augustan terms as (6.91–2):

must date in or after 7 BC, was a gesture in support of Augustus' marriage laws of 19 BC.

…Apollinea longas Concordia lauro
  nexa comas: placidi numen opusque ducis.

Concord, her long hair bound with Apollo's laurel: the deity and the work of
the chief of peace.

The laurel is not specifically Actian like that of Pax in book 1 nor is
the *dux* named. This could be an allusion to Numa, whom Ovid celebrates later in book 6 for his foundation of the cult of Vesta and her
temple, *regis opus placidi* (259); Numa is associated with Concordia
by an odd notice in Festus,[55] but if Ovid has him in mind he chose
the unspecific phrase in order to focus his readers on the peaceful
leader of the present time, be it Augustus or (perhaps) Tiberius.

As we have seen, Ovid's last recall of Concordia at 6.637–8 matches
his previous commemoration of Livia's dedication to the goddess at
1.649–50. The dedication in the Porticus Liviae is recorded by Dio as
a joint act of Livia and Tiberius, but Ovid uses the occasion to praise
Augustus for his forbearance as heir of the luxurious Pollio, and for
his exemplary severity as Censor. No sign here of late composition.
Rather it is the panel in book 1, honouring Tiberius with its Livian
coda, that is designed to balance this passage in book 6 and adapt it
to the political orientation of the new *princeps* in Ovid's last years.

It is possible, I believe, to trace the same evolution from the spatial
concept of the *domus Augusta*, enclosing its sacred precincts of Apollo
and Vesta on the Palatine, to the concept of the *domus* as an evolving
imperial family, even in the letters from Pontus. I have already cited
some of the enumerations of the family and its members spread
over three generations; but we also find celebration of the Palatine
complex as late as *Ex Ponto* 3.1.135: *cum domus Augusti, Capitoli
more colenda | laeta, quod est et sit, plenaque pacis erit | tum tibi di
faciant adeundi copia fiat* 'when Augustus' house, to be revered like
the Capitol, shall be happy (as it is now and I pray it may ever be)
and filled with peace, then may the gods grant you the opportunity
to approach'; or 3.3.87–91: *dum domus et nati, dum mater Liuia
gaudet, | dum gaudes patriae magne ducisque pater… | dum faciles
aditus praebet uenerabile templum* 'while the house and the children,

---

[55] Festus 372M (510L) *rem diuinam instituerit Marti Numa Pompilius pacis concordiae obtinendae gratia inter Sabinos Romanosque*, cited by Weinstock (1971) 261
n. 5.

while their mother Livia rejoices, while you, great father of our country and our leader, rejoice... while the holy temple offers an easy approach'; but the latter instance puts more stress on family than residence, and this is the tenor of every elegy in *Ex Ponto* 4, culminating in the physical embodiment of Ovid's domestic shrine. Ovid had thanked Cotta Maximus in *Ex Ponto* 2.8 for sending him the silver images of Augustus, Livia, and Tiberius, but in 4.9, the elegy celebrating his apotheosis of the *princeps*, we hear that he has added the next generation. The image of *diuus Augustus*, flanked by his wife and son, now has, *neu desit pars ulla domus* (4.9.109), a grandson on either side, Germanicus on the far side of Livia, and Drusus beside his father. To these images Ovid offers prayers every morning.

A corresponding change can be detected in the *Fasti*; we saw above how the fourth book ended in Ovid's prayers for the enduring survival of the Palatine residence with its divine triad (4.949–54, quoted above). At the corresponding position in his reworked first book, Ovid's *uota* are bound up with the services to peace of the generals of the Augustan house (Augustus, Tiberius, Germanicus), and his final injunction (1.721–2) urges the people to pray to the gods for their dynastic continuation:

utque domus quae praestat eam cum pace perennet
    ad pia propensos uota rogate deos.

ask of the gods, who are favourable to pious prayers, that the house that proffers peace may last forever in peace.

This finds a parallel in one other late example of such *uota*, the poet's prayer for Rome at the end of his narrative of the *urbis origo*, itself designed to recall Romulus' prayer within the narrative (4.859–62, recalling 831–2):

cuncta regas et sis magno sub Caesare[56] semper,
    saepe etiam plures nominis huius habe:

[56] I take *magno sub Caesare* as indefinite, 'under a great Caesar', since the hyperbole of *semper* referred to one living *princeps* would be excessive; this is borne out by the plural *plures nominis huius*, which seems to commend not only Tiberius as the *princeps*' adopted son, but the dual succession implicit in Tiberius' own adoption of Germanicus to become Iulius Caesar Germanicus along with his own son Drusus Caesar; the names apply any time after AD 4, but the emphasis is more in accord with

et quotiens steteris domito sublimis in orbe
omnia sint humeris inferiora tuis.

May you rule all and forever be subject to a great Caesar; often may you have more princes of that name. And whenever you stand high in the conquered world, may all things be lower than your shoulders.

Such *uota* for the nation and its first family are nowhere found in what survives of Callimachus' *Aitia*;[57] the Alexandrian reserves his vows for the duration of his own poetic achievement. But they form a natural conclusion to hymns and prose panegyrics.[58] It would be mistaken to postulate a single source or motivation for Ovid's adoption of the *uotum*; rather we should bear in mind the convergence of literary inheritance and of the recently formalized Roman practice of *publica uota*,[59] which began as *uota pro salute imperatoris* in the year after Actium and evolved into a full range of vows for the *princeps* and his family members on birthdays and other occasions. Ovid must have grown up with such public vows, and naturally absorbed them into his concept of loyalty; the *Fasti* offer a brief glimpse of how these vows came to be extended into the future and to incorporate the succession.

Tiberius' equal *imperium* in 13 or thereafter. For the arguments for and against the late date see Bömer ad loc.

[57] The only extant concluding wish in the *Aitia* is fr. 7.13–14, the prayer to the graces adapted by Ovid in his prayer to Flora at the end of their interview in *Fast.* 5.377–8 (see Pfeiffer on fr. 7).

[58] For such prayers and good wishes in hymns cf. Call. *H.* 1.85–8, 5.140, 6.134 ff., Theocr. 17, and for the prescribed prayer in panegyrics cf. Russell and Wilson (1981) 95: 'after this you must utter a prayer beseeching God that the Emperor's reign may endure long and the throne be handed down to his children and descendants'.

[59] On the *uota publica* and their development under Augustus see Daly (1950) 164–9. Ovid uses the term to characterize the wishes that end the Athenians' hymn to their hero Theseus in *Met.* 7.449–50, and perhaps echoes them in some of the simpler wishes of *Fasti*, for instance *Fast.* 1.603 *augeat annos* (a formula found in the Arval protocol, which Bömer ad loc. suggests was already semi-official in Ovid's lifetime): 2.65 *dent tibi annos*; and e.g. *Tr.* 2.261 *Liuia sic tecum sociales compleat annos*. Ovid ends the *Metamorphoses* with a combination of loyal prophecy (15.833–9) and *uota* to the Palatine deities (15.868–70), following them with his own Callimachean prayer for poetic survival. No opportunity is missed.

III

Examination of book 1 of the *Fasti* has illustrated a new stress on certain aspects of Augustan ideology centring on Pax, Concordia, and the *domus Augusta*, and we have seen that these late developments, dating from the time of Tiberius' adoption, or even after Ovid's relegation in AD 8, are scattered however sparsely throughout the poem. Another concept which came to prominence in Augustus' later years, to become associated with politically motivated prosecutions in Tiberius' principate, was *maiestas*. The *maiestas* of the emperor, first found in Horace's letter to Augustus of 13 BC,[60] was extended to his household and the phrase *sua domusque suae maiestas* in Suetonius *Augustus* 25 may cite the *princeps*' own words. In context it shows Augustus reacting against the populist affability of his sons-in-law when commanding the army; one thinks of Nero Drusus and his supposed republicanism,[61] but Suetonius' phrase *temporum quies* seems to fit any time between 20 BC and the Pannonian revolt of AD 5. There is a similar reference, not in Tacitus' introductory account of the charge of *maiestas* at *Annals* 1.72–4, but retrospectively when D. Silanus, exiled for adultery with Julia the younger, pleaded to return from exile. Tacitus comments (*Ann.* 3.24.3): 'By calling a vice so common among men and women by the awful name of sacrilege and treason, he went far beyond the indulgent spirit of our ancestors, beyond indeed his own legislation.' Velleius similarly condemns Iullus Antonius, the alleged lover of Julia the elder, as 'violator of his house' (2.100). Thus even before Tiberius 'had brought back the law of treason' (*Annals* 1.72)[62] Augustus was invoking the dignity of his

[60] *Ep.* 2.1.257–8: *sed neque paruum | carmen maiestas recipit tua, nec meus audet | rem temptare pudor.* On the relationship of *maiestas* and the *pudor* it inspires see below n. 70.

[61] Cf. Tac. *Ann.* 1.33.3 *Drusi magna apud populum Romanum memoria, credebaturque, si rerum potitus foret, libertatem redditurus.*

[62] On this misrepresentation of Tiberius' attitude to the *crimen maiestatis* and on its evolution under Augustus see Goodyear (1981) 172–5 and Levick (1976a) ch. 11. We should note how carefully Tacitus reports Tiberius' refusal to allow prosecution of the adulterous Varilla for *maiestas*: *quia probrosis sermonibus diuum Augustum ac Tiberium et matrem eius inlusisset Caesarique conexa adulterio teneretur* (*Ann.* 2.50). Levick argues that the appearance of both adultery at the senatorial level and *maiestas* before the same court had led to tacking the vaguer but more dangerous charge of *maiestas* on to lesser charges, but we may also read this case as an echo of the

household in connection with the scandals of either Julia the elder in 2 BC or her daughter, whose downfall seems to have entailed Ovid's own relegation. So it is particularly startling to find Ovid creating as part of his introductory panel on *mensis Maius* and its derivation an unprecedented myth as aition for the cult of *maiestas*; more than unprecedented, his myth seems to have had no sequel. Not only the new personification but many details in Ovid's presentation of this etymology and that relating *Maius* to *maiores* suggest that the whole panel opening book 5 may be late in composition, or at least substantially reworked.

Callimachus had let his muses—the same muses who met the Ascraean shepherd Hesiod by Hippocrene—narrate to him three *aitia* of the origins of the Graces, of which only fragments now remain.[63] Epigram 51 also shows that he could identify Queen Berenice with the Graces, and we might expect that his panel on the Graces opening *Aitia* 1 used the opportunity to pay a deft compliment to his patroness. This may be one reason why Ovid starts his fifth book of *Fasti* from an encounter with the Muses, and why in turn Polyhymnia, Urania, and Calliope offer three etymologies for the month, of which the first is historically associated with the imperial house: yet these historical associations are unexpectedly passed over, perhaps suppressed, in Ovid's text.

The Hesiodic allusion of book 5 is confirmed by Ovid's cross reference in book 6.13–14: *ecce deas uidi, non quas praeceptor arandi | uiderat, Ascraeas cum sequeretur oues* 'Lo, I saw goddesses, but not those whom the teacher of ploughing had seen when he was following his sheep on Ascra'. An earlier reference at 5.77–8 guarantees that he composed the two panels with their triad of etymologies to bind the months as a pair (Braun 1981: 1348–9). But although he may be imitating Callimachus' overall structure of the four-book *Aitia* with his successive pairs, Ovid's language at 5.7–8 is designed to recall Hesiod as strongly as it evokes Callimachus:

---

controversy over the elder and younger Julias, and interpret it as Tiberius' rejection of *maiestas domus Caesaris* as a political weapon.

[63] On the triple genealogy of the Charites see Call. *Aitia*, fr. 7 with the Florentine scholia (Pfeiffer p. 3 lines 29 ff.). On Berenice see fr. 112 and *Epigr.* 51 (*AP* 5.146) comparing a new statue of the Queen to a fourth Grace.

dicite quae fontes Aganippidos Hippocrenes
  grata Medusaei signa tenetis equi.[64]

Tell me, you who possess the fountains of Aganippean Hippocrene, the
pleasing traces of Medusa's steed.

The aition that follows is in fact a re-adaptation of Hesiod's creation
narrative from the *Theogony*,[65] Ovid matches each phase in Hesiod,
first describing Chaos (*Fasti* 5.11–12 = *Theogony* 116–17), then the
disposition of earth and sky (5.13–14, with 17–18 = 129–30) and
the role of Oceanus (5.21 = 133) and Themis (5.22 = 135). He
recalls Saturn/Kronos and his downfall (5.19–20 and 34 = 495–6)
and finally the Gigantomachy which ends in the victory of Jupiter
and the Olympians[66] (5.35–42 = 687 ff.). Ovid has already composed
two versions of the creation narrative, at *Metamorphoses* 1.1–160
and *Fasti* 1.103–12, both eclectic in origin but probably drawn from
Hellenistic sources. Only *Fasti* 5 returns to Hesiod in order to recreate
the sequence in social terms. We are shown the elements refusing to
keep their place as Earth will not give way to Sky, nor the stars to the
Sun (*Fasti* 5.17–18, to be contrasted with e.g. *Metamorphoses* 1.15–
20). This cosmos has no hierarchy: *par erat omnis honos*, and plebeian
gods usurp Saturn's magisterial chair while no one offers escort to old
father Ocean, and Themis is admitted last to the divine reception in
a parody of Roman *deductio* and *salutatio*.[67] To reform this anarchy
Ovid calls in, not divine Nature as in the *Metamorphoses*, but Maiestas, born in lawful wedlock of Reverentia and Honor. It is Maiestas
who takes on the function of the moderator, and *mundum temperat
omnem* (*Fasti* 5.25). At first she appears to be in supreme control,
holding jurisdiction with Pudor and Metus until Ovid reports that
Saturn grew old and is deposed. Apparently Maiestas, despite her

---

[64] Call. *Aitia*, fr. 2, repeated in part in Fr. 112, recalls Hesiod's encounter with the
Muses at Pegasus' fountain (παρ' ἴχνιον ὀξέος ἵππου) and the tale of the *Theogony*,
starting from the birth of Chaos, told ἐπὶ πτέρνης ὕδα [.

[65] This does not seem to have been noticed by commentators, though le Bonniec
and Bömer both note Ovid's debt to Verrius Flaccus for the equation of Janus with
Hesiodic Chaos at *Fast.* 1.103 ff., citing Festus 45M (52L). On Ovid's versions of the
creation narrative see Schwabl, *RE* Suppl. 9.1544 ff.

[66] For the association of the Gigantomachy as an epic theme with *laudes Augusti*
compare *Tr.* 2.67–72 and 333–8.

[67] Frazer (*Editio Maior* vol. 4 p. 3) oddly relates Ovid's allusion to *Il.* 15.87–8, where
Themis is first to greet Hera on her return to Olympus.

position *in medio... Olympo* arrayed in purple and gold, has coexisted with Saturn as ruler. With the challenge of the giants she is subordinated to Jupiter, and survives because of his protection: *his bene... armis defensa deorum* (5.43). In turn she attends the victor as *custos* and guarantees his continuance of power without recourse to violence (45–6).

At this stage in the allegory any reader would be reminded of Horace *Odes* 3.4, addressed to the Muses, who refresh Augustus the giant-killer in the Pierian grotto. The giants of this ode are Augustus' personal adversaries, destroyed by their own irrational violence: *uis consili expers mole ruit sua* (65). So in the *Fasti* Jupiter *uertit in auctores pondera uasta suos* (5.42) and maintains his authority *sine ui*. Ovid increasingly used the analogy between Jupiter as conqueror of the giants and Augustus, perhaps most conspicuously in *Tristia* 2 addressed to the *princeps*. In the *Fasti* the giants have not merely assaulted Olympus but have tried to violate Jupiter's house and family, *ausuros in Iouis ire domum* (5.36).

But at 5.47 Ovid brings his *aition* down to earth, tracing a historic cult of Maiestas to Romulus and Numa. The new, earthly Maiestas is not confined to enhancing the ruler; she protects *patres*, which the Romulean context might equate with the senate; then the addition of *matres... pueris uirginibusque* converts this into the spirit of respect within and towards the family. Ovid ends with a political application to the Curule magistrate and the *triumphator* (51–2).

This passage is quite extraordinary. Would anyone expect an Augustan poet who has committed himself to a national and monarchist panegyric to slide away from the Maiestas of Augustus and his family in order to praise the reverence due to Roman citizens and magistrates? But the almost republican effect of Ovid's account returns in a slightly different guise with the next etymology.

We know from Macrobius that Fulvius Nobilior's second-century *Fasti* derived Maius and Iunius from Romulus' division of the people into *maiores* and *iuniores*: *ut altera pars consilio altera armis rem publicam tueretur* (*Saturnalia* 1.12.16). So Ovid had a learned precedent for his etymology and for the association of *maiores* with the elders of the Senate: *uiribus illa minor nec habendis utilis armis | consilio patriae saepe ferebat opem* (*Fasti* 5.61–2). But he has shaped his tribute so as to reinforce the theme of Polyhymnia's Maiestasaition. Urania's story begins with the mother of Maiestas (*magna fuit quondam capitis reuerentia cani*, 57) and ends with her father, Honor (*nec leue propositi pignus successit honoris | Junius a iuuenum nomine dictus habet*, 77–8). There is another carry-over of motif; here as at 5.21 Ovid stresses the courtesy of walking on the outside of the older man: *et medius iuuenum, non indignantibus ipsis | ibat, et interior, si comes unus erat* (67–8). The courtesy denied to Ocean in the bad old days before Maiestas was properly paid to the *seniores* in Rome's past. Why this lingering on a detail of etiquette?

What I will argue is that the whole sequence reflects the move away from monarchy of Tiberius' early years, and that we can date this passage by details of its presentation that closely recall the motifs and diction of Ovid's last poems from Pontus. It is simplest to start from these echoes of diction. The detail of etiquette exploited negatively and positively in *Fasti* 5.21 and 67–8 is hardly found in other Augustan poetry except at *Ex Ponto* 4.9.17–18 where Ovid visualizes Graecinus, the consul suffect for AD 16, with his escort: *dumque latus sancti cingit tibi turba senatus | consulis ante pedes ire iuberer eques.*[68] The Pegasean fountain of Hippocrene is not much used by Ovid outside *Metamorphoses* 5 where its origin is explained by a Muse,[69] but, along with the allusions to Chaos and the Giants' assault, it recurs as an ornamental element in the elegy to Germanicus, *Ex Ponto* 4.8, and in context it increases the likelihood that Ovid is writing one passage with his eye on the other.

In *Ex Ponto* 4.8.55 Ovid makes the bold claim that poetry such as his *laudes Augusti* can make gods: *tantaque maiestas ore canentis eget.* Even the greatness of gods depends on the poet's voice. It is from poetry that men know of the reduction of chaos to order (57–8) and the defeat of the Giants' assault on Olympus, struck down by Jupiter's avenging fire (59–60). Ovid's next instances of the power of poetry are the conventional precedents for heroic apotheosis, Liber

---

[68] The only earlier reference seems to be Hor. *Sat.* 2.5.18 *utne tegam spurco Damae latus*, Palmer ad loc. quotes the scholiast on Juvenal 3.131 for *latus tegere | cludere* of walking on the honoured person's left side, and cites Suet. *Claud.* 24.3 *inde rursus reuertenti latus texit.*

[69] Compare *Met.* 5.256–7 *noui fontis...| dura Medusaei quem praepetis ungula rupit* and 312 *fonte Medusaeo.* Ovid gives the birth story of Pegasus and origin of Hippocrene *cum leuis Aonias ungula fodit aquas* at *Fast.* 3.449–58. Pfeiffer on *Aitia* fr. 2.1–2 notes the parallels from both *Metamorphoses* and *Fasti.*

and Hercules, leading to the climax at 63–4 with Germanicus' own grandfather whom Ovid's hymns have helped to consecrate. Line 64 rounds off the argument that began with gods and their *maiestas* in 55–6. The choice of chaos and the giants recalls the beginning and end of the Hesiodic *Theogony*, and Augustus is equated with Jupiter in the same context as the unkeyed allegory of *Fasti* 5.35–42. Was Ovid simply reading Hesiod or Callimachus at the time?

Certainly his description of Germanicus' poetic promise follows that of Hesiod's preface as well as Callimachus. Germanicus was to have been the greatest glory of the Pierides, and his Muse is enriched with the gifts of Jupiter (*Pont.* 4.8.77–8):

sic tibi nec docti nec desunt principis artes,
    mixta sed est animo cum Ioue Musa tuo.

So you lack the arts neither of the scholar nor of the prince, but in your mind the Muse and Jupiter are blended.

This allusion plays on Hesiod's distinction in *Theogony* 80–101 between men blessed by the Muses, whose role it is to hymn the Olympian gods (94–101), and those appointed by Zeus to be kings. Calliope also attends on revered kings (80) and the king whom the Muses honour is worshipped like a god in the assembly with sweet reverence (91–2), for poets come from the Muses, but kings are from Zeus. Thus both Zeus and the Muses share in honouring kings and giving them the *aidos* which makes them seem like gods among men. Such ideas spread widely in Hellenistic panegyric, but their concentration in *Ex Ponto* 4.8 is undiluted Hesiod. In him we have Ovid's precedent not only for Germanicus' equal share in the gifts of the Muses and of Jupiter but for the role which Ovid has given in the *Fasti* not to Reverentia,[70] the equivalent of *aidos*, but to Maiestas, because of its role in imperial ideology. And Ovid glances once more

---

[70] Bömer (1957–8) 292 on *Fast.* 5.23 compares Αἰδώς with *pudor* (seeing in *Pudor et Metus* the Homeric αἰδώς καὶ δέος *Il.* 15.657–8) and perhaps *reuerentia*. In Hesiod's account of the awe bestowed on Kings αἰδοῖος seems equivalent to *reuerendus* or *uenerandus* (as in *Fast.* 1.646) and we might compare *Pont.* 3.6.15–18: *cur, dum tuta times, facis ut Reverentia talis fiat in* Augustos *inuidiosa* deos? | *fulminis adflatos interdum uiuere telis* | *uidimus et refici, non prohibente Ioue.* The passage plays with the whole complex transference of reverence from Jupiter to his Augustan counterpart on earth.

at Hesiod in *Ex Ponto* 4.8, thanking Germanicus because his Muse has not driven Ovid away from the fountain *ungula Gorgonei quam caua fecit equi*; once more the Hesiodic-Callimachean rendezvous, and the learned allusion that we met in *Fasti* 5.7–8.

But Ovid could perfectly well have returned to Hesiod or to his own text of *Fasti* 5 after a lapse of years when he came to compose *Ex Ponto* 4.8; the resemblance does not determine chronology. For that we should recall the evolution of *maiestas* itself in Roman poetry and prose. It occurs in the earliest Roman author, apparently with royal associations; in Livius Andronicus *Trag.* 13, *maiestas mea* occurs in a speech of Agamemnon, just as *maiestatem uiri* in Accius *Trag.* 648 seems to refer to King Tereus as husband of Procne. In prose by contrast the earliest instances are the definitions of the offence *maiestatem populi Romani minuere* in *Rhetorica ad Herennium* 1.12.21 and 2.12.17 or *De Inuentione* 2.166. But just as *prouocatio* to the people was transformed into appeal to the *princeps*, so the *maiestas* of the people, for which Saturninus set up his standing court in 103 BC, gave way to the *maiestas* of the *princeps*. As Goodyear has shown in his extensive survey of the evidence (1981: 172–5), there is no reason to believe that the *lex Julia maiestatis* of Caesar was supplemented or replaced by an Augustan law. Ovid himself uses *maiestas* selectively, but not before *Ars Amatoria* 3. He indulges in malicious mockery of a rather Augustan Jupiter in *Metamorphoses* 2.846–7: *non bene conueniunt, nec in una sede morantur | maiestas et amor*; but chiefly applies it to the *princeps*: compare *Tristia* 2.512, *maiestas adeo comis ubique tua est*, or *Ex Ponto* 2.8.29–30, *perque tori sociam quae par tibi sola reperta est | et cui maiestas non onerosa tua est*, or 3.1.156 voicing his little book's awe of Livia's *maiestas*. We noted the *maiestas* of the gods in *Ex Ponto* 4.8.56; Ovid evokes it once more in his last elegy, *Ex Ponto* 4.9, congratulating Graecinus on his nomination by Tiberius for the consulship (67–8):

multiplicat tamen hunc grauitas auctoris honorem
   et maiestatem res data dantis habet.

The dignity of its sponsor multiplies this honour and the thing given has all the majesty of the giver.

This reflects a constitutionalism which is something new in Augustan poetry. Ovid is at pains to say that the consul shares as magistrate in the *maiestas* of the *princeps*. How did Tiberius look on his own *maiestas*? We know the Tacitean anecdote in which he refused to tolerate the prosecution of a man who had carelessly sullied the *maiestas* of the god Augustus by polluting his image: *deorum iniuriae dis curae*. But he not only played down the ruler's *maiestas*; he tried to convince the senate of its own dignity and the respect due to magistrates.[71] Two instances from Velleius show these dual aspects; the first speaks of Tiberius' *maiestas* at accession as a protection to the people (*tantaque unius uiri maiestas fuit ut nec pro bonis nec contra malos opus armis foret*, 2.124); later, describing the effect of his acceptance, of power, he declares: *accessit magistratibus auctoritas, senatui maiestas, iudiciis grauitas* (2.126). The same panegyric paragraph signals other themes that we have noted in the dedication to the *Fasti* and in later sections: the worldwide *pax Augusta* (2.126.3) and *honor dignis paratissimus*; compare 5.32, *fit pretium dignis, nec sibi quisque placet*, and contrast the deplorable *par honos* of 5.18. Velleius, with his caution that even apologizes *pace maiestatis eius* for a lurid metaphor in 2.129.3, reflects the climate in which Ovid wrote or rewrote the last lines of his *Fasti*.

To return for the last time to *Fasti* 5 and the aition of Maiestas: how shall we explain the *allegoria interrupta* which takes Ovid to the brink of celebrating the *maiestas* of Augustus and veers away to end with the *maiestas* of the consul and—exceptionally—the *triumphator*? I can only offer a speculative reconstruction, but I would assume that Ovid began book 5 while Augustus still lived, and was planning to honour the *princeps* at the climax of this aition alongside his mythical counterpart, Jupiter. The language of *Fasti* 5.36, *ausuros in Iouis ire domum*, might even suggest that Ovid composed the variant myth in allegorical repudiation of the adulterous or political conspiracy against the chosen heirs of Augustus in which he had been implicated at the time of his disgrace. But after he had embarked on his allegory Augustus died, and Tiberius showed a different, more republican, attitude to his relations with the senate and magistrates of Rome. Ovid turned back to this text and curtailed or reworked his hymn to imperial Maiestas so that it now culminated in the consul and *triumphator*, matching the actual achievements of his dedicatee Germanicus. He

---

[71] See Levick (1976*a*) 92 ff. and ch. 11. So too Suet. *Tib.* 30 *quin etiam speciem quandam libertatis introduxit* conservatis *senatui et magistratibus* et maiestate pristina et potestate.

went further and wrote or rewrote his etymological homage to the senate to emphasize the respect due to that body, fitting his panel to the mood of the new regime. Under the influence of this remodelling he composed the last two elegies, first honouring Germanicus with Hesiodic plumes borrowed from recent work on the *Fasti*, then transferring some of the new ideology into his congratulatory letter to Graecinus that ends with an indirect appeal to Tiberius (4.9.125–6) and his last direct address to the dead Augustus (4.9.133–4):

> auguror his igitur flecti tua numina, nec tu
>   immerito nomen mite parentis habes.

And so I prophesy that your will is yielding to these prayers, for you do not have the gentle name of 'Parent' undeservedly.

I have tried to survey the evidence that supports a later date for the present form of the Maius triptych, and relates it to the companion panel in June. There is intermittent evidence of late material in book 6, such as the final panel in honour of Marcia, wife of Fabius Maximus, from 799–812. Bömer cites editors' suggestions, on other grounds, that 6.237 (memories of the games on the Campus Martius), 219 ff. (referring to his daughter's happiness as sole reason for his survival), 666 (*exilium quodam tempore Tibur erat*), and 763–4 were added later (1957–8: 18–19). Most of these merely imply composition in exile or increasing age; only 763, *quamuis properabis uincere, Caesar*, bespeaks the last remodelling for Germanicus, since neither the 70-year-old Augustus nor the cautious Tiberius needed such restraint. We have noted two passages in book 6, at 92–3 and 637–8, where Ovid has focused on Augustus in contexts that could have been used to do honour to Tiberius; thus book 6 may have been left virtually unrevised, despite the evidence I have advanced for revision of book 5. Echoes and affinities with the poetry of exile are widely spread in the *Fasti*, but most conspicuous where we would expect them, in book 1. Yet I hope this examination has provided a clearer picture of the changing political and dynastic values behind Ovid's celebration of *Caesaris aras,* | *et quoscumque sacris addidit ille dies*.

18

Booking the Return Trip: Ovid and *Tristia* 1

Stephen Hinds

Two journeys are implied by the existence of *Tristia* 1: one, by a poet, from Rome to the gates of the Black Sea; the other, by a book, from the gates of the Black Sea back to Rome. Each of these journeys is explicitly, and prominently, discussed in *Tristia* 1; and each makes its presence felt in various ways throughout *Tristia* 1. Leaving for another day the outward voyage, described especially in the second, fourth, tenth, and eleventh poems, I am going to deal in this essay with the return trip of Ovid's book to Rome, as anticipated at some length in the very opening poem of the collection. And (because that is still a somewhat unwieldy topic) I am going to focus on the final destination of *Tristia* 1 *within* Rome, as specified in the last twenty lines or so of this first poem: viz: the bookcase in Ovid's Roman home. In these programmatically charged lines, the personified first book of exile poetry finds itself face to face with the poetry books written by Ovid before his exile. I want in the ensuing pages to take a closer look than is usually taken at some details of this and other encounters with Ovid's past writings in the first poems from exile; and my hope is that this analysis will tell us a few things along the way about how the poet is trying here to relate his literary present to his literary past.

(I)

Let us first find out a few basics about our personified traveller, by reminding ourselves of the very opening words of *Tristia* 1 (1.1–2):

parue (nec inuideo) sine me, liber, ibis in urbem:
  ei mihi, quod domino non licet ire tuo!

Little book, you will go without me (and I do not grudge it) to the city, where,
alas, your master may not go.

A poet takes leave of his book, speaking to it as master to slave, and
going on later in the poem to discuss how it will fare on its travels: the
commentators have not been slow to remark the parallel with the epilogue to Horace's first book of *Epistles* (a parallel whose claim on our
attention is strengthened by further evocation of *Epistles* 1 later in the
poem, where Ovid's advice to his book about approaching Augustus
echoes Horace in *Epistles* 1.13).[1] Note, however, the strangely inverted
nature of the master-slave relationship here in *Tristia* 1.1, evident in
this opening couplet. Ovid is the *dominus* and his book is the slave:
yet it is the slave who is free to go where he wants (line 1), and the
dominus who is not (line 2). The idea is taken up twice later in the
poem, each time with that same assonantal echo of *liber* in the verb
licet (15–16, 57–8)—

uade, *liber*, uerbisque meis loca grata saluta:
  contingam certe quo *licet* illa pede

Go, *my book*, and in my name greet the welcome places: at least I will reach
them with what foot I *may*.

tu tamen i pro me, tu, cui *licet*, aspice Romam:
  di facerent, possem nunc meus esse *liber*

But go, in my place, you who *may*, and look on Rome. I wish that the gods
would let me be my book now.

—something which perhaps makes one the more ready to discern
in the opening couplet a latent pun sharpening its paradox: the

---

[1] For the influence of Horace, *Epistles* 1.20, see e.g. Luck (1967–77), introduction to
Tristia 1.1; Nagle (1980) 35 and 83. For the influence of Horace, *Epistles* 1.13, see Luck
(1967–77) on *Trist.* 1.1.93–4, 101–2, 125–6; also, perhaps, in Ovid's twice repeated
uade (*Trist.* 1.1.3, 15) and four times repeated *caue* (*Trist.* 1.1.22, 25, 87, 104), there
is an acknowledgement of Horace's final exhortation *uade, uale, caue ne titubes . . . Ep.*
1.13.19).

book-slave is free where his master is constrained: the *lĭber* ('book') is the one who is truly . . . *lība̅r*('free').[2]

Right at the outset, then, elegant utterance is given to a brute fact which will determine Ovid's writing strategy for years to come, and of which he will never cease to remind us. The poet himself is stuck in exile: only through his books can he make his presence felt at Rome and argue there the case for his return (*Trist.* 1.1.3–4).

uade, sed incultus, qualem decet exulis esse;
  infelix habitum temporis huius habe.

Go, but be shabby, as suits an exile's book; wear an outfit that matches these days of mine.

The next twelve lines of the poem constitute an emphatic first statement of another inescapable fact of Ovid's writing from exile, viz. its constant insistence on its own shoddiness, which it puts down to the sad circumstances of its composition. Ovid keeps on telling us how substandard his exile poetry is: so persistently, indeed, does he tell us as to make us properly suspicious of his good faith in the matter. The self-criticism in this opening sally is ostensibly directed at the physical appearance of the book—which will, of course, be the first thing to be registered by the implied reader as he takes up the book and unrolls its first columns. In keeping with the circumstances of its master, the book is to be squalid and unkempt, *incultus* (a word which equally bodes ill for its content):[3] no purple-dyed wraps (5–6), no vermilion tinge to its title, no oil of cedar in its paper (7), no shining white *cornua* on its *frons* (8), and no polishing with pumice.

---

[2] A (false) etymology current in late antiquity actually *derives lĭber* from *liberatus*, in the context of the origin of the *lĭber* as 'bark' used for writing: Cassiodorus, *Inst.* 2. *praef.* 4 *liber autem dictus est a libro, id est arboris cortice dempto atque liberato*; cf. Isidore, *Orig.* 17.6.16 *liber est corticis pars interior, dictus a liberato cortice, id est ablato.* Perhaps, then, as often in Ovid (cf. n. 13 below), there is an etymological feel to the implicit pun in *Trist.* 1.1.1–2.

At the end of *Tristia* 3.1, the 'sequel' to the present poem (see n. 9 below), Ovid's personified book finds upon its arrival in Rome that it is not, after all, completely free; and the *lĭber | lība̅r* pun seems to me to be invoked again in an interesting way to mark the change (*Trist.* 3.1.71–4): *nec me, quae doctis patuerunt prima* libellis, | *atria* Libertas *tangere passa sua est. | in genus auctoris miseri fortuna redundat, | et patimur nati, quam tulit ipse, fugam.*

[3] For *incultus* as a literary term, see e.g. Horace, *Epist.* 2.1.233 *incultis . . . uersibus et male natis*, with Brink (1982) ad loc.; *OLD* s. v. *incultus* 3b.

The last-mentioned characteristic (11–12) has been recognized as pointing to an inversion here of Catullus' programmatic opening (Catullus 1.1–2);[4] but it is the next detail, in lines 13–14, which brings into prominence important fact number three about the exile poetry, viz. its pervasive debt to Ovid's own earlier writings.

The mention here of blots, *liturae*, caused by the writer's *lacrimae* constitutes an echo of the third line of one of Ovid's *Epistulae Heroidum*, the letter from Briseis to Achilles (*Trist.* 1.1.13–14, *Her.* 3.3):

neue liturarum pudeat; qui uiderit illas,
    de lacrimis factas sentiat esse meis.

Don't be ashamed of blots; let anyone who sees them feel that they were made by my tears.

quascumque aspicies, lacrimae fecere lituras

Whatever blots you see, her tears have made.

And the programmatic significance of this echo (which has, I think, been underestimated)[5] is doubled when we remember that the *Heroides* verse *itself* alludes to the second couplet of Propertius 4.3, the letter of a Roman matron who calls herself Arethusa to her absent husband Lycotas, often spoken of as the prototype for the *Heroides* (Anderson 1973: 67):

si qua tamen tibi lecturo pars oblita derit,
    haec erit e lacrimis facta litura meis

But if when you read it any portion is smudged and missing, this blot will have been caused by my tears.

The effect of the echo of the Propertian couplet in the *Heroides* line is to establish the *litura* as a sort of trademark of the elegiac epistle; so that Ovid's repetition of the motif here at the beginning of *Tristia* 1 is

---

[4] *Trist.* 1.1.11 *nec fragili geminae poliantur pumice frontes*; Catullus 1.1–2 . . . *lepidum nouum libellum | arida modo pumice expolitum*. For the allusion see Frécaut (1972) 311 n. 44; Evans (1983) 33–4.

[5] Amongst the commentators who note the echo of *Her.* 3.3, Nagle (1980) 84 and n. 27 is alone in cautiously seeing in it an 'indication . . . of the literary pedigree of the exilic elegies'.

immediately recognizable as a statement of literary alignment.[6] The statement does not lack its fulfilment: again and again in the poems which follow, the elegiac complaints sent by Ovid, stranded in exile, echo in general tone and in particular detail the elegiac complaints sent by his own earlier stranded heroines (Rahn 1958; Anderson 1973: 81). Even the love interest remains: just as the mythological women of the *Heroides* write to their distant husbands and lovers, so the real-life Ovid in *Tristia* 1.6 and in many later poems writes (reversing the sex roles) to his distant wife.

Note that in respect of its *dramatis personae* the elegiac epistle has here come full circle: in the *Heroides* Ovid transforms Propertius' tale of contemporary Roman married love into a series of tales of antique mythological love; now in the *Tristia* he reapplies the motifs of the mythological *Heroides* to *another* contemporary Roman married love, viz. his own. Perhaps, indeed, it is to draw attention to this reappropriation of the more remote model that his phrasing in *Trist.* 1.1.13–14 contains (as a close examination will reveal) specific verbal evocation of Propertius 4.3.4 over the head of *Her.* 3.3:[7] this kind of detailed double allusion to a nearer and a farther source is a standard technique of Augustan poetry.[8]

But it is the alignment with the *Heroides* which is most frequently reflected in the poems which follow; and, indeed, when in *Tristia* 3.1 (a poem written as a kind of sequel to *Tristia* 1.1)[9] the allusion to the beginning of *Heroides* 3 is picked up again, the exiled poet is found to have become even more like his mythological prototype there (*Trist.*3.1.15–18, *Her.* 3.1–4):

littera suffusas quod habet maculosa lituras,
    laesit opus lacrimis ipse poeta suum.

---

[6] Remember that elegy is the genre of weeping: thus a *litura* caused by the writer's tears is a most appropriate 'trademark' for epistles written in elegiac metre.

[7] With the collocation *Trist.* 1.1.14 *de lacrimis factas ... meis*, compare Propertius 4.3.4 *e lacrimis facta ... meis*. However, *Trist.* 1.1.13 *qui uiderit illas* perhaps looks rather towards *Her.* 3.3 *quascumque aspicies*, thus strengthening the strand of allusion which is more likely on general grounds to be immediate to the reader of *Tristia* 1.

[8] This principle of two-tier allusion is enunciated by Cairns (1979*b*) 121; cf., e.g., Kenney (1979) 106–12 with n. 31 on the sources of Virgil, *Aen.* 2.471–5 and 496–9.

[9] For the systematic recall of *Tristia* 1.1 in *Tristia* 3.1, see Frécaut (1972) 311–12, Evans (1983) 51–2, and the discussions of *Trist.* 3.1.71–2 in n. 2 above, and of 3.1.11–12 in section II below.

siqua uidebuntur casu non dicta Latine,
    in qua scribebat, barbara terra fuit.

If the letters are spotted and blurred with erasures, it is because the poet
himself has harmed his own work with tears. If by chance some phrases seem
not Latin, the land in which he wrote was barbarous.

quam legis, a rapta Briseide littera uenit,
    uix bene barbarica Graeca notata manu.
quascumque aspicies, lacrimae fecere lituras;
    sed tamen et lacrimae pondera uocis habent

The writing that you read comes from stolen Briseis, scarcely marked in
Greek by a barbarian hand. Whatever blots you see, her tears have made;
but tears, too, have none the less the weight of words.

Not only has he inherited her ink-blots (15–16 and *Her.* 3.3),[10] but
he has also, as a comparison of lines 17–18 with *Her.* 3.2 reveals,
inherited her other big difficulty: Briseis, a barbarian, has problems
writing good Greek; Ovid, stuck in a barbarian land, has problems
(or so he would have us believe) writing good Latin.

Returning to *Trist.* 1.1.13–14, we can use that couplet to recapitulate (in reverse order) on our three introductory facts of exile life:
1) The allusion to the *Heroides* verse offers an early indication of
Ovid's redeployment in exile of his own pre-exile poetry; 2) The
reference to *liturae* ends the first of many assertions of the shoddiness of this latest work, blamed on the poet's own sorry state; and
3) The invocation here of an *epistolary* model for the second time
in these opening lines—first Horace's *Epistles*, now Ovid's *Epistulae Heroidum*—draws attention to the fact that this is poetry which

---

[10] In *Trist.* 3.1.15 *littera suffusas quod habet maculosa lituras*, note that *littera* can
be interpreted either as 'a letter, a written character' (*OLD* s.v. *littera* 2), or as 'a letter,
an epistle' (*OLD* s.v. *littera* 7). Both usages are frequent in Ovid, as is the play between
them.

    Trist. 3.1.15 contains another interesting verbal detail too. If Ovid smudges with his
tears the *littera* that he is writing, what results, we read, is a *litura*. The paronomasia
between the two key words in the line may conceivably be felt to offer a *concrete
enactment* of the very relationship which they describe: for, if one of Ovid's tears
were to land in the middle of *the word littera itself*, as Ovid was writing it here in
Trist. 3.1.15, would not the resultant smudge (*littera . . . maculosa*) cause it to become
visually indistinguishable from . . . *the word litura*? One might perhaps argue for the
same reflexive twist in the earlier *Her.* 3.1 and 3 too.

is sent over a distance, poetry which has to speak for an absent writer.

It may be remarked, incidentally, in connection with number 3, that this epistolary programme for *Tristia* 1 has another aspect which turns out to be, if I may so put it, in part proleptic. The poems of *Tristia* 1 are in a *practical* sense epistles in that they have to be sent, in real life, over a distance to Rome (this, I have just argued, is the main point of Ovid's invocation of the epistle in this opening book). But in terms of internal, *literary* format, the typical elegy in *Tristia* 1 (or *Tristia* 3 or 4) is no more (or less) an epistle than any personal poem whatsoever with a named or implied addressee. And indeed *Tristia* 1 contains some poems which positively resist being interpreted as letters sent by one person to another: witness the second poem, which presents itself not as an epistle, but as a prayer directed to the gods. It is not until the fifth book of the *Tristia* that one meets many poems which are epistolary in the full sense, i.e. whose literary format demands that they be read as epistles (Duncan Kennedy's (1984) recent valuable observations on the epistolary mode should be recalled here: see ch. 3 above). An early example of this kind of poem is *Tristia* 3.3, with its overt designation of itself as an *epistula* (1), its use of the closing formula *uale* (87–8), and its other references at beginning and end to the business of letter-writing. What we see starting here, increasing in *Tristia* 5, and culminating in the switch from books of *Tristia* to a new collection of *Epistulae ex Ponto* with named addressees, is a belated assimilation of the internal, literary format of the exile poetry to the external, real-life fact of its always being written for posting. In effect, then, it is only in poems written long after *Tristia* 1 that this book's epistolary programme has its internal as well as its external consequences fully worked out.[11]

But that, as I say, is by the way. Our reading has brought us up to the eighth couplet of the opening poem. We have already had occasion to glance at this (*Trist.* 1.1.15–16):

uade, liber, uerbisque meis loca grata saluta:
  contingam certe quo licet illa pede

---

[11] John Henderson helped me to clarify this point.

Go, my book, and in my name greet the welcome places: at least I will reach
them with what foot I may.

The opening description of the book is over; and, after a slightly
contrived exploitation here of one of the most familiar puns in Latin
poetry, the one between *pes* 'human foot' and *pes* 'metrical foot', Ovid
proceeds to imagine what will happen when his book arrives in Rome.

   This is where *we* must speed up the action; and moving past all
the intermediate advice offered to the book—to tell the public that
Ovid is alive but far from well; to keep a low profile; to look for
toleration rather than praise from the critics; and, above all, to be very
circumspect in making any approach to Augustus—we find ourselves,
with the poet, in the final section of *Tristia* 1.1, anticipating the book's
ultimate destination, viz. the bookcase in Ovid's home.

(II)

cum tamen in nostrum fueris penetrale receptus,
   contigerisque tuam, scrinia curua, domum,
aspicies illic positos ex ordine fratres,
   quos studium cunctos euigilauit idem.
cetera turba palam titulos ostendet apertos,
   et sua detecta nomina fronte geret;
tres procul obscura latitantes parte uidebis:
   sic quoque, quod nemo nescit, amare docent.
hos tu uel fugias, uel, si satis oris habebis,
   Oedipodas facito Telegonosque uoces.
deque tribus, moneo, si qua est tibi cura parentis,
   ne quemquam, quamuis ipse docebit, ames (*Trist.* 1.1.105–16)

But when you've been received into my sanctuary and have reached your
own home, the round bookcases, you will see your brothers there arranged in
order, brothers whom the same midnight toil produced. The rest of the band
will display their titles openly, and will bear their names on their uncovered
edges, but you will see three at some distance trying to hide in a dark place—
even so they teach (what all know) how to love. These you should either avoid
or, if you can be so bold, see that you call them by the names of Oedipus or
Telegonus. And I warn you, if you have any regard for your parent, do not
love any of the three, though he himself will teach you how.

When the book reaches the *scrinia curua* (106), it will find lined up there Ovid's earlier books of poetry, its *fratres* (107): Ovid in this section (see also 115 *parentis*) presents us with a new image, destined to be used many times again, for his relationship with his books: no longer master and slave, but parent and son.[12] But (111–12) it will find skulking in the corner the three black sheep of the family, viz. the three books of the *Ars Amatoria*; and these our *liber* is to shun (113 *hos tu uel fugias*: an appropriate action, this, for an *exile* book); or, if it has the face, taking advantage of the failure of these books to display their titles openly like the rest (109–11), it is to try labelling them with a couple of new names: *Oedipodas facito Telegonosque uoces* (114).

Now Ovid, as the *Ibis* will subsequently show, is no slouch when it comes to dealing out a good literary insult; and this one looks as if it is meant to sting. Oedipus and Telegonus, the commentators explain, were parricides; and so, like the books of Ovid's *Ars Amatoria*, destroyed the author of their being (Luck 1967–77: on *Trist.* 1.1.113–14; Nagle (1980) 84). That is the gist of the insult: but it does not do full justice to its subtlety.

The father whom Telegonus killed was Ulysses; and the case of these new *Telegoni* is interestingly parallel. The parent whom *they* have destroyed is one who in the subsequent poems of *Tristia* 1, this book of voyaging, will align himself with one mythological character above all others: viz. the Neritian hero, Ulysses (Rahn 1958: 115–18; Evans 1983: 40). See especially the extended comparison in the final third of *Tristia* 1.5, which begins thus (*Trist.* 1.5.57–8):

pro duce Neritio docti mala nostra poetae
 scribite: Neritio nam mala plura tuli.

Write, poets, of my evils instead of the Neritian chief: for I have borne more evils than the Neritian.

And the allusiveness of this half of the insult extends also to include that old Ovidian mannerism for which J. C. McKeown has taught us to be ever vigilant, etymological play.[13] Ovid's new *liber* has been

---

[12] For the poet-parent image in Ovid's exile poetry, see now Davisson (1984); for the poet-parent image elsewhere in classical and post-classical literature, see Curtius (1953) 132–4 and Davisson (1984) 111.

[13] Ovid's liking for etymological word play has been demonstrated in detail in Dr McKeown's commentary on the *Amores* (1987; 1989). Such play is an important

instructed in 113 to give a wide berth to the books of the *Ars* (*hos tu uel fugias*). Now, in the following line, it is told to label the aberrant offspring with a name whose Greek formation very precisely picks up that policy of 'distancing': Τηλε-γόνους, *Telegonos.*[14]

One is prompted by this to consider the etymology of the first name thrown at the books of the *Ars*, viz. *Oedipodas*. The original Oedipus, as was common knowledge in antiquity, got his name from his *deformity of foot*—thus Οἰδί-πους (Soph. *Oed.* 1034–6; Sen. *Oed.* 812–13):

ΑΓ.   λύω σ᾽ ἔχοντα διατόρους ποδοῖν ἀκμάς.
ΟΙ.   δεινόν γ᾽ ὄνειδος σπαργάνων ἀνειλόμην.
ΑΓ.   ὥστ᾽ ὠνομάσθης ἐκ τύχης ταύτης ὃς εἶ.

Messenger: I freed you when you had your ankles pinned together.
Oedipus: It was a dread brand of shame that I took from my cradle.
Messenger: So much so that from that fortune you were called by that name which you still bear.

forata ferro gesseras uestigia,
tumore nactus nomen ac uitio pedum

You had ankles pierced by iron and took your name from the swollen deformity of your feet.

To the reader who knows his Ovid well, may not the books of the *Ars*, these latter-day parricides *in elegiac feet*, be thought of as being Οἰδί-ποδες in that same etymological sense? In an earlier introductory poem in his career which dealt in programmatic personification, *Amores* 3.1, Ovid had famously portrayed Elegy as a beautiful woman with one slight physical defect: namely, an irregularity of the *pes* (*Am.* 3.1.7–10):

uenit odoratos Elegia nexa capillos,
    et, puto, pes illi longior alter erat.
forma decens, uestis tenuissima, uultus amantis,
    et pedibus uitium causa decoris erat

feature of all learned poetry at Rome: cf. Cairns (1979*a*) 90–9 on Tibullus, Snyder (1980) on Lucretius.

[14] Many Greek names are compounded from τῆλε 'far': see Chantraine (1968–80) s.v.

There came Elegy, her coiled hair perfumed and, I think, she had one foot longer than the other. Her form was charming, her dress gauzy, her look loving; and her foot's deformity was part of her attraction.

The gallant Ovid of those days averred that the *uitium* just made her feet more attractive. Here in *Tristia* 1.1, as the poet reflects on his newly changed fortunes, his affair with the world of erotic elegy has gone a little sour; and the charming 'defect' characteristic of the elegiac *pes* (hexameter longer than pentameter) becomes, I suggest, fair game for covert personal invective: slight unevenness of length is caricatured as swollen deformity, and the troublesome elegiac books of the *Ars* find themselves labelled as Οἰδί-ποδες for more reasons than one.[15]

Again (lest you think that I am trying to lead you up an Alexandrian garden path) Ovid seems to point us towards the etymology: it is not just that Latin poets are always ready for *any* wordplay involving human and metrical feet; but that in this very poem, as we saw a few moments ago, Ovid has already, and with unusual explicitness, spelled out a *pes* pun for our benefit (line 16); so that the earlier, more straightforward 'foot' quibble, eight couplets into the poem, acts as a prompt to this later, more devious version, eight couplets from the end.

Furthermore, when Ovid systematically picks up the opening lines of *Tristia* 1.1 at the beginning of *Tristia* 3.1 (the sequel poem mentioned earlier), note how he varies the *pes* pun in 1.1.16 with a new 'foot' quibble in lines 11–12 of this poem:

clauda quod alterno subsidunt carmina uersu,
    uel pedis hoc ratio, uel uia longa facit,

If the lame poems hobble in alternate lines, either the metre's nature or the long journey is the cause.

A pick-up of the 'foot' quibble at *Trist.* 1.1.16, as the commentators say; an echo of the memorable conceit of the *uitium pedis* at *Am.*

---

[15] Note that the quibble works in Greek as well as in Latin translation: πούς admits precisely the same ambiguity between bodily and metrical feet as does *pes*. Greek poets do not seem to exploit this fact as frequently as do their Latin successors; but for two 'textbook examples' see Aristophanes, *Frogs* 1323–4, and Simias, *Egg* (= *AP* 15.27) 6 ff. pointed out to me by Neil Hopkinson.

3.1.7–10, as the commentators say;[16] but also, surely, an acknowl-edgement of that *other* 'foot' quibble within *Tristia* 1.1 itself, which has *already* brought the *uitium pedis* conceit into the picture.

By way of corollary, it may perhaps be suggested that *Trist.* 3.1.11–12 serves thus to highlight a touch of sly humour in Ovid's request to his exile book to address the books of the *Ars* as *Oedipodas*. It is one thing for *Ovid* to make fun (by my interpretation) of the *Ars*'s elegiac peculiarity of foot; but it is quite another for his exile book, which is itself, as those lines in *Tristia* 3.1 remind us, afflicted with precisely the same metrical *uitium*: Ovid is in effect asking a pot to call a kettle black.

Perhaps that is one of the reasons why in 113 he stipulates *si satis oris habebis*. At any rate that clause is one of two in this deprecation of the *Ars* which, as E. J. Kenney has remarked (1982: 446), manage to convey a simultaneous suggestion that deprecation is not really called for here. The other is the nicely ambiguous *quod nemo nescit* in 112. The clause can refer either, as the standard commentary takes it (Luck 1967–77: trans. of *Trist.* 1.1.112), to the notoriety of Ovid's didactic books: 'as everyone knows, they teach how to love'; *or* it can refer, as Professor Kenney takes it, to the fact that these books are simply telling people some facts of life with which they are already fully familiar: 'they teach (not that anyone needs a lesson) how to love'. In which latter case Augustus has been making rather a fuss about nothing in objecting to them.

These equivocations in 112 and 113 cannot be ignored; and, I think, there is a corresponding equivocation, which I have yet to remark on, in the mythological insults which follow in 114. Just as those jibes of *Oedipodas* and *Telegonos* contribute, more than has been realized, to the *attack* on the *Ars* in lines 111–16, so they make a simultaneous contribution, which has also gone largely unnoticed, to the quiet undercurrent here of *defence*. What exactly is it that Oedi-pus and Telegonus have in common? Recent commentators on the *Tristia* have responded as with one voice:[17] 'Both killed their fathers'. Good; but not good enough. For the answer which is really worth its

---

[16] So especially Nagle (1980) 22, who adds the observation that 'all Ovid's *pes*-puns contain a statement of poetics'.

[17] I am not quite fair here. Since I first drafted this section of my essay, two of my fellow participants in the boom in late-Ovidian studies have independently come up

alpha, one must go back to the author of the Bohn, Henry T. Riley of Clare Hall: 'Both killed their fathers . . . *unwittingly*' (Riley 1851: on *Trist.* 1.1.113–14). The fact is that, even while laying into the *Ars Amatoria*, Ovid tacitly acknowledges in the mythological references of 114 what he will go on to argue more forcibly and at greater length in *Tristia* 2: however bitter he may feel against them, ultimately his books are guiltless. They destroyed him; but they did so as a result of circumstances beyond their control.

(III)

Let us now follow our *liber* as it moves on its projected course to a happier part of Ovid's bookcase, where it will find the fifteen book-rolls of the *Metamorphoses*, designated in 117 through allusion to their opening sentence (*Trist.* 1.1.117–22):[18]

sunt quoque *mutatae*, ter quinque uolumina, *formae*,
    nuper ab exequiis carmina rapta meis.
his mando dicas, inter mutata referri
    fortunae uultum corpora posse meae.
namque ea dissimilis subito est effecta priori,
    flendaque nunc, aliquo tempore laeta fuit

There are also thrice five rolls of *changed forms*, a poem recently saved from my burial. I bid you say to them that the aspect of my fate can be reckoned among the changed bodies. For that aspect has suddenly become quite different from what it was before, and has become a cause of tears now, though formerly a source of joy.

The enclosed apposition in 117 perhaps carries a hint that the word *uolumina* is potentially as descriptive of the metamorphic *content* of this poetry as of the *paper* on which it is written.[19]

---

with the same improved answer given below: Posch (1983) 61 n. 118, and Davisson (1984) 112.

[18] *Met.* 1.1–2 *in noua fert animus mutatas dicere formas | corpora.*

[19] *uoluo* and its cognates often connote changeability in Latin: see especially *OLD* s.v. *uolubilis* 2b 'liable to change, unstable'. *uolumina* itself is thus used by Pliny, *Nat.* 7.147 *magna sortis humanae . . . uolumina.*

Ovid, we learn (119–22), wants to use his exile book to tell the volumes of the *Metamorphoses* about a new transformation which they can add to their collection. The 'aspect' of his own *fortuna*, the poet states, has suddenly become different from what it was before, a source of sorrow where it was once full of joy: therefore the *Tristia* book is to tell the books of the *Metamorphoses* that this *uultus* is one which merits inclusion in their catalogue of changed bodies.

The conceit, like others which we are going to examine shortly, presupposes some acquaintance with Ovid's great hexameter work itself. The reader will remember that in the proem of the *Metamorphoses* Ovid asks his inspiring deities to guide his poem from the first beginning of the universe down to his own times (*Met.* 1.3–4 ... *primaque ab origine mundi | ad mea perpetuum deducite tempora carmen*); and he will further remember that, when that final goal is reached in *Met.* 15.871–9, the *mea tempora* are celebrated in an exalted and exultant piece of writing in which Ovid sums up his achievement and predicts his own poetic immortality. The instruction at *Trist.* 1.1.119–22 is thus quite pointed. In asking the *Metamorphoses* to take on board the sudden transformation of the *uultus* of his own *fortuna*, Ovid clearly has his eye on that section of the *Metamorphoses* which *already has* his *fortuna* as its theme: viz. the poem's final nine lines. It is here, if anywhere, that the sorry tale of the change in Ovid's *fortuna* will have to be accommodated; and the effect will be, surely, to put something of a damper on the triumphant spirits of the epic's conclusion. Ovid's *mea tempora*, alas, are no longer what they were *aliquo tempore* (122); and the conceit in *Trist.* 1.1.119–22 suggests a way in which the end of the *Metamorphoses* can be rewritten to take account of the fact.

(IV)

Now, one important function of the trip to Ovid's bookcase, as has often been said (e.g. Kenney 1982: 446), is quite simply to serve as a reminder of the impressiveness of the poet's past achievements. It is the foremost literary figure of the day who has been banished; and it is vital to Ovid's strategy in exile that his Roman readers do not lose sight of this. The point is one which becomes fully explicit in a poem later in *Tristia* 1 which the present lines prefigure (or, if you like, recall, since *Tristia* 1.1 purports to be written after the rest of the book). In the seventh elegy of *Tristia* 1, even more powerfully than at the end of the first, Ovid brings us face to face once more with the output of his poetic past; and it is to *Tristia* 1.7 that we now turn.

Someone at Rome has a portrait of Ovid, an *imago* (1.7.1), in the form of a bust, or in the form of a ring: Ovid is grateful for the sign that he is not being forgotten. But for a *better* portrait of him, a *maior imago* (1.7.11), the addressee should turn to the *carmina* of the *Metamorphoses*: this is what Ovid really wants to be remembered by in his absence—even though, as he goes on to explain at some length, he has not had time to put the finishing touches to the poem.

Ovid's comments here on the allegedly unfinished state of the *Metamorphoses* have made this one of the most frequently anthologized and frequently talked about of all the exile elegies. The opening gambit of the post-biographical critic is by now a familiar one: 'What can *Tristia* 1.7 *really* tell us about the *Metamorphoses*?' Therefore, in search of originality, let us do a quick U-turn, and ask instead, 'What can the *Metamorphoses* really tell us about *Tristia* 1.7?' A new question and, I think, a promising one.

First, it can tell us some things that we may not have noticed about the most famous part of the elegy, in which Ovid claims to have burnt his copy of the *Metamorphoses* before going into exile (*Trist.* 1.7.15–20).

haec ego discedens, sicut bene multa meorum,
  ipse mea posui maestus in igne manu.
utque cremasse suum fertur sub stipite natum
  Thestias et melior matre fuisse soror,
sic ego non meritos mecum peritura libellos
  imposui rapidis uiscera nostra rogis

This when I departed, like so much that was mine, in sorrow I put in the fire with my own hand. Just as Thestius' daughter burned her own son, they say, in the branch and was a better sister than mother, so I placed the innocent books, my very vitals, on the devouring pyre to perish with me.

Taking as read the allusion (now universally acknowledged) to Virgil's dying wishes about the *Aeneid* (Grisart 1959; Evans 1983: 43–4), let us consider the simile in 17–20. Just as Thestias (i.e. Althaea) is said to have destroyed her son (i.e. Meleager) by burning the brand on which his life depended, so Ovid places on the devouring pyre the innocent books which are *his* offspring, his *uiscera*, to perish along with himself.[20]

We have returned, evidently (see also 35 *parente* below), to the parent-son image for Ovid's relationship with his books; except that the author who at the end of *Tristia* 1.1 was the victim of parricide (vis-à-vis the books of the *Ars*) is now himself in *Tristia* 1.7 (vis-à-vis the books of the *Metamorphoses*) the perpetrator of infanticide. However, let us confine ourselves to the question set. What can the *Metamorphoses* tell us about this simile for the burning of its own books?

Well, it can tell us that to find out more about the bizarre story of Meleager's fate we need look no further than the *Metamorphoses'* own *uolumina*, where that myth is handled at considerable length; and it can confirm that the *Metamorphoses* 8 account is indeed Ovid's immediate source here: there are clear verbal echoes in our simile.[21] That much has been noticed before. However, only when we view the Meleager episode in the context of the *Metamorphoses as a whole* will we see just how apt is the allusion to it here in this elegy from exile. What better way to illustrate this most crucial of all moments in the history of the *Metamorphoses*, this very crisis of its existence, than through a simile taken from what is, in terms of its position within the epic, the middle myth of the very middle book? Nothing could more clearly emphasize the threat to its survival— as recounted, one may add, in the centre of this elegy devoted to it.

---

[20] Note that as well as meaning 'my offspring, my flesh and blood' (*OLD* s.v. *uiscera* 5), as the context here demands, *uiscera nostra* can also contain a hint of 'my <own> vitals' (*OLD* s.v. *uiscus* 2): the language allows Ovid to identify for a moment with Meleager as well as with his mother.

[21] *Trist.* 1.7.18 *et melior matre fuisse soror*, *Met.* 8.463 *pugnat materque sororque*, 475 *esse tamen melior germana parente*. *Trist.* 1.7.17 *utque cremasse . . .*, 20 *imposui rapidis uiscera nostra rogis*, *Met.* 8.478 *rogus iste cremet mea uiscera*. For these echoes, see Grisart (1959) 127 and n. 3, Davisson (1984) 112.

A similar reward for reading this elegy about the *Metamorphoses* with the *Metamorphoses* in mind lies in store just below. Why did Ovid burn his masterpiece (*Trist.* 1.7.21–2)?

uel quod eram Musas, ut crimina nostra, perosus,
    uel quod adhuc crescens et rude carmen erat

Either because I had come to hate the Muses as the accusations against me, or because the poem was as yet growing and rough.

Either through hatred of the Muses (21); or (the reason he sticks with for the rest of the elegy) because the *Metamorphoses* was as yet a growing poem in a rough condition: *adhuc crescens et rude* (22). The description should ring another bell with the man who knows his *Metamorphoses*. The *carmen* is as yet *rude*—just as in the opening sentence of its own initial myth of Chaos (*Met.* 1.5–9) the *universe* is still a *rudis indigestaque moles*. The *carmen* is as yet *crescens*: in other words, it has failed to complete fully its projected (*Met.* 1.3–4) narrative journey to the poet's own day—from Chaos, the first beginning of the universe. Just above, the *Metamorphoses* was characterized in terms of its own *central* myth. Now, it is being characterized in terms of its own *opening* myth, the myth of the transformation of Chaos into an ordered universe; and, to drive the point home, not just the word *rude*, but also the words *adhuc* and *crescens* are drawn from the vocabulary of the opening lines of that myth (*Met.* 1.5–11):

ante mare et terras et quod tegit omnia caelum
unus erat toto naturae uultus in orbe,
quem dixere *Chaos*; *rudis* indigestaque moles
nec quicquam nisi pondus iners congestaque eodem
non bene iunctarum discordia semina rerum.
nullus *adhuc* mundo praebebat lumina Titan,
nec noua *crescendo* reparabat cornua Phoebe

Before the sea and the lands and the sky that covers all, in the whole world the appearance of nature was the same, which men have called *Chaos*: a *rough* and undivided mass, nothing else but an inert weight and warring seeds of ill-joined matter heaped together. *As yet* no Sun offered light to the world, nor did the moon renew her horns *by growing*.

After the evocation of the middle and the beginning of the *Meta-morphoses* comes, appropriately enough, an evocation of the end (*Trist.* 1.7.23–6):

quae quoniam non sunt penitus sublata, sed extant
  (pluribus exemplis scripta fuisse reor),
nunc precor ut uiuant et non ignaua legentum
  otia delectent admoneantque mei.

Since it was not utterly destroyed, but still exists (several copies were made, I think), now I pray that it may live, and that it may delight the lively leisure of readers and remind them of me.

Having told us what he did to his great poem, and why, Ovid now informs us that the *Metamorphoses* is still extant (23); because, apparently (as if he hadn't known it all along) there were multiple copies (24). Now, therefore, he prays that the poetry may live on: *nunc precor ut uiuant* (25). This time, the merest hint suffices. To live on, for the *Metamorphoses*, after the writer has gone to his metaphorical death (*Trist.* 1.7.19, cf. 38), will be to echo the final prediction of the hero of the *Metamorphoses'* own final myth: *Met.* 15.879, the very last word of the poem—*uiuam* (*Met.* 15.873–9):[22]

cum uolet, illa dies, quae nil nisi corporis huius
ius habet, incerti spatium mihi finiat aevi:
parte tamen meliore mei super alta perennis
astra ferar, nomenque erit indelebile nostrum,
quaque patet domitis Romana potentia terris,
ore legar populi, perque omnia saecula fama,
siquid habent ueri uatum praesagia, *uiuam*.

When it will, let that day, which has no claim but to this mortal body, end the span of my uncertain years. Still in my better part I shall be borne immortal above the lofty stars and my name shall be imperishable. Wherever Rome's power extends over the conquered world, my words will be on the lips of men; and, if the prophecies of bards have any truth, in fame through all the ages *I shall live*.

In this central section of *Tristia* 1.7, then, the story of the books of the *Metamorphoses* finds its metaphorical reflection in the stories of

---

[22] Luck (1967–77) on *Trist.* 1.7.25–6 appears to take the point.

the books' *own three pivotal myths*. The books of poetry consumed by flames are like Meleager in their own central volume consumed by flames; the poem in its rude state is like the universe at the beginning of *Metamorphoses* 1 in its rude state; and now, the poetry's future existence (if the prayer in *Trist.* 1.7.25 is answered) will be like the future existence of Ovid himself envisaged at the end of *Metamorphoses* 15. In this final case, however, the outer and inner stories coalesce. Ovid's future existence in the final myth of the *Metamorphoses* is, remember (see especially 15.875), an existence *through the survival of his poetry*: the subjects of the verbs *uiuant* in *Trist.* 1.7.25 and *uiuam* in *Met.* 15.879 are, ultimately, one and the same. The double story has found its climax.

Indeed, the last allusion is climactic in another way too. Ovid had begun that final myth of the *Metamorphoses* by proclaiming the durability of his work against the forces of nature (15.871–2):

iamque opus exegi, quod nec Iovis ira nec ignes
nec poterit ferrum nec edax abolere uetustas

And now I have completed my work, which neither the wrath of Jupiter, nor fire, nor sword, nor the devouring ages can destroy.

... *nec ignes*: the central section of *Tristia* 1.7 is precisely concerned with an attempt to nullify this by destroying the fifteen books of the *Metamorphoses* through fire; so that the eventual acceptance of the *Metamorphoses*' final life-affirming *uiuam* in 1.7.25 reads all the more pointedly.[23]

What else can the *Metamorphoses* tell us about *Tristia* 1.7? It can cast some light, I think, on the distinctive ring composition which encloses the elegy. As the commentators have observed (Evans 1983: 43), *Tristia* 1.7 begins and ends with a pair of contrasting requests (1–4; 33–4):

siquis habes nostri similes in imagine uultus,
    deme meis hederas, Bacchica serta, comis.
ista decent laetos felicia signa poetas:
    temporibus non est apta corona meis

---

[23] Simon Goldhill helped me to clarify this.

Whoever you may be who possess a portrait of my features, take the ivy,
Bacchus' garland, from my tresses. Those lucky symbols suit happy poets: a
wreath is not fitting for my brow.

hos quoque sex uersus, in prima fronte libelli
    si praeponendos esse putabis, habe.

Receive these six verses also, if you think that they should be placed at the
head of the first book.

The friend addressed should remove the Bacchic crown from Ovid's
bust (1–4); and he should add some explanatory verses to Ovid's
poem, the *Metamorphoses* (33–4). The bust is one kind of portrait of
the poet, one kind of *imago* (1); the poem, we remember, is a better
kind of portrait of the poet, a *maior imago* (11). The crown to be
removed from the bust connotes (3) poetic prosperity; the verses to
be added to the poem tell (as we shall see below) of poetic adversity.
Finally, the commentators note, a wordplay links beginning and end.
The crown is to be removed from the *tempora* of Ovid's bust, i.e. from
its 'forehead' (4); the verses are to be added to the *frons* of Ovid's
book, i.e. to its 'beginning' (33) . . . but also (as we perhaps recall from
the personifying tendencies of *Trist.* 1.1.8 and 11–12) to another word
which means 'forehead'.[24]

Thus Ovid's *imago* is to be changed, and the new *imago* will have a
new kind of *frons*: something of a transformation takes place between
the beginning of *Tristia* 1.7 and its end. In *Tristia* 1.1, it was the
uultus of Ovid's *fortuna* which, we were told (1.1.119–22), underwent
metamorphosis. Now it is the *uultus* of Ovid's *imago* (1.7.1) which are
likewise to be transformed; and the product of *this* metamorphosis,
the new *imago* of the poet which at the end of this elegy will replace
the old one, is, of course, nothing less than the *Metamorphoses* itself!

Tristia 1.7 is a remarkable monument in every way to the fifteen
books of the *Metamorphoses*. Not only does it tell the story of their
publication; not only does it contain pointed allusion to their opening, central, and final sections; but it is enclosed by a ring composition
which effectively enacts their very theme, viz. transformation.

---

[24] Note the further pun within *Trist.* 1.7.4 itself: *temporibus non est apta corona
meis* 'a crown does not befit *my temples*'; but also more than a hint of (cf. *Trist.* 1.1.4)
'a crown does not befit *my present circumstances*'.

For the second time in *Tristia* 1, then, Ovid openly reminds us of the existence of his greatest poem; and what is striking is that in both cases the reminder takes the form of a proposal that the poem itself be modified. In the first elegy, the *liber* of *Tristia* 1 was instructed to tell the *Metamorphoses*, when it made the acquaintance of that work, that it could make room within itself for a new metamorphosis, viz. the story of Ovid's change of *fortuna*:[25] as you will recall, we noted that this was likely to involve something of a rewriting of the poem's end. Now, in this second poetic return to the *Metamorphoses* in *Tristia* 1.7, a further piece of 'tampering with the text' is suggested, this time quite explicitly. The reader is to add (if he sees fit) six verses to the poem, given in lines 35–40; and these verses are to stand at the head of the *Metamorphoses as a new preface* (33–4). This is really quite extraordinary. First Ovid proposes to change the end of the *Metamorphoses*; now he proposes to change its beginning. What is going on? Why does Ovid insist on rewriting his epic each time that he summons it up in this first book of exile poetry?

The answer, I think, lies in the nature of the 'rewrite'. The new preface in *Trist.* 1.7.35–40, when transplanted to its intended site (where, of course, it will immediately feel at home, having spent its formative months in an elegy which is itself a microcosm of the *Metamorphoses*)—this new preface will first (35–6) allude to the fact that the *Metamorphoses* is poetry which represents an absent, exiled writer; and it will then (37–40) apologize for the poem's rough and unrefined state, which it will blame on the writer's sad circumstances:

'orba parente suo quicumque uolumina tangis,
    his saltem uestra detur in urbe locus.
quoque magis faueas, haec non sunt edita ab ipso,
    sed quasi de domini funere rapta sui.
quicquid in his igitur uitii rude carmen habebit,
    emendaturus, si licuisset, erat.'

[25] Note, incidentally, that this is not the only occasion in the first century AD when a new transformation is put up for membership of the *Metamorphoses*; and it may indeed be from *Trist.* 1.1.119–22 that Seneca gets the idea for his famous conceit in the *Apocolocyntosis*: 9.5 . . . *censeo uti diuus Claudius ex hac die deus sit ita uti ante eum quis optimo iure factus sit, eamque rem ad Metamorphosis Ovidi adiciendam.*

'You who touch these rolls bereft of their parent, let a place in your city be granted at least to them. Your indulgence may be the greater because these were not published by their master, but were taken from what might be called his funeral. And so whatever defect his rough poem may have he would have corrected, had it been permitted him.'

Coming after these depressing lines, *in noua fert animus . . .* (*Met.* 1.1) will no longer be able to engender quite the same *frisson* of excitement that it does in the original version of the *Metamorphoses*. And, like any preface, this new one will inevitably seek to exercise some influence over the poem as a whole: by re*writing* its opening lines, Ovid will force us to re*read* the entire poem in a slightly different light.

And it is this same kind of overall rereading that is implied by the rewriting of the poem's end, as proposed more obliquely in the first elegy. A sad ending can exercise a powerful retrospective influence over any narrative—think of the *Aeneid*—and a *Metamorphoses* whose final column incorporates a discussion of Ovid's ruined fortunes will not be the same *Metamorphoses* that it was before.

Ovid, then, offers in *Tristia* 1.7, as at the end of *Tristia* 1.1, a newly pessimistic way into the *Metamorphoses*; and the terms in which that pessimism is expressed are highly significant. What are the two constituent elements of the poem's proposed new preface at *Trist.* 1.7.35–40? First (we said) an allusion to the fact that the *Metamorphoses* is poetry which represents an absent, exiled writer; and second, an apology for the poem's shoddy state, ascribed to the writer's sad circumstances. We seem to have been here before. What (if we cast our minds back to the beginning of this essay) were the fundamental facts about Ovid's book *of exile poetry*, as established in the very opening lines of *Tristia* 1 itself? First, that it was poetry which spoke for an absent, exiled writer; and second, that it was poetry which made constant assertion of its own shoddiness, which it put down to its writer's sad circumstances.[26]

---

[26] With *Trist.* 1.1.1–2 and 15–16 compare in the '*Metamorphoses* preface' *Trist.* 1.7.35–6; with *Trist.* 1.1.46 *scriptaque cum uenia qualiacumque leget* compare in the main body of the seventh elegy *Trist.* 1.7.11–12 *carmina . . . | . . . quae mando qualiacumque legas* and 1.7.31 *ueniam pro laude peto*; and, amongst other elements which make one think of the *Tristia* 1.1 programme in connection with the *Metamorphoses*

Things begin to become clearer. The main argument of *Tristia* 1.7 has already told us that the job of the books of the *Metamorphoses* in these difficult times of exile is to function as a monument to the poet, as a reminder of his existence (1.7.11 *maior imago*; 1.7.26 *admoneantque mei*). What better way could they do this than by taking a lesson from the real professional at this job, viz. the book of exile poetry itself, whose essential strategy is to keep Ovid's case before the public eye by constantly drawing attention to his absence? Hence Ovid's 'rewrite': the *Metamorphoses* is to be given a new preface which will make pointed reference, like the beginning of *Tristia* 1 itself, to its author's exile; and which, again like the beginning of *Tristia* 1, will claim a reflection of the author's woes in the poem's own rough and unfinished state. And this new preface, combined with the new ending already proposed in the first elegy, will have the effect of making the *Metamorphoses as a whole* more pessimistic— more suited, in fact, to an age of *Tristia*.

Tristia 1.7, then, is not a poem about the *Metamorphoses per se*: it is a poem about how the *Metamorphoses* can be redeployed, how it can be rewritten, to reflect the circumstances of Ovid's exile, and thus, ultimately, to help him book his trip home.

Nor is the relevance of this conclusion about Ovid's proposals to rewrite the *Metamorphoses* to be limited to *Tristia* 1.7 (and the end of *Tristia* 1.1) alone. Remember important fact number three about Ovid's exile poetry, viz. its *pervasive* debt to his earlier works. *Tristia* 1 and the other books of *Tristia* and *Epistulae ex Ponto* which follow are full of echoes of the *Metamorphoses*. When to describe his voyage across the Adriatic in *Tristia* 1.2 Ovid alludes to his own account of the storm which kills Ceyx in *Metamorphoses* 11 (Evans 1983: 35 n. 9); when to describe Tomis in *Tristia* 3.10 he alludes to his own description of the abode of Hunger in *Metamorphoses* 8;[27] when to express his accumulation of woe after many

---

here, note especially the recurrence at *Trist.* 1.7.38 of the poet-*dominus* image found in *Trist.*1.1.1–2.

[27] *Trist.* 3.10.75 *aspiceres nudos, sine fronde, sine arbore campos*; *Met.* 8.789 *triste solum, sterilis, sine fruge, sine arbore tellus*, with Hollis (1970) ad loc. What is immediately striking is the recurrence of those adjectival phrases with *sine*; but the echo gains in piquancy if the reader of *Trist.* 3.10.75 happens to recall the first two words of the line being alluded to.

years in *Ex Ponto* 4.16 he echoes the speech of his own sorrowing
Hecuba in *Metamorphoses* 13;[28]—every time, in short, that Ovid
echoes his hexameter masterpiece in these elegies from the Black
Sea, what is he doing? Just as in the last six lines of *Tristia* 1.7, he
is *rewriting the Metamorphoses* to make statements about his own
exile.

(V)

In a pioneering paper on Ovid's exile poetry published under the
auspices of the Cambridge Philological Society exactly twenty years
ago, Professor Kenney offered a brief comment on *Tristia* 1.7 as an
appendix to a discussion of *Tristia* 1.6 (1965:39–42). I would now like
to invert the topos, and to conclude by offering a brief comment on
Tristia 1.6 as a pendant to *my* discussion of *Tristia* 1.7.

The elegy is addressed to Ovid's wife, and pays tribute to her
loyalty. It begins by comparing her with the women loved by the poets
Antimachus and Philetas (*Trist.* 1.6.1–4):

nec tantum Clario est Lyde dilecta poetae
    nec tantum Coo Bittis amata suo est,
pectoribus quantum tu nostris, uxor, inhaeres,
    digna minus misero, non meliore uiro.

Not so much was Lyde cherished by the Clarian poet, nor was Bittis so loved
by her Coan as you, my wife, cling to my heart, you who deserve a husband
not better, but less wretched.

and half way through it goes on to compare her with the great married
heroines of mythology, Andromache, Laudamia, and Penelope (*Trist.*
1.6.19–22):

---

[28] Martin Helzle drew my attention to the echo: *omnia perdidimus: tantummodo
uita relicta est,* | *praebeat ut sensum materiamque mali* (*Pont.* 4.16.49–50) and *omnia
perdidimus: superest, cur uiuere tempus* | *in breue sustineam, proles gratissima matri*
(*Met.* 13.527–8). The two laments are all the closer in that Hecuba is mistaken in her
flicker of optimism in *Met.* 13.527–8. She learns immediately after these lines that *her
proles gratissima*, Polydorus, is in fact dead: thus Ovid's version of her words in *Pont.*
4.16.49–50 can be felt to be a response to the full reality of her situation, of which she
has not yet been made aware.

nec probitate tua prior est aut Hectoris uxor,
aut comes extincto Laudamia uiro.
tu si Maeonium uatem sortita fuisses,
Penelopes esset fama secunda tuae.

Hector's wife does not exceed your virtue, nor Laodamia who shared her husband's death. If fate had given you the Maeonian bard, Penelope's fame would be second to yours.

This last reference (to Penelope: 21–2), by the way that it is phrased, subtly draws the two sets of comparisons together, viz. women loved by poets, and noble wives of myth: 'If you had been allotted Homer, Penelope's fame would be second to yours.'

In the final lines of the poem, Ovid goes on to regret that *his* poetic powers (as opposed to Homer's) are not equal to what his wife deserves; but he promises that, so far as his *carmina* have the power to effect it, she shall have her immortality (*Trist.* 1.6.29–36):

ei mihi, non magnas quod habent mea carmina uires,
nostraque sunt meritis ora minora tuis,
siquid et in nobis uiui fuit ante uigoris,
extinctum longis occidit omne malis.
prima locum sanctas heroidas inter haberes,
prima bonis animi conspicerere tui.
quantumcumque tamen praeconia nostra ualebunt,
carminibus uiues tempus in omne meis.

Alas, my poems have no great power and my words do not match your merits. If formerly I had some living vigour, it has all been extinguished by my long calamity. You would be the first to have a place among the sacred heroines, you would be the first to be seen for the qualities of your heart. Yet so far as my praise has power, you will live for all time in my poetry.

The elegy, as Professor Kenney rightly points out, is first and foremost a statement of what it means, even in exile, to be a poet.

My comment concerns line 33: *prima locum sanctas heroidas inter haberes*. Professor Kenney has a footnote: 'Mr G. R. Watson has suggested to me that there may . . . be a reference to Ovid's own poetry in *heroidas*'. Mr G. R. Watson has surely hit the mark[29]—for four

[29] The suggestion is reported at Kenney (1965) 40 n. 2. For the title *Heroides*, attested in Priscian, *Gramm. Lat.* ii.544 Keil, see Palmer (1898) x–xi. The probability

reasons. 1) The two couplets before the one with which we are concerned deal overtly with Ovid's own poetry, and so does the couplet
which follows it; 2) The immediately preceding couplet contains,
specifically, a contrast between Ovid's *present* poetic powers and his
past poetic powers; 3) We already know from the opening lines of
Tristia 1 that Ovid's present poetic project is a kind of return to the
past epistolary laments of his own *Heroides*; and number four, I think,
is the one that clinches it. Suppose that Ovid does mean an oblique
reference here to his own *Heroides*. What exactly would he then be
saying in line 33? 'You would be the *first* to have a place (*prima
locum . . . haberes*) amongst my *Heroides*'. If we have learnt anything
in the course of our discussion of *Tristia* 1.7, it is the importance of
bearing in mind the layout of Ovid's earlier poetry books when trying
to understand Ovidian allusion to those books. If Ovid's wife *were*
to be given first place amongst Ovid's *Heroides*, who would thereby
be relegated to *second* place in the collection? Why, none other than
Penelope, whose letter is currently the first in the collection. Ovid, in
fact, would be doing for his wife *exactly what he said Homer would
have done for her*, in line 22: *Penelopes esset fama secunda tuae*.[30]

    In the event, Ovid says that he is not up to the task of placing his
wife first amongst the revered[31] heroines. But perhaps the strongly
positive note of the final couplet (*Trist.* 1.6.35–6) makes one reflect
that, in a sense, he does achieve his desire. Even if Ovid's wife has
not made it to first position amongst the women of the *Heroides*, she
certainly, in poems like this one, makes it to first position amongst
the women of the *Tristia*. And what are the *Tristia* but (as we learnt
in 1.1.13–14) a rewriting in exile of the *Heroides*? Ovid's wife *shall* be
first; and Ovid's poetry, firmly rooted in its own past, shall live on.

is strong that both this and the longer form '*Epistulae Heroidum*' go back to
Ovid.

    [30] The fact that Ovid's Penelope in *Heroides* 1 is very closely modelled on Homer's
(see the brilliant discussion of Kennedy (1984, = ch. 3 above)) lends added point to
the conceit here. Incidentally, Jacobson (1974) 409, discussing the arrangement of the
Heroides, accounts for Penelope's pride of place in terms of this literary ancestry: as
the representative of Homer, the first poet, she is the one chosen by Ovid to begin the
collection.

    [31] Lee (1959) 407, also taking *heroidas* in 33 as a reference to Ovid's own poetry,
attractively interprets its epithet *sanctas* as an allusion to the fact that the mythological
characters of the *Heroides* boast a grander generic pedigree (epic, tragic) than do the
women found in conventional love elegy.

19

On Ovid's *Ibis*: A Poem in Context

Gareth D. Williams

In Propertius' reconstruction of the battle of Actium in 4.6, Apollo is pictured taking his place over Augustus' ship, braced for war (31–2):

non ille attulerat crinis in colla solutos
    aut testudineae carmen inerme lyrae.

He had not come with locks loosed over his shoulders or brought the (h)armless song of the tortoise lyre.

In the opening couplet of the *Ibis* Ovid repeats the words *carmen inerme* at the same point in the pentameter:

tempus ad hoc lustris bis iam mihi quinque peractis
    omne fuit Musae carmen inerme meae.

Up to this time, when I have already completed fifty years, every song of my Muse has been (h)armless.

In Propertius Apollo lays aside the peaceful lyre and takes up his bow to begin the onslaught (55) which will bring Augustus easy victory (57). By echoing Propertius' words Ovid signals his own move into bellicose poetics. But whereas Apollo is equally adept with the lyre and the bow, Ovid is a stranger to war and no more equipped to take up figurative arms in his unaccustomed hands (cf. 10) than he is to take up real arms in self-defence against the marauding hordes of Pontic barbarians (cf. *Tr.* 4.1.71–4). So why does Ovid have no option but to make war when, on his own admission, he is so ill equipped for the task? Why is he at such pains to stress his strangeness to arms?

442   *Gareth D. Williams*

The answer, in part, is to be found at *Tr.* 2.563–72, where Ovid closes his defence of the *Ars Amatoria* against the charge of immorality with a defence of his own character. He has never, he claims, either harmed or set out to harm anyone through venomous lampooning, and the only person who has ever suffered by his writings is himself, the victim of his own *Ars/ars* (565–8):

candidus a salibus suffusis felle refugi:
    nulla uenenato littera mixta ioco est.
inter tot populi, tot scriptis, milia nostri,
    quem mea Calliope laeserit, unus ero.

I am good-natured and have shunned wit steeped in gall: no writing of mine is infused with poisoned jest. Among so many thousands of our people, much as I wrote, I shall be the only one my Calliope has injured.

Now even if his salvoes against the likes of Dipsas in *Am.* 1.8 and Bagoas in *Am.* 2.3 are mere set pieces of contrived abuse, and even if he has manifestly avoided the poisonous mockery of particular victims (565), the fact remains that targeted wit can lack Hipponactean venom and yet still be subtly devastating. While such terms as *sales suffusi felle*, *laedere*, and *uenenatus iocus* indicate a malicious brand of humour which Ovid denies indulging, he can still lay claim to a more benign kind of humour, 'liberal' jesting as opposed to its 'illiberal' counterpart.[1] Perhaps Ovid is not quite whiter than white (cf. *candidus*, 565), a stranger to targeted wit, especially if one considers the many innuendoes which gently deflate his imperial panegyric in *Tristia* 2.[2] Augustus might reasonably absolve Ovid from the charge of poisonous wit and yet still disbelieve line 565 if he himself recognized these innuendoes; but Ovid can equally claim the alibi of not

---

[1] For the distinction see Cic. *Off.* 1.104, where two categories of jesting are distinguished—illiberal jesting and its urbane counterpart; on the history of the distinction in antiquity see Bramble (1974) 190 ff. The distinction is crucial to Horace's famous defence against the charge of malice in *S.* 1.4 (cf. *'laedere gaudes', inquit, 'et hoc studio prauus facis'*, 79–80), on which see Dickie (1981) 185–93 with Hunter (1985) 486–90. Cf. Bramble (1974) 200 on *Tr.* 2.563 and 565: 'more statements than disclaimers—if anything, iambic is envisaged rather than satire—these passages nonetheless derive from the sanctioned contrast between venomous and humane wit'.

[2] On various kinds of innuendo in *Tristia* 2 see Wiedemann (1975), Scott (1931) 293–6, Claassen (1986) 307–14, Focardi (1975), Vulikh 1968a and 1968b.

intending what he seems to imply in his innuendoes,[3] and for this reason it is with brazen confidence that he makes his last plea to the emperor, that his benevolent and harmless character (cf. *candor*, 574) be taken into account in deciding his ultimate fate. But after he has staked so much on his claim to *candor* at *Tr.* 2.563–72, what if someone should contest that claim? Ovid would be left to defend part of his own self-defence in *Tristia* 2; hence the gravity of his *iniuria magna* as described at *Ibis* 7–8, an attack on his *candor* by the man he terms Ibis.[4]

The real point of interest in this comparison with the end of *Tristia* 2 is not that it reveals a real, pragmatic reason for Ovid's writing of the *Ibis*, but that it offers an early illustration of the way in which the *Ibis* grows out of a thematic context already provided by the *Tristia*. An initial hint to this effect was given in the comparison drawn above between Ovid's enforced initiation into real war in Tomis and his equally enforced initiation into unaccustomed warfare in the *Ibis*. The hint is confirmed by the obvious correspondence between *Tr.* 2.563–72 and *Ibis* 1–10, where Ovid reiterates the innocence of his Muse and the fact that he is her only victim because of his *Ars* (3–6). Thematic correspondences of this sort immediately serve to qualify the commonly held view that the work is an aberration in which Ovid merely gives vent to years of stored-up learning in a mythological *tour de force* (Housman 1920: 317–18; Wilkinson 1955: 356–7; and Kenney 1982: 454). But my immediate priority is to examine Ovid's poetic programme in the *Ibis* and, in the light of the initial correspondences drawn thus far with the *Tristia*, to ask two questions. Is the *Ibis* really as novel a departure into an untried area of poetic experimentation as Ovid invites us to believe? And if not, could it be

---

[3] Cf. Hinds (1987*b*) 25–6 on Ovid's use of the 'hermeneutic alibi' of verbal ambivalence to evade the charge of deliberate flippancy in his treatment of Augustus in *Metamorphoses* 15.

[4] Who was Ibis? For various conjectures see Ellis (1881) xix–xxvii, La Penna (1957) xvi–xix and André (1963) xxiv–xxvi. But cf. Housman (1920) 316: Ibis 'is much too good to be true', born all too conveniently on the *dies Alliensis* (219–20) and in the African wilderness (221–2); 'nor does a man assail a real enemy, the object of his sincere and lively hatred, with an interminable and inconsistent series of execrations which can neither be read nor written seriously'. Like Wilkinson (1955: 355), I incline to Housman's view that Ibis is a fiction; but for an impartial summary of opinion on the whole controversy see Watson (1991) 130–1.

that the *Ibis* is ultimately an extension of an experiment with elegiac narrative which he has already undertaken in the *Tristia*?

Ovid hits back at his enemy with a programmatic statement of his poetic strategy in lines 45–64, and his earlier declaration that he is taking up arms in unaccustomed hands (10) is amplified in a number of ways. Ovid's military strategy begins on the wrong metrical footing:

prima quidem coepto committam proelia uersu,
     non soleant quamuis hoc pede bella geri. (45–6)

I will join the first battles in the measure I have begun, even though wars are not usually waged in this metre.

To the student of Roman elegy the soldier of love embarking on his erotic mission is a familiar figure (McKeown 1989: 258–9), but in the *Ibis* Ovid emphatically breaks generic convention by making elegy the medium for a different kind of warfare. According to the Roman generic code the obvious metre for war is of course the hexameter, and at first sight Ovid effects an extraordinary reconciliation in lines 45–6 between epic and elegy by crossing the metrical divide so clearly drawn in such *recusationes* as *Am.* 1.1 and 2.1 and Propertius 2.1, 3.1, 3.3, and 3.9. But in the light of lines 53–4 and Ovid's promise that an iambic riposte awaits his enemy if he perseveres in his attacks, the iambus is also implied in line 46 as the more usual medium for poetic battle. Whichever metre is eschewed in lines 45–6—the hexameter, the iambus, or both—the main point is that in the *Ibis* Ovid creates a correspondence between his own alleged unfamiliarity with abuse and the unfamiliar medium in which he presents that abuse.

This last point needs to be stressed if only to put into perspective the importance which has long been attached to Callimachus' *Ibis* and the extent of its influence on Ovid. The crucial text is *Ibis* 53–60:

postmodo, si perges, in te mihi liber iambus
     tincta Lycambeo sanguine tela dabit.
nunc, quo Battiades inimicum deuouet Ibin,
     hoc ego deuoueo teque tuosque modo,
utque ille, historiis inuoluam carmina caecis,

> non soleam quamuis hoc genus ipse sequi.
> illius ambages imitatus in Ibide dicar
>   oblitus moris iudiciique mei.

Afterwords, if you persist, my unrestrained iambus will hurl at you missiles tinged with Lycambean blood. Now, just as Battus' son curses his enemy Ibis, so do I curse you and yours. And like him, I will wrap my poem in impenetrable narratives, although I do not usually pursue this genre. It will be said that I imitated his riddling in the *Ibis*, forgetting my own style and taste.

A controversy of long standing concerns Ovid's choice of metre. According to one school of thought he adopts Callimachus' metre (Zipfel 1910: 9, Rostagni 1920: 8, Kolar 1933: 1244, Cahen 1929: 70), and he signals his debt with the word *modo* (56). But, counters Perrotta (1926: 147), how can Ovid be emulating Callimachus metrically in the light of his express statement in line 46 that war is not usually waged in elegiacs? How could Ovid make such a claim if Callimachus had already provided a precedent for elegiac warfare? Quite easily: Callimachus may have put elegy to the same unaccustomed use as does Ovid. At first sight, moreover, the contrast between *postmodo* (53) and *nunc* (55) might seem to endorse an accompanying metrical contrast between *iambus* (53) and *modo* (56): after threatening to launch an iambic attack in the future (*postmodo*), Ovid commits himself for the present (*nunc*) to a preliminary assault in the metre which Callimachus had deployed before him (55–6).

But standard Ovidian usage in fact tells against taking *modo* (56) in the sense of 'metre'. True, *modus* in the singular is well documented in other sources as a term denoting the rhythmical pattern, beat or measure of music and speech (*OLD* s.v. 7a), and it is so used by Ovid at *Am.* 2.17.21–2: *sed tamen apte | iungitur herous cum breuiore modo* 'and yet the heroic line is aptly joined to the shorter'. *Modus* refers here to the abbreviated metrical structure of the pentameter as opposed to the lengthier hexameter; but this use of *modus* does not justify *modo* in the sense of 'elegiac metre' at *Ibis* 56, for at *Am.* 2.17.22 *modus* is specifically applied to the pentameter alone, not to the composite elegiac formation.[5] Only in the plural does

---

[5] La Penna on *Ibis* 54 concedes this point even though on the strength of *Am.* 2.17.21–2 he writes of *modo* at *Ibis* 56 'non è impossibile intenderlo nel senso

modus find Ovidian parallels for the meaning ('elegiac metre') which is needed to make *Ibis* 55–6 an unambiguous statement of metrical affiliation with Callimachus' poem,[6] and for this reason the case for Ovid's adoption of the Callimachean metre is barely sustainable. The conclusion to be drawn is that even if Callimachus did in fact write in elegiacs, Ovid provides no clear proof to that effect. Certainly, *P. Sorbonn.* 2254 and *P. Brux.* 8934 provide evidence of an elegiac curse tradition to which Callimachus may have contributed in his *Ibis.*[7] But Euphorion's *Arai* and *Thrax* suggest that there was also a Hellenistic tradition of hexametrical cursing which was later emulated in the *Dirae;*[8] a confirmed Callimachean, Euphorion supports the possibility that Callimachus cursed Ibis in hexameters. If this is so, and if Callimachus thereby avoided the iambus like Ovid, a metrical contrast between *postmodo* (51) and *nunc* (53) need still not be ruled out: for the present Ovid writes in the Callimachean mode, if not the Callimachean metre, and the iambus remains the ultimate weapon to be wielded at a later date—just as it might have been the ultimate weapon for Callimachus.

While the debate rages about Callimachus' choice of metre and Ovid's possible subservience to his master,[9] one crucial point is beyond dispute. Whatever Callimachus' metre, in terms purely of Roman literary tradition Ovid's choice of metre in the *Ibis* breaks the generic rules.[10] He breaks his own rules, too, not only by turning

---

di "metro"'. The other example he cites, *rudem praebente modum tibicine Tusco* (*Ars* 1.111) is unhelpful because *modus* there clearly refers not to poetic metre, but to musical measure in accompaniment to Etruscan dance (see Hollis 1977: 54).

[6] See La Penna on 55–6 for examples; while he does not entirely rule out *modo* in the sense of 'metre' (cf. n. 5 above), he favours the sense of 'manner', 'mode'.

[7] Both papyri derive from the same roll. For the former see *SH* fr. 970 (Lloyd-Jones and Parsons 1983: 478–81); for the latter see Huys (1991). Barns and Lloyd-Jones (1963) suggest Phanocles as author of *P. Sorbonn.* 2254; Huys (1991) favours Hermesianax. In either case the fragments would predate Callimachus and possibly Moero as well (Watson 1991: 166), thus representing the early development of the Hellenistic (elegiac) curse tradition.

[8] So La Penna (1957) xliii. On the (doubtful) possibility that the *Arai* formed part of the *Chiliades*, see conveniently Watson (1991) 81 n. 103.

[9] For bibliography on the metrical issue see Watson (1991) 79 n. 92; for a summary of scholarly debate on the broader relationship between the two *Ibis* poems see Watson (1991) 79 n. 86.

[10] Cf. Horace, *Ars* 73–86: after generically delineating the epic hexameter (73-4), elegy (75–8), iambics (79–82), and lyric (83–5), Horace inveighs against ignorance of

to poetic invective for the first time, but by turning to Callimachus as his guide in a novel manner. Of course, Callimachus had already had a profound impact on Ovid's verse, most obviously in providing the starting point for the latter's *carmen perpetuum* in the *Metamorphoses* and for his aetiological treatment of the Roman calendar in the *Fasti*.[11] But in the *Ibis* Callimachus is announced as Ovid's guiding influence with a directness which is wholly new: never before has Ovid been so explicit in his call upon Callimachus, and never has the effect of that call been portrayed as so complete a betrayal of Ovid's poetic self (cf. *oblitus moris iudiciique mei*, 60). The *aemulatio* which Ovid announces in lines 55–6 is not just his victim's pseudonymity under the name provided by Callimachus (Herter 1937: 178), nor merely the adoption of the curse technique used by Callimachus;[12] with -*que* at the start of line 57 Ovid explains the *aemulatio* anticipated by the *quo* (*modo*) ... *hoc* ... *modo* construction in the previous couplet by stating that he, like Callimachus, will use dark obscurity to prophesy his victim's projected fate (*historiis inuoluam carmina caecis*, 57).[13] Herein lies Ovid's departure from what he portrays as his normal practice: *non soleam quamuis* (58) picks up *non soleant quamuis* in line 46 and connects Ovid's unaccustomed metre for war in the *Ibis* with his unaccustomed subject matter and style of writing.

generic divisions. Why should one be called a poet if one fails to observe generic and stylistic propriety (*descriptas ... uices ... operumque colores*, 86; for definition of these terms see Brink (1971) 171)? Why, on these Horatian criteria, should Ovid be hailed as a proficient poet when he fails to observe generic propriety in the *Ibis*? Mitigation for Ovid's seeming breach of generic protocol will be argued for below; but the Horatian passage serves to underline the generic novelty which the *Ibis* represents.

[11] On the former see Knox (1986*a*) 9 ff. and 23 nn. 1–2 and 9–10 for further bibliography on the Callimachean credentials of *Met.* 1.1–4; but cf. Kovacs (1987) for isolated opposition to the prevalent view of Ovid's Callimachean adherence. On Callimachean influence on the *Fasti* see Kenney (1982) 428–30.

[12] La Penna (1957) xxvii–xxix classifies the *Ibis* as a *deuotio*, detecting in lines 97–106 the human sacrifice standard to the ritual. But cf. Watson (1991) 208–9, arguing that since by Ovid's time the verb *deuoueo* was regularly used in the general sense of laying curses on someone (see *OLD* s.v. 3), the term cannot be restricted to the limited sense of ritualistic *deuotio*. The influence of *defixiones* or curse tablets has also been detected in the *Ibis*. See Zipfel (1910) 5–27 with La Penna (1957) xx–xxix for general discussion of the *defixio* tradition; but cf. Watson (1991) 194–216, arguing against anything more than the 'marginal influence' of *defixiones* on the Hellenistic literary curse tradition.

[13] See Watson (1991) 114–15 for a lengthier statement of this formulation with nn. 254–5 for a summary of divergent scholarship.

But does his emulation of Callimachus really mark such a complete desertion of his usual poetic practice?

Clearly, the sheer scale of Ovid's obscurantism in the *Ibis*, unparalleled elsewhere in his writings, marks a new departure. But in the context of his *oeuvre* as a whole, making new departures is hardly out of character. In the *Amores* he innovates by stretching the conventions of Roman love elegy; in the *Ars Amatoria, Medicamina Faciei* and *Remedia Amoris* he creates a fully developed genre of elegiac didacticism; in the *Heroides* he turns Propertius' experiment with epistolary elegy in 4.3 into a full-blown genre; in the *Fasti* he vies with and surpasses Propertius in making his own claim to the title of Rome's Callimachus; in the *Metamorphoses* he puts the heroic hexameter to novel use by redefining the thematic norms of the epic genre; and in the *Tristia* and *Epistulae ex Ponto* he takes elegy back to its alleged origin as a song of lament.[14] In the *Ibis* Ovid continues to experiment with generic innovation by creating a Roman mode of invective unprecedented in its complex obfuscation; and in this respect, at least, he is not quite as forgetful of his usual practice as he implies in line 60. Indeed, the very statement that he has 'forgotten' the tenets of his accustomed art is self-refuting, since it acknowledges that he is only too aware of the tenets from which he is now departing. The obvious question is why he should choose to make such a self-conscious departure. Of course, one reason is that the Hellenistic curse tradition held up obscurantism as the norm (Watson 1991: 103–13, 168–77). But every other Ovidian work shows that he was no slave to tradition: in what ways, then, does Ovid keep his distance from Callimachus' *Ibis*?

Various possibilities suggest themselves. One is that Ovid writes a curse poem which is intended to surpass the Callimachean original in scale and in the sheer ingenuity of its mythological repertoire. A key couplet in this respect is lines 449–50, where Ovid invokes Callimachus' curses:

et [eueniant uota] quibus exiguo uolucris deuota libello,
    corpora proiecta quae sua purgat aqua.

---

[14] On the disputed etymological origins of elegy as a song of lament (cf. *Am.* 3.9.3–4, *Tr.* 5.1.5–6) see conveniently Hinds (1987*a*) 103 and 160 n. 13 for further bibliography.

and [may the curses befall you] with which, in a little book, that bird is execrated which cleanses its body by throwing water on itself.

Ovid's characterization of Callimachus' *Ibis* as *exiguus libellus* (cf. 449) has been taken by some to mean that it was of meagre length (e.g. Perrotta 1926: 156; Cahen 1929: 70, 73; La Penna 1957: xli), perhaps even an epigram;[15] but the fact that both terms are key items in Roman literary vocabulary, indicating the small-scale quality of a poem rather than its length,[16] rules out any firm clue as to the size of Callimachus' poem. Even so, Ovid still magnifies his own achievement at Callimachus' expense in lines 449–50 by wishing on his enemy the curses which Callimachus had hurled in his *Ibis*. The immediate impression is that, even if we did not know it already, Ovid has a truly extraordinary breadth of mythological *doctrina*, one which far exceeds the Callimachean store—for the obvious implication of lines 449–50 is that none of Ovid's curses had already been hurled by Callimachus. This implication cannot, of course, be tested; but even if Ovid has drawn on Callimachus' *Ibis* at least in part, lines 449–50 still succeed in distancing the two poems, perhaps to grotesquely humorous effect: with Callimachean slimness of expression Ovid takes a single couplet to relaunch Callimachus' whole original broadside. But the possibility that Ovid aims in the *Ibis* to be a Pontic Callimachus of more than Callimachean stature passes completely unrecognized by Rostagni, who argues on the strength of *imitatus* (59) that Ovid's *Ibis* is a translation, and therefore declares lines 449–50 interpolated; how could Ovid invoke Callimachean curses when he is already translating them?[17] Quite easily, replies Housman (1921), if you modify the interpretation of *imitatus* and accept that there are modes of imitation other than translation.

---

[15] So Schneider (1873) 278 ff., but immediately countered by Riese (1874) 377–9.

[16] Cf. *Ibis* 51, 639, where Ovid terms his curse poem of 644 verses a mere *libellus*. For the word as a neoteric diminutive signalling the nature of a book's poetic content and not necessarily its size, see Quinn (1973) 89 on 1.1. For *exiguus* denoting generic humility as opposed to higher callings see Horace, *Ars* 77 with Brink (1971) 167 ad loc., Prop. 3.9.35–6, 4.1.59–60, Ovid, *Fasti* 2.3–4, 6.22, *Tr.* 2.329–30, 531–2, *Pont.* 3.3.33–4. On programmatic 'smallness' as basic to Hellenistic poetics see Cairns (1979a) 21 and n. 93 for additional bibliography.

[17] Rostagni (1920) 7–54, arguing further that since lines 299–300 refer to an event of the year 214 BC (the death of the Asian king Achaeus), the Greek poem which Ovid translated was the post-Callimachean work of an Alexandrian imitator.

A second technique by which Ovid could be distancing himself from Callimachus' *Ibis* is by deliberately invoking and adapting Callimachean works other than the *Ibis*. A number of the myths which Ovid adduces are traceable to the *Aetia* and *Hymns* (La Penna 1957: li–liv), and while these same myths could conceivably have been included in the Callimachean *Ibis*, a literal reading of lines 449–50 again suggests that they were not; if Ovid has steadfastly avoided repetition of the Callimachean curses, the natural implication is that material from the *Aetia* was not used in the Greek *Ibis*. True, in certain famous cases such as Saturn's mutilation of Uranus (273–4; cf. fr. 43.70–1 Pf.), Ovid may be indebted not to Callimachus exclusively but to a common source (cf. Hesiod, *Theog.* 179 ff.), and any argument for Ovid's pervasive exploitation of the Callimachean *oeuvre* has to be qualified accordingly (La Penna 1957: lvi–lxxi). But the plethora of coincidences with the *Aetia* in particular certainly suggests a roving debt to Callimachus; and Ovid's promise that his elegiac attack on his enemy is only a prelude to a full-blooded iambic assault (53–4) suggests one particular point of association with the *Aetia*—an association which, if valid, frees the Latin *Ibis* from strict subordination only to its Callimachean counterpart.

In *Am.* 3.1 Tragedy and Elegy compete for Ovid's attention, and Elegy wins the day—but with the promise that the poet will subsequently turn to the higher genre of Tragedy (69–70):

mota [Tragoedia] dedit ueniam. teneri properentur Amores,
    dum uacat: a tergo grandius urguet opus.

Tragedy was moved and granted my prayer. Let the tender Loves come quickly, while I am free: a greater work presses after me.

Ovid's threat in the *Ibis* of a future Hipponactean onslaught (53–4) modifies the generic contrast drawn in *Am.* 3.1 because elegy is now set against the iambic calling of invective, not of tragedy.[18] *Am.* 3.1,

---

[18] And iambic invective is not on the same elevated generic level as tragedy (cf. *grandius…opus*, *Am.* 3.1.70). For *grandis* marking an implicit contrast between elevated tragedy and lowly invective, cf. *Rem.* 375–8 (*grande sonant tragici*, 375) and Horace, *Ars* 79–80 (*grandes…coturni*, 80). Note also Callimachus, fr. 112.9 Pf., πεζὸν [ἔπ] ειμι νομόν, where πεζόν anticipates the *Iambi*. For this interpretation of πεζόν, supported by Horace's later use of *pedestris* of verse (*musa pedestris*, applied to his

then, is an inexact precedent for the contrast between elegiac and iambic which Ovid draws at *Ibis* 45–54; but other possibilities remain. At the end of the poem Ovid repeats his earlier warning of an iambic onslaught (643–4):

postmodo plura leges et nomen habentia uerum
    et pede quo debent acria bella geri.

You will read more later, bearing your true name and in the metre in which bitter wars ought to be waged.

It goes without saying that the effect of Ovid's iambic warning here is wittily ironic, for the reader who has just reached the end of the long catalogue of elegiac curses might well wonder how an iambic invective could be any more devastating. But where else in ancient literature does a poet close an elegiac work with the promise of a bellicose iambic sequel?

    Catullus' last poem, 116, is initially suggestive:

saepe tibi studioso animo uenante requirens
    carmina uti possem mittere Battiadae,
qui te lenirem nobis, neu conarere
    tela infesta <meum> mittere in usque caput,
hunc uideo mihi nunc frustra sumptum esse laborem,
    Gelli, nec nostras hic ualuisse preces.
contra nos tela ista tua euitamus amictu:
    at fixus nostris tu dabis supplicium.[19]

Often in the past I searched with earnest questing mind for how I could send to you the poems of the Battus' son, so that I might win you over to me and so you would not try to land deadly shafts upon my head; but now I see that I have undertaken this toil in vain, Gellius, and that in this my prayers have not availed. Those shafts of yours launched against me I parry by my garment; but you shall be pierced by mine and pay the penalty.

---

satires, *Sat.* 2.6.17; cf. *Ep.* 2.1.251, *Ars* 95), see Clayman (1988) 277–8; see also 288 n. 3 for the scholarly history of this interpretation and also for proponents of the now discredited view that at fr. 112.9 Callimachus alludes to his prose writings.

[19] In line 7 I follow most editors in reading *euitamus amictu*, thereby rejecting *euitabimus* as given in the MSS; but the latter is not out of place (cf. *dabis*, 8), though a conjecture such as Baehrens' *acta* is needed to retain it. I remain uncertain about my choice of reading, and no conclusions will be based upon it. For discussion of the difficulty see Fordyce (1961) 404–5.

With his peace offering of his own Callimachean renderings (*carmina...Battiadae*, 2) rejected by Gellius and hostilities set to continue (5–6), Catullus readies himself to fend off the shafts of his enemy's invective (7) and to retaliate with shafts of his own (8). Could Catullus' shafts be iambic? If the poem is taken to be a prelude to the elegiac shafts which Catullus directs at Gellius in poems 74, 80, and 88–91,[20] then certainly not. But if 116 is a prelude to Catullus' attacks on Gellius, why does the poem come after the attacks it introduces? The problem is not insurmountable if the position of 116 in the collection reflects its status as what Macleod (1973: 308 = 1983: 185) terms 'an inverted dedication'. Since 116 describes Catullus' futile attempt at dedicating a peace offering to Gellius, it reverses the dedicatory norms, and that reversal is reflected in its position: 'instead of opening a book, it concludes one' (Macleod 1973: 308 = 1983: 185).[21] But a further consequence if 116 is taken to be a prelude to the other Gellius poems, an elegiac piece introducing elegiac *tela*, is that Ovid's promised transition from elegy to iambics at *Ibis* 643–4 can owe nothing to Catullus. What, then, of the alternative that 116 be taken to follow the other Gellius poems chronologically (Ellis 1889: 500)? In that case it could be argued that after an initial elegiac attack in poems 74, 80, and 88–91 Catullus sues for peace and only when the attempt is thwarted does he, like Ovid later, issue the ultimate iambic threat to ward off Gellius.[22] But the simple fact is that at 116.7–8 there is no undeniable signal that Catullus is readying himself for a specifically iambic onslaught rather than a repetition of the elegiac insults he has already hurled.[23] However tempting at first glance, Catullus 116 cannot be adduced as

---

[20] Quinn (1973) 455 and Fordyce (1961) 403 are so inclined, but without insisting on the point. Cf. Macleod (1973) 308 = (1983) 185: 'it [116] has all the air of being a prelude to the other poems directed at him [Gellius]'.

[21] Cf. Schmidt (1973) 233 and Forsyth (1977) 352–3, taking *carmina...Battiadae* (116.2) to be a cross reference to 65.16 by which Catullus links the beginning and end of his elegiac book.

[22] Cf. Németh (1977) 27–30, detecting in Catullus' imagery of single combat at 116.4 and 7–8 an echo of his references to iambics at 36.5 and 40.2.

[23] But cf. Newman (1990) 67, detecting Archilochean influence in *tela* (116.7) on the grounds that tela (= βέλη) 'presupposes the derivation of *iambos* from βάλλω found, e.g., in the *Etymologicum Magnum* (p. 463–27)'. But see n. 24 below.

a clear precedent for Ovid's elegiac gesturing towards iambics in the
Ibis.[24]

A much more compelling parallel for Ovid's threatened transition
from elegiacs to iambics is provided by Callimachus' epilogue to
the *Aetia* (fr. 112.9 Pf.): αὐτὰρ ἐγὼ Μουσέων πεζὸν [ἔ]πειμι νομόν,
'but I will pass on to the prose pasture of the Muses'. Callimachus
foreshadows his *Iambi* by signalling his change to the plainer style of
the pedestrian Muse and his own resuscitation of the invective mode
of Hipponax.[25] True, Callimachus' *Iambi* do not share the ferocity
normally associated with Hipponax, but offer a change of ethos and,
in *Iambus* 1, a Hipponax whose tone is programmatically modified,
his sharpness blunted (Hutchinson 1988: 49 ff.); yet even so, the collection retains the polemical character of its genre.[26] Now it is not
impossible that Callimachus made a similar gesture towards iambic
vitriol in his (elegiac?) *Ibis*, and that Ovid's threat of iambics is modelled on that precedent. But Callimachus' movement from the *Aetia*
to the *Iambi*, from the elegiac polemic of his 'reply to the Telchines'
to polemical iambics, is one clearly re-enacted in Ovid's *Ibis* and
its promised iambic sequel. To what effect? The many mythological
parallels with the *Aetia* in Ovid's *Ibis* initially signal his exploitation

[24] Cf. Wiseman (1985) 186, citing Callimachus, fr. 112.9 as a tempting point of
comparison for 116.8, but then qualifying the parallel on the grounds that 'Catullus
has already given us iambics in the Callimachean style (especially scazons in the
manner of Hipponax) in the collection to which he is now saying farewell. They were
as finely polished as the rest of his poems, so Catullus can hardly be announcing
that genre with the breaking of "Callimachean" norms which lines 3 and 8 so conspicuously represent' (on this last point see Macleod (1973) 306–7 = (1983) 183–4).
Wiseman goes on to suggest (186 ff.) that instead of iambics Catullus threatens to
assail Gellius in iambic senarii and the genre of Laberian mime.

[25] For πεζόν denoting Callimachus' transition to the *Iambi* see n. 18 above.
On Callimachus' deliberate fusion of two distinct genres, elegiac and iambic, see
Clayman (1988) 277–86. Cf. Knox (1985) 59–65, arguing that the epilogue originally
concluded books 1–2 and was then moved to the end of 4 when the work was
expanded; by the time of that revision the promise of *Iambi* would already have been
met, rendering the epilogue in the revised version of the *Aetia* more a statement
of metrical versatility than of literary intent. If this is so, then at *Ibis* 643–4 Ovid
modifies the Callimachean nuance by making bellicose intent his priority, not metrical
versatility.

[26] Cf. Clayman (1980) 58: 'Callimachus' approach to invective is not so obviously
blunt as Hipponax's. It is nevertheless true that Callimachus' *Iambi* are full of personal
abuse directed at named or more probably pseudonamed individuals and that this
abuse sometimes has an obscene character.'

of more than one Callimachean source; and if the structural parallel with the *Aetia* and *Iambi* is accepted, the further implication is that Ovid resists complete subservience to Callimachus' *Ibis* by hinting at wider Callimachean allegiance.

Thus far the search for signs of Ovid's independence of his model has relied on assumptions about the size, mythological range and metre of Callimachus' *Ibis*, and on the presumption that Ovid's difference from his models in other works suggests the same quality of difference in his *Ibis*. But if it could be shown that Ovid's poetic programme in the *Ibis* is built on guidelines already established in the *Tristia*, we need no longer speculate on the nature of Callimachus' *Ibis* to find at least hints of Ovidian difference: even though an Ovidian work entitled *Ibis* inevitably signals *aemulatio* of Callimachus, proof of Ovid's independence of his model would lie in his loyalty to his own programmatic precedents, and not to that supplied by Callimachus. First, however, the date of the *Ibis* in relation to the *Tristia* has to be clarified in order to establish the latter's precedence.

The date of the *Ibis* is not certainly known, but it is generally agreed to have been written in about AD 11, on the grounds that Ovid, born in 43 BC (cf. *Tr.* 4.10.5–6), was not yet fifty-five when he composed it (cf. *Ibis* 1–2); on these criteria the poem could not be later than AD 12. If the poem extends the invective theme broached in *Tr.* 4.9, and if Ovid wrote *Tr.* 4.9 together with *Tr.* 4.7 two years into his exile (cf. *Tr.* 4.7.1–2), then AD 10 or 11 is a likely date (La Penna 1957: vii–xii; André 1963: vi–viii). Ovid's claim at *Pont.* 4.14.44 that he has as yet attacked no one in his exilic poetry need not affect this dating if his point there is that he has not attacked any of the Tomitans in his verse; his Roman addressees are another matter, although his claim to have harmed no one still stands if, as Housman argued (1920: 316), 'Ibis' never existed. That the *Ibis* is later than *Tristia* 2 is an obvious inference from Ovid's claim that he has hitherto injured only himself through his work (*Tr.* 2.563–72); were the *Ibis* earlier than *Tristia* 2, his claim would be patently false and hardly likely to impress Augustus. For this reason it would seem that Ovid had already made at least substantial progress with the *Tristia* before beginning the *Ibis*, and another factor supports this hypothesis: the poem brings to a climax the increasingly hostile tone of *Tr.* 1.8, 3.11,

4.9, and 5.8, surely suggesting that it was written as a sequel to those elegies.[27]

As for a *terminus ante quem* on the other hand, the *Ibis* could not have been written later than AD 14 on the grounds that Augustus was still alive when it was composed (cf. 23–8). But Ovid did not abandon invective after the *Ibis*. *Pont.* 4.3 revives the elegiac invective mode in a book thought to have been published posthumously. Since Tiberius is hailed as emperor in a poem written before *Epistulae ex Ponto* 4 (cf. *Pont.* 2.8.37–8), *Pont.* 4.3 has to be a post-Augustan poem and later than the *Ibis*, but it is no anticlimax; like *Pont.* 3.6, it has the novelty of being exceptional amongst the *Epistulae ex Ponto* in that its addressee is anonymous.

On the hypothesis that Ovid had completed most, if not all, of the *Tristia* by the time he composed the *Ibis*, I want now to identify one key aspect of his poetic programme in the *Tristia*, and so to establish an exilic precedent for a parallel programme in the *Ibis*. At *Tr.* 3.1.9–10 Ovid's *liber*, newly arrived at Rome, invites its reader to inspect its contents:

> inspice quid portem: nihil hic nisi triste uidebis,
>   carmine temporibus conueniente suis.

Examine what I bring: you will see nothing here except sadness, as the poem suit its state.

The correspondence drawn here between mood and subject matter is repeated at *Tr.* 5.1.5–6:

> flebilis ut noster status est, ita flebile carmen,
>   materiae scripto conueniente suae.

My state is mournful, mournful too my poem, as the writing suits its subject.

True to Horace's dictum in the *Ars Poetica* (89–118) that the poet, like the actor, must find the appropriate voice for his realistic projection

---

[27] Cf. André (1963) vi, identifying Ibis with the unnamed enemy (*nescioquis*) depicted at *Tr.* 1.6.13–14 and stating without argument that the *Ibis* predates *Tr.* 1.6. But even if André were right, his supposition that *Tr.* 1.6 is not necessarily an early poem (*'Trist.*, 1.6 ... passe, peut-être à tort, pour un des premiers poèmes') still allows the *Ibis* to follow *Tr.* 1.8, 3.1, 4.9, and 5.8 in chronological and thematic order.

of a given mood,[28] Ovid returns to this compatibility in *Pont.* 3.9 (35–6):

laeta fere laetus cecini, cano tristia tristis:
   conueniens operi tempus utrumque suo est.

For the most part when I was happy I sang of happy themes; now that I am sad, I sing sad ones: each time suits its own work.

When Ovid claims in defence of the *Ars* at *Tr.* 2.353–8 that there is a clear dividing line between his private life and public *persona*, between his own morality and the dubious morality of the *Ars*, between his private and poetic voices, the disconcerting implication is that the same could apply to his outpourings of perhaps less than totally authentic grief in the *Tristia*.[29] But if he is given the benefit of the doubt, Ovid achieves what Brink interprets as the Horatian ideal at *Ars* 89 ff.: his poetic voice truly reflects his woes,[30] and *conueniens*, the word which occurs in all three of the above couplets, summarizes the poetic programme which 'authenticates' those woes. His chosen mode of expression is generically appropriate because of elegy's alleged origin as a song of lament, the shabby appearance of his poetic book in *Tr.* 1.1 reflects his sad plight (cf. *infelix habitum temporis huius habe*, 1.1.4), the alleged defects of his exilic verse are made the symbol of poetic decline to match his personal decline amid the rigours of life in Tomis (cf. Williams 1992: 178–89). All these factors contribute to Ovid's attempt in the exile poetry at what Horace portrays in the *Ars Poetica* as 'wholeness', the overall consistency of a work of art which lacks contradictory or incompatible elements (Brink 1971: 117 and 484).

---

   [28] Cf. Brink (1971) 174: 'The key term throughout is appropriateness, τὸ πρέπον or the like.'

   [29] For the distinction between Ovid's private character and public *persona* cf. *Tr.* 1.9.59–60 and *Pont.* 2.7.47–50. The claim is frequently made from Catullus onwards: cf. Cat. 16.5–6, Apul. *Apol.* 11, Mart. 1.4.8, 11.15.13, Pliny, *Ep.* 4.14.4–5. Could Ovid be resorting to a Catullan trick to exculpate himself in *Tristia* 2?

   [30] Brink (1971) 482: 'H.'s psychology demands this close link between utterance and the emotion felt. Unless the emotion is genuine, diction will not sound true (108–10).' Cf. p. 188: 'His [H.'s] own concern is to link appropriateness of emotional styles with real emotion—a doctrine of poetic sincerity, a rarish thing in ancient literary criticism.' But on the problem of gauging artistic/rhetorical sincerity and on the difference between genuine emotion and 'genuinely' simulated emotion, see Rudd (1976) 145–81, esp. 171 ff.

This preoccupation with generic appropriateness is evident in Ovid's earliest writings. In *Am.* 1.1 he uses the word *conueniens* to describe his matching of epic theme and metre before Cupid diverts him to love elegy (1–2):

arma graui numero uiolentaque bella parabam
    edere, materia conueniente modis.

Arms and the violent deeds of war I was preparing to rehearse in weighty metre, with matter suited to the measure.

Cupid intervenes, snatches a metrical foot to create the pentameter, and brings about a generic crisis for the would-be epic poet (19–20):

nec mihi materia est numeris leuioribus apta,
    aut puer aut longas compta puella comas.

And yet I have no matter suited to lighter numbers, neither a boy nor a girl with long and lovely hair.

Ovid's epic subject matter has lost its natural mode of expression, and he has to resign himself to a change of theme to match the metrical change enforced by Cupid; hence he bids farewell to war (27–8) and gives way to love in his new elegiac mode. His erotic calling is generically humble, a lowly task which is contrasted at *Fasti* 2.3–4 with his more elevated attempt at rendering the Roman calendar in elegiacs:

nunc primum uelis, elegi, maioribus itis:
    exiguum, memini, nuper eratis, opus.

Now for the first time, my elegiacs, you sail with ampler canvas: as I remember, just recently you were a slender work.

This awareness of placing a greater strain than ever before on the lowly elegiacs arises from his change of subject matter from eroticism to the emperor Augustus (*Fasti* 2.15–16):

at tua prosequimur studioso pectore, Caesar,
    nomina, per titulos ingredimurque tuos.

But with an eager heart I describe your titles, Caesar, and begin with your claims to glory.

Ovid's penchant for generic experimentation reveals itself here in his method for circumventing a dilemma familiar in the Augustan elegists: if epic is the natural mode for celebrating an emperor of great stature, how is the lowly elegist to do him justice? One answer, provided by Propertius in 2.1, is to concede that the emperor is worthy of epic treatment but to declare oneself unable to rise to the higher genre. In *Fasti* 2, however, Ovid's tactic is to stretch generic protocol by undertaking a task which is notionally beyond elegy while acknowledging the licence he is taking. Hence at *Fasti* 2.125–6 Ovid is aware of the strain he is placing on his verse medium when he celebrates the anniversary of Augustus' accession to the title of *pater patriae* in 2 BC:

> quid uolui demens elegis imponere tantum
>   ponderis? heroi res erat ista pedis.

> Why in my madness did I want to impose so much weight on elegiacs? That was a subject for the heroic metre.

On this occasion Ovid overcomes the difficulty of paying Augustus epic respect in elegiacs by setting up a line-by-line syncrisis with Romulus and by favouring Augustus on every count (129–44).[31] And further evidence in the *Fasti* of Ovid's awareness of generic stratification comes in his treatment of Mars at the start of book 3. Introduced as *bellice* (1), the god is quickly disarmed (cf. *inermis*, 8) in programmatic accommodation to his new elegiac context (Hinds 1992: 88–90).

Thus Ovid is (or claims to be) acutely conscious of the limitations of the elegiac genre and the need for compatibility between form and subject matter. The same awareness might be expected in the *Ibis*; and so it proves. Not only does Ovid reflect his inexperience in invective by choosing a metre unaccustomed to the task; he also develops a key aspect of his exilic poetics by conforming to the principle stated at *Tr.* 5.1.6: *materiae scripto conueniente suae* 'as the writing suits its subject'. Ovid establishes this correspondence between his new subject matter and mode of expression in the *Ibis* by forging a parallel between the

---

[31] But for discordant hints in Ovid's seemingly effusive praise of Augustus here see Harries (1989) 166–7.

darkness in which he will shroud his curses and the dark fate which awaits his enemy (63–4):

utque mei uersus aliquantum noctis habebunt,
  sic uitae series tota sit atra tuae.

and just as my lines have something of the dark, so may your life's series be entirely black.

In the *Tristia* the sad complexion of Ovid's verse reflects his own sadness. In the *Ibis* Ovid momentarily throws off his mantle of grief and turns his self-destructive *ars* into a destructive one. Now the dark complexion of his verse—the obscurantism announced in *aliquantum noctis* (63)—is made to reflect his enemy's dark fate (cf. *atra*, 64) in a programmatic correspondence between his chosen theme and his mode of poetic expression. By this correspondence between Ibis' black destiny and the 'black' medium which describes it, Ovid returns to familiar ground, despite his claim that invective is alien to him. That same system of correspondence is basic to the *Tristia* and is portrayed as a central canon of literary theory in Horace's *Ars Poetica*: far from forgetting his established poetic practices and literary judgement in the *Ibis* (cf. 59–60), he remains committed to the rules of Roman generic protocol rather than flouting them.

By thus conforming to the *Tristia* Ovid proves not to be wholly subservient to Callimachus; his own brand of Callimachean imitation is tailored to the demands of his own poetic programme. That programme is announced in lines 63–4 and fully developed when Ovid embarks on the exempla of lines 251 ff. and fulfils his promise of Ibis' black fate in the sinister darkness of his *historiae caecae* (cf. 57); at an early stage in the catalogue (259–72) Ovid wishes on his enemy the blindness which afflicted such figures as Tiresias, Phineus, and Polyphemus, thereby adducing mythological *exempla* which literally bring about the *historiae caecae* promised earlier. But the black colour scheme of the *Ibis* is not restricted to lines 57–64, where the initial point of contact is made between the poem's darkness and Ibis' dark fate, and the great catalogue where Ovid's obscurantism enacts that fate. Occasional references to blackness in the intervening section, lines 65–250, where Ovid lays his curse in a massive extension of traditional formulae,[32] sustain the poem's colour scheme and coherence as a work which relies for its Horatian 'wholeness' on complementary shades of darkness.

Ovid's invocation of traditional magical practices contributes to this programmatic darkness. When, for example, he appeals to night to heed his imprecations (*nox... tenebrarum specie reuerenda tuarum* 'night...awful in the beauty of your shadows', 75), Canidia (cf. Horace, *Epod.* 5.51) and Medea (cf. *Met.* 7.192) are his magical informants; Ovid subsumes their dark influence. More unusual is the way in which Ovid casts a literally and figuratively dark shadow over every aspect of Ibis' life. The day of his birth was dark with massed clouds (*lux... natalis... inductis nubibus atra fuit*, 217–18); the nocturnal screech owl lent its pernicious influence to the scene (*sedit in aduerso nocturnus culmine bubo*, 223);[33] wrapped in swaddling clothes tinged with the dark hue of *ferrugo* (233), the ill-omened child bore the colour which both Virgil and Ovid associate with infernal gloom;[34] the Eumenides, located in Tartarus at *Ibis* 79–80, surface in line 225 to bathe the child in Stygian waters (226). His ominous origins are complemented by the dark fate which Clotho spins for him (cf. *stamina pulla*, 244), and the eventual fulfilment of that fate is prefaced by Ovid inviting the initiate audience to don the dark clothes of mourning appropriate to the sacrificial occasion (cf. *nigrae uestes*, 102).[35] Ibis' crime is to have disputed Ovid's claim to moral *candor* (cf. 7–8), and the poet's response is to curse him in a medium whose pervasive blackness reflects the lack of *candor* or goodwill in Ibis himself.[36]

---

[32] Zipfel (1910) 5–27 argues that *defixiones* formed Ovid's main source in lines 67–250; but cf. n. 12 *supra* and see *contra* Watson (1991) 200–8, where each of Zipfel's arguments is set out and countered.

[33] On the owl as a bird of ill omen in Latin literature see La Penna (1957) ad loc.

[34] Cf. *Met.* 5.404 (*ferrugo* applied to the reins of Pluto's chariot) and *Aen.* 6.303 (*ferrugineus* used of Charon's boat). For further examples see La Penna (1957) on 233, adding *Culex* 273.

[35] For black as a colour of mourning cf. Juv. 10.245, Stat. *Silv.* 2.1.19 and 5.1.19, and see Toynbee (1971) 46.

[36] Cf. also *candor* in the literary sense of stylistic lucidity (see *OLD* s.v. 5); so too *candidus* (see *OLD* s.v. 9, with further examples cited by Peterson (1891) 68). Ovid's diction in the *Ibis* lacks Alexandrian σκοτεινότης (on his 'insipid and colourless diction' see Watson 1991: 174–5), but his affected obscurantism nevertheless deprives the poem of stylistic *candor*. Could a fundamental irony of the *Ibis* be that Ovid defends his claim to moral *candor* (cf. 8) in a medium which incongruously lacks stylistic *candor*?

Or is it possible to define Ibis' character more stringently on the strength of the dark language which is applied to his birth and early development? A clue is offered by Ovid's portrayal of Ibis as dog-like in his vicious verbal assaults: *latrat... in toto uerba canina foro* 'he barks like a dog in the whole forum' (232). *Latrat* not only suggests that Ibis' crude outbursts are to be contrasted with the controlled *uox* of the refined Callimachean poet he attacks;[37] since to be termed dog-like is a standard item of abuse from Homer onwards,[38] Ovid's depiction of Ibis as an infant suckled on dog's milk (229) and as an orator of canine rabidness (cf. *rabiem*, 231) echoes a time-honoured insult.[39] But Ovid's canine slur also carries the implicit charge of *inuidia*. Beyond its role as a Cynic emblem (Dickie 1981: 207 n. 64; Lilja 1976: 105, 115–16), the growling, barking, biting dog regularly occurs as an emblemic symbol of wilful spite in ancient literature, though two examples of the phenomenon are particularly relevant for present purposes. The first is Horace's portrayal of his addressee in *Epode* 6 as a malicious dog (*canis*, 1). Horace threatens to bite back (cf. 3–4) with the ferocity of Archilochus and Hipponax (cf. 13–14) should he himself come under attack.[40] The charge of *inuidia* is explicitly made only in the penultimate verse (15): the tooth (*atro dente*) is standardly portrayed as the cutting edge of *inuidia*.[41] But the charge is implicitly made at the start of the poem, for by attacking the undeserving (cf. *immerentis hospites*, 1) and avoiding more formidable opposition in a cowardly fashion (cf. *lupos*, 2), the *canis* (1) reveals telltale signs

[37] For examples of *latro* applied to a crude oratorical manner see *OLD* s.v. 5b. For *caninus* applied to rabid oratory see the examples cited by La Penna (1957) on 232.

[38] For Homeric and later examples of κύων as an insult see *LSJ* s.v. II with Lilja (1976) 21–5 and index s.v. '"Dog" as term of abuse'. For *canis* as an insult in Roman comedy see Lilja (1965*b*) 33; see elsewhere Horace, *Epod.* 6.1, Petr. 74.9 with *OLD* s.v. *canis* 2a and b.

[39] The milk of wild animals (cf. 229) conventionally nurtures infants who will develop savage characters. Virgil's Camilla is a conspicuous example (*Aen.* 11.571); cf. Theocr. *Id.* 3.15-16, *Aen.* 4.367, Ovid, *Tr.* 1.8.43–4, 3.11.3 etc.

[40] Cf. Dickie (1981) 195–203, arguing that in *Epode* 6 Horace's representation of himself as the noble dog (cf. 5–6) confronting a malicious adversary (*canis*, 1) amounts to a programmatic denial that he, a new Archilocus or Hipponax (cf. 13–14), is an iambographer driven by wanton malice. He attacks only deserving targets.

[41] Cf. Cicero, *Balb.* 57, Horace, *Carm.* 4.3.16, Ovid, *Tr.* 4.10.123–4, *Pont.* 3.4.74, Seneca, *Phaed.* 492–3 etc.

of the *inuidus*.[42] By railing against the exiled poet who cannot defend himself at Rome, Ibis makes a similarly cowardly assault on Ovid; and in the light of Horace's depiction of the dog as a symbol of *inuidia* in *Epode* 6, Ovid's canine language at *Ibis* 232 implies a parallel charge of *inuidia*. My second example, drawn from Silius Italicus, supports this implication by connecting *inuidia* with the verb *allatrare* (8.290–1):

> nigro allatrauerat ore
> uictorem inuidia et uentis iactarat iniquis.[43]

envy had barked at the conqueror with her black mouth and had tossed him with unjust gales.

With *allatrauerat* Silius is surely alluding to the canine tradition of *inuidia* which Horace draws on in *Epode* 6; and the combined evidence of Silius and Horace underpins the connotation of *inuidia* at *Ibis* 232.

The conventional depiction of *inuidia* as dark of mouth in both Silius (*nigro ... ore*, 8.290) and Horace (*atro dente*, *Epod.* 6.15) allows a further point of comparison to be drawn between Invidia and Ibis. Ovid's depiction of the house of Invidia at *Met.* 2.760 ff. is suitably coloured in the language of darkness: set in the depths of a sunless valley (761–2) and ever shrouded in darkness (764), her dwelling is itself soiled with the black venom (*nigro ... tabo*, 760) which poisons her character.[44] The darkness which surrounds Ibis' birth and upbringing (*Ibis* 217 ff.) is not in itself enough to justify comparison with Invidia; but when the Furies are depicted as anointing Ibis' chest with poison (*pectora ... unxerunt Erebeae felle colubrae*, 229) and wrapping him in swaddling clothes tinged with the dark hue of *ferrugo* (233), Ovid's choice of language does indeed forge the comparison. Invidia's breast, like Ibis', is poisoned with venom (cf. *pectora felle uirent*, *Met.* 2.777), and her hand, like Ibis' swaddling clothes, is tinged with *ferrugo*

---

[42] For *inuidia* as unjust in attacking the undeserving see the examples cited by Dickie (1981) 204 n. 13; for cowardly *inuidia* see Dickie (1981) 202 with 204 n. 78.

[43] Cited by Dickie (1981) 201 in connection with canine *inuidia* in *Epode* 6.

[44] Note also *liuent rubigine dentes* (776), where the teeth of Invidia are suitably stained with the tartar of spite—an Ovidian variation on her *ater dens*. Martial 12 pr. 14 and Statius, *Silv.* 1.3.103 emulate Ovid in associating *liuor* with *rubigo*.

(cf. *manu ferrugine tincta*, *Met.* 2.798).[45] Through these associations Ibis is unmistakably infected with *inuidia*, and by disputing Ovid's claim to *candor* (cf. 7–8) Ibis reveals that aspect of his character: he attacks an innocent with the malicious intent of the true *inuidus*.

Ovid turns to the attack in the *Ibis* not with the rabid kind of verbal assault which his enemy launches (cf. 232), but with a measured assault which relates Ibis' dark character, his dark fate and the dark medium in which that fate is described to a coherent, all-embracing colour scheme. The insinuation of *inuidia* in the canine slur of line 232 blackens Ibis' character yet further by connecting him with the blackness traditionally associated with *inuidia*. If the rebuttal of *inuidia* is a conventional way for a poet to vindicate his own art (Nisbet and Hubbard 1978: 339–40), then Ovid's response to Ibis' own brand of *inuidia* vindicates not only his good character (cf. 7–8) but his art as well: Ovid's decision to embark on Callimachean obscurantism against his better judgement (cf. 59–60) is vindicated by the harmonious balance which he thereby effects between his subject matter and mode of narrative, between Ibis' dark destiny and its obscurantist expression. The same interaction between Ovid's subject matter and mode of expression was seen to be a central feature of the *Tristia*. The *Ibis* thus proves to be a development of Ovid's exilic poetics, even though he claims novelty for his enterprise (cf. 46, 58) against his usual practice (60). A key word in qualifying the extent of Ovid's departure from his own norms in the *Ibis* is *dicar* (59); the reader is made judge of the difference between Ovid's usual 'self' as revealed in his earlier works and the 'self' manifested in the *Ibis*. My contention is that the more discerning reader will not interpret Ovid's Callimachean obscurantism as a raw first attempt at poetic invective or as a complete departure from his own norms, but as a modification of norms applied in the *Tristia*. In short, the *Ibis* marks an Ovidian experiment with his own exilic poetics, and to ignore that poetics in assessing the place of the *Ibis* in the Ovidian *oeuvre* is to despatch the poem to its own form of exile.

---

[45] *ferrugo* itself carries the figurative connotation of envy; cf. *Laus Pis.* 107 (*animus… mala ferrugine purus*), Aus. 417.62.

20

Si licet et fas est: Ovid's *Fasti* and the Problem of Free Speech under the Principate

Denis Feeney

Silence, exile, cunning. (James Joyce, *Portrait of the Artist as a Young Man*)

The working title for the volume in which this paper originally appeared was, for a long time, *Poetry For and Against Augustus*. One reason why the title was eventually rejected was that this satisfyingly solid antithesis becomes less satisfying and less solid the more closely one examines it. With one marvellously acute question, C. R. Phillips (1983: 782) opens up many of the cracks in the edifice: 'Literary critics have usually not attended closely to the protean character of the principate—about what, precisely, were the authors ambivalent?'[1]

What Augustus 'was' cannot be regarded as a given in any context—not even at any one time, let alone over the fifty-six-and-a-half years in which Caesar's heir occupied centre stage in Roman life. The chronological transformations of Augustan ideology have recently received considerable attention. Hardie (1986: 136), for example, has described the difference between the classicizing 'calm simplicity of works like the Ara Pacis', and the 'violent subject-matter' of the much earlier reliefs on the doors of Apollo Palatinus. This whole subject has now been transformed by Zanker's

---

[1] On this matter, see also Kloft (1984); (1987: 77), criticizing, from the perspective of discourse theory, constructions of 'a monolithic Augustan ideology'.

study, in which the dramatic shifts in Augustan self-representation have been superbly analysed: in that work one may trace the changes from the exuberant, outrageously extravagant gestures of the triumviral period (1988: 33–77) to the comparatively restrained devices necessary for the 'first citizen' of the post-Actium period (79–100).

If Augustan ideological programmes in art and architecture were constantly evolving over time, we must also acknowledge that, at any given moment in his career, Augustus was a force which could not be pinned down by description. First of all, at a basic level of consistency, we observe that the régime was multifaceted in many ideological matters. For the *Fasti*, which has a primarily elegiac preoccupation with peace, and peaceful celebration, the most important example of this phenomenon is Augustus' simultaneous projection of both a martial and a pacific image.[2] There are many pressures on Ovid's peaceful project from Augustus' own constructions, and from Augustus' own record, to which the calendar may open itself at any point. A striking example of another poet's response to the multifaceted nature of Augustan ideology is to be found in Virgil's response to Augustus' Palatine complex in *Aeneid* 8, within the mythological framework of the Golden Age. Here one encounters a sustained engagement with the irreconcilable messages sent out by the coexistence of the literal goldenness of the temple of Apollo Palatinus, and the metaphorical goldenness of the conspicuously self-effacing dwelling of the *princeps*, inheritor of the moral values of poverty and self-denial embodied by Evander (Gransden 1976: 25–32, esp. 32, and notes on 99–100, 347–8). Magnificent splendour and praiseworthy *paupertas* ('poverty') are *both* Augustan; one may not slide out of the resulting quandary by saying that Augustus was promoting public splendour and private *paupertas*, since public/private was itself a dichotomy which the principate was collapsing, more dramatically in the Palatine complex than anywhere else.[3]

---

[2] See here, above all, Zanker's (1988: 194–201) fascinating exposition of the extreme complexity of the Mars Ultor programme. Mars himself becomes an amalgam of 'two different images - the fatherly protector and the mighty conqueror' (201). Hinds (1992) is an important discussion of these issues.

[3] On this process, see Millar (1977) 16, 189–201; Latte (1960) 305–6. On the physical linking of Augustus' residence with the temple of Apollo, see Zanker (1988) 51.

Besides such plain cases of internal inconsistency, it is necessary to take account of the larger problems involved in the impossible task which scholars often set themselves, of fixing what Augustus stood for at any given moment. Ovid's *Fasti* in particular, as we shall see, is acutely aware of the fact that what Augustus represented was a dynamic, a process which could not, in the last resort, be pinned down, as it made its way into every aspect of Roman life. However much the *princeps* protested his adherence to tradition, however much he attempted to present himself as a constant, bound into enduring Roman values, it was (and is) always possible to concentrate on the ways in which he was an anomaly, a novelty, a challenge to Roman powers of definition, occupying novel, uncategorizable conceptual areas. Two recent articles by Wallace-Hadrill chart some of these grey areas of nuance and imprecision. His study of Augustus' coinage in the 20s and 10s BCE (1986) reveals a marked degree of ambivalence between monarchical and Republican emblems of authority: the minters, the Senate, and the *princeps* himself were all feeling their way. Again, his study of the emperor's *ciuilitas* (1982) shows how impossible it was to fix the *princeps* definitively as either king or fellow citizen. Until at least the time of Trajan he was somewhere in between, and the indeterminacy of that 'somewhere' was a vital element of the ideology, for all concerned: pinning down such indeterminate points is something which modern scholars very much want to do, but if the Romans had done so, it would have wrecked the system, by forcing different groups with different interests to be explicit about something which most people found it convenient to leave outside the realm of public definition. Similar conclusions emerge from Price's invaluable investigations of ruler cult (1984: 220, 233): 'In Greece, as also in Rome, where no clear relationship was established between the categories of *deus* and *divus,* the institution of the imperial cult produced a system whose relationship to both gods and men was ambiguous'; 'The emperor stood at the focal point between human and divine.' The second of these sentences is quoted by Liebeschuetz in his review of Price's book (1985: 264), with the revealing comment: 'The difference between author and reviewer has shrunk to a disagreement over the location of this crucial "focal point".' That inability to agree on the focal point is the point.

However much modern observers need to refine definitions of 'Augustanism' for the purposes of analysis and pedagogy, we must bear in mind that 'Augustanism' was not a dogma conceived by a small band and handed down to a receptive, passive audience. Augustus and his apparatus represented a disorientating irruption into Roman value systems, yet he and his apparatus were themselves conditioned by responses, even initiatives, from 'below': the ideologies by which Romans constructed their world were a product of contestation and dialogue (Kennedy 1987: 72–7, esp. 77). One of the principal areas of contestation was an area in which much of Ovid's work located itself, the sphere of morals, marriage, and adultery. Augustus' persistent attempts to intervene in these matters encountered tenacious, widespread, and even successful resistance (Suet. *Aug.* 34; see Williams 1962; Brunt 1971: 558–66; Wiedemann 1975). From 18 BCE, when he passed his *Leges Iuliae*, to 9 CE, when demonstrations by the *equites* forced him to modify his earlier legislation with the diluted *Lex Papia Poppaea,* the *princeps* found himself entangled in a complicated tussle with important sections of opinion.[4] Paradoxically enough, one of the main grounds for the tussle was the fact that Augustus' very attempt to promote traditional Roman values clashed head-on with traditional Roman values, by obtruding the government into the *paterfamilias'* area of responsibility, and turning matters traditionally considered private into the subject of public purview.[5] Ovid's amatory poetry is part of a constellation of views which are not meshing with Augustus', and which are shaping what Augustus 'is' by means of that failure to mesh. We must resist the temptation to construct one set in which to place all those who are not at one with the *princeps*; the solid *equites* who demonstrated in 9 CE against Augustus' attempts to regulate their bedrooms would, no doubt, many of them, have regarded Ovid's poetry as so much piffle—if they had ever heard any of it.

If, therefore, we are very careful, as careful as Rudd in his essay on 'Ovid and the Augustan Myth' (1976), it is possible to isolate some part of what it might have been about the *Ars Amatoria,* for example,

---

[4] The supposed legislation of 28 BCE, an edifice erected on the basis of Prop. 2.7, has been demolished by Badian (1985).

[5] Tac. *Ann.* 3.24.2, adduced by Syme (1978) 200; cf. Brunt (1971) 559–60; Williams (1978) 59.

which enraged and provoked the *princeps* by its incongruence with
his own public ideals.[6] Yet we run the risk of allowing hindsight to
dominate our readings, as we look always to the catastrophe of 8
to provide a setting for our interpretations.[7] One of Ovid's cardinal
difficulties with Augustan ideology, in fact, and his greatest error, was
to overvalue one element of the dominant ideology, and not allow for
its changing in time: namely, its vaunted tolerance of free expression,
even of criticism. As Syme has clearly shown, the last years of the reign
saw a decisive shift towards intolerance, a shift which acted retrospectively against the *Ars Amatoria* and its poet (1978: 204–14; cf. Syme
1939: 486–7; 1986: 410–12; Wiedemann 1975: 267–8). This question
of the freedom to speak will be the main theme of the present paper,
so I want to delay documenting this element of Augustan ideology for
the moment, and note only that the *Ars* was tolerated on first publication, and even on second publication, if the theories of a second
edition are correct (Syme 1978: 13–20). What sort of (re-)reading
would Augustus have given the *Ars* without the focus provided by the
smarting humiliation of his daughter's catastrophe? We must allow
for shifts in the reading habits of Augustus himself (Rudd 1976: 12–
13)—or rather, in his *listening* habits, if we pay heed to Ovid, who
says that Augustus had never read the *Ars* (*Tr.* 2.237–40). It looks as
if a courtier culled through and read out choice excerpts which he
thought would upset the *princeps* (*Tr.* 2.77–80)—doing just what we
modern readers do when we set ourselves the task of investigating
Ovid's offence.

   Wallace-Hadrill concludes his paper on the *Fasti* by saying that the
reaction of modern readers to the poem's incorporation of Augustus
'will depend on our own values and estimation of Augustus' (1987:
229). The same is true, of course, of Ovid's original audience. Or
rather, we should say, of Ovid's original *audiences,* for there was a
multitude of them, Roman, Italian, international; throughout Ovid's

---

   [6] Following Rudd, I stress *public* ideals: 'there was...a tension, and in certain
matters a contradiction, between the private and public areas of Augustus' personality'
(8). It *is* necessary to be very careful. We are told by S. Lundström (1980: 25–7), for
example, that Augustus would have been angered to see his favourite god, Apollo,
slaughtering the Niobids in the *Metamorphoses.* Yet the slaughter of the Niobids
adorned the doors of Augustus' own temple of Apollo Palatinus: Prop. 2.31.14.
   [7] My phrasing is by no means intended to suggest that Rudd himself allows hindsight to dominate his readings: see his valuable comments on chronology, 12–13.

life, despite all Augustus' attempts to impose himself, society was more multivocal than we care normally to acknowledge.[8] Ovid's problems came when the special circumstances of the disaster of the year 8 meant that there was only one audience that mattered— Augustus—and when that one audience took to reading Ovid with the inquisitorial eye of a Rudd. The discrepancies between Augustus and Ovid need not have mattered, in other words; if either of them had died before the year 8, our accounts of Augustan tolerance would read very differently.

With such prolegomena on the problems of Augustan ideology behind us, we may turn to the *Fasti* itself, a poem which is more intimately involved with these problems than any other of Ovid's works. Even this introductory statement would be resisted by many, however; for Ovid's poetry, more than that of any other Augustan poet, is dogged by another antithesis, closely linked to that of 'Augustan/anti-Augustan': the antithesis between 'literature' and 'politics'.[9] Classicists have long been accustomed to allocating works and individuals to either one of these tidy compartments, mainly on the basis of a very rigid and restrictive definition of what 'political' is, together with a *topos*-orientated approach to 'literature'. The combination of these attitudes makes it all too tempting to see Roman literature as inward-turning, referring only to itself, as some kind of internally consistent, hermetically sealed system—or else Roman literature may be seen as referring to Greek literature, by a process which likewise becomes a self-sufficient explanation.

Whatever one decides about the larger issues, in the particular case of a poem about the Roman *fasti* the polarization of 'literary' and 'political' collapses immediately one considers the subject matter of the poem. Although the Roman calendar is described as 'safe subject matter', by Williams (1978: 95),[10] Beard (1987) has recently

---

[8] Hinds (1987*b*) 26: 'We should not fall into the trap of regarding the "Augustan reading public" as a monolith.'

[9] The polarization of 'literature' and 'politics' received its first extended treatment in Galinsky (1975) 210–61; cf. Williams (1978) 93–6. After Williams, the framework has been applied to the *Fasti* systematically by McKeown (1984). For criticisms of this framework, see, in brief, Wallace-Hadrill 1987: 221–3.

[10] Williams is led to this formulation by seeing 'religion' as the main subject matter of the poem; he is right, of course, but religion and politics are inextricable in Rome, at any period, and especially under Augustus.

demonstrated that the developed *fasti* were one of the main Roman
mechanisms for constructing their sense of identity, becoming a way
of reflecting, through the festivals and anniversaries, on what being
Roman meant. And if that were not 'political' enough, we must take
stock of the fact that, as Beard (1987: 7) puts it, the calendar 'did
not present a fixed, unchanging view of Romanness . . . it incorporated
new, changing, divergent images of what Rome was.' In the lifetime
of Ovid and his contemporaries, the calendar had undergone its
greatest transformation of all. The Roman *fasti* had become the Julian
calendar, and Augustus was imposing himself and his family on the
fasti as systematically as on every other area of Roman experience:
'The insertion of Augustus into all this', observes Wallace-Hadrill
(1987: 226),'. . . inserts Augustus into the very heart of this way of
representing what it meant to be Roman—under the new regime.'
The surviving *fasti*, as Wallace-Hadrill so clearly shows, bear eloquent testimony to the procedure: every few days, another imperial
anniversary, another commemoration of the *princeps* and his family,
a positive invasion, a planned and systematic act of intrusion which
has the cumulative effect of recasting what it means to be Roman.

Ovid captures perfectly the novelty and force of this invasion. The
subject matter of the poem, he explains to Germanicus, consists of
holy matters dug out of old annals (1.7)—*and* festival days of the
ruling house (*inuenies illic et festa domestica uobis*, 'you will find
there also the household festivals of your family', 8). In the address
to Augustus at the beginning of book 2, we learn that the Roman *fasti*
are now *nomina et tituli Caesaris* ('the names and titles of Caesar',
2.15–16). The prayer to Janus at the beginning of the work lays out the
new hierarchy: *dexter ades ducibus,* Ovid asks the god first ('attend the
chiefs with favour'), and only then comes the demoted SPQR: *dexter
ades patribusque tuis populoque Quirini* ('attend the senators with
favour too, and the people of Quirinus', 1.67–9). The very calendrical
time which is the backbone of the year has been appropriated by the
Caesars, and made theirs: time was out of order until Caesar took care
of it, along with so many other things (*errabant etiam nunc tempora,
donec | Caesaris in multis haec quoque cura fuit*, 3.155–6).[11]

---

[11] Cf. Wallace-Hadrill 1987: 224: 'Correlation of solar and civil years was only
made possible by Caesar's transformation of the Roman civil year.'

Ovid's poem, then, is intimately bound up with powerful ways of reflecting on the identity of Romanness, and it is inscribed into a system for doing that reflecting which was itself undergoing drastic change, in step with innumerable other drastic changes (involving Augustus and his family) to the identity of Romanness.[12] From this perspective, it is more interesting and more useful to start by seeing the *Fasti* as being 'about', or even as being part of, this process, implicated in it in order to explore it, than it is to hasten to the judgement of whether the poem is simply 'for' or 'against' it. I shall be arguing that there is a voice of protest in the poem, but if we listen to that voice only (just as if we listen to the affirmatory voice only) we will rob the poem of its ideological texture and rigour, its power to involve us as fully as possible in the metamorphosis of Roman norms.

The dichotomy between 'literature' and 'politics' falls to the ground before such considerations, and Wallace Hadrill (1987: 221–3) has made some very telling points on this score against McKeown, who has most recently applied the apparatus of this dichotomy to the *Fasti*. Although, however, Wallace-Hadrill's criticism of McKeown's use of the terms 'literary' and 'political' is telling, he does not do justice to the account McKeown gives of why Ovid wrote the *Fasti*; McKeown's position is actually more complex, and from my point of view more fruitfully complex, than it might seem at first. McKeown gives full weight to the political character of the subject matter.[13] Further, he sees the strongest possible political motivation for Ovid's choice of this particular subject, in the disgrace of the elder Julia in 2 BCE, with the death or exile of several leading nobles (McKeown

---

[12] The family element is vital, for the *Fasti* are truly imperial, and, in part, post-Augustan: the rededication of book 1 to Germanicus is a beautiful illustration of one of the poem's main interests, the interaction between cyclical and linear time—Augustus is dead. On the vexed question of the dating of the elements of the *Fasti*, see Fantham (1985, = ch. 17 above). Ovid is the first poet to write about one of the greatest novelties in Roman life, a novelty in some ways even greater than the principate itself: the succession to the principate (1.531–4).

[13] 'Such a choice of subject matter inevitably has considerable political implications, especially since the reform of the calendar in 46 BC had associated the organisation of the official year particularly with the *gens Iulia* and since Augustus, for political reasons, was conducting a campaign for religious restoration' (McKeown 1984: 169).

1984: 175–7).[14] Ovid, then, 'must have realised that *libertas* was dead' (177), and that his former style of poetry was no longer acceptable. At this point, McKeown's argument, very revealingly, becomes rather difficult to follow, since he seems fundamentally uncertain as to how to mesh this powerful political dimension with his conviction that 'the *Fasti* as a whole was inspired primarily by the literary tradition': the 'literature/politics' antithesis here reasserts its grip. But he is right, I think, to call attention to the importance of the question of *libertas* when considering the *Fasti,* for, as I hope to show, the question of what may be said, and when, and by whom, is one of the poem's key thematic preoccupations.

Freedom of expression under Augustus is a vexed issue, and some brief setting of the scene is necessary. There is, to begin with, a good deal of evidence for the *princeps'* toleration of outspokenness, even of personal criticism.[15] His most explicit statement of his policy comes (appropriately enough) in a private letter, to Tiberius: *aetati tuae, mi Tiberi, noli in hac re indulgere et nimium indignari quemquam esse, qui de me male loquatur; satis est enim, si hoc habemus ne quis nobis male facere possit* ('Don't, my Tiberius, let your youth get the better of you in this matter by getting too upset about the fact that there is someone who should speak ill of me; it's enough if we achieve the aim of not having anyone *do* ill to us', Suet. *Aug.* 51.3). In this respect he emulated his father (Suet. *Jul.* 73); an aspect of noble arrogance resided precisely in the ability 'to take these things gracefully' (Syme 1939: 152). This edifying picture needs considerable qualification, however, and the first obvious qualification is that of chronology. Under the triumvirate it was plainly dangerous to speak freely, as is attested by Pollio's famous reply to Octavian's Fescennine attacks: *at ego taceo. non est enim facile in eum scribere qui potest proscribere* ('but I keep silent; it isn't easy to write against some one who can write you

---

[14] Cf. Littlewood (1981) 381–95, 382 on the importance of Julia's disgrace in 2 BCE. On these transactions, see Syme (1978) 193–7.

[15] Syme (1939) 481–6; Galinsky (1975) 212–14. Suetonius has a chapter illustrating Augustus' ability to put up with such things (*Aug.* 51); Macrobius has a lengthy collection of similar anecdotes (*Sat.* 2.4.19–31). See Wallace-Hadrill (1982) 38, on how it is common policy in the early principate for the rulers to 'advertise the restoration of freedom of speech by setting their faces against *adulatio,* and enduring critical remarks'.

off').[16] And at the end of the reign, by a process which Griffin (1984: 215) calls a 'fearful symmetry', the old man's vindictiveness and petulance brought back an atmosphere in which *libertas* was once again severely circumscribed, with the extension of the laws of *maiestas* to cover speech, with the burning of the histories of T. Labienus, and the banishment of Cassius Severus—and of Ovid: 'freedom of speech was now curbed and subverted under pretext of social harmony'.[17]

It is the middle period of Augustus' reign, from Actium to the disgrace of his daughter, that provides the bulk of the evidence for his tolerance and *comitas* ('geniality', 'affability'). Yet the early part even of this period saw the suicide of Gallus, who could not hold his tongue when he was in his cups (Ov. *Tr.* 2.446). Further, the *libertas* enjoyed even by the highest members of society had suffered irrevocable infringement, as everybody knew, although nobody could pin down quite where the boundaries were (I do not mean to imply that it had ever been possible to pin down those boundaries). Syme (1939: 482) praises his hero, Pollio, for his exercise of *libertas,* but one's doubts about Pollio's Republican freedom of speech are confirmed by a reading of Seneca's superb account of the conversation between Augustus and Pollio about the rabid historian Timagenes, who was using Pollio's house as a base for his attacks on the *princeps* (*De Ira* 3.23.7–8). In Seneca's passage one can sense the two men testing the ring of the circle within which they must operate; the crucial point, however, is that Pollio does say that he will forbid Timagenes his house 'if Augustus gives the order' (*si iubes, Caesar*). In the end, as with everything else in the principate, it was up to the *princeps,* in each particular case, to draw the line in the sand. O. S. Due (1974: 174 n. 92), with his customary insight, catches the essence of the matter: 'The strength of his power enabled him to permit a certain freedom of speech but he arbitrarily and unpredictably reserved for himself the right of determining the limits of it, and in his later years he was narrowing those limits.' This arbitrary and unpredictable element is

---

[16] Macr. *Sat.* 2.4.21; it is fascinating to observe that Macrobius tells this story as his second example of Augustus' restraint when he was the butt of other people's wit.

[17] Syme (1978) 214; 212–14 on the events mentioned in the text. Galinsky (1975) 256, on 'the late Augustan reign', would have it that 'free speech was as rampant as ever and so was its toleration'.

the key, as it is in every aspect of imperial power (Millar 1977: 9–10, 74, 112–13, 300, 527).

In accordance with the usual habit of regarding these issues as a one-way imposition of rules from the top, it is often forgotten that Augustus himself could not simply say whatever he felt like: the novel circumstances demanded that Augustus curb his own utterance in ways which a Republican noble would not have tolerated. The death of Gallus, early in the reign, illustrates Augustus' recognition of the lethal power of his tongue. When the *princeps*' declared wrath led inexorably to the harassment of his former friend by prosecutors and senatorial decrees, and to his suicide, 'Augustus wept and bemoaned his lot, because he was the only person who could not be as angry as he liked against his friends' (*quod sibi soli non liceret amicis, quatenus uellet, irasci*, Suet. *Aug.* 66.2). Whatever judgement we make on these tears, and whatever judgement contemporaries may have made, they reveal a chasm which the system normally tried very hard to paper over, and it is too easy to write off Augustus' lamentations as mere hypocrisy.[18]

The case of his friend Asprenas Nonius is even more revealing (Suet. *Aug.* 56.3). When this man was accused by Cassius Severus, Augustus consulted the Senate for advice: if he appeared in Nonius' defence, the case would be as good as won for him, and it would look as if Augustus were above the law, yet if he didn't, people would think he was abandoning his friend and condemning him in advance. The compromise position arrived at by *princeps* and Senate is a beautiful illustration of the novel tact and self-advertising self-effacement which the novel circumstances required: *consentientibus uniuersis sedit in subselliis per aliquot horas, uerum tacitus et ne laudatione quidem iudiciali data* ('with unanimous agreement he sat on the bench in the court for some hours, but in silence, without even making the usual speech of character reference'). The openly discussed

---

[18] Seneca lays out these paradoxes very clearly in his address to Nero in the *De Clementia*, where he says that humble people may indulge themselves by fighting and quarrelling, while the king must govern even his speech: *graue putas eripi loquendi arbitrium regibus, quod humillimi habent. 'ista,' inquis, 'seruitus est, non imperium'* ('you think it's a serious thing that kings should have snatched away from them the power of speech, which the lowest of the low have got. "That", you say, "is to be a slave, not a ruler"', 1.7.4–5).

decision to smother the speech of the *princeps* finds eloquent emblem in the silently observing figure on the bench. The need for Augustus to put limits on his own forms of self-expression, while finding ways of calling attention to his self-denial, is most strikingly exemplified in his *Res Gestae*, where he openly boasts of the fact that he rebuilt the temple of Jupiter and the theatre of Pompey *sine ulla inscriptione nominis mei* ('without putting my name on any inscription', 20.1). One thinks, similarly, of the Ara Fortunae Reducis, a monument erected to trumpet the *princeps'* modesty in not claiming a triumph after his return to the city in 19 BCE (*Res Gestae* 11; see Torelli 1982: 28–9).

What we are dealing with, then, is not straightforward repression or straightforward tolerance, but, as always, a developing and shifting relationship, without any precedents, where all the parties involved are feeling their way; habits and patterns of behaviour firm up as time goes on, of course, but it remains an essentially provisional and improvisatory atmosphere. Apart from Ovid, the poet who most effectively catches the mood is Horace, in whose poetry one sees an acute sensitivity to the transformations of *libertas* under the triumvirate and principate. DuQuesnay's fundamentally important essay on *Sermones* 1 sheds much light here, especially in its analysis of Horace's awareness of the difference between his *libertas* and that of Lucilius; Republican *libertas* can now manifest itself only as the offensive and indecorous proceedings which Horace shows us in *Sat.* 1.7.[19] When, much later in his career, Horace presents his potted history of Latin literature to Augustus, his starting-point is the curbing of *licentia*, excessive *libertas*, through legislation (*Ep.* 2.1.145–55).[20]

---

[19] DuQuesnay (1984) esp. 27–32, and 37 on 1.7. *Sat.* 1.7 shows *licentia*, not *libertas*: on the distinction, see Wirszubski (1950) 7. As Duncan Kennedy points out to me, one man's *licentia* is another man's *libertas*; the terms are always contested.

[20] Of course Horace here is assimilating Latin literary history to Greek, on analogy with the laws supposedly passed at Athens to curb Old Comedy: cf. *Ars* 281–4, with Brink ad loc. But the important question to ask is 'Why did Horace need to see the history of Latin literature as virtually co-extensive with the history of censorship?' I may take the opportunity here to point to an example of Virgil's sensitivity to what may and may not be said, and to correct a gross blunder which I perpetrated (1986). At *Aen.* 6.841 Anchises asks *quis te, magne Cato, tacitum aut te, Cosse, relinquat?* I still believe that the question form makes us wonder whether the elder or younger Cato is the greater, and that 'the question of whether to leave Cato the younger unmentioned was…not untopical' (1986: 13). I cannot understand, however, how I referred in

Ovid's poem has an intense interest in the conditions of speech determined by the principate, but, in accordance with its general plan, the poem maps these questions on to the very broad backdrop provided by Roman customs and Roman history. The problem of what may be said, by whom, where, and when, is one which the reader encounters before even reading any of the poem, in the title itself: *dies fasti*, after all, are *dies quibus fari licet* ('days on which it is allowable to speak', Varro, *Ling.* 6.29). The poet soon expounds the articulation of time and allowed legal forms of speech which controls the Roman system of days (1.45–52):

> ne tamen ignores uariorum iura dierum,
>   non habet officii Lucifer omnis idem.
> ille nefastus erit, per quem tria uerba silentur:
>   fastus erit, per quem lege licebit agi.
> nec toto perstare die sua iura putaris:
>   qui iam fastus erit, mane nefastus erat;
> nam simul exta deo data sunt, licet omnia fari,
>   uerbaque honoratus libera praetor habet.

To make sure you're acquainted with the prerogatives of the various days: every day does not have the same official function. That day will be a 'no-speaking' day through the course of which the three words are unspoken; it will be a 'speaking' day through the course of which it will be allowable by law for business to be conducted. And don't think that a day's prerogatives persist through the whole day: the day that will now be a 'speaking' day was a 'no-speaking' day in the morning; for as soon as the inwards have been given to the god, it is allowable to speak everything, and the honoured praetor has free words.

Coming through this description of the calendrical constraints upon the praetor's right to adjudicate with his three words, *do, dico, addico*, one sees an emblem of a totally characteristic Roman way of proceeding. At no period of Roman history was it possible simply to say what you liked, when you liked.[21] The Athenian herald's equestion to the ecclesia, *tis agoreuein bouletai?* ('Who wishes to speak?'), is

footnote 65 to 'the unproblematic Cossus', for Livy 4.20.5–11 shows that the person who was not leaving Cossus silent was Augustus himself.

[21] Powerfully stated by Momigliano (1942: 124). On Roman control of speech, see Daube 1951; G. W. Williams has a valuable article on 'Libel and Slander in Rome' in *OCD*[2].

inconceivable in a Roman context. *Quis dicere uult?* would be a shocking thing to hear in a *contio*, but even in the Senate, where discussion was guided by the chairman, the consul, these words are unimaginable. Wherever speech of a public character is at issue in Rome, we find the state systematically involved, marking off appropriate times and places—even to the extent of allowing for periods of true licence, when jokes and obscenities were permitted.[22] Ovid takes the opportunity to mark three important festivals where such licence was allowed: Anna Perenna, on March 15 (3.675–96); Floralia, at the end of April and beginning of May (4.946, 5.331–2); Lesser Quinquatrus, on June 13–15 (6.691–2). Prostitutes and low people were accorded strict segments of time in which to exercise *libertas*, or rather, *licentia*; the *libertas* of the upper orders was more extensive in time, but less extensive in scope.

By Ovid's presentation, allowing different periods for different forms of speech is one aspect of what he casts as the characteristically Roman obsession with imposing order and control on natural time. The full synchronization of Roman time and natural time only comes, as we have seen, with Julius Caesar's reforms, whereby Roman time and natural time merge (as Roman space and natural space merge; 1.85–6, 2.683–4); but Ovid concentrates on the way in which Caesar's reforms are the culmination of Roman methods of organizing time which go all the way back to the founder, Romulus. An extensive passage in book 3 describes how the stars were free (*libera*) before Romulus' ten-month calendar (3.111–12), which itself needed correction by Numa (151–4), who still did not get things quite right, so that Caesar had to take care of matters (155–6). Between Romulus and Caesar, we hear of other reforms, by the *decemuiri* (2.53–4), and by the Roman government in 153 BCE (3.147–8 and Bömer 1957–8: ad loc.).

If the Roman state has always organized time, and times for speech, the conditions of speech are not always the same. Every Roman schoolboy knew that the beginning of *libertas* was the expulsion of the kings, and Ovid takes the opportunity to focus on the story of

---

[22] Such carnivalesque periods of licence were discussed at length by J. G. Frazer (1913: 306–411). Since the influential work of M. M. Bakhtin (1968), there has been much important work: see Stallybrass and White (1986); especially Castle (1986), with bibliography at 350 n. 15.

Tarquin, Lucretia, and Brutus through the perspective of silence and speech. The establishment of Libertas becomes, in Ovid, an act of *libertas,* an act of outspokenness, following a traumatic silence. Ovid's account of the rape of Lucretia and the establishment of the Republic (2.685–852) is very closely modelled on the account of Livy (1.57.6–60.3). He veers away from Livy, however, after the moment of the rape. In Livy, Lucretia immediately sends a messenger to her father and husband, saying that something terrible has happened (1.58.5). When they arrive, she straight away says what has happened, naming Tarquin (58.7–8), and then commits suicide. In Ovid, she sends a messenger, but when her relatives arrive, she says nothing for a long time (2.819–20). Three times she tries to speak, and fails (823–4)—finally (825–8):

'hoc quoque Tarquinio debebimus? eloquar' inquit,
    'eloquar infelix dedecus ipsa meum?'
quaeque potest, narrat; restabant ultima: fleuit,
    et matronales erubuere genae.

'Shall I owe this too to Tarquin? Shall I pronounce,' she says, 'shall I, unhappy one, myself pronounce my own disgrace?' She tells what she can; the last bit was still remaining; she wept, and her matronly cheeks blushed.

Lucretia can barely escape silence, and remains at the end trapped in silence.[23] Brutus, the mute man, then belies his name (*animo sua nomina fallit,* 2.837), and does speak the unspeakable, *nefanda,* instituting the *annua iura* of the Republic—the *fasti* (2.849–52):

          Brutus clamore Quirites
  concitat et regis facta nefanda refert.
Tarquinius cum prole fugit: capit annua consul
  iura: dies regnis illa suprema fuit.

Brutus with a shout summons the citizens and relates the unspeakable deeds of the king. Tarquin flees with his children: the consul assumes the annual authority: that day was monarchy's last.

---

[23] In the rape scene itself, Ovid likewise stresses her silence (2.797–810), in contrast to the emphatic speech act of the rapist: '*ferrum, Lucretia, mecum est* | ... *Tarquiniusque* loquor' ('I have a sword with me, Lucretia, and it is Tarquin who *speaks*', 2.796).

Speech in Republican time is qualitatively different, then, from speech under the monarchy, and it issues from the dumb man's daring to speak the unspeakable. Speaking out of turn, however, is normally fatal in the world of the *Fasti*. At the comic level, we have the double story of Priapus' attempted rape of Lotis in book 1 and of Vesta in book 6. Each time he is interrupted by the braying of Silenus' donkey, which is punished by death (Lotis: 1.433–40: Vesta: 6.341–6). In book 1, this aetiology of animal sacrifice is followed immediately by another, when we are told that birds are sacrificed *quia linguae crimen habetis,* | *dique putant mentes uos aperire suas* ('because you are guilty of having a tongue, and the gods think that you open up their minds', 1.445–6). At the tragic level, we have the most shattering story in the *Fasti*, the story of the goddess with the extraordinary name of Tacita, the Dea Muta. Her mother kept telling her to hold her tongue, but she warned Juturna and Juno of Jupiter's plans (2.601–6), whereupon Jupiter ripped out the tongue which she had used without restraint (*quaque est non usa modeste* | *eripit huic linguam,* 2.607–8). Worse follows, as the tongueless creature is handed over to Mercury, to be taken to the Manes, 'the right place for silent ones' (*locus ille silentibus aptus,* 2. 609). Mercury rapes her *en route* (2.613–16):

uim parat hic, uoltu pro uerbis illa precatur,
  et frustra muto nititur ore loqui,
fitque grauis geminosque parit, qui compita seruant
  et uigilant nostra semper in urbe Lares.

He gets ready to rape her, she prays with her expression in place of words, and in vain struggles to speak with her mute mouth, and she becomes pregnant, and gives birth to twins, who keep the crossroads, and are wakeful in our city always, the Lares.

These watchful children of the mute goddess are the Lares Compitales, one of the most important focuses for the cult of Augustus in the city of Rome. He added the cult of his Genius to these Lares, so that each *uicus* in the city had a group of three statues, the Lares Compitales flanking the Genius Augusti; indeed, the Lares Compitales came to be thought of as the Lares Augusti (Liebeschuetz 1979: 70; Bömer 1957–8: ad 5.140). Ovid's story, by linking these little deities to his fictions about excessive speech, enforced muteness, and rape, transforms them into an ever-present warning of the dangers of using your tongue without restraint.[24] This story comes seventy lines before the larger story of rape and silence, the story of Lucretia.

The poem, then, shows diverse interest in the regulation of speech, and in the occasions of speech. For a poet with the sensitivity to genre of Ovid, the implications for himself as a creator of *Fasti* are not going to pass unmarked. At one level, and with certain examples, this is a field for fine, self-referential, generic play. When Numa wishes to learn how to expiate Jupiter's thunderbolts, he chains Faunus and Picus in order to force them to divulge their wisdom (3.323–6):

> emissi laqueis quid agant, quae carmina dicant,
>   quaque trahant superis sedibus arte Iouem
> scire *nefas* homini. nobis concessa canentur
>   *quaeque* pio *dici* uatis ab ore *licet.*

What they do when they are let out of their nets, what songs they sing, and by what art they drag Jupiter down from his abode above, it is wrong (*no-speak*) for man to know. My song shall deal with authorized subject-matter, *things which are allowed to be said* by a bard's pious mouth.

quae dici licet ('things which are allowed to be said') are, very precisely, *fasti,* and Ovid is using the Silenus story of Virgil's sixth *Eclogue* in order to define the boundaries of his new genre: his self-imposed *lex operis* dictates here that he keep to his account of state cult and aetiology, without following his model into larger vistas of poetics and cosmology.[25] Again, when he comes to the Liberalia on 17 March, he lists all the topics connected with Liber which he is going to pass over in silence (and which are treated in the *Metamorphoses*)—Semele, the miraculous birth, Eastern triumphs, the death of Pentheus, Lycurgus (3.715–22). I would like, he says, to tell of the sailors turned into fish—*sed non est carminis huius opus* ('but that is not the job of this poem', 723–4). What is the *opus* of this *carmen*? State cult: *carminis huius opus causas exponere quare | uilis anus populos ad sua liba uocet* ('it is the job of this poem to lay out

---

[24] On Ovid's inventions here, especially in making Lara/Tacita the mother of the Lares, see Fauth (1978) 143–4; Porte (1985) 448–51.

[25] And what is *Eclogue* 6 but metamorphosis? That is the *other* poem.

the reasons why the paltry little old lady summons the peoples to her cakes', 3.725–6).

Besides the generic constraints upon what Ovid may and may not say, there are other constraints, of tact, and of Augustan sensibility. The Ides of March are the feast day of Anna Perenna, a day of unusual licence of speech, when girls from the lower orders sing obscene songs and jokes (3.675–6, 695). Immediately after telling us about this custom, Ovid finds himself faced with another noteworthy fact about the Ides of March, and his first reaction is to pass over it in silence (3.697–9):

praeteriturus eram gladios in principe fixos,
    cum sic a castis Vesta locuta focis:
'Ne dubita meminisse ...'

I was going to pass over the swords stuck in the *princeps,* when Vesta spoke these words from the chaste hearths: 'Don't hesitate to mention ...'

We achieve nothing by affixing the label 'anti-Augustan' to this display of the dilemmas of tact thrown in the poet's path by the progression of the calendar: the sheer difficulty of speech on such a theme, such a *nefas* (3.705), is obstacle enough for the poet to negotiate.

In book 4, the constraints of tact combine with the laws of the genre to force silence upon the poet. Ovid explains the contribution of Greek culture to Roman life by giving a list of Greeks (and Trojans) who came to Italy. The first on the list is the exile Evander (4.65), and the last is Aeneas' companion, Solimus, eponymous founder of Ovid's own town, Sulmo (4.80–4):

    a quo Sulmonis moenia nomen habent,
Sulmonis gelidi, patriae, Germanice, nostrae.
    me miserum, Scythico quam procul illa solo est!
ergo ego tam longe—sed supprime, Musa, querellas:
    non tibi sunt maesta sacra canenda lyra.

... from whom the walls of Sulmo have their name, cold Sulmo, the fatherland, Germanicus, of me. Unhappy me, how far that fatherland is from Scythian soil! So I, so far away—but quell these laments, Muse: you shouldn't sing holy subject matter with a sad lyre.

The celebratory mode of the *Fasti* squeezes out the personal disaster of the poet; what should be sung *maesta lyra* ('with a sad lyre') is, of course, *Tristia,* the work upon which he was engaged at the time he wrote these lines for the *Fasti.* [26]

It is, naturally, the personal disaster of the poet, Ovid's exile, which constitutes the poem's principal reflection on the right to speak. The status of the *Fasti* in the exile years is a matter of considerable dispute (Bömer 1957–8: i.16–22; cf. Bömer 1988, Fantham 1985, = ch. 17 above). In *Tristia* 2, Ovid represents his exile as cutting off his two greater works, the *Fasti* and the *Metamorphoses* (*Trist.* 2.549–52, 555–6):

sex ego Fastorum scripsi totidemque libellos,
    cumque suo finem mense uolumen habet,
idque tuo nuper scriptum sub nomine, Caesar,
    et tibi sacratum sors mea rupit opus . . .
dictaque sunt nobis, quamuis manus ultima coeptis
    defuit, in facies corpora uersa nouas.

I wrote six little books of *Fasti,* and the same number again; and each volume terminates with its own month, and this work, recently written with your name at the head, Caesar, and dedicated to you, my disaster interrupted . . . And I had also composed (although the undertaking lacked the final touch) bodies turned into new appearances.

In fact, as Hinds (1987*a*: 10) puts it, 'one suspects . . . that the *Metamorphoses* was rather more, and the *Fasti* rather less, finished than Ovid seems to claim'. There is no doubt that portions of the *Fasti* were written after Ovid's exile, even after Augustus' death (Williams 1978: 84–5; Fantham 1985, = ch. 17 above). But we have no more than six books, and there is no reason to believe we have lost the second block of six; it is generally taken that Ovid's *scripsi* in his letter to Augustus refers to a draft or sketch of the last six books.[27] The poem, then, is unfinished; what is more, in the light of the annual format,

[26] At *Pont.* 3.4.45–6, Ovid faces the opposite problem, when he wishes to sing of the triumph of Tiberius: *adde quod assidue domini meditata querellas | ad laetum carmen uix mea uersa lyra est* ('add the fact that my lyre, after busily practising the complaints of her master, has turned with difficulty to a happy poem').

[27] Bömer (1957–8) I.20–1. Williams (1978: 84) and Hinds (1987*a*: 137 n. 23) both make the convincing suggestion that (as Hinds puts it) Ovid's phrasing 'may be designed to hold out a promise to Augustus that clemency for the poet will result

it is nakedly and glaringly unfinished, poised at the halfway mark, on the brink of the month of July (6.797–8):[28]

tempus Iuleis cras est natale Kalendis:
  Pierides, coeptis addite summa meis.

Tomorrow is the day that gives birth to the Kalends of July. Muses, add the final touch to my undertakings.

A number of scholars have commented on the implicit promise in this point of break-off: the very months which Augustus should be most interested in are just around the corner—July, and, of course, August (Williams 1978: 84; Hinds 1987*a*). This is a very valuable perspective, but I wish to concentrate on the implicit *reproach* in this point of break-off, by looking at the ways in which the poem refers to its own premature ending after the imposition of silence. There has been much speculation about why and when Ovid decided not to carry on from book 6 (Syme 1978: 34; Fantham 1983: 210–15; Bömer 1988: 221). I have no suggestion to offer on this score (although, as a devout admirer of this extraordinarily intelligent poem, I am sure that the poet's boredom had nothing to do with it). What I do want to suggest is that important sections of the poem were rewritten from exile so as to make the *Fasti* read like a poem whose *licentia* has been suppressed, which has not been allowed to keep speaking, which has become *nefas*.

The dedication to Germanicus which opens the poem was composed in exile (Fantham 1985: 243–56, see ch. 17 above); amid a generally apprehensive atmosphere,[29] the opening reveals an anxiety on

almost immediately in the completion of the one Ovidian work which should really appeal to him'.

[28] An Ennian reference may help accentuate the fact that we have an ending here, which should be picked up by a continuation. Ovid ends with the restoration of the *aedes Herculis Musarum* by L. Marcius Philippus. Now, it appears that the original climax of Ennius' *Annales* was the founding of this temple by M. Fulvius Nobilior in 187 BCE: see Skutsch (1985) 553. The point is that this was the end of book 15 of the *Annales,* and that Ennius began afresh with a continuation, with the opening of book 16 containing the poet's declaration of why he is beginning again (XVI. i–ii, Skutsch).

[29] Note especially *pacato uoltu ... timidae nauis* ('with a placated expression, ... timid ship', 1.3–4); *pauidos metus ... da mihi te placidum* ('quaking fears, ... give yourself to me in a placid spirit', 16–17).

the question of whether the project will be brought to a completion (1.25–6):

si licet et fas est, uates rege uatis habenas,
    auspice te felix totus ut annus eat.

If it is allowable and right ('speakable'), as a bard yourself guide the reins of your bard, so that the whole year may go fortunately along under your auspices.

It proved, in fact, not to be *fas* to *fari* until the *Fasti* were complete, until the whole year was done. This key language is picked up and heightened in a crucial passage at what is now the halfway point, in the conversation with Venus which opens book 4. The goddess affects to be surprised that Ovid wants anything to do with her, now that he is engaged on greater projects (4.3–4). Having deftly reminded her that she too has been an epic character,[30] the poet defends his earlier love poetry as being *sine crimine* ('without crime', 9), an apologia which must have been written after his banishment for *carmen et error* ('a poem and a blunder,).[31] After Ovid has told Venus of his new subject, she tells him *coeptum perfice... opus* ('finish off the work you have begun', 4.16). His response is cautious (17–18):

sensimus, et causae subito patuere dierum:
    dum licet et spirant flamina, nauis eat.

I felt her inspiration, and the explanations for the days were suddenly open to me: while it is allowed and the breezes blow, let the ship go on.

First, we note the same provisional language as in the opening to book 1: here, Ovid says *dum licet* ('while it is allowed'); there, *si licet et fas est* ('if it is allowed and right/speakable', 1.25). The language which Venus addresses to Ovid is also vital: *coeptum perfice... opus* ('finish off the work you have begun'); *opus* ('work') and *coeptum/a* ('beginnings/undertakings') have been key items of diction in Ovid's earlier

---

[30] Such is the point of line 5, *scis, dea, ... de uolnere* ('you know, goddess, about wounds'), a reference to (among other things) her wounding by Diomedes in *Iliad* 5 (330–40).

[31] Even Bömer (1957–8), who attributes as little of the poem as possible to a date after exile, thinks it is 'possible' to see such a reference here. We are less than eighty lines away from Ovid's explicit reference to his place of exile, after talking of Solimus (4.82–4).

poetry. This is not the first time Ovid has called on Venus to help him with *coepta*. At the beginning of the *Ars,* Ovid asks her: *coeptis, mater Amoris, ades* ('attend, mother of love, my beginnings/undertakings', 1.30). The crucial point to note is the way in which this language is picked up throughout the *Ars* until a definitive end is reached. At the end of the first book, we read *pars superest coepti, pars est exhausta, laboris* ('part of the work I have undertaken still remains, part is done', 1.771); at the end of the work as a whole, we are told that we have reached the end: *lusus habet finem* ('the game has an end', 3.809). Similarly, in the *Amores,* Cupid gives Ovid an *opus* to sing at the beginning of the collection (*'quod'que 'canas, uates, accipe' dixit 'opus',* 1.1.24), and the completion of the *opus* is marked by the final line, and final word, of the collection (*post mea mansurum fata superstes opus,* 'a work which will remain to survive me after my death', 3.15.20). At the beginning of the *Remedia,* Cupid asks Ovid to carry the proposed *opus* to completion: *et mihi 'propositum perfice' dixit 'opus'* ('and he said to me, "finish off the proposed work"', 40); at the end, the completion of the *opus* is announced: *hoc opus exegi: fessae date serta carinae;* | *contigimus portus, quo mihi cursus erat* ('this is the work I have erected: put garlands on the tired ship; we have reached the port which was my goal', 811–12). Finally, the *Metamorphoses* begins with a prayer to the gods to breathe favourably upon the *coepta* (1.2–3), and ends with a declaration that the *opus* has been achieved (*iamque opus exegi,* 15.871).

When Venus, then, at the beginning of *Fasti* 4, tells Ovid to bring to completion the work which he has begun (*coeptum perfice... opus*), she is speaking in the same way as her son has spoken before; but the poet replies with caution (*dum licet... nauis eat*); the ship of the *Remedia* gets to port at the end, but the ship of the *Fasti* never does. The *opus* is never *perfectum,* it never gets beyond the *coepta* stage. At the end of *Fasti* 6, at the end of the work as we have it, we are still at the end of the beginning, with an invocatory appeal to the Muses to reinforce the sense of shock at finding ourselves at the end (6.797–8):

tempus Iuleis cras est natale Kalendis:
    Pierides, coeptis addite summa meis.
dicite, Pierides...

Tomorrow is the day that gives birth to the Kalends of July. Muses, add the final touch to my undertakings. Tell, Muses...

The broken-off atmosphere which Ovid thus creates for his poem is enhanced by the presence of forward references to months which the poem never reaches.[32] All of these references, it is interesting to observe, are to two months and no others, months which are crucial for different reasons: August, the month in which Augustus should have most interest, and December, the end of the poem. At 3.199–200 Ovid points forward to both of these months, when he says that Consus will explain his feast when we get there: there were Consualia both on 21 August and on 15 December. At 5.145–8 Ovid says that he will talk about Augustus' Lares Compitales when he arrives in Augustus' month. From the perspective of the truncation of the poem, however, the most interesting forward reference comes in book 3, when Ovid touches on the finding of Romulus and Remus by Faustulus and his wife, Larentia (55–8):

non ego te, tantae nutrix Larentia gentis,
　　nec taceam uestras, Faustule pauper, opes:
uester honos ueniet, cum Larentalia dicam:
　　acceptus geniis illa December habet.

I will not, Larentia, nurse of such a great people, I will not be silent about you, nor will I be silent about your aid, Faustulus. Your honour will come when I speak of the Larentalia; December, home to the genial spirits, has that festival.

In fact, he *will* be silent about Larentia, and her festival, and December. Although the poem never manages to arrive at the Larentalia, that festival would have been, for numerous reasons, the ideal ending; it is the assumed ending which Ovid is creating in his reader's mind for his unfinished work. First of all, Ovid would have had one more chance to retell the story of Romulus and Remus from yet another point of view, for the fifth or sixth time. Then, the Larentalia, on 23 December, are the last festival of the year, an ideal place to stop. The Larentalia were also the last day of the Saturnalia, which lasted from 17–23 December. This would not only have been

---

[32] There are two forward references which are picked up within the poem as we have it: 3. 791 is picked up by 5.621 ff.; 4.947 by 5.183 ff.

Ovid's last chance to retell the story of Saturn for the third or fourth time; the Saturnalia would have provided him with a culminating opportunity for presenting the exercise of *licentia* (following on from his images of Anna Perenna, Floralia, and Lesser Quinquatrus), for the Saturnalia were the quintessential festival of *licentia* when even slaves could speak freely, where *ioci* and *libertas* ruled (Scullard 1981: 206–7). Far from being able to complete his work with a final description of Roman *licentia*, however, Ovid has had his own *licentia* stifled in mid-course. The silent image of the December licence which will never be described hangs over the finale of the fragment which the *Fasti* has now become. The work ends not in licence, but silence, as the poet tells us forty lines from the end of book 6: *tempora labuntur, tacitisque senescimus annis* ('time's passage is slipping by, and I grow old in silent years', 771). Two days before the Larentalia, two days before the end of the Saturnalia, one finds the festival of Diva Angerona, who may fill the void as the poem's last presiding deity. Her statue showed her with a bandage tied over her mouth—or with a finger on her lips, admonishing silence.[33]

Ovid, then, has three poetic strategies from exile. His first and most important is the exile poetry itself, where he asserts and justifies himself in the face of his smothering catastrophe, vindicating his right

---

[33] Plin. *HN* 3.65; Macr. *Sat.* 3.9.4. I had made this (I confess, rather flippant) reference to Diva Angerona before reading the fascinating speculations on Angerona and Larentia in Coarelli 1983: 255–82; Coarelli argues that there are extremely tight links in space, time, and cult between Diva Angerona and Acca Larentia. Their shrines are adjacent, on the flank of the Palatine at the north-eastern boundary of the Velabrum; their feast days straddle the winter solstice (22 December); they are linked temporally and spatially with Saturn, whose extended festive period comprehends both theirs, and who borders the north of the Velabrum; their cults are involved with the Lares. The result is a constellation of associations with midwinter, year-end, and rites of the dead. This cluster is itself linked with another cult of the dead, the Feralia, which comes exactly ten months before the day of Angerona, on 21 February (258). This day is the feast day of Tacita, the Dea Muta, likewise linked with the Lares, and Coarelli stresses the twinning of Tacita and Angerona (259). The curtailment of the *Fasti* leaves me wondering what Ovid, who makes so much of Tacita, would have made of this second silent goddess (now perpetually left in silence), so intimately involved with the Larentalia which he promises (and fails) to describe. Could he, further, have passed up the opportunity to make mention of another shrine not twenty yards away, a shrine in tight connection with Angerona and Larentia (Coarelli, 261, 275)? I mean the shrine of Aius Locutius, the personified act of speech.

to speak, maintaining his voice. [34] Then he has two uses of the two masterpieces which (so he would have it) were not quite finished when his sentence came. The *Metamorphoses*, as Hinds has shown, has its beginning and end rewritten from exile so as to become itself an 'exile-poem' (1985: 20–1, 25–7, see ch. 18 above). The unfinished *Fasti* he turns into the obverse of the self-assertive exile poetry, so that its failure to reach its goal stands as an actualization of one of its main thematic preoccupations, becoming a mute reproach to the constraints set upon the poet's speech. The silent second half of the work has, in its own way, as much to say about the principate and its ideology as the vocal first half.

---

[34] Syme (1978) 215–29; note esp. *Tr.* 3.7. 47–8 (cited by Syme, 227): *ingenio tamen ipse meo comitorque fruorque:* | *Caesar in hoc potuit iuris habere nihil* ('my genius is my companion and my resource: Caesar has not been able to have any jurisdiction over *that*').

Acknowledgements

1. Stephen Hinds, 'Generalizing about Ovid', reprinted from *Ramus* 16 (1987) 4–31.
2. Niklas Holzberg, 'Playing with his Life: Ovid's "Autobiographical" References', reprinted from *Lampas* 30 (1997) 4–19.
3. Duncan F. Kennedy, 'The Epistolary Mode and the First of Ovid's *Heroides*', reprinted from *The Classical Quarterly* 34 (1984) 413–22.
4. John F. Miller, 'Ovidian Allusion and the Vocabulary of Memory', reprinted from *Materiali e discussioni per l'analisi dei testi classici* 30 (1993) 153–64.
5. James J. O'Hara, 'Vergil's Best Reader? Ovidian Commentary on Vergilian Etymological Wordplay', reprinted from *The Classical Journal* 91 (1996) 255–76.
6. Philip Hardie, 'Lucretius and the Delusions of Narcissus', reprinted from *Materiali e discussioni per l'analisi dei testi classici* 20–1 (1988) 71–89.
7. Sergio Casati, 'Other Voices in Ovid's "Aeneid"', translation of 'Altre voci nell' Eneide di Ovidio', in *Materiali e discussioni per l'analisi dei testi classici* 35 (1995) 59–76, incorporating the author's revisions.
8. Maria Wyke, 'Reading Female Flesh: *Amores* 3.1', reprinted from A. Cameron (ed.), *History as Text* (London: Duckworth 1989) 111–43.
9. Barbara Weiden Boyd, 'The Death of Corinna's Parrot Reconsidered: Poetry and Ovid's *Amores*', reprinted from *The Classical Journal* 82 (1987) 199–207.
10. R. Alden Smith, 'Fantasy, Myth, and Love Letters: Text and Tale in Ovid's *Heroides*', reprinted from *Arethusa* 27 (1994) 247–73.
11. Alison R. Sharrock, 'Ovid and the Politics of Reading', reprinted from *Materiali e discussioni per l'analisi dei testi classici* 33 (1994) 97–122.
12. E. J. Kenney, 'Ovidius Prooemians', reprinted from *Proceedings of the Cambridge Philological Society* 22 (1976) 46–53.
13. Alessandro Barchiesi, 'Voices and Narrative "Instances" in the *Metamorphoses*', translation of 'Voci e istanze narrative nelle Metamorfosi di Ovidio', from *Materiali e discussioni per l'analisi dei testi classici* 23 (1989) 55–97, in *Speaking Volumes* (London: Duckworth 2001) 49–78.
14. Peter E. Knox, 'Pyramus and Thisbe in Cyprus', reprinted from *Harvard Studies in Classical Philology* 92 (1988) 315–28.

15. Gianpiero Rosati, 'Form in Motion: Weaving the Text in the *Metamorphoses*', reprinted from P. Hardie, A. Barchiesi, and S. Hinds (eds.), *Ovidian Transformations* (Cambridge: Cambridge Philological Society 1999) 240–53.

16. Carole Newlands, 'Ovid's Narrator in the *Fasti*', reprinted from *Arethusa* 25 (1992) 33–54.

17. Elaine Fantham, 'Ovid, Germanicus, and the Composition of the *Fasti*', reprinted from *Papers of the Liverpool Latin Seminar* 5 (1985) 243–81.

18. Stephen Hinds, 'Booking the Return Trip: Ovid and *Tristia* 1', reprinted from *Proceedings of the Cambridge Philological Society* 31 (1985) 13–32.

19. Gareth D. Williams, 'On Ovid's *Ibis*: A Poem in Context', reprinted from *Proceedings of the Cambridge Philological Society* 38 (1992) 171–89.

20. Denis Feeney, '*Si licet et fas est* : Ovid's *Fasti* and the Problem of Free Speech under the Principate', reprinted from A. Powell (ed.), *Roman Poetry and Propaganda in the Age of Augustus* (London: Bristol Classical Press 1992) 1–25.

References

Journal abbreviations follow those in *L' Année Philologique*.

Abbot, R. (1966). 'Ovid: Poet of Immorality and Non-Conformity', *Pegasus* 5: 3–9.

Ahl, F. M. (1976). *Lucan: An Introduction*. Ithaca and London: Cornell University Press.

—— (1985). *Metaformations: Soundplay and Wordplay in Ovid and Other Classical Poets*. Ithaca and London: Cornell University Press.

—— (1989). 'Homer, Vergil, and Complex Narrative Structures in Latin Epic: An Essay', *ICS* 14: 1–31.

Albrecht, M. von (1961). 'Zum Metamorphosenprooem Ovids', *RhM* 104: 269–78.

—— (1963). *Die Parenthese in Ovids Metamorphosen and ihre dichterische Funktion*. Hildesheim: Olms.

—— and Zinn, E. (eds.) (1968). *Ovid*. Darmstadt: Wissenschaftliche Buchgesellschaft.

Alison, J. (2001). *The Love Artist: A Novel*. New York: Farrar Straus Giroux.

Allen, C. (2002). *Ovid and Art*, in Hardie (2002*b*) 336–67.

Alpers, J. (1912). *Hercules in Bivio*. Göttingen: Dieterich.

Altman, J. G. (1982). *Epistolarity: Approaches to a Form*. Columbus, Ohio: Ohio State University Press.

Alton, E. H., Wormell, D. E. W., and Courtney, E. (1978). *P. Ovidi Nasonis Fastorum Libri Sex*. Leipzig: Teubner.

Anderson, W. S. (1958). 'Juno and Saturn in the *Aeneid*', *Stud. in Philol.* 60: 519–32.

—— (1964). 'Hercules exclusus: Propertius IV.9', *AJPh* 85: 1–12.

—— (1972). *Ovid's Metamorphoses: Books 6–10*. Norman, OK: University of Oklahoma Press.

—— (1973). 'The *Heroides*', in Binns (1973) 49–83.

—— (1977). *Metamorphoses*. Leipzig: Teubner.

—— (1990). 'The Example of Procris in the *Ars amatoria*', in M. Griffith and D. J. Mastronarde (eds.), *Cabinet of the Muses: Essays on Classical and Comparative Literature in honor of Thomas G. Rosenmeyer*. Atlanta: Scholars Press, 131–45.

—— (ed.) (1995). *Ovid*. New York and London: Garland.

André, J. (1963). *Ovide: Contre Ibis*. Paris: Collection Budé.

André, J. (1975). 'Ovide Helléniste et Linguiste', *RPh* 49:191–5.

Apter, T. E. (1982). *Fantasy Literature: An Approach to Reality*. Bloomington: Indiana University Press.

Aulock, H. von (1963). 'Die Münzprägung der kilikischen Stadt Mopsus', *A&A*: 231–78.

Austin, R. G. (ed.) (1971). *P. Vergili Maronis Aeneidos Liber Primus*. Oxford: Clarendon Press.

Badian, E. (1984). 'Three Non-Trials in Cicero. Notes on the Text, Prosopography and Chronology of *Diuinatio in Caecilium* 63', *Klio* 66: 291–309.

—— (1985). 'A Phantom Marriage Law', *Philologus* 192: 82–98.

Bakhtin, M. M. (1968). *Rabelais and his World*. Trans. H. Iswolsky. Cambridge, Mass.: M.I.T. Press.

Bal, M. (1985). *Narratology: Introduction to the Theory of Narrative*. Trans. C. van Boheemen. Toronto: University of Toronto Press.

Baldassarre, I. (1981). 'Piramo e Tisbe: dal mito all'immagine', in *L'art décoratif à Rome à la fin de la République et au début du Principat. Table ronde organisée par l'École française de Rome (Rome, 10–11 mai 1979)*. Paris: de Boccard, 337–51.

Baldo, G. (1995). *Dall'Eneide alle Metamorfosi*. Padua: Imprimitur.

Balty, J. (1982). 'La Mosaïque au Proche-Orient I', *ANRW* 2.12.2: 347–429.

Barchiesi, A. (1984). 'Narratività e convenzione nelle *Heroides*', *MD* 19: 63–90.

—— (1988). 'Ovid the Censor', *AJAH* 13: 96–105.

—— (1991). 'Discordant Muses', *PCPhS* 37:1–21.

—— (1992). *P. Ovidii Nasonis: Epistulae Heroidum 1–3*. Florence: Le Monnier.

—— (1993). 'Insegnare ad Augusto: Orazio *Epistole* 2.1 e Ovidio, *Tristia* II', *MD* 31: 149–84. Trans. in Barchiesi (2001) 79–103.

—— (1997). *The Poet and the Prince: Ovid and Augustan Discourse*. Berkeley: University of California Press.

—— (1999). 'Venus' masterplot: Ovid and Homeric Hymns', in Hardie et al. (1999) 112–26.

—— (2001). *Speaking Volumes*. London: Duckworth.

—— (2002). 'Narrative Technique and Narratology in the *Metamorphoses*', in Hardie (2002*b*) 180–99.

Barchiesi, M. (1962). *Nevio epico*. Padua: Cedam.

Barkan, L. (1986). *The Gods made Flesh: Metamorphosis and the Pursuit of Paganism*. New Haven and London: Yale University Press.

Barnes, T. D. (1974). 'The Victories of Augustus', *JRS* 64: 21–6.

Barns, J. W. B. and Lloyd-Jones, H. (1963). 'Un nuovo frammento papiraceo dell'elegia ellenistica', *SIFC* 35: 205–72.

Bartelink, G. J. M. (1965). *Etymologisering bij Vergilius*. Amsterdam: Noord-Hollandsche Uitg. Mij.

Barthes, R. (1979). *A Lover's Discourse: Fragments*. London: Cape.

Bassett, E. L. (1966). 'Hercules and the Hero of the *Punica*', in L. Wallach (ed.), *The Classical Tradition: Literary and Historical Studies in Honor of Harry Caplan*. Ithaca: Cornell University Press, 258–73.

Beard, M. (1987). 'A Complex of Times: No More Sheep on Romulus' Birthday', *PCPhS* 33: 1–15.

Bennett, A. W. (1968). 'The Patron and Poetical Inspiration, Prop. 3.9', *Hermes* 96: 319–40.

Berger, J. (1972). *Ways of Seeing*. Harmondsworth: Penguin.

Berman, K. E. (1975). 'Ovid, Propertius and the Elegiac Genre: Some Imitations in the *Amores*', *Rivista di Studi Classici* 23: 14–22.

Bertini, F. (1983). *Ovidio: Amori*. Milan: Garzanti.

Bing, P. (1981). 'The Voice of Those Who Live in the Sea: Empedocles and Callimachus', *ZPE* 41: 33–6.

Binns, J. W. (ed.) (1973). *Ovid*. London: Routledge and Kegan Paul.

Blodgett, E. D. (1973). 'The Well-Wrought Void: Reflections on the *Ars Amatoria*', *CJ* 68: 322–33.

Bloom, H. (1973). *The Anxiety of Influence. A Theory of Poetry*. New York: Oxford University Press.

Blümner, H. (1872). *Technologie und Terminologie der Gewerbe und Künste bei Griechen und Römern*. Leipzig: Teubner.

Bömer, F. (1957–8). *P. Ovidius Naso: Die Fasten*. Heidelberg: Winter.

—— (1968). 'Ovid und die Sprache Vergils', in Albrecht and Zinn (1968) 173–202.

—— (1969). *P. Ovidius Naso Metamorphosen Buch I–III*. Heidelberg: Winter.

—— (1976). *P. Ovidius Naso: Metamorphosen. Buch IV–V*. Heidelberg: Winter.

—— (1982). *P. Ovidius Naso: Metamorphosen. Buch XII–XIII*. Heidelberg: Winter.

—— (1986). *P. Ovidius Naso: Metamorphosen. Buch XIV-XV*. Heidelberg: Winter.

—— (1988). 'Über das zeitliche Verhältnis zwischen den *Fasten* und den *Metamorphosen* Ovids', *Gymnasium* 95: 207–21.

Boucher, J.-P. (1965). *Études sur Properce: problèmes d'inspiration et d'art*. Paris: de Broccard.

Boyd, B. W. (1983). '*Cydonea Mala*: Vergilian Word-play and Allusion', *HSPh* 87: 169–74.

—— (1990). '*Non hortamine longo*: An Ovidian "Correction" of Virgil', *AJPh* 111: 82–5.

Boyd, B. W. (1997). *Ovid's Literary Loves: Influence and Innovation in the Amores*. Ann Arbor: University of Michigan Press.

_____ (ed.) (2002). *Brill's Companion to Ovid*. Leiden: Brill.

Boyle, A. J. and Woodard, R. D. (2004). *Ovid: Fasti. Translated and Edited with an Introduction and Notes*. London: Penguin.

Braccesi, L. (1984). *La leggenda di Antenore da Troia a Padova*. Padua: Signum.

Bramble, J. C. (1974). *Persius and the Programmatic Satire*. Cambridge: Cambridge University Press.

Brandt, P. (1911). *P. Ovidi Nasonis Amorum libri tres: Text und Kommentar*. Leipzig: Dieterich.

_____ (1963). *P. Ovidi Nasonis Amorum libri tres*. Hildesheim: Georg Olms.

Braun, L. (1981). 'Kompositionskunst in Ovids *Fasti*', *ANRW* 2.31.4: 2344–85.

Brenkman, J. (1976). 'Narcissus in the Text', *Georgia Review* 30: 293–327.

Bretzigheimer, G. (1991). 'Exul ludens: Zur Rolle von *relegans* und *relegatus* in Ovids *Tristien*', *Gymnasium* 98: 39–76.

_____ (2001). *Ovids* Amores: *Poetik in der Erotik*. Classica Monacensia 22. Tübingen: G. Narr.

Bright, D. F. (1978). *Haec mihi fingebam: Tibullus in his World*. Leiden: Brill.

Brink, C.O. (1971). *Horace on Poetry: The Ars Poetica*. Cambridge: Cambridge University Press.

_____ (1982). *Horace on Poetry: Epistles Book II: The Letters to Augustus and Florus*. Cambridge: Cambridge University Press.

_____ (1985). *Horace on Poetry II: The Ars Poetica*. 2nd edn. Cambridge: Cambridge University Press.

Brown, R. D. (1987). *Lucretius on Love and Sex. A Commentary on* De rerum natura *IV, 1030–1287*. Leiden: Brill.

_____ (1990). 'The Homeric Background to a Vergilian Repetition (*Aeneid* 1.744 = 3.516)', *AJPh* 111:182–6.

Brown, S. A. (1999). *The Metamorphosis of Ovid: Chaucer to Ted Hughes*. London: Duckworth.

Bruère, R. T. (1959). '*Color Ovidianus* in Silius *Punica* 8–17', *CPh* 54: 228–45.

Brugnoli, G. and Stok, F. (1992). *Ovidius παρῳδήσας*. Pisa: ETS.

Brunt, P. A. (1971). *Italian Manpower 225 BC–AD 14*. Oxford: Oxford University Press.

Bryson, N. (1994). 'Philostratus and the Imaginary Museum', in S. Goldhill and R. Osborne (eds.), *Art and Text in Ancient Greek Culture*. Cambridge: Cambridge University Press, 255–83.

Buchan, M. (1995). 'Ovidius Imperamator: Beginnings and Endings of Love Poems and Empire in the *Amores*', *Arethusa* 28: 53–85.

Buchheit, V. (1972). *Der Anspruch des Dichters in Vergils Georgika*. Darmstadt: Wissenschaftliche Buchgesellschaft.

Büchner, K. (1957). *Humanitas Romana*. Heidelberg: Winter.

Butler, H. E. and Barber, E. A. (1933). *The Elegies of Sex. Propertius*. Oxford: Clarendon Press.

Cahen, E. (1929). *Callimaque et son oeuvre poétique*. Paris: E. de Boccard.

Cahoon, L. (1983). 'Juno's chaste festival and Ovid's wanton loves. *Amores* 3.13', *Classical Antiquity* 2: 1–8.

——— (1984). 'The Parrot and the Poet: the Function of Ovid's Funeral Elegies', *CJ* 80: 27–35.

Cairns, F. (1979*a*). *Tibullus: A Hellenistic Poet at Rome*. Cambridge: Cambridge University Press.

——— (1979*b*). 'Self-Imitation within a Generic Framework: Ovid, *Amores* 2.9 and 3.11 and the *renuntiatio amoris*', in West and Woodman (1979) 121–41.

——— (1984). 'Propertius and the Battle of Actium', in Woodman and West (1984) 129–68.

Calza, G. (1940). *La Necropoli del Porto di Roma nell' Isola Sacra*. Rome: La libreria dello stato.

Cameron, A. (1968). 'The First Edition of Ovid's *Amores*', *CQ* 18: 320–33.

——— (2004). *Greek Mythography in the Roman World*. New York: Oxford University Press.

Cameron, Averil (ed.) (1989). *History as Text: The Writing of Ancient History*. London: Duckworth.

Camps, W.A. (1967). *Propertius: Elegies Book II*. Cambridge: Cambridge University Press.

Canciani, F. (1981). 'Aineias', in Boardman, J. et al. (1981–), *Lexicon Iconographicum Mythologiae Classicae* 1.1: 381–96.

Casali, S. (1995). *Heroidum Epistula: Deianira Herculi*. Florence: Felice Le Monnier.

——— (1999). '*Facta Impia* (Virgil, *Aeneid* 4.596–9)', *CQ* 49: 203–11.

——— (2003). 'L'errore di Anchise e altre correzioni ovidiane all'*Eneide*', in L. Landolfi and P. Monella (eds.), *Ars adeo latet arte sua: riflessioni sull'intertestualità ovidiana*. Palermo: Flaccovio, 81–101.

——— (2004). 'Terre mobili: la topografia di Azio in Virgilio (*Aen.* 3.274–89), in Ovidio (*Met.* 13.713–5) e in Servio', in F. Stok and C. Santini (eds.), *Hinc Italae gentes: geopolitica ed etnografia italica nel commento di Servio all'Eneide*. Pisa: ETS, 45–74.

——— (2004–5). 'Further Voices in Ovid, *Heroides* 7', *Hermathena* 177–8: 141–58.

Càssola, F. (1991). 'Le origini di Roma e l'età regia in Diodoro', in E. Galvagno and C. Molè Ventura (eds.), *Mito storia tradizione: Diodoro Siculo e la storiografia classica.* Catania: Prisma, 273–324.

Castiglioni, L. (1906). *Studi intorno alle fonti e alla composizione delle Metamorfosi di Ovidio.* Pisa: Nistri.

Castle, T. (1986). *Masquerade and Civilization: The Carnivalesque in Eighteenth-century English Culture and Fiction.* Stanford: Stanford University Press.

Chantraine, P. (1968–80). *Dictionnaire étymologique de la langue grecque, histoire des mots.* Paris: Klincksieck.

Chwalek, B. (1996). *Die Verwandlung des Exils in die elegische Welt: Studien zu den* Tristia *und* Epistulae ex Ponto *Ovids.* Studien zur klassischen Philologie, 96. Frankfurt am Main: P. Lang.

Claassen, J.-M. (1986). *Poeta, exsul, vates: A Stylistic and Literary Analysis of Ovid's Tristia and Epistulae ex Ponto.* Diss. Stellenbosch.

_____ (1990). 'Ovid's Poetic Pontus', *PLLS* 6: 65–94.

_____ (1999). *Displaced Persons: The Literature of Exile from Cicero to Boethius.* London: Duckworth.

Clausen, W. (1964). 'Callimachus and Latin Poetry', *GRBS* 5: 181–95.

_____ (1982). 'Theocritus and Vergil', in Kenney and Clausen (1982) 310–19.

_____ (1994). *A Commentary on Virgil: Eclogues.* Oxford: Oxford University Press.

Clauss, J. J. (1988). 'Vergil and the Euphrates Revisited', *AJPh* 109: 309–20.

Clayman, D.E. (1980). *Callimachus' Iambi.* Leiden: E. J. Brill.

_____ (1988). 'Callimachus' Iambi and Aitia', *ZPE* 74: 277–86.

Coarelli, F. (1983). *Il foro romano, periodo arcaico.* Rome: Quasar.

Conington, J. (1883). *The Works of Virgil.* 4th edn. rev. by H. Nettleship. London: Whittaker.

Connors, C. M. (1989). *Petronius' 'Bellum Civile' and the poetics of discord.* Diss. Michigan.

Conte, G. B. (1974). *Memoria dei poeti e sistema letterario.* Turin: Einaudi.

_____ (1984). *Virgilio: Il genere e i suoi confini.* Milan: Garzanti.

_____ (1986). *The Rhetoric of Imitation: Genre and Poetic Memory in Virgil and Other Latin Poets.* Ithaca and London: Cornell University Press.

_____ (1989). 'Love without Elegy: The *Remedia Amoris* and the Logic of a Genre', *Poetics Today* 10: 441–69. (Reprinted (1994) in *Genres and Readers: Lucretius, Love Elegy, Pliny's Encyclopedia.* Trans. by G.W. Most. Baltimore: Johns Hopkins University Press.)

_____ (1990). 'Insegnamenti per un lettore sublime'. Introduction to L. Canali, G. B. Conte, and I. Dionigi (eds.), *Lucrezio, La natura delle cose.* Milan: Rizzoli.

Cook, J. M. (1973). *The Troad*. Oxford: Clarendon Press.

Courtney, E. (1969). 'Three Poems of Propertius', *BICS* 16: 73–87.

Culler, J. (1975). *Structuralist Poetics: Structuralism, Linguistics, and the Study of Literature*. Ithaca: Cornell University Press.

Cunningham, M. P. (1949). 'The Novelty of Ovid's *Heroides*', *CPh* 44: 100–6.

Curran, L. C. (1975). 'Nature to Advantage Dressed: Propertius 1.2', *Ramus* 4.1: 1–16.

Curtius, E. R. (1953). *European Literature and the Latin Middle Ages*. Trans. W. Trask. New York: Pantheon.

Daly, L. W. (1950). '*Vota publica pro salute alicuius*', *TAPhA* 81: 164–8.

Daube, D. (1951). '*Ne quid infamandi causa fiat*: The Roman Law of Defamation', *Atti del congresso internazionale di diritto romano e di storia del diritto, 1948*. Milan: A. Giuffrè, 3.411–50.

Davies, J. (1653). *The Extravagant Shepherd: The Anti-Romance. Or, the History of the Shepherd Lysis*. London: Thomas Heath.

Davis, G. (1978). 'Ovid's *Metamorphoses* 3.442 ff. and the Prologue to Menander's *Misoumenos*', *Phoenix* 32: 339–42.

——— (1983). *The Death of Procris: 'Amor' and the Hunt in Ovid's Metamorphoses*. Rome: Ed. dell'Ateneo.

Davis, J. T. (1981). 'Risit Amor: Aspects of Literary Burlesque in Ovid's *Amores*', *ANRW* 2.31.4: 2460–506.

——— (1989). *Fictus Adulter: Poet as Actor in the* Amores. Amsterdam: J. C. Gieben.

Davisson, M. H. T. (1984). 'Parents and Children in Ovid's Poems from Exile', *CW* 78: 111–14.

Day, A. A. (1938). *The Origins of Latin Love-Elegy*. Oxford: Blackwell.

DeBrohun, J. B. (1994). 'Redressing Elegy's *Puella*: Propertius IV and the Rhetoric of Fashion', *JRS* 84: 41–63.

Deremetz, A. (1995). *Le miroir des Muses: poétiques de la réflexivité à Rome*. Villeneuve d'Ascq: Presses Universitaires du Septentrion.

Derrida, J. (1981). *Dissemination*. Trans. B. Johnson. Chicago: University of Chicago Press.

Desmond, M. (1993). 'When Dido Reads Ovid: Gender and Intertextuality in Ovid's *Heroides* 7', *Helios* 20: 56–68.

Dickie, M. (1981). 'The Disavowal of *Invidia* in Roman Iamb and Satire', *PLLS* 3: 183–208.

Diggle, J. (1967). 'Notes on the Text of Ovid's *Heroides*', *CQ* 17: 136–44.

Diller, H. (1934). 'Die dichterische Eigenart von Ovids Metamorphosen', *Hum. Gymn.* 45: 25–37.

Dixon, S. (1988). *The Roman Mother*. London: Croom Helm.

Dixon, S. (2001). *Reading Roman Women: Sources, Genres and Real Life*. London: Duckworth.

Döpp, S. (1969). *Virgilischer Einfluss im Werk Ovids*. Munich: UNI-Druck.

—— (1991). 'Vergilrezeption in der Ovidischen "Aeneis"', *RhM* 134: 327–45.

—— (1992): *Werke Ovids: Eine Einführung*. Munich: Deutscher Taschenbuch Verlag.

Dörrie, H. (1968). *Der Heroische Brief: Bestandaufnahme, Geschichte, Kritik einer humanistische-barocken Dichtgattung*. Berlin: De Gruyter.

—— (1971). *P. Ovidii Nasonis Epistulae Heroidum*. Berlin: De Gruyter.

—— (1975). *P. Ovidius Naso: Der Brief der Sappho an Phaon mit literarischem und kritischem Kommentar im Rahmen einer motivgeschichtlichen Studie*. Munich: Zetemata 58.

Duckworth, G. E. (1931). 'ΠΡΟΑΝΑΦΩΝΗΣΙΣ in the Scholia to Homer', *AJPh* 52: 320–38.

Due, O. S. (1973). 'Zur Etymologisierung in der Aeneis', in O. S. Due, N. Friis Johansen, and B. Dalsgaard Larsen (eds.), *Classica et mediaevalia F. Blatt septuagenario dedicata*. Copenhagen: Gyldendal, 270–9.

—— (1974). *Changing Forms: Studies in the* Metamorphoses *of Ovid*. Copenhagen: Gyldendal.

Duke, T. T. (1971). 'Ovid's Pyramus and Thisbe', *CJ* 66: 320–7.

Du Quesnay, I. M. LeM. (1973). 'The *Amores*', in Binns (1973) 1–48.

—— (1981). 'Vergil's First Eclogue', *PLLS* 3: 29–182.

—— (1984). 'Horace and Maecenas: The Propaganda Value of *Sermones* 1', in Woodman and West (1984) 19–58.

Durante, M. (1976). *Sulla preistoria della tradizione poetica greca*. Rome: Edizioni dell' Ateneo.

—— (1977). *Sulla preistoria della tradizione poetica greca. Parte seconda: risultanze della comparazione indoeuropea*. Rome: Ateneo & Bizzarri.

Durling, R. M. (1958). 'Ovid as *Praeceptor Amoris*', *CJ* 53: 157–67.

Dyson, J. T. (1997). 'Birds, Grandfathers, and Neoteric Sorcery in *Aeneid* 4.254 and 7.412', *CQ* 47: 314–15.

Edmunds, L. (2001). *Intertextuality and the Reading of Roman Poetry*. Baltimore and London: The Johns Hopkins University Press.

Edwards, C. (1993). *The Politics of Immorality in Ancient Rome*. Cambridge: Cambridge University Press.

Ehwald, R. (ed.) (1915). *Metamorphoses*. Leipzig: Teubner.

Eisenhut, W. (1961). '*Deducere carmen*: ein Beitrag zum Problem der literarischen Beziehungen zwischen Horaz und Properz', in G. Radke (ed.), *Gedenkschrift für G. Rohde*. Tübingen: Niemeyer, 91–104 (= W. Eisenhut (ed.) (1975). *Properz*. Darmstadt: Wissenschaftliche Buchgesellschaft, 247–63.)

Eliades, G. S. (1982). *Die Villa mit den Mosaiken von Nea Paphos: Das Haus des Dionysus*, 2nd edn. Paphos: G.S. Eliades.

Elliott, R. C. (1982). *The Literary Persona*. Chicago and London: University of Chicago Press.

Ellis, Robinson (1876). *A Commentary on Catullus*. Oxford: Clarendon Press.

—— (1881). *P. Ovidii Nasonis Ibis*. Oxford: Clarendon Press.

—— (1889). *Catulli Veronensis Liber*. 2nd edn. Oxford: Clarendon Press.

Evans, H. B. (1983). *Publica Carmina: Ovid's Books from Exile*. Lincoln: University of Nebraska Press.

Ewbank, W.W. (1933). *The Poems of Cicero*. London: University of London Press.

Fairweather, J. (1987). 'Ovid's Autobiographical Poem, *Tristia* 4.10', *CQ* 37: 181–96.

Fantham, R. E. (1972). *Comparative Studies in Republican Latin Imagery*. Toronto: University of Toronto Press.

—— (1982). *Seneca's Troades, a Literary Introduction, Text and Commentary*. Princeton: Princeton University Press.

—— (1983). 'Sexual Comedy in Ovid's *Fasti*: Sources and Motivation', *HSPh* 87: 185–216.

—— (1985). 'Ovid, Germanicus and the Composition of the *Fasti*', *PLLS* 5: 243–81.

—— (1992). 'Ceres, Liber and Flora: Georgic and Anti-georgic Elements in Ovid's *Fasti*', *PCPhS* 38: 39–56.

—— (1998). *Ovid, Fasti: Book IV*. Cambridge: Cambridge University Press.

Fantuzzi, M. (1980). '*Ek Dios archomestha*. Arat. *Phaen*. 1 e Theocr. XVII 1', *MD* 5: 163–72.

Fauth, W. (1978). 'Römische Religion im Spiegel der *Fasti* des Ovid', *ANRW* 2.16.1: 104–86.

Fears, J. R. (1981). 'The Cult of Virtues and Roman Imperial Ideology', *ANRW* 2.17.2: 827–948.

Fedeli, P. (1980). *Sesto Properzio: Il primo libro delle elegie*. Florence: Olschki.

—— (1985). *Properzio: Il libro terzo delle elegie*. Bari: Adriatica Editrice.

—— (1986). 'La matrona di Efeso', in L. Pepe (ed.), *Semiotica della novella latina*. Rome: Herder, 9–35.

—— and Dimundo, R. (eds.) (1988). *Petronio Arbitro, I racconti del 'Satyricon'*. Rome: Salerno.

Feeney, D. C. (1986). 'History and Revelation in Vergil's Underworld', *PCPhS* 32: 1–24.

—— (1989). Review of Conte (1986). *JRS* 79: 206–7.

—— (1991). *The Gods in Epic: Poets and Critics of the Classical Tradition*. Oxford: Oxford University Press.

Feichtinger, B. (1989). 'Poetische Fiktion bei Properz', *GB* 76: 143–82.

Ferguson, J. (1960). 'Catullus and Ovid', *AJPh* 81: 337–57.

Fetterley, J. (1978). *The Resisting Reader: A Feminist Approach to American Literature.* Bloomington, Indiana: Indiana University Press.

Fishwick, D. (1969). '*Genius* and *Numen*', *HThR* 62: 356–67.

Fleisher, U. (1957). 'Zur Zweitausendjahrfeier Ovids', *A&A* 6: 27–59.

Flory, M. (1984). '*Sic exempla parantur*: Livia's shrine to Concordia and the Porticus Liviae', *Historia* 33: 309–30.

Flynn, St. J. E. (1997). 'The saint of the womanly body: Raimon de Cornet's fourteenth-century male poetics', in Gold et al. (1997) 91–109.

Focardi, G. (1975). 'Difesa, preghiera, ironia nel II libro dei *Tristia* di Ovidio', *SIFC* 47: 86–129.

Forbes Irving, P. M. C. (1990). *Metamorphosis in Greek Myths.* Oxford: Clarendon Press.

Fordyce, C. J. (1961). *Catullus: A Commentary.* Oxford: Clarendon Press.

Forster, L. (1969). *The Icy Fire: Five Studies in European Petrarchism.* Cambridge: Cambridge University Press.

Forsyth, P. Y. (1977). 'Comments on Catullus 116', *CQ* 27: 352–3.

Fränkel, H. (1945). *Ovid: A Poet Between Two Worlds.* Berkeley: University of California Press.

Frazer, J. G. (1913). *The Golden Bough. Vol.* 9. *The Scapegoat,* 3rd edn. London: Macmillan.

—— (1931). *Ovid's* Fasti. Cambridge, Mass.: Harvard University Press.

Frécaut, J.-M. (1972). *L' esprit et l'humour chez Ovide.* Grenoble: Presses universitaires de Grenoble.

Fredrick, D. (1997). 'Reading Broken Skin: Violence in Roman Elegy', in Hallett and Skinner (1997) 172–93.

Fredericks, B. R. (1976). '*Tristia* 4.10: Poet's Autobiography and Poetic Auto-biography', *TAPhA* 106: 139–54.

Freund, E. (1987). *The Return of the Reader.* London: Methuen.

Fulkerson, L. (2005). *The Ovidian Heroine as Author: Reading, Writing, and Community in the Heroides.* Cambridge: Cambridge University Press.

Fyler, J. M. (1971). '*Omnia Vincit Amor*: Incongruity and the Limitations of Structure in Ovid's Elegiac Poetry', *CJ* 66: 196–203.

Gabba, E. (1967). 'Considerazioni sulla tradizione letteraria sulle origini della Repubblica', in *Entretiens Hardt sur l'antiquité classique* 13. Geneva: Vandoeuvres, 135–74.

_____ (1976). 'Sulla valorizzazione politica della leggenda delle origini troiane di Roma fra III e II secolo a.C.', in M. Sordi (ed.), *I canali della propaganda nel mondo antico*. Milan: Vita e pensiero, 84–101.

Gaertner, J. F. (2005). *Ovid:* Epistulae ex Ponto, *Book I*. Oxford: Oxford University Press.

Galasso, L. (1995). *P. Ovidii Nasonis Epistularum ex Ponto Liber II*. Florence: Felice Le Monnier.

_____ (2000). *Ovidio: Opere 2. Le metamorfosi*. Turin: Einaudi.

Galinsky, K. (1969*a*). *Aeneas, Sicily and Rome*. Princeton: Princeton University Press.

_____ (1969*b*). 'The Triumph Theme in the Augustan elegy', *WS* 3: 75–107.

_____ (1972). *The Herakles Theme: The Adaptation of the Hero in Literature from Homer to the Twentieth Century*. Oxford: Blackwell.

_____ (1974). 'Ovid's Metamorphosis of Myth', in K. Galinsky (ed.), *Perspectives of Roman Poetry: A Classics Symposium*. Austin: University of Texas Press, 105–27.

_____ (1975). *Ovid's* Metamorphoses: *An Introduction to the Basic Aspects*. Berkeley and Los Angeles: University of California Press.

_____ (1996) *Augustan Culture: An Interpretive Introduction*. Princeton: Princeton University Press.

Galletier, E. (1922). *Étude sur la poésie funéraire romaine d'après les inscriptions*. Paris: Hachette.

Gallo, I. and Nicastri, L. (eds.) (1995). *Aetates Ovidianae: lettori di Ovidio dall' antichità al Rinascimento*. Naples: Edizioni Scientifiche Italiane.

Gauly, B. M. (1990). *Liebeserfahrungen: Zur Rolle des elegischen Ich in Ovids Amores*. Studien zur klassischen Philologie, 48.Frankfurt am Main: Lang.

Genette, G. (1976). *Figures III*. Paris: Éditions du Seuil.

_____ (1980). *Narrative Discourse: An Essay in Method*. Trans. J. E. Lewin. Ithaca: Cornell University Press.

_____ (1983). *Nouveau discours du récit*. Paris: Éditions du Seuil.

Georgii, H. (1891). *Die antike Äneiskritik*. Stuttgart: Kohlhammer.

Giangrande, G. (1981). 'Hellenistic Topoi in Ovid's *Amores*', *Museum Philol. Lond.* 4: 25–51.

Gibson, R. K. (2003). *Ovid, Ars Amatoria: Book 3*. Cambridge: Cambridge University Press.

Gigon, O. (1956). *Kommentar zum zweiten Buch von Xenophons Memorabilien*. Schweizerische Beiträge zur Altertumswissenschaft, Heft 7. Basel: Verlag Friedrich Reinhardt.

Gilbert, C. D. (1976). 'Ovid, *Met.* 1.4', *CQ* 26: 111–12.

Gildenhard, I. and Zissos, A. (1999). '"Somatic Economies": Tragic Bodies and Poetic Design in Ovid's *Metamorphoses*', in Hardie et al. (1999) 162–81.

Gold, B. K., Miller, P. A., and Platter, C. (1997). *Sex and Gender in Medieval and Renaissance Texts: The Latin Tradition.* Albany: State University of New York Press.

Goodyear, F. R. D. (1981). *The Annals of Tacitus, Vol. II (Annals 1.55–81 and Annals 2).* Cambridge: Cambridge University Press.

Goold, G. P. (1977). *Manilius: Astronomica.* Cambridge, Mass.: Harvard University Press.

—— (1983). 'The Cause of Ovid's Exile', *ICS* 8: 94–107.

Gordon, R. (1990). 'From Republic to Principate: Priesthood, Religion, and Ideology', in M. Beard and J. North (eds.), *Pagan Priests.* London: Duckworth, 179–98.

Gorni, G. (1979). 'La metafora di testo', *Strumenti Critici* 38: 18–32.

Gow, A. S. F. and Page, D. L. (eds.) (1965). *The Greek Anthology: Hellenistic Epigrams.* Cambridge: Cambridge University Press.

—— (1968). *The Greek Anthology: The Garland of Philip.* Cambridge: Cambridge University Press.

Graf, F. (1988). 'Ovide, les *Métamorphoses* et la véracité du mythe', in C. Calame (ed.), *Métamorphoses du mythe en Grèce antique.* Geneva: Labor et Fides, 57–70.

Gransden, K. W. (1976). *Virgil: Aeneid VIII.* Cambridge: Cambridge University Press.

Green, P. (1982*a*). *Ovid: the Erotic Poems. Translated with an Introduction and Notes.* Harmondsworth: Penguin.

—— (1982*b*). '*Carmen et Error*', *Classical Antiquity* 1: 202–20.

—— (2005). *Ovid. The Poems of Exile: Tristia and Black Sea Letters.* Berkeley: University of California Press.

Green, S. J. (2004). *Ovid, Fasti 1: A Commentary.* Leiden: Brill.

Greene, E. (1998). *The Erotics of Domination: Male Desire and the Mistress in Latin Love Poetry.* Baltimore: Johns Hopkins University Press.

—— (2000). 'Gender Identity and the Elegiac Hero in Propertius 2.1', *Arethusa* 33: 241–61.

Griffin, J. (1984). 'Augustus and the Poets: "*Caesar qui cogere posset*"', in F. Millar and E. Segal (eds.), *Caesar Augustus: Seven Aspects.* Oxford: Oxford University Press, 189–218.

—— (1985). *Latin Poets and Roman Life.* London: Duckworth.

Grisart, A. (1959). 'La publication des Métamorphoses: une source du recit d'Ovide', in Paratore (1959) 125–56.

Gross, N. P. (1975–6). 'Ovid, *Amores* 3.11A and B: a literary mélange', *CJ* 71: 152–60.

Guthmüller, B. (1981). *Ovidio metamorphoseos vulgare: Formen und Funktionen der volkssprachlichen Wiedergabe klassischer Dichtung in der italienischen Renaissance*. Boppard am Rhein: Boldt.

Habinek, T. N. (1998). *The Politics of Latin Literature: Writing, Identity, and Empire in Ancient Rome*. Princeton: Princeton University Press.

Hallett, J. P. and Skinner, M. B. (eds.) (1997). *Roman Sexualities*. Princeton: Princeton University Press.

Hardie, P. R. (1986). *Virgil's* Aeneid: *Cosmos and Imperium*. Oxford: Oxford University Press.

——— (1991). 'The Janus Episode in Ovid's *Fasti*', *MD* 26:47–64.

——— (1992). 'Augustan Poets and the Mutability of Rome', in A. Powell (ed.), *Roman Poetry and Propaganda in the Age of Augustus*. London: Bristol Classical Press, 59–82.

——— (1993). *The Epic Successors of Virgil: A Study in the Dynamics of a Tradition*. Cambridge: Cambridge University Press.

——— (1998). 'Fame and Defamation in the *Aeneid*: the Council of Latins (*Aeneid* 11.225–467)', in H.-P. Stahl (ed.), *Vergil's Aeneid: Augustan Epic and Political Context*. London: Duckworth, 243–70.

——— (2002*a*). *Ovid's Poetics of Illusion*. Cambridge: Cambridge University Press.

——— (ed.) (2002*b*). *The Cambridge Companion to Ovid*. Cambridge: Cambridge University Press.

——— Barchiesi, A., and Hinds S. (eds.) (1999). *Ovidian Transformations: Essays on Ovid's* Metamorphoses *and its Reception*. Cambridge: Cambridge Philological Society.

Harries, B. (1989). 'Causation and the Authority of the Poet in Ovid's *Fasti*', *CQ* 38: 164–85.

——— (1990). 'The Spinner and the Poet: Arachne in Ovid's *Metamorphoses*', *PCPhS* 36: 64–82.

Hartman, J. J. (1905). *De Ovidio poeta commentatio*. Leiden: E.J. Brill.

Harvey, E. D. (1989). 'Ventriloquizing Sappho: Ovid, Donne, and the Erotics of the Feminine Voice', *Criticism* 31: 115–38.

Harvey, P. (1937). *The Oxford Companion to Classical Literature*. Oxford: Oxford University Press.

Harvey, S. (1980). 'Woman's Place: The Absent Family of Film Noir', in E. A. Kaplan (ed.), *Women in Film Noir*. London: British Film Institute, 22–34.

Haupt, M. (1876). *Opuscula*. Leipzig: Hirzel.

Haupt, M., Korn, O., Ehwald, R., and von Albrecht, M. (1966). *P. Ovidius Naso, Metamorphosen*. Zurich-Dublin: Weidmann.

Heath, M. (1985). 'Hesiod's didactic Poetry', *CQ* 35: 245–63.

Heinze, R. (1915). *Vergils epische Technik*. Leipzig: Teubner.

——— (1919). 'Ovids elegische Erzählung'. *Sitzungsberichte der Sächsischen Akademie der Wissenschaften, phil.-hist. Kl.* 71,7.Leipzig. (= Heinze (1960) 308–403.)

——— (1960). *Vom Geist des Römertums*, ed. E. Burck. 3rd edn. Stuttgart: Teubner.

Heldmann, K. (1994). 'Ovids Sabinus-Gedicht (*Am.* 2,18) und die "Epistulae Heroidum"', *Hermes* 122: 188–219.

Helzle, M. (2003). *Ovids Epistulae ex Ponto, Buch I-II: Kommentar*. Heidelberg: C. Winter.

Henderson, A. A. R. (1969). 'Tibullus, Elysium and Tartarus', *Latomus* 28: 649–53.

Henderson, J. (1986). 'Becoming a Heroine (1st): Penelope's Ovid . . .', *LCM* 11.1: 7–10.

——— (1999). 'Ch-ch-ch-changes', in Hardie et al. (1999) 301–23.

Herbert-Brown, G. (1994). *Ovid and the* Fasti: *An Historical Study*. Oxford: Oxford University Press.

——— (ed.) (2002). *Ovid's* Fasti: *Historical Readings at its Bimillennium*. Oxford: Oxford University Press.

Herescu, N. I. (1958). *Ovidiana: recherches sur Ovide*. Paris: Les Belles Lettres.

Herrlinger, G. (1930). *Totenklage um Tiere in der antiken Dichtung*. Stuttgart: W. Kohlhammer.

Herrmann, P. and Bruckmann, F. (1906). *Denkmäler der Malerei des Altertums*. Munich: F. Bruckmann.

Herter, H. (1937). 'Bericht über die Literatur zur hellenistischen Dichtung aus den Jahren 1921–35', *Bursians Jahresb.* 255: 65–226.

——— (1948). 'Ovids Kunstprinzip in den Metamorphosen', *AJPh* 69: 129–48. (= Albrecht and Zinn 1968: 340–61.)

——— (1981). 'Ovidianum Quintum', *ICS* 6: 319–55.

Heydenreich, T. (1970). *Tadel und Lob der Seefahrt: Das Nachleben eines antiken Themas in der romanischen Literatur*. Studien zum Fortwirken der Antike, 5. Heidelberg: Winter.

Heyne, Chr. G. (ed.) (1833). *P. Vergilius Maro*. 4th edn. by G. P. E. Wagner. Leipzig: Hahn.

Hinds, S. (1982). 'An Allusion in the Literary Tradition of the Proserpina Myth', *CQ* 32: 476–8.

——— (1985). 'Booking the Return Trip: Ovid and *Tristia* 1', *PCPhS* 31: 13–32 (= ch. 18 of this volume).

——— (1987*a*). *The Metamorphosis of Persephone: Ovid and the Self-Conscious Muse*. Cambridge: Cambridge University Press.

_____ (1987*b*). 'Generalising about Ovid', *Ramus* 16: 4–31.

_____ (1992). '*Arma* in Ovid's *Fasti*—Part I: Genre and Mannerism', *Arethusa* 25: 81–112; 'Part II: Genre, Romulean Rome and Augustan Ideology', *Arethusa* 25: 113–53.

_____ (1993). 'Medea in Ovid: Scenes from the Life of an Intertextual Heroine', *MD* 30: 9–47.

_____ (1998). *Allusion and Intertext: Dynamics of Appropriation in Roman Poetry*. Cambridge: Cambridge University Press.

_____ (1999). 'After Exile: Time and Teleology from *Metamorphoses* to *Ibis*', in Hardie et al. (1999) 48–67.

Hofmann, H. (1986). 'Ovid's *Metamorphoses: carmen perpetuum, carmen deductum*', *PLLS* 5: 223–41.

Hofmann, M. and Lasdun, J. (eds.) (1994). *After Ovid: New Metamorphoses*. London: Faber.

Hollander, J. (1981). *The Figure of Echo. A Mode of Allusion in Milton and After*. Berkeley: University of California Press.

Holleman, A. W. J. (1971). 'Ovid and Politics', *Historia* 20: 458–66.

_____ (1973). 'Ovid and the Lupercalia', *Historia* 22: 260–8.

Hollis, A. S. (ed.) (1970). *Ovid: Metamorphoses, Book VIII*. Oxford: Oxford University Press.

_____ (1973). 'The *Ars Amatoria* and *Remedia Amoris*', in Binns (1973) 84–115.

_____ (1977). *Ovid: Ars Amatoria, Book I*. Oxford: Oxford University Press.

_____ (1983). *Ovid: Metamorphoses, Book VIII*, 2nd edn. Oxford: Oxford University Press.

_____ (1992). 'Hellenistic Colouring in Virgil's Aeneid', *HSPh* 94: 269–85.

Holzberg, N. (1981). 'Ovids erotische Lehrgedichte und die römische Liebeselegie', *WS* 15: 185–204.

_____ (1990). Rev. 2nd edn. (2001). *Die römische Liebeselegie: Eine Einführung*. Darmstadt: Wissenschaftliche Buchgesellschaft.

_____ (1995). 'Enkomionstruktur und Reflexe spätrepublikanischer Realität in der Atticus-Vita des Cornelius Nepos', in P. Neukam (ed.), *Anschauung und Anschaulichkeit*. Dialog Schule–Wissenschaft, 29. Munich: Bayerischer Schulbuch-Verlag, 29–43.

_____ (1997). *Ovid: Dichter und Werk*. Munich: C. H. Beck.

Hopkinson, N. (1988). *A Hellenistic Anthology*. Cambridge: Cambridge University Press.

Horsfall, N. M. (1979). 'Some Problems in the Aeneas-Legend', *CQ* 29: 372–90.

_____ (1986). 'The Aeneas Legend and the *Aeneid*', *Vergilius* 32: 8–17.

_____ (1991*a*). *Virgilio: l'epopea in alambicco*. Naples: Liguori.

Horsfall, N. M. (1991*b*). 'Virgil and the Poetry of Explanations', *G&R* 38: 203–11.

—— (2000). *Vergil: Aeneid 7. A Commentary.* Leiden: E.J. Brill.

Houghton, L. B. T. (2000). 'Ovid's Dead Parrot Sketch: *Amores* II, 6', *Mnemosyne* 53: 718–20.

Housman, A. E. (1897). 'Ovid's *Heroides*', *CR* 11: 102–6 (= J. Diggle and F. R. D. Goodyear (eds.), *The classical papers of A. E. Housman* (Cambridge, 1972) 380–7).

—— (1899). Review of Palmer (1898), *CR* 13: 172–8 (= *Classical Papers* 470–80).

—— (1920). 'The *Ibis* of Ovid', *JPh* 35: 287–318 (= *Classical Papers* 1018–42).

—— (1921). 'Review: A. Rostagni, Ibis', *CR* 35: 67–8 (= *Classical Papers* 1049–51).

Hubbard, M. (1974). *Propertius.* London: Duckworth.

Hughes, T. (1997). *Tales from Ovid.* London: Faber.

Hunter, R. L. (1985). 'Horace on Friendship and Free Speech', *Hermes* 113: 486–90.

Hutchinson, G. O. (1988). *Hellenistic Poetry.* Oxford: Clarendon Press.

—— (2006). 'The Metamorphosis of Metamorphosis: P. Oxy. 4711 and Ovid', *ZPE* 155: forthcoming.

Huys, M. (1991). *Le Poème élégiaque hellénistique P. Brux. Inv. E. 8934 et P. Sorbonn. Inv. 2254.* Brussels: *Papyri Bruxellenses Graecae* vol. II.22.

Imhoof-Blumer, F. (1924). *Fluss- und Meergotter auf griechischen und römischen Münzen.* Geneva: Au siège de la Société.

Innes, D. C. (1979). 'Gigantomachy and Natural Philosophy', *CQ* 29: 165–71.

Jacobs, J. (1890). *De progymnasticorum studiis mythographicis.* Diss. Marburg.

Jacobson, H. (1974). *Ovid's Heroides.* Princeton, NJ: Princeton University Press.

Jal, P. (1961). 'Pax Civilis-Concordia', *REL* 39: 210–31.

Janan, M. (1994). *'When the Lamp is Shattered': Desire and Narrative in Catullus.* Carbondale: Southern Illinois Press.

—— (1998). 'Refashioning Hercules: Propertius 4.9', *Helios* 25: 65–77.

—— (2001). *The Politics of Desire: Propertius IV.* Berkeley: University of California Press.

Jost, F. (1966). 'Le roman épistolaire et la technique narrative au XVIIe siècle', *Comparative Literature Studies* 3: 397–427.

Junod, H. (1991). '*Barbarus ensis* (*Met.* 14.574) ou les ambiguïtés de l'Énéide ovidienne', *EL* 1991: 43–75.

Kaplan, E. A. (ed.) (1980). *Women in Film Noir.* London: British Film Institute.

Karageorghis, V. (1963*a*). 'Chronique des fouilles et découvertes archéologiques à Chypre en 1962', *BCH* 87: 383–5.

_____ (1963*b*). 'Ten Years of Archaeology in Cyprus, 1953–1962', *A&A*: 498–501.

Kaster, R. A. (1995). *Suetonius Tranquillus: De Grammaticis et Rhetoribus.* Oxford: Clarendon Press.

Keith, A. M. (1991). 'Etymological Play on *Ingens* in Ovid, Vergil, and *Octavia*', *AJPh* 112: 73–6.

_____ (1992*a*). *The Play of Fictions: Studies in Ovid's* Metamorphoses *Book* 2. Ann Arbor: University of Michigan Press.

_____ (1992*b*). '*Amores* 1.1 : Propertius and the Ovidian Programme', in C. Deroux (ed.), *Studies in Latin Literature and Roman History VI.* Brussels: Latomus, 327–44.

_____ (1994). '*Corpus Eroticum*: Elegiac Poetics and Elegiac *Puellae* in Ovid's *Amores*', *CW* 88.1: 27–40.

_____ (1999). 'Slender Verse: Roman Elegy and Ancient Rhetorical Theory', *Mnemosyne* 52.1: 41–62.

_____ (2000). *Engendering Rome: Women in Latin Epic.* Cambridge: Cambridge University Press.

Kennedy, D. F. (1984). 'The Epistolary Mode and the First of Ovid's *Heroides*', *CQ* 34: 413–22 (= ch. 3 of this volume.)

_____ (1987). Review of H.-P Stahl, *Propertius: 'Love' and 'War'* (Berkeley 1985), *LCM* 12: 72–7.

_____ (1993). *The Arts of Love: Five Studies in the Discourse of Roman Love Elegy.* Cambridge: Cambridge University Press.

_____ (2002). 'Recent Receptions of Ovid', in Hardie (2002*b*) 320–35.

Kenney, E. J. (1958). 'Nequitiae Poeta', in Herescu (1958) 201–9.

_____ (1961). *P. Ovidi Nasonis Amores, Medicamina Faciei Femineae, Ars Amatoria, Remedia Amoris.* Oxford: Oxford University Press.

_____ (1965). 'The Poetry of Ovid's Exile', *PCPhS* 11: 37–49.

_____ (1970). 'In parenthesis', *CR* 20: 291.

_____ (1973). 'The style of the *Metamorphoses*', in Binns (1973) 116–53 (= B. Boyd (ed.) (2002). *Brill's Companion to Ovid.* Leiden: E. J. Brill, 27–89.)

_____ (1976). 'Ovidius prooemians', *PCPhS* 22: 46–53 (= ch. 12 of this volume).

_____ (1979). '*Iudicium transferendi*: Virgil, *Aeneid* 2.469–505 and its Antecedents', in West and Woodman (1979) 103–20.

_____ (1982). 'Ovid', in Kenney and Clausen (1982) 420–57.

_____ (1986). Introduction and Notes to Melville (1986).

_____ (1990). *Apuleius: Cupid and Psyche.* Cambridge: Cambridge University Press.

Kenney, E. J. (1996). *Ovid: Heroides XVI-XXI*. Cambridge: Cambridge University Press.

—— and Clausen, W. (eds.) (1982). *Cambridge History of Classical Literature, Vol. II*. Cambridge: Cambridge University Press.

Keul, M. (1989). *Liebe im Widerstreit. Interpretationen zu Ovids Amores und ihrem literarischen Hintergrund*. Europäische Hochschulschriften, Reihe XV: Klassische Sprachen und Literaturen, 43. Frankfurt am Main: P. Lang.

Kiessling, A. and Heinze, R. (1968). *Q. Horatius Flaccus, Oden und Epoden*. Zurich and Dublin: Weidmann.

King, J. K. (1980). 'Propertius 2.1–12: His Callimachean Second Libellus', *WJA* 6: 61–84.

—— (1981). 'Propertius 2.2: A Callimachean "multum in parvo"', *WS* 15: 169–84.

Kinsley, J. (1958). *The Poems of John Dryden*. Oxford: Clarendon Press.

Kirfel, E.-A. (1969). *Untersuchungen zur Briefform der Heroides Ovids*. Noctes Romanae Band 11. Bern: Haupt.

Kloft, H. (1984). 'Aspekte der Prinzipatsideologie im frühen Prinzipat', *Gymnasium* 91: 306–26.

Knauer, G. N. (1981). 'Vergil und Homer', *ANRW* 2.31.2: 870–918.

Knox, B. M. W. (1968). 'Silent Reading in Antiquity', *GRBS* 9: 421–35.

Knox, P. E. (1985). 'The Epilogue to the *Aetia*', *GRBS* 26: 59–65.

—— (1986*a*). *Ovid's Metamorphoses and the Traditions of Augustan Poetry*. Cambridge: Cambridge Philological Society.

—— (1986*b*). 'Ovid's *Medea* and the Authenticity of *Heroides* 12', *HSPh* 90: 207–23.

—— (1988). 'Phaethon in Ovid and Nonnus', *CQ* 38: 536–51.

—— (1995). *Ovid: Heroides. Select Epistles*. Cambridge: Cambridge University Press.

—— (2004). 'The Poet and the Second Prince: Ovid in the Age of Tiberius', *Memoirs of the American Academy in Rome* 49: 1–20.

Kolar, A. (1933). 'Inwieweit ist Ovids *Ibis* von der *Ibis* des Kallimachos abhängig?', *PhW* 53: 1243–8.

Kondoleon, C. (1995). *Domestic and Divine: Roman Mosaics in the House of Dionysos*. Ithaca: Cornell University Press.

Korzeniewski, D. (1964). 'Ovids elegisches Proömium', *Hermes*: 92: 182–213.

Kovacs, D. (1987). 'Ovid, *Metamorphoses* 1.2', *CQ* 37: 460–2.

Kraus, W. (1958). 'Der Forschungsbericht: Ovid. I. Bericht, 1. Teil', *AAHG* 11: 129–46.

—— (1968): 'Ovidius Naso', in Albrecht and Zinn (1968) 67–166.

Kroll, W. (1924). *Studien zum Verständnis der römischen Literatur*. Stuttgart: Metzler.

Kuntz, M. (1994). 'The Prodikean "Choice of Herakles". A Reshaping of the Myth', *CJ* 89: 163–81.

Labate, M. (1975). 'Amore coniugale e amore "elegiaco" nell' episodio di Cefalo e Procri', *ASNP* ii. 5: 103–28.

_____ (1984). *L'arte di farsi amare: Modelli culturali e progetto didascalico nell'elegia ovidiana*. Pisa: Giardini.

_____ (1991). 'Città morte, città future: un tema della poesia augustea', *Maia* 43: 167–84.

Lachmann, K. (1969). *Kleinere Schriften*. Berlin: De Gruyter.

Laird, A. (1993). 'Sounding out Ecphrasis: Art and Text in Catullus 64', *JRS* 83: 18–30.

Lamacchia, R. (1960). 'Ovidio interprete di Virgilio', *Maia* 12: 310–30.

_____ (1969). 'Precisazioni su alcuni aspetti dell'epica ovidiana', *Atene e Roma* 14: 1–20.

La Penna, A. (1957). *Publi Ovidi Nasonis Ibis*. Florence: La Nuova Italia.

_____ (1963). *Orazio e l'ideologia del principato*. Turin: Einaudi.

Latte, K. (1960). *Römische Religionsgeschichte*. Munich: Beck.

Leach, E. W. (1964). 'Georgic Imagery in the *Ars Amatoria*', *TAPhA* 95: 142–54.

Le Boeuffle, A. (1975). *Germanicus: Les Phénomènes d'Aratus*. Paris: Les Belles Lettres.

Le Bonniec, H. (1965). *P. Ovidius Naso Fastorum Liber Primus*. Paris: Presses universitaires de France.

_____ (1969). *P. Ovidius Naso Fastorum Liber Secundus*. Paris: Presses universitaires de France.

Lee, A. G. (1953). *P. Ouidi Nasonis Metamorphoseon Liber I*. Cambridge: Cambridge University Press.

_____ (1958). 'The Authorship of the *Nux*', in Herescu (1958) 457–71.

_____ (1959). 'The Originality of Ovid', in Paratore (1959) 405–12.

_____ (1962) 'Tenerorum lusor amorum', in J. P. Sullivan (ed.), *Critical Essays on Roman Literature: Elegy and Lyric*. London: Routledge and Kegan Paul, 149–79.

_____ (1968). *Ovid's Amores*. English trans. with Latin text. London: John Murray.

Lefèvre, E. (1976). 'Die Lehre von der Entstehung der Tieropfer in Ovids Fasten 1 335–456', *RhM* 123: 39–64.

_____ (1980). 'Die Schlacht am Cremera in Ovids Fasten 2, 195–242', *RhM* 123: 152–62.

Lefkowitz, M. R. (1981). *Heroines and Hysterics*. London: Duckworth.

Levi, D. (1947). *Antioch Mosaic Pavements*. Princeton: Princeton University Press.

Levick, B. M. (1975). 'Julians and Claudians', *G&R* 22: 29–38.

——— (1976*a*). *Tiberius the Politician*. London: Thames and Hudson.

——— (1976*b*). 'The Fall of Julia the Younger', *Latomus* 35: 301–39.

——— (1983). 'The Senatus Consultum from Larinum', *JRS* 73: 97–115.

Lieberg, G. (1969). 'Seefahrt und Werk: Untersuchungen zu einer Metapher des antiken, besonders der lateinischen Literatur', *GIF* 21: 209–40.

Liebeschuetz, J. H. W. G. (1979). *Continuity and Change in Roman Religion*. Oxford: Oxford University Press.

——— (1985). Review of S. R. F. Price, *Rituals and Power: The Imperial Cult in Asia Minor*. *JRS* 75: 262–4.

Lightfoot, J. L. (1999). *Parthenius of Nicaea: The Poetical Fragments and the Ἐρωτικὰ Παθήματα*. Oxford: Oxford University Press.

Lilja, S. (1965*a*). *The Roman Elegists' Attitude to Women*. Helsinki: Suomalainen Tideakatemia. Reprinted New York 1978.

——— (1965*b*). *Terms of Abuse in Roman Comedy*. Helsinki: Suomalainen Tiedeakatemia.

——— (1976). *Dogs in Ancient Greek Poetry*. Helsinki: Societas Scientiarum Fennica.

Lindheim, S. H. (1998). 'Hercules Cross-Dressed, Hercules Undressed: Unmasking the Construction of the Propertian *Amator* in Elegy 4.9', *AJPh* 119: 43–66.

——— (2003). *Mail and female : epistolary narrative and desire in Ovid's Heroides*. Madison: University of Wisconsin Press.

Lipshitz, S. (ed.) (1978). *Tearing the Veil: Essays on Femininity*. London: Routledge and Kegan Paul.

Littlewood, R. J. (1975*a*). 'Ovid's Lupercalia (*Fasti* 2.267–452): A Study in the Artistry of the *Fasti*', *Latomus* 34: 1060–72.

——— (1975*b*). 'Two Elegiac Hymns: Propertius 3.17 and Ovid, *Fasti*, 5.663–692', *Latomus* 34: 662–74.

——— (1980). 'Ovid and the Ides of March (*Fast.* 3.523–710)', in C. Deroux (ed.), *Studies in Latin Literature and Roman History II*. Brussels: Latomus, 301–21.

——— (1981). 'Poetic Artistry and Dynastic Politics: Ovid at the *Ludi Megalenses. Fasti* 4.179–372', *CQ* 31: 381–95.

Lloyd-Jones, H. and Parsons, P. (eds.) (1983). *Supplementum Hellenisticum*. Berlin and New York: De Gruyter.

Luck, G. (1958). 'Zum Prooemium von Ovids Metamorphosen', *Hermes* 86: 499–500.

——— (1967–77). *P. Ovidius Naso, Tristia*. Heidelberg: Winter.

Lundström, S. (1980). *Ovids* Metamorphoses *und die Politik des Kaisers*. Uppsala: Uppsala universitet.

Lyne, R. (2001). *Ovid's Changing Worlds. English Metamorphoses, 1567–1632.* Oxford: Oxford University Press.

Lyne, R. O. A. M. (1974). '*Scilicet et tempus ueniet . . .* Virgil, *Georgics* I.463–514', in A. J. Woodman and D. A. West (eds.), *Quality and Pleasure in Latin Poetry.* Cambridge: Cambridge University Press, 47–66.

——— (1978). *Ciris. A Poem Attributed to Vergil.* Cambridge: Cambridge University Press.

——— (1980). *The Latin Love Poets from Catullus to Horace.* Oxford: Oxford University Press.

——— (1983). 'Lavinia's Blush. Vergil, *Aeneid* 12.64–70', *G&R* 30: 55–64.

——— (1987). *Further Voices in Vergil's Aeneid.* Oxford: Oxford University Press.

——— (1989). *Words and the Poet: Characteristic Techniques of Style in Vergil's Aeneid.* Oxford: Oxford University Press.

Maas, P. (1935). Review of J. Braune, *Nonnos und Ovid* (Greifswald 1935). *Byz. Zeitschr*; 35: 385–7.

Mack, S. (1988). *Ovid.* New Haven: Yale University Press.

Macleod, C. W. (1973). 'Catullus 116', *CQ* 23: 304–9.

——— (1983). *Collected Essays.* Oxford: Clarendon Press.

Mair, G. R. (1921). *Callimachus, Lycophron, Aratus.* Cambridge, Mass.: Harvard University Press.

Malouf, D. (1978). *An Imaginary Life: A Novel.* London: Picador.

Maltby, R. (1991). *A Lexicon of Ancient Latin Etymologies.* Leeds: Francis Cairns.

Manlove, C. N. (1982). 'On the Nature of Fantasy', in R. Schlobin (ed.), *Aesthetics of Fantasy Literature and Art.* Notre Dame: University of Notre Dame Press, 16–35.

Manuwald, B. (1975). 'Narcissus bei Konon und Ovid. (Zu Ovid met. 3,339–510)', *Hermes* 103: 349–72.

Marrou, H. I. (1956). *A History of Education in Antiquity.* Trans. G. Lamb. New York: Sheed and Ward.

Martin, Charles (2003). *Ovid: Metamorphoses.* New York: Norton.

Martin, Christopher (1985). 'A Reconsideration of Ovid's *Fasti*', *ICS* 10: 261–74.

——— (1998). *Ovid in English.* Harmondsworth: Penguin.

Martindale, C. (ed.) (1988). *Ovid Renewed : Ovidian Influences on Literature and Art from the Middle Ages to the Twentieth Century.* Cambridge: Cambridge University Press.

——— (1993). *Redeeming the Text: A Study in the Dynamics of a Tradition.* Cambridge: Cambridge University Press.

Maurach, G. (1978). *Germanicus und sein Arat. Eine vergleichende Auslegung von V. 1–327 der Phaenomena.* Heidelberg: Winter.

McGinn, T. A. J. (1998). *Prostitution, Sexuality, and the Law in Ancient Rome.* New York: Oxford University Press.

McKeown, J. C. (1984). 'Fabula proposito nulla tegenda meo', in Woodman and West (1984) 169–87.

——— (1987). *Ovid: Amores. Text, Prolegomena and Commentary in Four Volumes.* I: *Text and Prolegomena.* Leeds: Francis Cairns.

——— (1989). *Ovid: Amores. Vol. II: A Commentary on Book One.* Leeds: Francis Cairns.

——— (1994). 'Sound-imitation: A Neglected Technique in Ovid and Other Roman Poets'. Paper delivered at the One Hundred Twenty-Fifth Annual Meeting of the American Philological Association, Atlanta.

——— (1998). *Ovid: Amores. Vol. III: A Commentary on Book Two.* Leeds: Francis Cairns.

McNamee, K. (1993). 'Propertius, Poetry, and Love', in M. M. DeForest (ed.), *Woman's Power, Man's Game: Essays on Classical Antiquity in Honor of Joy K. King.* Wauconda, Il.: Bolchazy-Carducci, 215–48.

Melville, A. D. (1986). *Ovid, Metamorphoses.* Oxford: Oxford University Press.

——— (1990). *Ovid: The Love Poems.* Oxford: Oxford University Press.

——— (1992). *Ovid: Sorrows of an Exile (Tristia).* Oxford: Oxford University Press.

Millar, F. (1977). *The Emperor and the Roman World (31 BC–AD 337).* Ithaca: Cornell University Press.

Miller, J. F. (1980). 'Ritual Directions in Ovid's *Fasti*', *CJ* 75: 203–14.

——— (1982). 'Callimachus and the Augustan Aetiological Elegy', *ANRW* 2.30.1: 371–417.

——— (1983). 'Ovid's Divine Interlocutors in the *Fasti*', in C. Deroux (ed.), *Studies in Latin Literature and Roman History III.* Brussels: Collection Latomus, 156–92.

——— (1988). Review of Conte (1986). *Vergilius* 33: 118–21.

——— (1991). *Ovid's Elegiac Festivals: Studies in the Fasti.* Frankfurt and N.Y.: Lang.

——— (1992). 'The *Fasti* and Hellenistic Didactic: Ovid's Variant Aetiologies', *Arethusa* 25: 11–31.

——— (1993). 'Ovidian Allusion and the Vocabulary of Memory', *MD* 30: 153–64.

Miller, P. A. (1997). 'Laurel as the Sign of Sin: Laura's Textual Body in Petrarch's *Secretum*', in Gold et al. (1997) 139–63.

_____ (2001). 'Why Propertius is a Woman: French Feminism and Augustan Elegy', *CPh* 96: 127–46.

Momigliano, A. (1942). '*Terra marique*', *JRS* 32: 53–64.

Morgan, K. (1977). *Ovid's Art of Imitation: Propertius in the Amores*. Leiden: Brill.

Moskalew, W. (1990). 'Myrmidons, Dolopes, and Danaans: Wordplay in *Aeneid 2*', *CQ* 40: 275–9.

Murgatroyd, P. (1994). *Tibullus: Elegies II*. Oxford: Oxford University Press.

_____ (2005). *Mythical and Legendary Narrative in Ovid's* Fasti. Leiden: Brill.

Myerowitz, M. (1985). *Ovid's Games of Love*. Detroit: Wayne State University Press.

Myers, K. S. (1990). 'Ovid's *tecta ars*: *Amores* 2.6, Programmatics and the Parrot', *EMC* 34: 367–74.

_____ (1992). 'The Lizard and the Owl: An Etymological Pair in Ovid, *Metamorphoses* Book 5', *AJPh* 113: 63–8.

_____ (1994). *Ovid's Causes: Cosmogony and Aetiology in the Metamorphoses*. Ann Arbor: University of Michigan Press.

_____ (1999). 'The Metamorphosis of a Poet: Recent Work on Ovid', *JRS* 89: 190–204.

_____ (2002). '*Psittacus Redux*: Imitation and Literary Polemic in Statius, *Silvae* 2.4', in J. F. Miller, C. Damon, and K. S. Myers (eds.), *Vertis in usum: Studies in Honor of Edward Courtney*. Munich and Leipzig: Teubner, 189–99.

Mylne, V. (1981). *The Eighteenth-century French Novel: Techniques of Illusion*, 2nd edn. Cambridge: Cambridge University Press.

Mynors, R. A. B. (1958). *C. Valerii Catulli Carmina*. Oxford: Clarendon Press.

_____ (1969). *P. Vergili Maronis Opera*. Oxford: Clarendon Press.

Nadeau, Y. (1982). '*Caesaries Berenices* (or, the Hair of the God)', *Latomus* 41: 101–3.

Nagle, B. R. (1980). *The Poetics of Exile: Program and Polemic in the* Tristia *and* Epistulae ex Ponto *of Ovid*. Collection Latomus, 170. Brussels: Latomus.

Németh, B. (1977). 'To the Evaluation of Catullus 116', *ACD* 13: 23–31.

Nethercut, W. R. (1983). 'Recent Scholarship on Propertius', *ANRW* 2.30.3: 1813–57.

Newlands, C. E. (1992). 'Ovid's Narrator in the *Fasti*', *Arethusa* 25: 33–54.

_____ (1995). *Playing with Time: Ovid and the* Fasti. Ithaca, New York, and London: Cornell University Press.

Newman, J. K. (1990). *Roman Catullus and the Modification of the Alexandrian Sensibility*. Hildesheim: Weidmann.

Nikolaou, K. (1963). 'The Mosaics at Kato Paphos', *RDAC* 1963: 56–72.

Nikolaou, K. (1966). 'Archaeology in Cyprus, 1961–66', *AR* 12: 39–40.

Nisbet, R. G. M. and Hubbard, M. (1970). *A Commentary on Horace, Odes Book I*. Oxford: Clarendon Press.

——— (1978). *A Commentary on Horace, Odes Book II*. Oxford: Clarendon Press.

Norden, E. (1927). *P. Vergilius Maro, Aeneis Buch VI*. 3rd edn. Leipzig: Teubner.

O'Hara, J. J. (1990*a*). *Death and the Optimistic Prophecy in Vergil's Aeneid*. Princeton: Princeton University Press.

——— (1990*b*). 'The Significance of Vergil's *Acidalia mater*, and *Venus Erycina* in Catullus and Ovid', *HSPh* 93: 335–42.

——— (1990*c*). 'Etymological Wordplay in Apollonius of Rhodes, *Aeneid* 3 and *Georgics* 1', *Phoenix* 44: 370–6.

——— (1990*d*). 'Homer, Hesiod, Apollonius, and *Neritos ardua* at *Aeneid* 3.271', *Vergilius* 36: 31–4.

——— (1992). 'Naming the stars at *Georgics* 1.137–138 and *Fasti* 5.163–183', *AJPh* 113: 47–61.

——— (1996*a*). *True Names: Vergil and the Alexandrian Tradition of Etymological Wordplay*. Ann Arbor: University of Michigan Press.

——— (1996*b*). 'Vergil's Best Reader? Ovidian Commentary on Vergilian Etymological Wordplay', *CJ* 91: 255–76 (= ch. 5 of this volume).

Oltramare, A. (1926). *Les origines de la diatribe romaine*. Lausanne: Payot.

O'Neill, K. (1999). 'Ovid and Propertius: Reflexive Annotation in *Amores* 1.8', *Mnemosyne* 52: 286–307.

Otis, B. (1938). 'Ovid and the Augustans', *TAPhA* 69: 188–229.

——— (1966). *Ovid as an Epic Poet*. Cambridge: Cambridge University Press.

——— (1970). *Ovid as an Epic Poet*. 2nd edn. Cambridge: Cambridge University Press.

Owen, S. G. (ed.) (1915). *P. Ovidi Nasonis Tristium Libri Quinque, Ibis, Ex Ponto Libri Quattuor, Halieutica, Fragmenta*. Oxford: Clarendon Press.

Page, D. L. (1941). *Select Papyri*, III. Cambridge, Mass.: Harvard University Press.

Palmer, A. (1898). *P. Ovidi Nasonis Heroides*. Oxford: Clarendon Press.

Panofsky, E. (1930). *Hercules am Scheidewege*. Leipzig: Teubner.

Papponetti, G. (ed.) (1991). *Ovidio poeta della memoria*. Rome: Herder.

Paratore, E. (ed.) (1959). *Atti del convegno internazionale ovidiano*. Rome: Istituto di Studi Romani.

Parsons. P. J. (1977). 'Victoria Berenices', *ZPE* 25: 1–50.

Paschalis, M. (1986). 'Virgil and the Delphic Oracle', *Philologus* 130: 44–68.

Pasquali, G. (1942). 'Arte Allusiva', *L'Italia che Scrive* 25: 185–7 (= (1951). *Stravaganze quarte e supreme*. Venice: N. Pozza, 275–83).

Pearson, C. S. (1980). 'Simile and Imagery in Ovid *Heroides* 4 and 5', *ICS* 5: 110–29.

Pease, A. S. (1955). *M. Tulli Ciceronis De Natura Deorum.* Cambridge, Mass.: Harvard University Press.

Perdrizet, P. (1932). 'Légendes babyloniennes dans les Métamorphoses d' Ovide', *RHR* 105: 193–228.

Perkell, C. (1981). 'On Creusa, Dido, and the Quality of Victory in Virgil's *Aeneid*', in H. P. Foley (ed.), *Reflections of Women in Antiquity.* New York: Gordon & Breach Science Publ., 355–77.

Perrotta, G. (1926). 'Studi di poesia ellenistica vi. L'Ibis di Callimaco', *SIFC* n.s. 4: 140–201.

Peterson, W. (1891). *Quintilian: Book X.* Oxford: Clarendon Press.

Pfeiffer, R. (1949–53). *Callimachus.* 2 vols. Oxford: Clarendon Press.

Phillips, C. R. (1983). 'Rethinking Augustan Poetry', *Latomus* 42: 780–818.

Pianezzola, E. (1972). 'Conformismo e anticonformismo politico nell'Ars Amatoria di Ovidio', *Quad. Ist. filol. Lat.* 2: 37–58 (= (1999). *Ovidio. Modelli retorici e forma narrativa.* Bologna: Pàtron, 9–27).

——— (1979). 'La metamorfosi ovidiana come metafora narrativa', in D. Goldin (ed.), *Retorica e poetica. Atti del III Convegno Italo-tedesco (Bressanone 1975).* Padua: Liviana Ed., 77–91 (= (1999). *Ovidio. Modelli retorici e forma narrativa.* Bologna: Pàtron, 29–42).

Pichon, R. (1902). *Index verborum amatoriorum de sermone amatorio apud Latinos elegiarum scriptores.* Paris: Hachette.

Pillinger, H. E. (1969). 'Some Callimachean Influences on Propertius Book 4', *HSPh* 73: 171–99.

Porte, D. (1985). *L' Étiologie religieuse dans les Fastes d'Ovide.* Paris: Les Belles Lettres.

Posch, S. (1983). *P. Ovidius Naso. Tristia I: Interpretationen (Die Elegien 1–4).* Innsbruck: Universitätsverlag Wagner.

Pöschl, V. (1959). 'Kephalos und Procris in Ovids *Metamorphosen*', *Hermes* 87: 328–43.

——— (1964). *Die Hirtendichtung Virgils.* Heidelberg: Winter.

Postle, M. (1995). *Sir Joshua Reynolds: The Subject Pictures.* Cambridge: Cambridge University Press.

Powell, A. (ed.) (1992). *Roman Poetry and Propaganda in the Age of Augustus.* London: Bristol Classical Press.

Preston, K. (1916). *Studies in the Diction of the Sermo Amatorius in Roman Comedy.* Chicago: George Banta.

Price, S. R. F. (1984). *Rituals and Power: The Roman Imperial Cult in Asia Minor.* Cambridge: Cambridge University Press.

Primmer, A. (1982). 'Datierungs- und Entwicklungsfragen bei Vergil und Ovid', *WS* 16: 245–59.

Pulbrook, M. (1977). 'The Original Published Form of Ovid's *Heroides*', *Hermathena* 122: 29–45.

——(1985). *Nux Elegia.* Maynooth: Maynooth University Press.

Putnam, M. C. J. (1972). 'The Virgilian Achievement', *Arethusa* 5: 53–70.

——(1976). 'Propertius 1.22: A Poet's Self-Definition', *QUCC* 23: 93–123.

——(1994). 'Structure and Design in Horace *Odes* 1.17', *CW* 87: 357–75.

Quadlbauer, F. (1968). 'Properz 3.1', *Philologus* 112: 83–118.

——(1970). '*Non humilem . . . poetam*: zur literaturgeschichtlichen Stellung von Prop. 1,7,21', *Hermes* 98: 331–9.

Quinn, K. (1963). *Latin Explorations: Critical Studies in Roman Literature.* London: Routledge.

——(1973). *Catullus: The poems.* 2nd edn. London: Macmillan.

Raeburn, D. (2004). *Metamorphoses: A New Verse Translation.* London: Penguin.

Rahn, H. (1958). 'Ovids elegische Epistel', *A&A* 7: 105–20.

Ransmayr, C. (1988). *Die Letzte Welt.* Nördlingen: Greno.

Reeve, M. D. (1973). 'Notes on Ovid's *Heroides*', *CQ* 23: 324–38.

Rehm, B. 1932. *Das geographische Bild des alten Italiens in Vergils Aeneis.* Leipzig: Dietrich.

Reinach, S. (1922). *Répertoire de peintures grecques et romaines.* Paris: E. Leroux.

Reitzenstein, E. (1931). 'Zur Stiltheorie des Kallimachos', in E. Fraenkel and H. Fränkel (eds.), *Festschrift Richard Reitzenstein.* Leipzig: Teubner, 23–69.

——(1935). 'Das neue Kunstwollen in den Amores Ovids', *RhM* 84: 62–88.

Richardson, N. J. (1974). *The Homeric Hymn to Demeter.* Oxford: Clarendon Press.

——(1980). 'Literary Criticism in the exegetical Scholia to the *Iliad*: a Sketch', *CQ* 30: 265–87.

Richlin, A. (1983). *The Garden of Priapus: Sexuality and Aggression in Roman Humor.* New Haven: Yale University Press. Revised edn. (1992). New York: Oxford University Press.

Richmond, J. (1981). 'Doubtful Works Ascribed to Ovid', *ANRW* 2.31.4: 2744–83.

——(1990). *Ovidius: Ex Ponto Libri Quattuor.* Leipzig: Teubner.

Riese, A. (1874). 'Zur Beurteilung von Ovidius und Kallimachos *Ibis*', *Jahrb. f. class. Philol.* 109: 377–81.

Riley, H. T. (1851). *The Fasti, Tristia, Pontic Epistles, Ibis and Halieutica of Ovid.* London: H. G. Bohn.

Rizzo, G. E. (1929). *La pittura ellenistico-romana.* Milan: Fratelli Treves.

Rohde, A. (1929). *De Ovidi arte epica capita duo*. Berlin: Ebering.

Rosati, G. (1976). 'Narciso o l'illusione dissolta (Ovidio, *Metam.* III, 339–510)', *Maia* 28: 83–108.

——— (1983). *Narciso e Pigmalione: Illusione e Spettacolo nelle Metamorfosi di Ovidio*. Florence: Sansoni.

——— (1989). *Lettere di eroine*. Milan: B.U.R.

——— (2002). 'Narrative Techniques and Narrative Structures in the *Metamorphoses*', in Boyd 2002: 271–304.

Roscher, W. H. (ed.) (1884–1937). *Ausführliches Lexicon der griechischen und römischen Mythologie*. Leipzig: Teubner.

Rosen, R. M. and Farrell, J. (1986). 'Acontius, Milanion and Gallus: Vergil *Ecl.* 10.52–61', *TAPhA* 116: 241–54.

Ross, D. O. (1973). 'The Tacitean Germanicus', *YClS* 23: 209–27.

——— (1975a). *Backgrounds to Augustan Poetry: Gallus, Elegy and Rome*. Cambridge: Cambridge University Press.

——— (1975b). 'The *Culex* and *Moretum* as post-Augustan literary parodies', *HSPh* 79: 235–63.

——— (1987). *Virgil's Elements: Physics and Poetry in the Georgics*. Princeton: Princeton University Press.

Rostagni, A. (1920). *Ibis. Storia di un poemetto greco*. Florence: F. Le Monnier.

Rousset, J. (1962). 'Une Forme littéraire; le roman par lettres', in *Forme et signification: essais sur les structures littéraires de Corneille à Claudel*. Paris: J. Corti, 65–108.

Rudd, N. (1976). *Lines of Enquiry: Studies in Latin Poetry*. Cambridge: Cambridge University Press.

Ruiz de Elvira, A. (1972). 'Cefalo y Procris: Elegia y epica', *Cuadernos de Filologia clásica* 2: 97–123.

Russell, D. A. and Wilson, N. G. (1981). *Menander Rhetor*. Oxford: Oxford University Press.

Rutledge, E. S. (1980). 'Ovid's Informants in the *Fasti*', *Latomus* 168: 322–31.

Sabot, A.-F. (1976). *Ovide: poète de l'amour dans ses oeuvres de jeunesse*. Paris: Ophrys.

Santirocco, M. (1969). 'Metamorphosis in Ovid's *Amores*', *CB* 45: 83–4.

Sauvage, A. (1970). 'Les insects dans la poésie romaine', *Latomus* 29: 269–96.

——— (1975). *Étude de thèmes animaliers dans la poésie latine*. Brussels: Latomus.

Scheid, J. and Svenbro, J. (1996). *The Craft of Zeus. Myths of Weaving and Fabrics*. Cambridge, Mass.: Harvard University Press.

Schickel, J. (1962). 'Narziss. Zu Versen von Ovid', *Antaios* 3: 486–96.

Schiesaro, A. (1984). '*Nonne vides* in Lucrezio', *MD* 13: 143–57.

Schlunk, R. R. (1974). *The Homeric Scholia and the* Aeneid. Ann Arbor: University of Michigan Press.

Schmidt, E. A. (1973). 'Catulls Anordnung seiner Gedichte', *Philologus* 117: 233.

Schmitzer, U. (1997). 'Gallus im Elysium: Ein Versuch über Ovids Trauerelegie auf den toten Papagei Corinnas (*Am.* 2, 6)'. *Gymnasium* 104: 245–70.

——— (2002). 'Neue Forschungen zu Ovid', *Gymnasium* 109: 143–66.

Schneider, O. (1873). *Callimachea II.* Leipzig: Teubner.

Schoonhoven, H. (1992). *The Pseudo-Ovidian ad Liviam de morte Drusi* (Consolatio ad Liviam, Epicedium Drusi). *A Critical Text with Introduction and Commentary.* Groningen: E. Forsten.

Schrader, H. (1890). *Porphyrii quaestionum Homericarum ad Odysseam pertinentium reliquiae.* Leipzig: Teubner.

Schrijvers, P. H. (1976). '*O tragedia tu labor aeternus.* Études sur l'élégie III, 1 des Amours d'Ovide'. In J. M. Bremer, S. L. Radt, and C. J. Ruijgh (eds.), *Miscellanea tragica in honorem J. C. Kamerbeek.* Amsterdam: Hakkert, 405–24.

Schumann, Otto. (1979–83). *Lateinisches Hexameter Lexicon: Dichterisches Formelgut von Ennius bis zum Archipoeta*, 7 vols. Munich: Monumenta Germaniae Historica.

Scivoletto, N. (1976). *Musa Iocosa: Studio sulla poesia giovanile di Ovidio.* Rome: Elia.

Scott, K. (1931). 'Another of Ovid's Errors?', *CJ* 26: 293–6.

Scullard, H. H. (1981). *Festivals and Ceremonies of the Roman Republic.* London: Thames and Hudson.

Seager, R. (1972). *Tiberius.* London: Methuen.

Segal, C. (1975). 'Ovid's Cephalus and Procris: Myth and Tragedy', *GB* 7: 175–205.

——— (1989). *Orpheus: The Myth of the Poet.* Baltimore and London: Johns Hopkins University Press.

Shackleton Bailey, D. R. (1956). 'Maniliana', *CQ* 6: 81–6.

Sharrock, A. (1994). *Seduction and Repetition in Ovid's* Ars Amatoria 2. Oxford: Clarendon Press.

Shechter, S. 1975. 'The Aition and Virgil's Georgics', *TAPhA* 105: 346–91.

Shotter, D. C. A. (1968). 'Tacitus, Tiberius and Germanicus', *Historia* 17: 194–214.

Skinner, M. (1997). 'Introduction: *Quod multo fit aliter in Graecia . . .*', in Hallett and Skinner (1997) 3–25.

Skinner, V. (1965). 'Ovid's Narcissus. An Analysis', *CB* 41: 59–61.

Skutsch, O. (1956). 'Zu Vergils Eklogen', *RhM* 99: 193–201.

_____ (1959). 'Notes on Metempsychosis', *CPh* 54: 114–16.

_____ (1968). *Studia Enniana*. London: Athlone.

_____ (1985). *The* Annals *of Quintus Ennius*. Oxford: Oxford University Press.

Slater, N. (1990). *Reading Petronius*. Baltimore and London: Johns Hopkins University Press.

Slavitt, D. R. (1994). *The Metamorphoses of Ovid*. Baltimore and London: Johns Hopkins University Press.

Smith, K. F. (1913). *The Elegies of Albius Tibullus*. New York: American Book Company.

Smith, R. A. (1994). 'Epic Recall and the Finale of Ovid's *Metamorphoses*', *MH* 51: 45–53.

_____ (1997). *Poetic Allusion and Poetic Embrace in Ovid and Virgil*. Ann Arbor: University of Michigan Press.

Snyder, J. M. (1980). *Puns and Poetry in Lucretius' De Rerum Natura*. Amsterdam: Grüner.

_____ (1981). 'The Web of Song: Weaving Imagery in Homer and the Lyric Poets', *CJ* 76: 193–6.

Solmsen, F. (1961). 'Propertius in his Literary Relations with Tibullus and Virgil', *Philologus* 105: 273–89.

Solodow, J. (1988). *The World of Ovid's Metamorphoses*. Chapel Hill: University of North Carolina Press.

Spentzou, E. (2003). *Readers and Writers in Ovid's Heroides : Transgressions of Genre and Gender*. Oxford: Oxford University Press.

Spinazzola, V. (1953). *Pompei alla luce degli scavi nuovi di Via dell' Abbondanza*. Rome: Libreria dello Stato.

Spoth, F. (1992). *Ovids Heroides als Elegien*. Munich: C. H. Beck.

Stack, V. E. (1969). *The Love-Letters of Robert Browning and Elizabeth Barrett*. London: Heinemann.

Stallybrass, P. and White, A. (1986). *The Politics and Poetics of Transgression*. Ithaca: Cornell University Press.

Stapleton, M. L. (1996). *Harmful Eloquence: Ovid's* Amores *from Antiquity to Shakespeare*. Ann Arbor: University of Michigan Press.

Starr, R. (1987). 'The Circulation of Literary Texts in the Roman World', *CQ* 37: 213–23.

Steinmetz, P. (1987). 'Die Literarische Form der Epistulae Heroidum Ovids', *Gymnasium* 94: 128–45.

Sternberg, M. (1978). *Expositional Modes and Temporal Ordering in Fiction*. Baltimore: Johns Hopkins University Press.

Stirrup, B. E. (1976). 'Ovid's Narrative Technique: A Study in Duality', *Latomus* 35: 97–107.

Stitz, M. (1962). *Ovid und Vergils Aeneis: Interpretation Met. 13.623–14.608.* Diss. Freiburg.

Stroh, W. (1971). *Die römische Liebeselegie als werbende Dichtung.* Amsterdam: Hakkert.

——— (1979). 'Ovids Liebeskunst und die Ehegesetze des Augustus', *Gymnasium* 86: 323–52.

——— (1991). 'Heroides Ovidianae cur epistulas scribant', in Papponetti, G. (ed.), *Ovidio poeta della memoria. Atti del Convegno Internazionale di Studi, Sulmona, 19–21 ottobre 1989.* Rome: Herder, 201–44.

Sullivan, J. P. (1961). 'Two Problems in Roman Love Elegy', *TAPhA* 92: 522–36.

Sumner, G. V. (1967). 'Germanicus and Drusus Caesar', *Latomus* 26: 413–35.

Suter, A. (1989). 'Ovid, from Image to Narrative: *Amores* 1, 8 and 3, 6', *CW* 83: 15–20.

Syme, R. (1939). *The Roman Revolution.* Oxford: Oxford University Press.

——— (1974). 'History or Biography', *Historia* 23: 481–96.

——— (1978). *History in Ovid.* Oxford: Oxford University Press.

——— (1986). *The Augustan Aristocracy.* Oxford: Oxford University Press.

Tarrant, R. J. (1975). *Seneca: Agamemnon.* Cambridge: Cambridge University Press.

——— (1982). 'The Editing of Ovid's *Metamorphoses*: Problems and Possibilities'. *CPh* 77: 342–60.

——— (2002). 'Ovid and Ancient Literary History', in Hardie (2002*b*) 13–33.

——— (2004). *P. Ovidi Nasonis Metamorphoses.* Oxford: Clarendon Press.

Thibault, J. C. (1964). *The Mystery of Ovid's Exile.* Berkeley and Los Angeles: University of California Press.

Thomas, E. (1965). 'A Comparative Analysis of Ovid, *Amores*, II, 6 and III, 9', *Latomus* 24: 599–609.

Thomas, R. F. (1982*a*). *Lands and Peoples in Roman Poetry: The Ethnographical Tradition.* Cambridge: Cambridge Philological Society.

——— (1982*b*). 'Catullus and the Polemics of Poetic Reference', *AJPh* 103: 144–54.

——— (1983). 'Callimachus and Roman Poetry', *CQ* 33: 92–113.

——— (1986). 'Virgil's *Georgics* and the Art of Reference', *HSPh* 90: 171–98.

——— (1988). *Virgil: Georgics*, 2 vols. Cambridge: Cambridge University Press.

——— (2001). *Virgil and the Augustan Reception.* Cambridge: Cambridge University Press.

——— and Scodel, R. (1984). 'Vergil and the Euphrates', *AJPh* 105: 339.

Thompson, Sir D'A. W. (1936). *A Glossary of Greek Birds,* 2nd edn. London: Oxford University Press.

Timpanaro, S. (1986). *Per la storia della filologia virgiliana antica*. Rome: Salerno Editrice.

—— (2001). *Virgilianisti antichi e tradizione indiretta*. Florence: Leo S. Olschki Editore.

Tissol, G. (1993). 'Ovid's "Little Aeneid" and the Thematic Identity of the *Metamorphoses*', *Helios* 20: 69–79.

—— (1997). *The Face of Nature: Wit, Narrative, and Cosmic Origins in Ovid's Metamorphoses*. Princeton: Princeton University Press.

Todorov, T. (1967). *Littérature et signification*. Paris: Larousse.

Tompkins, J. P. (ed.) (1980). *Reader Response Criticism: From Formalism to Post-Structuralism*. Baltimore: Johns Hopkins University Press.

Torelli, M. (1982). *Typology and Structure of Roman Historical Reliefs*. Ann Arbor: University of Michigan Press.

Toynbee, J. M. C. (1971). *Death and Burial in the Roman World*. London: Thames and Hudson.

Traina, A. (1965). '*Si numquam fallit imago*. Riflessioni sulle Bucoliche e l'epicureismo', *A&R* 10: 72–8.

Tränkle, H. (1960). *Die Sprachkunst des Properz und die Tradition der lateinischen Dichtersprache*. Wiesbaden: F. Steiner.

—— (1963). 'Elegisches in Ovids Metamorphosen', *Hermes* 91: 459–76.

Traube, L. (1911). 'Einleitung in die lateinischen Philologie des Mittelalters', in F. Boll (ed.), *Vorlesungen und Abhandlungen*, vol. 2. Munich: Beck.

Trypanis, C. (1968). *Callimachus: Aetia Iambi Hecale and other Fragments*. Cambridge, Mass.: Harvard University Press.

Ussani, V. (1947). 'Enea traditore', *SIFC* 22: 108–23.

—— (ed.) (1952). *Eneide libro II*. Rome: Vittorio Bonacci.

Verducci, F. (1985). *Ovid's Toyshop of the Heart: Epistulae Heroidum*. Princeton: Princeton University Press.

Vermeule, C. (1976). *Greek and Roman Cyprus*. Boston: Museum of Fine Arts.

Versini, L. (1968). *Laclos et sa tradition*. Paris: Klincksieck.

Veyne, P. (1983). *L'Élégie érotique romaine: l'amour, la poésie et l'occident*. Paris: Éditions du Seuil. Reprinted in 1988 in English trans. by D. Pellauer as *Roman Erotic Elegy: Love, Poetry, and the West*. Chicago: University of Chicago Press.

Viarre, S. (1987). 'Des poèmes d'Homère aux "Héroïdes" d'Ovide: Le récit épique et son interprétation élégiaque', *Bulletin de L'Association Guillaume Budé*: 2–11.

Vinge, L. (1967). *The Narcissus Theme in Western European Literature up to the Early Nineteenth Century*. Lund: Gleerup.

Vollgraff, W. (1909). *Nikander und Ovid*. Groningen: J. B. Wolters.

Vollmer, F. (1891). *Laudationum funebrium Romanorum historia et reliquarum editio.* Leipzig: Teubner.

——— (1898). *Silvae.* Leipzig: Teubner.

Vulikh, N. V. (1968*a*). 'Ovid and Augustus', *VDI* 103: 151–60.

——— (1968*b*). 'La révolte d'Ovide contre Auguste', *LEC* 36: 370–82.

Wallace-Hadrill, A. (1982). '*Civilis princeps:* Between Citizen and King', *JRS* 72: 32–48.

——— (1986). 'Image and Authority in the Coinage of Augustus', *JRS* 76: 66–87.

——— (1987). 'Time for Augustus: Ovid, Augustus and the *Fasti*', in M. Whitby, P. Hardie, and M. Whitby (eds.). *Homo Viator: Classical Essays for John Bramble.* Bristol: Bristol Classical Press, 221–30.

Warner, M. (1976). *Alone of all her Sex.* London: Weidenfeld and Nicolson.

Watson, A. (1967). *The Law of Persons in the Later Roman Republic.* Oxford: Clarendon Press.

Watson, L. (1991). *Arae: The Curse Poetry of Antiquity.* Leeds: Francis Cairns.

Weinreich, O. (1928). *Studien zu Martial.* Stuttgart: W. Kohlhammer.

Weinstock, S. (1971). *Divus Julius.* Oxford: Clarendon Press.

Wellmann-Bretzigheimer, G. (1981). 'Ovids "ars amatoria"', in H. G. Rötzer and H. Walz (eds.), *Europäische Lehrdichtung: Festschrift für W. Naumann.* Darmstadt: Wissenschaftliche Buchgesellschaft, 1–32.

Wendorf, R. (1996). *Joshua Reynolds: The Painter in Society.* London: National Portrait Gallery.

West, D. A. and Woodman, A. J. (eds.) (1979). *Creative Imitation and Latin Literature.* Cambridge: Cambridge University Press.

Wheeler, A. L. (1925). 'Topics from the Life of Ovid', *AJPh* 46: 1–28.

Wheeler, S. (1993). 'Lost Voices: Vergil, *Aeneid* 12.718–19', *CQ* 43: 451–4.

——— (1999). *A Discourse of Wonders: Audience and Performance in Ovid's Metamorphoses.* Philadelphia: University of Pennsylvania Press.

——— (2000). *Narrative Dynamics in Ovid's Metamorphoses.* Tübingen: Narr.

Whitfield, J. H. (1963). 'La belle charité: the Italian pastoral and the French seventeenth century', *Italian Studies* 18: 33–53.

Wiedemann, T. (1975). 'The Political Background to Ovid's *Tristia* 2', *CQ* 25: 264–71.

Wiggers, N. (1976–7). 'Reconsideration of Propertius II.1', *CJ* 72: 334–41.

Wilkinson, L. P. (1955). *Ovid Recalled.* Cambridge: Cambridge University Press.

——— (1956). 'Greek Influence on the Poetry of Ovid', in J. Bayet (ed.), *L'influence grecque sur la poésie latine de Catulle à Ovide*, Entretiens Hardt sur l'antiquité classique 2. Geneva: Vandoeuvres, 221–43.

——— (1966). 'The Continuity of Propertius ii.13', *CR* 16: 141–4.

Williams, F. (1981). 'Augustus and Daphne: Ovid *Metamorphoses* 1, 560–63 and Phylarchus *FGrH* 81 F 32 (b)', *PLLS* 3: 249–57.

Williams, G. D. (1992). 'Representations of the Book-roll in Latin Poetry: Ovid, *Tr.* 1, 1, 3–14 and Related Texts', *Mnemosyne* 45: 178–89.

―――― (1994). *Banished Voices: Readings in Ovid's Exile Poetry.* Cambridge: Cambridge University Press.

―――― (1996). *The Curse of Exile: A Study of Ovid's Ibis.* Cambridge: Cambridge Philological Society.

Williams, G. W. (1962). 'Poetry in the Moral Climate of Augustan Rome', *JRS* 52: 28–46.

―――― (1968). *Tradition and Originality in Roman Poetry.* Oxford: Oxford University Press.

―――― (1969). *The Third Book of Horace's Odes.* Oxford: Clarendon Press.

―――― (1978). *Change and Decline: Roman Literature in the Early Empire.* Berkeley and Los Angeles: University of California Press.

Wimmel, W. (1960). *Kallimachos in Rom: Die Nachfolge seines apologetischen Dichtens in der Augusteerzeit.* Wiesbaden: Steiner.

Wirszubski, C. (1950). *Libertas as a Political Ideal at Rome during the Late Republic and Early Principate.* Cambridge: Cambridge University Press.

Wiseman, T. P. (1969). *Catullan Questions.* Leicester: Leicester University Press.

―――― (1985). *Catullus and his World.* Cambridge: Cambridge University Press.

Woodman, A. J. (1977). *Velleius: the Tiberian Narrative.* Cambridge: Cambridge University Press.

Woodman, A. J. and West, D. (eds.) (1984). *Poetry and Politics in the Age of Augustus.* Cambridge: Cambridge University Press.

Woytek, E. (1995). 'Die unlauteren Absichten eines Ehrenmannes (Zur Doppelbödigkeit von Ovid, Amores 1, 3)', *WS* 108: 417–38.

Wright, E. (1984). *Psychoanalytic Criticism: Theory in Practice.* London: Methuen.

Wyke, M. (1987). 'Written Women: Propertius' *scripta puella*', *JRS* 77: 47–61.

―――― (2002). *The Roman Mistress: Ancient and Modern Representations.* Oxford: Oxford University Press.

Zanker, P. (1966). '*Iste ego sum.* Der naive und der bewusste Narziss', *Bonner Jahrbücher* 166: 152–70.

―――― (1988). *The Power of Images in the Age of Augustus.* Ann Arbor: University of Michigan Press.

―――― (1989). *Augusto e il potere delle immagini.* Turin: Einaudi.

Zetzel, J. E. G. (1981). 'On the Opening of *Aitia* II', *ZPE* 42: 31–33.

_____ (1982). 'The Poetics of Patronage in the Late First Century B.C.', in B. K. Gold (ed.), *Literary and Artistic Patronage in Ancient Rome*. Austin: University of Texas Press, 87–102.

_____ (1996). 'Poetic Baldness and its Cure', *MD* 36: 73–100.

Zeydel, E. H. (ed.) (1944). *The Ship of Fools by Sebastian Brant*. New York: Columbia University Press.

Zimmermann, B. (1994): '*Ille ego qui fuerim, tenerorum lusor amorum*. Zur Poetik der Liebesdichtungen Ovids', in M. Picone and B. Zimmermann (eds.), *Ovidius redivivus: Von Ovid zu Dante*. Stuttgart: M & P, 1–21.

Zimmerman, M. (2002). *Metamorphoses: A Play*. Evanston: Northwestern University Press.

Ziolkowski, T. (2005). *Ovid and the Moderns*. Ithaca: Cornell University Press.

Zipfel, K. (1910). *Quatenus Ovidius in Ibide Callimachum aliosque fontes inprimis defixiones secutus sit*. Diss. Leipzig.

Index of Passages from Ovid

General Index

Italic numbers denote references to illustrations.